THE STUDY OF AMERICAN FOLKLORE

AN INTRODUCTION

FOURTH EDITION

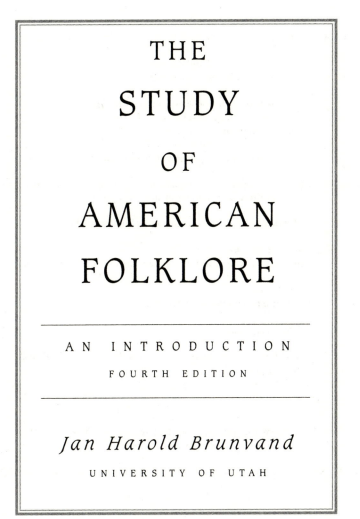

THE
STUDY
OF
AMERICAN
FOLKLORE

AN INTRODUCTION

FOURTH EDITION

Jan Harold Brunvand

UNIVERSITY OF UTAH

W. W. NORTON & COMPANY

NEW YORK • LONDON

The text of this book is composed in Granjon
with the display set in Caxton
Composition and manufacturing by PennSet, Inc.
Book design by JAM Design
Manufacturing by Courier Companies

Since this page cannot legibly accommodate all the copyright notices, pp. 615–16
constitute an extension of the copyright page.

Library of Congress Cataloging-in-Publication Data

Brunvand, Jan Harold.
   The study of American folklore : an introduction / Jan Harold
Brunvand. — 4th ed.
     p.   cm.
   Includes bibliographical references and index.

   ISBN 0-393-97223-2

     1. Folklore—United States.   2. United States—Social life and
customs.   I. Title.
GR105.B7   1997
398'.0973—dc21   97-26188
                                                       CIP

W. W. Norton & Company, Inc., 500 Fifth Avenue, New York, N.Y. 10110
www.wwnorton.com

W. W. Norton & Company Ltd., Castle House, 75/76 Wells Street, London W1T 3QT

8 9 0

To Richard Mercer Dorson
1916–1981
from whom I received my own
introduction to American folklore

CONTENTS

PREFACE TO THE
FOURTH EDITION

Since the publication of the first edition of this textbook in 1968, the study of folklore in the United States has advanced greatly. Changes in the second edition (1978) reflected the growth in American folklore studies, and the third edition (1986) brought the book into line with the latest scholarship and enhanced both its pedagogic and its reference uses. This fourth edition, while retaining the organization by major genres of folklore and folklife, and updating the bibliographic notes, has other, more radical changes. The four sample studies in the appendix have been dropped, and in their place—or rather throughout the book—"Focus" points have been added that contain brief examples of American folklore materials or interpretations along with discussion topics. The bibliographic notes have been pruned of items superseded by more-recent writings. Finally, to improve the book's readability and to stimulate class discussions, the format has been enlarged and redesigned and numerous illustrations have been added.

The basic purpose of *The Study of American Folklore* remains the same—to pave the way for deeper studies of the subject by clearly and systematically presenting the types of folklore found in the United States. A guide for beginning students to genres of American folklore, to theories and methods of research, and to major publications in the field, the book is organized around three groupings of folk materials—oral, customary, and material. Each chapter begins with definitions of the type involved, and continues with a delineation of subtypes, a selection of examples, and discussion of research methods or theories appropriate to that type. Although the bulk of the examples are Anglo-American, and often *modern*, folklore, for many categories some older lore and some representative traditions of ethnic and racial minorities are included.

The philosophy behind these features is that Anglo-American folklore is a coherent and familiar body of material with a huge bibliography of studies behind it; once understood, the Anglo-American material provides a basis for further studies of the folklore of other groups, either in the United States or elsewhere. In other words, I expect many students using this book to approach American folklore via their own traditions, or at least via traditions with which they are familiar, without losing sight of American history or of the diversity of subcultures that this country embraces. As for theory, I have provided an eclectic overview of modern theories rather than narrowing the book by following a single contemporary approach.

Professional folklorists will find (as in earlier editions) that I have generalized their findings as published in the professional literature, citing sources in the text or in the notes. I seldom list the same works more than once, although many publications have a bearing on more than one kind of folklore. For ease of reference, the major generic and theoretical terms introduced appear in boldface or italic type.

A good supplement to this book is my *Readings in American Folklore* (New York: W. W. Norton, 1979), a collection of thirty-six essays selected from folklore journals and provided with introductory headnotes. These readings are grouped as collectanea, studies in context, interpretations, and essays in theory. Items in the bibliographic notes of the present work that are reprinted in the first edition of the *Readings* are so indicated.

Several general surveys and textbooks are recommended for students' further introduction to folklore. *Folklore and Folklife: An Introduction* (Chicago: University of Chicago Press, 1972), edited by Richard M. Dorson, surveys folklore types internationally. Folklorists from several countries contributed to this collection, and Dorson provided the introduction to folklore definition, theory, and method. Another important reading supplementary to this textbook is *Folk*

Groups and Folklore Genres: An Introduction (Logan: Utah State University Press, 1986), edited by Elliott Oring and containing ten chapters focused on folklore topics and folk groups. Especially valuable for the student is William A. Wilson's chapter "Documenting Folklore." Accompanying the latter book, also edited by Oring, is *Folk Groups and Folklore Genres: A Reader* (Logan: Utah State University Press, 1989), a compilation of three dozen essays from scholarly sources.

Barre Toelken's *The Dynamics of Folklore* (1979; revised and expanded edition, Logan: Utah State University Press, 1996), a well-written and fully illustrated work on the behavioral, contextual, communicative, and functional aspects of folklore analysis, draws examples largely from American folklore, including immigrant and native American material. *Folkloristics: An Introduction*, by Robert A. Georges and Michael Owen Jones (Bloomington: Indiana University Press, 1995), reviews folklore "as historical artifact, as describable and transmissible entity, as culture, and as behavior," with numerous and well-chosen examples. The book gives equal attention to modern and older folklore traditions and theories. A practical approach to learning about folkloristics is represented by *The Emergence of Folklore in Everyday Life: A Fieldguide and Sourcebook*, edited by George H. Schoemaker (Bloomington, Ind.: Trickster Press, 1990). This volume was compiled by advanced graduate students at Indiana University to guide undergraduates in basic folklore classes as they collect, document, and interpret the traditions of their own lives and surroundings. Three sample fieldwork papers by IU students are included.

Two major reference books in American folklore belong in every college and university library and should be consulted by anyone doing research in the subject. First is the *Handbook of American Folklore* (Bloomington: Indiana University Press, 1983), edited by Richard M. Dorson. It contains sixty-plus chapters by as many contributors, and it covers "Topics of Research, Interpretations of Research, Methods of Research, [and] Presentation of Research." The second, and most recent, basic reference is *American Folklore: An Encyclopedia* (New York: Garland Publishing Company, 1996), edited by Jan Harold Brunvand. This comprehensive work contains more than five hundred entries written by leading folklorists on American folklore genres, groups, theories, scholars, and performers.

Since material in both the *Handbook* and the *Encyclopedia* is pertinent to virtually every topic in the present textbook, the chapters and entries are not cited individually in the bibliographic notes of *The Study of American Folklore*.

Many years of planning the original textbook, using it myself in the classroom, collecting comments from other teachers and students, revising, rewriting, and supplementing the text, updating the bibliographies, and endlessly cutting, pasting, and tinkering—first with scissors and tape, later on computers—have gone into this edition, which I trust will be found by teachers and students of American folklore to be the best yet in the ongoing series.

Salt Lake City, Utah
April 1997

ABBREVIATIONS USED IN THE BIBLIOGRAPHIC NOTES

AA	*American Anthropologist*
AFFWord	(journal of "Arizona Friends of Folklore"; replaced by *SWF* in 1977)
AQ	*American Quarterly*
ArQ	*Arizona Quarterly*
AS	*American Speech*
BJA	*British Journal of Aesthetics*
CA	*Current Anthropology*
C&T	*Culture and Tradition*
CFQ	*California Folklore Quarterly* (later *WF*)
CL	*Comparative Literature*
EM	*Ethnomusicology*
FF	*Folklore Forum*
FFC	*Folklore Fellows Communications* (Helsinki)
FFemC	*Folklore Feminists Communication* (after 1977, *FWC*)
FFMA	*The Folklore and Folk Music Archivist*
FFV	*Folklore and Folklife in Virginia*
FMS	*Folklore and Mythology Studies* (UCLA)
Folk Life	(full title of the journal of the [English] Society for Folk Life Studies)
Folklore	(full title of the journal of the [English] Folklore Society)

FWC	*Folklore Women's Communication* (until 1977, *FFemC*)
GR	*Geographical Review*
HF	*Hoosier Folklore*
HFB	*Hoosier Folklore Bulletin*
IF	*Indiana Folklore*
IFR	*International Folklore Review*
IMH	*Indiana Magazine of History*
IY	*Idaho Yesterdays*
JAC	*Journal of American Culture*
JAF	*Journal of American Folklore*
JAMS	*Journal of the American Musicological Society*
JEGP	*Journal of English and Germanic Philology*
JFI	*Journal of the Folklore Institute* (after 1982, *JFR*)
JFR	*Journal of Folklore Research* (before 1982, *JFI*)
JGLS	*Journal of the Gypsy Lore Society*
JIFMC	*Journal of the International Folk Music Council*
JOFS	*Journal of the Ohio Folklore Society*
JPC	*Journal of Popular Culture*
JSP	*Journal of Social Psychology*
KF	*Keystone Folklore* (until 1973, *KFQ*; in 1982 began a new series with vol. 1)
KFQ	*Keystone Folklore Quarterly* (after 1973, *KF*)
KFR	*Kentucky Folklore Record*
KR	*Kenyon Review*
LFM	*Louisiana Folklore Miscellany*
MAF	*Mid-America Folklore* (until 1978, *MSF*)
MC	*Material Culture* (until 1984, *PA*)
MF	*Midwest Folklore*
MFR	*Mississippi Folklore Register*
MFSJ	*Missouri Folklore Society Journal*
MH	*Minnesota History*
MJLF	*Midwestern Journal of Language and Folklore*
MLN	*Modern Language Notes*
MLQ	*Modern Language Quarterly*
MLW	*Mountain Life and Work*
MP	*Modern Philology*
MQ	*Musical Quarterly*
MSF	*Mid-South Folklore* (after 1978, *MAF*)
NCF	*North Carolina Folklore* (after 1973, *NCFJ*)

NCFJ	*North Carolina Folklore Journal* (until 1973, *NCF*)
NEF	*Northeast Folklore*
NEQ	*New England Quarterly*
NH	*Nebraska History*
NJF	*New Jersey Folklore*
NMFR	*New Mexico Folklore Record*
NWF	*Northwest Folklore*
NYF	*New York Folklore* (until 1975, *NYFQ*)
NYFQ	*New York Folklore Quarterly* (after 1975, *NYF*)
OFB	*Oregon Folklore Bulletin*
PA	*Pioneer America* (after 1984, *MC*)
PADS	*Publications of the American Dialect Society*
PF	*Pennsylvania Folklife*
PMLA	*Publications of the Modern Language Association*
PTFS	*Publications of the Texas Folklore Society*
SF	*Southern Folklore* (earlier *SFQ*)
SFQ	*Southern Folklore Quarterly* (later *SF*)
SWF	*Southwest Folklore* (replaced *AFFWord* in 1977)
TAW	*The American West*
TFSB	*Tennessee Folklore Society Bulletin*
TQ	*Texas Quarterly*
TSL	*Tennessee Studies in Literature*
TSLL	*Texas Studies in Literature and Language*
UHQ	*Utah Historical Quarterly*
UHR	*Utah Humanities Review*
WAL	*Western American Literature*
WF	*Western Folklore* (earlier *CFQ*)

COLLECTIONS CITED IN NOTES
BY TITLE ONLY

Abrahams, Roger D., ed. *Fields of Folklore: Essays in Honor of Kenneth S. Goldstein*. Bloomington, Ind.: Trickster Press, 1995.

Beck, Horace P., ed. *Folklore in Action: Essays for Discussion in Honor of MacEdward Leach*. Bibliographical and Special Series. Vol. 14. Philadelphia: American Folklore Society, 1962.

Bendix, Regina, and Rosemary Lévy Zumwalt, eds. *Folklore Interpreted: Essays in Honor of Alan Dundes*. New York: Garland, 1995.

Bronner, Simon J., ed. *Creativity and Tradition in Folklore: New Directions (A Festschrift for W. F. H. "Bill" Nicolaisen)*. Logan: Utah State University Press, 1992.

Brunvand, Jan Harold. *Readings in American Folklore*. New York: Norton, 1979.

Burlakoff, Nikolai, and Carl Lindahl, eds. *Folklore on Two Continents: Essays in Honor of Linda Dégh*. Bloomington, Ind.: Trickster Press, 1980.

Dégh, Linda, Henry Glassie, and Felix J. Oinas, eds. *Folklore Today: A Festschrift for Richard M. Dorson*. Bloomington: Research Center for Language and Semiotic Studies at Indiana University, 1976.

Dorson, Richard M. *American Folklore and the Historian*. Chicago: University of Chicago Press, 1971.

———*Folklore: Selected Essays*. Bloomington: Indiana University Press, 1972.

———*Folklore and Fakelore: Essays toward a Discipline of Folk Studies*. Cambridge, Mass.: Harvard University Press, 1976.

Dundes, Alan. *The Study of Folklore*. Englewood Cliffs, N.J.: Prentice-Hall, 1965.

———*Analytic Essays in Folklore*. The Hague and Paris: Mouton, 1975.

———*Interpreting Folklore*. Bloomington: Indiana University Press, 1980.

———*Folklore Matters*. Knoxville: University of Tennessee Press, 1989.

Goldstein, Kenneth S., and Neil V. Rosenberg, eds. *Folklore Studies in Honour of Herbert Halpert*. St. John's, Newfoundland, Canada: Memorial University of Newfoundland, 1980.

Jackson, Bruce, ed. *Folklore and Society: Essays in Honor of Benj. A. Botkin*. Hatboro, Pa.: Folklore Associates, 1966.

Pound, Louise. *Nebraska Folklore*. Lincoln: University of Nebraska Press, 1959.

Richmond, W. Edson, ed. *Studies in Folklore: In Honor of Distinguished Service Professor Stith Thompson*. Folklore Series. No. 9. Bloomington: Indiana University Press, 1957.

Walls, Robert E., and George H. Schoemaker, eds. *The Old Traditional Way of Life: Essays in Honor of Warren E. Roberts*. Bloomington, Ind.: Trickster Press, 1989.

I

INTRODUCTION

1.

INTRODUCTION

1

THE FIELD OF FOLKLORE

WHAT IS FOLKLORE?

Folklore comprises the unrecorded traditions of a people; it includes both the form and content of these traditions and their manner of communication from person to person. The study of folklore (or "folkloristics") records and attempts to analyze these traditions (both content and process) so as to reveal the common life of the human mind apart from what is contained in the formal records of culture that compose the heritage of a people.

This type of research has been carried out in the United States in an organized way since the late nineteenth century. Writing in the first issue of *The Folklore Historian*, a newsletter begun in 1984, folklorist W. K. McNeil gave this capsule account of the founding of the American Folklore Society (AFS) nearly a century before:

In the summer of 1887 several scholars resident in the United States received a letter proposing the formation of an American folklore society modeled somewhat on the organization established in England nine years earlier [1878]. A few months later, in October, a second letter containing 104 names from different areas of the United States and Canada was distributed. As a result, a number of people gathered in University Hall at Harvard University on January 4,

1888, to officially establish the American Folklore Society. . . . Although the new organization selected the eminent ballad scholar Francis James Child president, the real moving force behind the Society was William Wells Newell, the secretary and, for many years, editor of the *Journal of American Folklore*.

The goals of the society were well expressed in the description of "a journal of a scientific character" that appeared in the first number of the journal itself:

(1) For the collection of the fast-vanishing remains of Folk-Lore in America, namely:
    (a) Relics of Old English Folk-Lore (ballads, tales, superstitions, dialect, etc.).
    (b) Lore of Negroes in the Southern States of the Union.
    (c) Lore of the Indian Tribes of North America (myths, tales, etc.).
    (d) Lore of French Canada, Mexico, etc.
(2) For the study of the general subject, and publication of the results of special students in this department.

The accomplishments of some of the founders and early leaders of American folklore study are discussed in appropriate chapters of this book: Child in chapter 12, Newell in chapter 18, Archer Taylor's work on riddles in chapter 6, Stith Thompson's motif and tale-type indexes in chapters 8 and 10, Wayland D. Hand's studies of superstitions in chapter 14, and so forth. Still other American folklorists' names come up in briefer notices: see, for example, the index references to John Lomax, A. H. Krappe, Louise Pound, Olive Dame Campbell and Cecil J. Sharp, Vance Randolph, and others. Thanks to these and many other scholars whose works are mentioned in the bibliographic notes, the study of American folklore grew from the concern of a handful of enthusiasts to a secure part of the current academic scene, although it was not until the 1950s that advanced degrees in folklore began to be offered at American universities. The original goals of the founders of AFS remain primary—to collect and study folklore in America and to publish it in the *Journal of American Folklore* (*JAF*) and elsewhere. The notions that folklore is "fast vanishing" and that only "relics" remain have proven false, however, as this book amply documents. At the 1988 centennial of AFS, folklore study was vigorous, and, just as the creation and dissemination of folklore are thriving, the field of folklore in the United States continues to grow.

Unfortunately, the field of folklore tends to be narrowly understood by many people who may have been attracted to it through treatments in the popular media, where the word "folklore" is loosely applied, or who may know the word only with reference to children's literature or in the sense of rumor, hearsay, or error. However, it is in the scholarly sense of "oral and customary tradition" that we are employing the word "folklore" here. Archer Taylor put it succinctly in 1948: "Folklore is the material that is handed on by tradition, either by word of mouth or by custom and practice."

The chief difficulty in defining "folklore" more completely and scientifically is that the word has acquired varying meanings among the different scholars and writers who use it. The word itself is not a "folk word"; it was coined by a nineteenth-century English scholar, W. J. Thoms, to supply an Anglo-Saxon word to replace the Latin-based term "popular antiquities," referring to the intellectual "remains" of earlier cultures surviving in the traditions of the peasant class. Modern folklorists avoid the peasant connotations of the original term, but they still use it to signify that portion of any culture that is passed on in oral

Traditional image of Paul Bunyan and his blue ox, Babe, used to illustrate Daniel G. Hoffman's 1952 book *Paul Bunyan: Last of the Frontier Demigods*. Hoffman identified the largely popular-culture sources for the stories, leading folklorists of the time to label them fakelore.

or customary tradition. Folklorists, at least until recently, tended to exclude as spurious or contaminated any supposed folklore that was transmitted largely by print, broadcasting, or other commercial and organized means without an equally strong interpersonal circulation. American folklorists have sometimes used the term "fakelore" (coined by Richard M. Dorson in 1950) to disparage the professional writers' contrived inventions and rewritings—like many Paul Bunyan stories—that are foisted on the public as genuine examples of native folk traditions, but that have only a thin basis of real tradition underlying them. More recently, however, American folklorists have begun to analyze even fakelore itself as a reflection of traditional culture.

"Folk" is a somewhat misleading and ambiguous term in an academic context, and thus some folklorists have suggested substitutes

FOCUS: FAKELORE AND NATIONALISM

Fakelore apparently fills a national, psychic need: namely, to assert one's national identity, especially in a time of crisis, and to instill pride in that identity. . . . It may be true that ideally folklore serves the cause of national identity cravings, but where folklore is deemed lacking or insufficient, individual creative writers imbued with nationalistic zeal have felt free to fill in that void. They do so by creating a national epic or national "folk" hero ex nihilo if necessary, or what is more usual, they embroider and inflate fragments of folklore into fakeloristic fabrications.

. . . Folklorists have long realized the connection between nationalism and folklore, but what has not been perceived is the possible relationship between feelings of national inferiority and the tendency to produce fakelore. If folklore is rooted in nationalism, I believe fakelore may be said to be rooted in feelings of national or cultural inferiority.

Source: Alan Dundes, "Nationalistic Inferiority Complexes: A Reconsideration of Ossian, the Kinder- und Hausmärchen, the Kalevala, and Paul Bunyan," JFR 22 (1985): 5–18.

DISCUSSION TOPICS:

1. Look at some examples of American folklore included in educational materials or in the popular media. To what extent are these items fakelore, according to the definitions given by Dorson and Dundes?

2. In what sense might Americans be said to suffer from "feelings of national or cultural inferiority" that have inspired them to create fakelore?

for the word "folklore," such as "hominology" or simply "lore." But "hominology" is just another word for "anthropology" and has achieved no currency; the term "lore" itself is no improvement, since it is hard to justify including behavioral and material data under that heading, and it is still necessary to differentiate traditional "lore" from other aspects of culture. The anthropological terms "folk culture" and "verbal arts" have also been proposed as better names for folklore, but neither seems adequate for the full range of topics studied by folklorists; furthermore, "folk culture" implies specific social and economic conditions that are not found in most of the settings folklorists study. The most successful candidate for a term to replace "folklore" is "folklife," about which see chapter 19 below. Perhaps the best approach, still, for understanding the scholarly field of American folklore/folklife seems to be to state as clearly as possible the concepts folklorists themselves hold, for, as one frustrated definer of the term finally put it, "Folklore is what folklorists study."

FOCUS: FOLKLORE ANSWERS QUESTIONS

Folklore sometimes provides traditional answers to questions that otherwise seem to have no ready answers, such as:

How do you cure the hiccups (or a hangover, a cold sore, a wart)?

What do you do at a birthday party (or a wedding shower or baby shower)?

What is done with the bride's bouquet?

How can you magically predict the sex of an unborn baby?

What do you do with a baby tooth when it falls out?

How do you make "somemores?" What other names do they have?

How do you build a snowman?

How do you know how long to wait for a professor who is late to class?

What gesture do you use to signal "Everything's OK"?

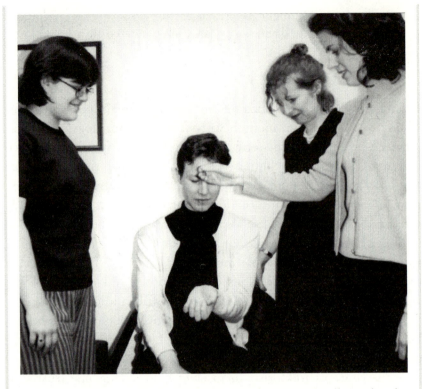

Four women demonstrate the use of a pendulum to magically predict the sex of an unborn baby. A ring on a thread is suspended over the hand of the pregnant woman.

DISCUSSION TOPICS:

1. What are *your* answers to these questions, and how do other people answer them differently?

2. What other questions are answered by folklore?

3. At what point, and with which questions, might someone turn to an official or institutional source for answers to the same questions? (For example, when would you consult a doctor for hiccups, or read an etiquette book for help in planning a wedding?)

FOLK, NORMATIVE, ELITE

Folklore is the traditional, unofficial, noninstitutional part of culture. It encompasses all knowledge, understandings, values, attitudes, assumptions, feelings, and beliefs transmitted in traditional forms by word of mouth or by customary examples. Many of these habits of thought are common to all human beings, but they always interact with and are influenced by the whole cultural context that surrounds them. Folklore manifests itself in many oral and verbal forms ("mentifacts"), in kinesiological forms (customary behavior, or "sociofacts"), and in material forms ("artifacts"), but folklore itself is the whole traditional complex of thought, content, and process—which ultimately can never be fixed or recorded in its entirety; it lives only in its performance or communication, as people interact with one another. An international committee of leading folklore scholars formed by UNESCO to discuss means of "safeguarding folklore" issued in 1987 this useful definition of "folklore":

a group-oriented and tradition-based creation of groups or individuals reflecting the expectations of the community as an adequate expression of its cultural and social identity; its standards and values are transmitted orally, by imitation or by other means. Its forms include, among others, language, literature, music, dance, games, mythology, rituals, customs, handicrafts, architecture and other arts. (Quoted in Nordic Institute of Folklore "Newsletter" no. 3, 1987)

It is instructive to represent all of these generalizations and terms in a chart, with typical labels for the supposed levels of culture (or behavior) on one axis and the kinds of traditional materials (or products) on the other:

	Products:		
	ORAL/VERBAL	CUSTOMARY	MATERIAL
Levels:	(Mentifacts)	(Sociofacts)	(Artifacts)
Elite (academic, progressive, etc.)			
Normative (popular, mass, mainstream, etc.)			
Folk (conservative, traditional, etc.)			

In general, the elite and normative traditions are transmitted mainly in print or by other formal means, while the folk tradition relies on oral or customary circulation, although there are always exceptions. If we try now to isolate one specific human need or desire for each level and its typical products, we arrive at a set of samples like this:

	ORAL/VERBAL (entertainment)	CUSTOMARY (cure)	MATERIAL (housing)
Elite	serious novel	doctor's care	architect's design
Normative	popular romance	nonprescription drug	tract development house
Folk	tall tale or joke	home remedy	log cabin or saltbox house

Such a chart and samples are oversimplifications of very complex phenomena, and an important part of many research projects in folklore is sorting out the various threads of influence and the interweavings in one level from another. For example, while most movies are popular art, some serious works of "cinema" appeal to an elite audience; musical comedy would seem to be a mass-culture variant of opera. Similarly, bluegrass music has roots in folk music, but most of its development is in popular music; and Paul Bunyan stories span the same two categories. In general, the movement of ideas tends to be from top to bottom, as when Greek Revival architecture became a popular style for banks and survived later as a traditional decorative style on houses. Other materials and ideas, however, have stayed in place (many barn types), or moved upward ("folk" clothing and dances becoming "fashionable"), or skipped steps ("folk" arts appealing to "elite" art critics). The study of folklore itself is, of course, "elite." Most important to bear in mind is that individuals may be aware of, influenced by, and participate in any level of culture during their lifetime, or even during the course of a particular day.

ORAL, CUSTOMARY, MATERIAL

The materials and manifestations of folklore are extremely wide-ranging and diverse; their genres may be identified as either *ethnic (or native) categories*, those of the people themselves (like "old wives' tales" or the generic term "jokes"), or *analytical categories*, those of research scholars (like "Child ballads" or the specific term "riddle-jokes"). For the purpose of an orderly presentation of American folklorists' research, we will treat the types of folklore here, using typical analytical categories, in three groups, according to their modes of existence: *oral, customary, or material.*

Oral folklore, the type most commonly studied until fairly recently in the United States, may be conveniently arranged and listed from the simplest to the most complex varieties. At the level of the individual word is folk *speech*, including dialect and naming. Traditional phrases and sentences make up the area of folk *proverbs* and *proverbial sayings*, while traditional questions are folk *riddles*. Next are folk *rhymes* and other traditional poetry, then folk *narratives* of all kinds, and finally folk *songs* and folk *ballads* with their music.

Customary folklore, which often involves both verbal and non-verbal elements, includes folk *beliefs* and *superstitions*, folk *customs* and *festivals*, folk *dances* and *dramas*, traditional *gestures*, and folk *games*.

Material folk traditions include folk architecture, crafts, arts, costumes, and food.

These categories and subcategories overlap, but such a three-part classification emphasizes elements that comprise folklore and shows how individual items and performances may be roughly sorted on the basis of their major modes of existence. Placing a folksinger's lyrics in one category, his or her guitar-playing style and melody in another, and the call and figures of a dance done to the same song in a third is not intended to lead to fragmentation of either the tradition involved or the study of it. The classification is only a means of clarifying and organizing the processes and materials that are to be observed and analyzed. Without an awareness of these elements of a traditional performance, there would be a tendency simply to tape-record "the song" without capturing its context or the nonverbal nuances. Similarly, because folktales are basically verbal folklore, folklorists should not overlook collecting and studying such nonverbal elements as facial expressions, gestures, and audience reactions while tales are being told. The ideal study is one that takes into account the entire traditional event, which is what we are referring to here as a "performance."

DEFINITIONS: WHAT FOLKLORE IS AND WHAT IT ISN'T

The foregoing discussion identifies mainly the materials that circulate in folk tradition; we can extract from these materials some common qualities that will provide us with a useful general definition of the subject. Folklorists generally associate five qualities with true folklore: (1) its content is oral (usually verbal), or custom-related, or material; (2) it is traditional in form and transmission; (3) it exists in different versions; (4) it is usually anonymous; and (5) it tends to become formularized. Each of these terms is used in a broad sense, and the first three qualities are the primary ones to be considered in arriving at a clear definition of folklore.

Folklore is oral or custom-related in that it passes by word of mouth and informal demonstration or imitation from one person to another and from one generation to the next. Much folklore is "aural," reaching the ear either from voices or from musical instruments. While written folklore (such as graffiti or autograph rhymes) is verbal without being oral, its transmission is customary, not institutionalized. The same is true for learning to produce or use folk artifacts, such as whittled wooden chains, hand-sewn quilts, or traditional log cabins. Folklore is never transmitted entirely in a formal manner through printed books, phonograph records, school classes, church sermons, or by other learned, sophisticated, and commercial means.

Folklore is traditional in two senses in that it is passed on repeatedly in a relatively fixed or standard form, and it circulates among members of a particular group. Traditional form or structure allows us to recognize corresponding bits of folklore in different guises. The characters in a story, the setting, the length, the style, even the language may vary, but we can still call it the "same" story if it maintains a basic underlying form. Think, for example, of "Cinderella," which would probably be recognizable even in a comic-

Traditional tale-teller Ray Hicks of Beech Mountain, North Carolina, performing at a recent National Storytelling Festival in Jonesborough, Tennessee.

strip parody if the characters were made modern teenagers, or in the movies if the parts were acted by Hollywood stars in a big-city setting.

But comic strips and movies are not folklore, and this leads to the observation that the first two qualities must be found together to define folklore. For example, some things, like conversations, are oral but not traditional. (Entire conversations are not passed on among members of a group in a relatively fixed or standard form and repeated over and over again.) Other things, like legal processes, are largely traditional but not oral. (The proceedings in courts of law are preserved in print, not by word of mouth. Law precedents must be followed precisely, but folk performers [sometimes called "informants"] seldom refer to printed collections of folklore.) Only those aspects of culture that are both oral or customary and traditional may be folklore; thus, there may be traditional folk stories, proverbs, or gestures passed on either in conversations or in courtroom arguments and testimony. These items are legitimate examples of folklore. The possibility of "new traditions" developing is illustrated in discussions elsewhere in this book of such material as "Xeroxlore," "(computer) Netlore," and the folklore of academe.

FOCUS: CREATING A RITE OF PASSAGE

After 27 years at Vesterheim [The Norwegian-American Museum in Decorah, Iowa], *Lila and I felt that our moment of passage should be marked by some rite. We worked frantically at the museum until 6:00 p.m. on December 30th, just completing the move of the furniture and fine arts into the new storage area, and headed that night for Minneapolis. At 7:30 the next morning we flew to New York and were among the tens of thousands on Times Square to watch the ball of the old year and a good portion of our lives descend.*

What happens on Times Square at midnight on New Year's Eve is a powerful document of tradition and the desire of human beings to assemble for support at moments of change. There is nothing else to bring them, no speeches, no choirs, no bands, just tradition and wanting to be with others when the old passes and new must be faced. It felt good to share in something so fundamental, to lose ourselves if only for a moment in a solid mass of flesh and blood spreading for blocks without distinctions in color and creed. We realized that on entering our new lives we would again fall into the old distinctions we had come to take for granted, but we also felt that the experience would help remind us what a small drop the sphere to which we relate is in the great ocean of humanity.

Source: A form letter dated February 18, 1992, sent by Marion Nelson to Vesterheim members upon his retirement as director of the museum.

New York City's Times Square (shown here on January 1, 1996) is the traditional focus of New Year's Eve celebrations in the United States.

DISCUSSION TOPICS:

1. What elements would or would not support our seeing the New Year's Eve gathering at Times Square as a traditional folk event?

2. What other similar traditional gatherings can you think of? Have you observed other traditional ways to celebrate retirement?

3. What did *you* do last New Year's Eve? What traditions did you follow (or invent)?

The American "folk groups" from which major bodies of tradition have been identified are discussed in chapter 3. Much controversy has centered on the meaning of the "folk" in "folklore," but perhaps it is sufficient to say here that we should not think only of quaint, rustic tradition-bearers, but rather of any group that has distinctive oral traditions, which is to say, just about any group. ("Hackers" and others involved in computerized communication are a leading contemporary example.)

Oral transmission of folklore invariably creates different versions of the same text, and these versions or "variants" are the third defining characteristic of folklore. Folklorists often speak of individual recordings of folklore as either "texts" or "versions," reserving the term "variants" for texts that deviate more widely from the common standard. A story, proverb, or other text is living folklore only as long as it continues to circulate orally in different traditional variations. "The Three Bears," for instance, except in oral parodies, has always been more a literary tale than a folktale; "Home on the Range" was collected as an oral folksong but, after the influence of wide reprinting, is now learned from books or sheet music in a standardized form.

Generally speaking, then, folklore may be defined as *those materials in culture that circulate traditionally among members of any group in different versions, whether in oral form or by means of customary example, as well as the processes of traditional performance and communication.*

Although oral or customary tradition and the presence of different versions serve to define folklore, the two other qualities, anonymity and formularization, are important enough to belong in a complete description of typical folk material. Folklore is usually anonymous simply because authors' names are seldom part of texts that are orally transmitted and folk artifacts are seldom signed, although occasion-

ally a ballad may contain the supposed name or initials of its composer in the last verse and sometimes local tradition preserves the
name of a notable folk composer or artisan. On occasion, too, research has unearthed the identity of a creator of folklore; but the
majority of folklore bears no trace of its authorship, and even the
time and place of its origin may be a mystery.

Most folklore tends to become formularized—that is, it is expressed partly in commonplace terms or patterns. These may range
in complexity from simple set phrases and patterns of repetition to
elaborate opening and closing devices or whole passages of traditional verbal stereotypes. Furthermore, there are different bodies
of formularized language in different countries and for different
kinds of folklore, so that we can distinguish between English and
American ballads, for example, partly on the basis of the different
formulas used in each. Nonverbal folklore, too, makes use of stereotyped habits, gestures, patterns, designs, and the like. One interesting area of folklore research is the identification and attempted
explanation of this recurring formularization.

The criteria for identifying authentic folklore and the specific definition of "folklore" given in this chapter are not meant to exclude
other views or other formulations by different folklorists. There is
something to be learned both about folklore and the history of its
study in the United States from every definition, ranging from
C. F. Potter's metaphorical one, "a lively fossil which refuses to die"
(1949), and Alan Dundes's "definition consisting of an itemized list
of the forms of folklore" (1965), to Dan Ben-Amos's elegant and
concise "performance" definition of folklore as "artistic communication in small groups" (1971). More-recent definitional statements
attempt to reconcile the older generic approach to folklore with the
current emphasis on context, communication, and performance.
Thus we have Barre Toelken's cautious statement, "We might characterize or describe the materials of folklore as 'tradition-based communicative units informally exchanged in dynamic variation through
space and time'" (1979). And we also have Robert Georges's similar
careful reference to folkloristics as the study that concentrates on
"continuities and consistencies in human behavior . . . what human
beings express and the ways they express themselves during face-to-
face interaction" (1980).

Turning to the American Folklore Society itself for an "official" definition of "folklore/folklife" we find this wording in a booklet published by AFS in 1984: "expressive and instrumental activities of all kinds learned and communicated directly or face-to-face in groups ranging from nations, regions, and states through communities, neighborhoods, occupations, and families." (The concept of variation is conspicuously absent here!)

Even more official, perhaps, is the definition of "American folklife" contained in Public Law 94-201, dated January 2, 1976, the "American Folklife Preservation Act." Quoting selectively:

> the traditional expressive culture shared within the various groups in the United States [including] . . . a wide range of creative and symbolic forms . . . mainly learned orally, by imitation, or in performances, and . . . generally maintained without benefit of formal instruction or institutional direction.

The American Folklife Center, established in the Library of Congress by the above-named Act of Congress, defined the term "folklife" more concisely—after listing many specific examples—in a 1991 publication as "community life and values, artfully expressed in myriad forms and interactions."

The boundaries of the field of folklore laid out in this chapter do not take in all of the various recent uses to which the terms "folk" and "lore" have been put. They do, however, delimit rather broadly the scholarly area that folklorists have staked out for their studies. It bears repeating that this study is one of prime significance for our fuller understanding of human behavior and culture. Certainly the popularization and sometimes banalization of folklore in the United States, the creation of American fakelore, and even utter misapplication of the term "folklore" (i.e., to mean simply "falsehood," as in "that's just folklore!"), also reveal important things about culture and behavior, and these deserve study, too. These are subject matter for which a survey of the major folklore types like the present one is probably a necessary prerequisite.

BIBLIOGRAPHIC NOTES

The Victorian gentleman-scholar W. J. Thoms suggested the term "folklore" in a letter, signed "Ambrose Merton," published in *The Athenaeum* in 1846; see Duncan Emrich, " 'Folk-Lore': William John Thoms," *CFQ* 5 (1946): 355–74. Twenty-one definitions by modern folklorists are gathered in *Funk & Wagnalls Standard Dictionary of Folklore, Mythology, and Legend*, 2 vols. (New York: Funk & Wagnalls, 1949; rev. 1 vol. ed., 1972). The Thoms letter and a discussion of the dictionary definitions are reprinted in Dundes's *The Study of Folklore*, which contains other important articles (including Archer Taylor's, quoted in this chapter) on the problem of defining folklore. Richard M. Dorson introduced the word "fakelore" in an article in *The American Mercury* 70 (March 1950): 335–43, and he furnished the background for his coinage in an article in *Zeitschrift für Volkskunde* 65 (1969): 56–64 (reprinted in *American Folklore and the Historian*, pp. 3–14). Writing "In Defense of Paul Bunyan" in *NYF* 5 (1979): 43–51, Edith Fowke criticized writings (including earlier editions of this textbook) that branded Paul Bunyan a complete fakelore invention, pointing out that there are reliable sources dated before 1910 from at least eight locations proving a Bunyan oral tradition before popularizing began. Fowke likened the early popularizers' works to the printed sheets ("broadsides") that once helped to disseminate ballads. However, this reasonable argument does not obviate the need for the term "fakelore" itself. Alan Dundes reviewed the whole question in an international context in an article discussing "nationalistic inferiority complexes" in *JFR* 22 (1985): 5–18 (quoted in Focus: Fakelore and Nationalism).

"A Forum on the Term 'Folklore' " appeared in *JFR* 33:3 (Sept.–Dec. 1996): 185–264. This special issue usefully reprinted Thoms's 1846 proposal, plus all definitions from the *Funk & Wagnalls Standard Dictionary* along with commentaries by eight modern folklorists.

Bruce Jackson criticized the term "folkloristics" in *JAF* 98 (1985): 95–101, tracing its history and usage. Several responses followed in the pages of *JAF*, including one that showed a Yiddish prototype for the term.

Three addresses by former presidents of the American Folklore Society are important statements on the field of folklore. They are Herbert Halpert's "Folklore: Breadth versus Depth," *JAF* 71 (1958): 97–103; Wayland D. Hand's "American Folklore after Seventy Years: Survey and Prospect," *JAF* 73 (1960): 1–11; and William Bascom's "Folklore, Verbal Art, and Culture," *JAF* 86 (1973): 374–81. Three professional assessments of the state of American folklore studies are Tristram P. Coffin's "Folklore in the American Twentieth Century," *AQ* 13 (1961): 526–33; Francis Lee Utley's "The Academic Status of Folklore in the United States," *JFI* 7 (1970): 110–15; and Richard M. Dorson's "Is Folklore a Discipline?" *Folklore* 84 (1973): 177–205.

The history of American folklore study itself and how it bears on ongoing research was taken up in the special "American Folklore Historiography" issue of *JFI* 10 (June/August 1973): 1–128, which had essays on figures such as William Wells Newell, A. L. Kroeber, George Lyman Kittredge, and Phillips Barry, as well as theoretical and bibliographical articles. Important backgrounds to American folklore studies in the work of their English predecessors are contained in Richard M. Dorson's *The British Folklorists: A History* (Chicago: University of Chicago Press, 1968). Dorson's own work was evaluated in two special issues of folklore journals: *WF* 48 (1989) and *JFR* 26 (1989).

Other individual folklorists' works are evaluated in such studies as Dudley C. Gordon's "Charles F. Lummis: Pioneer American Folklorist," *WF* 28 (1969): 175–81; Rosemary Lévy Zumwalt's *Wealth and Rebellion: Elsie Clews Parsons, Anthropologist and Folklorist* (Urbana: University of Illinois Press, 1992); and Jeanne Patten Whitten's "Fannie Hardy Eckstorm: A Descriptive Bibliography of Her Writings, Published and Unpublished," *NEF* 16 (1975). The title of Angus K. Gillespie's *Folklorist of the Coal Fields: George Korson's Life and Work* (University Park: Pennsylvania State University Press, 1980) speaks for itself, as does Robert Cochran's *Vance Randolph: An Ozark Life* (Urbana: University of Illinois Press, 1985). The special issue of *JFI* (vol. 16, nos. 1–2 [1979]) dedicated to Harry Middleton Hyatt contains a good analysis of the work of the compiler (with his sister Minnie Hyatt Small) of *Folklore from Adams County, Illinois* and other works. Doubtless of great future interest for historians of American folkloristics will be *Roads into Folklore*, no. 14 in the *Folklore Forum* Bibliographic and Special Series (Bloomington, Ind.: 1975), which contains anecdotal accounts of how they got into folklore by forty of Richard M. Dorson's students, with a bonus of one parody entry credited to "Gregor Isomotif."

For statements on the discipline of folklore in the United States made two decades apart by the dean of American folklore scholars see Stith Thompson's "American Folklore after Fifty Years," *JAF* 51 (1938): 1–9, and "Folklore at Midcentury," *MF* 1 (1951): 5–12. Jan Harold Brunvand reviewed Thompson's evaluations in the light of another twenty years' progress in "New Directions for the Study of American Folklore," *Folklore* 82 (1971): 25–35 (repr. in *Readings in American Folklore*, pp. 416–26). A politically oriented critique by John Alexander Williams entitled "Radicalism and Professionalism in Folklore Studies: A Comparative Perspective" was published in *JFI* 11 (1974 [misdated 1975]): 211–34, and answered by Richard M. Dorson in the same journal, pp. 235–39. And a philosophical critique, mainly of American folklore studies, is Kenneth Laine Ketner's "Identity and Existence in the Study of Human Traditions," *Folklore* 87 (1976): 192–200. Invoking Plato, Wittgenstein, and others, Ketner finds so many logical flaws in the assumptions underlying folklore studies that one wonders how the field has managed to survive at all.

In "American Folklore vs. Folklore in America," *JFI* 15 (1978): 97–111, Richard M. Dorson urged scholars to "relate folkstuff to the American historical experience," as he found most earlier studies sadly lacking in this regard. His particular demand for a chronological framework for true "American folklore" studies drew a rebuttal from Stephen Stern and Simon J. Bronner entitled "Comment—American Folklore vs. Folklore in America: A Fixed Fight?" *JFI* 17 (1980): 76–84; Dorson replied in the same journal (pp. 85–89) that such scholars "lock themselves into a parochial present and blind themselves to the buried treasure in America's past." Dorson edited a special double issue of *JFI* (vol. 17, nos. 2–3 [1980]) on "The American Theme in American Folklore," with articles on American outlaws, biography, folklore in literature, folk religion, sports, urban legends, and (inevitably) fakelore.

Alan Dundes presented "The American Concept of Folklore" in *JFI* 3 (1966): 226–45, repr. in *Analytic Essays in Folklore*, pp. 3–16. The same author speaks for many, perhaps most, of his compatriots in his 1977 essay "Who Are the Folk?" (reprinted in *Interpreting Folklore*, pp. 1–19) when he answers "Among others, *we* are!" Taking a comparative approach, Américo Paredes discussed "Concepts about Folklore in Latin America and the United States" in *JFI* 6 (1969): 20–38.

That North American folklorists have widened their traditional view of folklore as oral literature and are embracing the concept of folklore as including folklife —the totality of traditional life—is indicated by the greatly expanded coverage of folklife topics possible in this textbook since its first publication in 1968. The journal *Pioneer America*, devoted to American material-culture studies, spanned about the same period, having started in 1969; the cumulative index for volumes 1 through 10, published in volume 11 (1979), shows a great number and variety of studies in this periodical alone. (In 1984 the title of the journal was changed to *Material Culture*.) Henry Glassie is a prime mover among American material-culture scholars; his general appraisal of the cultural roles of handmade things appears in "Artifacts: Folk, Popular, Imaginary, and Real," published in Marshall Fishwick and Ray B. Browne's *Icons of Popular Culture* (Bowling Green, Ohio: Bowling Green State University Popular Press, 1970), pp. 103–22. Simon Bronner has contributed much to the incorporation of folklife into American folklore studies: see his *Grasping Things: Folk Material Culture and Mass Society in America* (Lexington: University Press of Kentucky, 1986) and "The Fragmentation of American Folklife Studies," *JAF* 103 (1990): 209–14. Twenty chapters by a pioneer American folklife scholar (teacher of both Glassie and Bronner) is Warren Roberts's *Viewpoints on Folklife: Looking at the Overlooked* (Ann Arbor, Mich.: UMI Research Press, 1988). Roberts coined the term "OTWOL," or "Old Traditional Way of Life," for the folklife traditions of a bygone era in the United States.

Theoretical problems in distinguishing folklore types and categories were taken up in a "Symposium on Folk Genres" conducted by Dan Ben-Amos in the journal *Genre* 2 (1969): 1–301; of particular importance is Ben-Amos's own essay there, "Analytical Categories and Ethnic Genres," pp. 275–301. These essays were reprinted in book form as *Folklore Genres*, ed. Dan Ben-Amos, American Folklore Society Bibliographic and Special Series, no. 26 (Austin, Texas: 1976). Alan Dundes identifies "Some Minor Genres of American Folklore" (envelope sealers, evasive answers, feigned apologies, etc.) in *SFQ* 31 (1967): 20–36. A good example of how the social context in which a folkloric item is communicated determines its genre is Ronald L. Baker's note "'Hogs Are Playing with Sticks—Bound to Be Bad Weather': Folk Belief or Proverb?" *MJLF* 1 (1975): 65–67 (repr. in *Readings in American Folklore*, pp. 199–202). Several fine examples of how folklore mutates in an international context are presented in Wolfgang Mieder's *Tradition and Innovation in Folk Literature* (Hanover, N.H.: University Press of New England, 1987).

Richard M. Dorson's 1973 paper "Folklore in the Modern World," reprinted in *Folklore and Fakelore*, pp. 33–73, outlines the traditional and "revised" concepts of what folklore is, putting the emphasis in the "new" definition on the influences of industry and technology, the mass media, nationalism, and the like. In " 'For Want of a Nail': A Synthesis of Metaphorical Definitions," *TFSB* 46 (1980): 1–15, Mariella Hartsfield proves with multiple examples how folklorists have drawn on metaphors of warfare, flowing water, mirrors, fields, games, and especially plants—particularly trees and their wooden products—in conceptualizing the subject matter and methodology of folklore and its study. (For example, this textbook and the accompanying *Reader* originally had a wood-grained dust-jacket design, Dorson's *American Folklore* cover shows a rail fence, Krappe's *The Science of Folklore* [1930] used twiglike lettering, and so forth; the language of folklore definitions is often similarly treelike, or at least plantlike.)

Probably the most influential publication directed to the strong desire to redefine "folklore" along contextual or behavioristic lines is Dan Ben-Amos's "Toward a Definition of Folklore in Context," pp. 3–15, in "Toward New Perspectives in Folklore," ed. Américo Paredes and Richard Bauman, *JAF* 84 (1971): iii–172, and in the American Folklore Society Bibliographic and Special Series, no. 23 (1972). The "new perspectives" question was revisited in an AFS symposium comprising fourteen essays published in *WF* 52 (1993), nos. 2, 3, and 4, edited by Charles Briggs and Amy Shuman. See also Charles E. Warshaver, "On Postmodern Folklore," *WF* 50 (1991): 219–29.

In an earlier attempt to reformulate the concept of folklore, *Folklore Forum* devoted no. 12 in its 1975 Bibliographic and Special Series to fourteen articles on "Conceptual Problems in Contemporary Folklore Study"; the most lucid of these (despite its title) was Gerald Cashion's "Folklore, Kinesiological Folklore, and the Macro-Folklore Complex," pp. 24–35. An equally well-written and clarifying essay is Kay L. Cothran's "Participation in Tradition," *KF* 18 (1973): 7–13 (repr. in *Readings in American Folklore*, pp. 444–48).

The unattributed definitions of "folklore" quoted in this chapter are from the *Standard Dictionary of Folklore* (Potter), *The Study of Folklore* (Dundes), Ben-Amos's article cited above, *The Dynamics of Folklore* (Toelken), and Georges's 1980 article on the text/context controversy cited in the notes to chapter 2.

2

—

THE STUDY OF FOLKLORE

Folklore is fascinating to study because people are fascinating creatures. It is a diversified and complex subject because it reflects the
whole intricate mosaic of the rest of human culture. Folklore is part
of culture, but it seems elusive, flowing along separately from the
mainstream of the major intellectual attainments of humanity. In
traditional lore, however, there are counterparts for literary and representational art, philosophical speculations, scientific inquiries, historical records, social attitudes, and psychological insights. Thus, the
study of folklore is part of the broader study of people and their
works, and as such, folklore research has much in common with
both the humanities and the social sciences.

From the humanistic point of view past folklore research tended
to emphasize the "lore," often taking a literary approach to the recorded "texts" of verbal traditions; from the social-science point of
view folklore research emphasized the "folk," often taking an anthropological (or "functional") approach to the full cultural significance of traditions. Thus, to a humanist, proverbs were "folk
philosophy," riddles were "traditional metaphorical questions," and
folktales were "oral literature," but to an anthropologist these forms
were rather educational tools, social controls, or status markers. Seen
from either viewpoint, the materials of folklore afford the unique

Idaho folklorist Louie Attebery interviews Jim Bentz of Drewsey, Oregon, in 1976. Bentz shows with his fingers how narrow a strip of rawhide should be for the reata he is making.

opportunity of studying what exists and persists in culture largely without the support of established learning, religion, government, and other formal institutions. Folklore represents what people preserve in their culture through the generations by custom and word of mouth when few other means exist to preserve it. The discovery of the historical depth and the geographical breadth of some of these traditional "survivals" (as they were once called) is what first gave the study of folklore much of its fascination.

Nowadays, there is much more interest than previously in the present functions and meanings of folk traditions; thus, the literary and anthropological approaches to folklore study have merged as a new "folkloristic" study develops. A statement from an AFS symposium of 1992 on "the culture of politics" (or "the politics of culture"), reflecting the influence of "cultural studies" on folkloristics, described folklore as "a discipline concerned with the study of traditional, vernacular, and local cultural productions [including] the ways in which traditionalizing (identifying aspects of the past as significant in the present) [is] a dynamic cultural process." Most significantly, the same statement challenged "the authority of any nation, group, gender, or class to represent the experience of an-Other." In other words, who really has the right to define and study the folklore of somebody else?

What humanists and social scientists share when they study folklore is an interest in finding out how, why, and which traditional cultural mentifacts, sociofacts, and artifacts develop, vary, and are passed on. From observations and records of these materials folklorists hope to reconstruct something of the unrecorded intellectual life of people of the past and present. The findings of such folklore research are applicable to many fields. Some literary scholars are interested, for instance, in the folk roots of epic and other narrative poetry and in the stylistic or thematic use of folklore in literature. Students of the fine arts may similarly consider the background of their subjects in folk music and folk art. Historians find that oral traditions, although seldom factually accurate in all details, furnish insights into grassroots attitudes toward historical events. Psychologists have long held that folklore, in common with dreams and other manifestations of fantasy, contains clues to the subconscious. Sociologists may study folklore (especially protest lore) along with other data on group life and behavior. While some applications of folklore study to other fields (such as the natural sciences) are still in an early stage, other and new applications (such as studying the efficacy of folk medicine) are also emerging. In fact, probably every field of study involving people and their works will in some way eventually make use of evidence from folklore as folklorists continue to refine and publicize their work. And the unified (or holistic) approach of recent folklore research holds even more promise for the application of findings to other fields.

SOME FUNDAMENTAL QUESTIONS

Modern folklore study embraces oral, customary, and material aspects of tradition equally, and it makes eclectic use of theoretical and methodological approaches from anthropology, linguistics, communications, psychology, and other relevant areas. While several distinct theoretical approaches and schools of thought have developed within folklore studies, most folklore research may still be thought of as an attempt to answer certain fundamental questions:

Definition (what folklore is)
Classification (what the genres of folklore are)
Source (who "the folk" are)
Origin (who composed folklore)
Transmission (how folklore is carried, how fast, and how far)
Variation (how folklore changes and for what reasons)
Structure (what the underlying form of folklore is and the relation
    of form to content)
Function (what folklore means to its carriers and how it serves them)
Purpose and *meaning* (what the performer intends to convey and the
    intended effect; what folklore may symbolize or otherwise represent in a metaphorical way)
Use and *application* (what should be done with folklore and in what
    other areas of study it is useful).

Ideally, no folk product or performance would be considered fully understood until answers had at least been suggested for all such questions. In practice, however, because past folklorists have tended to be specialists in one genre or region or technique, studies seldom considered more than one or two of these matters at a time, and very few aspects of folklore have been subjected to more comprehensive research. The assumption that underlies all research in folklore is that, since nothing in culture is meaningless or random, folklore—as a part of culture—inevitably has some function or meaning for those who create it and transmit it. Often the key to unlocking the meanings of folklore is the identification of habits of thought or formal patterns that both the items and the performances of folklore display.

The linguist Allen Walker Read described the process of studying folklore concisely, in an essay on graffiti as a field for research: "[The

folklorist] can take unpromising, trivial details,* organize them into
an orderly body of material, and from them derive significant findings in the interpretation of human life." This statement introduces
the three typical stages of folklore research that give us a convenient
framework to survey this scholarship—*collection, classification, and
analysis.*

COLLECTING FOLKLORE

The raw materials of oral folklore research are texts (or "records of
mentifacts"). It is axiomatic that these texts must be collected verbatim from oral sources; editorial additions to or "improvements"
in the texts have no part in honest research. Most folklorists today
seek out promising informants and use tape or video recorders to
collect the exact words of the informants, practicing a variety of
interview techniques to achieve a relaxed atmosphere and a natural
response. Not only the most skilled "active" informants are sought,
but also the relatively "passive" informants who may remember interesting lore, although they impart it only in garbled or fragmentary
form. Often collectors will make several visits to their best informants, sometimes over a long span of time, recording familiar material
and asking for new items.

Besides verbatim texts, folklorists record data about the informants themselves (age, occupation, national origin, etc.) and gather
background on the families and communities of the informants. An
informant's gestures and facial expressions should be described as an
integral part of the performance, and these aspects of style (or "texture") may be captured with candid photographs, movie films, or
videotapes.

*In "On the Future of American Folklore Studies: A Response," *WF* 50 (1991): 75–81,
Elliott Oring considered the "trivial" nature of folklore data: "the public's perception that
folklore deals with 'trivialities' is in some measure legitimate, because triviality is one of
the few conceptual categories capable of encompassing the miscellany that passes for folkloristic inquiry. . . . As folklorists, we have the license to study virtually anything we want
from whatever perspective we deem worthwhile. This is the outstanding benefit conferred
by liminality [i.e., marginality of folklore as a discipline]."

FOCUS: COLLECTING FOLKLORE

Today most folklorists are so accustomed to using portable tape recorders that they regard it as unbelievable that in my first few years of fieldwork I should have collected dozens of interviews and brief life histories, as well as hundreds of song texts and tales, by writing them down from dictation. In those days I not only could write very rapidly, but I also had developed one helpful trick. It was, of course, extremely rare to find a singer who could recite a song text that he or she was used to singing. In collecting a song text, I would sing back to the singer the last words I had written down; with such a cue, most could continue singing from that point. I adapted a version of this device in writing down interviews and tales. I would repeat aloud the last few phrases I had written, imitating as closely as possible the informant's tone in saying them. Most could then complete the thought and go on from there.

Source: Herbert Halpert, "Coming Into Folklore More Than Fifty Years Ago," *JAF* 105 (1992): 453.

Herbert Halpert transcribing a narrative from James L. Conklin in the Western Catskill Mountains, New York, 1946.

DISCUSSION TOPICS:

1. What are some disadvantages of Halpert's method of cuing informants?

2. How did Halpert try to minimize one potential bad effect of such cuing?

3. Compare Halpert's method of collecting with those of Randolph and Lomax described later in this chapter.

4. Compare a fieldwork method sometimes used among the Utah Mormons by Austin and Alta Fife: Austin would interview an informant while Alta took down the conversation in shorthand.

The texts and texture of folklore always exist in a specific context, and this, too, needs to be carefully documented. Field-workers must note the setting for the performance (time, place, and situation), the participants and their responses to the performer, and the "frame" for the folk event (what preceded and followed the performance of folklore). The context may be natural—just something that happened in a traditional way—or it may be induced by the collector, who sets up a more or less artificial situation of "collecting folklore." Probably the closer collectors are to blending in with the folk as participant-observers themselves, the better and less self-conscious the performances will be. Contexts may be summarized in general terms ("Where do you usually tell this kind of story?" etc.) or may be described from immediate observation ("How the children played jump rope this afternoon"). In the most penetrating studies, informants may be asked to discuss or interpret their texts (providing "oral-literary" criticism), and experiments using "planted" folk materials have been attempted with some informants and their audiences. Another kind of data to collect, suggested by folklorist Alan Dundes, is "metafolklore" (folklore about folklore; e.g., proverbs about proverbs, or a folktale about a traditional prank).

FOCUS: METAFOLKLORE

For good Ole and Lena stories, one goes to Norwegian communities in the Dakotas or Minnesota, where a promise of "a new joke" is understood to mean a new Ole and Lena story.

Metafolklore is folklore about folklore; in this example, we have an Ole and Lena story about Ole and Lena stories:

Ole likes to tell them Ole and Lena stories but now and then he offends some of his Norwegian countrymen. One day the Lutheran preacher takes Ole aside and tells him he should be a little more diplomatic about them stories and maybe even do what the preacher does. Whenever he wants to use a Norwegian story or a Polack or Bohunk joke, he changes the name of the group over to some ancient biblical people like the Hittites, so's he can avoid any problem of offending someone. Ole thanks him for the advice and promises to use the idea the next time a chance comes up, and sure enough, that night in the town tavern, the boys get to telling stories, and so when Ole's turn comes around he remembers what the preacher told him and he starts off, "Okay, there was these two Hittites . . . named Ole and Lena, and they was going to Fargo one day . . ."

Source: Roger L. Welsch's "Science Lite" column in *Natural History*, February 1993, p. 22, headlined "Of Light Bulbs and Shaggy Dogs: Is laughter a universal language?"

DISCUSSION TOPICS:

1. Alan Dundes coined "metafolklore" on the analogy of the word "metalanguage." What do you think "metalanguage" means?

2. Find other examples of metafolklore.

3. Collect other joke cycles in which two stereotyped characters have set names.

4. Explain the terms "Polack" and "Bohunk." Do you know other similar terms?

5. Why does Welsch write his paraphrase in ungrammatical English ("them stories," "so's he can," "he starts off," etc.; note also the spelling "lite" in the column's title)?

Questionnaires have long been successfully used for folklore collecting in Europe, generally with trained semiprofessional fieldworkers asking the questions of residents in their own region. Mailed questionnaires allow researchers to cover a wider area than they might conveniently visit in person, but this technique also limits the inquiry to a specific subject and eliminates the free association that is often the most productive part of direct collecting. Only a few studies of American folklore have made use of questionnaires, but they seem to hold promise, particularly for accurate distributional and variation studies of folk speech, customs, and artifacts.

Folklore texts or descriptions of customs and artifacts may sometimes be collected from handwritten sources, such as diaries, letters, and notebooks, or from printed matter, such as books, magazines, and newspapers. For instance, many colonial "divine providences" collected and printed by Puritan writers were probably old popular beliefs and superstitions; some Civil War folksongs survived in soldiers' writings, and American regional newspapers in the nineteenth century preserved much traditional native humor that has not been fully explored. Current popular periodicals also occasionally print items of folklore that have been reported either as rumors or as actual events. (See "Urban Legends" in chapter 9.)

A beginning folklore collector can learn much about field problems and techniques by reading accounts of fieldwork by veteran collectors. For example, the works of Richard M. Dorson, one of the most active and successful American collectors, are rich in anecdotes and suggestions. In his *Negro Folktales in Michigan* (Cambridge, Mass.: 1956) two prefatory chapters analyze the communities and informants visited and include several photographs of narrators in action. In one case, the leather patches on Dorson's jacket sleeves convinced an informant that Dorson was really a "writer feller" and not, as some others in the town thought, an FBI agent.

In *Bloodstoppers and Bearwalkers* (Cambridge, Mass.: Harvard University Press, 1952) Dorson described how he pieced together the Upper Peninsula legend of "The Lynching of the McDonald Boys" from numerous incomplete reports and offhand allusions. "Old-timers have spun the grisly yarn . . . to pop-eyed youngsters for more than sixty years . . . [but] no two granddads tell quite the same story, for this is strictly a family tradition, never frozen in print, and unceasingly distorted with the vagaries that grow from hearsay and surmise." Turning to a completely different subject near the end of his life—the urban center as a field for folklore collecting—Dorson described his techniques for "doing fieldwork in the city." He located informants by haunting the same hangouts as his sources and by following the leads of people he called "bridge contacts," who introduced him to good performers. With his equipment always at the ready, Dorson tape-recorded numerous everyday conversations, life histories, and personal experiences; he supplemented these sound records by keeping a daily field diary in which he recorded "ethnographic observations of the urban scene." The results of his fieldwork appeared in the book *Land of the Millrats* (Cambridge, Mass.: Harvard University Press, 1981).

The Ozark collector Vance Randolph was as industrious and successful in the field as Dorson, but more casual in his approach; he generally included in his books a prefatory note something like the following from his collection of Ozark jokes, *Hot Springs and Hell* (Hatboro, Pa.: Folklore Associates, 1965):

> Some of these items were recorded on aluminum discs, but most of them were set down in longhand and typed a few hours later while the details were still fresh in my mind. They are not verbatim transcripts, but every one of them is pretty close to the mark. They are not literary adaptations. I did not add any characters or incidents, or try to improve the narrator's style. I did not combine different versions, or use material from more than one informant in the same tale. Many backwoods jokes are nonverbal anyhow, and some folk humor is too subtle for print, just as certain folk tunes cannot be compassed by the conventional notation. I just set down each item as accurately as I could and let it go at that.

Unorthodox collecting methods sometimes yield good results when conventional approaches fail. Some folklorists, for instance, have tried rocking an empty rocking chair, opening an umbrella in the house, or violating some other superstitious taboo in order to elicit a response about bad luck. Others have had success singing a song or telling a tale in garbled form so that intended informants will correct them. Kenneth S. Goldstein once devised a field experiment that led two Scottish women unself-consciously to tell their versions of a previously tape-recorded family legend in the presence of the other. He later asked them to retell the legend on the pretense that he had accidentally erased the tape. He discovered that each storyteller had somewhat modified her own telling, influenced by what she had heard from the other narrator. An excellent collection of Norwegian tall tales was made by a paint company through a contest advertised in popular periodicals. Similarly, I found a rich stock of shaggy-dog stories that had been collected by a network radio program devoted to answering listeners' questions. A student based a fascinating term project on the following topic, presented with teachers' cooperation to several classes of elementary-school children: "Write down your favorite jump-rope rhyme and tell why you like it." (Some specific hints on tape-recorder technique are in-

cluded in chapter 13, and on collecting with camera or sketch pad
in chapter 19.)

Whatever the collecting methods employed, and however ingenious or well prepared the collector may be, persistence and a willingness to adapt to the informants' habits and moods will pay off
in the long run. The following quotation from John A. Lomax's
autobiographical *Adventures of a Ballad Hunter* (New York: 1947) is
illustrative:

> It was cowboy songs I most wished. . . . These I jotted down on a
> table in a saloon back room, scrawled on an envelope while squatting
> about a campfire near a chuck wagon, or caught behind the scenes
> of a broncho-busting outfit or rodeo. To capture the cowboy music
> proved an almost impossible task. The cowboys would simply wave
> away the large horn I carried and refused to sing into it! Not one
> song did I ever get from them except through the influence of gen-
> erous amounts of whiskey, raw and straight from the bottle or
> jug.

An important, but sometimes neglected, aspect of folklore fieldwork is the ethical dimension—the responsibilities and liabilities of
a folklorist with regard to informants and their material, especially
when embarrassing, antisocial, or illegal material is involved. Unless
clear legal limits of access to and liability for collected information
are established, the folklorist would do well to code his or her
sources or to give pseudonyms to the human sources of such lore—
for example, that concerning drug use, moonshining, telephone or
machine fraud, tax evasion, and the like. But even less criminal
subjects may raise ethical questions, such as whether informants
should be compensated for their cooperation, by whom collected
material may be used and for what purposes, and whether published
material should be specifically credited to informants. It is never a
good idea to record folklore surreptitiously unless the informants are
advised of the act later and allowed to review the material, and
archives should always insist upon some kind of informants' and
collectors' release forms accompanying any filed material and clearly
outlining any conditions to be imposed on it.

CLASSIFYING FOLKLORE

Collected folklore texts, descriptions of customs, or artifacts are of little use to a scholar until identified by category and arranged systematically in an archive (or museum) or published. Classification of the myriad forms of folklore facilitates their study just as classification systems do for the natural sciences: without standardized terminology and arrangement, we could not communicate effectively or gather data from archives and published collections. The difficulty (as pointed out in chapter 1) is that ethnic or "native" categories for folk materials differ a great deal from culture to culture or even from person to person. The more abstract "analytical" categories devised by scholars have not always yielded mutually exclusive systems, nor have they won universal scholarly acceptance. Any classification, it should be borne in mind, is always for a purpose; and, for the purpose of organizing data for analysis, certain traditional categories have become established in the voluminous reference works for motifs, tales, ballads, superstitions, riddles, proverbs, and other forms. These classification systems, whatever their shortcomings, have yet to be superseded; they structure the balance of this book and are cited in the appropriate bibliographic notes.

Folklore materials are usually arranged by genre and subgenre within a regional or folk-group framework in the published or archived collections. Thus, the proverbs of Illinois might be divided into full sentences ("true proverbs") versus phrases ("proverbial phrases and comparisons") and then listed alphabetically by the first noun or other significant word if there is no noun (see chapter 5). Superstitions collected from fishermen might be divided as "signs or magic" and then subdivided into such categories as "equipment," "good luck," "winds and weather," and "taboos" (see chapter 14). Such systems of organization are useful for bringing like materials together, and with proper cross-references other groupings are possible. But for the needs of analysis or interpretation the folklorist may wish to sort the data by other criteria, using headings such as recreational traditions (games, dances, and so forth), educational lore (instructive stories, songs, or sayings), practical skills (crafts, cooking, and the like), and artistic creations (folk arts, crafts, music, etc.). The

Robert Winslow Gordon, first archivist (appointed 1928) of the Archive of American Folk Song at the Library of Congress. He is shown here, about 1930, with wax-cylinder recordings and archive recording equipment.

specific manner of classifying a folklore collection depends mainly on the interests and needs of researchers, which, when we start using publications and archives, usually means simply being able to find what we need to carry the research further. However, it is also important to consider how the informants themselves view the categories of their own lore.

Since much American folklore has been collected by university folklorists or by their students, the largest folklore archives in this country are on campuses. Although there is no national folklore archive in the United States, nor even a uniform archiving system in use, individual archivists can still consult the standard reference works to arrange and annotate their materials. Folklore journals and other publications rely on the same indexes. Most archivists and editors also make some attempt to cross-index materials by informants, by region, or by ethnic background, and sometimes even by collector. But since no one can anticipate all the possible research needs future users of an archive may have, the chief frustration of archivists is probably locating among their varied holdings all the materials potentially useful for a particular project. Some archives have tried to increase their flexibility and usefulness by publishing catalogs of their holdings or by computerizing materials. To their tasks of acquisition, cataloging, storage, and retrieval, folk museums must add the challenges of display and interpretation for the public, needs that few folklore archives even attempt to meet.

ANALYZING: COMPARATIVE STUDY

In the past it was assumed that only when folklore had been collected in some quantity, classified in considerable detail, and made generally available to scholars could any significant analysis take place. In general, for historical and transmission studies, this still holds true. The oldest, and still perhaps the most common, technique of folklore analysis is comparison, usually comparing different versions of the same item. This approach requires many recorded examples arranged in workable categories by type. The most elaborated form of this kind of research, the **historic-geographic method** (or "Finnish method"), introduced into American folklore study by Archer Taylor and Stith Thompson, is described in chapter 10 as it applies to folktale analysis.

Another avenue of comparative research followed by some American folklorists is to bring their viewpoint to bear on other closely related scholarly fields. For example, such material traditions in the United States as homemade cabins, houses, and barns have been investigated for some time by American folklorists and cultural geographers, the former concerning themselves mainly with the survival and variation of traditional patterns, and the latter with regional distribution and the explanations for it. To some degree, architectural historians have also been involved, fitting "vernacular" styles in with the sequence of high or academic design. Henry Glassie, an eclectic American folklorist (see chapter 20), has acquaintance with all three fields, plus solid field experience. He attempts to frame a unified explanation for certain kinds of traditional buildings, adding to this his **cross-cultural comparisons** to prototypical building types found in Europe.

Even a beginning student not specializing in folklore might, for example, comparatively study common attitudes toward geography as found in folk speech, proverbs, place-names, legends, tall tales, jokes, folksongs, or other genres. A student trying this project might consider the cartographic suggestions of such expressions as "up North" and "down South," the historical suggestions of "out West," and the difference between "back East" and "down East"; then the student might assemble variant folk sayings referring to geographic features—"to be sold down the river" as opposed to "to cross that river when we come to it"; and "as old as the hills" versus "over the hill." Such an approach could be revealing of regional culture in relation to physical geography. Other geographic lore would seem to derive from old schoolroom drills. One orally collected song, for instance, describes numerous geographic features of oceans and shorelines, always returning in the refrain to "Green Little Islands." Another song, collected in the Ozarks, names and accurately characterizes thirteen Texas rivers and streams. Probably from the schoolroom come several variants of a sentence for remembering how to spell the word "geography" itself: "George Elliot's old grandmother rode a pig home yesterday." Similar comparative research projects could be done with folklore references to such fields as journalism, law, business, or politics.

ANALYZING: SOME MAJOR SCHOOLS

While students' own research in folklore may be limited by time or availability of published references, the folklore student should at least become aware of the range and diversity of recent scholarship as it extends far beyond collection, classification, and comparative analysis. For a guide to some major scholarly trends as they have affected the study of American folklore, see the notes to this chapter. The following summary descriptions of schools of folklore analysis refer to some specific parts of this book in which theory and method are demonstrated in concise practical applications, but to understand folklore theory well there is no substitute for reading the published works of analysis themselves.

A **literary or esthetic approach** to folklore, typical of humanists, may take the form either of analyzing the poetics of oral style or of charting the influence of folk traditions upon works of literature and the fine arts. A taste of the first application is provided in chapters 11 ("Folksongs") and 12 ("Ballads"), where art songs are distinguished from popular songs and folksongs. The second application of an esthetic approach is best represented in longer studies (such as the essays and books on folklore in American literature mentioned in the notes). The broader relation of American folklore to American studies and cultural history, what Richard Dorson called the **hemispheric approach,** is demonstrated in this book in connection with local and historical legends in chapter 9. Also see the discussions of historic American folk costumes and foods in chapters 22 and 23.

The **functional or anthropological approach** to American folklore, typical of scholars with a background in the social sciences, examines the roles of folklore in culture in order to determine meanings and functions. Building upon earlier **anthropological approaches,** most folklorists agree that "folklore" exists not just as a fixed set of abstract genres, verbal or otherwise, but as traditional patterns of thought and behavior manifested in various ways during acts of communication between people. This constitutes an approach, variously called **contextual, behavioral, rhetorical,** or **performance-oriented.** The works of several champions of this theoretical orientation are listed in the notes.

The **psychological approach** to interpreting meanings in folklore, often Freudian or Jungian in orientation, has been advocated by David Hufford and Alan Dundes, among others. Here either the habits of mind underlying folk belief are investigated (see chapter 14, "Superstitions"), or the symbolic and metaphorical patterns in folk traditions are decoded (as with urban legends in chapter 9). What Dorson called an **ideological approach** to the symbolic interpretation of folklore (Marxist, capitalist, Christian, etc.) so far has not had many adherents in American folklore, but this may be changing.

Another interpretive method advocated by Alan Dundes is the **formal** or **structural** one. Linguistic structuralism (the analysis of grammar according to patterns of speech) flowered into several approaches toward a true folkloristic structuralism based on the patterns in folklore, rather than those in language itself. This is touched on in chapter 5, with a simple fixed-phrase oral form (proverbs), and in chapter 10, with more complex oral narratives (folktales). Another brand of formal text analysis—the **oral-formulaic theory**—was developed by Harvard University folklorists Milman Parry and Albert B. Lord. Although the "Parry-Lord" system of analyzing thematic formulas and rhythmic patterns was created for the study of Balkan epic songs, it has also been applied to Anglo-American ballads (see notes to chapter 12) and to American folk sermons (see Bruce Rosenberg's work mentioned in the notes to this chapter).

Besides these long-established theories and methodologies of folklore research a number of approaches are evolving in American folkloristics. A specific **mass-cultural school**, for instance, may develop out of the work of several American folklorists studying interrelations of oral and customary traditions with the mass media and advertising. The particular interests and scholarly styles of specialists in material culture (those with a **folk-cultural approach**) are yielding a coherent body of research with distinctive goals and techniques. What was once called **applied folklore**—the viewpoint that folklore study can make specific contributions to knowledge and progress in other fields—has evolved into **public-sector folklore**, more commonly called just **public folklore** work, often focusing on the presentation of folk performances to a wider audience. One of the most vigorous new directions in American folkloristics is **feminist folkloristics**—a special approach both to aspects of women's folklore as such and to the production of scholarship countering the male biases evident in many earlier studies.

FOCUS: FEMINIST FOLKLORISTICS

There was much discussion at the 1985 American Folklore Society meetings about authenticity as a Eurocentric category imposed upon indigenous production, but in none of the panels I attended was it mentioned that this was a masculine script. Authenticity, I suggest, like the emphasis on tradition and repertoire and the endless pursuit of origins in folklore studies, is probably a displacement of patrilineal anxiety. Pater semper incertus est. And that reminds me of a story: While superintending Pueblo pottery revivals, Kenneth Chapman of the Museum of New Mexico insisted that Maria Martinez authenticate and increase the value of her pottery by signing it—something that Pueblo potters had never done. When the other potters in the village realized that pots with Maria's signature commanded higher prices, they asked her to sign their pots as

*well and she freely did so until the Santa Fe authorities realized what
was happening and put an end to this semiotic riot.*

Source: Barbara A. Babcock, "Taking Liberties, Writing From the Margins, and
Doing It With a Difference," *JAF* 100 (1987): 394–95.

DISCUSSION TOPICS:

1. Translate the short sentence written in Latin, and explain the
words "Eurocentric," "authenticate," and "semiotic."

2. Is Babcock's illustrative story *folklore?* If so, is it also
metafolklore?

3. What are some implications of this story for her general point
about authenticity as a "masculine script"?

4. For other discussion topics, consult the special issue of *JAF* titled
"Folklore and Feminism," in which this quotation appears in the
introduction.

The study of American folklore, either in its own boundaries or
as applied to outside subjects, is still a relatively young and flexible
academic discipline. Almost every new folklore journal or conference
suggests some new approaches or theories for future research, and
even the categories of folklore themselves are being continually expanded. The history of American folklore studies has only recently
been written, and the dimensions of such fields as urban folklore,
obscene folklore, and women's folklore have only been sketched out.
The appointment of several "state folklorists" holds great promise
for future regional research, just as the passage of the American
Folklife Preservation Act in 1976 (creating the American Folklife
Center in the Library of Congress) did for national study. To keep
abreast of such developments, the reader should follow current
publications and use the bibliographic tools listed following the chapters in this book.

BIBLIOGRAPHIC NOTES

Two books that trace the history of American folkloristics are Simon J. Bronner's
American Folklore Studies: An Intellectual History (Lawrence: University Press of
Kansas, 1986) and Rosemary Lévy Zumwalt, *American Folklore Scholarship: A Di-
alogue of Dissent* (Bloomington: Indiana University Press, 1988). See also Alan

Jabbour, "On the Values of American Folklorists," *JAF* 102 (1989): 292–98; and Robert A. Georges, ed., "Taking Stock: Current Problems and Future Prospects in American Folklore Studies," a special issue of *WF* 50 (1991): 1–126.

Richard M. Dorson surveyed "Current Folklore Theories" in *CA* 4 (1963): 93–112. His essay was updated and expanded as the introduction to the excellent general textbook *Folklore and Folklife: An Introduction* (Chicago: University of Chicago Press, 1972), which contains specialized chapters by folklorists mostly associated in one way or another with the graduate program at Indiana University. The collections of essays listed in the front of the present book and in its preface contain many useful discussions of folklore genres, theories, methodology, interpretation, and more. An idiosyncratic but intriguing approach is taken by Munro S. Edmonson in *Lore: An Introduction to the Science of Folklore and Literature* (New York: Holt, Rinehart and Winston, 1971); the author identifies his subject as "connotative semantics and analogic systems of thought" and he pursues it widely through world literature and oral tradition.

Archer Taylor outlined "The Problems of Folklore" in *JAF* 59 (1946): 101–7. Louise Pound's thorough survey, "The Scholarly Study of Folklore," *WF* 11 (1952): 100–8, was reprinted in *Nebraska Folklore*, pp. 222–33. Stanley Edgar Hyman defined the questions of origin, structure, and function in folklore studies and criticized some popularized anthologies in "Some Bankrupt Treasuries," *KR* 10 (1948): 484–500. Other general discussions of approaches to folklore are reprinted in Dundes's *The Study of Folklore*.

Techniques of collecting folklore are expertly treated in the introduction to Richard M. Dorson's *Buying the Wind* (Chicago: University of Chicago Press, 1964). Rosalie H. Wax's *Doing Fieldwork: Warnings and Advice* (Chicago: University of Chicago Press, 1971), although written for anthropologists, offers good examples and advice for folklorists as well. Kenneth S. Goldstein's manual *A Guide for Field Workers in Folklore* was published by the American Folklore Society (Philadelphia: Memoirs of AFS, vol. 52, 1964). An important supplement to Goldstein's book is *People Studying People: The Human Element in Fieldwork*, by Robert A. Georges and Michael O. Jones (Berkeley and Los Angeles: University of California Press, 1980). Several regional fieldwork guides have been published, but they may be considered effectively replaced by Bruce Jackson's comprehensive book *Fieldwork* (Urbana: University of Illinois Press, 1987).

Edward D. Ives's *The Tape-recorded Interview: A Manual for Field Workers in Folklore and Oral History* (Knoxville: University of Tennessee Press, 1980) is an expansion of a widely used work originally published in 1964 mainly for folklorists working in the Northeast. Considering its purpose—to dispense technical information and helpful advice to inexperienced field-workers using tape recorders—this book is surprisingly engaging and encouraging. It covers basic information, often overlooked in other manuals, such as how a tape recorder works, how to interview people with a tape recorder, and the "processing" of the collected material (transcription, archiving, analysis, etc.) after field research is finished.

The field experiences of two folksong collectors are preserved in W. Roy Mackenzie's *The Quest of the Ballad* (Princeton: Princeton University Press, 1919) and

John A. Lomax's *Adventures of a Ballad Hunter* (New York: Macmillan, 1947). Lomax's work is reconsidered in Jerrold Hirsch's "Modernity, Nostalgia, and Southern Folklore Studies . . ." *JAF* 105 (1992): 183–207; Nolan Porterfield's *Last Cavalier: The Life and Times of John A. Lomax* (Urbana: University of Illinois Press, 1996) is a detailed biography. The results of many years of devoted collecting in the Ozarks are gathered in the numerous books edited by Vance Randolph, in the prefaces and notes to which are many insightful comments on the art of unobtrusive collecting. Experiences collecting urban folklore are presented in two works based on the same project: "Folklorists in the City: The Urban Field Experience," ed. Inta Gale Carpenter, a special issue of *FF* (vol. 11, no. 3 [1978]), which contains eight articles by members of "The Gary [Indiana] Gang" of fieldworkers; and Richard M. Dorson's "Doing Fieldwork in the City," *Folklore* 92 (1981): 149–54.

Gender-related issues in folklore fieldwork are discussed in a special issue of *SF* (vol. 47, no. 1 [1990]), "Folklore Fieldwork: Sex, Sexuality, and Gender." Other aspects of field success and of interpretive approaches to collected material are found in Susan L. Scheiberg's "A Folklorist in the Family: On the Process of Fieldwork Among Intimates," *WF* 49 (1990): 208–14; and Elaine J. Lawless's " 'I was afraid someone like you . . . an outsider . . . would misunderstand': Negotiating Interpretive Differences Between Ethnographer and Subjects," *JAF* 105 (1992): 302–14.

My own manual for folklore researchers, *Folklore: A Study and Research Guide* (New York: St. Martins, 1976), is directed more to the library than to fieldwork. It contains selected bibliography; a history and survey of folkloristics; directions for taking notes, outlining, and actually writing a research paper (precomputer, however!); and a sample folklore paper written by an undergraduate student. Her subject was folk narratives from a southern Utah town.

The chief example of a comprehensive American regional collection, fully classified and annotated, is the seven-volume *The Frank C. Brown Collection of North Carolina Folklore*, edited by a committee of specialists (Durham, N.C.: Duke University Press, 1952–64). Analyses of folklore in a specific regional tradition are found in such books as Emelyn E. Gardner's *Folklore from the Schoharie Hills* (Ann Arbor: University of Michigan Press, 1937) and Richard M. Dorson's *Negro Folktales in Michigan* (Cambridge, Mass.: Harvard University Press, 1956). The last, for instance, contains not only the verbatim texts, classified and fully identified with background data, but also chapters on "The Communities and the Storytellers" and "The Art of Negro Storytelling" as well as four pages of photographs.

From 1958 to 1968, *The Folklore and Folk Music Archivist*, published by Indiana University, provided a quarterly forum for articles on collecting, documenting, indexing, and cataloging folklore. The editor, George List, published "A Statement on Archiving" in *JFI* 6 (1969): 222–31. A finding list, *Folklore Archives of the World*, ed. Peter Aceves and Magnus Einarsson-Mullarký, constituted the first number of the *Folklore Forum* Bibliographic and Special Series (Bloomington: 1968). One model for catalogs of folklore archival holdings is Florence Ireland's "The Northeast Archives of Folklore and Oral History," *NEF* 13 (1972). Important legal questions were raised in an American Folklore Society symposium of 1971, published as "Folklore Archives: Ethics and the Law," *FF* 6 (1973): 197–210. Directions for modernizing archival techniques are discussed by Robert A. Georges, Beth Blumenreich, and Kathie O'Reilly in "Two Mechanical Indexing Systems for Folklore Archives: A Preliminary Report," *JAF* 87 (1974): 39–52. Problems of computerizing folklore data are regularly discussed by folklorists at conferences or on the Internet, but no single acceptable and widely used system has yet emerged.

A necessary skill of the folklorist—identifying folklore lodged in print—is demonstrated in George G. Carey's "Folklore from the Printed Sources of Essex County, Massachusetts," *SFQ* 32 (1968): 17–43. An important methodological essay on studying folklore in literature is Alan Dundes's "The Study of Folklore in Literature and Culture: Identification and Interpretation," *JAF* 78 (1965): 136–42, repr. in *Analytic Essays in Folklore*, pp. 28–34. MacEdward Leach surveyed "Folklore in American Regional Literature" in *JFI* 3 (1966): 376–97; but Roger D. Abrahams found the "lore-in-literature" approach insufficient and proposed other kinds of analysis in "Folklore and Literature as Performance," *JFI* 9 (1972): 75–94. Essays on folklore in individual American authors abound in the journals; a book-length study admirable for its sound approach and full details is Ronald L. Baker's *Folklore in the Writings of Rowland E. Robinson* (Bowling Green, Ohio: Bowling Green State University Popular Press, 1973). Attempts at a wider synthesis are Daniel Hoffman's *Form and Fable in American Fiction* (New York: Oxford University Press, 1961; Norton paperback ed., 1973), Gene Bluestein's *The Voice of the Folk: Folklore and American Literary Theory* (Amherst: University of Massachusetts Press, 1972), and Bruce A. Rosenberg's *Folklore and Literature: Rival Siblings* (Knoxville: University of Tennessee Press, 1991). As background for this whole subject, students should read William A. Wilson's essay "The Deeper Necessity: Folklore and the Humanities," *JAF* 101 (1988): 156–67.

Richard M. Dorson suggested projects involving "Folklore and Cultural History" in *Research Opportunities in American Cultural History*, ed. John Francis McDermott (Lexington: University of Kentucky Press, 1961), pp. 102–23. An important theoretical discussion of folklore and history, citing mostly African examples, is Jan Vansina, *Oral Tradition*, trans. H. M. Wright (Chicago: Aldine, 1965). Articles on folklore and history appeared in *JFI* 1 (1964). Richard M. Dorson collected a dozen of his essays from journals in *American Folklore and the Historian*, including the important "A Theory for American Folklore" from 1959 and his thoughts on the "Theory . . . Reviewed" from 1969, both originally published in *JAF*. William A. Wilson takes a Western perspective in "Folklore and History: Fact amid the Legends," *UHQ* 41 (1973): 40–58, repr. in *Readings in American Folklore*, pp. 449–66. Two exemplary books on the subject are William Lynwood Montell's *The Saga of Coe Ridge: A Study in Oral History* (Knoxville: University of Tennessee Press, 1970) and Gladys-Marie Fry's *Night Riders in Black Folk History* from the same publisher (1975).

An important handbook for American folklore/history studies was published in 1981: Barbara Allen and William Lynwood Montell's *From Memory to History:*

Using Oral Sources in Local Historical Research (Nashville, Tenn.: American Association for State and Local History). See also Montell's book *Don't Go up Kettle Creek: Verbal Legacy of the Upper Cumberland* (Knoxville: University of Tennessee Press, 1983). In the field of family-folklore research, Margaret R. Yocom's "Family Folklore and Oral History Interviews," *WF* 41 (1982): 251–74, gives excellent guidance and advice.

A bibliographic survey on "American Folklore and American Studies" by Richard Bauman, Roger Abrahams, and Susan Kalčik, in *AQ* 28 (1976): 360–77, has a historical framework and strives to "delineate the conceptual organizing principles of the field" rather than simply listing major sources. Consequently, this is a useful introduction to the subject as well as a guide to published sources. For connections between "Folklore and Communications," see a special issue of that title edited by Elizabeth C. Fine: *SF* 49 (1992): 1–72. José E. Limón discussed "Western Marxism and Folklore" in *JAF* 96 (1983): 34–52.

On "The Comparative Method in Folklore," see a special issue of that title edited by Linda Dégh: *JFR* 23, nos. 2/3 (1986). Robert A. Georges discussed "The Folklorist as Comparatist" in *WF* 45 (1986): 1–20.

Kenneth S. Goldstein described his innovative research methods in "Experimental Folklore: Laboratory vs. Field," in *Folklore International*, ed. D. K. Wilgus (Hatboro, Pa.: Folklore Associates, 1967), pp. 71–82. Theoretical backgrounds for such studies are given in Kenneth Laine Ketner's "The Role of Hypotheses in Folkloristics," *JAF* 86 (1973): 114–30; an opposing view appears in Anne Cohen and Norm Cohen, "A Word on Hypotheses," *JAF* 87 (1974): 156–60. Alan Dundes pointed to what he saw as a limiting mind-set for research in "The Devolutionary Premise in Folklore Theory," *JFI* 6 (1969): 5–19, repr. in *Analytic Essays in Folklore*, pp. 17–27. Responses to this came from Ronald Grambo in *FF* 3 (1970): 57–58, William M. Clements in *NYFQ* 29 (1973): 243–53, and Elliott Oring in *WF* 34 (1975): 36–44, among others. Oring discussed "Three Functions of Folklore: Traditional Functionalism as Explanation in Folkloristics" in *JAF* 89 (1976): 67–80; comments and a response then appeared in *JAF* 90 (1977): 68–77.

David J. Hufford provides an overview of another analytic approach in "Psychology, Psychoanalysis, and Folklore," *SFQ* 38 (1974): 187–97. Paulo de Carvalho-Neto's *Folklore and Psychoanalysis*, originally published in 1956, was issued in its first English translation in 1972 (Coral Gables, Fla.: University of Miami Press) with a foreword by Alan Dundes, a leading North American advocate of psychoanalytic interpretations of folk tradition; see for example, Dundes's 1976 article "Projection in Folklore: A Plea for Psychoanalytic Semiotics," in *Interpreting Folklore*, pp. 33–61. A representative psychological analysis is illustrated in Eric Berne's "The Mythology of Dark and Fair: Psychiatric Use of Folklore," *JAF* 72 (1959): 1–13. A sociopsychological study is Brian Sutton-Smith's "A Formal Analysis of Game Meaning," *WF* 18 (1959): 13–24. One sociological approach to folk belief and behavior is *Water Witching U.S.A.* by Evon Z. Vogt and Ray Hyman (Chicago: University of Chicago Press, 1959).

Two pacesetting early treatments of folklore in its cultural context were by William Hugh Jansen: "A Culture's Stereotypes and Their Expression in Folk

Clichés," *Southwestern Journal of Anthropology* 13 (1957): 184–200; and "The Esoteric-Exoteric Factor in Folklore," *Fabula* 2 (1959): 205–11, repr. in *The Study of Folklore*, pp. 43–51. An early advocate of this "contextual" or "behavioral" approach to folklore was Roger D. Abrahams, three of whose influential articles are: "Folklore in Culture: Notes toward an Analytic Method," *TSLL* 5 (1963): 98–110, repr. in *Readings in American Folklore*, pp. 390–403; "Introductory Remarks to a Rhetorical Theory of Folklore," *JAF* 81 (1968): 143–58; and "A Rhetoric of Everyday Life: Traditional Conversational Genres," *SFQ* 32 (1968): 44–59. Abrahams's pioneering study *Deep Down in the Jungle: Negro Narrative Folklore from the Streets of Philadelphia* appeared in 1964 (Hatboro, Pa.: Folklore Associates) and in a revised edition in 1970 (Chicago: Aldine Press). Another representative study from this viewpoint is Richard Bauman's "Verbal Art as Performance," *AA* 77 (1975): 290–311. A group of articles on folklore and culture appeared in *JFI* 2 (1965).

One of the most enduring early articles advocating more attention to the contexts in which folklore is performed is Alan Dundes's 1964 essay "Texture, Text, and Context," repr. in *Interpreting Folklore*, pp. 20–32. Identifying "folklore about folklore" as a traditional practice worthy of more study, Alan Dundes proposed "Metafolklore and Oral Literary Criticism," a concept quickly seized upon by folklorists, in *The Monist* 50 (1966): 505–16 (repr. in *Analytic Essays in Folklore*, pp. 50–58, and in *Readings in American Folklore*, pp. 404–15). A published debate—typical of much of the oral debate conducted at professional conferences—concerning the contextual approach to folklore pitted Steven Jones against Dan Ben-Amos in the "Topics and Comments" section of *WF* 38 (1979): 42–55; much depends upon just what the scholars mean by the term "traditional" in analyzing folklore. Robert A. Georges attempted ". . . A Resolution of the Text/Context Controversy" in *WF* 39 (1980): 34–40; he prefers to be called a "behaviorist," and he denies that there is any "war" between factions of contextualist and noncontextualist schools. Rebutting Georges is Yigal Zan's "The Text/Context Controversy: An Explanatory Perspective," *WF* 41 (1982): 1–27. More interesting, perhaps, to a beginning folklore student than these abstract essays would be Georges's article "Feedback and Response in Storytelling," *WF* 38 (1979): 104–10, in which a specific instance of context affecting text and performance is described in concrete terms. See also Katharine Young, "The Notion of Context," *WF* 44 (1985): 115–22.

A useful general discussion of the structural approach to folklore is Butler Waugh's "Structural Analysis in Literature and Folklore," *WF* 25 (1966): 153–64. In *Structural Models in Folklore and Transformational Essays* (The Hague: Mouton, Approaches to Semiotics 10, 1971), Pierre and Elli [Köngäs] Maranda provided a systematic presentation of an important structural theory and method. This is a revised version of an essay first published in *MF* (1962), supplemented by new studies of myth and riddle. The Marandas' anthology *Structural Analysis of Oral Tradition* (Philadelphia: University of Pennsylvania Press, 1971) contains eleven essays by various scholars analyzing myth, ritual, drama, folktale, riddle, and folksong. The contributors include most of the leading contemporary structuralists who produced folklore studies.

An imaginative application of the oral-formulaic theory to American materials is found in Bruce A. Rosenberg's *The Art of the American Folk Preacher* (New York: Oxford University Press, 1970), revised as *Can These Bones Live?* (Urbana: University of Illinois Press, 1989). A related analytic approach is found in Bennison Gray's "Repetition in Oral Literature," *JAF* 84 (1971): 289–303; and another is William M. Clements's "The Rhetoric of the Radio Ministry," *JAF* 87 (1974): 318–27.

A pioneering essay on the esthetic standards of the folk themselves is Kenneth S. Goldstein's "Notes Toward a European-American Folk Aesthetic: Lessons Learned from Singers and Storytellers I have Known," *JAF* 104 (1991): 164–78; one conclusion is that "Big is Beautiful." A detailed study of one text in its performances is Charles L. Perdue's " 'What Made Little Sister Die?': The Core Aesthetic and Personal Culture of a Traditional Singer," *WF* 54 (1995): 141–63.

Brief notes on traditional "Geographic Sayings from Louisiana" were published by Fred Kniffen in *JAF* 67 (1954): 78. He distinguished those sayings that "attribute qualities to specific areas" ("the ozone belt") from those "based on a striking natural process in geography" ("My grandfather crossed there on a plank"). One is reminded of numerous sayings elsewhere in the United States that fall into the same classes—"the banana belt," for instance, for unusually mild climates in northern regions, and "You can set your watch by it," referring (inaccurately) to Old Faithful. Two discussions of general relationships for cooperation are Roger T. Trindell's "American Folklore Studies and Geography," *SFQ* 34 (1970): 1–11; and W. F. H. Nicolaisen's "Folklore and Geography: Towards an Atlas of American Folk Culture," *NYFQ* 29 (1973): 3–20. An excellent example of a specific application of geographic and folkloristic methods is E. Joan Wilson Miller's study "Ozark Superstitions as Geographic Documentation," *The Professional Geographer* 24 (1972): 223–26.

A groundbreaking panel, "Folk Literature and the Obscene," sponsored by the American Folklore Society, was published in a special issue of *JAF* (75 [1962]: 189–282) edited by Frank A. Hoffmann; speakers included Herbert Halpert, Horace Beck, Alan Dundes, and Gershon Legman. *The Horn Book: Studies in Erotic Folklore and Bibliography* (New Hyde Park, N.Y.: University Books, 1964) by Legman is a basic scholarly reference in this area. Kenneth S. Goldstein discusses a process common to handling of obscene folk materials in "Bowdlerization and Expurgation: Academic and Folk," *JAF* 80 (1967): 374–86; and Mac E. Barrick presents some traditional erotic materials that appear in written form as "The Typescript Broadside," *KFQ* 17 (1972): 27–38.

The interrelations of folklore with mass culture were discussed by a few past scholars. Priscilla Denby surveyed "Folklore in the Mass Media" in *FF* 4 (1971): 113–25. Alan Dundes's "Advertising and Folklore," *NYFQ* 19 (1963): 143–51, may be compared with Tom E. Sullenberger's "Ajax Meets the Jolly Green Giant: Some Observations on the Use of Folklore in American Mass Marketing," *JAF* 87 (1974): 53–65. Other mass-cultural studies are Tom Burns's "Folklore in the Mass Media: Television," *FF* 2 (1969): 90–106; and John T. Flanagan's "Grim Stories: Folklore in Cartoons," *MJLF* 1 (1975): 20–26. The first major work on the broader subject is Linda Dégh's *American Folklore and the Mass Media* (Bloomington: Indiana University Press, 1994).

Dick Sweterlitsch edited nine "Papers on Applied Folklore" in *FF*, Bibliographic and Special Series, no. 8 (1971). See also Mary Ellen B. Lewis's "The Feminists Have Done It: Applied Folklore," *JAF* 87 (1974): 85–87. Among works in the large, and rapidly growing, literature of American feminist folkloristics are: Rosan A. Jordan and Susan J. Kalčik, eds., *Women's Folklore, Women's Culture* (Philadelphia: University of Pennsylvania Press, 1985); "Folklore and Feminism," a special issue of *JAF* 100 (1987): 387–588 (also published in book form); "Feminist Revisions in Folklore Studies," edited by Beverly J. Stoeltje as a special issue of *JFR* 25 (1988): 141–241; and Mary Ellen Brown, "Women, Folklore and Feminism," *JFR* 26 (1989): 259–64, a review article on five books published from 1985 to 1988.

Barbara Kirshenblatt-Gimblett's essay "Mistaken Dichotomies," *JAF* 101 (1988): 140–55, disputes the supposed distinction between "pure" and applied folklore study. An important anthology on the subject, edited by Robert Baron and Nicholas R. Spitzer, is *Public Folklore* (Washington, D.C.: Smithsonian Institution, 1992). "Cultural conservation" in public-sector work is the subject of a book of essays edited by Burt Feintuch (Lexington: University Press of Kentucky, 1988) and of an article by Alf H. Walle in *WF* 49 (1990): 261–75. A specific case from the past is presented in Simon J. Bronner's *Popularizing Pennsylvania: Henry W. Shoemaker and the Progressive Uses of Folklore and History* (University Park: Penn State University Press, 1996).

Perhaps the most common application of folklorists' studies is in teaching, for which see "Folklore and Education: A Selected Annotated Bibliography of Periodical Literature" (by five compilers) in *KF* 22 (1978): 53–85; Dorson's *Handbook of American Folklore* also has several chapters on teaching folklore. A special issue of *SF* (48: 1 [1991]) edited by Nancy J. Nusz contained eight essays and a bibliography concerning folklife in education. Bruce Jackson edited *Teaching Folklore* (Buffalo, NY: Documentary Research for AFS, 1984), with thirteen essays on the subject. Ronald L. Baker surveyed folklore teaching in American and Canadian colleges and universities first in *JAF* 99 (1986): 50–74, with periodic updates in *JAF*.

The invaluable bibliographic notes in Richard M. Dorson's *American Folklore* (updated in his 1977 ed.) should be supplemented in any search for references to a particular topic in American folklore by the analytic indexes to folklore journals (*FF, JAF, JFI, WF, PTFS*, etc.). An annual AFS bibliography was published in the Supplement to *JAF* until 1963, when it was shifted to the new journal *Abstracts of Folklore Studies*. When *Abstracts* ceased publication in 1969, its important bibliographic function was filled by the expanded folklore section of the huge Modern Language Association bibliography appearing annually in *PMLA*. *The Journal of American Folklore* itself was reindexed as an AFS Centennial Project and published as *JAF*, vol. 101, no. 402 (1988); see Michael Taft's "Supplements" to the Index in *JAF* 102 (1989): 299–314, and in *JAF* 107 (1994): 479–536, which updates the series from the issues of 1988 through 1994. An important American folklore bibliography was published annually in *SFQ* from 1937 to 1973, then continued in book form by Merle E. Simmons for two years by the Folklore Institute (Bloomington, Indiana), and thereafter by the Institute for the Study of Human Issues (Philadelphia). This bibliography's founder, Ralph Steele Boggs, also published the useful *Bibliography of Latin American Folklore* (New York: H. W. Wilson Co., 1940). Charles Haywood's *A Bibliography of North American Folklore and Folksong* is unusual in that it includes much Native American material; originally published in 1951, it was reprinted in two volumes by Dover Books in 1961, but unfortunately none of the numerous factual errors in citations of the first edition was corrected. Another guide to check for references is Cathleen C. Flanagan and John T. Flanagan's *American Folklore: A Bibliography, 1950–1974* (Metuchen, N.J.: Scarecrow Press, 1977). For most purposes, the beginning student's best bibliographic aid will simply be the general references mentioned in the preface, plus the notes to each chapter of this textbook. In going beyond the sources listed here, researchers must consult the computerized databases increasingly becoming available at most libraries or online.

3

FOLK GROUPS: BEARERS OF
AMERICAN FOLK TRADITION

DOES AMERICA HAVE A FOLKLORE?

Depending upon how it was defined, "American" folklore has been pictured as nonexistent, relatively rare, or extremely common. As late as 1930 Alexander H. Krappe, a prominent American folklorist of the time, was still European-oriented enough to take the extreme position that there was no such thing as American folklore, but only a few folkloric importations that eventually lost themselves in our mechanized age. The American Folklore Society itself, as described in chapter 1, was formed in 1888 partly to collect the "fast-vanishing remains" of foreign (including African-American) folklore in the United States; as for the phrase "American Folklore," that referred to the Native Americans, or to the nationality of members of the society. Published collections of American folklore still occasionally appear prefaced with gloomy essays about disappearing traditions and the rapid loss of our meager folklore. The other extreme is reached by the many popular books and records that try to boost every scrap of Americana in sight—old or new—as another example of our profuse national folklore. Most of these publications are heavy on fakelore—that is, imitation folklore attributed to a group that never possessed it.

One should not be dogmatic about whether American folklore

exists in abundance until the terms "American" and "folklore" are explained. Our criteria for "folklore" are oral, customary, and material tradition, appearing in variants, while for "American" an inclusive definition would be "found in the United States," and a restrictive one might be "originated in the United States." Most American folklorists incline toward the inclusive view, as far as theory is concerned, although their field-collecting often has emphasized older American, or at least Americanized, material. For example, while some American folklore collectors have realized that there exist traditional songs unique to the United States—songs of protest, industries, parody, pornography, and the like—what they have collected most vigorously in the past have been old British traditional ballads and lyrical songs.

American folklore research has amply demonstrated that a substantial body of oral, customary, and material tradition is circulating in the United States, some of it homegrown and some transplanted from other cultures. Of course, individual folk practices do fade away, but new ones are constantly appearing, so that the report of the demise of American folklore, as Mark Twain said about the report of his own death, has been "greatly exaggerated." In a general sense we can say that some types of folklore (such as folk drama) are now rather rare in the United States, some types survive vigorously in quite ancient forms (such as superstitions), some types have been revived for a popular audience (folk dances and songs), and some types are still being invented along contemporary lines (jokes and urban legends).

To assert that folklore is regularly being created and transmitted in modern American culture is to suggest that "the folk" must now exist in a modern guise. While most attempts to characterize the sources of folklore have emphasized isolation, lack of sophistication, and groups with relative homogeneity, the materials that folklorists collect and study prove that such qualities are not essential to fostering folklore. The American "folk" are certainly not comparable to the "peasant societies" studied in Europe and elsewhere. On the contrary, folklore flourishes among some of the most sophisticated and mobile Americans—teenagers, entertainers, athletes, professors, and members of the armed forces. Strict preconceived notions of who "the folk" are have led to much disputing in folklore research when energy might better have been devoted to fieldwork and comparative studies to learn just how folklore actually is developed and put into circulation. To begin such studies, no better definition of "folk" would seem necessary than "anyone who has folklore."

THEORIES OF THE FOLK
AND FOLK GROUPS

On the general level, four basic theories were offered by past scholars to explain who the folk are and how their lore originates. The **communal theory** held that the folk were unsophisticated peasants who composed folklore as a group effort. The **survivals theory** pushed the origin of folklore back to a "savage stage" of civilization and maintained that contemporary folklore was an inheritance or "survival" from the past. The theory of ***gesunkenes Kulturgut*** (German for "debased elements of culture") reversed the direction of diffusion—folklore had sunk from its high origin as "art" or "learning," to become "tradition" among the common people. Finally, the theory of **individual origins and communal re-creation,** probably accepted by most modern folklorists (whether they use these precise terms or not), held that an item of folklore most likely had a single inventor, who could have lived at any level of society, but that each item was repeatedly revised (or "re-created") as it was transmitted by word of mouth. Each of these theories was applied to specific types of American folklore, and each perhaps has some validity in particular cases, as is pointed out in later chapters. (See, for example, the arguments about communal origins versus communal re-creation of ballads in chapter 12, about survivals exhibited in myths in chapter 8, and about *gesunkenes Kulturgut* applied to superstitions in chapter 14.)

The focus on specific creators and performers of traditions usually involves identifying these individuals with what have been called **folk groups.** The acceptance of traditions by these groups usually implies some degree of conformity with group tastes and values. (There are exceptions, however, both in individual traditional creators with no strong group affiliation and in folklore that is subversive of group values.) While some such groups may be identified simply in terms of obvious social, political, or geographic factors, they are often identified for folklore purposes first by their distinctive folk speech and other traditions—the lingo and customs that set one group apart from others. Thus, among themselves, loggers talk about "widow makers" (dangerous dangling tree limbs) and may sing ballads about woods disasters. Children playing independently from adult supervision may cry "King's X" (a "truce term" in a game like tag) and play a game like Anthony Over (a ball game played around a garage or other small building). Family members may use nicknames for each other and celebrate holidays with practices learned from the grandparents. Girls may know the terms for playing jacks ("taps," "baskets," etc.) or the variations of playing jump rope better than the boys, who may be better informed about marble terms ("fudgies," "changies," etc.) and mumbletypeg (a game played with a pocketknife). Residents of southern Illinois may speak of themselves as living in "Egypt" and give varying legendary explanations for the name based on supposed parallels to the history of the old-world country in biblical times; and Finns in America tell stories from both the old country and the new, mixing their native tongue with English into "Finglish."

The examples summarized above suggest six major kinds of American folk groups—*occupational groups, age groups, family groups, gender-differentiated groups, regional groups,* and *ethnic or nationality groups.* Folk groups may also be distinguished according to religion, education, hobbies, neighborhood, and even military or prison residence, as well as other factors, such as blindness or deafness. This viewpoint makes clear that folk groups need not be composed only of rural people living in remote locations and that a person may belong to several folk groups at the same time. A Polish steelworker in Gary, Indiana, for instance, may know distinct types of ethnic, industrial, and regional lore, and if he happens to be a second-generation American he may also know immigrant lore unknown to his own parents. As a child he surely participated in different traditions than he has as a man, and as a man he likely knows some folklore that is not familiar to or popular with his mother, sisters, or wife. Still, in his own family the steelworker shares a body of traditional lore that is not exactly duplicated in any other family. The first test a folklorist could make of membership in a folk group is the members' awareness of shared traditions; then the background of this heritage can be investigated.

Navajo "codetalkers" with the U.S. Marines, on the western Pacific island of Saipan during World War II (date of photo unknown). Using their native language for radio and telephone communications, the Navajo Indians confounded the Japanese with a "code" that was never broken.

FOCUS: ETHNIC/OCCUPATIONAL FOLK SPEECH

Recently, on a trip to New York City I took a taxi from Manhattan to the John F. Kennedy International Airport to catch my flight home. While edging his car along in the late-afternoon traffic, the cabdriver spoke on his radio to the dispatcher. He was not speaking English, and I asked him what language he was using.

"That was Greek," he said. "A lot of the drivers for this company are Greeks. I was telling the dispatcher that I'm going out to JFK, and then after I get a fare back to the city I'll be going off duty."

"I don't know any Greek," I said, "but I didn't recognize your saying 'Kennedy,' or 'JFK' or 'airport.' Are there different Greek words for things like that?"

The cabbie replied, "No, and I didn't use any of those words you used either. I just told him I was going to *mega*, you know: 'the big one.'"

"Then what do you call La Guardia Airport [New York City's other major airport]?" I asked.

"*Micro*," he said, pronouncing it "mē'-crow." "You know: 'the little one.'"

I had just learned a couple of terms that are part of a regional/ethnic/occupational folk-speech tradition.

Source: Jan Harold Brunvand's field notes.

DISCUSSION TOPICS:

1. Once the terms *mega* and *micro* are explained, why are their meanings perfectly clear to one who does not understand Greek?

2. To what folk groups does the cabdriver belong? What about the passenger? (Do these groups seem to overlap in any way?)

3. What other "folk" terms or practices might be typical of cabdrivers?

4. Collect similar examples of folk speech in other contexts.

OCCUPATIONAL GROUPS

Among **occupational groups** in the United States, the old rugged outdoor callings are associated with vigorous oral traditions: ax logging, raft and barge freighting, sailing before the mast, and running cattle were all activities rich in folklore. The long exposure of small bands of toughened men to the elements led them to fall back on their stocks of stories and songs for entertainment, and the dangers inherent in the work produced superstitions like the "Flying Dutchman" and the "ghost herd." But the present has its comparable groups, too, with their own folklore, as studies of mining, railroading, oil pumping, and other industries have shown. To some degree, the modern armed forces retain typical traditions of the older (then all-male) labor groups, as do prisons. However, physical strain is no necessary accompaniment to occupational folklore; jet pilots, journalists, tour guides, and even members of the clergy (including seminarians) have esoteric oral traditions of language and lore that are little known outside these groups. Nor have the domestic scene and the other usual workplaces of American women in the past lacked folklore; folk traditions surround cooking, childbearing and child raising, and household crafts as well as the traditional jobs for women in schools, offices, or libraries. The folklore of women in professional fields, where they more and more have starring roles, is probably no less rich than for the comparable positions held by men, but it has been less often collected and studied.

So rapidly does folklore develop around new jobs and products that there is already a considerable cycle of *exoteric* (that is, told by outsiders) oral stories circulating about computers and their designers, programmers, and users, as well as a rich set of *esoteric* (inside) terms, stories, and pranks that are known among the "hackers" (computer buffs) themselves. The whole computer industry is loaded with rumors and legends, often about future products and their alleged features (for example, "vaporware" is promised future software, which sometimes never does reach the market). This kind of lore once characterized the American automobile industry, when the technology was evolving and annual major model changes were highly publicized. The folklore of many other modern occupations has been recognized, if not studied in detail, including lore of assembly and processing plants, of government service, of science, and of academic life. Among the possibilities of the latter are stories of eccentric and absentminded professors, of master cheaters in the student body, of prudish deans, and of administrators and their vagaries.

AGE GROUPS

The distinctive folklore of different **age groups** is becoming better understood as folklorists pursue the topic. Beyond the general notion of children growing from one stage to another, shedding layers of folklore as they go and acquiring new ones, we have to consider the differing folklore of genders at the same time, for the rigid patterns of child behavior (who plays which games when or tells which stories to whom or uses which terms) are bound by both age and gender. Children's folklore offers a particularly interesting field for research, since it derives from an almost pure field situation in which some items are transmitted completely by word of mouth in an atmosphere of great textual conservatism—as any adult who has changed the wording of a bedtime story or tried to instruct a child in the "right way" to play a game like kick-the-can knows. American children's folklore has been collected in some quantity, and analysis has begun, considering such factors as its distribution, variants, or function. Past collecting tended to be from grownups recalling their youth, but today most of the collected material comes from observations of youths. Still, the results tend to be spotty—we have the singing games but few of the jokes of small children; we have the jargon but little of the sexual or alcoholic lore of teenagers; and so forth.

School folklore has a close connection to age-related traditions. The rather innocuous traditional rhymes of elementary schoolchildren, for example ("School's out, school's out / Teacher let the fools out"), later yield to the more shocking and sophisticated chants of their older colleagues ("East High School's my prison / Room 30 is my cell. / Miss Parsons is my warden / And she can go to Hell!"). The folklore of schooling extends to virtually every topic that a student encounters, from academic fields and teachers to school lunches and organized sports. College and university students, as mentioned above, have no less rich a body of folklore, from fraternity and sorority lore to legends about campus buildings and even nicknames for courses (some examples of which are quoted in the next chapter).

FOCUS: MULTICULTURAL SCHOOL JOKE

There's this well-meaning new teacher in an inner-city school—in an ethnic neighborhood, you know. And on the first day of school she's trying to learn every kid's name and how to pronounce them all. So she goes around the class and asks each kid, "What's your name?" and "What's your name?"

But one little boy doesn't answer her, or even say a thing when she asks "What's your name?" a couple of times. And this other kid speaks up, and he says, "Oh, he's Italian; he doesn't understand English."

And the teacher says, "Oh, well, is there anyone here who can speak any Italian who can ask him his name?" And this kid in the back row says, yeah, he can speak Italian, so he'll help her out.

The kid in the back row walks up to the quiet little boy, and he stands in front of him and looks him straight in the eye, and he says "Hey! What's-a your name?"

Source: Told by a college student from New York City in a University of Utah class.

DISCUSSION TOPICS:

1. What are some typical stylistic features of oral joke-telling in the above story?

2. What's the significance in school folklore that the wiseguy character is often "a kid in the back row"? What does his body language in the story suggest about his personality?

3. What does this joke have to say about multiculturalism and language diversity, especially in the classroom?

Age-related folklore continues to develop distinctive forms and styles throughout peoples' lives, and "the folklore of aging" has become a popular research topic. Not only do elders provide much of the folk cultural heritage learned by their juniors, but as their own lives reach the last cycle, elders may return to folk customs and practices they previously abandoned and even create new folklore forms in response to their social situations. Folk medicine, storytelling, proverbial lore, and traditional crafts are among the items that folklorists have pursued among the elderly.

FAMILY GROUPS

The folklore of **family life** is rich in traditional texts, customs, and artifacts in which folklorists have increasingly become interested, often beginning with the exploration of their own family's lore. Family members frequently communicate using a set of abbreviations, terms, allusions, and coinages that seldom appear to them as special or different from other families' traditions. One good example is a particular call or whistle used to get the attention of other family members in a crowd; another is the "punch line" of a favorite anecdote about a family member that is repeated without further explanation (e.g., "I'll hang the picture if you'll drive the nail"). Some typical subjects of family folklore include the background of the family surname, family misfortunes ("we'd be rich today if only . . ."), stories of travel and vacations, memories of the family's fa-

vorite car or pet or piece of furniture, and tales of eccentric or notable relatives. Family reunions and major holiday celebrations are
excellent occasions to collect family folklore; scrapbooks, photo albums, home movies, and videotapes are sources that deserve study,
along with the oral and customary traditions of family life.

GENDER-DIFFERENTIATED GROUPS

The specific folklore of **gender-differentiated groups** is strongly influenced by the typical roles assigned to each gender by the culture.
Thus, American women were the midwives in pioneer communities
and may have told more supernatural legends or sung most of the
lullabies, while men were expected to be the blacksmiths and may
have swapped mostly brags and tall tales among themselves. Wom-
en's versus men's folklore repertoires seem fairly fixed in the published collections, but to some extent this reflects the biases of
collectors who expected women to know the charms or to do the
needlework and expected men to know the hunting lore and to do
heavy outdoor work. Research has revealed instances when people
crossed these barriers—such as when men participated in quilting and cooking or women told bawdy jokes and sang dirty songs.
More study needs to be done on the functional aspects of traditional
gender-related lore—for instance, how quilting bees were the settings for exchanging supportive women's lore, while men met their
cronies and got positive reinforcement at livery stables or barber-
shops. Both kinds of groupings prefigured the encounter groups and
"rap sessions" advocated by recent psychologists and spokespersons
for women's liberation. The functions of gender-related modern stories also need more documentation; these would probably include
men boosting their egos with memories from military or sports experiences, and women warning other women by describing encounters with male "putdowns" or experiences with street crimes. Along
with changing attitudes toward such folklore and new avenues for
research, there are gradual changes in the very language of discussing the subject—we speak of "spokespersons" and "chairpersons,"
of "women" (not "girls") and "artisans" (not "craftsmen").

Besides the subject of women's folklore as such, the negative views
of many men (who were often the folklorists) regarding these

traditions are revealed in a number of ways. At a folk level, male chauvinism takes such forms as antifeminist proverbs ("Keep her barefoot and pregnant") or proverbial warnings to women ("A whistling woman and a crowing hen will always come to some bad end"). Or the community might brand some women with supposed special powers as "witches," and call some of women's traditional talk mere (malicious?) "gossip"; but at the same time men who are gifted with alleged supernatural skills might be called "wizards" or "healers," and some men's talk might be regarded as mere (harmless?) "windies" or "yarns." It is also necessary to study how certain traditional tale or ballad themes—such as bride tests versus hero tests or seductions versus faithful love—were altered in the American oral tradition. When folklore is presented to mass audiences, sex-role stereotypes are perpetuated by such matters as which European fairy tales are usually translated (and how) and which ones are turned into popular films.

FOCUS: FEMINIST FOLKLORE FIELDWORK

Rangeley, Maine, is awash with gender issues. The work worlds of men and women, for example, especially among logging families, are quite separate. The men work in the woods all day, usually from about six in the morning to three or four in the afternoon. Working with other men, they labor hard with weather, trees, and heavy machinery and live every day with the threat of injury and death. They go to the women's places of work to rest and refresh.

The women work part-time, usually in restaurants and motels. They stay in town, indoors, doing the same activities that they do in their homes: cleaning and cooking and caring for others. Women are responsible for all the housework at home and for all the child care. They also do much charity work at the church and at the auxiliaries of fraternal organizations like the American Legion.

As if to dramatize the already strongly bifurcated gender roles, Rangeley residents enact gender differences over and over. On the Fourth of July, little girls wheel their fancifully decorated doll carriages down Main Street in the Doc Grant Doll Carriage Parade. At the Logging Festival in July, women throw rolling pins at a scarecrow dressed as a man. A store window once hung with a T-shirt bearing the slogan: "Take my wife not my gun." And on Valentine's Day evening, the owners of Doc Grant's Res-

taurant offer free beers to any man who will come dressed as a woman.
Doing fieldwork in this town as a woman and a feminist is not easy.

Source: Margaret R. Yocom, "Fieldwork, Gender and Transformation: The Second Way of Knowing," *SF* 47 (1990): 33–44.

Participant in the Doc Grant Doll Carriage Parade on Children's Day in Rangeley, Maine (date unknown).

DISCUSSION TOPICS:

1. Do the expressions of gender issues in Rangeley, Maine, differ much from similar expressions of such issues in other American communities?

2. What aspects of the Rangeley expressions of gender issues seem to be genuine examples of folklore, folkways, or folklife?

3. Yocom continues her essay by pointing out that her "first way" of knowing was via the "prescriptive methods" taught in folklore classes and fieldwork manuals. The "second way," she describes as "unintentional," and more a process than a method, reflecting "an evolving relationship" between collector and subjects of study. How may you apply these two principles to your own collecting?

Important to consider with gender-differentiated folklore is the lore of homosexuals in American society, which until relatively recently was known only to insiders or in the form of exaggerated stereotypes of gay speech and behavior. Recent studies have detailed a complex network of gay and lesbian folk traditions involving not only traditional texts (names, sayings, stories, parodies, etc.) but also aspects of custom, belief, and festival. A favorite gay joke refers to one popular notion about the origin of homosexuality: One gay man says to another, "My mother made me a homosexual." The listener replies, "If I buy her the yarn will she make me one too?"

REGIONAL GROUPS

Regional groups have yielded some of the most bountiful harvests of folklore material in this country, because geographic features tend to create relative isolation and encourage a community spirit that sustains long-standing traditions. The major folklore regions that American folklorists have described so far are New England, the Southern Appalachians, the Midwest, the Ozarks, the South, and the Southwest. Some folkloristic subregions that have been studied are Schoharie County, New York; Brown County, Indiana; the Upper Peninsula of Michigan; and the Mormon-settled Great Basin. State and other political boundaries have little effect on the types of folklore and its distribution, although many state collections have been brought together, mostly as a convenience for publishing. Studies of regional folk groups offer an excellent chance for cooperative projects by folklorists working with historians, geographers, linguists, and others; certainly a thorough understanding of settlement history and the national backgrounds of immigrants should underlie any study of their folklore. Although such cross-disciplinary research has been unusual in this country, it has been done for some time in Europe.

Several American folklorists began working at the regional level and later branched out to broader comparative studies, just as some regional folklore journals have expanded their coverage. Thus *Midwest Folklore* (1951), formerly *Hoosier Folklore Bulletin* (1942) and *Hoosier Folklore* (1946), became the more international *Journal of the Folklore Institute* (1964), which was renamed *Journal of Folklore Re-*

search in 1982; and in 1968 an entirely new journal, *Indiana Folklore*, began. The *California Folklore Quarterly* (1942) became *Western Folklore* (1947), and *Southern Folklore Quarterly* (1937) was revived (combined with *Kentucky Folklore Record*) as *Southern Folklore* (1989); not every article published in these journals has a regional slant, although special issues are sometimes regionally aimed. On the other hand, new regional journals devoted mostly to their own territories have sprung up, including *Northeast Folklore* (1958) and *Mid-South Folklore* (1973), which became *Mid-America Folklore* in 1978.

ETHNIC, NATIONALITY, AND
RELIGIOUS GROUPS

Ethnic, nationality, and religious groups have a folklore as rich and varied as the multicultural American population itself. Again, only a fraction of this lore has been recorded or studied. The folktales, songs, proverbs, and other folklore of Native Americans, however, have been intensively studied for generations, partly by folklorists but mostly by anthropologists with special linguistic and ethnographic training. There has been very active folklore collecting and research among American blacks, both in the Deep South and in the northern settlements, as African-American folk music, then tales and other lore have interested scholars. The early studies were concerned mainly with tracing African survivals in America, but folklorists increasingly dealt with the psychological and sociological functions of folklore among blacks. Perhaps the best-documented nationality group in the United States is also an important regional group—the so-called Dutch (i.e., Deutsch) of German Pennsylvania, about whom there are numerous articles and books. Good studies are also available about the folklore of other groups such as Jewish people in big cities, the Spanish in the Southwest, the Cajuns in Louisiana, and the Scandinavians in the Midwest. Some other urban nationality groups that have been approached are the Greeks in Tarpon Springs, Florida; the Finns in Astoria, Oregon; the Poles in Hamtramck, Michigan; and the Spanish in Denver, Colorado. Among the many other groups awaiting more attention are the Basques in the Far West, the Puerto Ricans in New York City, the Norwegians in the Northwest (including Alaska), the Bohemians in

Nebraska, the Cubans in Florida, and the Southeast Asians in many cities.

Often the study of immigrant folklore has resulted from the devoted work of a scholar who is himself or herself a fairly recent arrival. One such notable collector is the Lithuanian-American Jonas Balys. Another is the Hungarian-American Linda Dégh. In other groups an American-born descendant of immigrants takes up folklore collecting, such as Warren Kliewer among Low-German-speaking Mennonites, Robert Georges among Greeks, and Larry Danielson among Swedes. Non-European groups have been studied relatively little, but they could be; one good possibility is in the "Chinatowns" of several cities, and another is the Japanese of California and other states. In a sense, the United States is a prime multicultural meeting ground of foreign folklores and thus provides an ideal arena for observing the survival of old traditions and the assimilation of new ones. American Christmas customs, for example, are a curious blend of several European sources, while immigrant folksong repertoires tend to be influenced by country-western, Tin Pan Alley, blues, and even cowboy songs. The scope of possibilities can be imagined when the largest nationality groups are considered—Irish, Italian, German, Scandinavian, and especially the most prominent group, the Anglo-Americans.

This chapter has only sketched in rough outline some few American folk groups, and it has referred to only a fraction of their folklore. To treat fully the oral traditions of even one such group would require a full volume or more, preceded by extensive fieldwork. Essentially, the following chapters should be regarded as a survey of English-language folklore in America. Most of it, naturally, is Anglo-American in character if not in origin, but many of the groups mentioned above have been referred to and their traditions sampled.

BIBLIOGRAPHIC NOTES

Alexander H. Krappe discussed " 'American' Folklore" in *Folk-Say: A Regional Miscellany* (Norman: University of Oklahoma Press, 1930), pp. 291–97, but he strongly denied that there was any. Krappe maintained that there were only imported traditions in this country and that the culture of the immigrant was lost after he or she became Americanized. Three studies of contemporary individual creators of folk traditions (from New York, Maine, and Newfoundland) are printed in *Folksongs and Their Makers*, edited by Henry Glassie, Edward D. Ives, and John F. Szwed (Bowling Green, Ohio: Bowling Green State University Popular Press, 1970).

American folklore from an occupational group context is collected in Tristram Potter Coffin and Hennig Cohen's *Folklore from the Working Folk of America* (New York: Doubleday, 1973; Anchor paperback, 1974). In 1978 two special issues of folklore journals concentrated on occupational folklore: "Working Americans: Contemporary Approaches to Occupational Folklore," *WF* 37, no. 3 (1978), edited by Robert H. Byington, contained five articles, and "Occupational Folklore and the Folklore of Working," *FF* 11, no. 1 (1978), edited by Catherine Swanson and Philip Nusbaum, contained seven articles. A decade later, occupational folklore was the topic of *NYF* 14, nos. 1–2 (1988), which contained eight essays. Many individual articles, too numerous to list here, on occupational folk traditions continued to appear. Book-length studies include Mody C. Boatright's *Folklore of the Oil Industry* (Dallas: Southern Methodist University Press, 1963); George Korson's *Black Rock: Mining Folklore of the Pennsylvania Dutch* (Baltimore: Johns Hopkins Press, 1960); Horace Beck's *Folklore and the Sea* (Middletown, Conn.: Wesleyan University Press, 1973); Patrick B. Mullen's, *I Heard the Old Fishermen Say: Folklore of the Texas Gulf Coast* (Austin: University of Texas Press, 1978; rev. ed. Logan: Utah State University Press, 1988); Howard W. Marshall and Richard E. Ahlborn's *Buckaroos in Paradise: Cowboy Life in Northern Nevada* (Washington, D.C.: Library of Congress, 1980), essentially the catalog of an exhibit of cowboy artifacts; Jack Santino's *Miles of Smiles, Years of Struggle: Stories of Black Pullman Porters* (Urbana: University of Illinois Press, 1989); and Archie Green's *Wobblies, Pile Butts, and Other Heroes: Laborlore Explorations* (Urbana: University of Illinois Press, 1993). See also the works on occupational customs listed in the notes to chapter 14.

American children's lore has been gathered in countless journal articles, such as Nancy C. Leventhal and Ed Cray, "Depth Collecting from a Sixth-Grade Class," *WF* 22 (1963): 159–63 and 231–57. (Articles dealing with individual genres of childlore are listed in the appropriate bibliographic notes that follow.) An excellent book-length treatment drawn from research among English children reveals many parallels in American lore; see Iona Opie and Peter Opie's *The Lore and Language of Schoolchildren* (New York: Oxford University Press, 1959). For a comparison based on the Opies' work see Loman D. Cansler, "Midwestern and British Children's Lore Compared," *WF* 27 (1968): 1–18. Two comprehensive books on American children's folklore are Mary and Herbert Knapp's *One Potato, Two Potato: The Secret Education of American Children* (New York: Norton, 1976) and Simon J. Bronner's *American Children's Folklore* (Little Rock: August House, 1988), which was published in both a trade edition and a fully annotated scholarly edition. The autobiographical book *Dorothy's World* (Englewood Cliffs, N.J.: Prentice-Hall, 1977) by the American-children's folklorist Dorothy Howard includes lore from her childhood in the Sabine-bottom area of Texas in the early twentieth century. In 1980 two folklore journals published important special issues on children's folklore: *SWF* 4, nos. 3–4, had twelve articles, and *WF* 39, no. 3, had six articles and a good bibliography.

Brian Sutton-Smith, who has published many good studies of children's games, discusses "Psychology of Childlore: The Triviality Barrier," in *WF* 29 (1970): 1–8. An interesting analysis based on a verbatim tape-recorded storytelling session with five boys is given in Steve Bartlett, "Social Interaction Patterns of Adolescents in a Folklore Performance," *FF* 4 (1971): 39–67. In Angus K. Gillespie, ed., "Teaching and Collecting Folklore at a Boys' Prep School," *KFQ* 15 (1970): 55–113, the folklore of adolescents is collected and studied. Individual studies of child-lore continue to appear in *Children's Folklore Review*, the journal of the Children's Folklore Section of the AFS. Just one good example of a study of folklore and aging is Patrick B. Mullen's *Listening to Old Voices: Folklore, Life Stories, and the Elderly* (Bloomington: Indiana University Press, 1992).

For a good survey with numerous examples of the folklore of academe, see Simon J. Bronner's *Piled Higher and Deeper: The Folklore of Campus Life* (Little Rock: August House, 1990).

Two excellent books on family folklore are *A Celebration of American Family Folklore*, edited by Steven J. Zeitlin, Amy J. Kotkin, and Holly Cutting Baker (New York: Pantheon, 1982) and Elizabeth Stone's *Black Sheep and Kissing Cousins—How Our Family Stories Shape Us* (New York: Times Books, 1988). Kathryn L. Morgan's autobiographical study *Children of Strangers: The Stories of a Black Family* (Philadelphia: Temple University Press, 1980) demonstrates how her family stories—particularly those about a resolute female ancestor—served as "buffers" against the forces of racial prejudice in the modern world. Larry Danielson edited a special issue of *WF* (vol. 51 [1994]) on family folklore. Reducing the topic to perhaps its smallest common denominator, Elliott Oring discussed "Dyadic Traditions" [interactions between two individuals] in *JFR* 21 (1984): 19–28, a notion further pursued by Regina Bendix in "Marmot, Memet, and Marmoset: Further Research on the Folklore of Dyads," *WF* 46 (1987): 171–91. William A. Wilson proposes a longer family-folklore form in his article "Personal Narratives: The Family Novel," *WF* 50 (1991): 127–49, while Anne F. Hatch links family traditions to a piece of furniture in "The Beehive Buffet," *WF* 50 (1991): 421–30.

A special issue of *JAF* (vol. 88, no. 347 [1975]) highlighted "Women and Folklore"; Claire R. Farrer was the editor. A critical response to that material and its handling, by Rosan A. Jordan, was published in *FFemC*, no. 8 (Winter 1976): 4–5. In the renamed version of this journal—*FWC* (no. 20, Winter 1980: 16–22)—Elizabeth Starr commented "On Sexism in Folklore Scholarship," citing specific examples from the publications of several male American folklorists. Alan Dundes's essay "The Crowing Hen and the Easter Bunny: Male Chauvinism in American Folklore," first published in 1976, was reprinted in *Interpreting Folklore*, pp. 160–75; it is not surprising to find here that American folklore reflects the traditional biases of American history and culture. Specific categories and styles of women's folklore as such have been emerging in scholarly studies such as Susan Kalčik's " '. . . Like Ann's Gynecologist or The Time I Was Almost Raped': Personal Narratives in Women's Rap Groups," on pp. 3–11 in the "Women and

Folklore" issue of *JAF* mentioned above. A related kind of warning story is found in Eleanor Wachs's " 'With My Heart in My Throat and My Whistle in My Hand': Women's Crime-Victim Narratives from the Urban Setting," *NYF* 6 (1980): 11–26. (Additional writings on feminist folkloristics are listed in the bibliographic notes to chapter 2.)

A good example of the data of cultural geography used to differentiate a regional folk group is found in E. J. Wilhelm, Jr., "Folk Settlement Types in the Blue Ridge Mountains," *KFQ* 12 (1967): 151–74. The Ozarks, a prime American folk enclave, is discussed in E. Joan Wilson Miller's "The Ozark Culture Region as Revealed by Traditional Materials," *Annals of the Association of American Geographers* 58 (1968): 51–77. The riches of material already collected there are indexed in Vance Randolph's *Ozark Folklore: A Bibliography*, Folklore Institute Monograph Series, vol. 24 (Bloomington: Indiana University Press, 1972), which extends only up to 1964 and yet lists 2,489 items. Volume 3, no. 3 (Winter 1975), of *MSF* was a special issue dedicated to Vance Randolph, with essays about and dedicated to the regional folklorist.

One model study of a region and its folk groups, prefaced by a discussion of "the folk" in the United States, is Richard M. Dorson's *Bloodstoppers and Bearwalkers: Folk Traditions in the Upper Peninsula* (Cambridge, Mass.: Harvard University Press, 1952; paperback repr., 1972). A fine Western counterpart is Austin and Alta Fife's *Saints of Sage and Saddle: Folklore among the Mormons* (Bloomington: Indiana University Press, 1956).

There are many large popularized anthologies of American folklore, most of them either arranged or cross-indexed by regional groups, and many of them probably trading on the success of B. A. Botkin's inclusive but somewhat unscholarly *A Treasury of American Folklore* (New York: Crown Publishers, 1944) and Botkin's several regional "treasuries." Tristram P. Coffin and Hennig Cohen's *Folklore in America* (Garden City, N.Y.: Doubleday, 1966; Anchor paperback, 1970) draws all of its examples from *JAF*, but often without the annotations or analyses originally provided there. Duncan Emrich's *Folklore on the American Land* (Boston: Little, Brown and Company, 1972) includes some extraneous editorializing by the compiler, but the sources and bibliography are clearly stated, and the illustrative photographs of Americans from the 1930s and 1940s are excellent.

A popularized anthology from one important region is Richard Chase's *American Folk Tales and Songs . . . as Preserved in the Appalachian Mountains . . .* (New York: New American Library, 1956; Dover Books repr., 1971). John Greenway's *Folklore of the Great West* (Palo Alto, Calif.: The American West Publishing Co., 1969) is drawn from the pages of *JAF* but presented in an essentially nonscholarly format. Similarly, Jan Harold Brunvand's "Folklore of the Great Basin," *NWF* 3 (1968): 17–32, is written for a nonprofessional audience, although based on scholarly sources and fieldwork. Perhaps the best introduction to regional American folklore is Dorson's *Buying the Wind* (Chicago: University of Chicago Press, 1964; paperback ed., 1972), which presents folklore from seven regions to illustrate the corresponding discussion in chapter 3 of his *American Folklore* (Chicago: University of Chicago Press, 1959).

Supplementary to Frank C. Brown's collection of North Carolina folklore mentioned in the notes to chapter 2 is Charles Bond's article "Unpublished Folklore in the Brown Collection," *NCF* 20 (1972): 11–20, which catalogs and offers a few samples from materials on file in the Duke University Library (repr. in *Readings in American Folklore*, pp. 5–15). Other state anthologies include Earl J. Stout's *Folklore from Iowa*, American Folklore Society Memoir, vol. 29 (New York, 1936); Harold W. Thompson's *Body, Boots and Britches* (on New York State) (Philadelphia: J. P. Lippincott, 1940); George Korson's *Pennsylvania Songs and Legends* (Philadelphia: University of Pennsylvania Press, 1949); Samuel J. Sackett's *Kansas Folklore* (Lincoln: University of Nebraska Press, 1961); Roger L. Welsch's *A Treasury of Nebraska Pioneer Folklore* (Lincoln: University of Nebraska Press, 1966); three works by George G. Carey: *Maryland Folklore and Folklife* (Cambridge, Md.: Tidewater Publishers, 1970), *Maryland Folk Legends and Folk Songs* (Cambridge, Md.: Tidewater Publishers, 1971), and *A Faraway Time and Place: Lore of the Eastern Shore* (on Chesapeake Bay) (Washington, D.C., and New York: Robert B. Luce, 1971); and R. Gerald Alvey's *Kentucky Bluegrass Country* (Jackson: University Press of Mississippi, 1992). In *Sang Branch Settlers: Folksongs and Tales of a Kentucky Mountain Family*, American Folklore Society Memoir, vol. 61 (Austin, Tex., 1974), Leonard Roberts presents a family tradition within a regional context.

Further collections and studies of regional folklore are Robert D. Bethke's *Adirondack Voices: Woodsmen and Woods Lore* (Urbana: University of Illinois Press, 1981); Francis Harper and Delma E. Presley's *Okefinokee Album* (Athens: University of Georgia Press, 1981); the Wisconsin folklore issue of *MJLF* (vol. 8, no. 1) published in 1982 and edited by James P. Leary, with a bibliography of more than two hundred items; Marta Weigle and Peter White's *The Lore of New Mexico* (Albuquerque: University of New Mexico Press, 1989); W. K. McNeil and William M. Clements's *An Arkansas Folklore Sourcebook* (Fayetteville: University of Arkansas Press, 1992); and Américo Paredes's *Folklore and Culture on the Texas-Mexican Border* (Austin: University of Texas Center for Mexican American Studies, 1993).

Discussions of regionalism itself are Suzi Jones's "Regionalization: A Rhetorical Strategy," *JFI* 13 (1976): 105–20; W. F. H. Nicolaisen's "The Folk and the Region," *NYF* 2 (1976): 143–49; William M. Clements's "The Folklorist, the Folk, and the Region," *MFSJ* 1 (1979): 44–54; and Barbara Allen and Thomas J. Schlereth, eds., *Sense of Place: American Regional Cultures* (Lexington: University Press of Kentucky, 1990). A study of prime importance to the whole subject is David E. Whisnant's *All That Is Native and Fine: The Politics of Culture in An American Region* (Chapel Hill: University of North Carolina Press, 1983). *The Encyclopedia of Southern Culture* (Chapel Hill: University of North Carolina Press, 1989; paperback ed., Two Harbors, Minn.: Anchor Books, 1991), edited by Charles Reagan Wilson and William Ferris, includes a strong emphasis on folk traditions of all kinds.

For information about regional folklore journals, see William J. Griffin's article "The TFS Bulletin and Other Folklore Serials in the United States: A Preliminary Survey," *TFSB* 25 (1959): 91–96. *Indiana Folklore: A Reader*, edited by Linda Dégh

(Bloomington: Indiana University Press, 1980), contains fifteen essays from the pages of the journal *Indiana Folklore*.

Publications on Native American folklore, including the vast anthropological literature, are far too numerous and varied to be represented here by a few citations. The notes to chapter 8 list some key works on Native American oral narratives, but the bibliography *Native American Folklore, 1879–1979*, by William M. Clements and Frances M. Malpezzi (Athens, Ohio, London, and Chicago: Swallow Press and Ohio University Press, 1984), contains more than five thousand entries.

For backgrounds to African-American folklore see Ruth Finnegan's comprehensive survey *Oral Literature in Africa* (New York: Oxford University Press, 1970). Volume 1 of *Afro-American Folk Culture: An Annotated Bibliography* (Philadelphia: Institute for the Study of Human Issues, 1978), compiled by John F. Szwed, Roger D. Abrahams, and others, is devoted to North America; volume 2, to the West Indies and Central and South America. Papers of the African Folklore Conference held at Indiana University in 1970 were published in *African Folklore*, ed. Richard M. Dorson (Bloomington: Indiana University Press, 1972). A particularly valuable collection that places African-American folklore in a historical context is Bruce Jackson's *The Negro and His Folklore in Nineteenth-Century Periodicals*, American Folklore Society Bibliographic and Special Series, vol. 18 (Austin, Tex., 1967). *African Folklore in the New World*, ed. Daniel J. Crowley (Austin: University of Texas Press, 1977), contains five essays on the topic and reveals some spirited debate among the contributors. Roger D. Abrahams's *Positively Black* (Englewood Cliffs, N.J.: Prentice-Hall, 1970) offers interpretive social and cultural comments on his own and others' recent studies. Alan Dundes's *Mother Wit from the Laughing Barrel: Readings in the Interpretation of Afro-American Folklore* (Englewood Cliffs, N.J.: Prentice-Hall, 1973) anthologizes many important essays on the subject. An often unappreciated cross-ethnic pattern of borrowing is treated in Alan Dundes's "African Tales among the North American Indians," *SFQ* 29 (1965): 207–19. Lawrence W. Levine's *Black Culture and Black Consciousness: Afro-American Folk Thought from Slavery to Freedom* (New York: Oxford University Press, 1977) is a successful application of African-American folklore studies to writing the history of this people. More-recent studies of importance include Charles Joyner's *Down by the Riverside: A South Carolina Slave Community* (Urbana: University of Illinois Press, 1984) and Roger Abrahams's *Singing the Master: The Emergence of African American Culture in the Plantation South* (New York: Pantheon, 1992). See also the bibliographic notes for individual genres throughout the present book.

The distinguished Canadian folklorist C. Marius Barbeau discussed "The Field of European Folk-Lore in America" in *JAF* 32 (1919): 185–97; Reidar Th. Christiansen, while professor of folklore at the University of Oslo, wrote "A European Folklorist Looks at American Folklore," *PTFS* 28 (1958): 18–44. Christiansen's full discussion, *European Folklore in America*, was published as number 12 of Studia Norvegica (Oslo, 1962). W. John Rowe placed more emphasis on material traditions than on verbal folklore in "Old-World Legacies in America," *Folk Life* 6 (1968): 68–82. *The Folklore of Texas Cultures*, ed. Francis Edward Abernethy, *PTFS* 38 (1974), is a good compilation of lore from two dozen groups found in the Lone Star State, with illustrations drawn from both old and recent photographs of each group.

An invaluable aid to immigrant-American folklore studies is Robert A. Georges and Stephen Stern's *American and Canadian Immigrant and Ethnic Folklore: An Annotated Bibliography* (New York: Garland, 1982), classified by groups (Armenian through Yugoslavian) and cross-indexed by folklore forms, regions, and authors. There are about nineteen hundred entries, though some are multiple listings. An older but still-worthy book-length work on an immigrant group's folklore is Phyllis H. Williams's *South Italian Folkways in Europe and America* (New Haven, Conn.: Yale University Press, 1938); a recent counterpart is Carla Bianco's *The Two Rosetos* (Bloomington: Indiana University Press, 1974), a comparison of folkways in Roseto Valfortore, Italy, and Roseto, Pennsylvania. Other book-length studies include Mac E. Barrick's *German-American Folklore* (Little Rock: August House, 1987); Frances M. Malpezzi and William M. Clements's *Italian-American Folklore* (Little Rock: August House, 1992); Ronald L. Baker's *French Folklife in Old Vincennes* (Terre Haute: Indiana Council of Teachers of English, 1989); and *Studies in Italian American Folklore* (Logan: Utah State University Press, 1993), edited by Luisa Del Giudice.

Representative journal articles on immigrant folklore are Henry R. Lang, "The Portuguese Element in New England," *JAF* 5 (1892): 9–18; Robert A. Georges, "Matiasma: Living Folk Belief [Greek]," *MF* 12 (1962): 69–74; Warren Kliewer, "Collecting Folklore among Mennonites," *Mennonite Life* 14 (July 1961): 109–12 (repr. in *Readings in American Folklore*, pp. 22–30); Arthur L. Campa, "Spanish Folksongs in Metropolitan Denver," *SFQ* 24 (1960): 179–92; Rosan Jordan DeCaro, "Language Loyalty and Folklore Studies: The Mexican-Americans," *WF* 31 (1972): 77–86; Pat Bieter, "Folklore of the Boise Basques," *WF* 24 (1965): 263–70; Alixa Neff, "Belief in the Evil Eye among the Christian Syrian-Lebanese in America," *JAF* 78 (1965): 46–51; Yvonne R. Lockwood, "The Sauna: An Expression of Finnish-American Identity," *WF* 36 (1977): 71–84; Dennis J. Clark, "Our Own Kind: Irish Folk Life in an Urban Setting" [Philadelphia], *KF* 23 (1979): 28–40; and "Sally Peterson, "Translating Experience and the Reading of a [Laotian Hmong] Story Cloth," *JAF* 101 (1988): 6–22.

Theoretical and methodological matters underlying immigrant folklore studies are taken up in Elli Kaija Köngäs, "Immigrant Folklore [Finnish]: Survival or Living Tradition?" *MF* 10 (1960): 117–23; and Linda Dégh, "Approaches to Folklore Research among Immigrant Groups," *JAF* 79 (1966): 551–56. A special issue of *WF* (vol. 36, no. 1 [1977]), "Studies in Folklore and Ethnicity," edited by Larry Danielson, contains an introduction and five articles. A reverse view—of the tales of emigrants returning to Norway from America—appears in Knut Djupedal's article "Tales of America," *WF* 49 (1990): 171–89.

The long tradition of folklore studies among Canada's diverse ethnic and regional groups was continued and consolidated in the Canadian Centre for Folk Culture Studies at the National Museum of Man in Ottawa. A useful introduction to their research was provided by Carmen Roy in Paper No. 7 of their Mercury Series (Ottawa, 1973); a representative commissioned report is Jan Harold Brunvand, *Norwegian Settlers in Alberta*, Paper No. 8 of the Mercury Series (Ottawa, 1974). Robert B. Klymasz's *An Introduction to the Ukrainian-Canadian Immigrant Folksong Cycle* (Ottawa: National Museums of Canada, Bulletin no. 234, Folklore Series no. 8, 1970) is a model study with texts in two languages, music, illustrations, and three small discs of recorded examples. An essay with implications for the future of this research is Klymasz's "From Immigrant to Ethnic Folklore: A Canadian View of Process and Tradition," *JFI* 10 (1973): 131–39.

For decades American folklore continued to be thought of only in a rural or small-town setting; a special issue of *JAF* devoted to "The Urban Experience and Folk Tradition" (vol. 83, no. 328 [April–June, 1970]; Bibliographical and Special Series no. 22 [1971]), ed. Américo Paredes and Ellen J. Stekert, indicated that attitudes were changing. Richard M. Dorson's contribution to this publication, "Is There a Folk in the City?" (pp. 185–228), elicited much discussion along with the eventual expansion of his thesis in Bruce E. Nickerson's "Is There a Folk in the Factory?" *JAF* 87 (1974): 133–39. A special issue of *NYF* (vol. 4, nos. 1–4 [1978]), edited by Susan G. Davis, described "The Utica Project," in which a number of folklorists analyzed traditions of that city. The urban-folklore research of Richard Dorson's Indiana University folklore graduate students in the Calumet Region of the north of the state is described in a special issue of *IF* (vol. 10, no. 2 [1977]). Dorson fully treats the results of this project in his *Land of the Millrats* (Cambridge, Mass.: Harvard University Press, 1981).

An unsuspected field for modern folklore studies is revealed in Mac E. Barrick's "Folktales from the Institute at Duke," *NCFJ* 23 (1975): 75–81, which contains traditional material heard from some fifty scholars assembled for the Sixth Southeastern Institute of Medieval and Renaissance Studies. That modern and urban folklore is by no means exclusively an American phenomenon is indicated by Stewart Sanderson's article "The Folklore of the Motor-Car," in *Folklore* 80 (1969): 241–52. A useful reference is Camilla Collins's "Bibliography of Urban Folklore," *FF* 8 (1975): 57–125. See also the discussion of urban legends in chapter 9 and the accompanying references.

Modern technology spawns folklore rather than replacing it or rendering it obsolete. Among others, Michael J. Preston has published examples of "Xeroxlore" in *KF* 19 (1974): 11–26; and in *JOFS* 3 (1975): 27–30. The first book-length collection and commentary was offered in Alan Dundes and Carl R. Pagter, *Urban Folklore from the Paperwork Empire*, American Folklore Society Memoirs, vol. 62 (Austin, Tex.: 1975), republished by Indiana University Press as *Work Hard and You Shall Be Rewarded* (1978). Dundes and Pagter have followed this book with three other anthologies. In 1976, two large collections of Xeroxlore were published in actual photocopy format by Xerox University Microfilms of Ann Arbor, Michigan: *Urban Folklore from Colorado: Typescript Broadsides*, ed. Cathy M. Orr and Michael J. Preston, and *Urban Folklore from Colorado: Photocopy Cartoons*, ed. Cathy M. Orr and Michael J. Preston. For a postmodernist look at American folklore, see John Dorst's "Tags and Burners, Cycles and Networks: Folklore in the Telectronic Age," *JFR* 27 (1990): 179–90.

Alan Dundes documents an old but prevailing mind-set of Americans (reflected frequently even in this textbook!) in an essay first published in 1968: "The Number Three in American Culture," reprinted in *Interpreting Folklore*, pp. 134–59. The sometimes quick reaction of modern folklore to current events is shown in Yvonne J. Milspaw's "Folklore and the Nuclear Age: 'The Harrisburg Disaster' at Three Mile Island," *IFR* 1 (1981): 57–65, as well as numerous other jokelore studies of recent years.

Contemporary social concerns reflected in folklore are the subjects of such essays as Norine Dresser's " 'The Boys in the Band Is Not Another Musical': Male Homosexuals and Their Folklore," *WF* 33 (1974): 205–18; Eve Mitchell's "Folklore of Marijuana Smoking," *SFQ* 34 (1970): 127–30; and many others listed in the bibliographic notes to subsequent chapters. The first book-length folklore study of its kind is Joseph Goodwin's *More Man Than You'll Ever Be: Gay Folklore and Acculturation in Middle America* (Bloomington: Indiana University Press, 1989). Folklore of the Vietnam War was discussed in four articles in *JAF* 102, no. 406 (1989). Illustrating just one of the "miscellaneous" minor folk groups possible to distinguish is Gary Alan Fine's article on the traditional humor of mushroom collectors, published in *WF* 47 (1988): 177–94.

Folklore collected from the folk group of folklorists themselves makes one wonder where it will all end. See Richard A. Reuss, " 'That Can't Be Alan Dundes! Alan Dundes is Taller Than That!' The Folklore of Folklorists," *JAF* 87 (1974): 303–17. This essay was supplemented by Regina Bendix's chapter on "Dundesiana," included in the Alan Dundes Festschrift listed under "Collections" at the beginning of the present book.

II

ORAL
FOLKLORE

The lore that circulates from person to person by word of mouth includes most traditions originally associated with the term "folklore." Most of it is *oral* (one may quibble about exactly how human speech is produced, and we make an exception for instrumental music); a good part of it is *verbal*. But all of it is *aural*. Calling it all "oral folklore" is something of a simplification, but to do so has been traditional for a long time in folklore studies. In an analogy with literary and language studies, these types of folklore are set up in collections, archives, and studies usually in terms of their relative linguistic or stylistic complexity—from words, names, phrases, and sentences, to questions (i.e., "riddles"), rhymes, stories, songs, and ballads. While beginning students should find this a convenient approach (especially as they peruse older folklore studies), they should always bear in mind that any given folklore performance is more than the automatic transmission of "text," more even than text-in-context, but is in fact a complex communicative event in which "oral folklore" items are only one conspicuous component.

Music is included in this section because so often in American folk tradition it coexists and interacts with words. Instead of separating purely instrumental tradition for discussion purposes, chapter 13 sketches out the whole topic of folk music.

4

FOLK SPEECH AND NAMING

The simplest level of verbal folklore is the traditional word, expression, usage, or name that is current in a folk group or in a particular region. When a Southerner says "y'all," or a Missourian pronounces his state name ending in "uh" [məz' ərə],* or an Easterner differs with a Midwesterner over what a soda and a cruller are, or a child names a puppy Rex, Prince, or Queenie, we have instances of what the folklorist calls **folk speech**. Strictly speaking, these subjects are in the domain of *linguistics* (especially dialect study, or "linguistic geography") and of *onomastics* (the study of names), but the folklorist has a legitimate and somewhat specialized interest in them, too.

DIALECTS AND SPEECH VARIATIONS

Dialect—the traditional deviation from standard speech—includes variations in *grammar* (both *morphology* and *syntax*), *pronunciation*, and *vocabulary*. While only trained linguists have the special ability and techniques needed to collect and study dialect in a rigorously scientific manner, they usually focus their attention on typical informants in one region who are interviewed on the basis of a formal

* The International Phonetic Alphabet (IPA) spelling to indicate pronunciation.

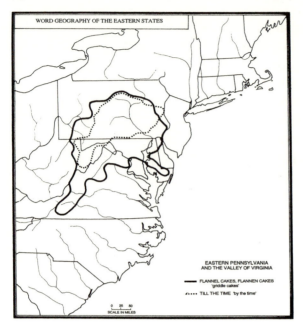

Dialect boundaries, or isoglosses, show the overlapping distribution of two folk expressions in the eastern United States.

questionnaire. Then "isoglosses," or dialect boundaries, may be mapped to show the distribution of certain usages, and these maps are potential guides for folklore collecting. But a "linguistic atlas" does not serve all the needs of research in folk speech. For one thing, some distinction should be made between standard regional dialects and special regional or social folk dialects.

Folklorists also concern themselves with the dialects of different groups, but they usually study deviations from standard speech as they are embedded in folktales, songs, rhymes, and other traditional contexts. Folklorists are interested in the use of dialect within groups, the retention of outmoded dialect forms in folk texts, and the linguistic changes that take place as texts are transmitted orally. Similarly, the naming that a folklorist studies is that which is traditional and which appears in the context of other folklore. Whatever their separate specialties, then, folklorists should be aware of some terms and techniques for collecting and studying folk speech, while students of dialect or names may benefit from an awareness of folklore research methods and of folk materials.

Variations of grammar in folk speech may consist of nonstandard word forms (morphology) or word order (syntax); collectors of folklore should carefully record both kinds without exaggerating their occurrence. Also they should note whether some expressions used in folklore are missing in everyday speech. There are countless variations possible, but space permits illustrating only a few. The past tense of verbs, for instance, is frequently nonstandard in regional folk speech, so that informants may say "It *snew* yesterday," "I *seen* him," or "He *drownded*"; the past tense of climb may be *clim* or *clum*, and such distinctions as *hung/hanged* or *lay/laid* made in polite speech may be disregarded. Some speech forms such as *boughten, enthused, being as,* or *different than* have become so common as to be almost respectable now, while others such as *fotch* (past of *fetch*) and *hit* (for *it*) linger only in isolated regions like the Southern Appalachians. Many modern folk expressions such as *I could care less* and *Tell it like it is*, although "ungrammatical," are heard in daily usage.

Dialect forms may be coined to fit a familiar pattern: the Ozark hillman has his combined verbs *house-clean, target-practice,* and many others like them, as do many other American groups. The college student has *proficiency-out* (to substitute a proficiency examination for a course; sometimes *test-out*) and *brown-nose* (to flatter an instructor). The combinations with *-ify* follow another favorite pattern; they range from *prettify* and *speechify* to *rectify* (to correct school homework) and *witchify* (to apply witchcraft to). Accounts of children's talk may qualify as folklore when they achieve oral circulation as part of a family's anecdotes: "It's *winding*" (on the analogy of *raining* and *snowing*), "I *hood* it from you" (nonstandard past tense of *hide*), and "We're *undusting*" (i.e., removing the dust).

Syntactical variations are often heard in the speech of nonnative-speaker groups, such as the Pennsylvania Germans, who are credited (in what is sometimes referred to as "ferhoodled English") with sentences like "Make the window up," "Don't eat yourself done, there's a pie back," "The off is on" (i.e., "The vacation has begun"), "Throw Mama from the train a kiss," and "Outen the lights." Often vocabulary plus word form or syntax vary simultaneously, as shown in the last example and in a sentence based on the word *liver-out* for "hired girl"—"Is your liver-out in?" Anecdotes based on expressions such as these are a form of folklore themselves, and they are more likely traditional tales than authentic incidents. Nevertheless, such speech does occur, and even in relatively sophisticated American circles one may occasionally hear syntactical oddities learned by imitation, not classroom instruction, such as "I can't remember things like I used to could." (The author once heard a professor shout, in an outburst of unreflective "folk speech," "Where you stayin' at, Jack?" in an elevator that was crowded with delegates to a national Modern Language Association convention.)

For a folklore collector untrained in linguistics, the phonetic transcription of dialect pronunciations may be too demanding, but a satisfactory substitute for most purposes is the use of rhyming words. Thus, for local community names, the pronunciation of *Moscow* [máskow] in Idaho may be reported as rhyming with *toe*; *Spokane* [spowkǽn] in Washington rhymes with *can* rather than *cane*; some residents of Indiana call their city of *Brazil* [bréyzəl] by a name rhyming with *hazel* (which may be closer to *gray zeal*, with almost no syllable accent); and *Versailles*, Indiana (also Kentucky), often rhymes with *curtails*. *Berlin*, New Hampshire, is accented on the first syllable, and the *Thames River* in Connecticut is pronounced *Thayms*, not *Temms*. The people of Utah speak of *Zion's Park* instead of Zion National Park. Such pronunciations as these for place-names may prove useful for defining the boundaries of folk regions.

Sometimes a dialect pronunciation may creep into spelling, as in the sign painted by a Southerner peddling "Red Haven" peaches who wrote "Raid Haven Peaches." Another handmade notice spotted one winter offered to shovel snow off "rooves." Or the college freshman frequently must be taught not to spell *athlete* as he or she carelessly pronounces it—*athalete*. A lengthy "manuscript of the folk language" laboriously typed out by an uneducated man for folklorist Duncan Emrich began in this manner:

> In Writing This Book I Have Carictorized It In The Best Manner Posible For Me To Remember As I Am A Man of 66. Years Of Age And Did Nevver Keep No Dairie Of The Dayley Happenings As I Should Of Did But Nevver Thinking Of Writing This Book, I Just Have To Go Back In Memory As Fare As Posible And Give The Facts As Best I Can Remember.

Especially when the point of a folk story turns on a certain pronunciation, it is important for the collector to record sounds carefully; such texts indicate folk recognition of dialect. Examples of this are jokes about Swedes confusing *jail* with *Yale*, or Finns praising the two American cars that begin with *P*—"the *Puiks* and the *Packards*." (The last instance might also be dated by the demise of the Packard.)

VOCABULARIES

Regional variations in **dialect vocabulary**—such as *earthworm, angleworm, night crawler, night walker, mud worm,* and *fish worm*; or *rootbeer float, black cow,* Boston cooler, and *Alaskan milkshake*—have been extensively mapped by linguistic geographers. Workers on the *Dictionary of American Regional English (DARE)*, a research project of many years' duration (which began partial publication in 1985), found more than 175 ways that Americans describe a downpour, including *hay rotter, duck drencher, tree bender, chunk floater, sewer clogger, clod roller, toad strangler,* stumpwasher, and *goosedrowner.*

goose-drowder n Also *gosling-drownder, goose-strangler,* ~ (or *duck*)*-drencher, duck-drownder, chicken-*~, *hen-*~ [*drownd* (at **drown 1**)] **chiefly Midl See Map Cf fish-drownder, frog-strangler**
A heavy rain, downpour.
   1929 *AmSp* 5.180 Ozarks, *Goose-drownder. . .* A very heavy rain, a cloudburst. **1933** Williamson *Woods Colt* 73 Ozarks, A reg'lar old goose-drowneder [sic] of a rain, this un is. **1939** *AmSp* 14.90 TN, The rain was a goose drownder. **1944** *AmSp* 19.205 cwIN, *Goose-drownder.* **1950** *PADS* 14.32 eSC, *Goose drownder.* **1953** Randolph–Wilson *Down in Holler* 248 Ozarks, Oh Lord, send us rain! We don't want no *drizzle-drozzle,* Lord. We don't want no *gully-washer,* nor no *fence-lifter.* What we need is a regular old *goose-drownder,* Lord! **1954** *WELS Suppl.* Milwaukee WI, "Goose drownder" . . an unusually heavy rain. **1960** Criswell *Resp. to PADS* 20 Ozarks, *(A heavy, continuous rain)* Hen-drownder. **1962** Atwood *Vocab.* TX 38, Duck drencher. **1965–70** *DARE* (Qu. B25, *. . Joking names . . for a very heavy rain*) 13 Infs, **chiefly N Midl,** Goose-drownder; IL81, IN29, Gosling-drownder; IL114, Goose-strangler; OH69, Goose-drencher; KY72, Goosedrownder, duck-drownder; WV4, 5, 8, Duck-drownder; KY28, Chicken-drownder; KS5, Hen-drownder; (Qu. B24, *. . A sudden, very heavy rain*) Infs NE9, OH36, 61, Goose-drownder. **1969** *Daily Progress* (Charlottesville, Va.) 22 Aug. 4/6 *(OEDS),* Other two-word names for a heavy rain . . are: bresh- or brush-mover, bridge-lifter, goose drownder, gully-washer, sand-packer, toad-strangler, and trash-mover. **1971** Bright *Word Geog. CA & NV* 113 cwCA, Gosling drownder—1 [inf]. **1983** *MJLF* 9.1.41 ceKY, *Goose drownder . .* a rain heavier than a *gulley washer.*

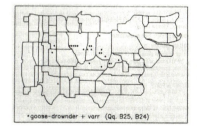

goose-drownder + varr (Qq. B25, B24)

Dictionary of American Regional English (DARE) entry, including a distribution map, for the term *goose-drownder* and its variations.

Focus: Hornswoggle

1. To embarrass, disconcert, confuse. . . . Also harnswaggle, hornscriggle, hornsnoggle, hornswaggle, hornswargle.

She's like a cow has tried to jump a high fence and has got hung up on it—she's hornswoggled. (1933)
2. To cheat or trick; to swindle . . .
   Them town fellers done hornscriggled ol' man Barton out'n his farm. (*1933*)
3. In phrase "I'll be hornswoggled" . . . expression of surprise, amazement, disgust.

Well, I'll be hornswoggled—look who's here! (1975)

Source: Vol. II of the *Dictionary of American Regional English* (*DARE*). Sense no. 1 is recorded from 1829, no. 2 from 1860, and no. 3 from 1834. Sense 3 also has the variant *dingswizzled.*

DISCUSSION TOPICS:

1. Are *hornswoggle* or its variations still current in American speech? What examples can you locate?

2. Some desk dictionaries attempt to link *hornswoggle* with cuckoldry, which in the past was associated with the image of "wearing horns" to signify one's embarrassment at being fooled in marriage. Another source claims that the word refers to the actions of a roped steer. Do the *DARE* quotations support these or other etymologies?

3. A dictionary of British dialect says that *hornswoggle* is an Americanism meaning to humbug, to delude, or to seduce. Similar terms used in England are listed: to *gammon, bamboozzle, flummox, put the kibosh on, slumbuzzle,* or *take in.* Are these terms, or others, still current in Great Britain or in the United States?

Folklorists tend to concern themselves less with the language of regions than with that of occupational and social folk groups. As a result, numerous glossaries have been compiled from such groups as actors, children, construction workers, homosexuals, jazz musicians, miners, railroad workers, and truck drivers, to name but a few. Euphemisms (for diarrhea or pregnancy, for instance) are a form of folk speech; for the former we hear *Delhi Belly, Montezuma's Revenge, the big D,* and *quick step,* and for the latter the most common allusion is to *having one in the oven.* Also part of folk speech are intensifiers like *hogwash, tarnation,* and *oh, fudge,* or such sham-swearing expressions (called "Missionary Swearing" in Utah) as

Cheese and rice got damp in the cellar. Other alternatives to "real" swearing include terms like *bull pucky* and *horse's patoot*. Actual profanity, blasphemy, cursing, and other "maledicta" are, of course, largely folk language, learned orally and practiced traditionally as well as varying according to time, place, and social situation.

The easiest test of a folk group's existence is to identify a specialized informal vocabulary; an important early step in any fieldwork project is to compile a glossary of the distinctive terminology of the group under study. By way of example, consider college students, who may at first appear not to have any significant oral traditions but from whom in a short time one might easily collect such terms (heard in the Northwest in 1961–63) as *high-school Harry*, *pasture function* (night picnic with beer), *pig pot* (money collected for the escort of the ugliest partner at an "exchange party"), *troll* (plain or ugly girl), and *wimp* (coward). These examples are possibly all now forgotten, and some have entered standard American English usage, but such campus language is being updated constantly, and students of folklore should collect their own current slang. Sometimes folk usage may become standard within the very institution where it first developed: for instance, the word *sluff* (for skipping school classes, i.e. "playing hookey," in older usage) became accepted as both a verb ("to sluff a class") and a noun ("how many sluffs do you allow?") among students, faculty, and administrators in at least one big-city school system. Eventually the school's official handbook provided information on "sluffs," and when a local newspaper reported on missed classes, it quoted "sluffing" as an explanation for a student's remark about "blowing off a class."

Even highly technical and specialized fields have their in-group folk expressions. Among themselves medical personnel speak of *gomers* (difficult and uncooperative patients, usually elderly), *blue bloaters* (sufferers from chronic emphysema), *crispy critters* (burn victims), and cases of *NAT* ("nonaccidental trauma," such as physical abuse by family members). A sick child, as yet undiagnosed, may be dubbed an *FLK*, or "funny-looking kid," in folk-medical shorthand. Such usages, it seems clear, are partly mechanisms for countering, via humor, some of the stresses of working daily with the sick and wounded. On the folk-medical level, a person may speak of having *spranged* his ankle or suffering *stomach flu*. Traditional terminology of illegal drug use includes *turn on, trip, speed, grass, pot, roach clip* (a holder for a marijuana cigarette), *blunt, cook, smack, spliff,* and many more words and phrases. Folk language of space flight includes *A-OK, blast off* (or *lift off*), *cherry picker, gantry, docking,* and nicknames for crew members, rockets, and moon-exploration vehicles. Computers have yielded a rich new vocabulary of *bits, bytes, glitches, crashes, hackers,* and the acronym *GIGO* (the programmer's maxim for "garbage in, garbage out"). More recently, such expressions as *surf the Web, hypertext,* and *WYSIWYG* ("What you see is what you get") have emerged, and there is a whole new vocabulary used in electronic mail (e-mail), including acronyms like *BTW* ("By the way") or *RTM* ("Read the manual") plus a vast number of variations on "smiley faces" composed of keyboard symbols (to be viewed sideways), such as :-)

The supposed explanations of acronyms for common short words are usually pure fantasy, unprovable at best. These folk etymologies include "port out, starboard home" (for *posh*), "constable on patrol" (for *cop*), "for unlawful carnal knowledge" (not hard to figure out), and "boys' ventilated drawers" (for the trade name *BVDs*). Sets of initials not forming words, used as signals in family folklore, are *FHB* (for "family hold back"—i.e., abstain from eating too much when guests are present), *LSF* ("lick and save fork"), and *PMIK* ("plenty more in the kitchen").

Not uncommonly, a traditional folk term acquires a new meaning as times change. The word *twofer*, for example, long used (and still sometimes used) in theater lore to mean "two tickets for the price of one," has lately also been employed as bureaucratic-personnel jargon for the appointment of a black woman to a government position. And *longhair*, once widely applied to lovers or performers of classical music, currently is more likely to refer to long-haired youth with rebellious or antisocial attitudes. (Some rebellious folk, on the other hand, shave their heads, becoming *skinheads*.)

Military-service personnel in general quickly learn to converse in their group's traditional terms, such as *KP* ("Kitchen Police"), *SOP* (standard operating procedure), *no sweat, deuce and a half* (for a two-and-a-half-ton truck), and *the old man*. When folk jokes based on a specialized vocabulary occur, we again have the phenomenon of folk commenting on their own distinctiveness. One such *GI* (Government Issue) story concerns a *USO* (United Service Organizations) entertainer who was asked whether she preferred "to *mess* with the officers or the men"; she responded, "Makes no difference, but can I eat first?" As official military terminology changes, so does the folk speech: *C-Rations* of World War II, the butt of many jokes, became *Meals Ready to Eat* by the time of the Gulf War, and soldiers soon said that *MRE* stood for "meals rejected by Ethiopians."

Among nationality groups in the United States a whole conglomerate dialect language sometimes develops in the first generation. Norwegians tell about an emigrant joyfully greeting his mother back in the old country with "How's my *gamle mor?*" (The Norwegian words mean "old mother," the only words she would understand in the sentence.) Another Norwegian-American is supposed to have remarked, describing a disastrous drought, *"Jeg luse hele kroppen,"* meaning, to him, "I lost my whole crop"; but in Norwegian the sentence sounds more like "I have lice on my entire body." In "Finglish" the word *nafiksi* sometimes occurs—nonexistent in native Finnish but derived in the United States from the English *enough*. A Finnish-American storyteller might also end a text with the sentence *"Ne sanot että se oli tosi stori"* ("They said it was a true story"), using the final English word in an otherwise Finnish context. In the "Tex-Mex" spoken in the bilingual Southwest, one might hear *"Dame mi pokebuk"* ("Give me my pocketbook") or *"Es un eswamp"* ("It's a swamp").

"Pig Latin" and other secret languages of children deserve study. These include "backwards talk," "Double Dutch," "G-talk," "King Tut," sign languages, and certain orthographic codes for writing secret messages. Even more peculiar is a regional "slanguage" discovered in Boonville, California, and dubbed "Boontling." Here a language of apparently nonsensical words was invented by children, but later spread to adults of the community. At first, the parents picked up the expressions in an attempt to understand and communicate with their children. Then others found in them a way to express what they felt was the uniqueness of Boonville, unrecognized and unappreciated by outsiders. The language includes many nouns, such as *gannow* ("apple"), *beemsh* ("show"), and *higg* ("money"); verbs such as *dehigg* ("spend money") and *deek* ("learn"); and a few adjectives, such as *ball* ("fine"). The "Boontling" terms, together with local nicknames, are used in oral communication only and intermixed with otherwise conventional English. The following sentences are typical: "We have ball gannows here in Boont. Why don't we dehigg ourselves and have a beemsh so people will deek how ball our gannows are?"

FOCUS: BUCK FANSHAW'S FUNERAL

After Buck Fanshaw's inquest . . . a committee of one was deputed to call on the minister, a fragile, gentle spirituel [sic] new fledgling from an eastern theological seminary, and as yet unacquainted with the ways of the mines. The committeeman, "Scotty" Briggs, made his visit; and in after days it was worth something to hear the minister tell about it.
    . . . "Are you the duck that runs the gospel-mill next door?"
    "Am I the—pardon me, I believe I do not understand?"
    With another sigh and a half-sob, Scotty rejoined, ". . . [are you] the head clerk of the doxology-works next door."
    "I am the shepherd in charge of the flock whose fold is next door. . . . I am a clergyman—a parson."
    "Now you talk! You see my blind and straddle it like a man. . . . We're in a power of trouble. You see, one of the boys has gone up the flume—"
    "Gone where?"

"Up the flume—throwed up the sponge, you understand."

"Thrown up the sponge?"

"Yes—kicked the bucket—"

"Ah—has departed to that mysterious country from whose bourne no traveler returns."

"Return? I reckon not. Why pard, he's dead!"

"Yes, I understand."

"Oh, you do? Well I thought maybe you might be getting tangled some more."

Source: Chapter 47 of Mark Twain's *Roughing It* (1872), based on Western travels of 1861 onward.

DISCUSSION TOPICS:

1. How would you characterize the speech patterns of "Scotty" versus the parson (elaborated throughout this chapter of *Roughing It*)? Which expressions can be validated as folk speech, and which seem to be Mark Twain's comic invention?

2. Are these traditional euphemisms for death still current? What other such expressions are used nowadays?

Folklorists' studies of American folk speech have usually been mere collections, although sometimes these have been imaginative ones. George W. Boswell extracted folk etymologies from folksong diction, finding such onomatopoetic terms as *trinkling* ("Her life's blood came *trinkling* down"), oral mistakes like "He dressed himself in a *tie* [for *attire*] of blue," and irregular verb forms: "I *tuck* her by her yellow hair / I *drug* her 'round and 'round." In a closer analysis of traditional speech patterns, Alan Dundes recognized three kinds of reduplicative phrases—*identical* (*din din* or *goody goody*), *ablaut* (*zigzag*), and *rhyming* (*mumbo jumbo*)—with a marked preference in American English for the third type. The "Henny Penny phenomenon" of initial-consonant alternation appears in many verbal folk forms, often as /h/:/p/ (*henpecked*), or /t/:/l/ (*Turkey Lurkey, toodle-loo*), and even in such commercial brand names as Hotpoint and Hush Puppies (already a folk term).

NAMING

Folk naming practices present a broad field for collecting as well as some interesting possibilities for interpretation, since there are certain traditional names or nicknames for almost anything that can be given a name, ranging from family members and domestic animals to vacation cottages, apartment houses, family cars and sports cars, rifles, and elusive game fish. As in some primitive cultures in which one's "real" name is earned by a great deed or perhaps even a shortcoming, American folk practice is to name children for some notable man or woman, to give names of positive connotation, to avoid giving names thought inappropriate for the child's sex, or to select someone's nickname because of his or her appearance, behavior, or background.

Place-names—both for geographic features and for communities —have been more thoroughly researched than any other branch of name lore, but even here vast areas remain unexplored. From the folklorist's point of view (but not the historian's or the cartographer's) the legendary folk etymologies for place-names are of prime concern. Thus the folk imagination can be counted on to concoct a story about gnawing on bones to explain a town name like *Gnawbone* (Indiana), whereas the likely origin is a corruption of the displaced French name *Narbonne*. Also having traditional roots are regional nicknames like *Hoosier*, *Sooner*, or *Webfoot*.

Studies have been made of such subjects as folk names for cats (*Tabby, Tom*, etc.), for plants (*piss fir, spear grass*, etc.), for pioneer foods (*hush puppies, hoe cakes, pluck and plunder stew*, etc.), and even for automobiles (*Blue Boy, Magnificent Six, Little White Dove, Travellin' Man*, etc.). Traditional variations in a folk name are demonstrated in those used for a favorite picnic dessert made from toasted marshmallows, graham crackers, and a chocolate bar: *somemores, Brownie Delights, angels on horseback, angels with dirty faces, heavenly hoboes*, and *heavenly hash*. (The latter is also sometimes applied to a whipped-cream and fruit-cocktail salad, and it has been used as a name for a commercial ice-cream flavor.) In using traditional names like these, people are sometimes only following tradition or habit (*Tabby*); other times they may be rendering judgment (*piss fir*), alluding to a legend (*hush puppies*), revealing a mood (*Blue Boy*), or creating metaphysical images (*angels with dirty faces*).

Names play a traditional role—though not always an apparent one—in such folk sayings as "robbing *Peter* to pay *Paul*," "every *Tom, Dick*, and *Harry*," "The real *McCoy*," and "quicker than you can say '*Jack Robinson*.'" Certain names recur in folk ballads (*Pretty*

Loggers in Harlan County, Kentucky, whipsawing logs and "scoring lumber"—
that is, grading, sorting, and tallying the wood (ca. 1890–1903).

Polly), folktales (*Jack*), and legends (*Old Scratch* and *Old Nick*), while
other names creep into everyday usage in remarks like "sign your
John Hancock" (or, mistakenly, "your *John Henry*") and in sample
addresses to *John Doe* or *John Q. Citizen*. Finally, ethnic names and
place-names are employed as slurring adjectives in such terms as
Dutch treat, *Irish lace* (spider webs), *Mexican credit card* (a hose for
stealing gasoline), *Indian giver*, *Puerto Rico Pendleton* (an old work
shirt), *Swedish fiddle* (either a crosscut saw or an accordion), *French
screwdriver* (a hammer), *Jewish penicillin* (chicken soup), and *Vatican
roulette* (the "rhythm" birth-control method).

The vocabulary and traditional naming habits of one folk group
can be a fascinating subject for a limited folklore study. Northwest
loggers offer a convenient example, for nearly every aspect of their
life and work has acquired a distinctive folk term. There are terms
for pieces of equipment (*A-frame*, *bells and buttons*, *gut wrappers*),
terms for particular jobs (*cat skinner*, *choker setter*, *pond monkey*),
terms for trees and logs (*widow maker*—a dangerously leaning or
hanging tree or limb; *barber chair*—a split-cut stump), and even
special terms for some foods (*saddle blankets* for hotcakes, *chokum*
for cheese, *excelsior* for noodles, *bear sign* for blackberry jam).

Some of these loggers' terms have either penetrated to more general usage by other groups or have acquired specialized meanings in
the woods, and it is often impossible to tell which way a term has
gone. *Haywire*, for instance, has long been used by loggers to refer

to any lightweight wire (also called *straw wire*), and when such wire was frequently used for general camp repairs, it became a *haywire outfit*—a patched-together and mixed-up camp. An alternative explanation is that when one cuts baling wire loose from a bale, the wire goes every which way in a tangled mess. These may be either the origins of or only offshoots from the generally used expression "to go haywire." Similarly, the logger uses *hoosier* not for a resident of Indiana, necessarily, but for any greenhorn in the woods. A *gypo outfit* in loggers' parlance is not a company that "gyps" customers, but simply a company, especially a small one, that logs on contract. The term *skid road*, used originally for a log-skidding road, then for the tough streets in West Coast towns, has been altered to *skid row* in general usage. (The loggers consider the term as phony as *lumberjack*, the term applied to the loggers by almost everyone but themselves.)

Names and naming contribute further to the flavor of woods terminology. Corn bread may be designated *Arkansaw wedding cake*; a homemade lantern is a *palouser* (from the "Palouse" region of eastern Washington and northern Idaho); the Chinook word *Potlatch* (a gift-exchange festival) appears in the company name "Potlatch Forests Incorporated" (called P.F.I. or "Pin Feathers, Inc." locally), as well as in place-names and in such terms as *Potlatch turkey* (crow) and *Potlatch tram* (a type of logging tramway). The American loggers' *peavey*, used all over the country, supposedly was developed by J. H. Peavey of Bangor, Maine, but a *Jacob's staff* and a *Johnson bar* are other tools not clearly traceable to sources. Loggers have christened their trucks and other modern equipment with such nicknames as *The Monster, Old Asthma, Road Runner*, or *Widow Maker*, just as fellow workers bear such descriptive nicknames as *White Pine Joe, The Galvanized Swede, Cruel-Jimmy Holmes*, and *Greasy Pete*.

A similar collecting project might successfully focus on any occupational group. Thus, the house painter's "haywire outfit" is a *Joe McGee rig*, although just why this name refers to makeshift equipment is unclear. (From the term come the verbs *Joe McGee it* or simply *McGee it*.) Paint cans are always *pots*, thinner of any kind is *turps*, the last coat of paint applied is *the third coat*, and so forth. With the popularity of citizens-band two-way radios spreading from truckers to the general public, the esoteric "CB" language became better known: *the dirty side* refers to the eastern United States, *clean side* to the West. A highway patrolman is *Smoky the Bear*, and when he is checking traffic speeds, "Smoky's in the woods taking pictures." Furniture trucks are *bedbug haulers*, and a truckload of new cars is a *future junk yard*. In the folk language of some college students the course names may be humorously replaced: Abnormal Psychology becomes *Nuts and Sluts*; Introductory Geology is *Rocks for Jocks*; Military History is *Tanks and Jeeps*; *Play a Day* refers to English Drama; and *Darkness at Noon* fits an art-history class held in the middle of the day and largely devoted to showing slides of the works studied.

Every trade, every hobby, every age group, and every region has a dialect of its own, most still awaiting the thorough collector of folk speech. When such linguistic strayings from the standard speech are purely ephemeral or technical, they may be regarded as *slang* or *jargon*, respectively; but when such language is longer-lived and more generally used, it becomes traditional speech of prime interest to the folklorist.

BIBLIOGRAPHIC NOTES

Linguistic, onomastic, and folkloristic studies of folk speech are scattered through the professional books and journals of all three disciplines. A good general survey of the subject is Raven I. McDavid's chapter "The Dialects of American English," in W. Nelson Francis's *The Structure of American English* (New York: Ronald Press, 1958), pp. 480–543. McDavid also provides a comprehensive view of the two related disciplines in "Linguistic Geography and the Study of Folklore," *NYFQ* 14 (1958): 242–62. For the folklorist's point of view, see Louis Pound's "Folklore and Dialect," *CFQ* 4 (1945): 146–53, reprinted in *Nebraska Folklore*, pp. 211–21. Jay Robert Reese made specific suggestions for cooperative studies in "Dialectology and Folklore: Woodscolts in Search of Kin," *TFSB* (1979): 48–60.

Two useful general reference works are *A Dictionary of Americanisms on Historical Principles*, ed. M. M. Mathews (Chicago: University of Chicago Press, 1951), and *Dictionary of American Slang*, ed. Harold Wentworth and Stuart Berg Flexner (New York: Crowell, 1960; reissued with supplement, 1967). The basic background study for all such research is H. L. Mencken's *The American Language*, first published in 1919, issued in a rewritten and enlarged edition in 1936, with supplements added in 1945 and 1948, and subsequently many times reprinted (New York: Alfred A. Knopf).

Linguistic geographer Frederic G. Cassidy reviews the history of a proposed "Dictionary of American Regional English" in "The ADS Dictionary—How Soon?" *PADS* no. 39 (1963): 1–7. The *DARE* project was accepted in 1964 as a cooperative research project of the Department of Health, Education, and Welfare;

the American Dialect Society; and the University of Wisconsin. Volume I of the
DARE, including letters A through C, appeared in 1985; volume II, letters D
through H, appeared in 1991. A thorough study in one state's folk speech is E.
Bagby Atwood's *The Regional Vocabulary of Texas* (Austin: University of Texas
Press, 1962).

Most folk-speech studies by folklorists concern vocabulary; three exceptions alluded to in this chapter are Gordon Wilson's "Some Folk Grammar," *TFSB* 33
(1967): 27–35; George W. Boswell's "The Operation of Popular Etymology in
Folksong Diction," *TFSB* 39 (1973): 37–58; and Alan Dundes's "The Henny Penny
Phenomenon: A Study of Folk Phonological Esthetics in American Speech," *SFQ*
38 (1974): 1–9.

Dundes documents what he calls "future orientation in American worldview"
largely from folk speech in an essay entitled "Thinking Ahead" (in *Interpreting
Folklore*, pp. 69–85). Yet another approach was taken by Duncan Emrich in "A
Manuscript of the Folk Language," *WF* 11 (1952): 266–83, wherein he presents a
verbatim transcript of a "folk" speaker just as the speaker wrote (or rather typed)
out his reminiscences, spelling and punctuating the words and sentences exactly
as they sounded to him.

An imaginative study by Howard Wight Marshall and John Michael Vlach
demonstrates the relationship between folk dialect and folk architecture; see "Toward a Folklife Approach to American Dialects," *AS* 48 (1973): 163–91. In Wayland D. Hand's "From Idea to Word" (*AS* 48 [1973]: 67–76), several folk words
and expressions that derive from folk beliefs and customs are explained.

The best dialect survey of an American folklore region is Vance Randolph and
George P. Wilson's *Down in the Holler: A Gallery of Ozark Folk Speech* (Norman:
University of Oklahoma Press, 1953; paperback repr., 1979). Ramon Adams's three
books on Western folk speech, *Cowboy Lingo* (Boston: Houghton Mifflin, 1936),
Western Words (Norman: University of Oklahoma Press, 1944: rev. ed., 1968), and
The Cowboy Says It Salty (Tucson: University of Arizona Press, 1971) are author-
itative and highly readable. On Western American folk speech see also Richard
Poulsen, "Black George, Black Harris, and the Mountain Man Vernacular," *Ren-
dezvous* 8 (Summer 1973): 15–23.

For a discussion of "Spanglish" in Puerto Rico see Rose Nash in *AS* 45 (1970):
223–33; the same author discusses "Englañol" [Spanishized English] in *AS* 46
(1971): 106–22.

Children's folk speech, a neglected subject, is treated in Rochele Berkovits's
"Secret Languages of Schoolchildren," *NYFQ* 26 (1970): 127–52; her examples
include sign languages, bop talk, pig Latin, girl talk, boy talk, and an orthographic
code traceable back to sixteenth-century Italian practice. Mary and Herbert Knapp
discuss "Tradition and Change in American Playground Language" in *JAF* 86
(1973): 131–41; they analyze truce terms, terminology in games of tag, and a
ceremony performed after children accidentally say the same thing and shout
"jinx."

"Boontling," first reported in a folklore journal in the 1940s, has been widely
discussed since. Charles C. Adams gathers most references and presents a detailed

study in *Boontling: An American Lingo* (Austin: University of Texas Press, 1971), which should be supplemented with E. N. Anderson, Jr., and Marja C. Anderson, "The Social Context of a Local 'Lingo,'" *WF* 29 (1970): 153–65.

Fully documented historical studies of individual expressions are well represented by Allen Walker Read's "The Folklore of O.K.," *AS* 39 (1964): 5–25; and Peter Tamony's " 'Hootenanny': The Word, Its Content and Continuum," *WF* 22 (1963): 165–70. The general language of American labor is glossed in an appendix to Archie Green's article "John Neuhaus: Wobbly Folklorist," *JAF* 73 (1960): 189–217. The following works are only a few of the many that deal with vocabulary in a particular occupation: Walter F. McCulloch, *Woods Words: A Comprehensive Dictionary of Loggers' Terms* (Portland: Oregon Historical Society, 1958); Roberta Hanley, "Truck Drivers' Language in the Northwest," *AS* 36 (1961): 271–74; John F. Runice, "Truck Drivers' Jargon," *AS* 44 (1969): 200–9; Terry L. McIntyre, "The Language of Railroading," *AS* 44 (1969): 243–62; T. G. Lish, "Word List of Construction Terms," *PADS* no. 36 (1961): 25–31; Barbara P. Harris and Joseph F. Kess, "Salmon Fishing Terms in British Columbia," *Names* 23 (1975): 61–66; Gerald E. Warshaver, "Schlop Scholarship: A Survey of Folkloristic Studies of Lunchcounter and Soda Jerk Operatives," *FF* 4 (1971): 134–45; Marvin Carmony, "The Speech of CB Radio: Observations on Its Past, Present, and Future," *MJLF* 4 (1978): 5–17; Roberta Krell, ". . . The Technical Language of Pitchmen," *FMS* 4 (1980): 26–32; and two by Kelsie B. Harder: "The Vocabulary of Hog-Killing," *TFSB* 25 (1959): 111–15; and "Hay-Making Terms in Perry County," *TFSB* 33 (1967): 41–48.

Further references suggest some folk-speech topics outside of strictly regional or labor terminology: S. J. Sackett, "Marble Words from Hays, Kansas," *PADS* no. 37 (1962): 1–3; R. T. Prescott, "Calls to Animals," *SFQ* 2 (1938): 39–42; Gertrude Churchill Whitney, "New England Bird Language," *WF* 20 (1961): 113–14; C. Douglas Chrétien, "Comments on Naval Slang," *WF* 6 (1947): 157–62; Richard K. Seymour, "Collegiate Slang: Aspects of Word Formation and Semantic Change," *PADS* no. 51 (1969): 13–22; Paul A. Eschholz and Alfred F. Rosa, "Course Names: Another Aspect of College Slang," *AS* 45 (1970): 85–90; Julia P. Stanley, "Homosexual Slang," *AS* 45 (1970): 45–59; Sterling Eisiminger, "Acronyms and Folk Etymology," *JAF* 9 (1978): 582–84; and Sidney I. Landau, "Popular Meanings of Scientific and Technical Terms," *AS* 55 (1980): 204–9.

The folk speech of medical personnel is the focus of three publications: Victoria George and Alan Dundes, "The Gomer: A Figure of American Hospital Folk Speech," *JAF* 91 (1978): 568–81; C. J. Scheiner, "Common Patient-directed Pejoratives Used by Medical Personnel," *Maledicta* 2 (1978): 67–70; and Lois Monteiro, "Not Sticks and Stones, but Names: More Medical Pejoratives," *Maledicta* 4 (1980): 53–58.

Names, published quarterly as the journal of the American Name Society, since 1953, is the major organ for onomastic activities and studies in this country. The society's pamphlet publication, *Theory of Names*, by Ernst Pulgram (Berkeley: 1954), is a solid introduction to the field.

George R. Stewart's frequently reprinted book *Names on the Land* (New York:

Random House, 1945; 4th ed., San Francisco: Lexikos, 1982) is the basic introduction for American place-name studies, many of which have been carried out
in great detail for individual states; two good ones that have been recently revised
are Lewis A. McArthur's *Oregon Geographic Names* (1928), 3rd ed. (Portland: 1952),
and Will C. Barnes's *Arizona Place Names* (1935), rev. and enl. Byrd H. Granger
(Tucson: University of Arizona Press, 1960). A newer volume is Ronald L. Baker's
From Needmore to Prosperity: Hoosier Place Names in Folklore and History (Bloomington: Indiana University Press, 1995). E. Joan Wilson Miller, a geographer with
folklore training, discusses "The Naming of the Land in the Arkansas Ozarks: A
Study in Cultural Processes" in *Annals of the Association of American Geographers*
59 (1969): 240–51. Terry L. Alford's article "An Interesting American Place-
Name," in *MFR* 2 (1968): 76–78, concerns the name "Indianola," seventeen examples of which in the United States he attributes to the origin in Texas, renamed
from "Powderhorn" in 1849, and not because of an Indian maiden named "Ola,"
as is sometimes reported. W. F. H. Nicolaisen treated "Some Humorous Folk-
Etymological Narratives" in *NYF* 3 (1977): 1–13. Robert M. Rennick discussed in
general "The Folklore of Place-Naming in Indiana" in *IF* 3 (1970): 35–94, while
Ronald L. Baker discusses the Indiana place named "Monsterville" in *Names* 20
(1972): 186–92. Audrey R. Duckert identifies eight varieties of "Place Nicknames"
in *Names* 21 (1973): 153–60. An article by Hazel E. Mills, "The Constant Webfoot," in *WF* 11 (1952): 153–64, traces the history of Oregon's state nickname.

   The general role of names and naming in folklore is taken up by Robert M.
Rennick in "The Folklore of Curious and Unusual Names (A Brief Introduction
to the Folklore of Onomastics)," *NYFQ* 22 (1966): 5–14; and by Jan Harold Brunvand in the introduction to a special folklore issue of *Names*: 16 (Sept. 1968): 197–
206. Byrd Howell Granger surveys a subarea in her article "Naming: In Customs,
Beliefs, and Folktales," *WF* 20 (1961): 27–37. Warren E. Roberts, in a review of
P. H. Reaney's book *The Origin of English Surnames* (FF 14 [1981]: 41–50), provides
a good argument and excellent examples for folklorists' interest in this category
of naming. See also Robert M. Rennick, "Successive Name-Changing: A Popular
Theme in Onomastic Folklore and Literature," *NYFQ* 25 (1969): 119–28; O. Paul
Straubinger, "Names in Popular Sayings," *Names* 3 (1955): 157–64; and Archer
Taylor, "The Use of Proper Names in Wellerisms and Folktales," *WF* 18 (1959):
287–93. Nicknames (among Amish) are the subject of studies by Maurice A. Mook
in *Names* 15 (1967): 111–18; (among prison inmates) by Bruce Jackson in *WF* 26
(1967): 48–54; and (in an immigrant community) by Rosemary Hyde Thomas in
"Traditional Types of Nicknames in a Missouri French Creole Community,"
MFSJ 2 (1980): 15–25.

   J. L. Dillard's *Black Names* (Contributions to the Sociology of Language 13
[The Hague and Paris: Mouton, 1976]) traces patterns of African usage in black
American naming. He considers personal names, musical-group names, church
names, vehicle names, and names in trade and business. A comprehensive view
of naming practices by Leonard R. N. Ashley has the inevitable title *What's in a
Name . . . Everything You Wanted to Know* (Baltimore: Genealogical Publishing
Co., 1989).

A study of the term preferred by an ethnic group for self-reference is José E. Limón's "The Folk Performance of 'Chicano' and the Cultural Limits of Political Ideology," included in *"And Other Neighborly Names . . . ,"* ed. Richard Bauman and Roger D. Abrahams (Austin: University of Texas Press, 1981), pp. 197–225.

A miscellany of name studies for specific subjects includes blooming plants— Lalia Phipps Boone in *SFQ* 19 (1955): 230–36; cats—Wendell S. Hadlock and Anna K. Stimson in *JAF* 59 (1946): 529–30, and Archer Taylor in *JAF* 60 (1947): 86; cars—Jan Harold Brunvand in *Names* 10 (1962): 279–84, and *WF* 23 (1964): 264–65; apartment houses—Elli Kaija Köngäs in *JAF* 77 (1964): 80–81; tobacco— Kathrine T. Kell in *JAF* 79 (1966): 590–99.

House painters' jargon of the kind quoted in this chapter is collected by Donald M. Hines in *AS* 44 (1969): 5–32, and by John Michael Bennett in *SFQ* 33 (1969): 313–16.

Ed Cray discusses "Ethnic and Place Names as Derisive Adjectives" and gives numerous examples in *WF* 21 (1962): 27–34. David J. Winslow takes a more specialized approach in "Children's Derogatory Epithets," *JAF* 82 (1969): 255–63. George Monteiro's examples are "Chinese Fire Drill," "French Screw Driver" (a hammer), and "Jewish Penicillin" (chicken soup) in his note published in *WF* 34 (1975): 244–46. The best summary of scholarship and most systematic approach to this whole subject is found in Alan Dundes's "Slurs International: Folk Comparisons of Ethnicity and National Character," *SFQ* 39 (1975): 15–38.

The founding of the journal *Maledicta* in 1977 specifically to publish studies of cursing and other aggressive language signaled a new wave of interest in this area of research. Some samples of essays published there are Reinhold Aman's (editor of *Maledicta*) "An Onomastic Questionnaire," in 1 (1977): 83–101; David L. Closson's "The Onomastics of the Rabble" (nicknames in a predominantly black male liberal arts college), in 1 (1977): 215–33; Sterling Eisiminger's "A Glossary of Ethnic Slurs in American English," in 3 (1979): 153–74; and Gary Alan Fine's "Rude Words: Insults and Narratives in Preadolescent Obscene Talk," in 5 (1981): 51– 68. Of related interest is Sandra K. D. Stahl's "Cursing and Its Euphemisms: Power, Irreverence, and the Unpardonable Sin," *MJLF* 3 (1977): 54–68. (The unpardonable sin, she finds, is blasphemy directed against the Holy Spirit.)

5

PROVERBS AND PROVERBIAL LORE

A proverb is a popular *saying* in a relatively *fixed form* that is, or has been, in *oral circulation*. Many attempts have been made to define proverbs more precisely than this, usually in terms of their origin ("the wisdom of many, the wit of one"), their nature (sayings that "sum up a situation . . . characterize its essence"), or their function ("to provide an argument for a course of action which conforms to community values"); but the three qualities italicized above are basic to all. First, the proverb must be a saying, not merely a traditional word like "fiddlesticks" or "phooey." Second, the proverb exists in a somewhat standardized form; "sour grapes" is proverbial, but not "bitter grapes," or "acid grapes," or "sweet grapes." Third, a proverb must have had some oral vitality as distinguished from the written clichés of poetry, advertising, sports reporting, and the like. The combination of all three features is what makes "Waste not, want not!" or "Keep your eye upon the donut and not upon the hole" or "If you're going to talk the talk you have to walk the walk" proverbs.

Proverbs are perhaps the most common and familiar form of *conversational folklore* (oral traditions that occur frequently in everyday situations of communication); but proverbs are much more than mere quotable quotes, wise sayings, or memorable phrases. People employ proverbial expressions to pass judgment on events, to give advice, to rationalize their own actions, or to criticize and praise others. Proverbs provide a "name" or a category for situations that recur in life, saying, in effect, something like "That's a matter of a little knowledge being a dangerous thing" or "You shouldn't judge a book by its cover, you know." And proverbs come to mind not only when speaking conversationally but also in teaching, preaching, counseling, political persuasion, advertising, and many other situations of communication and personal interaction. Both the events that we recognize as being part of the common human experience and the sayings that we traditionally draw upon to describe these situations have become "proverbial." For unclear reasons, some authored epigrams, like "I'd rather be right than be President" or "History is bunk," have never become proverbial, while many others, like "Pride goeth before a fall" or "Something is rotten in Denmark," have, though (as here) these are generally misquoted. Four major categories of proverbs and proverbial lore, with several subdivisions, plus a broad classification of miscellaneous sayings, may be distinguished in American tradition, and most of these are paralleled in folk sayings throughout the world.

TRUE PROVERBS

The **true proverb** is always a complete sentence, varies slightly in form, and usually expresses some general truth or wisdom. Such sayings are termed "fixed phrase" kinds of oral folklore, and the variation comes in their meanings and uses in particular contexts. Some true proverbs are simple sententious comments such as "Live and let live," "Absence makes the heart grow fonder," and "Accidents will happen." A few of these leave part of the sentence (here the verb) unstated but understood: "No fool like an old fool," "Penny-wise and pound-foolish," etc. Other true proverbs are based on Aesop's fables or similar old stories—for example, "Don't count your chickens before they hatch" and "Don't kill the goose that lays the golden egg." But the majority of true proverbs are metaphorical descriptions of an act or event applied as a general truth; examples are numerous: "A burnt child dreads the fire," "A new broom sweeps clean," "A rolling stone gathers no moss," etc. The "wisdom" expressed in a true proverb, rather than being in the form of a serious adage, may employ irony or other wit, as in "Marry in haste, repent at leisure" or "Be true to your teeth or they will be false to you."

PROVERBIAL PHRASES

Proverbial phrases, on the other hand, are never complete sentences, regularly vary in form as they are used, and seldom express any generalized wisdom; nearly all of them are metaphorical. Proverbial verb phrases vary in number and tense and permit the addition of adverbial modifications. Such traditional phrases are often anthologized as infinitives ("to be in hot water," "to raise the roof," "to cut off one's nose to spite one's face"), although they do not occur in speech that way ("He's in hot water now!" or "You're going to get in hot water doing that!"). Phrases without a verb are equally common, such as "behind the eight ball," "from A to Z" (a modernization of "from Alpha to Omega"), and "a song and dance." Some proverbial phrases allow for extensions, either of images or applications. For instance, "up a creek" may add "without a paddle," and the creek may be named.

The meanings of traditional proverbial phrases are usually clear, even if the exact image intended or the origin of the expression is unknown. For example, the well-known phrase "to have one's ducks in a row" may have originally referred to actual baby ducklings lined up, to adult ducks flying in a line and being hunted, to model ducks lined up in a shooting gallery, or (the most likely etymology) to the wooden pins arranged for play in the bowling game called "skittles" or "duck pins." These variant meanings matter little when a person admits in conversation "I didn't have my ducks in a row" (i.e., "I wasn't very well organized or prepared for that situation.") or when a company brags in an advertisement "We've got our ducks in a row" (i.e., "We are well prepared to serve the public.") Is "ducks in a row" an old traditional proverb? Possibly not, as the earliest citation of the phrase in the *Dictionary of American Regional English* is from a 1944 issue of *Newsweek*, where the saying is described as "a bit of business vernacular."

(Above) A popular proverbial phrase used in an advertisement promises to organize borrowers' finances and provide preapproved home mortgages (America First Credit Union, Salt Lake City, Utah). *(Below)* A cartoon directed at academics parodies the popular proverbial phrase "to get my ducks in a row."

PROVERBIAL COMPARISONS

While proverbial phrases are traditional metaphors, **proverbial comparisons** are traditional similes, usually expressed in the "like" or
"as" form. A proverbial comparison may be logical and direct ("red
as a beet," "go like blazes," "greedy as a pig"), or it may be ironic
("as clear as mud," "a face like a can full of worms," "as little chance
as a snowball in Hell"). Often there is humorous particularization
or exaggeration in American proverbial comparisons; "go like
blazes," for instance, becomes "go like blue blazes," or a person's
luck is described in terms of the chances of "a celluloid cat chased
by an asbestos dog in Hell." Some comparisons are formally grammatical ("cool as a cucumber"), but others are not ("quick like a
bunny"). Many American proverbial comparisons are graphic and
quite variable: "slick as snot," for example, though meaningful
enough as it stands, gains even more effect when further terms are
added. The saying becomes "slick as snot on an ax handle" (or "on
a new ax handle"), "slick as snot on a doorknob" (or "a brass doorknob"), and, in its ultimate slickness, "slick as snot on a new glass
doorknob." Sayings may be stated in comparative form ("tighter
than a drum," "lower than a snake's belly," "blacker than a stack
of black cats") or in the "so . . . that" or "more . . . than" pattern:
"so tight he screaks," "so slow you have to set a stake to see him
move," "more nerve than Carter has Little Liver Pills," "more trou-
bles than you can shake a stick at," and so on.

A form of comparative expression popularized in recent years, *the
metaphorical putdown*, often follows the pattern "[he or she] is some
X short of a full Y," as in "He's a few pickles short of a barrel."
Variations include "He's two bricks shy of a load," ". . . a few
sandwiches short of a picnic," and ". . . one French fry short of a
Happy Meal." The older equivalent saying was ". . . not playing
with a full deck," and contemporary variations on the idea, if not
the structure, of the putdowns include "He's got a bad spot on his
disk," ". . . doesn't have all his groceries in the same bag," ". . .
doesn't have all the dots on his dice," ". . . is all booster, no payload,"
and "The cheese has slid off his cracker."

WELLERISMS

The **Wellerism** (or "Quotation Proverb"), named for Charles Dickens's character Sam Weller, in *Pickwick Papers* (1837), who often used them, is a fourth major kind of proverb. Wellerisms—actually much older than their nineteenth-century namesake—are easy to identify but harder to imagine from their definition: "a saying in the form of a quotation followed by a phrase ascribing the quotation to someone who has done something humorous and appropriate." For example: " 'Everyone to his own taste,' [quotation] as the old lady said [ascription] when she kissed the cow [action]." A subvariant involves someone spoken to: " 'There's always a first time,' as the actress said to the bishop." Other familiar Wellerisms are " 'Neat but not gaudy,' said the Devil, as he painted his tail blue," and " 'It won't be long now,' as the monkey said when he backed into the electric fan." Some Wellerisms involve puns, sometimes with grammatical change (" 'I see,' said the blind man, as he picked up his hammer and saw"), and a few of them are completely obscure in meaning (" 'Aha!' she cried, as she waved her wooden leg and died.") Another curious fact about Wellerisms is that the speaker in them is frequently an old woman, the Devil, a monkey, or a blind man.

SAYINGS

Variations of **miscellaneous proverbial sayings** are innumerable, and many of them tend to come into and go out of fashion quickly. A few long-term popular types include:

- *Insults, retorts, and wisecracks* (sometimes called "slam sayings")— "He's all right in his place, but that hasn't been dug yet"; "You make a better door than you do a window"; and "He couldn't be elected dogcatcher in a ward full of cats."
- *Sarcastic interrogatives*—"Does a dog have fleas?"; "Is the Pope a Catholic?"
- *Euphemisms*—"It's snowing down south" (meaning, "Your slip is showing"); "There's a star in the East" (meaning, "Your fly is unzipped").

- *National and ethnic slurs*—"The British have taken to Scotch; the French have taken to cognac; the Italians have taken to port."
- *Authors and titles*—"*School Dinners*, by Major Sick." (A related category is *Records and artists*—"'On the Sunken Side of the Street,' by the Earthquakes.")
- *Confucius say*—"Girl in stretch pants get stern look."
- *She was only*—"the stableman's daughter, but all the horsemen knew her."
- *Tom Swifties* (Wellerism-like often-adverbial puns based on a familiar expression in the old Tom Swift boys' books)—"'Only seven more days,' Tom said weakly."

FOCUS: "IT AIN'T OVER . . ."

BARCELONA—Whoever said, "it ain't over till the fat lady sings" obviously has never attended an Olympic opening ceremonies in Barcelona. No less than three fat ladies and a few fat men sang before the ceremonies came to an end, and by then our deodorant and our desire to stay standing had long since expired.

*

Life is full of surprises.
How could Midvale [Utah]-born Dick Motta have known in 1978, when he coined the phrase "It ain't over till the fat lady sings," that he might be describing Roseanne Barr's career 11 years later?

*

One of the late-night talk-show hosts—either Jay Leno or David Letterman—commented the day after the 1996 presidential election, "Election night turned out to be a quiet one at Bob Dole's campaign headquarters. That's all there was—Dole, a few volunteers and a fat lady, singing."

Sources: Top—marathon runner Ed Eyestone, special correspondent for the *Salt Lake City Deseret News*, "The fat ladies sing, but ceremonies go on and on," July 28, 1992. Middle—television editor Harold Schindler of *The Salt Lake Tribune*, "Now Roseanne's Facing the Music For Her Off-Key, Unfunny Song," August 7, 1990. Bottom—Jan Brunvand's notes.

The fat lady sings: Roseanne Barr shouting the National Anthem at the 1990 World Series. Several commentators on her performance quoted the proverbial "It ain't over . . ." saying. Barr was probably unaware that she was holding her hands in much the same position as that used while performing the southern "swamp holler" (see chapter 11).

DISCUSSION TOPICS:

1. Dick Motta, then coach of the NBA Washington Bullets, did indeed say "The opera ain't over till the fat lady sings" during the 1978 playoffs; but he was quoting *San Antonio Express-News* columnist Dan Cook, who in 1975 was responding to someone else saying "The rodeo ain't over till the bull riders ride." Check reference works on familiar quotations for other variations and attributions.

2. How appropriate is the proverb to the situation Harold Schindler is referring to?

3. "It ain't over . . ." has become a popular saying in sports and politics. In 1992 tennis player Andre Agassi commented, "I didn't hear the fat lady humming yet"; and Paul Tully, political director of the Democratic National Committee, said, "We've got the fat lady tapping the mike, getting ready to sing." What were these speakers referring to, and how did the saying function as a proverb?

ANALYZING AND RESEARCHING PROVERBS

Because they are short, pithy, common, and extremely varied, proverbs offer many interesting possibilities for analysis that often lead to better understanding of other aspects of culture. The contents of proverbs, for instance, which may suggest their origin, are wide-ranging. There are proverbs based on beliefs ("Rats leave a sinking ship"), proverbs based on weather signs ("All signs fail in a dry season"), proverbs based on medical lore ("An apple a day keeps the doctor away"), proverbs based on business ("Out of debt, out of danger"), proverbs based on folk law ("Two wrongs don't make a right"), proverbs deriving from historical events or slogans ("Old soldiers never die; they just fade away"), and many proverbs referring to household or farm tasks ("A watched pot never boils," "Make hay while the sun shines," etc.). America's pioneer past is suggested by such proverbs as "to come down like Davy Crockett's coon," "to see the elephant" (a popular frontier expression meaning "to see everything worth seeing"), "dry as a powder horn," "to play possum," "to go on the warpath," and "The only good Indian is a dead Indian."

Numerous proverbs are really familiar quotations, usually misquoted, especially from the Bible, from Shakespeare, or from other well-known literary sources. These are called *geflügelte Worte*—German for "winged words"—and they often are used by people without reference to any source. Biblical proverbs include "Money is the root of all evil" (misquoted from 1 Timothy 6:10) and the phrase "to cast bread upon the waters" (from Ecclesiastes 11:1). Shakespeare has given us "What's in a name," "The wish is father to the thought," and scores of other proverbs, while other important literary sources include Alexander Pope ("Fools rush in where angels fear to tread"), William Congreve ("Hell hath no fury like a woman scorned"), Samuel Johnson ("Patriotism is the last resort of a scoundrel"), and William Wordsworth ("The child is father to the man"). The extent to which our daily speech may be colored by such literary borrowings, often with some traditional variation, is indicated by the following common sayings, all of which gained their currency from *Hamlet* and probably take their origin from that play as well: "A method in his madness," "brevity is the soul of wit," "to know a hawk from a handsaw," "suit the action to the words," "sweets to the sweet."

Many proverbs come from classical Greek and Roman sources ("Love is blind," "The die is cast," "Many men, many minds"), or they contain references to classical mythology and history ("to cross the Rubicon," "as rich as Croesus," "Rome was not built in a day"). Similarly, some proverbs refer to biblical or legendary characters, including "Adam's off ox," "poor as Job's turkey," " 'round Robin Hood's barn," and "as bare as Mother Hubbard's cupboard." However, many personal references in proverbs are irretrievably lost in history; who, we may wonder, are "Sam Hill," "Jack Robinson," "George" (as in "Let George do it"), and the trio "Tom, Dick, and Harry"? ("George" may refer to the tradition of calling railroad porters by this name.) There may be an echo of saints' names in expressions such as "for the love of Mike," "for Pete's sake," and "rob Peter to pay Paul," but conclusive evidence for such origins has yet to be presented.

Proverbs exhibit most of the stylistic devices of poetry. They have *meter* ("You can leád a horse to wáter, but you cán't máke him drínk"), *rhyme* ("Haste makes waste"), *slant rhyme* ("A stitch in time saves nine"), *alliteration* ("Live and let live"), *assonance* ("A rolling stone gathers no moss"), *personification* ("Necessity is the mother of invention"), *paradox* ("No news is good news"), *parallelism* ("Man proposes; God disposes"), and other poetic characteristics. Many figures of speech occur not only in proverbial phrases and proverbial comparisons but also in true proverbs.

The philosophy expressed in proverbs introduces yet another area of inquiry. In the first place, it is easy to think of proverbs that contradict one another yet are current simultaneously: "Look before you leap" versus "He who hesitates is lost." Many proverbs offer conservative advice such as "Don't bite off more than you can chew" or "Experience is the best teacher," while others are more cynically inclined, such as "It's not what you know, but who you know" or "If you can't be good, be careful." On the whole, judging from several representative collections, the subjects of well-known American proverbs tend to come from homey, simple, familiar, natural, and domestic topics. Nouns such as "dog," "man," "cat," "bird," "wind," "bear," and "day" appear more frequently than any others;

a somewhat contradictory fact, however, is that in collections, references to the Devil in American proverbs usually outnumber those to God by about four to one. The most popular individual proverbs in American sayings tend to create a picture of optimism and a Puritanical social code; in nineteenth-century Indiana novels, for instance, the chief favorites were "to build castles in the air," "Honesty is the best policy," and "to turn over a new leaf."

Although all of these topics (and many more) challenge the student of proverbs, many past studies have consisted only of collecting, and too often collections made only from literary or other printed sources. Gradually, oral proverbs are also being collected, sometimes to be printed in regional folklore journals or in book-length dictionaries of proverbs. Oral collections are important for several reasons. They help to validate supposed proverbs from print, they are the only way to include off-color proverbs, they show which ancient proverbs still live in tradition, and they may allow us to capture the process of proverb making as it occurs.

A case in point is the discussion that ensued when a spokesperson for the planning committee of a local celebration in a large Western American city responded to criticism that too few ethnic or religious minorities had been appointed by saying "If you hung some people with a new rope, they'd complain." Minority representatives quickly objected that the saying was offensive, reminding them of past lynchings of slaves as well as of such expressions as "Give them enough rope and they'll hang themselves." Others in the community, however, defended the saying as simply an old Western (or one claimed Canadian) proverb or "an old joke," usually phrased, perhaps punningly, as "You'd kick if you were hung with a new rope." A search of the published literature, however, reveals that the saying is neither very common nor particularly regional. In fact, only two citations were found: the "You'd kick" form occurs in an Illinois collection, and "He's so cantankerous he'd complain if they hung him with a new rope" was collected in the state of Washington. A tentative conclusion might be that the saying is indeed traditional; since it may be inoffensive only if used within a particular community or with a clearly exaggerated-to-be-humorous intent, a modern urban bureaucrat would be well advised to avoid the expression in situations where it might be taken literally or as an expression of his or her general views toward other people.

Fully documented collections both from print and from oral tradition are needed before folklorists will be able to evaluate the numerous and often highly imaginative explanations that have been proposed for some proverbs. The expression "Mind your Ps and Qs," for example, has had at least five different explanations; it is often said to refer to penmanship, to typesetting, to measurements ("pints and quarts"), to dancing instruction (*pied et queue*, that is, "foot and pigtail"), and to religion (Puritan and Quaker). The most fanciful (and completely undocumented) explanation suggested, by just one source, is that Ps referred to sailors' pea coats while Qs referred to their pigtails, and the full saying warned them not to get the tar used to shape their hairstyle onto their coat collars. Without full collections of dated texts, it is impossible to accept any such etymologies.

Another such puzzle, a proverbial saying with internal rhyme, containing a national slur, has now been identified as an immigrant-American coinage. The saying is "Ten thousand Swedes ran through the weeds, chased by one Norwegian" (sometimes continued as a quatrain with "It weren't no use, 'cause they had no snoose at the battle of Copenhagen" or "Ten thousand Jews jumped out of their shoes; they smelled them frying bacon"). Norwegian-American informants associated the saying with a seventeenth-century military engagement against Sweden, but, significantly, they never quoted the rhyme in Norwegian; as a matter of fact, the saying would not form a rhyme in Norwegian. One scholar concluded that most likely the rhyme was invented in the United States by Norwegians carrying on the traditional Old World rivalry with Swedes; they probably patterned it after the similar Anglo-Irish rhyme "Ten thousand micks [Irishmen] got killed with picks at the Battle of Boyne Water."

Individual English proverbs may be traced through several historical dictionaries of them, sometimes even back to the Middle Ages (see the bibliographic notes for references). A sampling of these shows how deceptively "modern" an old saying might sound; the still-current "penny-wise and pound-foolish," for example, was already recorded in the seventeenth century. "The coast is clear" and "Beggars cannot be choosers" were both known in the sixteenth century, "To eat one out of house and home" in the fifteenth century, "A short horse is soon curried" and "Look before you leap" in the fourteenth century, and the proverb about leading a horse to water but failing to make him drink in the late twelfth century.

Other dictionaries of proverbs allow us to compare the sayings of different cultures concerning the same theme. S. G. Champion's *Racial Proverbs*, for instance, lists these, among others, under the heading "Celibacy": "old maids lead apes in Hell" (English), "old maids and young dogs should be drowned" (Romanian), "a bachelor and a dog may do everything" (Polish), "an old spinster is not worth more than an unposted letter" (Hungarian), "a bachelor is never sent as a 'go-between' " (Russian), "no man too old for old maid" (Jamaican), and "an old bachelor compares life to a shirt-button, because it so often hangs by a thread" (Chinese).

Another avenue of research is to collect proverbs in foreign languages that are still current among immigrant Americans. Sometimes these, too, have their parallels in English sayings. For instance, an American Mennonite proverb in a Low-German dialect, *"Waut dee Maun met dem Ladawoage nenbringe kaun, daut kaun dee Fru met dem Schaldoak erut droage"* ("What the husband can bring in with the wagon, the wife can carry out with her apron"), is matched by Anglo-American sayings in which the man uses a wheelbarrow or shovel and the wife a spoon. (The wife might find her rejoinder, then, in a proverb like "A man may work from sun to sun, but woman's work is never done!") One of my mother's favorite Norwegian sayings, *"Fra barn og fyllefolk skal du høre sannheten"* ("From children and drunks you hear the truth"), is partly matched in English by the proverbs "Kids say the darndest things" (or "Out of the mouths of babes") and "It's the whiskey talking."

A comprehensive study of American authors' interest in and use of proverbs would provide some new insights into American literature. From the beginning, American authors have cited proverbs; William Bradford's *Of Plymouth Plantation*, begun in 1630 and chronicling the Pilgrims' first settlement, contained "last and not least," "tide stops for no man," "one swallow makes no summer," and others. Benjamin Franklin was famous for the proverbs he employed in his *Poor Richard's* almanac (1732–57) and *The Way to Wealth* (1757), although he seems to have coined only one that passed into oral circulation on its own—"Three removes [that is, moves to a new household] is worse than a fire." James Fenimore Cooper's novels were rich in proverbs; Ralph Waldo Emerson quoted proverbs, altered them, and even tried to invent them; and Carl Sandburg wove proverbs, wisecracks, and other folk speech into *The People, Yes* (1936).

Of course, proverbs derived from authors' coinages may change as they enter oral tradition. The last time I saw Franklin's "three removes" saying quoted, it was in the form "Three moves are equal to one fire" and attributed to a popular newspaper advice columnist. Similarly, when proverbs are used commercially, they may be altered or merely alluded to. A reply card querying about the quality of service on a Volkswagen car was headed "Thanks for letting us fix your wagen." The television sitcom title "Three's Company" varies the old proverb "Two's company, three's a crowd," while the title "All in the Family" takes the proverbial phrase straight. The name "Rolling Stones," as in the rock band, alludes to a true proverb, using just two of its words. One of the most popular "new" American proverbs, "Different strokes for different folks," also gave its name to a television sitcom.

STRUCTURES AND CONTEXTS OF PROVERBS

Alan Dundes advocates study of the "folkloristic structure" of proverbs (as distinguished from the linguistic structure of their grammar). Such patterning is independent of the various languages in which a proverb may appear, and its analysis should allow eventually for a true structural definition of the proverb and its subtypes. Dundes begins with the observation that all proverbs contain a topic (A) and a comment (B), so that simple equational proverbs such as "Boys will be boys," "Business is business," or "Coffee boiled is coffee spoiled" might all be represented as an $A = B$ equation. Other proverbs are oppositional, asserting a contrast or a lack of equivalence, such as "A fair exchange is no robbery," "One swallow does not make a summer," or "Two wrongs don't make a right," all of which suggest the $A \neq B$ formula. Still other patterns are possible: "His eyes are bigger than his stomach" is $A > B$; "Half a loaf is better than no bread" might be $A/2 > (B)$, and "Two heads are better than one" $2A > B$, although essentially both are still $A > B$. Many multidescriptive element proverbs (whether oppositional or non-oppositional) are based on traditional semantic contrastive pairs (few-many, young-old, before-after, etc.): "Like father, like son" is a nonoppositional example, and "Man works from sun to sun, but woman's work is never done" is oppositional. A limited number of such structural types exist, with some types being more popular in one culture than in another.

The functions or uses of proverbs, although seldom studied in American folklore, would offer a fruitful field for research. As Roger Abrahams has pointed out, "The strategy of the proverb . . . is to direct by appearing to clarify; this is engineered by simplifying the problem and resorting to traditional solutions." The philosophy of a single prolific informant might be investigated by means of his proverbial stock. The use of proverbs in advertising ("When it rains it pours," etc.) could be studied. Parodies of proverbs are specially popular nowadays, either as separate utterances ("Absence makes the heart go wander," "Don't enumerate your fowl until the process of incubation has materialized," "Familiarity breeds attempt," "A stitch in time gathers no moss," "You've buttered your bread, now lie in it," "That's the way the cookie bounces") or as the punch lines of so-called shaggy-dog stories ("People who live in grass houses shouldn't stow thrones"). Generally the proverb parody seems to mock the very notion of giving "good advice" in a sententious form, but sometimes (as in "An ounce of contraception is worth a pound of cure") the old reliable advice is simply updated and rephrased.

FOCUS: PROVERB VARIATION

[Background: During a particularly difficult day in a university departmental office, while working on an extremely frustrating and complex problem of setting up faculty schedules, "Dolly," the person in charge of the project, commented on her plight by coining a proverb.]

After someone called her to make the fifth change that day, "Dolly" hung up the telephone, threw down the printout she had been scribbling on in exasperation, and said to me disgustedly, "It's like pulling hens' teeth to get this done!"

I don't know if she realized that she had combined two proverbial phrases—"like pulling teeth" and "scarce as hens' teeth"—but the resulting proverb actually works quite well. Her version strengthens the implication of a difficult task into the implication of an almost impossible task.

Source: A paper by University of Utah student Julia West, Spring 1992.

DISCUSSION TOPICS:

1. To what category of proverbial lore do the two parts of the new proverb belong?

2. Why is the combined proverb more effective than either of its parts?

3. Is this combined proverb unquestionably part of folklore? Why or why not?

4. Probably most people have altered a traditional saying— whether deliberately or not—at some time. Collect further examples.

The specific meanings and functions of particular proverbs should always be determined within the individual contexts where the sayings occur. Something like "Apple pie without some cheese is like a kiss without a squeeze" may be used to justify one's preference for a food combination, to request that particular combination, or to offer these foods to a diner. When printed on a restaurant napkin or placemat, the proverb notifies customers that such a food preference may indeed be satisfied here; and when the proverb is alluded to ("I'll have to give you the kiss without the squeeze"), the speaker assumes common knowledge of the food preference and the related saying, but might also be making a flirtatious remark.

Apple pie without

some cheese

Is like a Kiss

without a squeeze

MARIE CALLENDER'S ®
PIES

A restaurant's printed paper napkin quotes a traditional food proverb.

Even international relations and political tensions might be better understood, at least one scholar has suggested, through *paremiology* —the study of proverbs. The former Soviet premier Nikita S. Khrushchev was inclined to pass judgment on events in terms of proverbs; he once expressed his belief in peaceful coexistence with the United States, for instance, with the Russian proverb "When you live with a goat, you must get used to the bad smell." Other world leaders may quote proverbs of their peoples in order to justify policy or characterize a viewpoint on some international issue. Among proverbs quoted recently by national American political leaders were "You do dance with those what brung you," used to justify support for an issue with local appeal, and "A rising tide does raise all boats," quoted to support the idea of a balanced budget. Thus, proverbs and proverbial lore reach from the common folk to the elite political leader, all of whom, to some extent, behave very traditionally when speaking proverbially.

FOCUS: A POLITICAL PROVERB

In the spring of 1989, First Secretary and President Mikhail Gorbachev, while presiding over the demise of the Communist Party and also of the Soviet Union itself, visited Cuba. Journalists from around the world watched and listened closely during his visit to see if Fidel Castro, who presided over one of the world's last surviving Communist regimes, would give any sign of cracking under the events and this international scrutiny.

Clearly upset by this attention, Castro finally snapped at a group of reporters, "What did you want—a fifth leg on a cat?"

Source: Paraphrased from news reports datelined Havana and published on April 4, 1989.

DISCUSSION TOPICS:

1. How would you decode or translate the meaning of Castro's remark?

2. Try to determine by consulting reference books whether Fidel Castro was quoting a traditional proverbial saying or coining a new phrase. (Perhaps Spanish-speaking students know this saying or a variation.)

3. Search news reports of the same period for instances of Gorbachev or other Soviet leaders resorting to proverbial language. (Re-

member the example quoted from Nikita S. Khrushchev in this chapter.)

4. Some have suggested that Castro might have been alluding to the Chernobyl accident. Why is this idea unlikely? What is the typical folklore of nuclear disasters, such as those at Chernobyl and at Three Mile Island?

BIBLIOGRAPHIC NOTES

An excellent older introduction to the nature and study of proverbs is Margaret M. Bryant's "Proverbs and How to Collect Them," *PADS* no. 4 (1954), a handbook prepared for the collectors in the ADS project to compile a *Dictionary of American Proverbs*. It is instructive to compare Archer Taylor's even older survey, "Problems in the Study of Proverbs," *JAF* 47 (1934): 1–21, with his new foreword to the second edition of his 1931 classic, *The Proverb* (Hatboro, Pa.: Folklore Associates, 1962). Taylor, the chief early American authority on proverbs, also outlined "The Study of Proverbs" in *Proverbium* no. 1 (1965): 1–10. This bulletin was distributed free by the Society of Finnish Literature to libraries, institutes, and active proverb scholars until no. 25 (1975). *Proverbium* was revived as a yearbook of paremiological research in 1984, published by the Ohio State University and later the University of Vermont. Archer Taylor's other contributions to the original *Proverbium* included "The Collection and Study of Proverbs," in no. 8 (1967): 161–76, and "Method in the History and Interpretation of a Proverb," in no. 10 (1968): 235–38 (repr. in *Readings in American Folklore*, pp. 263–66). The fifteenth number of *Proverbium* (1970) was "Essays in Honor of Archer Taylor on his Eightieth Birthday," with a bibliography of Taylor's writings on proverbial lore. *Selected Writings on Proverbs by Archer Taylor* (FFC 216 [1975]) was edited by Wolfgang Mieder, editor of the new *Proverbium*.

Mieder, who followed Taylor as the leading American proverb scholar, published two volumes of important essays on the genre: *American Proverbs: A Study of Texts and Contexts* (Bern, Frankfort, New York, and Paris: Peter Lang, 1990) and *Proverbs Are Never Out of Season: Popular Wisdom in the Modern Age* (New York: Oxford University Press, 1993).

The basic American proverb dictionary for the early period is Archer Taylor and Bartlett Jere Whiting's *A Dictionary of American Proverbs and Proverbial Phrases, 1820–1880* (Cambridge, Mass.: Harvard University Press, 1958); the introduction to this work is very useful, and the reference bibliography includes all of the important American collections in book or periodical form at the time of publication. Three inclusive state collections are B. J. Whiting's "Proverbs and Proverbial Sayings," in *The Frank C. Brown Collection of North Carolina Folklore*, vol. I (Durham, N.C.: Duke University Press, 1952), pp. 331–501; Jan Harold Brunvand's *Proverbs and Proverbial Phrases from Indiana Books Published before 1890*, Indiana University Folklore Series no. 15 (Bloomington, 1961); and Frances

M. Barbour's *Proverbs and Proverbial Phrases of Illinois* (Carbondale and Edwards-ville: Southern Illinois University Press, 1965). The bibliographies in these works may now be supplemented with F. A. DeCaro and W. K. McNeil's *American Proverb Literature: A Bibliography*, Bibliographic and Special Series no. 6, Folklore Forum (1970). Bringing the references up to date are two important works, Bart-lett Jere Whiting's *Modern Proverbs and Proverbial Sayings* (Cambridge, Mass.: Har-vard University Press, 1989) and Wolfgang Mieder and Stewart A. Kingsbury, eds., *A Dictionary of American Proverbs* (New York: Oxford University Press, 1992).

Proverbs circulating in the United States in languages other than English may be found in such journal articles as Rubén Cobos, "New Mexican Spanish Prov-erbs," *NMFR* 12 (1969–70): 7–11; Anna Mary Boudreux, "Proverbs, Metaphors and Sayings of the Kaplan Area [Vermillion Parish, Louisiana]," *LFM* 3 (April 1970): 16–24; and those in a special issue of *NJF* (vol. 1, no. 1) published in 1976. (The latter includes Polish, Italian, Hungarian, Gaelic, German, and Russian examples.)

In "The Proverbial Three Wise Monkeys," *MJLF* 7 (1981): 5–38, Wolfgang Mieder traces a familiar saying, often illustrated ("See no evil, hear no evil, speak no evil"), to its apparent Japanese source and through its Western circulation since at least the 1920s. Mieder researched "A Picture Is Worth a Thousand Words" in *SF* 47 (1990): 207–25, and "Don't throw out the baby with the bath water" in *WF* 50 (1991): 361–400, as well as several other familiar proverbs in his other published essays. See also Shirley L. Arora's "On the Importance of Rotting Fish: A Proverb and Its Audience," *WF* 48 (1989): 271–88, which begins with the prov-erb about fish rotting first from the head as it was quoted during an American presidential campaign.

The only book-length collection of proverbial comparisons is Archer Taylor's *Proverbial Comparisons and Similes from California*, Folklore Studies no. 3 (Berkeley, 1954). More California comparisons are printed in *WF* 17 (1958): 12–20. James N. Tidwell discusses the special language of American proverbial comparisons in "Adam's Off Ox: A Study in the Exactness of the Inexact," *JAF* 66 (1953): 291–94; and in "Folk Comparisons from Colorado," *WF* 35 (1976): 175–208, Cathy M. Orr presents a computer-aided study of some forty-five hundred items coded by age and sex.

C. Grant Loomis gathered various miscellaneous kinds of nineteenth-century proverbial sayings in three articles in *Western Folklore:* Wellerisms and Yankeeisms are in *WF* 8 (1949): 1–21; epigrams and perverted proverbs in *WF* 8 (1949): 348–57; and such types as definitions, literal clichés, naming, and occupational punning are in *WF* 9 (1950): 147–52. Wayland D. Hand lists more perverted proverbs in *WF* 27 (1968): 263–64: "Familiarity breeds attempt," "A stitch in time gathers no moss," and so forth. In Charles Clay Doyle's "Title-Author Jokes, Now and Long Ago," *JAF* 86 (1973): 52–54, this minor proverbial genre is related to a mid-seventeenth-century English fashion for book-title jokes. The same author com-ments on "Sarcastic Interrogative Affirmations and Negatives ['Is the Pope a Catholic?' or 'Does a chicken have lips?']," in *MJLF* 1 (1975): 33–34, and in *Maledicta* 1 (1977): 77–82. Wellerisms are collected in a dictionary, the first of its kind, edited by Wolfgang Mieder and Stewart A. Kingsbury and published by Oxford University Press in 1993.

Adding to the sources of proverbs described in Taylor's *The Proverb*, Frances M. Barbour gave examples, in *MF* 13 (1963): 97–100, from songs (i.e., "babes in the woods"), from echoes of other proverbs (i.e., "easy as falling off a diet"), and from advertising (i.e., "good to the last drop"). C. Grant Loomis discussed other "Proverbs in Business" in *WF* 23 (1964): 91–94. In *Names* 6 (1958): 51–54, Archer Taylor concluded that the phrase "Tom, Dick, and Harry" was an Americanism of the early nineteenth century based upon antecedents reaching back three centuries; later, however, he found the same expression in earlier sources from England.

The relationships of proverbs to poetry are analyzed in detail by S. J. Sackett in "Poetry and Folklore: Some Points of Affinity," *JAF* 77 (1964): 143–53. B. J. Whiting extracted proverbial material from popular ballads for an article in *JAF* 47 (1934): 22–44. The unraveling of the background of "Ten Thousand Swedes" was accomplished by the Norwegian-American sociologist Peter A. Munch, who published his findings in *MF* 10 (1960): 61–69.

Two good reference works for tracing English proverbs are G. L. Apperson's *English Proverbs and Proverbial Phrases: A Historical Dictionary* (London: J. M. Dent, 1929; repr. Detroit: Gale Research Co., 1969) and W. G. Smith and J. E. Heseltine's *The Oxford Dictionary of English Proverbs* (Oxford: Oxford University Press, 1935, 3d ed.; rev. by F. P. Wilson, 1970). S. G. Champion's *Racial Proverbs* (London: Routledge, 1938; rev. 1950) is perhaps the most reliable of several similar compilations of proverbs from many lands to be found in most large libraries.

On proverbs in literature, see Wolfgang Mieder, "The Essence of Literary Proverb Studies," *NYFQ* 30 (1974): 66–76 (also published in *Proverbium* no. 23 [1974]: 888–94). Mieder surveyed "The Proverb and Anglo-American Literature" in *SFQ* 38 (1974): 49–62. Four good individual studies are Stuart A. Gallacher's "Franklin's Way to Wealth: A Florilegium of Proverbs and Wise Sayings," *JEGP* 48 (1949): 229–51; Warren S. Walker's "Proverbs in the Novels of James Fenimore Cooper," *MF* 3 (1953): 99–107; J. Russell Reaver's "Emerson's Use of Proverbs," *SFQ* 27 (1963): 280–99; and Joseph Moldenhauer's "The Rhetorical Function of Proverbs in *Walden*," *JAF* 80 (1967): 151–59.

Structural analysis of proverbs was suggested by Alan Dundes in *MF* 12 (1962): 31–38, in a review of *Trends in Content Analysis* (1959), ed. Ithiel de Sola Pool. Another approach was taken by G. B. Milner in "Quadripartite Structures," *Proverbium* no. 14 (1969): 379–83; Dundes subsequently reconsidered the matter and expanded upon his own proposal in "On the Structure of the Proverb," *Proverbium* no. 25 (1975): 961–73, repr. in *Analytic Essays in Folklore*, pp. 103–18.

The majority of past studies of proverbs by literary folklorists have been collections or source searches, an exception that deals with functions being Joseph Raymond's "Tensions in Proverbs: More Light on International Understanding," in *WF* 15 (1956): 153–58. Representative of the functional or communications approach taken by some anthropological folklorists is E. Ojo Arewa and Alan Dundes's "Proverbs and the Ethnography of Speaking Folklore," *AA* 66 (1964): 70–85.

Recent studies that pay more attention to the contexts of proverbs' uses and meanings are Richard Bauman and Neil McCabe's "Proverbs in an LSD Cult," *JAF* 83 (1970): 318–24; James P. Leary's " 'The Land Won't Burn': An Esoteric American Proverb and Its Significance," *MJLF* 1 (1975): 27–32; and Rosan A. Jordan's "Five [Mexican-American] Proverbs in Context," *MJLF* 8 (1982): 109–15.

In an essay entitled "The Use of Proverbs in Psychological Testing," *JFI* 15 (1978): 45–55, Wolfgang Mieder provides a bibliography of forty-nine items, discusses how proverbs have been used in this way, outlines hazards of such uses, and calls for better communication between folklorists and psychologists in such testing. In "Proverbial Speech in the Air," *MJLF* 7 (1981): 39–48, Robert A. Georges draws on examples of proverbial speech overheard during a cross-country airplane trip to illustrate persuasive uses of proverbs in a conversational context.

Alan Dundes's discussion of the proverb "Seeing is believing" (*Natural History* 81, May 1972; repr. in *Interpreting Folklore*, pp. 86–92) stresses the apparent primacy of sight data in the American worldview as revealed in traditional speech patterns. However, Simon J. Bronner disputes the point in an essay entitled, from the traditional completion of the proverb, ". . . Feeling's the Truth," *TFSB* 48 (1982): 117–24; the sense of touch, he says, is sometimes primary. Bronner presents the theoretical background for his argument in "The Haptic Experience of Culture," *Anthropos* 77 (1982): 351–62.

6

RIDDLES AND OTHER VERBAL PUZZLES

Folk riddles are traditional questions with unexpected (albeit traditional) answers—usually verbal puzzles (some involving gestures or writing) that demonstrate the cleverness of the questioner and challenge the wit of the audience. The practice of riddling can be traced to the dawn of literary expression; it is referred to in the most ancient Asian and Sanskrit writings, in the Bible, in classical legends and myths, in European folktales and ballads, and in some of the earliest manuscripts of medieval literature. Compilations of riddles were among the first printed books in the Middle Ages, and books of literary riddles remained popular well into the Renaissance. Since the beginning of professional interest in folklore in the nineteenth century, massive collections of folk riddles have been published in most European countries and in many other countries. Riddles have been found in the native cultures of most peoples, including the Native Americans, who were once thought to possess only a few, which had been borrowed from Europeans.

Not only is riddling widespread, but the variety of actual riddles in collections is dazzling. Yet the basic forms that riddles take seem to be relatively limited, and many individual riddles have persisted with little essential change for centuries. A striking example is the "Sphinx riddle" from the Greek legend of Oedipus—"What walks on four legs in the morning, on two in the afternoon, and on three in the evening?" This riddle, whose answer is "man" (that is, human beings, who crawl in infancy, walk upright in adulthood, and lean on a cane when aged), is only the best-known of many riddles with the same answer, all based on related puzzling questions that are common in Western tradition and scattered through the rest of the world. Literature has helped to keep the riddle of the Sphinx alive from the beginning, but its oral circulation has never ceased. It has been found in English in Great Britain, Canada, the United States, and the West Indies. One version, collected from a fifteen-year-old schoolgirl in Scotland, is rendered in rhyme without the metaphor of times of day, but with the added detail of man's decreasing vigor; yet it is still clearly recognizable as the same enigma that challenged Oedipus on the outskirts of Thebes:

> Walks on four feet,
> On two feet, on three.
> The more feet it walks on,
> The weaker it be.

Studies of riddles date from the late 1800s in European languages and were pioneered in English by the American folklorist Archer Taylor, whose work began in the 1930s and culminated in the publication of his *English Riddles from Oral Tradition* in 1951. In addition to the basic bibliography and methodology for riddle studies, Taylor gave us the important distinctions between the "true riddle" and others, as well as an ingenious scheme of classification.

TRUE RIDDLES

The **true riddle** is essentially a comparison between the unstated answer and something else that is described in the question. This description usually has two parts, one general and one straightforward, such as "Little Nancy Eddicote, in a white petticoat, and a red nose," followed by a more precise but apparently contradictory part: "The longer she stands, the shorter she grows." The answer to this common English riddle is "a candle," and the riddle can be regarded as a *comparison* of a candle to a little girl or a *description* of a candle in terms of a little girl.

An American variant of this riddle adds a further contradictory detail but retains the same descriptive method:

> Little Miss Etticoat in a white petticoat
> Shorter and shorter she grows.
> Oh, how she suffers while we with the snuffers
> Are nipping her little red nose.

These two basic parts of a true riddle were called by Taylor the *description* and the *block*, and they may be observed in a great variety of texts. Many riddles have only these two parts plus an answer, as in the following:

Robbers came to our house and we were all in; [description]
the house leapt out the windows and we were all taken. [block]
Answer: Fish in a net (The "house" is the water; "windows" are holes in the net).

It is possible for a true riddle to have six distinct parts, which may be designated:

Introduction	As I went over London Bridge
Description	I met my sister
Name	Jenny;
Block	I broke her neck and drank her blood
	And left her standing empty.
Close	Answer me if you can.
Answer	A bottle of wine.

Few riddles collected from oral tradition, however, have all six parts.

Attempts to classify true riddles by their answers long frustrated folklorists, because the answers may vary considerably from text to text and quite different riddles may have the same answers. Instead, Archer Taylor's system classifies riddles by the nature of the item described in the question, using seven general categories:

I. Comparisons to a Living Creature (e.g., the Sphinx riddle)
II. Comparisons to an Animal
III. Comparisons to Several Animals

IV. Comparisons to a Person (e.g., "Little Nancy Eddicote," "Sister Jenny," and "Humpty Dumpty")
V. Comparisons to Several Persons (e.g., the fish-in-a-net riddle)
VI. Comparisons to Plants
VII. Comparisons to Things
   The man who made the coat didn't use it; the man who bought it didn't want it; the man who used it didn't know it.—A coffin.

In the four further categories of Taylor's classification, the principle behind the puzzling question is an enumeration of details rather than the description of a recognizable item. With examples for each, these are:

VIII. Enumerations of Comparisons
   Round as a hoop, deep as a cup; all the king's oxen can't pull it up.—A well.
IX. Enumerations in Terms of Form or of Form and Function
   Patch on patch and has no seams.—Cabbage. [form]
X. Enumerations in Terms of Color
   Throw it up green, comes down red.—A watermelon.
XI. Enumerations in Terms of Acts
   With what vegetable do you throw away the outside, then cook the inside, then eat the outside, and throw away the inside?—Corn.
   I went into the woods and got it; I set me down on a log to look for it; and then I brought it along home with me because I couldn't find it.—A splinter.

Most English true riddles are very old, and their counterparts may be found somewhere among Taylor's 1,749 individual types. The following, for example, learned in San Francisco about 1932 and collected in Idaho in 1964, is Taylor's riddle type number 1,727 (category XI), first reported from the British West Indies in 1921:

What does a man love more than life, hate more than death or mortal strife? That which contented men desire, the poor have, the rich require. The miser spends, the spendthrift saves, and all men carry to their graves?—Nothing!

Occasionally a new riddle will be invented, such as:

> What is round and has squares [the block]; it lived once upon a time. You see it every day, and most every home has it?—A roll of toilet paper.

(Despite the apparent "newness" of the reference to toilet paper, the sequence of "once alive, now dead" to describe paper is actually a very old metaphor in traditional riddling.)

One riddle based on comparisons (category VIII) refers to a unique American animal and so far has been reported only from Mississippi:

> Hands like a man, ears like a bat, tail like a rat; guess what it is and I'll give you my hat.—An opossum.

One special category, sometimes included with true riddles, is the **neck riddle**, so called because it is usually attributed in folktales and legends to a condemned prisoner who to "save his neck" must pose a riddle that no one can solve. His riddle refers to a scene that he, and he only, has observed and can identify from the cryptic description given. Samson's riddle in the Bible (Judges 14:14) is a neck riddle of this kind:

> Out of the eater came forth meat, and out of the strong came forth sweetness.—Honeycomb in a lion's carcass.

One American counterpart of this "living in the dead" neck riddle is from Texas:

> Six set and seven sprung, from the dead they live and run. What is it?—One quail that hatched six quails out of a dead cow's skull.

One of the most common *story riddles* in the United States concerns a desperate prisoner—a Confederate captive during the Civil War, according to an Ozark version—who declared:

> Corn et corn in a high oak tree, if you guess this riddle, you kin hang me!

The Union captors, however, could not guess that his name was
Corn and that he had been eating parched corn while sitting up in
a tree before being captured. (In other versions, his name is Horn,
he had gnawed on a cow's horn, and his riddle begins "Horn ate
horn.") In another favorite American story riddle, the prisoner has
had his dog named "Love" killed; its skin is made into leather for
use in a glove, a shoe, and part of his saddle. The riddle he poses
is "On love I ride, on love I stand, and I hold love in my right
hand."

FOCUS: RIDDLES BASED ON FAMILY RELATIONS

Here are three examples of a confusing question that sometimes
occurs in the "neck riddle" frame:

> It wasn't my sister, nor my brother,
> But still was the child of my father and mother.
> Who was it?

*

> Brothers and sisters have I none,
> Yet this child's father was my mother's son.
> Relation?

*

> Brothers and sisters have I none,
> But this man's father is my father's son.
> Who is he?

Sources: "Genealogical Riddles" in vol. I of *The Frank C. Brown Collection of North
Carolina Folklore* and Archer Taylor, "Riddles Dealing with Family Relationships,"
JAF 51 (1938): 25–37.

DISCUSSION TOPICS:

1. What are the answers of these riddles? Who is the speaker in
each case? Do you know other riddles of this type?

2. Draw a diagram to illustrate the pattern of these genealogical
riddles. Do these riddles have a description and a block?

3. How do the international counterparts for these riddles, cited
by Taylor in *JAF* 51, either parallel or differ from the English-
language examples?

The two other story-riddle types both involve tricky language—
the first kind substituting the part for the whole (*synechdoche*) and

the second using "queer words," or nonsense syllables that approximate the sound of the answer. An example of the first, from Southern black tradition:

> Two legs sat on three legs; up jumped four legs and grabs one leg.
> —Man sitting on a three-legged stool; up jumps a dog and grabs ham on the table.

And a version of the second type, from Indiana:

> My mother went over to your mother's house to borrow a wim babble, wam bobble, a hind body, fore body, whirl-a-kin nibble.—A spinning wheel.

The **pretended obscene riddle** is another special subtype, often of the comparative or enumerative variety. Here the description suggests something risqué, usually sexual, but the correct answer is quite tame. For example, the question "What is a man called who marries another man?" has the bland solution "a minister." Other pretended obscene riddles seem to be describing sexual intercourse, but actually refer to scrubbing clothes, chewing gum, picking fruit, making a bed, and other innocuous acts. Compare, too, this attempt to lead a listener into speaking a taboo word: "What has four letters, starts with an F, gives old folks a backache and young folks pleasure?"— A Ford (car).

A variation of the old "Ford" riddle, above, usually appears with three other pretended obscene riddles on membership cards for the so-called Turtle Club. Members of this old American mock organization, which remains popular in the military services, must know the "right" answers to riddles such as "What is a four-letter word ending in K that means the same as intercourse?" (answer: talk) and "What is it a man can do standing up, a woman sitting down, and a dog on three legs?" (answer: shake hands). Once a new Turtle is initiated into the mysteries of such riddles, he or she is given a personal membership card signed by the poser of the riddles and is then required to answer the question "Are you a Turtle?" with the invariable answer "You bet your sweet ass I am." Failure to give the proper answer requires the member to provide a beverage of choice to the asker. The whole routine of asking the riddles, issuing

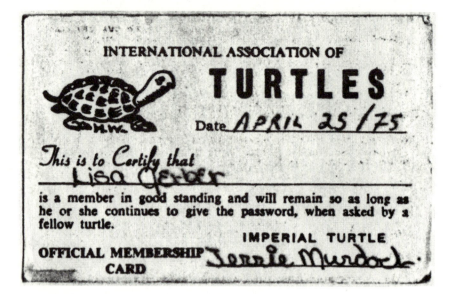

Typical Turtle Club membership card. The wording and art vary on the fronts of these cards, but the backs are always printed with three pretended obscene riddles, usually the same ones.

the cards, and quizzing others for their membership is often performed in bars.

FOCUS: WHO HAS A LONG ONE?

Arnold Schwarzenegger has a long one.
Michael J. Fox [or Jay Leno] has a short one.
Madonna doesn't have one.
And the Pope has one, but doesn't use it.
    What is it?

*

President Gorbachev has a long one.
President Bush has a short one.
The Pope has one, but doesn't use it.
    What is it?

*

President Echevarria has a long one.
President Nixon has a short one.
Liberace doesn't have one.
And the Pope has one but doesn't use it.
    What is it?

Source: Oral tradition; notes taken by Jan Harold Brunvand over the years.

DISCUSSION TOPICS:

1. There is a single correct—and nonsexual—answer to each of these riddles. What is it? But what sexual answer is implied? What male anxiety is alluded to?

2. What is the pattern of content and of format in these riddles? (What are the consistent and variable elements?)

3. Can you approximately date these three variations on the basis of the named characters?

4. What other pretended obscene riddles have you heard? In what contexts? Were they answered with the sexual solution, the nonsexual solution, or both?

In all of the riddle types presented thus far, the facts for answering are well contained within the questions themselves; when a person understands how true riddles operate, he or she can learn to solve them. But many traditional riddles do not follow such a predictable pattern, and they can be solved only by means of special knowledge or wit. These can be placed in several distinct categories.

RIDDLING QUESTIONS AND OTHER NONPREDICTABLE RIDDLES

The **riddling question** (or "clever question") is the general type of nonpredictable riddle. The "Riddle Song" of British balladry is made up of these: the first question in it, "How can there be a cherry without a stone?" is answered, "A cherry when it's blooming, it has no stone." There are countless other such riddles: "How deep is the ocean?—A stone's throw"; "How many balls of string to reach the moon?—One, if it's long enough"; "Where was Moses when the lights went out?—In the dark"; "What do they call little black cats in England?—Kittens"; "What lives in a stable, eats oats, and can see as well out of one end as the other?—A blind horse"; and so forth. One riddling question is answered with a sound rather than a word: "What makes a horse go, a dog come, and a man stay?" For the answer, the sound of a kiss is made.

The **conundrum** is a riddle based on punning or other wordplay. The pun may occur in the answer ("When is a ship not a ship?—

When it's *afloat*") or in the question ("What has four wheels and
flies?—A garbage truck"). Often the conundrum asks why one thing
is like another: "Why is a thief in the attic like an honest man?—
Because he's above doing a mean thing" and "Why is coffee like the
soil? It is ground." Some conundrums develop double or larger multiple puns: "What's the difference between a ball and a prince?—
One is thrown in the air; the other is heir to the throne" and "What
is the difference between a jeweler and a jailer?—One sells watches
and the other watches cells." A few that form a spoonerism* in the
answer may be termed *spooneristic conundrums*: "What's the difference between the clown at the circus and a guilty conscience?—One
is a cute amuser, the other a mute accusor."

The general terms **puzzle** and **problem** may be applied to a host
of traditional questions involving special biblical, arithmetical, genealogical, or practical knowledge for an answer. These may be
posed seriously for an attempted solution, or they may be completely
whimsical. For example, there are serious arithmetical riddles involving weights and measures, ages, or monetary figures that can be
solved by an acute mind, but the following Ozark text is pure
whimsy:

> If it takes a peckerwood eight months t' peck a four-inch hole in a
> gum-tree that would make 250 bundles o' good shingles, how long
> would it take a wooden-legged grasshopper t' kick all th' seeds out'n
> a dill pickle seven inches long an' an inch and a quarter thick?—
> There ain't no answer, you fool!

Some problems involve the practical enigmas of transporting incom-
patible creatures across a river in a small boat, or picking a matched
set of socks out of a drawer in the dark, and the like. But one is a
sort of anagrammatic problem, requiring the solver to find four letters that will make five words to fill the blanks:

> An _____ old woman of _____ intent
> Put on her _____ and away she went.
> "Come _____ my son," she was heard to say.
> "We'll _____ on the fat of the land today."

---

*Named for the Reverend W. A. Spooner (1844–1930), an Englishman famous for unin-
tentionally interchanging the sounds of words in sayings.

(As soon as a person recognizes that the fourth line of the verse incorporates a variation of a familiar proverbial phrase, he or she can easily solve the puzzle.)

Some traditional questions are really not intended to be answered at all; they are merely **catch questions**, designed to embarrass the unwary. A boy asks a girl, "Do you know what virgins eat for breakfast?" and all she need do is respond "No, what?" to bring his laugh and her blush. A child asks, "What comes after seventy-five?" and if a person is gullible enough to say "seventy-six," he gleefully shouts, "That's the spirit!" In a more elaborate catch someone asks, "What's the first sign of insanity?—Hair growing on your knuckles." Then, as the dupe sneaks a look at the back of his hand, the riddler asks, "What's the second sign?—Looking for it."

A prolific modern form of riddle, usually just termed a "joke" in folk tradition, is the **riddle-joke**. Riddle-jokes come and go in fad cycles, usually centering on a single theme while they last. Popular in the 1950s were the so-called *moron jokes* with their outrageous puns: "Why did the little moron cut a hole in the rug?—To see the floorshow." Another favorite cycle dwelt upon foods (grapes, pickles, bananas, etc.): "What's purple and conquers continents?—Alexander the Grape"; "What's green, bumpy, and floats around in the ocean?—Moby Pickle." One variant of the fruit joke asks, "What's purple and has twenty-seven wives?—Brigham Plum" (playing on the name of Brigham Young, the Utah Mormon leader during the period of polygamy in the Church of Jesus Christ of Latter-day Saints). Dialogue riddle-jokes called *knock-knocks* were the rage for a while, followed by *elephant jokes*, *sick jokes* (macabre humor), *wind-up-doll jokes*, *celebrity riddle-jokes* (later including O. J. Simpson jokes), *AIDS jokes*, *Challenger jokes*, *Ethiopian jokes*, and on and on.

Numskull riddle-jokes often center on particular ethnic or regional groups ("Aggies," "Newfies," "Italians," etc.), but huge cycles once highly popular, such as the *lightbulb jokes*, may be aimed (beamed?) at just about anybody: "How many psychologists does it take to change a lightbulb?—Just one, but the lightbulb has to want to change." An even larger group of riddle-jokes had the Polish-American as its target: "How do you tell the groom at a Polish wedding?—He's the one with a clean bowling shirt on." Then with the election of a Pope who came from Poland, we began to hear Polish-Pope riddle-jokes: "Did you hear about the new Pope's first miracle?—He made a blind man lame." And "Did you hear about his second one?—He bowled a three-oh-five." Yet another joke on this theme claimed that the Polish Pope built a tavern behind the Vatican palace so he would have a place to cash his paycheck. A few Polish jokes (which most people seem to tell without any specific denigration of Polish-Americans in mind) have some narrative content, and some are based on a photocopied sketch or diagram, such as the "Polish Computer System" for "output processing," an elaborate drawing that folds down to a picture of a simple toilet. At this point the riddle-joke form has overlapped both with folktale and Xeroxlore.

FOCUS: INITIALISMS

Sometimes joking explanations for acronyms are used in a riddling context. (The device is similar to the folk etymologies mentioned in chapter 4 for posh, cop, BVDs, etc.) The question is asked, tongue-in-cheek, "What do these names or initial letters really stand for?" The answers are, of course, fictitious:

BMW	Big Money Wasted
Bud	Best until drunk
FBI	Fat Bored and Impotent
FIAT	Fix It Again, Tony
FORD	Fix Or Repair Daily
IBM	Itty Bitty Morons (or International Business Mistakes)
IRS	Infernal Revenue Service (or Internal Robbery Service)
NASA	Need Another Seven Astronauts
PhD	Piled higher and Deeper
SDT (Sigma Delta Tau fraternity)	Seldom Dated Twice

Source: Selected from Nicholas Howe, "Rewriting Initialisms: Folk Derivations and Linguistic Riddles," *JAF* 102 (1989): 171–82.

DISCUSSION TOPICS:

1. What are the actual meanings of each of the above words and initials? Do you know other joking explanations for these or for other terms? In what contexts does this tradition occur?

2. From what areas of life do the joking initialisms come? Is there any apparent meaning to the range of sources?

3. See also Sterling Eisiminger, "Acronyms and Folk Etymology," *JAF* 91 (1978): 582–84. Do the examples in these two articles overlap? Do you think folk etymologies became riddles since this article was published, or were they likely circulating as riddles then as well?

NON-ORAL RIDDLES

Two special kinds of riddles are **non-oral**, involving as they do either gestures or drawings. The *non-oral riddle* itself (or sometimes "facial droodle") has only the question "What's this?" accompanied by a gesture, such as waving the hand and snapping fingers (a butterfly with hiccups), or holding fingertips of both hands together palm to palm with fingers flexing (a spider doing push-ups on a mirror). The *droodle*, which was briefly syndicated in many newspapers but was initially derived from folklore, asks "What's this?" about sketches like these:

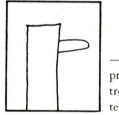

—A man
practicing his
trombone in a
telephone booth.

—A girl with a pony-
tail in a bubble bath
practicing the trumpet.

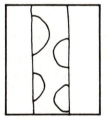

—A bear climbing
a tree. (Variant:
a giraffe's neck.)

As in most oral riddles, the droodle basically involves seeing something from an unusual point of view. The persistence of this prin-

ciple in droodle art across a span of some three hundred years is
illustrated in the two examples below, the right-hand one from an
Italian source of 1678, and the left-hand one from the United States
about 1950:

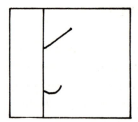

—A soldier and his dog,
just disappearing around
a corner.

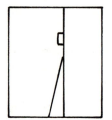

—A blind beggar with cup
and stick, just coming around
a corner.

OTHER VERBAL PUZZLES

The complicated riddlelike **question guessing game** that John F.
Kennedy's aides reportedly played during dull moments in the 1960
presidential campaign is also based on taking an unusual viewpoint.
Here the quizzer gave an answer and the players tried to find a
question to match. To the answer "9-W," for example, the proper
question was "Is your name spelled with a 'V,' Mr. Wagner?" The
answer—"Nein, 'W.'"

Among the other types of traditional verbal puzzles and tricks
are some that require a written rather than purely oral presentation.
The **palindrome** is a sentence that reads the same backward or forward, such as "Madam, I'm Adam" (what Adam said to Eve), "Able
was I ere I saw Elba" (referring to Napoleon), and "A man, a plan,
a canal: Panama" (an allusion to Theodore Roosevelt's backing for
the Panama Canal). The **all-letter sentence** is just what its name
implies—a sentence containing all the letters of the alphabet, such
as "William F. Jex quickly caught seven dozen Republicans." Such
sentences were once used by teletype operators and typewriter re-
pairmen to test their equipment, and many people immediately rap
out "The quick brown fox jumps over the lazy dog" when trying

out a new keyboard. A sentence that contains all the letters only once each is "J. Q. Vandz struck my big fox whelp." The **over-and-under sentence** depends upon written position for its meaning; the following, allegedly used as an address, is translated "John Underwood, Andover, Massachusetts":

Wood
John
Mass.

Analogous to this are the following two over-and-under renderings (and there are many more) of traditional phrases:

Well
My word
        ("Well upon my word")

Once
4 p.m.
        ("Once upon a time")

Other written puzzles employ different positional clues:

("Laying it on the line")

("Grapes in season")

Such graphic and orthographic puzzles have proliferated in recent years (or perhaps folklorists have just begun to notice them). Examples like the following are sometimes set up on sheets labeled

"Entrance Exam" or "Brain Teasers" containing about one or two dozen such enigmas, but seldom the explanations:

BEN

("Big Ben")

|R|E|A|D|I|N|G|

("Reading between the lines")

("Crossroad")

SAND on SiO₂

("Sandbox")

BL(OUSE)

("See-through blouse")

("Walk around the block")

Another variety of puzzle/test, often duplicated, involves cryptic letter-and-number statements like these:

  26 = L. of the A. (26 letters of the alphabet)
  88 = P. K. (88 piano keys)
200 = D. for P. G. (200 dollars for passing Go [in Monopoly])
   8 = S. on a S. S. ([you figure it out])

One very curious traditional guessing item is based on the following numbers and letters written on a sheet of paper: 3909 Ǝ H T.

The question is then asked, "If this many nuns went to Rome, who would be the happiest?" The answer is discovered by holding the paper up to the light backward and reading through it—"The Pope."

The **tongue-twister** is a verbal puzzle requiring agility in pronouncing difficult sounds, rather than in providing answers. The best known is probably "Peter Piper picked a peck of pickled peppers," which is only the sentence for "p" from a whole tongue-twister alphabet once popular in elocutionist handbooks. Many tongue-twisters have a kind of surrealistic quality: "Seven slick slimy snakes sliding slowly southward" or "Two toads totally tired tried to trot to Tadbury." Campus favorites are those tongue-twisters that may lead the unwary into uttering an off-color word or expression: "She slit a sheet, a sheet she slit, and in her slitted sheet she'd sit." There are also tongue-twister songs of this type, such as the one beginning "Sarah, Sarah, sitting in a shoeshine shop. / All day long she sits and shines, / All day long she shines and sits." Also likely to be heard in college are tongue-twisters used to teach proper pronunciation of foreign languages, or at least to exercise the language student in the characteristic sounds of another tongue.

Finally, traditional **mnemonic devices** might be considered a subtype of the verbal puzzle; these are rhymes, sayings, words, or other expressions intended to aid the memory. There are mnemonic devices for remembering spellings, geographic facts, scientific principles, navigational rules, and many other matters. Some are very simple, such as the acronym "Roy G. Biv" for remembering the colors in the spectrum in order (*R*ed, *O*range, *Y*ellow, *G*reen, *B*lue, *I*ndigo, and *V*iolet), while some are more complex, as in the sentences used for remembering the twelve cranial nerves from "olfactory" to "hypoglossal" ("*O*n *o*ld *O*lympus' *t*owering *t*ops, *a* *F*inn and *G*erman *v*iewed *s*ome *h*ops") or for the scale of hardness for geological analysis from "talc" to "diamond" ("*T*roy *g*irls *c*an *f*lirt *a*nd *o*ther *q*ueer *t*hings *c*an *d*o").

ANALYZING RIDDLES

Many English and American riddles of all varieties have been collected and published, providing rich possibilities for analysis. One interesting observation that can be verified simply from the index of answers in Taylor's classification is that the subjects of true riddles tend to come from the world of a farm woman looking out her kitchen window; thus, the most characteristic answers to riddles are berries, fruits, garden vegetables, the stars and the moon, the well, a needle and thread, cooking utensils, clothing, and the like. Furthe more, in common with many proverbs, riddles are essentially metaphorical, and they exhibit other stylistic features of poetry, especially meter and rhyme. Sometimes, too, archaic words and expressions are preserved in riddle texts.

The structure of true riddles interested folklorists Robert Georges and Alan Dundes, who pointed out that the same basic "topic-comment" form exists in them as in some proverbs. They defined the riddle structurally as containing "one or more descriptive elements . . . the referent [to which] is to be guessed." They determined that the description may be either *oppositional* or *nonoppositional* (that is, may or may not contain the "block" element), and either *literal* or *metaphorical*. Riddles with blocks (oppositional) are almost always metaphorical and may exhibit one of three kinds of opposition: *antithetical* (only one part can be true), *privational* (the second part denies a logical or natural attribute of the first), or *causal* (the first part consists of an action denied by the second). To this Roger Abrahams has added the identification of three techniques employed in riddling: *incomplete detail* (not enough information provided for the parts to fit together clearly), *too much detail* (inconsequential details that bury the important traits), and *false Gestalt* (commonly leading to off-color answers in catches and pretended obscene riddles). These approaches (and others have extended them) help to tie up loose ends of earlier definitions, furnishing more concrete and specific descriptions of what riddles really are.

The symbolism and functions of riddles in folk tradition raise further questions. Do riddles mask meanings not immediately apparent in their literal wording? How can these meanings be discovered? What roles do riddles play in folk groups as entertainment and as educational devices? Are riddles primarily children's folklore, and how long do they circulate them? What are the favorite times for asking riddles, besides parties, dances, "bees," wakes, and other social occasions during which they have previously been observed? Is riddling usually engaged in as a "concert" (one riddler performing for the others) or as a "contest" (riddlers taking turns and matching question for question)? What are the usual practices of guessing riddles? Do these matters all vary from region to region, family to family, period to period? Do the uses of riddles in folktales and ballads reflect their earlier functions in courtship, initiation, legal processes, and the like?

One study of the riddles included in British and Anglo-American traditional ballads concluded that all of them include thinly veiled sexual symbolism. The sequence of answers in the widely known "Riddle Song," for instance—cherry, egg, ring, baby—suggests impregnation, an interpretation also supported by both context and variants of the ballad. Another pioneering field study carried out in the United States and Scotland resulted in the first systematic observations of riddling customs in these areas. While riddles in American tradition tended to occur only incidentally, the riddle session or contest was still occasionally discovered in Scotland; in one such session the collector recorded sixty-five riddles from five persons during an evening. Such studies begin to answer questions about riddles and riddling, and they point the way for many other possible analyses of these eternally fascinating enigmas. The continued popularity of trivia books and games and of TV quiz and game shows proves how durable the charm is of trying to solve (or guess at) the puzzling problems and queries posed by others.

BIBLIOGRAPHIC NOTES

Archer Taylor surveyed "Problems in the Study of Riddles" in *SFQ* 2 (1938): 1–9; and he compiled "A Bibliography of Riddles" in *FFC* no. 126 (1939). His *English Riddles from Oral Tradition* (Berkeley: University of California Press, 1951) established the basic corpus of English and Anglo-American true riddles. A succinct essay on the types of riddles is Taylor's "The Riddle" in *CFQ* 2 (1943): 129–47. A similar statement is his "The Riddle as a Primary Form," published in *Folklore in Action*, pp. 200–7. An article in a popular vein that incorporates folkloristic concepts is Duncan Emrich's "Riddle Me, Riddle Me, What Is That?" in *American Heritage* 7 (Dec. 1955): 116–19.

In more-recent years several American folklorists have explored new definitions and analytic approaches for riddles. The special issue "Riddles and Riddling" of *JAF* 89, no. 352 (1976), edited by Elli Köngäs-Maranda, contains six articles, among them an important study of riddles in context by David Evans (pp. 166–88). Thomas A. Green and W. J. Pepicello proposed a strictly linguistic approach in "The

Folk Riddle: A Redefinition of Terms," *WF* 38 (1979): 3–20, and their joint work resulted in their 1984 book *The Language of Riddles: New Perspectives* (Columbus: Ohio State University Press). Another important book is John Holmes McDowell's *Children's Riddling* (Bloomington: Indiana University Press, 1979).

The supposed nonexistence of Native American riddles was challenged by three articles in *JAF:* Archer Taylor's "American Indian Riddles" in 57 (1944): 1–15; Charles T. Scott's "New Evidence of American Indian Riddles" in 76 (1963): 236–41; and David P. McAllester's "Riddles and Other Verbal Play among the Comanches," in 77 (1964): 251–57.

The true riddles themselves from collections in English up to 1951 are all included in Archer Taylor's classification, but three representative articles from mid-America might be listed for reference to their original publication with notes: Vance Randolph and Isabel Spradley published "Ozark Mountain Riddles" in *JAF* 47 (1934): 81–89; Randolph and Taylor published more "Riddles in the Ozarks" in *SFQ* 7 (1944): 1–10; and Paul G. Brewster published "Riddles from Southern Indiana" in *SFQ* 3 (1939): 93–105. A group of 143 items of riddling lore, including forty-eight true riddles, from the state of Mississippi was analyzed in George W. Boswell's "Riddles in the WPA-collected Folklore Archives," *MFR* 3 (1969): 33–52.

Various riddle types are often intermixed in the published collections, such as Catherine Harris Ainsworth's "Black and White and Said All Over," *SFQ* 26 (1962): 263–95, containing 535 miscellaneous texts collected by mail from ninth-grade and tenth-grade students in seven states. The conundrum alluded to in Ainsworth's title is discussed in many different contexts, variants, and offshoots in Mac E. Barrick's note "The Newspaper Riddle Joke," *JAF* 87 (1974): 253–57. Another large riddle collection from schoolchildren is Meryl Weiner's "The Riddle Repertoire of a Massachusetts Elementary School," *FF* 3 (1970): 7–38, in which about 260 students from first through fifth grades contributed examples.

Roger D. Abrahams's monograph "Between the Living and the Dead," *FFC* 225 (1980), the completion of a work begun by Archer Taylor, contains a survey and analysis of neck riddles with a catalogue of 423 types arranged in the three subcategories described in this chapter. The quoted examples come from this study as well. For riddles in English from the West Indies, see Abrahams's "A Riddling on St. Vincent," *WF* 42 (1983): 272–95.

Two articles explored the dynamics of the so-called pretended obscene riddles and paid particular attention to what a culture senses as being obscene and how a particular folklore genre operates with these assumptions: see Jan Hullum, "The 'Catch' Riddle: Perspectives from Goffman and Metafolklore," *Folklore Annual* 4–5 (1972–73): 52–59; and Waln K. Brown, "Cognitive Ambiguity and the 'Pretended Obscene Riddle,' " *KF* 18 (1973): 89–101. Use of pretended obscene riddles in a prank or initiation context is discussed by Richard Bauman in "The Turtles: An American Riddling Institution," *WF* 29 (1970): 21–25.

Conundrums from nineteenth-century American newspapers were compiled by Archer Taylor in *CFQ* 5 (1946): 273–76, and by C. Grant Loomis in *WF* 8 (1949): 235–47. Donald M. Hines culled 230 examples from regional newspaper files in

"Rare Blooms from a Rude Land: Frontier Riddles from the Inland Pacific Northwest," *IF* 6 (1973): 205–40; he discovered only nineteen that were "true riddles."

In "American Numskull Tales: The Polack Joke," *WF* 26 (1967): 183–86, Roger L. Welsch directed folklorists' attention to a new popular cycle of ethnic riddlejokes. In 1969 William M. Clements published *The Types of the Polack Joke*, a comprehensive catalog, as Bibliographical and Special Series no. 3 of *FF* (a supplementary list appeared in *FF* 4 [1971]: 19–29). Mac E. Barrick compared "Racial Riddles and the Polack Joke" in *KFQ* 15 (1970): 3–15, and Kathleen A. Preston and Michael J. Preston discussed the "Visual Polack Joke" in *JAF* 86 (1973): 175–77.

Reports on two large collections of ethnic riddle-jokes are Michael J. Preston's "A Typescript Ethnic Joke Anthology," *NYF* 1 (1975): 223–34; and Linda T. Humphrey's " 'It Ain't Funny, Buster': The Ethnic Riddle-Joke at Citrus Community College," *SWF* 4 (1980): 20–25, concerning a collection of over five hundred individual jokes.

Three articles that concentrate on interpretive analysis of more than one cycle of racial or ethnic joke are Jan Harold Brunvand, "Some Thoughts on the Ethnic-Regional Riddle Jokes," *IF* 3 (1970): 128–42; Nathan Hurvitz, "Blacks and Jews in American Folklore," *WF* 33 (1974): 301–25; and Alan Dundes, "A Study of Ethnic Slurs: The Jew and the Polack in the United States," *JAF* 84 (1971): 186–203.

Another cycle of numskull jokes in riddle form that may denigrate ethnic minorities is introduced in Judith B. Kerman's "The Light-Bulb Jokes: Americans Look at Social Action Processes," *JAF* 93 (1980): 454–58, and Alan Dundes's "Many Hands Make Light Work, or Caught in the Act of Screwing in Light Bulbs," *WF* 40 (1981): 261–66. Dundes asserts that these jokes are essentially about sexual and political impotence. Yet another cycle of numskull/ethnic/riddle-jokes is the subject of Alan Dundes's "Polish Pope Jokes," *JAF* 92 (1979): 219–22, and Lydia Fish's "Is the Pope Polish? Some Notes on the Polack Joke in Transition," *JAF* 93 (1980): 450–54. The Pope referred to was elected in October 1978, the first Pole to hold the office and thus the most obvious target for a new round of "Polack" jokes. ("Why does the Pope have 'TGIF' embroidered onto his slippers?" "It means 'Toes go in first,' " and so forth.)

The first article in a folklore journal on another popular riddle-joke genre was Alan Dundes's "The Elephant Joking Question," *TFSB* 29 (1963): 40–42. More analysis was offered in Roger D. Abrahams's "The Bigger They Are the Harder They Fall," *TFSB* 29 (1963): 94–102. A brief list of examples was printed in *WF* 23 (1964): 198–99, and a gathering of them was made by Mac E. Barrick in "The Shaggy Elephant Riddle," *SFQ* 28 (1964): 266–90. Another large collection was Ed Cray and Marilyn Eisenberg Herzog's "The Absurd Elephant: A Recent Riddle Fad," *WF* 26 (1967): 27–36. Roger D. Abrahams and Alan Dundes offered further interpretive suggestions in "On Elephantasy and Elephanticide," *The Psychoanalytic Review* 56 (1969): 225–41, reprinted in *Analytic Essays in Folklore*, pp. 192–205.

Two folklorists subjected the "sick joke" of the late 1950s to some analysis;

Brian Sutton-Smith published " 'Shut Up and Keep Digging': The Cruel Joke Series," *MF* 10 (1960): 11–22, and Roger D. Abrahams published "Ghastly Commands: The Cruel Joke Revisited," *MF* 11 (Winter 1961–62): 235–46. Then as further sick-joke subgenres emerged, folklorists were quick to study them. See Alan Dundes, "The Dead Baby Joke Cycle," *WF* 38 (1979): 145–57; Mac E. Barrick, "The Helen Keller Joke Cycle," *JAF* 93 (1980): 441–49; and Barrick, "Celebrity Sick Jokes," *Maledicta* 6 (1982): 57–62 (Dolly Parton, Natalie Wood, John Belushi, and others). Maurice D. Schmaier discussed "The Doll Joke Pattern in Contemporary American Oral Humor" in *MF* 13 (Winter 1963–64): 205–16. Robin Hirsch also treated this form in an article in *WF* 23 (1964): 107–10. Further essays on riddle-jokes are László Kurti's "The Politics of Joking: Popular Response to Chernobyl," *JAF* 100 (1988): 324–34, Alan Dundes's "Six Inches from the Presidency: The Gary Hart Jokes as Public Opinion," *WF* 48 (1989): 43–51, and Alan Dundes and Carl Pagter's "The Mobile SCUD Missile Launcher and other Persian Gulf Warlore: An American Folk Image of Saddam Hussein's Iraq," *WF* 50 (1991): 303–22.

A small collection mainly of arithmetical puzzles gathered by a radio station in Lafayette, Indiana, was annotated by Ray B. Browne for *MF* 11 (1961): 155–60. A page of short written "Verbal Puzzles" appeared in *NCFJ* 23 (1975): 112. Sixteen examples of what some people call "logic problems," short puzzling narratives with cryptic solutions, were published by Danny W. Moore in "The Deductive Riddle: An Adaptation to Modern Society," *NCFJ* 22 (1974): 119–25.

Non-oral riddles were printed in *WF* 17 (1958): 279–80 and *WF* 19 (1960): 132–33. David Bowman asks the questions "Whatever Happened to Droodles? Whatever Happened to Roger Price?" in *JPC* 9 (1975): 20–25. He provides useful information about their popularization in the United States during the early 1950s by Roger Price's publications, but he fails to identify the droodle itself (not the name) as a much older form. Four examples of "pictorial riddles" drawn for amusement by seventeenth-century Italian painters are reproduced as Figure 55 and mentioned on pp. 65–66 in Donald Posner, *Annibale Carracci*, vol. I (London: Phaidon Press, 1971). These were originally published by Carlo Cesare Malvasia in Bologna in 1678. A semiotic analysis of droodles ("visual descriptive riddles") was published by Danielle M. Roemer in *JAF* 95 (1982): 173–99. Visual riddles in a scientific community are collected in Gail Matthews's "Mercedes Benzene: The Elite Folklife of Physical Chemists," *FF* 19 (1986): 153–74. Other riddles involving writing or drawing are the subjects of articles by Thomas A. Green and W. J. Pepicello, "Sight and Spelling Riddles," *JAF* 93 (1980): 23–34; and Michael J. Preston, "The English Literal Rebus and the Graphic Riddle Tradition," *WF* 41 (1982): 104–38.

Tongue-twisters are sometimes printed as fillers in folklore journals or in general folklore anthologies. One specialized article, however, is Maurice A. Mook's "Tongue Tanglers from Central Pennsylvania," *JAF* 72 (1959): 291–96; the article is followed by a tongue-twister song from collegiate tradition (pp. 296–97). Another popular article, by Duncan Emrich, is "The Ancient Game of Tongue-Twisters," *American Heritage* 6 (Feb. 1955): 119–20. A children's book of tongue-twisters, but with a useful bibliography, is Alvin Schwartz's *A Twister of Twists, a Tangler of Tongues* (Philadelphia and New York: J. B. Lippincott, 1972). An article by Marilyn Jorgensen, "The Tickled, Tangled, Tripped, and Twisted Tongue: A Linguistic Study of Factors Relating to Difficulty in the Performance of Tongue Twisters," *NYF* 7 (1981): 67–81, offers not only a technical analysis but also some strategies for reciting tongue-twisters correctly. A richly annotated article on mnemonic devices was published by Alan Dundes in *MF* 11 (1961): 139–47.

A structural analysis of true riddles was made by Robert A. Georges and Alan Dundes and published in *JAF* 76 (1963): 111–18, reprinted in *Analytic Essays in Folklore*, pp. 95–102. Dundes and Roger D. Abrahams survey riddles from a structural and typological viewpoint in their chapter "Riddles" in Dorson's textbook *Folklore and Folklife: An Introduction* (Chicago: University of Chicago Press, 1972), pp. 129–43.

J. Barre Toelken examined the riddle ballads in "Riddles Wisely Expounded," *WF* 25 (1966): 1–16. "Riddling Traditions in Northeastern Scotland" were described by Kenneth S. Goldstein in *JAF* 76 (1963): 330–36.

7

RHYMES AND FOLK POETRY

Rhyme is a basic stylistic device of verbal folklore, and it occurs in many types besides the rhyming proverbs and riddles already mentioned. There are some rhymes in folktales—the dialogues in "The Three Little Pigs" and the giant's threats in "Jack and the Beanstalk," for example. Folk beliefs may be expressed in rhyme:

> Mole on the neck, trouble by the peck,
> Mole on the face, suffers disgrace.

Or the card players' rule:

> Cut 'em thin, sure to win,
> Cut 'em deep, sure to weep.

A traditional rhyme may serve as a characterizing or mnemonic device:

> Low and lazy,
> High and crazy,
> Broad and hazy.

This refers to the Episcopal Church services, "low" (no kneeling, hence "lazy"), "high" (formal and full of symbolism, or "crazy"), and "broad" (a "hazy" mixture of low and high). A schoolroom mnemonic rhyme (about how to divide by a fraction) combines information with commentary and is a parody of lines from Tennyson's poem "Charge of the Light Brigade":

> Ours is not to reason why,
> Just invert and multiply.

Another teaching rhyme instructs a person in the polite way to eat soup:

> As a ship goes out to sea,
> I dip my spoon away from me.

A belief-rhyme regarded as having magical power is called a *verbal charm*, the best known being the "Star light, star bright" verse used in wishing on a star. Many charms are intended to affect the transference of some ailment:

> Sty, sty, leave my eye;
> Take the next one passing by.

Other charms may make butter come in a churn, remove warts, stop bleeding in a wound, or drive the rain away to "come again another day." Good advice is sometimes transmitted in a rhyme, such as the following one for hours of sleep:

> Nature needs but five.
> Custom gives thee seven.
> Laziness takes nine,
> And wickedness eleven.

In addition to such uses of rhyme in other kinds of folklore, numerous independent rhymes, largely circulated by children, are chanted, whined, sung, shouted, muttered, or otherwise recited at suitable occasions. These bits of fluid folklore are highly elusive and have not been systematically collected or arranged on a large scale in the United States; thus, this chapter can only indicate some basic types of folk rhymes and suggest possible subdivisions. In general, there are four major categories of American folk rhymes—*nursery rhymes*; rhymes of play, games, and fun (including "the dozens," or "jiving"); *rhymes of work*; and *written traditional rhymes*. A few longer rhymed texts (including epic toasts, or "toasties") qualify for the rather vague title *folk poetry*.

NURSERY RHYMES

Nursery rhymes, although usually British in origin and often printed in their transmission, still play a role in American oral folklore. Parents may read "Mother Goose" to children out of books, but book versions vary significantly from text to text, and children alter them further as they repeat them.

At first, as children learn the rhymes by heart, they tend to rebel at any variation introduced into their favorites. Later, however, they may delight in parodies of nursery rhymes, which range from such innocent humor as the spider saying to Miss Muffet, "Pardon me, is this seat taken?" or "Mary Mary, quite contrary" finding in her garden "one lousy petunia," all the way to obscene parodies and grotesqueries such as:

> Little Jack Horner
> Sat in a corner
> Eating his sister.

What may be the best-known verse in the English language, "Mary Had a Little Lamb," is also probably the most often parodied. Composed by Mrs. Sarah Josepha Hale of Boston in 1830, it appeared in journalistic parodies by 1871 in the United States and by 1886 in England—a sure sign that readers were expected to be familiar with it. The themes of printed parodies clustered around subjects like Mary having different pets or new clothes, desiring special food or drink, and the like; only a few suggested the risqué twist that oral parodies have taken. The following, for example, is from a college humor magazine of 1928:

Mary had a little dress
It was so light and airy;
It never showed a speck of dust,
But it showed just lots of Mary.

This has its counterpart in the oral parody:

Mary had a little lamb,
She also had a bear;
I've often seen her little lamb,
But I've never seen her bear [bare].

Persistence of tradition is illustrated in the "Mary" parodies. The earliest recorded reference to the rhyme was a note in *Harper's Weekly* in 1869, discovered by folklorist C. Grant Loomis, in which a child was reported to be confused about the "fleas as white as snow." Still known in oral tradition is the parody:

Some folks say that fleas are black,
But I'm not sure they know.
Cause Mary had a little lamb,
Whose fleas were white as snow.

A full collection of children's oral parodies of "Mary" would reveal some of their preoccupations. For instance, delight in wordplay and a dawning awareness of the facts of life are suggested in

Mary had a little lamb
(Boy was the doctor surprised!)

Or observe the abrupt shift from playing with a pet at home to the real business of going off to school (initiated by the domineering figure of a parent and supported by vigorous vernacular language) in

Mary had a little lamb,
Her father shot it dead.
Now Mary takes her lamb to school,
Between two hunks of bread.

A favorite form of adult parody of nursery rhymes consists of changing the direct simple language of the original into abstract or pseudoscientific language, as in the following partial examples:

A research team proceeded toward the apex of a natural geological protuberance, the purpose of their expedition being the procurement of a sample of fluid hydride of oxygen in a large vessel. ("Jack and Jill")

A chronologically enhanced mother named Hubbard removed herself to her cupboard with the intention of procuring her canine companion a byte or two of ossified matter. ("Old Mother Hubbard")

The contents of Mother Goose rhymes, as Archer Taylor has pointed out, are extremely broad, reflecting a range of traditional sources that include lullabies ("Bye Baby Bunting"), finger rhymes ("Pat a Cake"), bouncing rhymes ("To Market, to Market, to Buy a Fat Pig"), story rhymes ("Old Mother Hubbard"), games ("Here We Go 'round the Mulberry Bush"), riddles ("Humpty Dumpty"), limericks ("Hickory Dickory Dock"), and even such types as charms, street cries, mnemonic devices, and traditional prayers. Ingenious and sometimes fantastic theories and interpretations have been offered for the origin and meaning of nursery rhymes, but about all that might be safely said is that many of them are very old, and some of them were certainly used (and perhaps invented) for political and social satire in Great Britain.

FOCUS: MOTHER GOOSE BECOMING LAME DUCK?

GLENSIDE, Pa. (AP)—Jack and Jill went up the hill to fetch a pail of water, but then what did Jack do? Many youngsters didn't know, said a researcher who is worried that the nation may be forgetting Mother Goose.

. . . [Bette] Goldstone surveyed 150 pre-schoolers in suburban Philadelphia during the past two years to determine their knowledge of six basic Mother Goose rhymes. . . . Nearly a third of the youngsters didn't know all of "Jack and Jill."

. . . Here is part of the quiz:

1. Where did Polly Flinders sit?

2. *What time did the clock strike in Hickory Dickory Dock?*
3. *What problem did the little old lady who lived in a shoe have?*
4. *What do beggars wear?*
5. *Who is Tom, Tom's father?*

Source: Associated Press report published under the above headline in *The Salt Lake Tribune* on May 2, 1991.

DISCUSSION TOPICS:

1. Answer the questions and complete "Jack and Jill" (both verses!). If you do not already know the answers, look them up in *The Oxford Dictionary of Nursery Rhymes*, cited in the bibliographic notes to this chapter.

2. Even if preschoolers do not know Mother Goose well, how might older children be likely to acquire knowledge of these rhymes?

3. What positive things might children learn from Mother Goose, and what negative elements do some of the rhymes contain? Taken together, do you think the influence of Mother Goose rhymes on children is desirable or not?

Most of the "explanations" offered for English nursery rhymes turn out to be what the best authorities on the genre (Iona and Peter Opie) characterize as "the work of the happy guessers." For instance, "Mary, Mary, quite contrary" is said to refer to Mary Queen of Scots and her ladies-in-waiting (the "four Marys" of balladry); the "cockleshells" are said to be decorations on a particular dress of the queen's. One problem with this theory is that no version of the rhyme was found until some 150 years after Mary's beheading. On the other hand, there are some examples of "political squibs" in nursery rhymes, such as the use of "Jack Spratt" to ridicule an Archdeacon Pratt in the seventeenth century and a popular rhyme that emerged in 1914 as a political cartoon with this text (parodying "Goosie Goosie Gander"):

Kaiser, Kaiser-gander, where do your men wander?
Upstairs, downstairs, in my lady's chamber,
Burning their cathedrals till they couldn't say their prayers,
Then there came the British troops who flung them down the stairs.

RHYMES OF PLAY, GAMES, AND FUN

Play rhymes begin a baby's social life with such highly amusing (to infants) activities as bouncing, finger and toe counting, and tickling to the accompaniment of chants such as "This Is the Way the Farmer Rides," "Here Is the Church; Here Is the Steeple," "This Little Piggy," and

> Ticklee, ticklee on the knee,
> If you laugh, you don't love me.

All these rhymes are performed with gestures or other actions, thus combining simple motor activity with rhythmic verse. The parent chants, "Round a bit, round a bit, like a wee mouse," while circling his or her finger in baby's palm; then says, "Up a bit, up a bit, into the house," while running his or her fingers up baby's arm to tickle the baby under the chin. Later, the baby learns to perform the rhyme on him- or herself or on others. Another favorite group of rhymes assigns comical names to the features of the face—"chin-chopper" and "eyewinker." In finger-and-toe-counting rhymes, with their simple narrative plots, the child probably is expected to identify with the smallest digit, who not only "cried 'wee, wee, wee,' all the way home," but in other versions and other lands may be chastised as a glutton, a crybaby, a tattletale, a prig, or a noisy nuisance who wakes up the big, strong thumb. As children grow more adept in their motions, they master the more complex gestures that accompany rhymes like "Pease Porridge Hot," "Two Little Blackbirds," or "Eensy Weensy Spider."

Next, what one collector has called "the *ars poetica* of children" manifests itself in **game rhymes**. Simplest is the basic *amphimacric beat* (unstressed syllable between two stressed syllables) of a bounce-ball-catch rhyme ("Ivory soap / See it float"), followed in complexity by the rhymes that involve both bouncing and patting the ball, then making leg-lifting movements ("O Leary") and pantomime gestures or bouncing the ball to another child. The word "a-lery" (i.e., holding one's leg crooked so as to appear crippled) has been found in a fourteenth-century manuscript, leading one American folklorist to remark about the "O Leary" rhyme that "although children obviously use [the word] correctly, not one of them can say what it means."

When competitive games begin, the counting-out rhyme appears for choosing "it." The one beginning "Eeny, meeny, miney, mo" is at once the most common and the most obscure in meaning of all counting-out rhymes, and no convincing origin for it has yet been proposed. The rhyme has changed to suit the times, so that the offensive word "nigger" has yielded to "chigger," "tiger," "froggy," or "lawyer," who is caught by the toe. Children of many countries know variants fully as complicated as this American one:

Eentery, meentery, cutery corn
Apple seed and apple thorn
Wire, briar, limber lock,
Three geese in a flock.
One flew east, and one flew west.
One flew over the cuckoo's nest.
O-U-T spells "out goes she!"

After choosing "it" and before beginning the game, children may chant a "locking" verse in order to fix the number of players, excluding any children who show up later:

Tick Tock, the game is locked
And nobody else can play.
If they do, we'll take their shoe,
And keep it for a day or two.

Jump-rope rhymes exhibit astonishing variety within a limited number of basic forms, and they frequently contain perceptive commentaries from a child's-eye view of the world. The simplest pattern is the *plain jump* game, in which a child simply chants a rhyme to the rhythm of her jumping. More demanding is the endurance jump based on an open-end rhyme that continues until the jumper misses:

I love coffee; I love tea,
How many boys are stuck on me?
One, two, three, four . . .

Endurance jumps frequently use *prophetic rhymes*, as above, or end "Yes-no-maybe," or with a series of colors, or with the alphabet. Social comment is specific in the following example, in which the young jumper is watching her older sister primp:

> Grace, Grace, dressed in lace,
> Went upstairs to powder her face.
> How many boxes did she use?
> One, two, three, four . . .

The game of *speed jump* is set off by such words as "pepper," "hot," or "fire" in a rhyme; then the rope is twirled with ever-increasing speed until the jumper misses. Most complicated of all are *action rhymes* that require the jumper to imitate the behavior of the subject of the verse—usually "Teddy Bear"—as he touches the ground, turns around, goes upstairs, says his prayers, and so forth. Finally, there are *call-in, call-out rhymes* to signal changing jumper during a group game.

The list of characters frequently mentioned in jump-rope rhymes is peculiar. While "Mickey Mouse" and "Teddy Bear" (or sometimes "Yogi Bear") seem suitable for the context, what is the reason for the continuing popularity of "Shirley Temple," "Betty Grable," and that shadowy figure in popular rhymes, "the lady with the alligator purse"? Several past motion-picture stars and other historical personages, too early for most of today's rope-jumpers to remember in action, live on in their rhymes:

> Charlie Chaplin went to France,
> To teach the ladies how to dance;

It is clear that "Teddy Bear" (originally referring to a bear hunted by Theodore Roosevelt) is now to the jump-rope rhymes what the littlest pig is to the toe-counting verse. The child sees himself and his beloved stuffed toy being suppressed in a world tyrannically ruled by harsh adults, in a rhyme like

> Teddy on the railroad, pickin' up stones,
> Along came a train and broke Teddy's bones.

"Oh," said Teddy, "that's not fair!"
"Oh," said the engineer, "I don't care!"

And for a nutshell summary of the conventional course of life, what could be clearer than

First comes love, then comes marriage,
Then comes Judy with a baby carriage.

Rhymes too numerous to list accompany other games and recreations; they are usually gathered and studied in connection with the games themselves. A typical game of hide-and-seek illustrates this. First there is a counting-out rhyme to select "it." The designated child then covers his or her eyes and counts in a formulaic manner to a specified number before calling out "Bushel of wheat, bushel of rye / Who's not ready holler 'I' " or "Bushel of wheat, bushel of clover / Who's not ready can't hide over." When the designated child tags a hider, "it" calls out one saying or rhyme; but a hider who slips in safely can cry a rhyme of his or her own, calling the others

Fourth graders in Blue Ridge [Virginia] Elementary School perform a hand-clapping routine called "My Left, My Left." This routine came into the mountain community from New York, via a cousin of the girl on the right.

in "free." Other games may have more or less rhyme content than this, but nearly all active folk games have some rhyme attached to them. Amusements like the following are little more than a rhyme followed by appropriate behavior:

> Order in the courtroom, monkey wants to speak.
> First one to speak is a monkey for a week.

A vast number of rhymes have no connection with organized play or games at all, but are simply recited for the fun of it. Even so, there may be some underlying sense to the most nonsensical of them:

> I sent my boy to college,
> With a pat on the back.
> I spent ten thousand dollars,
> But I got a quarterback.

*

> Marriage for me in '93
> Marriage for sure in '94
> Anything alive in '95

Many are **topical rhymes:**

> Reagan's in the White House
> Waiting to be elected.
> Mondale's in the garbage can,
> Waiting to be collected.

(Whether this rhyme, modifying an earlier presidential verse, was updated beyond the Reagan era is uncertain.)

Some fun rhymes are **parody rhymes,** often of religious texts such as prayers, hymns, and blessings:

> Good food, good meat,
> Good God, let's eat!

*

> Now I lay me down to sleep,
> Bedbugs all around me creep.

> If they bite before I wake,
> I pray the Lord their jaws will break.

Some parodies of old school recitations are in rhyme:

> The boy stood on the burning deck,
> Melting with the heat.
> His big blue eyes were filled with tears,
> And his shoes were full of feet.

Other rhymed recitations are pure nonsense rather than parodies:

> Ladies and gentlemen, hoboes and tramps,
> Crosseyed mosquitoes, bowlegged ants,
> I now tell you something I know nothing about.
> Last night about 3 o'clock this morning,
> An empty truckload of bricks drove up my front back alley,
> And ran over my poor dead cat and half killed her.
> I rushed her to the hospital as slow as I could go,
> And there I saw Gene Autry eating vinegar with a pitchfork.

But most **nonsense orations** are composed in a sort of surrealistic free verse:

> Ladies and jellyfish, I come here not to dress you or undress you, but to address you as to how Christopher Cockeyed Cucumber crossed the Missisloppi River with the Declaration of Indigestion in one hand and the Star Speckled bannaner in the other.

Missionaries for the Church of Jesus Christ of Latter-day Saints (Mormons) have made up a sort of nonsense oration that parodies the rhetoric of the standard opening statement they use when going door-to-door with the church's message. Called "A Poor Green Missionary's First Day," the oration begins

> Good Madam Morning! How do you do? I'm Joseph Smith from Salt Lake City. I mean, I'm a mission mormonary representing the Church of Jesus Christ of Rattle-Day Snakes. I'm traveling without body parts or passions, and I represent a God without a purse or script.

Athletic cheers form a pattern for further rhyme parodies, such as this effete revision of a popular one:

> Retard them, retard them
> Make them relinquish the ball.

Or this bilingual (Norwegian-American) gem from Wisconsin:

> *Lutefisk, lefse,*
> *Takk skal du ha.*
> Stoughton High School
> Rah! Rah! Rah!

Many fun rhymes reflect nothing more than pure boredom, day-dreaming, and release:

> Spring is sprung, the grass is riz, I wonder where the birdies is.

*

> Squirrel, squirrel on the ground,
> You don't make a single sound.
> I know why so still you are,
> You've been flattened by a car.

*

> Said Aaron to Moses,
> "Let's cut off our noses."
> Said Moses to Aaron,
> "It's the fashion to wear 'em."

Other nonsense rhymes are circular rhymes. Among the best known are the dialect pieces beginning "My name is Yon Yonson" and "Where do you worka John?" which advance a story for a few lines that lead right back to the opening line and repetitions ad infinitum.

A curious form of nonsense rhyme is the so-called **spelling-riddle,** really only another fun rhyme. "How do you spell 'snapping turtle'?"

> Snopey, snappin'
> Fat an' tickin'

Tortle, tortle,
Snappin' turtle.

Rhymes of derision may be classified as fun rhymes, fun at least
for the ones who chant them against fat kids, skinny kids, weak
kids, foreign kids, kids who wear glasses, sissies, tattletales, and all
the other unfortunates of a child's world. Let a youngster acquire a
sweetheart, and someone is sure to sing "Johnny's got a girlfriend"
to a well-known tune, or recite the rhyme

Johnny's mad, and I'm glad,
And I know what'll please him.
A bottle of ink to make him stink
And _____ to squeeze him.

Similarly, **rhymed retorts** (compare "catches" in chapter 6) are
delivered:

What's your name?
—Puddin-tane
Ask me again and I'll tell you the same.

*

Do you like Jelly?
—I'll punch you in the belly.

*

See my finger?
See my thumb?
See my fist?
You'd better run!

Ritualized **rhymed insults,** usually directed at another's mother,
are common in the black tradition of "sounding" or "playing the
dozens," but such verses have also been collected from whites. Mild
examples of dozens, which are often quite obscene (the "dirty dozens"), are:

I can tell by your eyes,
You've been eatin' welfare pies.

*

I can tell by your hair,
Your father was a grizzly bear.

*

Fee, fie, fo, fum,
Your mother's a bum.

*

I can tell by your toes,
Your mother wears brogues.

A second type of mostly black folk verse is the "toast," not primarily a drinking stanza or compliment as much as a longer narrative or editorial rhymed recitation.

Of course, the drinking toast itself is also folklore, whether it be the simple compliment "Cheers!" or "Bottoms up!" or the longer verse. Analogous to rhymed toasts are verses like the following, used when a particular product is served:

Carnation Milk in a little red can,
Best tasting milk in the whole wide land.
No tits to squeeze, no tail to twitch,
Just punch a little hole in the son of a bitch.

(According to a traditional story about the Carnation Milk verse, a rancher's daughter composed the first two lines to send in as an entry in a slogan contest. But the cowboy who mailed her postcard thought her verse was too tame to win, so he added the second two lines. One variant of line three is "No tits to pull, no hay to pitch.")

WORK RHYMES

What might be called **work rhymes** are gradually disappearing from American life, and they have always tended to shade off into folksongs. This category includes various rhymes associated with a particular trade, craft, or calling; they serve as advertising, or to retain useful information, to maintain the rhythm of work, or simply to ease strain and weariness.

Peddlers' cries (or "street cries") and **newsboys' calls**—chanted or sung—were once heard regularly on many American streets from fresh-fruit and vegetable sellers, rag and bone collectors, fishmongers, refreshment dispensers, and other wandering hawkers. In recent years street selling seems to have been replaced by supermarkets or convenience stores, and old-time peddlers' cries are rarely heard. Only an occasional informant recalls how these cries used to sound. The words were generally very simple—mere lists of the goods offered:

> Green corn and tomatoes
> Sweet and Irish potatoes.

> *

> Blackberries, blackberries,
> Fresh and fine,
> Just off the vine.

The rhymes were often imperfect, the form loose, and the words improvised from a stock of commonplaces. Sometimes a claim for the product's qualities was included in the cry:

> Hot tamales, floatin' in gravy,
> Suit your taste and I don't mean maybe.

> *

> Watermelons, come and see,
> Every one sold with a guarantee.

> *

> Ice cold lemonade!
> Freeze your teeth, curl your hair,
> Make you feel like a millionaire.

In Texas, and perhaps elsewhere, the story was told of an Italian street peddler who was weak in English and so followed an American hawker around calling out, "Same-a-ting! Same-a-ting!"

Yet even in the modern age some work traditions of rhythmic

"Old Rags." An early New York street peddler advertises his services—collecting reusable trash—with a street cry (undated engraving).

expressive speech continue, especially at auctions, carnivals, circuses, and among some small-scale retailers. As recently as 1978 at the Maine Avenue Fish Wharf in Washington, D.C., a vendor used a microphone to pitch his products in a lengthy chant that began

> People walk on down
> If you want to see the largest crabs in town.
> Fresher fish cannot be found. . . .
> Yes if it swims in the sea
> You can believe me
> I got it on sale right here at the back boat today.

Planting rhymes have also been driven aside by automation; no powered corn drill needs anyone to chant "One for the blackbird / One for the crow" or any of its numerous continuations and variants. Other such rhymes contained the traditional dates for planting certain crops, information now secured from a government bulletin or a county farm adviser:

Plant pumpkin seeds in May,
And they will all run away.
Plant pumpkin seeds in June,
And they will come soon.

Verses for rhythmic group work—sea chanteys, chain-gang hollers, chopping and pounding songs, and so forth—usually were delivered in a two-part call-and-response pattern, with a leader
initiating the call or song and the community of workers chorusing
back the response. One African-American rhyme for lining railroad
ties went

Oh, shove 'em up solid,
Up solid and sound,
So the big Nine-Hundred, boys,
Cannot whop him down.

Although many of these types of rhymes are dead or dying now,
circus roustabouts used them until recently when hoisting the big
tops. And one such practice remains in **military cadence chants:**

Leader: You had a good home but you left.
    Chorus: You're right!
Leader: Jody was there when you left.
    Chorus: You're right!

The "left-rights," of course, must fall on the proper feet for the
march; the name "Jody," which occurs frequently, represents the
civilian men back home who enjoy the good life that soldiers secure
for them. Comments on army life and discipline are also popular:

Ain't no need in lookin' down,
Ain't no discharge on the ground.

(A version, heard in Joseph Wiseman's film *Basic Training*:

Uncle Dicky, drop the bomb—
I don't want to go to "Nam.")

*

> Airborne, airborne, where you been?
> Round the world and gone again.
> What you gonna do when you get back?
> Run again with a full field pack.

Some traditional admonitions in rhyme (often incorporating folk beliefs) might simply be termed **rhymed advice,** such as these instructions for buying a horse:

> If he has one white foot, buy him,
> If two, try him,
> Three, deny him,
> Four white feet and a white nose,
> Take off his hide and feed him to the crows.

WRITTEN TRADITIONAL RHYMES

Although they are seldom transmitted orally, certain **written rhymes** qualify as folklore on the grounds of traditionality, variation, and anonymity. For example, verses found carved on old powder horns often turn out to be variants of this one:

> I powder with my brother ball,
> A hero like I conquer all.
> The rose is red, the grass is green,
> The years are past which I have seen.

Other powder-horn rhymes commemorate the designer or owner of the horn and may advertise the latter's prowess:

> The man who steals this horn,
> Will go to Hell, so sure as he is born.
> I James Fenwick of Ogdensburg
> Did the year of 1817 kill 30 wolf,
> 10 bear, 15 deer
> And 46 partridges.

Similar traditional verses are sometimes found on hope chests, jewel boxes, snuffboxes, and the like.

Epitaphs, especially facetious or ironic ones, may be traditional, as is the following:

> Pass on stranger, don't waste your time,
> O'er bad biography or bitter rhyme,
> For what I am this crumbling clay insures,
> And what I was is no concern of yours.

Sometimes the verses stitched into old samplers (needlework exercises for girls) resembled epitaphs in their pious and sententious language, as in this example from England, which has counterparts in American sampler verse:

> Mary Purmtum is my name.
> And England is my nation.
> Danvers is my dwelling place,
> And Christ is my salvation.
> When I am dead and laid in my grave,
> And all my bones are rotten,
> When this you see, remember me,
> That I may not be forgotten.

Another and simpler piece of sampler verse is

> This I have done
> To let you see
> What care my parents
> Took of me.

The flyleaves of old textbooks are another source of written traditional rhymes. **Flyleaf inscriptions** may be simple statements like "In case of flood, stand on this; it's dry"; but often they are traditional admonitions in rhyme:

> If by chance this book should roam,
> Box its ears and send it home.

*

Don't steal this book,
My little lad,
For fifty cents
It cost my dad;
And when you die
The lord will say,
"Where is that book,
You stole one day?"
And when you say
You do not know,
The lord will say,
"Go down below!"

One curious inscription found written over the Ten Commandments in a schoolbook dated 1832 reveals its rhymed message when a letter "e" is inserted for each dot:

P.RS.V.R.Y.P.RF.CTM.N
.V.RK..PTH.S.PR.C.PTST.N

Sometimes envelope sealers and inscriptions have a similar form. The familiar "SWAK" (sealed with a kiss) may be expanded to "SWALCAKWS" (sealed with a lick 'cause a kiss won't stick). An admonition to the postman is "PMPMDBS / BLEGMG" (Postman, postman, don't be slow, / Be like Elvis, "Go, man, go!!"). And even more complicated is this one:

D-liver
D-letter
D-sooner
D-better
D-later
D-letter
D-madder
I-getter

Envelope sealers from Scotland (where "D-liver D-letter" also appears) include

Postie, Postie, dinna dither
If Isobel's nae in, gie it tae her mither.

*

Postie, Postie, do your stuff
Take this to my wee cream puff.

Graffiti—writings on public walls—are frequently traditional, sometimes rhymed, but most often take the form of witty prose commentaries:

Death is nature's way of telling you to slow down.

*

Ask God in prayer and she will answer.

Public-restroom graffiti ("latrinalia"), a common form in more ways than one (they tend to be profane, sexual, and scatological), have been widely collected and studied. Their earthy language, in contrast to the euphemisms often used in speech, led linguist Allen Walker Read to comment: "That anyone should pass up the well-established colloquial words of the language and have recourse to the Latin *defecate*, *urinate*, and *have sexual intercourse*, is indicative of grave mental unhealth."

A related form, **desktop inscriptions** (or "horizontal graffiti"), may comment on the school or college situation:

I came, I saw, I laughed.

*

Professional absentee sits here.

Or the desktop inscription involves some whimsical trick writing:

THGUAC M'I PLEH
REDNU GNIHTEMOS NO
KSED SIHT

Autograph rhymes (or "friendship verses") constitute the largest, most varied, and most enduring category of written American folk rhymes, although traditional inscriptions include prose as well as verse. Enjoying a great vogue in the late nineteenth century, autograph books then were elegant; the writings in them tended to be pious and sentimental:

Remember well and bear in mind,
A constant friend is hard to find,
But when you get one kind and true,
Forsake not the old one for the new.

*

Our lives are albums written through,
With good or ill, with false or true,
And as the blessed Angels turn,

Rhyme, dated 1883, from an autograph album belonging to George Steinmetz. The book's inscriptions were written in English and German, with one phrase here (written sideways) in Greek. "When you throw a glance / Upon these lines, / Do you also sometimes think / Back to the time // When we typeset the 'Courier' / Busily, day and night, / And occasionally refreshed ourselves / By making pie? // Oh, if, without effort and pain, / You should remember / The beautiful 'devil' days, / Then think also of me. / —Hermann Hoffmann / Independence, Jan. 27th 1883 'Know thyself!'" "Devil" refers to a "printer's devil," a printshop apprentice who does chores and often becomes very black with dust or ink, while "pie" (usually spelled "pi") is printers' jargon for spilled or mixed-up type.

The pages of your years,
God grant they read the good with smiles,
And blot the bad with tears.

But even then whimsical verses began to appear—often comments on the act of writing such verses or on marriage:

Some write for pleasure,
Some write for fame,
But I write simply,
To sign my name.

*

When you get married and cannot see,
Put on your specks and think of me!

*

As you slide down the bannister of life,
I hope you don't get a splinter in your career.

The "When you get married" verse with the "Yours 'til" signoff is still a favorite autograph gimmick, rivaled recently by such novelty inscriptions as

I'd cross the hottest desert,
I'd swim the deepest sea,
I'd climb the highest mountain,
But I can't come over tonite, 'cause it's raining.

*

Two sat in a hammock
About to kiss,
When all of a sudden,
It went like sıɥʇ.

*

Don't be #
Don't be ♭
Just be ♮

*

Y Y U R [i.e., "too wise (two Ys) you are"]
Y Y U B
I C U R
Y Y 4 Me

*

U R 2 good 2 B 4 got 10

The enduring long-term favorite autograph-book rhyme, whether "straight" or in parody, begins "Roses are red / Violets are blue."

FOLK POETRY

FOCUS: FOLK POETRY ON THE INTERNET

Too Bee Oar Knot Two Bee

I have a spelling checker,
It came with my PC.
It plainly marks four my revue
Mistakes witch I can not sea.

I've run this poem threw hit,
I wood bee sure your pleased too no,
Its letter perfect in it's weigh,
My checker tolled me sew.

A Ballad

Father, dear Father, come home with me now,
The clock in the steeple strikes one.
You promised to come straight home from the lab,
As soon as your home page was done.

Source: Various e-mails and chat groups on the Internet.

DISCUSSION TOPICS:

1. The first poem requires being *written* for its effect, and the subject is computer word processing. Its medium of circulation is electronic. Is it still folklore?

2. Does anyone nowadays not recognize the terms "Internet,"

"spelling checker," "PC," or "home page"? What are other traditions of "the information superhighway"?

3. The "ballad" begins with an allusion to an old sentimental ("folk"?) poem or song. Can you find a text of this item? What was the father's addiction in the original?

4. Look at some home pages of individuals on the World Wide Web (among university students or faculty members, for example). What clichés or "traditions" seem to have developed for this new medium of self-expression?

The term **folk poetry** has been very broadly applied, ranging from a description of the proverb as "a one-line folk poem" to consideration of lengthy folksong texts as poems. A reasonable limitation of the term might be to use it for "longer" folk rhymes (usually more than one stanza), especially those not connected with a specific game or work; for instance, many African-American toasts, like "Shine" and "The Titanic," reach nearly epic proportions. The traditional *limerick*, which is usually off-color and hence circulated orally, is a familiar example of folk poetry:

> There was an old lady from Kent,
> Whose nose was most awfully bent,
> She followed her nose,
> One day I suppose,
> And nobody knows where she went.

The Spanish-American *memoria*—newspaper verses memorializing the dead—are also considered folk poetry. Folklorist T. M. Pearce, an investigator of this and other local verse, proposed this definition of a folk poet:

He writes often of community events and personalities associated with them and of manifestations of natural forces with effects upon society. He writes of the experiences of individuals when such happenings offer occasion for joy or sorrow to groups of relatives and friends or acquaintances. His poetic forms (metrical and stanzaic) are traditional, sometimes irregular or modified in the direction of informal and freer communication. His poetic idiom is stamped with expressions describing group feeling and thought.

This definition could embrace the soldiers of World War I who composed rhymed chronicles of their experiences, such as the following fragments of a long piece written in a notebook by a retired Indiana railroad man:

> In the year of 1918, April the 26th day,
> I joined the American army to help whip Germany.
> I spent four weeks at camp Taylor in the city of Louisville,
> There they dressed me in khaki and taught me how to drill.

*

> In fourteen days I had eight meals,
> And most of them, I fed the seals.
> Most of the way it was very cool.
> July the 10th we arrived at Liverpool.

*

> There we seen hard fighting, also done our bits,
> Sending over three-inch shells, making each one a good hit.
> For two weeks we advanced continually through the Hindenburg line,
> And our intentions were very great for reaching the River Rhine.
> The huns made no resistance, they knew they couldn't win.
> They kept right on retreating away from us fighting men.

*

> The 11th of November we had them on the hop
> When they gave us orders at eleven o'clock to stop.
> But we were not sorry, a happy bunch were we,
> To know the war was over and we had won the victory.

This poem ended with a reference to returning to the job back home in Indiana:

> I'm no poet, just a railroad man,
> And I work between Lafayette and Bloomington.
> When I am back home you'll find me without doubt,
> Someplace up and down the dear old Monon route.

That compositions like this one are traditional is suggested by parallels such as these lines from a Pennsylvania logger's recitation:

> I'm only just a raftsman
> From up Clearfield way
> I been up in the mountains
> E'r since the last o' May.
> Peelin' oak and hemlock
> And skiddin' yeller pine
> And I just come down the river
> To have a little 'shine. . . .
> And off we go once more
> Gellahootin' through the chute
> Bound for Jersey Shore.

Cowboy poetry and logger poetry, old frontier traditions, have been rediscovered in recent years, making some of their practictioners famous even on a national level. Besides celebrating the rugged outdoor life and the jobs that had to be done on the frontier, these poets often comment on contemporary America, as in this portion of a poem by Everett Brisendine titled "The Subdivisions":

> Up on the ridge was a big fog of dust
> There was a fellow plowin' and scrapin'
> He was really tearin' up the grass
> For something he called lanscapin'
>
> After lookin' around I turned away
> From country I had loved so well
> Some call this progress, but looks to me like
> This country is sure goin' to Hell.

One long poetic text in free verse—the Twenty-third Psalm— has inspired many full-length parodies. Certainly a traditional process is operating when so many different versions of this verse circulate around themes such as the Model-T Ford ("The Ford is my auto, I shall not want another / It maketh me to lie down in mud puddles"), the Great Depression ("Mr. Roosevelt is my shepherd, I am in want / He maketh me to lie down on park benches" or "The Welfare Board is my shepherd, I shall not want another / It maketh me work in the road ditches"), and so forth. Most of the Twenty-third Psalm parodies are conservative, pious, and anti–big government in tone; several of them are commentaries on American presidents as recent as Lyndon Johnson and Richard Nixon. (True to form, as the present edition of this textbook was being prepared a parody mentioning President Clinton began circulating. It ended, "We shall live in a rented mobile home, eating Spam and Hamburger Helper forever.")

Clearly the folk poets of our culture, whoever they are, in common with the recognized art poets, respond to both personal emotions and social conditions in their works. And at the present, when formal poetry has discarded most restraints of the past masters and when popular-music composers—often employing folksong forms —may touch upon the most serious and immediate problems, it becomes virtually impossible to draw hard and fast lines around art, popular, or folk poetry.

BIBLIOGRAPHIC NOTES

There is no book-length collection of general American folk rhymes to compare with Thomas Talley's specialized work *Negro Folk Rhymes* (New York: Macmillan, 1922); an expanded edition with music was published in 1991 by the University of Tennessee Press (Knoxville). Duncan Emrich's *American Folk Poetry* (Boston: Little, Brown, 1974) is really an anthology of the lyrics of American folksongs. Interesting popular collections are Carl Withers's *A Rocket in My Pocket: The Rhymes and Chants of Young America* (New York: Henry Holt, 1948), Lillian Morison's *A Diller a Dollar: Rhymes and Sayings for the Ten o'Clock Scholar* (New York: Crowell, 1955), and Ian Turner's *Cinderella Dressed in Yella: Australian Children's Play-Rhymes* (Melbourne: Heinemann Educational Publications, 1969), which has a good introduction, thorough annotation, and a surprising number of parallels to American rhymes.

Some general compendiums of folklore have sections of rhymes; Paul G. Brewster edited them for the *Frank C. Brown Collection of North Carolina Folklore*, vol. I (Durham, N.C.: Duke University Press, 1952), pp. 160–219. *Kansas Folklore* (Lincoln: University of Nebraska Press, 1961), edited by Samuel J. Sackett and William E. Koch, has two chapters of folk verse (pp. 116–37). A representative special collection is Ruth Ann Musick and Vance Randolph's "Children's Rhymes from Missouri," *JAF* 63 (1950): 425–37.

Mary Anne Spiller offers "Some Contrasts in Rhymes Related by Children and Remembered by Adults in the San Gabriel Valley" in *FMS* 3 (1979): 47–64. She presents fifty-three examples, comparing those collected from children and adults. In a chapter coauthored with Mary Sanches, Barbara Kirshenblatt-Gimblett discusses "Children's Traditional Speech Play and Child Language," which appears in a book edited by Kirshenblatt-Gimblett, *Speech Play* (Philadelphia: University of Pennsylvania Press, 1976), pp. 65–110. An appendix identifies thirteen classic rhetorical patterns in children's folk rhymes.

Iona and Peter Opie's *The Oxford Dictionary of Nursery Rhymes* (New York: Oxford University Press, 1951) is the standard work on that genre, providing bibliography and evaluations of the many interpretations of Mother Goose. Archer Taylor's succinct and useful survey "What Is 'Mother Goose'?" appeared in *NMFR* 2 (1947–48): 7–13. *The Annotated Mother Goose* by Wm. and Cecil Baring-Gould (New York: Bramhall House, 1962) contains many odd and unusual variations, plus explanatory notes. Another approach is taken by Lucy Rollin in *Cradle and All: A Cultural and Psychoanalytic Reading of Nursery Rhymes* (Jackson: University Press of Mississippi, 1992). Nursery-rhyme parodies are discussed by C. Grant Loomis in "Mary Had a Parody: A Rhyme of Childhood in Folk Tradition," *WF* 17 (1958): 45–51; and by Joseph Hickerson and Alan Dundes in "Mother Goose Vice Verse," *JAF* 75 (1962): 249–59.

Sam M. Shiver's "Finger Rhymes," in *SFQ* 5 (1941): 221–34, presents an interesting comparative survey of foreign, mostly German, and some English texts. Marian Hansen gathers "Children's Rhymes Accompanied by Gestures" in *WF* 7 (1948): 50–53. Dorothy Howard has written many fine articles on children's folklore, among them "The Rhythms of Ball-Bouncing and Ball-Bouncing Rhymes," *JAF* 62 (1949): 166–72.

Counting-out rhymes held the interest of some early folklorists in America, among them Henry Carrington Bolton, who published a classic book, *The Counting-Out Rhymes of Children* (New York: Appleton, 1888; repr. Detroit: Singing Tree Press, 1969); Bolton published an article with the same title during the same year in volume 1 of *JAF* (31–37). Later notes on counting-out rhymes appeared in *JAF* 2 (1889): 113–16 and *JAF* 10 (1897): 313–21. Still later, Emelyn E. Gardner published "Some Counting-Out Rhymes in Michigan," *JAF* 31 (1918): 521–36. These and many other sources were consulted for Roger D. Abrahams and Lois Rankin's invaluable *Counting-Out Rhymes: A Dictionary* (Austin, Texas: AFS Bibliographic and Special Series, vol. 31, 1980).

Roger D. Abrahams's *Jump-Rope Rhymes: A Dictionary* (Austin, Texas: AFS Bibliographic and Special Series, vol. 20, 1969) gathers numerous examples and compiles a thorough bibliography of previously published sources (not listed here). The classification of jump-rope rhymes used in this chapter was suggested by Bruce R. Buckley in *KFQ* 11 (1966): 99–111. Ed Cray includes previously unpublished variants (which, therefore, are not listed in Abrahams's work) in "Jump-Rope Rhymes from Los Angeles," *WF* 29 (1970): 119–27.

Paul G. Brewster collected " 'Spelling Riddles' from the Ozarks," in *SFQ* 8 (1944): 301–3. Kenneth W. Porter collected references from earlier published notes, and he classified various texts of "Circular Jingles and Repetitious Rhymes" in *WF* 17 (1958): 107–11; George Monteiro performed the same service for "Parodies of Scripture, Prayer, and Hymn" in *JAF* 77 (1964): 45–52. See also Kenneth W. Porter, "Humor, Blasphemy, and Criticism in the Grace before Meat," *NYFQ* 21 (1965): 3–18, and Monteiro's "Religious and Scriptural Parodies," *NYF* 2 (1976): 150–66.

The game of playing the dozens is discussed by Roger D. Abrahams in *JAF* 75 (1962): 209–20, and by Guy Owen in *NCFJ* 21 (1973): 53–54. Some similar material from white informants was included in Anna K. Stimson's "Cries of Defiance and Derision, and Rhythmic Chants of West Side New York City, 1893–1903," *JAF* 58 (1945): 124–29, and in Millicent R. Ayoub and Stephen A. Barnett's "Ritualized Verbal Insult in White High School Culture," *JAF* 78 (1965): 337–44. The publications dealing with toasts are listed in the bibliography of Bruce Jackson's collection and study entitled *Get Your Ass in the Water and Swim Like Me: Narrative Poetry from Black Oral Tradition* (Cambridge, Mass.: Harvard University Press, 1974). Jackson's negative response to the article by Dennis Wepman, Ronald B. Newman, and Murray B. Binderman, "Toasts: The Black Urban Folk Poetry," in JAF 87 (1974): 208–24, appeared in the next volume of *JAF* along with a rejoinder by the original authors. The first article to get much beyond toast texts and functions is David Evans's "The Toast in Context," *JAF* 90 (1977): 129–48.

Street cries have been published in numerous scattered sources. Among them are Elizabeth Hurley's Texas collection "Come Buy, Come Buy," *PTFS* 25 (1953): 115–38; Edward Pinkowski's "Philadelphia Street Cries," *KFQ* 5 (1960): 10–12; Laurilynn McGill's "The Street Cry as an Artistic Verbal Performance," *Folklore Annual* 3 (1971): 17–25; Richardson L. Wright's *Hawkers and Walkers in Early America* (New York: Ungar, 1927; repr. 1965), ch. XV; Simon J. Bronner's "Street Cries and Peddler Traditions in Contemporary Perspective," *NYF* 2 (1976): 2–15; and Anne Warner's "Fresh Peanuts Is the Best of All: A Street Cry from Suffolk, Virginia," *FFV* 1 (1979): 68–72. An excellent survey of the whole subject by Amanda Dargan and Steven Zeitlin is "American Talkers: Expressive Styles and Occupational Choice," *JAF* 96 (1983): 3–33.

Kenneth Porter discusses the familiar "Corn-planting Rhyme" ["One for the blackbird"] in *WF* 17 (1958): 205–7. A collection of African-American work chants is William R. Ferris, Jr., "Railroad Chants: Form and Function," *MFR* 4 (1970): 1–14. George G. Carey, himself a former paratrooper, prepared "A Collection of Airborne Cadence Chants" for *JAF* 78 (1965): 52–61. See also Susanna Trnka, "Living a Life of Sex and Danger: Women, Warfare, and Sex in Military Folk Rhymes," *WF* 54 (1995): 232–41.

Rhymes from old powder horns were illustrated and discussed by W. M. Beauchamp in *JAF* 2 (1889): 117–22 and *JAF* 5 (1892): 284–90. Epitaphs were discussed by D. P. Penhallow in *JAF* 5 (1892): 305–17; northern-California epitaphs were printed by Kenneth W. Clarke in *WF* 20 (1961): 238 and *WF* 21 (1962): 146. An interesting chapter on "Flyleaf Scribblings" was included in Clifton Johnson's *Old-Time Schools and School-Books* (New York: Macmillan, 1904; reissued in paperback by Dover, 1963); the chapter was also reprinted in *What They Say in New England*, compiled from Clifton Johnson's various folklore publications by Carl Withers (New York: Columbia University Press, 1963), pp. 196–206. An early note on the same subject was Fanny D. Bergen's "Flyleaf Rhymes and Decorations," *New England Magazine*, n.s. 23 (1901): 505–11, which contains variants of several references quoted by Johnson. A more recent discussion is Robert H. Woodward's "Folklore Marginalia in Old Textbooks," *NYFQ* 18 (1962): 24–27.

Graffiti have been the subject of both scholarly and popularized treatments. A casual survey of much typical wall writing is Norton Mockridge's *The Scrawl of the Wild: What People Write on Walls—and Why* (Cleveland and New York: World, 1968). A lavish production with examples in color and an interpretation written by Norman Mailer is *The Faith of Graffiti* (New York: Praeger, 1974). Alan Dundes studied just toilet graffiti, coining a new term for them, in "Here I Sit—a Study of American Latrinalia," *Kroeber Anthropological Society Papers* no. 34 (Spring 1966): 91–94, reprinted in *Analytic Essays in Folklore*, pp. 177–91. In "The Growth of Graffiti," *FF* 7 (1974): 273–75, Mac E. Barrick analyzes thirty-two additions to a single graffito written in a men's room of the Duke University library; further campus examples are discussed in Patricia A. Mastick, "The Function of Political Graffiti as Artistic Creativity," *NYFQ* 27 (1971): 280–96; Charlene Gates, "Graffiti and Environment of the Folk Group: University Music Majors," *FF* 9 (1976): 35–42; Gregory J. Longenecker, "Sequential Parody Graffiti," *WF* 36 (1977): 354–64; and Don L. F. Nilsen, "Sigma Epsilon XI: Sex in the Typical University Classroom" (desktop graffiti), *Maledicta* 5 (1981): 79–91.

Terrance L. Stocker, Linda W. Dutcher, Stephen M. Hargrove, and Edwin A. Cook present a comprehensive bibliography of studies and a most ambitious analysis in their article "Social Analysis of Graffiti" in *JAF* 85 (1972): 356–66. Introducing a category of graffiti neither obscene nor humorous is Sylvia Ann Grider, "Con Safos: Mexican-Americans, Names and Graffiti," *JAF* 88 (1975): 132–42, reprinted in *Readings in American Folklore*, pp. 138–51. The pioneering work by Allen Walker Read originally entitled *Lexical Evidence from Folk Epigraphy in Western North America* (1935) was reissued with the straightforward title *Classic American Graffiti* by Maledicta Press (Waukesha, Wis., 1977). Read's excellent statement "Graffiti as a Field of Folklore" was published in *Maledicta* 2 (1978): 15–31. A theoretical advance in studies of graffiti is represented by George Gonos, Virginia Mulhern, and Nicholas Poushinsky's "Anonymous Expression: A Structural View of Graffiti," *JAF* 89 (1976): 40–48. Notes on male versus female graffiti (mostly latrinalia) are found in *JAF* 90 (1977): 188–91 and *Maledicta* 2 (1978): 42–59. In "Folk Epigraphy by Subtraction," *MJLF* 7 (1981): 49–50, Charles Clay Doyle reveals how latrinalia may be formed by scraping away letters on a set of stenciled instructions found on hand dryers ("Push Button" becomes "Push Butt," etc.). A sort of roadside graffiti is described by Thomas H. King in "Roadside Rock Art," *JAF* 93 (1980): 60; desert stones are arranged along a Utah freeway to spell out names and inscriptions.

Alan Dundes thoroughly surveyed the earlier writings on friendship verses in "Some Examples of Infrequently Reported Autograph Verse," *SFQ* 26 (1962): 127–30. Two representative older collections are Vance Randolph and May Kennedy McCord's "Autograph Albums in the Ozarks," *JAF* 61 (1948): 182–93, in which a useful classification of these rhymes is offered; and Lelah Allison's "Traditional Verse from Autograph Books," *HF* 8 (1949): 87–94, in which Gay Nineties and modern verse are compared. W. K. McNeil has published three important articles on the subject: "The Autograph Album Custom: A Tradition and Its Scholarly Treatment," *KFQ* 13 (1968): 29–40; "From Advice to Laments: New York Autograph Album Verse: 1820–1850," *NYFQ* 25 (1969): 175–94; and the continuation of the latter article to 1850–1900 in *NYFQ* 26 (1970): 163–203. Stephen Stern reports on interviews with those who write in and collect autograph books in his article "Autograph Memorabilia as an Output of Social Interactions and Communication," *NYFQ* 29 (1973): 219–39. Two other articles on the subject are Sylvia C. Henricks, "The Gentle Pastime," *IF* 11 (1978): 161–73, and Meguido Zola, " 'By Hook or by Crook': New Look at the Autograph Book," *NYF* 6 (1980): 185–94. Thomas A. Green and Lisa Devaney discussed "Linguistic Play in Autograph Book Inscriptions" in *WF* 48 (1989): 51–58. Related areas of tradition are described in Steven J. Zeitlin's "As Sweet As You Are: The Structural Elements in the Signed High School Yearbook," *NYFQ* 30 (1974): 83–100, and Toni Flores Fratto, " 'Remember Me': The Sources of American Sampler Verses," *NYF* 2 (1976): 205–22.

Jeanne Soileau makes a case for "Children's Cheers as Folklore" in *WF* 39 (1980): 232–47; her texts come from black and white children in Louisiana in 1975–76. Susan Gelman has an impressive collection of what she calls "postal graffiti" (envelope sealers, etc.) in an article in *WF* 36 (1977): 102–18.

The quotation from T. M. Pearce in this chapter comes from his "What Is a Folk Poet?" in *WF* 12 (1953): 242–48; Rubén Cobos supplemented some of Pearce's assertions in "The New Mexican memoria, or In Memoriam Poem," *WF* 18 (1959): 25–30. Further examples of Mexican-American folk poetry appear in Inez Cardozo-Freeman, "Arnulfo Castillo, Mexican Folk Poet in Ohio," *JOFS* 1 (1972): 2–28, and John Donald Robb, "H. V. Gonzales: Folk Poet of New Mexico," *NMFR* 13 (1973–74): 1–6. The leading scholar of folk poetry is Canadian folklorist Pauline Greenhill; in addition to several articles, she has published a book, *True Poetry: Traditional and Popular Verse in Ontario* (Montreal: McGill-Queen's University Press, 1989).

The passages quoted above from the World War I rhymed chronicle were collected by me from Clarence E. ("Old Hickory") Pierson in Bloomington, Indiana, on August 8, 1959; Elsie Clews Parsons discussed similar folk poems in her note "War Verses," *JAF* 47 (1934): 395. Américo Paredes reviewed the concept of folk poetry in his article "Some Aspects of Folk Poetry" in *TSLL* 6 (1964): 213–25; he saw the subject as ranging from the proverb to the folksong and drew comparisons between "The Maid Freed from the Gallows" and Shakespeare's Sonnet 73 ("That time of year thou mayst in me behold") to illustrate his points. Two studies of individual folk-poetry composers are Edward D. Ives's *Laurence Doyle, the Farmer Poet of Prince Edward Island* (Orno, Me.: University of Maine Studies, no. 92, 1971) and Steven A. Schulman, "Howess Dewey Winfrey: The Rejected Songmaker," *JAF* 87 (1974): 72–84.

The growth of interest among American folklorists in cowboy poetry owes much to the pioneering work of Hal Cannon, founder and director of the annual Cowboy Poetry Gathering in Elko, Nevada. Cannon's book *Cowboy Poetry: A Gathering* (Salt Lake City: Peregrine Smith Books, 1985) includes representative samples of earlier poems plus a long bibliography. This work was followed by many other books, articles, and tapes documenting the ongoing creation of poems by cowboys and other workers of ranch, forest, and field. The quoted example in this chapter is from James S. Griffith's "The Cowboy Poetry of Everett Brisendine: A Response to Cultural Change," *WF* 42 (1983): 38–45.

An example of the traditional recitation, long a neglected genre of folk poetry, was given in *AFFWord* 2 (1972): 38–39—the piece was "The Volunteer Organist." The same journal, renamed *Southwest Folklore*, devoted an entire issue (vol. 2, no. 4 [1978]: 63 pp.) to "Uncle Horace's Recitations," a set of notes to accompany a recording of a dozen texts from one informant. The subject had come into its own as an area for study with the "Monologues and Folk Recitations Special Issue" of *SFQ* (vol. 40, nos. 1–2 [1976]), edited by Kenneth S. Goldstein and Robert D. Bethke. Keith Cunningham's *The Oral Tradition of the American West* (Little Rock: August House, 1990) is an anthology and discussion of traditional recitations from one important region.

G. Legman published his essay "The Limerick: A History in Brief" in *The Horn Book* (New Hyde Park, N.Y.: University Books, 1964), pp. 427–53. Legman's definitive collection, *The Limerick: 1700 Examples, with Notes, Variants, and Index*, originally published in France and long a rare book, was reprinted in 1974 (New York: Bell). A most engagingly written popular survey is William S. Baring-Gould's *The Lure of the Limerick: An Uninhibited History* (New York: Clarkson N. Potter, 1967). A traditional erotic poem is studied by Ronald L. Baker in "Lady Lil and Pisspot Pete," *JAF* 100 (1987): 191–99.

The presidential parody of the Twenty-third Psalm appears in Ed Cray, "The Quadrennial Perennials," *WF* 24 (1965): 199–201. Further examples appear in Gary Alan Fine, "In Search of the Quadrennial Perennials," *FF* 7 (1974): 203–5, and in Mac E. Barrick, "The Presidential Psalm," *FF* 8 (1975): 357–60. Fine mentions this and other pieces of typescript political satire in "Recurring Political Satire," *Maledicta* 6 (1982): 71–74. The Bill Clinton variant began circulating in typescript and on the Internet soon after he took office in 1992.

8

—

MYTHS AND MOTIFS

Traditional prose narratives in oral circulation are often loosely termed "folktales"; such stories constitute one of the largest and most complex branches of folklore. These narratives include stories regarded as true, called "myths" and "legends," and stories regarded as fictional, properly called "folktales" (discussed in chapter 10). Myths are distinguished from legends (as anthropologist William Bascom formulated it) by the attitudes of storytellers toward them, the settings described in them, and their principal characters. Myths are regarded as sacred, and legends as either sacred or secular; myths are set in the remote past, the otherworld, or an earlier world, and legends are set in the historical past; myths have as their principal characters gods or animals, while legends (discussed in chapter 9) generally have humans in the major roles.

Myths have been defined as "traditional prose narratives, which, in the society in which they are told, are considered to be truthful accounts of what happened in the remote past." Typically, they deal with the activities of gods and demigods, the creation of the world and its inhabitants, and the origins of religious rituals. Whenever myths purport to account for such matters as origins of geographic features, animal traits, rites, taboos, and customs, they are known as *explanatory* or *etiological narratives*.

NATIVE AMERICAN MYTHS AND TALES: PROBLEMS IN CATEGORIZATION

There is some difficulty in using these terms and distinctions, because the word "myth" has acquired other specialized meanings among literary critics, historians, and philosophers. Also, among the general public, and encouraged by journalism, the term "myth" (like the word "folklore") often denotes simply error or misinformation, as in expressions like "It's a myth that lightning never strikes twice in the same place."

It is not always possible to establish clearly whether a given oral narrative should be termed myth, legend, or folktale. With traditions outside our own, it is particularly artificial to make such distinctions. Native American narratives, for instance, which have been collected in large numbers over a long period of time, constitute an impressive body of what is often loosely termed "myth"; but such a designation takes little account of the native tellers' actual attitudes, their oral style, or even of the stories' typical elements. Native American narratives often freely mix human and animal characters, and the animals may have both human and godlike qualities (both physical and

Johnnie Moses, Native American storyteller, performing at a recent National Storytelling Festival in Jonesborough, Tennessee.

mental). The stories tend to combine believable and fantastic elements, and even when they seem to be explanatory in purpose, the specific facts of life "explained" may not be as apparent to the non-Indian reader of published stories as they were to the original audiences for their oral performances. These stories were often told in a dramatic oratorical or poetic manner, employing some language forms used only in storytelling. What we have, then, in our older compilations of English prose translations of Native American myths—as numerous and varied as they are—is only an approximation of a rich and diverse repertoire of poetic oral texts.

Three short excerpts from English prose translations of Indian narratives in Stith Thompson's *Tales of the North American Indians* (1929)—all of them involving animals—demonstrate both the applicability of the myth, legend, and folktale categories and the problems associated with them. The first excerpt was collected from Pacific Coast Indians (Tahltan) and published in *JAF* in 1919:

> Once Porcupine and Beaver quarreled about the seasons. Porcupine wanted five winter months. He held up one hand and showed his five fingers. He said, "Let the winter months be the same in number as the fingers on my hand." Beaver said, "No," and held up his tail, which had many cracks or scratches on it. He said, "Let the winter months be the same in number as the scratches on my tail." Now they quarreled and argued. Porcupine got angry and bit off his thumb. Then, holding up his hand with the four fingers, he said emphatically, "There must be only four winter months." Beaver became a little afraid, and gave in. For this reason porcupines have four claws on each foot now.
>
> [The story continues to explain how Raven came to consider the arguments and decided that Porcupine had been right, though the number of winter months was then set to be only approximately four months henceforth.]

This story is a typically "mythic" one, serving to explain features of nature as supposedly determined by the actions of primeval animals.

The second story was collected from Central Woodlands Indians (Menomini) and published in a Bureau of American Ethnology report in 1896:

There was a large settlement on the shore of a lake, and among its people were two very old blind men. It was decided to remove these men to the opposite side of the lake, where they might live in safety, as the settlement was exposed to the attack of enemies, when they might easily be captured and killed. So the relations of the old men got a canoe, some food, a kettle, and a bowl and started across the lake, where they built for them a wigwam in a grove some distance from the water. A line was stretched from the door of the wigwam to a post in the water, so they would have no difficulty in helping themselves. . . . One day a raccoon, which was following the water's edge looking for crawfish, came to the line which had been stretched from the lake to the wigwam. The raccoon thought it rather curious to find a cord where he had not before observed one. . . . Wishing to deceive the old men, [the raccoon] untied the cord from the post, and carried it to a clump of bushes.

[The story continues with the raccoon continuing to shift the cord around and to play tricks on the two blind men until they accuse each other of stealing food. Then the raccoon criticizes the blind men for finding fault with each other so easily, and returns to his crawfish hunting along the shore.]

This narrative is more characteristically "legendary," since it deals with a realistic human problem solved in a nonsupernatural way, although an oddly anthropomorphic (humanlike) animal enters the story in the role of a trickster.

The third story is an Eskimo tale published in *JAF* in 1899:

A man who was walking, once upon a time, came to a pond, where there were a number of geese. These geese had taken off their garments and had become women, and were now swimming in the pond. The man came up to them without being seen, and seized their feather-garments. He gave them all back but two, whereupon the women put them on and flew away. Finally he gave one of the two remaining ones hers, whereupon she also flew off. The last woman, however, he kept with him, took to his house, and married. Soon she became pregnant and gave birth to two children.

[The story continues with the wife and children putting on feathers and flying away, the husband going on a long quest to find them, and his eventual killing of the wife and driving off of the children.]

This story has the "folktale" qualities (indicated by the translator's use of "once upon a time") of magical themes that are treated fictionally.

The original texture, or style, of such ancient narratives, which were once told widely by Native Americans, is lost to us in these renderings into standard written English. (The situation is worse with literary treatments like Longfellow's *Song of Hiawatha*, or storybook versions, sometimes given in pseudoscriptural prose.) An even greater loss in our appreciation of Native American narrative tradition is any clear sense of the ultimate meanings of the stories to their owners. Just how literally are we expected to take the adventures of these animals? Are the plots merely vehicles for various "lessons," rather than accounts of events that were really believed in? Thus, it has become crucially important in the study of Native American narratives to work with the few remaining speakers of the hundreds of aboriginal languages and dialects of the continent, and to uncover through close linguistic and ethnographic analysis the layers of meaning that the stories contain. This study is complicated, because the themes and plots of American Indian narratives are often close enough to European folk stories to raise the possibility of borrowing. (Oral stories about the deception of blind persons and the existence of "Swan Maidens," for example, have international distribution, as the *Motif-Index* [see below] indicates.)

FOCUS: LOVER'S LEAPS

Monument Mountain, a picturesque height in the Berkshires, is faced on its western side by a precipice, from which an Indian maiden flung herself because the laws of her tribe forbade her marriage with a cousin to whom she had plighted troth.

*

An Indian brave [living near Hot Springs, N.C.] *wished to marry a girl of a tribe with which his own had been immemorially at war. The match was opposed on both sides, so he scaled the rock in her company and leaped with her into the stream. They awoke as man and wife in the happy hunting-ground.*

*

Rising, with her eyes toward heaven, and murmuring her last prayer to God, she [a Spanish belle kidnapped in Texas to become a Comanche warrior's bride] *plunged headlong down the precipice and struck the rocks below, mangled, bleeding, and dead!*

Sources: Top and middle—from Charles M. Skinner, *Myths and Legends of Our Own Land* (1896; repr. Detroit: Singing Tree Press, 1969). Bottom—an 1874 text, from Flora Eckert, "Lover's Leap in Kimble County," *PTFS* 3 (1924).

"Valley of Nacoochee" [Georgia], named to commemorate the fatal leap of Nacoochee, a Cherokee "princess," and her lover, Sautee, a Choctaw brave, when their marriage was forbidden by chiefs of the rival tribes. Melodramatic Victorian writings claimed that the star-crossed lovers leapt from nearby Mount Yonah.

DISCUSSION TOPICS:

1. Judging from these and other versions of Lover's Leap legends, what are their typical features of language and content? (Some versions have even been versified or set to music.)

2. Why were many folklorists reluctant to label such stories unequivocally as fakelore?

3. Considered as supposed Native American oral-narrative texts (or paraphrases), these stories are extremely doubtful, but perhaps they have a function as the "local legends" of whites. See Francis A. de Caro's suggestion in "Vanishing the Red Man . . . ," *IFR* 4 (1986): 74–80.

Because of the extremely wide range of Native American customs, languages, and traditions, plus the sheer numbers of collected narratives, it is difficult to generalize about their themes and plots. It is possible to say, however, that all Native groups used stories to explain the creation of the world and its transformation into the condition in which we know it. Most groups, too, had stories of heroes and the tests they underwent, of supernatural journeys, and of animal husbands and wives. Comparing the many bodies of Native American narratives, scholars have also distinguished cycles of stories with widespread variants across the continent and sometimes beyond; these are referred to with such conventional titles as "The Earth Diver," "The Theft of Fire," "The Star Husband," "The Arrow Chain," and "The Sun Snarer."

The most characteristic group of Native North American narratives is the *trickster cycle*, a lengthy series of adventures experienced by a character who is a sort of combined man/animal, god/human, benefactor/enemy figure known by the general name of "Trickster." The trickster appears in various different forms, such as the human Manabozho in the Central Woodlands region, Coyote in the Plains and Western regions, and Raven, Mink, or Blue Jay in the North Pacific. (Some of these figures are creators or transformers as well, and their specific names and epithets vary a good deal from group to group.) Tricksters engage in all manner of outrageous, dangerous, and even obscene behavior, often injuring themselves as well as others. Their antisocial behavior provides negative models for conduct and the release of tensions via fantasy—that is, the stories show the Indian audiences how not to behave, but they also afford a release through humor from the strain of maintaining proper behavior. The consequences of the trickster's acts are often simple realities of everyday life, as in this Uintah Ute coyote story published in *JAF* in 1910:

> Long ago Wildcat had a long nose and tail. One day he was sleeping on a rock when Coyote came along. He pushed Wildcat's nose and tail in, and then went home. At noon Wildcat woke up, and noticed his short nose and tail. "What's the matter with me?" he asked. Then he guessed the cause. "Oh! Coyote did that," he said, and he hunted for him.
>
> Now, Coyote was sleepy and had lain down. Wildcat came and

sat down beside him. He pulled Coyote's nose and tail and made them long. They were short before. Then he ran off. After a while Coyote woke up and saw his long nose and tail.

Probably a non-Native reader of this story would conclude, "So that's how the Indians thought these animals' appearances got that way." But a Paiute Indian woman, telling another version of the same story, remarked, "This story carried an admonition for us not to do things to our brothers and sisters out of anger. Fights between brothers and sisters ended by grandfather saying, 'All right, Coyote and Bobcat!' That stopped everything."

The repertoire of Native American narratives also includes adaptations of stories originally told by missionaries, as well as traditional Indian stories that have been turned into satiric commentary upon the invading whites. Here are two short examples of such stories:

Almost everything was Coyote's way. The Indian planted the apple. When he planted it, he said for all the Indians to come and eat. When he told them that, all the people came. The white man was a rattlesnake then, and he was on the tree. The white people have eyes just like the rattlesnake. When the Indians tried to eat the apples, that snake tried to bite them. That's why the white people took everything away from the Indian; because they were snakes. If that snake hadn't been on that tree, everything would have belonged to the Indians. Just because they were snakes and came here, the white people took everything away. They asked the Indians where they had come from. That's why they took everything and told the Indians to go way out in the mountains and live.

[A Northern Paiute telling of the Adam and Eve story, published in *JAF* in 1938]

*

Once they were making a railroad through Coyote's place. "I don't want it. Take it away; take your tools and go away," he said. "Don't pay any attention to him," the people said. "Just go ahead and lay the tracks." The workers paid no attention to Coyote and laid the tracks. When Coyote saw it, he said, "Oh, there's a train going through my place now." "Stay right where you are," he said to the train. Then the train and all the people inside it turned into a rock right on the spot. "You must stay there forever; you will never move again," Coyote said.

[A Northern Pacific (Coast Salish) story collected in the early twentieth century and published in 1934]

MOTIFS AND THE *MOTIF-INDEX*

Despite the remoteness of myths, in both time and cultural distance, from mainstream modern American folklore, there are good reasons for American folklorists to be concerned with myths, including the so-called primitive myths of prehistoric cultures and modern preliterate peoples, the myths of India and the Far East, or the more familiar myths of the classical world and ancient northern Europe. Among these three bodies of world myth are themes that recur again and again, raising difficult questions of origin and dissemination. These themes include the creation of the world and the shaping of it to the present form, the origin of death or of fire, the consequences of rivalries between or among individuals and peoples, the arrival of heroes who save their people from enemies or disasters, and the resurrection of slain gods or kings to become mythic personalities. For centuries writers, artists, and composers—as well as most educated people—drew inspiration from the great bodies of world mythology. Although knowledge of and interest in mythology had declined by the start of the twentieth century, the subject has enjoyed a resurgence with the recent interest in "New Age" philosophy and lifestyles.

Fantastic and grotesque elements that have widespread distribution in myths are puzzling factors in the interpretation of myths. Do these elements, which include cannibalism, shape shifting, marriage between different species, and descriptions of many kinds of mutants and monsters, reflect reality, mental problems, fear, or some other origin? Another enigma is the relatively limited number of distinct forms of myths, the texts of which may vary greatly in their specific details. For example, the story of a destruction of the world's creatures by a flood and the beginning of a new cycle of life after one remaining creature enters the void and returns with a scrap of the old world (such as an olive branch or a handful of mud) has international circulation in myths, though the specifics (cause of the flood, nature of the creature, method of restoring life, etc.) are extremely variable.

The rich variety of myths is demonstrated by one of the most comprehensive general reference works in folklore studies, Stith Thompson's *Motif-Index of Folk-Literature* (1955–58). The contents and the broad scope of this encyclopedic six-volume work are indicated in its subtitle, *A Classification of Narrative Elements in Folk-tales, Ballads, Myths, Fables, Mediaeval Romances, Exempla, Fabliaux, Jest-Books and Local Legends.* A **motif,** or "narrative element," from these traditional texts is any striking or unusual unit recurring in them; it may be an object (such as a magic wand), a marvelous animal (such as a speaking horse), a concept (such as a taboo or forbidden act), an action (such as a test or a deception), a character (such as a giant, an ogre, or a fairy godmother), a character type (such as a fool or a prophet), or a structural quality (such as formulistic numbers or cumulative repetition). Thousands of such elements are arranged in the *Motif-Index* according to a systematic plan, along with bibliographic references to their occurrences in collected texts. (A fair number of motifs, however, also exist as separate oral narratives, sometimes termed "one-motif tales.") Use of the *Index* is facilitated by detailed synopses before each of the twenty-three lettered chapters; numerous cross-references to the numbered individual motifs throughout; and an alphabetical index to the *Index,* in the sixth volume. Although the *Motif-Index* is used primarily in studies of folktales (see chapter 10), it is inclusive of world mythology and thus has important applications for analyzing myths.

Motifs from myths are scattered throughout the *Index,* which is organized in sections lettered from A to Z, then subdivided by numbers, using an expandable decimal system. The predominantly "Mythological Motifs" are contained in section A under the following broad divisions:

A0– A99.	Creator
A100– A499.	Gods
A500– A599.	Demigods and culture heroes
A600– A899.	Cosmogony and cosmology

A900– A999. Topographical features of the earth
A1000–A1099. World calamities
A1100–A1199. Establishment of natural order
A1200–A1699. Creation and ordering of human life
A1700–A2199. Creation of animal life
A2200–A2599. Animal characteristics
A2600–A2699. Origin of trees and plants
A2700–A2799. Origin of plant characteristics
A2800–A2899. Miscellaneous explanations

These thirteen general categories of mythological motifs are sub-divided into numerous specific categories that are numbered (as in all sections of the *Index*) in groups of tens. For example, A1200–A1299, "Creation of man," is broken down as follows in the synopsis:

A1210. Creation of man by creator
A1220. Creation of man through evolution
A1230. Emergence or descent of first man to earth
A1240. Man made from mineral substance
A1250. Man made from vegetable substance
A1260. Mankind made from miscellaneous materials
A1270. Primeval human pair
A1290. Creation of man—other motifs

As can be seen above between A1270. and A1290., Thompson sometimes skipped numbers in the *Motif-Index* to allow for adding further groups of motifs. Also, within each chapter (which in this instance contains 279 pages of closely printed motif entries) the sub-divisions are made infinitely expandable by a system of "points." Thus Motif A1226. is "Man created after series of unsuccessful experiments," and A1226.1. is the more specific motif "Creator makes man out of butter first; it would not stand up and melted." If a new myth were discovered in which humanity were made out of margarine first, then, considering margarine as a variant of butter, the number *A1226.1.1. could be added; but if a new material, say chocolate, were used for a succession of creations, number *A1226.2. would be appropriate. (Whenever a new motif number is created, it is designated with an asterisk until it appears in a revised edition of the master index.) Also note that two cross-references appear under

A1226.: numbers A630., "Series of creations," and A1401., "Culture originated by previous race of man." Thompson's bibliographic references indicate that the concept of a series of unsuccessful experiments to create humanity is found in myths from Greece, Latin America, and the Banks Islands in the Pacific New Hebrides; the unsuccessful creation out of butter is found in a myth from India. The references do not establish any historical relationship among these similar myth motifs, although further research may suggest one.

The assorted materials out of which humanity is said to have been made illustrate the varied and sometimes fantastic nature of mythological motifs. The mineral substances include sand sprinkled with water, earth reddened with animal blood, stones, ice, shells, and metals. Vegetable substances include trees and wood, fruit, nuts, seeds, sugar-cane stalks, ears of corn, herbs, and grass. In some mythological explanations, the raw material comes from the body of the creator: sweat (the Lithuanians), spittle (the Lithuanians and in Oceanic myths), or even a broken-off toenail (the Indians of Brazil). The *Motif-Index* lists parallels for the Judeo-Christian explanation that humanity was made from clay or other earth in Hindu, Babylonian, Greek, Irish, Siberian, Chinese, Polynesian, Indonesian, Australian, Eskimo, North and South American Indian, and Aztec mythology. Again, listing such parallels does not presuppose any necessary historical connection among these bodies of mythology. Some of these particular parallels, in fact, must predate Judaism and Christianity, while others were probably influenced directly by missionaries.

USING THE *MOTIF-INDEX*

The *Motif-Index*, less a theoretical work than simply a massive catalog of traditional narrative elements with bibliographic references, has applications in folklore study far beyond myth comparisons. The term "motif," it should be remembered, refers in this special folkloristic sense only to units of traditional narratives, not to other patterns evident in folklore. Motifs are often international in distribution, but similar motifs are not necessarily related historically. In the *Index*, motifs are usually somewhat generalized and simplified for their listings. Mastery of the *Motif-Index* is important to much folklore scholarship, and this skill may be acquired best through working with the *Index* listings and references, and by observing how motif numbers may be applied to collected folklore examples or in folklore studies.

FOCUS: ESCAPE BY REVERSING SHOES

"Your horses the wrang way maun a' be shod." [Your horses the wrong way must all be shod.]

*

Rogers's Slide . . . a lofty precipice at the lower end of Lake George. . . . On March 13, 1758, while reconnoitring near Ticonderoga with two hundred rangers, [Major Rogers] was surprised by a force of French and Indians. But seventeen of his men escaped death or capture, and he was pursued nearly to the brink of this cliff. During a brief delay among the red men, arising from the loss of his trail, he had time to throw his pack down the slide, reverse his snow-shoes, and go back over his own track to the head of a ravine before they emerged from the woods, and seeing that his shoe-marks led to the rock, while none pointed back, they concluded that he had flung himself off and committed suicide to avoid capture. Great was their disappointment when they saw the major on the frozen surface of the lake beneath going at a lively rate toward Fort William Henry. He had gained the ice by way of the cleft in the rocks, but the savages, believing that he had leaped over the precipice, attributed his preservation to the Great Spirit and forbore to fire on him.

*

To the people of northern New York the favorite story [about Robert Rogers the Ranger (1731–1795)] concerns a place on the west side of Lake George known as Rogers Slide or Rogers Rock, immortalized by an exploit of the spring of 1758 when the Ranger escaped death by a characteristic stratagem. . . . Rogers found himself alone at the top of a lofty precipice overlooking Lake George, with certain death before and behind him. Loosening his pack, he pushed it over the slide to make a track which resembled the fatal fall of a man. Then putting his snowshoes on backward he descended to the ice-covered lake by a roundabout path, reversed his snowshoes, picked up his pack, and started for Fort William Henry. When the Indians arrived, they found tracks leading to the edge of the slide, and looking over the precipice they saw a valiant figure headed southward on the lake. A brief consultation decided that Rogers was under the protection of the Great Spirit; the lonely figure was permitted to disappear in the direction of the British stronghold.

Sources: Top—advice to a horseman escaping enemies in the Scottish ballad "Jock O' the Side" (Child No. 187). Middle—Charles M. Skinner's *Myths and Legends of Our Own Land* (1896). Bottom—Harold W. Thompson's *Body Boots and Britches* (1940).

DISCUSSION TOPICS:

1. See Motif K534.1., "Escape by reversing horse's (ox's) shoes," with many Old World examples cited by Thompson. Baughman's *Index* (see bibliographic notes) has three English references from 1883–1901 plus these two American references under K534.2., "Escape by reversing snowshoes." Collect and compare further examples of these motifs and of K534.4., "Hero walks backwards," recorded only from an African source. Do all of these motifs seem to be historically connected, or are they perhaps instances of polygenesis?

2. The two American "legends" are heavily rewritten in a poetic style. How convincing are these texts as genuine folklore? How could the survival of this motif in New World tradition be validated?

3. A friend of the author wrote, "In Romania I kept hearing this story about Vlad Tepes [the historical prototype for Dracula]. He was about to be attacked by the Turks when some village elders advised that he take off the horses' shoes and put them on in reverse to make the enemy think they were just arriving instead of just leaving the fortress." What do you think of this story?

4. Child commented on the ballad motif, "This device, whether of great practical use or not, has much authority [i.e., many folkloric examples] to favor it." How reasonable does the device seem, as a method of escaping? Do snowshoes seem more or less likely to succeed than horseshoes or boots worn backward?

As a guide for approaching the *Index*, here is a synopsis of the twenty-three lettered chapters,* with one or more examples of motifs from each section, plus a few parenthetical comments:

A. Mythological Motifs
A1150. Determination of seasons. [See story quoted earlier.]
A2214.3. Unicorn thrown from ark and drowned; hence no longer exists.

* There are no chapters for the letters I, O, and Y.

B. Animals

B422. Helpful cat. [As in "Puss in Boots"]

C. Tabus

C480.1.1. Tabu: whistling in mine.

D. Magic

D361.1. Swan Maidens [See story quoted earlier.]

D1323.1. Magic clairvoyant mirror. [As in "Snow White"]

E. The Dead

E332.3.3.1. The Vanishing Hitchhiker.

E332.3.3.2. Deity as ghostly rider. [I.e., Jesus as the hitchhiker]

F. Marvels

F511.2.2. Person with ass's (horse's) ears. [I.e., King Midas]

G. Ogres

G303.4.5.3.1. Devil detected by his hoofs. [The Devil may have horse's hoofs, goat's feet, claws, chicken's feet, etc. In some recent legends he shows up at a disco, where he is finally recognized by his deformed feet.]

H. Tests

H542. Death sentence escaped by propounding riddle that a king (or judge) cannot solve. [I.e., a neck riddle]

J. The Wise and the Foolish

J121. Ungrateful son reproved by naive action of his own son. [In one version the son carves a wooden cup —in imitation of his father, who had made one for his own father's use at mealtimes—so the palsied old man will not break the china when his hand trembles.]

J1741.3.1. Stupid scholar memorizes set answers to oral examination in Latin. The questions are not given in the order he expects; comic results. [This medieval story is also

A modern version of the "Devil with Chicken's Feet," locating his appearance on Halloween in "Latin nightclubs in South Texas."

told in the American Northwest about an Indian trying to pass an exam given orally in English.]

K. Deceptions

K333. Theft from blind person. [See story quoted earlier.]

K581.1. Briar-patch punishment for rabbit.

K581.2. Burying the mole as punishment.

K584. Throwing the thief over the fence.

L. Reversal of Fortune

L50. Victorious youngest daughter.

L100–199. Unpromising hero (heroine). [I.e., the Cinderella figure]

M. Ordaining the Future

M312.0.1. Dream of future greatness.

N. Chance and Fate

N338.3. Son killed because mistaken for someone else.

P. Society

P314. Combat of disguised friends. [A motif found in one Civil War ballad]

Q. Rewards and Punishments

Q386. Dancing punished.

R. Captives and Fugitives

R41. Captivity in tower (castle, prison). [I.e., as in "Rapunzel"]

S. Unnatural Cruelty

S262. Periodic sacrifices to a monster.

T. Sex

T554. Woman gives birth to animal.

T562. White woman bears black child.

U. The Nature of Life

U111. Many books do not make a scholar. [A "folk idea"]

U147. Animals try unsuccessfully to exchange food. [As in Aesop's fable of the fox and heron]

V. Religion

V81.2. Tails fall off mountain spirits when they are baptized.

V221.3. Saint cures leprosy.

W. Traits of Character

W111. Laziness.

W111.3.6. "Who will not work, shall not eat."

W111.5.4. Lazy dog wakes only for his meals.

W111.5.13. Man weeds garden from cushioned rocking chair, using fire tongs to reach weeds.

X. Humor

X900–1899. Humor of lies and exaggerations.

X905.4. The liar: "I have no time to lie today"; lies nevertheless. [A very popular one-motif tall tale]

X115.1. Fisherman catches fish with amazing contents.

Z. Miscellaneous groups of motifs

Z13.2. Catch tale: teller is killed in his own story.

Z71.1. Formulistic number: three.

"OUR OWN" MYTHS

The study of myths and motifs raises the question of how to regard "our own" myths, that is, the symbolic or metaphorical stories told and interpreted among Christians, Jews, Moslems, and members of other major religions. These include the biblical accounts of the Creation, the Great Flood, the Last Supper, and the Resurrection, and the numerous written and traditional backgrounds of other religions' diverse beliefs and practices. On the one hand, the unvarying scriptural basis for "organized religions" would argue against regarding them as folk-related; yet the cross-cultural and cross-denominational variations that exist do remind us of folk tradition. (See also the discussions of "religious legends" in chapter 9 and of "folk religion" in chapter 14.) Furthermore, to some extent even modern children learn the sacred stories of their culture by traditional means, such as family conversations or celebrations of religious holidays, rather than by strictly institutionalized means, such as Sunday-school lessons or Bible-study classes. Another consideration must be the uses to which people put their religious narratives—as guides for living, charters for belief, means of evaluating others' actions, and the like. These functions and attitudes are not unlike those related to myths in primitive cultures, and it ought not to damage the religious convictions of students of American folklore to regard their own system as part of a continuum of worldwide tradition rather than a set of unique literal and inviolable truths. Only the culturally naive could regard all of "our" beliefs and religious narratives as literally true in every detail, but regard the beliefs of "others" as myths, superstitions, and mere folklore. As the folklorist Dell Hymes wrote, after years of studying Northwestern Indian myths and their counterparts elsewhere, "The shaping of deeply felt values into meaningful, apposite form, is present in all communities, and will find some means of expression among all." In other words, with regard to contemplating their relationship to a larger reality and expressing their beliefs in narrative "mythical" form, the world's people, however advanced their cultures, are all "folk."

Another aspect of modern folk thought that resembles mythmaking is what might be called "mythic traditions" in American history. Archetypal images found in our culture, such as the country bumpkin (Brother Jonathan in colonial times), the city slicker (for example, in "The Arkansas Traveler"), and our national symbols (like Uncle Sam, the Statue of Liberty, and even the flag) have become metaphors for concepts about our past. The same is true for the "myths" surrounding events, like the fall of the Alamo, Custer's Last Stand, and the assassinations of presidents. Also mythic in this sense are the stereotyped plots of romance and legend—"from rags to riches" or "virtue is rewarded." To a large extent, myth- and image-making of this kind underlie our sense of national identity, and even influence our social and political decisions.

THEORIES AND THE ORIGIN OF MYTHS

The history of scholarly theories about traditional myth origins is essentially the history of attempts to account for similar elements in different bodies of mythology and similarities between myths and folktales. In story after story, whether myth or tale, heroes are set difficult tasks to perform—they slay monsters, and they receive royal gifts as rewards; humans sometimes marry animals that often turn out themselves to be transformed humans; food or other necessities are magically provided; and characters go on long voyages and sometimes return unrecognized. Basically, only two explanations are possible for such parallels: they may be the result of *polygenesis*, the independent invention of the same materials in different places, or of *diffusion*, the single invention at one place of an item that was then transmitted to other regions.

Pioneer folktale scholars Jacob and Wilhelm Grimm, of nineteenth-century Germany, perceived both possibilities and selected diffusion, which still has more favor among folklorists, as the better explanation. The Brothers Grimm theorized that folktales, such as those they collected in Germany, were *broken-down myths* that had originated among the prehistoric Indo-European tribes and had been disseminated during their migrations throughout Europe.

A second nineteenth-century theory drew further on the advancing study of comparative linguistics for its evidence. It was championed by a German "philologist," or what we would now call a linguist, Max Müller, an Oxford University professor. When Sanskrit came to be recognized as the key language of the Indo-European family, Müller compared the names of gods in various bodies of mythology with the names of heavenly bodies in Sanskrit; he concluded that all of the principal gods' names had originally stood for solar phenomena. His theory, which came to be called *solar mythology*, regarded myths as essentially accounts of the recurrence of day and night; the European folktales presumably were descended from myths and conveyed the same symbolism.

Followers of Max Müller, both in England and in the United States, carried solar (and also lunar) explanations of myths to great lengths, applying them to texts from around the world. Similar research also produced a "zoological" interpretation, which read animal symbolism into myths, and a sweeping "Indianist" theory, which traced all European folktales back to India.

The solar mythologists were opposed by the so-called *English anthropological school* of comparative mythologists. Their theoretical foundation was the idea of cultural evolution, patterned on the biological evolution that Charles Darwin had described in *The Origin of Species* in 1859. Assuming that all cultures, like plants and animals, had evolved in stages from lower to higher forms, these anthropologists postulated that the primitive and peasant cultures of today retain "survivals" of the "savage stage" of modern civilization. E. B. Tylor's landmark book *Primitive Culture* (1871) articulated this theory of survivals, and the following passage from Andrew Lang's

Custom and Myth (1884) describes the method by which it was applied.

> The student of folklore is led to examine the usages, myths, and ideas of savages, which are still retained, in rude enough shape, by the European peasantry. . . .
>
> The method is, when an apparently irrational and anomalous custom is found in any country, to look for a country where a similar practice is found, and where the practice is no longer irrational and anomalous, but in harmony with the manners and ideas of the people among whom it prevails. . . . Folklore represents, in the midst of a civilised race, the savage ideas out of which civilisation has been evolved.

With Lang as their standard-bearer, the English anthropologists waged a devastating campaign against the solar mythologists, even to the extent of using Müller's own method to prove that Müller himself was a sun god. One monument of Victorian scholarship, Sir James G. Frazer's *The Golden Bough* (first published in 1890 and expanded to twelve volumes by its final revision in 1915), was essentially a massive assemblage of evidence of the worldwide persistence of folk beliefs, myths, and customs that was taken by some readers to support the theory of survivals of culture.

The suggestion of several nineteenth-century German scholars that the fantasy world of dreams might have given rise to myths anticipated the *psychoanalytic approach to myths* introduced by Sigmund Freud. This school, like that of the English anthropologists, assumed that polygenesis explained widespread myth parallels. The Freudian explanation drew on the study of dreams, neuroses, and complexes to unravel the workings of the unconscious or subconscious mind and their Oedipal, phallic, and other symbolism. Carl Jung, who introduced the term "collective unconscious" to account for generalized cultural patterns, and Otto Rank, author of *The Myth of the Birth of the Hero* (1914), made major contributions to this type of interpretation.

As early as the fourth century B.C. the idea arose that myths were actually based on historical traditions and that mythic heroes were real people. The theory was known as *euhemerism* after the Sicilian philosopher Euhemerus, who proposed it, and who held, in effect, that humanity had made gods in its own image. A kind of "new euhemerism" constituted the *heroic-age theory* set forth by H. M. and N. K. Chadwick in their work *The Growth of Literature* (3 volumes, 1932–40). They asserted that mythical heroes such as England's Beowulf, Germany's Siegfried, France's Roland, and Ireland's Cuchulain were based on actual chieftains who had led roving bands of warriors across prehistoric Europe; historical accounts of their deeds had been passed down as heroic legends and myths. Recently the theory was applied by Richard M. Dorson to the American frontier, with Davy Crockett as a heroic-age figure.

Exactly the opposite assumption—that the basis of myth is never history—underlies the *myth-ritual theory* advanced by Lord Raglan in his work *The Hero* (1936). Like Otto Rank and others before him, Lord Raglan schematized a large number of mythical biographies into a monomyth. Raglan's analysis then held that no myth, legend, or folktale that significantly matched this pattern could preserve any history. Instead, religious ritual was the source of all myths, and myths preceded all genuine folklore. The myth-ritual theory has been strongly criticized in the United States, but has also had a vigorous defense in the writings of Stanley Edgar Hyman.

Although all of these theories of myth origins once had their firm adherents, most of them claim only a few serious advocates among folklorists today. But the theories introduced in these early studies continue to influence folklore scholarship. The question of polygenesis versus diffusion must still be dealt with; the concepts of folktales as "broken-down myths" and of all folklore as cultural "survivals" are far from dead. Psychoanalytic theory has gained some disciples among professionally trained folklorists, as has euhemerism. Many terms introduced in the nineteenth-century studies are still employed by writers, and several anthropological folklorists have tried to combine what they consider the best features of several schools of analysis and interpretation into new, more comprehensive explanations of myths.

The materials outlined and sampled in this chapter, together with the bibliographic notes that follow, give only a skeletal idea of myths in the fullness of their narrative and symbolic development and of motifs in the fineness of their distinctions among myriad narrative elements. Because myth and motif are fundamental aspects of folklore material and analysis, the student should explore these subjects further both by reading the scholarly literature and by using reference works.

BIBLIOGRAPHIC NOTES

J. R. Rayfield's "What Is a Story?" in *AA* 74 (1972): 1085–1106, establishes criteria by which listeners accept or reject a telling as conforming to their idea of what constitutes a story. A voluminous literature is devoted to the same question. Two important works that make generous reference to it are Margaret K. Brady, "Narrative Competence: A Navajo Example of Peer Group Evaluation," *JAF* 93 (1980): 158–81, and Brian Sutton-Smith and others, *The Folkstories of Children*, AFS Publications, New Series, vol. 3 (Philadelphia, 1981).

William Bascom's formulation of definitions for "The Forms of Folklore: Prose Narratives" (quoted in this chapter) appeared in *JAF* 78 (1965): 3–20. Stith Thompson's *The Folktale* (New York: Dryden Press, 1946) is a basic older survey of traditional prose narratives and their study; part 3, "The Folktale in a Primitive Culture," surveys North American Indian traditional narratives. J. L. Fischer's article "The Sociopsychological Analysis of Folktales," *CA* 4 (1963): 235–95, is important, with a valuable bibliography and comments by seventeen anthropologists and folklorists. Like Thompson, Fischer and others use the general term "folktale" for all traditional prose narratives. The introduction by Bødker in *European Folk Tales*, ed. Laurits Bødker, Christina Hole, and G. D'Aronco (Copenhagen: Rosenkilde and Bagger; and Hatboro, Pa.: Folklore Associates, 1963), compares similar motifs in folktales and myths.

For nearly one hundred examples of Native American traditional prose narratives taken from the older collections and with voluminous notes, see Stith Thompson's *Tales of the North American Indians* (Cambridge, Mass.: Harvard University Press, 1929; paperback ed. Bloomington: Indiana University Press, 1966). The first four stories quoted in this chapter come from Thompson's anthology. Alan Dundes's "The Morphology of North American Indian Folktales," in *FFC* no. 195 (1964), discusses the structural approach to myths and establishes some basic forms of Indian narratives. Levette J. Davidson quotes some interesting examples of "White Versions of Indian Myths and Legends" in *WF* 7 (1948): 115–28. Links between Asiatic and American Indian mythology were considered in Gudmund Hatt's monograph *Asiatic Influences in American Folklore*, Det. Kgl. Danske Videnskabernes Selskab, Historisk-Filologiske Meddelelser, 31:6 (Copenhagen, 1949). Another specific case is taken up in E. Adamson Hoebel's "The Asiatic Origin of a Myth of the Northwest Coast," *JAF* 54 (1941): 1–9. I make reference to an Old Norse myth to explain a recent American joke in a note, "Thor, the Cheechako and the Initiates' Tasks: A Modern Parallel for an Old Jest," *SFQ* 24 (1960): 235–38.

"Myth: A Symposium," edited by Thomas A. Sebeok for *JAF* (October–December 1955), reprinted in 1958 by Indiana University Press, contains nine important articles on theories of myth, including Richard M. Dorson's "The Eclipse of Solar Mythology" and Thompson's "Myths and Folktales." William Bascom discussed "The Myth-Ritual Theory" in *JAF* 70 (1957): 103–14, and set off a wave of responses, favorable and hostile, in the following issues of the journal. Two later important contributions to evaluating the myth-ritual and other monomyth theories are Archer Taylor's "The Biographical Pattern in Traditional Narrative," *JFI* 1 (1964): 114–29 and Herbert Weisinger's "Before Myth," *JFI* 2 (1965): 120–31. Two other good anthologies of myth studies are "Myth and Mythmaking," ed. Henry A. Murray, in *Daedalus* (Spring 1959), and the January–March 1966 special issue of *JAF*, ed. Melville Jacobs, called "The Anthropologist Looks at Myth." Jacobs's methods of myth analysis were criticized in a review of *The People Are Coming Soon: Analyses of Clackamas Chinook Myths and Tales* (Seattle: University of Washington Press, 1960), by Sven Liljeblad in *MF* 12 (1962): 93–103. In "Five Interpretations of a Melanesian Myth," *JAF* 86 (1973): 3–13, Elli Köngäs-Maranda subjects the same text to analysis in terms of (1) Myth and Ritual, (2) Reflection of Culture, (3) Charter of Society, (4) Freudian and Jungian Symbolism, and (5) Structure.

Although a wealth of Native American narrative texts was available in government reports, museum bulletins, journals of folklore and anthropology, etc., since the late nineteenth century, the integration of these traditions with mainstream American folklore studies has been slow. In older collections like Harold W. Thompson's *Body, Boots, and Britches* (1940), for example, the chapter "Injun-Fighters" is *about* New York State Indians rather than based on their own traditions. In George Korson's *Pennsylvania Songs and Legends* (1949), one chapter concerns a single Indian personality—the Seneca chief "Cornplanter"—and the traditions surrounding his people. Richard M. Dorson's *Bloodstoppers and Bear-walkers* (1952) devoted one section (three chapters) to "The Indian Tradition" of Michigan's Upper Peninsula, contrasting the "stuffed" Indian of tourist-promotional literature and other published sources with the "live" Indians of everyday Peninsular life and history. (Full references to these three collections are given in the notes to chapter 3.) Roger L. Welsch provides twenty-three Plains Indian texts in English translations in his *Treasury of Nebraska Pioneer Folklore* (Lincoln: University of Nebraska Press, 1966), pp. 176–238. On "Indian" Lover's Leap legends, see John A. Burrison's "Sautee and Nacoochee: Anatomy of a Lovers' Leap Legend," *SF* 47 (1990): 117–32. One convenient source is a paperback collection of fifty-two texts, selected from the vast anthropological literature, in Susan Feldman's *The Storytelling Stone: Myths and Tales of the American Indians* (New York: Dell-Laurel, 1965). This handy volume also contains a bibliography.

Readings in American Folklore includes Roland B. Dixon's "Some Coyote Stories from the Maidu Indians of California" (pp. 16–21), which came from *JAF* of 1900, and which contains four texts in English without comment; and Judy Trejo's "Coyote Tales: A Paiute Commentary" (pp. 192–98), from *JAF* of 1974, which also has four tales but includes an insider's comments on their style, performance, and meaning. (One of Trejo's comments is included in this chapter, following the story of Wildcat and Coyote.)

Stith Thompson's "The Star Husband Tale," a classic study of a widespread Native American narrative, first published in 1953, is conveniently reprinted in Dundes's *The Study of Folklore*, pp. 414–74. Two studies reviewing the same material are George W. Rich's "Rethinking the Star Husbands," *JAF* 84 (1971): 436–41, and Frank W. Young, "Folktales and Social Structure: A Comparison of Three Analyses of the Star Husband Tale," *JAF* 91 (1978): 691–99.

The Native American "Adam and Eve" story quoted in this chapter comes from Jarold Ramsey's article "The Bible in Western Indian Mythology," *JAF* 90 (1977): 442–54, quoted there from *JAF* of 1938. The quoted Coyote story adapted to criticize the white man comes from Madronna Holden's article " 'Making All the Crooked Ways Straight': The Satirical Portrait of Whites in Coast Salish Folklore," *JAF* 89 (1976): 271–93, quoted there from an earlier book. A study of related material is Keith H. Basso's *Portraits of "The Whiteman": Linguistic Play and Cultural Symbols among the Western Apache* (London and Cambridge: Cambridge University Press, 1979).

Two essays in Richard M. Dorson's *Handbook of American Folklore* (see preface for reference) briefly discuss the shortcomings of previous scholarship in this area and some promises for the future. Elaine Jahner, in "Finding the Way Home: The Interpretation of American Indian Folklore" (pp. 11–17), demonstrates "micro-analysis" of texts with a Sioux story of a rescue aided by wolves. George Lankford, in "The Unfulfilled Promise of North American American Indian Folklore" (pp. 18–23), advocates an exhaustive study of "local rules for tale-telling" among Indian groups.

Barre Toelken's work with Navajo storytelling offers an excellent example of folklorists' concern with close reading of texts plus full attention to contexts and styles. Toelken gives a detailed account of his fieldwork and findings among Navajo storytellers in *The Dynamics of Folklore* (see preface). Toelken's essay "*Ma'i Jaldloshi*: Legendary Styles and Navaho Myth" appeared in *American Folk Legend: A Symposium*, ed. Wayland D. Hand (Berkeley and Los Angeles: University of California Press, 1971), pp. 203–11. The next stage of Toelken's analysis resulted in the essay "The 'Pretty Languages' of Yellowman: Genre, Mode, and Texture in Navaho Coyote Narratives," included in *Folklore Genres*, ed. Dan Ben-Amos, American Folklore Society Bibliographic and Special Series, vol. 26 (Austin: University of Texas Press, 1976), pp. 145–70. Then Toelken's retranslation and reevaluation of Yellowman's stories appeared as an essay cowritten with Tacheeni Scott in the collection *Traditional American Indian Literatures: Texts and Interpretations*, ed. Karl Kroeber (Lincoln: University of Nebraska Press, 1981), pp. 65–116. (This same volume contains important chapters by Kroeber, Jarold Ramsey, Dennis Tedlock, and Dell Hymes.) Toelken reviews all the lessons of his Navajo research in "Fieldwork Enlightenment," *Parabola* (Summer 1995): 28–35, an essay expanded for the book *The World Observed: Reflections on the Fieldwork Process*, eds. Bruce Jackson and Edward D. Ives (Urbana: University of Illinois Press, 1996).

At the forefront of scholars and critics promoting a fresh awareness of the artistic qualities of Native American narratives is Jarold Ramsey. His essay "The Wife Who Goes Out Like a Man, Comes Back as a Hero: The Art of Two Oregon Indian Narratives" broke new ground by appearing in the leading American journal of literary scholarship, *PMLA* 92 (1977): 9–18. The same year, Ramsey published a volume of texts, *Coyote Was Going There: Indian Literature of the Oregon Country* (Seattle: University of Washington Press). Related writings by other scholars are John Bierhorst's "American Indian Verbal Art and the Role of the Literary Critic," *JAF* 88 (1975): 401–8, and "Folklore and Literary Criticism: A Dialogue," *JFI* 18 (1981): 97–156, which contains a study of two English renderings of a single story by Karl Kroeber with commentary by five scholars and a rejoinder by Kroeber.

An excellent introduction to the problem of the translation of Indian texts is Dennis Tedlock's "On the Translation of Style in Oral Narrative," *JAF* 84 (1971): 114–33. Tedlock points out specific shortcomings in the translations given in classic collections of Zuñi narratives such as Ruth Benedict's *Zuñi Mythology* (1935), then presents principles for retranslating texts as dramatic poetry, with a few passages of example. More of Tedlock's translations are given in his anthology *Finding the Center: Narrative Poetry of the Zuñi Indians* (1972; repr. with a new preface, Lincoln: Bison Books, University of Nebraska Press, 1978).

The most impressive body of recent work on Native American texts—both in subtlety of analysis and in sheer volume—is that of Dell Hymes on Northwest Indian material. Hymes's essay "Folklore's Nature and the Sun's Myth" (quoted in this chapter), originally a presidential address to the American Folklore Society, was published in *JAF* 88 (1975): 345–69. It presents Hymes's conception of the discipline of folklore set forth partly in the form of an Oregon Indian text as rendered into poetic lines. Hymes's book *In Vain I Tried to Tell You* (Philadelphia: University of Pennsylvania Press, 1981) reprints ten of his earlier "Essays in Native American Ethnopoetics" (the subtitle) and contains a good bibliography of ethnopoetics. Keith Cunningham presents a narrative ethnography of everyday stories told in English by modern Southwest Native Americans in *American Indians' Kitchen-Table Stories* (Little Rock: August House, 1992).

Some materials relating to mythic traditions in American history and culture are contained in E. McClung Fleming's essay "Symbols of the United States: From Indian Queen to Uncle Sam," in *Frontiers of American Culture*, ed. Ray B. Browne, Richard H. Crowder, and Virgil L. Stafford (Lafayette, Ind.: Purdue University Studies, 1968), pp. 1–24. See also the section "American Cultural Myths" in Dorson's *Handbook of American Folklore*. Perry McWilliams, in "The Alamo Story: From Fact to Fable," *JFI* 15 (1978): 221–33, delineates what he terms "the process of enfablement." Karl G. Heider shows how three generals of the American Revolution were transformed into mythic figures in folk and popular sources in his essay "The Gamecock, the Swamp Fox, and the Wizard Owl: The Development of Good Form in an American Totemic Set," *JAF* 93 (1980): 1–22. Daryl Dance considers some mythic aspects of African-American narratives in his essay "In the Beginning: A New View of Black American Etiological Tales," *SFQ* 40 (1977): 53–64.

Stith Thompson's *Motif-Index of Folk-Literature* appeared in its revised definitive six-volume edition between 1955 and 1958 (Copenhagen and Bloomington,
Ind.: Indiana University Press); it was recently reissued on CD-ROM in the IBM
computer format. For American folklore, it is essential to consult Ernest W.
Baughman's *A Type and Motif Index of the Folktales of England and North America*
(The Hague: Indiana University Folklore Series no. 20, 1966); Thompson simply
cites all Anglo-American motif occurrences to the original unpublished dissertation
of Baughman's now-published work.

9

LEGENDS AND ANECDOTES

MYTH, LEGEND, ANECDOTE

Legends, the second large category of traditional prose narratives, resemble myths in that they are stories regarded by their tellers as true, despite being partly based on traditional motifs or concepts. Unlike myths, however, legends are generally secular and are set in the less remote past in a conventional earthly locale. Legends are sometimes referred to as *folk history*, although actual history is soon distorted by oral transmission. Because many legends reflect folk beliefs, the term "belief tale" is also applied to them; and just as myths serve the function of validating religious rites in a primitive culture, legends are often told to validate superstitions or other traditional beliefs in modern folklore. Since the spread of legends is analogous to the dissemination of *rumors* (unverifiable reports of supposed events), some sociological rumor theories have been applied to legends as well. Rumors may swell to legend proportions as they develop a specific narrative content. Single-episode belief tales, especially those centering on individuals, are termed *anecdotes* and constitute a large and common genre of legendary lore in modern America.

Rumors, anecdotes, and legends alike are concerned with remarkable, even bizarre, events that allegedly happened to ordinary people in everyday situations. These reports and stories are recounted, usually in conversation, as a way of explaining strange things that occur—or are thought to have occurred—and they are passed on in order to warn or inform others about these unprovable events. The structure of legends is loose. In effect, each version is a re-creation of the story by the teller using the basic elements of its traditional content. As Linda Dégh has pointed out, legends seem believable to their tellers and audiences because they contain two kinds of "reality factors": a verifiable fact combined with "an illusion commonly believed to be true." Furthermore, often legends are given the added support of certain "validating formulas," such as "This happened in our neighborhood" or "I heard this from a friend of mine who knows the person it really happened to" or "I read this in the paper once" or "I think I heard about this on the radio." Indeed, the subject matter of legends is the same sort of event that makes news; so in modern folklore the mass media often contribute to the spread of rumors and legends.

Legends are usually *migratory*—widely known in different places—but when texts become rooted and adapted to a particular place, they are said to be *localized*. For example, the widespread legend about a new member of a college secret society accidentally killed during an initiation has been localized on many campuses to a particular fraternity and a specific kind of ceremony or prank. The motif that a Judas figure within a group was responsible for the betrayal and death of the hero gets attached to every outlaw whom the folk admire, from Robin Hood to Jesse James and beyond. (A localized variant of a folklore item is sometimes called—adapting a term from biology—an "ecotype" or an "oikotype"; thus the process of localization may be called "ecotypification" or "oikotipification.")

Summarizing the vast bibliography of legend theory, Timothy R. Tangherlini suggests this general characterization of the narratives folklorists identify as legends:

> typically a short (mono-) episodic, traditional, highly ecotypified, historicized narrative performed in a conversational mode, reflecting on a psychological level a symbolic representation of folk belief and collective experiences and serving as a reaffirmation of commonly held values of the group to whose tradition it belongs.

Often legends are circulated in *cycles*, or groups of narratives relating to one event, person, or theme. Among these stories there may be both long, well-developed accounts and mere fragments of rumor and hearsay. For this reason the classification of legends has been a vexing matter; as the folklorist Wayland D. Hand, who has wrestled with the problem, wrote, "For the systematizer, folk legends seem endless in bulk and variety, and they are often so short and formless as to defy classification." For discussion purposes, however, five groups of legends may be established on the basis of their primary concern with religion, the supernatural, urban settings, individual persons, or localities and their histories.

RELIGIOUS LEGENDS

Religious legends include the narratives to which the term "legend" in Europe originally applied exclusively—stories of the lives of Christian saints. Many such stories belong to official religious literature when they have been attested by an official investigation and are entered in printed accounts, but some legends remain folklore while they circulate orally in traditional varying versions. Even the sanctioned "lives of saints" in print contain numerous traditional motifs from folk sources, and saintly influences continue to be manifested, according to folk accounts from both Europe and the United States, in many cases never officially validated by the Church. A counterpart tradition in an American-originated church is that of the miraculous appearances of the three "Nephites" who have aided Mormons in time of need by bringing them food, comforting them, rescuing them, and sometimes healing them.

FOCUS: BIRTH OF A NEPHITE "LEGEND"

In July of 1986 I convinced my dad to go with me and my two sons on a fishing trip in the Uintah mountains of Utah. I had been on vacation for about two weeks and had grown a beard during that time. We had to hike about three miles through a wilderness area, and in the late afternoon, a ten-year-old boy approached me and said he had been lost all day. He was supposed to be with a troop of scouts at Camp Steiner, ten miles from where we were.

My father agreed to watch my kids while I returned this lost kid to his camp. I was a little perturbed that people would let a ten-year-old wander off, and I asked him who was in charge of his troop. He told me his dad was the scoutmaster and that was why he was allowed on the camp, but I was more interested in who had sponsored their troop, and he told me, "Our high councilman is Bill Evans." I knew an electrician named Bill Evans, so I told the boy that Bill would know me, and that my name was Alma.

We hiked to the highway, got into my car, and I drove to the scout camp where we had to hike for another mile. As we approached the camp, a man saw us and asked the boy if he was the lost kid everybody was looking for. I said I had found him at Kamas Lake.

"Kamas Lake? That's ten miles from here!"

"Tell me about it."

He took the boy's hand and said, "Well, OK," turned and walked away. I left in a hurry because I didn't want to have to hike to our camp in the dark. I heard the rest of the story a week later when I called my office.

I was working temporarily in the Los Angeles office of System Parking, Inc., and I needed to call my assistant in Salt Lake City. When he answered the phone, he was laughing so hard he could barely speak. He explained that Bill Evans had come by and described how his scout troop had lost a boy in the mountains. They had spent most of the day looking for him, and finally they gathered the whole camp together to pray for help. Immediately after the prayer, Bill said, they separated to continue the search. Almost immediately one of the adult leaders brought the lost boy into the camp.

When they asked him how he got back, he said, "It was some guy with a beard named Nephi, or Alma." The camp of Mormon scouts and leaders recognized these as names of prophets from the Book of Mormon, and someone gasped, "One of the three Nephites!" Bill Evans knew me, but he also knew that my employer didn't allow beards, so he thought he'd wait until he could see if I had a beard. I guess the boy didn't think to explain that we covered most of the miles in a 1985 Oldsmobile.

A few weeks later, my brother's scout troop returned from Camp Steiner, where they too had heard the story told of the mysterious bearded stranger with a Nephite name.

Source: As retold by Alma Allred, Director of Parking Services at the University of Utah, in November 1996; he had originally told it to Jan Brunvand in 1989. (Many Boy Scout troops in Utah are sponsored by the Church of Jesus Christ of Latter-day Saints, or Mormon Church. A "High Councilman" is an official of an LDS "stake," a unit comparable to a Roman Catholic diocese.)

DISCUSSION TOPICS:

1. What do the Nephites of legend look like, and how do they usually behave in the legends? (See William A. Wilson's 1969 article on the Three Nephites, cited in the bibliographic notes. Although there are said to be three helpful Nephites, they are not individually identified, nor do they usually appear together.)

2. What categories of folk narrative were A) the boy's experience as he told it, B) the experience as it was interpreted by some of the Scout leaders, and C) Alma Allred's retelling of his experience?

3. Alma Allred jokingly claims that his family motto is "Any story is worth telling better," but he insists that this tale is strictly factual. Still, what elements of effective oral style are apparent in this account?

The term "legend" now refers to many more kinds of stories than just *saints' legends*, and even the term "religious legends" includes other types, which we might place under the rubric *blessings and miracles*. Traditional stories about miracles, revelations, answers to prayers, marvelous icons, and blessings bestowed upon the faithful may all be called religious legends if their dissemination is largely oral and some of their motifs are traditional. To say such stories are legendary is not necessarily to say they are of doubtful veracity, for folklore may be true as well as false. Thus, a legend about a group of nuns who retreat to prayerful sanctuary before an advancing forest fire and emerge later to find that the fire has miraculously bypassed them may be perfectly true, although divine intercession is unprovable. Still, it is a religious legend as long as traditional oral versions continue to circulate.

A third category of religious legends is *the Bible of the folk*—a cycle of stories that fill the blanks of, or extend, biblical narratives. For example, the term "Adam's apple" refers to legendary accounts of the apple sticking in Adam's throat when he took it from Eve and ate it. The dog is said to have a cold nose because he was late coming to the ark and had to ride next to the rail. Gypsies are allowed to roam the whole Earth, according to legend, because one of them stole the nail forged for Christ's heart when He was nailed to the cross. Various animals or plants are rewarded or formed as they are because of some legendary connection with the life of the Savior. Flies that gathered on the body of Christ at His Crucifixion looked like nails and prevented more nails from being driven, and therefore they may dine at kings' tables—while various trees (the aspen, poplar, and others) are said to be "cursed" for supplying wood for His cross. All of these examples, it should be noted, are etiological legends and to many tellers may even function as myths—that is, as charters for religious faith. The folklorist Francis Lee Utley referred to this area of religious legends as "an uncharted wilderness" that requires the use of numerous sources, both written and oral, for its successful exploration.

SUPERNATURAL LEGENDS

Supernatural legends generally take the form of supposedly factual accounts of occurrences and experiences that seem to validate folk beliefs and superstitions. For the simplest of these, a kind of prelegend that is merely a "narrative of a personal happening," the useful term *memorate* was coined by the Swedish folklorist C. W. von Sydow. Memorates are firsthand descriptions of personal experiences with the supernatural, although a story about a remarkable (non-supernatural) personal experience could be thought of as a "secular memorate." While a memorate might be repeated by a second or third person, more commonly the story would either remain with its original subject as a personal narrative or become detached, acquire further traditional elements, and grow into a legend proper.

The folklorists Linda Dégh and Andrew Vázsonyi have isolated an even more basic unit they call the *proto-memorate*, referring to any "credibility-seeking utterance like folk belief itself" that may precede or provide background for legend formation. The true legend must be a traditional rather than just a personal narrative, but the proto-memorate and memorate, though influenced by folk belief, mainly describe a purely personal experience of the narrator's. All such stories are told, at least in part, to give credence to folk beliefs. Yet, as Patrick B. Mullen points out, sometimes the "basic narrative value" of a legend may keep it alive in tradition long after anyone seriously believes it. Supernatural legends may be grouped according to such categories of superstition as beliefs in supernatural creatures, in returning spirits of the dead, in magic, and in supernatural signs.

European legendry is full of stories of supernatural creatures, both evil ones, such as vampires, werewolves, trolls, and other monsters, and the partly helpful ones, such as elves, brownies, fairies, *nisser*, and other "little people." But very few of these creatures migrated to the New World, where immigrant life lacked the settings and family traditions to maintain this lore. We can collect legends of "bearwalkers" and other shape shifters, and of occasional zombies, deformed maniacs, ape men, "Bigfoots," and other monsters, but usually just in isolated pockets of folk culture, especially where Indian, African-American, or certain immigrant tradition is strong. A hotbed of creaturelore—some joking, some told in earnest—is the adolescent summer camp, where stories of fearsome folk figures are told to wide-eyed campers gathered around the nightly bonfire. Other supernatural legends—often told as personal experiences— describe UFO visitations, alien abductions, cattle mutilations, and mysterious "Men in Black" who are assumed to be part of some huge international (possibly intergalactic) conspiracy.

Legends of witchcraft, a staple of colonial American folklore, are still circulated in modern America, though mostly in the backwoods or rural towns. The following slightly condensed account collected by Leonard Roberts in Kentucky shows a typical mix of community beliefs and personal narrative. The first episode is essentially a memorate, while the character's powers are illustrated with two legendary episodes; the story concludes with a paraphrase of the character's own account of how he acquired his powers:

When I was a small girl there was an old man named George. The folks around home said he was a witch. . . .

One day I was in the barn milking when I suddenly heard a noise. I went to see what it was, of course. There stood George with his old crooked cane pointing at our old red cow. . . . She turned around and walked right up the ladder into the barn loft. Well, we had a time getting her down from there.

A while after that my mother was churning but was not getting much butter to come. George came along and wanted to churn, so mother let him take the dasher. Well, he churned about five minutes and he had that churn full of butter. My mother was afraid to use the butter, so she gave it to our twelve hogs and they everyone died as dead as a wedge.

Old George used to tell people how he become a witch. He said that he went to the top of the mountain before the sun rose and prayed to the Devil and cursed the Lord.

Magically influencing animals, controlling the formation of butter in a churn, and praying to the Devil are all typical motifs of witchcraft.

Supernatural legends concerning the returning spirits of the dead, a major category in world folklore, are equally common and varied in the United States. The term *ghost stories* for such narratives suggests bloodcurdling scare tales about white-sheeted or invisible spooks who are out to destroy humankind. But most ghosts in American legends are lifelike in appearance and come back from the dead only to set right an error or finish a task. A better term for these creatures is *revenants*, or "returners"—those who return from the world of the dead, usually only temporarily. Their reasons for coming back are numerous, and harmless to anyone with a clear conscience. Only a few spirits return for revenge, and they always have justification; more commonly they return for such a purpose as to reveal hidden treasure, to ask that a crooked limb in the coffin be straightened, or to reveal the cause of death. A common motif in these legends is E402: "Mysterious ghostlike noises heard." These sounds include calls, moans, snores, sobs, sighs, footsteps, and sometimes even that old standby of Hollywood horror films, chain rattling. Often a brave person can communicate with the spirit by means of these noises, asking for one for "yes" and two for "no," to discover the reason for the haunting. Besides human spirits, the ghosts of animals may come back to torment the living, but more often they come to assist. The ways by which ghosts may be summoned, the reasons they come, their appearance, the attempts to placate them, and the variants of tales about encounters with them constitute a fascinating study within a region or for a particular folk group. For example, often it is ghost stories that teenagers continue to tell, with varying degrees of belief or disbelief, while participating in the custom of "legend-tripping" (see chapter 15).

Another approach to legend research, suggested by John M. Vlach, is to distinguish from serious supernatural belief tales the *humorous antilegends* told mostly by children and adolescents to evoke simultaneous fear and laughter. Serving a more sinister purpose were the stories of "Night Riders" and "Night Doctors" told by Southern whites to intimidate their black slaves by encouraging superstitious fear of ghosts and bogies. A study by Gladys-Marie Fry based on ex-slave narratives and oral history interviews reveals how actual mounted white patrols and units of the Ku Klux Klan served to lend credence among blacks to the rumors spread by whites about ghostly spirits and human body-snatchers who would capture the slaves if they ventured forth after dark. Thus a cycle of created legends was used for social control and racial suppression.

Memorates of supernatural signs and magic are probably more common than full-scale legends concerning them, although memorates have not been collected as frequently as legends have by American folklorists. Yet, one often hears first-person accounts of folk cures that worked, wishes that came true, warnings of death that were fulfilled, bad luck that followed a traditional omen, prophetic dreams, and so forth. As one analysis has described the forming sequence, "primary stimuli," such as folk superstitions (i.e., "Bad luck comes in threes") encounter the "releasing stimuli" involved in an actual situation (three unlucky things happen to someone); the event is interpreted ("That saying is true!"); and then that happening is narrated to others as a memorate. Repeated transmissions of the memorate in turn support the folk belief.

Personal narratives of supposed cases of prenatal influence demonstrate this process at work. One informant stated the well-known belief "If you are suddenly startled by something while you are pregnant and then touch your body, your baby will be marked in that same spot." Then she related this secondhand memorate as evidence:

> My aunt had this experience. She was startled by a rabbit while working in her garden one day. The rabbit suddenly jumped out near her and she hit herself quite hard on the thigh in reaction to the scare. Her baby girl was born with a birthmark on her thigh in the shape of a rabbit in the exact spot where she had hit herself.

But not every story with similar content is a memorate. The following, though told in a serious manner and referring to the same belief, is really a parody of a belief tale:

> Many people today don't believe when a pregnant woman gets scared that an imprint of this goes on the child. But I know of an

actual case. This lady was at the Bronx Zoo just before she was to have her baby, and she got scared by a bear. And sure enough when the child was born, it had bare feet!

URBAN LEGENDS

A convenient subject in which the student might observe the growth of legends is the so-called **urban legend**—a story in a contemporary setting (not necessarily a big city), reported as a true individual experience, with traditional variants that indicate its legendary character. Urban legends (also called "contemporary legends" and "modern legends") typically have three good reasons for their popularity: a suspenseful or humorous story line, an element of actual belief, and a warning or moral that is either stated or implied. Only a few urban legends contain supernatural motifs, but all of them include at least highly unnatural details. This fact shakes popular belief in them not a bit, for people in all walks of life credit such stories, and various publications frequently reprint them—or radio commentators report them—as the truth. In recent years urban legends have been much repeated and discussed on the Internet, often regarded there by the discussants as mere "jokes."

One of the oldest American urban legends, and a rare supernatural example, is "The Vanishing Hitchhiker" (Motif E332.3.3.1.), in which the spirit of a young girl tries to hitchhike home annually on the anniversary of her death. More recently the hitchhiker who vanishes suddenly is said to be a wholesome-looking young man who announces that Jesus is coming soon. In both versions the hitchhiker vanishes suddenly from the moving car, often leaving behind some token or article of clothing as proof of his or her existence. Another favorite car legend based on presumed facts concerns "The Death Car," a late-model automobile selling for a song because the smell of a corpse cannot be eradicated from it. Still other modern car legends play on possible dangers met with while driving (i.e., "The Hook" [maniac's hook hand torn off by car doorhandle] and "The Killer in the Backseat" [assailant hidden in car]) or else on the theme of inexpensive cars (i.e., "The Economical Carburetor" and "The Fifty-Dollar Car" [man's car sold cheaply by his spurned wife]).

FOCUS: LIGHTS OUT!

10/29/93   **ALERT**

This information was received from Fox Chase Cancer Center via St. Mary's Hospital in Langhorne, Pa.

PLEASE READ THIS !!!

If you are driving at night and see a car
without their headlights on,
DO NOT FLASH YOUR HIGH BEAMS
signalling them to turn on their lights.

Two separate Pennsylvania Police Departments have been contacting businesses in the Langhorne area with the following information. The street gang known as the "Bloods" has a new initiation practice. They drive around without their headlights on and follow the first car to "flash" its high beams with the intent to kill the driver.

BE CAREFUL OUT THERE !!!

BEWARE !!

There is a new "Gang Initiation" !!!!!

This new initiation of MURDER is brought about by
Gang Members driving around at night with their car
lights off. When you flash your car lights to signal
them that their lights are out, the Gang members take
it literally as "LIGHTS OUT", so they are to follow you
to your destination and kill you!! That's their
initiation.

Two families have already fallen victim to this
initiation ritual. **BE AWARE AND INFORM YOUR
FAMILIES AND FRIENDS.**
DON'T FLASH YOUR CAR LIGHTS FOR ANYONE.

THIS INFORMATION WAS PROVIDED BY THE
CHICAGO POLICE DEPARTMENT

THIS IS NOT A JOKE

Source: Anonymous fliers faxed around the United States in autumn 1993.

DISCUSSION TOPICS:

1. These warning notices and many similar ones were fictional in nearly every detail, as news reports and police statements explained. Yet many people took them seriously, adding written comments like "Better safe than sorry" and "This is not a joke" to the fliers before faxing them onward. What "reality factors" made the warnings believable?

2. What stylistic features make these warnings unlikely as official police statements?

3. See Jan Harold Brunvand, " 'Lights Out!': A Faxlore Phenomenon," *Skeptical Inquirer* 19:2 (March/April 1995): 32–37, with added comments in *SI* 19:4 (July/August 1995): 61–62 in which a possible origin for the warnings is proposed and denied. What do you think?

In some urban legends an original supernatural element was rationalized. "The Robber Who Was Hurt," for example, is told nowadays about a would-be intruder who is badly burned when he tries to enter a woman's home and she thrusts a hot iron or poker against his hand. When she asks a neighbor woman for help, the neighbor says that she has to tend to her husband, who just returned home with a burned hand. This legend seems to be a revision of an old witchcraft story about a supernatural intruder in animal form who is injured in the paw; later a neighbor found to have a cut or burned hand is detected as the culprit. Another supernatural connection is found in recent rumors and legends about the Procter & Gamble company trademark—a man in the moon and thirteen stars enclosed in a circle. This innocent design was claimed by some to be a satanic symbol adopted by the company when the founder made a Faustlike pact with the Devil to secure his financial success.

Many urban legends, though they may display the coloration of other national folklore, are really international in their distribution. The story of "The Hairy-armed Hitchhiker," known in England during the 1977–78 "Yorkshire Ripper" scares (ultimately springing from a tale known there for more than a century), migrated to the United States by spring 1983. Rather than being recognized as a man in woman's clothing by his hairy arms or hands, as in England, the threatening figure now was unmasked when his wig fell off during a struggle with a shopping-mall security guard. In either version a hatchet or an ax was later found in the stranger's handbag, left in the intended victim's car. This legend adapted easily to the American scene, where stories of crime in shopping centers are common. Eventually the story developed variations in which the threatened woman driver worked out her own rescue instead of calling on a man (police, security guard, etc.) for help.

Occasionally it may appear that an urban legend has sprung from verifiable history. Richard M. Dorson thought he had traced "The Death Car" to a 1938 incident in the small town of Mecosta, Michigan, but later study turned up prototypical elements earlier in Europe. (A legend about a hotel room contaminated with the smell of death has circulated more recently in the United States.) The legend about a husband who fills a Cadillac parked in front of his house with cement, thinking that the owner is seducing his wife, seemed to have been verified by a newspaper article. Folklorist Louie W. Attebery found such an event reported in a Denver, Colorado, newspaper in 1960; the cemented vehicle in this instance was a 1946 DeSoto, but there was no jealousy motive. The same legend, however, had been heard in Texas some four months earlier, suggesting that life may sometimes imitate folklore, a process called *ostention* or *ostensive action* by folklorists.

The urban legend about a woman's dead cat wrapped for burial in a neat package, which is then pilfered by a shoplifter while the owner pauses in a department store on the way to meet a friend, has been reported by newspapers in different cities for at least thirty-five years. Possibly such an event did happen somewhere once, but not all the times and not in all the places to which it has been attributed. Besides, once again, oral tradition has carried the same story for several decades longer than the news media have known it. For example, the legend about a grandmother's corpse stolen from the car-top rack when a vacationing family was driving her home from Mexico for burial seems to be a mere re-creation of the same stolen-corpse plot, but with different details. ("The Runaway Grandmother" was also originally a European story.)

Another variation on the dead-cat theme involves guests at a dinner party who rush to a hospital to have their stomachs pumped when the family pet, earlier caught nibbling at the poached salmon, is found dead on the back porch. The next day a neighbor confesses that he ran over the cat in the driveway and left the corpse on the porch rather than interrupting the party. (A variation of this "Poisoned Pussycat" story involves a family testing some mushrooms they have picked by feeding them to their pet.) Yet another treatment of the suffering-pet idea involves an animal put into a microwave oven to be dried after a bath, whereupon the creature explodes. (In a horrific variation, a baby is put into the microwave by a babysitter who has taken drugs.) Still other suffering pets are eaten in Chinese-American restaurants, or served to their owners in a Hong Kong restaurant, or pounded flat under a newly laid carpet (a parakeet or a gerbil), or flushed down the toilet in New York City (baby pet alligators). Probably all of these creatures of legend to some degree represent mistreated family members, an idea made explicit in the grandmother-heist story.

Basic modern anxieties often lie behind popular urban legends. An instance of this is fear of contamination from manufactured goods. A favorite story in this category is about a girl who sickens and sometimes dies because black-widow spiders have infested her sprayed hairdo; there are counterpart tales of insects living in skin boils, under plaster casts, or in the sinus cavities. A similar story describes a girl who is embalmed alive in a "poisoned dress" that had been taken from a corpse and resold. Vague rumors about foreign matter contaminating food, another frequent motif, may develop into narratives about a mouse in a soda bottle, worms in hamburgers, a dead rat floating in a chocolate company's vats, a batter-fried rat, and so forth. That successful lawsuits have been brought against companies for selling food or drink contaminated in similar ways does not prevent the stories from qualifying as folk-lore, for the traditional versions are highly stylized in both form and content, and they seldom concern specific documented cases. Instead, the legends mention the familiar and unreliable "friend of a friend" (FOAF) validation of other urban lore.

An antibusiness viewpoint may be revealed in urban legends, such as the Procter & Gamble story mentioned above. Defective or accidentally released experimental products (like the economical carburetor) crop up repeatedly—a bathing suit becomes transparent, a lightbulb or razor blade never wears out, a tin-can speedometer casing is found on an early Japanese car, and so forth. Well-known establishments may become associated with a particular legend. The Waldorf-Astoria hotel, for example, was named as the business where a secret recipe for "Red Velvet Cake" was sold to a woman for an outrageous price. In revenge, she distributed the "secret" ("Add one-quarter cup of red food coloring to the batter") widely among her friends. The management of the Waldorf cannot explain why, but this legend has stuck with them for decades, though no such cake was ever featured on their menus. Later, a variation of the story was applied to Mrs. Fields Chocolate Chip Cookies and to Neiman Marcus department stores; both of these variations have had a very active life on the Internet.

In another business-legend cycle, one discount store from a particular chain (often Kmart) is said to be the place where a woman was bitten by a poisonous snake sewn into the sleeve or lining of an imported coat. Or it may be misuse of a product, rather than a defect or other shortcoming, that causes an accident. This idea appears in legends about contact lenses sticking to the cornea after a welding accident, superglue bonding parts of the body together, power-lawnmower blades hacking off fingers when the running mower is lifted to trim a hedge, or butane cigarette lighters exploding in a pocket and injuring someone.

Anxiety about being caught in the nude or otherwise embarrassed is projected in several migratory legends of wide circulation in the United States. In a railroading version, a traveling businessman wearing only pajamas is enticed into a young woman's Pullman compartment, where he awakens alone the next morning; his clothes and luggage are back in his own Pullman car, which had been disconnected from the train during the night. In a mobile-home variation, the man is napping nude in the trailer while his wife drives; at a sudden stop for a traffic light he groggily arises and steps outside, only to be left behind when the light changes. A cycle of "nude surprise party" stories describes a serviceman or businessman misunderstanding the secretive arrangements of his girlfriend or secretary for a dinner party at her home; he removes his clothes in anticipation of lovemaking only to discover that the event is really a surprise welcome-home party or an office party thrown in his honor. Another surpriser-surprised tale describes a housewife caught doing her laundry in the nude by the gas-meter reader, or a babysitter and her boyfriend caught frolicking in the nude. In a flatulent form of the same theme, a girl breaks wind in the front seat of her date's car, unaware that the couple they are double-dating with are already sitting in the back seat.

Aspects of modern technology (microwave ovens, contact lenses, etc.) sometimes seem to substitute in urban legends for the supernatural threats of older belief tales. In one favorite story among teenagers, an assailant threatens a babysitter by calling her from the extension telephone in the same home she is working in, but she foils him by having the calls traced and then escaping. Other telephone legends involve a celebrity offering his credit-card number for fans to make unlimited free calls on, and a woman unable to report a fire in her home because she cannot find the number 11 on her dial in order to call the 911 emergency code. Plots like these—as well as others involving computers—can generally be shown to be unverifiable and probably fictional.

Research on the "new" urban legends that crop up usually reveals older prototypes. A prime instance involves the "Choking Doberman" story that raced across the country beginning in 1981. Here a guard dog was discovered with two or three fingers stuck in its throat, and an injured intruder was found hiding in the house. Comparisons with many other legends about dogs, fingers, assailants, and the like linked the Doberman story with centuries-old traditional plots involving similar motifs, as well as with several other new legends in simultaneous circulation. Central in this history of an urban legend was the notion of a pet found in puzzling or compromising circumstances that were later explained as proving the pet's heroic defense against an intruder in the master's home (e.g., a guard dog with a bloody mouth has really killed an attacking wolf, from which the dog had defended the master's child). The hidden burglar in the modern story replaced an attacking beast (usually a snake or a wolf) that was repelled by the dog in the earlier versions. The severed-fingers (or -hand) motif had been lifted without alteration from other older narratives. Only the recombination of traits and the addition of some contemporary themes (often racial, sexist, or technical) could be said to distinguish the "new" story of the choking guard dog from the older versions.

PERSONAL LEGENDS

Personal legends are stories attached to individuals and told as true. In Old World folk tradition, cycles of ancient hero legends described

an impressive catalog of national champions such as Roland, Char-
lemagne, Saint Patrick, King Arthur, and Robin Hood; in American
folklore the hero legend has been manifested first in such frontier
figures as Davy Crockett and the keelboatman and scout Mike Fink,
later in regional characters like Johnny Appleseed and Billy the Kid,
and in the twentieth century in the largely fakelore elaboration of
Paul Bunyan and the characters created in imitation of him. Scattered narratives, sometimes heroic, also circulate about gangsters
(John Dillinger), sports stars (Babe Ruth, John L. Sullivan, Jim
Thorpe), martyrs (Martin Luther King Jr., John F. Kennedy), and
military leaders (Generals Doolittle, Patton, and MacArthur), as well
as others. But the stories concerning such figures do not compare in
number and national folk circulation to the European heroic-legend
cycles, and no greater misconception exists about American folklore
than the notion that we as a people have continually created and
celebrated epic folk heroes. The vaunted "heroes" of juvenile literature and chamber-of-commerce boosting are often inventions of
professional writers and public-relations people, not of the folk
groups to which they are attributed.

FOCUS: HOW BRONKO NAGURSKI WAS DISCOVERED

According to football lore, [early star Bronko Nagurski] *was discovered in 1925 when Minnesota coach Doc Spears drove past a farm and
saw a muscular boy plowing a field—without a horse. Spears supposedly
asked Nagurski directions, and Bronko picked up the plow and pointed.*

*

*He's got the biggest hands I've ever seen. He was so strong that, in
Southern Illinois, when someone would ask Jerry Sloan* [present coach
of the Utah Jazz] *for directions, he would point a plow.*—Frank Lay-
den [former coach of the Utah Jazz]

Source: First quotation from the Associated Press story on Nagurski's death in January 1990; second quotation from an interview published in *Private Eye Weekly* of
Salt Lake City, March 24, 1993.

DISCUSSION TOPICS:

1. Other Midwestern versions of this story appear in Ronald Baker's *Hoosier Folk Legends* (1982) and in Richard M. Dorson's Michigan
collection, *Bloodstoppers and Bearwalkers* (1952); see the bibliographic
notes. Compare these variants to the above.

Bronko Nagurski in the uniform of the Chicago Bears, 1943.

2. "Strong man lifts plow" is Motif F624.4. with references to Danish and German sources (see Grimm Tale No. 90, "The Young Giant"). Curiously, the motif does not appear in Baughman's *Index*, so the reference works are not perfect. Do you know other motifs concerning athletic ability or strength that may or may not appear in the motif indexes?

3. Some European versions of the story concern recruiting for the military; American versions are often about athletic recruitment. Why is the story not likely to survive, in either form, much longer?

One typical hero of genuine indigenous oral tradition in the United States is not the brawling frontier trailblazer or the giant mythical laborer but rather the local tall-tale specialist who has gathered a repertoire of traditional exaggerations and attached them all to his own career. Figures like John Darling of New York State, Abraham "Oregon" Smith of southern Indiana and Illinois, and Len Henry of northern Idaho were famous yarnspinners in their own regions who have been the subjects of study by folklorists but who have no popular reputations beyond their own communities, where they were celebrated fondly as "the biggest liars in seven counties." These figures might, like John Darling, be pictured mainly as powerful men or great hunters, or they might possess a special repertoire, like Oregon Smith's travel yarns. Smith also had a reputation as a folk doctor, hence his other nickname, "Sassafras," from his favorite source of a curative potion. Almost invariably the story is told about someone approaching the local liar to ask him to "Tell the biggest lie you know!" The vaunted liar, however, says he is too busy to tell a lie; "old man so-and-so just died and I have to go order a coffin for him." When people call on the widow, they discover that the liar has indeed told them a big one, for there is old man so-and-so, rocking on the front porch. Although this story is reported as a tribute to the yarnspinner's quick wit, actually it is a traditional tale that has been widely collected both in Europe and America.

First-person reminiscences and family stories have long puzzled American folklore collectors and scholars. How many repetitions are needed, or how widely must a personal narrative be spread for it to qualify as folklore? How can we distinguish between unstructured musings, polished retellings of events, memorates, personal narratives, and personal legends? Every folklorist who has tape-recorded good informants has had to deal with such questions. It has been asserted, with some convincing examples, that family traditions constitute a traditional category with subcategories, including courtship stories, misfortune stories, favorite anecdotes about eccentric relatives, and often-repeated—and somewhat embellished—experiences. Such stories tend to develop specific themes: family-misfortune stories might explain "Why we are not a rich family today," "How Grandpa lost his fortune or failed to capitalize on his invention," or "The time someone failed to marry money." Courtship stories may follow such themes as "love at first sight" or "meant for each other," or be interlarded with fairy-tale or romance conventions.

Nicknames and distinctive verbal expressions used within a family group might be the subject of other stories. Jimmy Durante's famous sign-off, for instance, "Good night, Mrs. Calabash, wherever you are!" is said to refer to a pet name he used for his first wife. In one family a whining child was always called "Ransey Sniffle." Why do children in one family say "We need a tombstone, Mom!" when they need to find a restroom on an auto trip? The family's oral tradition preserves the answer: because one time on a trip they were sent into a roadside cemetery to "find a tombstone" behind which to relieve themselves. In another family the expression "off towards Kelsey's" is used to describe having a coverlet or tablecloth on crooked; the story explains that one time they lived across the street at a diagonal ("kitty-corner") from a family named Kelsey.

Longer narrative traditions than these bits and pieces may preserve a good deal of family history. In some Texas families, the folklorist Mody Boatright reported, members cherish traditional accounts (which he proposed calling "family sagas") of how their pioneer forebears behaved and why they came to Texas. Richard M. Dorson suggested the term "sagaman" for the old-timer who spins long, fantastic yarns about his own exploits, in which "he plays an heroic role, overmastering the hazards and outwitting the dangers presented by vicious men, ferocious beasts, and implacable nature." Personal reminiscences of these kinds furnish background for the other folklore texts of gifted informants, and for this reason also they ought to be collected.

Not all personal experiences that become "folklorized" during retellings into personal narratives are necessarily family stories. Individuals may repeat, embellish, and dramatically perform stories about close calls, embarrassing situations, coincidences, lucky occurrences, accidents, crimes directed against them, run-ins with government authorities, and a host of other topics common to everyday conversation. As such narratives enter the teller's repertoire of set pieces, they may be drawn forth time and again at the requests of his or her acquaintances, who will listen for the pleasure the performance gives, long after any suspense about the outcome of the story is gone. And when traditional groupings of tellers and listeners form, the topics of personal narratives tend to fall into patterns. For example, Susan Kalčik found that the narratives told in women's rap groups (consciousness-raising groups developed by the women's liberation movement) usually drew from four subjects—men in gen-

eral, other women, mothers, and male doctors. These stories, Kalčik
felt, served usually as strategies to cope with the oppression of
women or else as devices of self-discovery.

The *anecdote* proper is a short personal legend, supposedly true
but generally apocryphal, told about an episode in the life of either
a famous individual or a local character. (Sometimes the term "anecdote" is also loosely applied to any single-episode story about a
place or event.) The anecdote about George Washington and the
cherry tree ("I cannot tell a lie; I did it with my little hatchet!"),
though concocted by Parson Weems, an early Washington biogra-
pher, remains a traditional story to illustrate the first president's
perfect honesty, and it is repeated both in print and orally. An anecdote about a famous intellectual and a chorus girl has the folkloric
credentials of being attached to various individuals. In one version
it is George Bernard Shaw, who is propositioned thus: "You have
the greatest brain in the world. I have the most graceful body. Let
us then produce the perfect child." Shaw responds, "But suppose the
child had my body and your brain!" In other accounts Albert Einstein is the man named, but the episode has ultimately been found
in an Old French manuscript dated 1319, and it was reprinted several times in the eighteenth and nineteenth centuries.

FOCUS: FOLKLORISTS RELATE AN ANECDOTE

In mid-October, 1991, at the annual meeting of the American
Folklore Society I mentioned to a friend one morning that I was on
my way to attend a session devoted to proverb studies in order to
hear a talk on the history and variations of the saying "Early to bed
and early to rise makes a man healthy, wealthy, and wise."

My friend commented, "I wonder if the speaker will mention Oscar Wilde's parody of that proverb: 'Early to rise and early to bed
makes a man healthy, wealthy, and dead.'"

The speaker did indeed quote that variation, but he attributed it
to James Thurber.

Whichever writer uttered that witticism, if in fact either one did,
we have in the story the essence of what folklorists call an anecdote
—a concise account of some well-known person who supposedly said
or did something rather wise or witty.

Or, as another wit defined the genre, "An anecdote is a brief account of an incident that has never occurred in the life of some famous person."

Source: From Jan Harold Brunvand's "Urban Legends" column, United Feature Syndicate, release date December 2, 1991, titled "Celebrities and the Tales They Can't Shake."

DISCUSSION TOPICS:

1. Do the published sources on "familiar quotations"—or the biographies of writers—support the attribution of the "Early to rise" parody to Wilde, to Thurber, or to other people?

2. Can you locate the source of the witty definition of "anecdote" quoted above?

3. How is the term "anecdote" used and misused by writers and speakers of English? What is the etymology of the term?

4. Collect other doubtful tales that celebrities (and others) can't shake. Are there others about witty restatements of traditional proverbs? What makes these tales so appealing and so persistent?

Another persistent anecdote about a famous person deals with the supposed derivation of John Philip Sousa's surname from the initials S. O. (said to stand for Siegfried or Sigismund Ochs, presumably a German name) and the letters U.S.A. stenciled on his baggage when he traveled to (or from) the United States; another version claims that "John Phillipso USA" was the baggage marking. Sousa was actually born in Washington, D.C., and the family name was Sousa (a Portuguese name) from the start. Tales of this sort circulate especially about political figures, scientists, criminals, show-business personalities, professional athletes, and military men, and they should be distinguished from *jokes* about personalities. While jokes are obviously false but do reveal popular attitudes toward public figures, anecdotes always have the air of truth about them, and they supposedly demonstrate how people have revealed their own personalities.

Anecdotes about local characters emphasize supposed mental, ethical, and personality traits of their subjects in stories presumed to be true by most of the local populace, but local-character anecdotes often contain motifs found in other regions as well. The local miser pays his son a penny for going to bed without supper, then charges him a penny for breakfast. The town's laziest man wins a load of corn in a contest and asks, "Is it shelled?" The village dolt is eating his first banana on a train ride; the train goes through a tunnel, and he cries out that the fruit has blinded him. The clever rascal, on the other hand, plays dumb and always picks the big coin (a nickel) instead of the little one (a dime) because, "Otherwise those smart alecks would quit asking me to choose." The absentminded professor is a frequent target of local-character anecdotes on college campuses. He forgets that he has driven to the campus and walks home; when he gives a speech, he sometimes reads both the original and the photocopy of each page; and when he reaches into his pocket for the frog he caught for dissection class, he finds instead the sandwich he thought he had eaten for lunch.

The comical Indian, sometimes foolish but more often shrewd, was the subject of a long cycle of racist anecdotes from early American history that still echoes through modern jokebooks and in oral folklore. The white man shivers in his heavy winter clothing while the Indian is comfortable in only a blanket, because, as he explains it, "Me all face." (This story has been traced to a late-classical Greek source that came via French and English literary versions to the United States.) In other anecdotes Indians turn the tables on whites by using the whites' own law and religion against them, or a white settler frightens the Indians by removing his wig, wooden leg, glass eye, or other artificial body part. A common theme in these anecdotes is feeding the Indians; for instance, the Indians arrive at a farm or ranch to beg for food, and the settler watches in dismay as a whole platter of fried eggs disappears down the gullet of one brave, while all of the others demand the same size serving. The Indians may stand around the molasses barrel, dipping their fingers into it and licking off the sweet. One brave is said to have eaten a whole pot of half-cooked beans one day; he was found dead the next day with his stomach distended. An anecdote about Indians offering to trade many horses or other valuables for a blonde white girl is related as true in several accounts of early Western travel, but a historian's study of them indicates that "Goldilocks on the Oregon Trail" is a legendary story stemming from traditional sources rather than from firsthand experience. An old Navajo living on the tribal reservation in Arizona is the subject of another local-character anecdote. He walks to town to pick up his monthly government check, stopping overnight at several hogans of kinsmen on the way. By the time he has gone in and back, it is time to begin going in again for the next check.

LOCAL LEGENDS

Local legends are closely associated with specific places, either with their names, their geographic features, or their histories. Presumably these legends are unique regional creations, but in reality many of them are simply localized versions of migratory legends; even a story that originates from a local feature or event tends to spread outward, changing and being localized as it moves. A good example of the transplanted migratory legend is the Maine-woods story of "The Man Who Plucked the Gorbey" (Canada jay); the man's own hair was later plucked while he slept. This tale evidently goes back to a Scottish and North-Country English legend about plucking a sparrow, but it has become solidly entrenched in Maine and New Brunswick, being locally credited there to some thirty different characters.

A good example of a legend spawned by technology that became localized as a historical tradition is "The Image on Glass" story analyzed by folklorist Barbara Allen. Evidently the idea that a flash of lightning could cause a photographic image to form on an ordinary windowpane or a mirror arose from people's misunderstanding in the late nineteenth century of the nature of the emerging science of photography. Stories that grew out of this concept usually referred to criminals, murder victims, or even Christ leaving an image on the glass. Specific rootings of these general accounts became local legends, as illustrated by the version from Carrollton, Alabama, about a black prisoner whose face was allegedly engraved by lightning onto a window while he awaited trial in 1878 for burning a courthouse. The name of the prisoner, the date, and the facts of his crime are matters of record, but the oral legend developed numerous variations of detail as it circulated in and around Carrollton, and the lightning-image motif appeared in local legends in other regions, eventually fading away in the late 1880s as photography became less of a novelty and as flexible films were introduced to replace glass plates.

Sometimes stories that seem to be reliable accounts of local incidents, even being carried by newspapers, have legendary plots with a long history in tradition. A good example is the urban legend about a child nearly abducted or actually mutilated or killed by a group of assailants in the restroom of a department store or shopping center. The earliest known version of the story circulated in Rome in the second and third centuries A.D., claiming that the Christians were ceremonially murdering non-Christian children in their initiation rites. (Possibly the legend grew from misunderstanding the nature of the Holy Eucharist in Christian belief and practice.) By the fifth century there is evidence of a revision of the story: in Syria, it was said, a group of Jews had tortured and murdered a Christian child in mockery of Christ. This accusation against the Jews in the form of legend ("The Blood Libel") was common in the Middle Ages, and it has been revived frequently ever since. The British-American traditional ballad "Little Sir Hugh" is one variant, and Chaucer's "Prioress's Tale" is another. In Nazi Germany it was a common piece of anti-Semitic propaganda, and by 1933 it had turned up in American hate literature. In the 1960s the plot took a new twist as the urban legend in which an assault upon a white child was attributed either to blacks, homosexuals, or Hispanics. Reports of the story, often detailed as to supposed time, place, and result, are circulated by print and word of mouth; they serve to reinforce prejudice and encourage persecution of the falsely accused minority group.

Local place-name etymologies (mentioned in chapter 4) often have their parallels and close variants in other places. Numerous puzzling town names, for example, are explained as being made up on the basis of early settlers' initials, or as coming from some final act of desperation like pointing out a name from a map of Europe while blindfolded or taking a name from the side of a provisions box. Also, folk etymologies often disagree about the origin of the same name. One version may try to make sense out of the name spelled backward, while another maintains that United States Post Office officials either misread the handwritten name that townspeople submitted or made an error while taking it down.

Several of these processes are illustrated in Idaho place-name stories collected by students. *Emida* is said to be derived from the names of three early settlers, East, Miller, and Dawson; but other informants point out that "It's 'a dime' spelled backwards, and that's about what it's worth!" *Moscow* is usually associated with the Russian capital, leading to the mistaken notion that many Russians settled that part of Idaho, but sometimes stories are developed around phrases such as "Ma's cow" or "the moss cow." *Tensed*, Idaho, is near the old Desmet mission, named for its founding father; one folk etymology maintains that spelling the mission name backward for the village name was not acceptable to the Post Office, so officials in Washington changed the "m" to "n" on their own. Other people say that a telegraph operator or a writer mistook the letter while sending the name in for registry. Stories like these abound in every region, and the collector can usually assume that hardly any oral explanation for a place-name will actually convey historical truth.

Striking geographical features are frequently the subjects of local legends. The readiness of the American public to believe the hundreds of phony "Indian" Lover's Leap legends is just a sentimental fancy, but it does point up the folklore-attracting qualities of dramatic geography. (See chapter 8, Focus: Lover's Leaps.) Scores of deep, dark, cold lakes are supposed to be bottomless, and a number of them are also said to have monsters lurking in them. Some lakes have underground connections with other lakes, complete with currents strong enough to pull a drowned person from one to the other. Most large caves were robber hideouts and have treasure stashed away inside somewhere, or else someone was trapped there once and starved to death before rescuers arrived. Western deserts contain hidden oases, known to early explorers but never found since. Mountain ranges are sprinkled liberally with "lost mines" or, in California and the Southwest, with lost Spanish missions crammed with treasure. Several American cities are honeycombed underground by secret tunnels used to smuggle slaves and other fugitives to safety.

Outstanding human-made features like bridges, railroad and highway tunnels, dams, and precipitous mountain highways acquire legendary lore about such things as their designers' methods ("His six-year-old son really drew the original plans") or accidents during construction ("There's a workman's body inside that concrete!"). The "haunted house" tradition, which includes many other kinds of buildings besides houses, is a good example of a migratory supernatural motif that becomes localized in regional legends; another is "The Graveyard Wager" (Motif N384.2., "Death in the graveyard;

person's clothing is caught"; Tale Type 1676B, "Clothing caught in graveyard"), which is generally told about a specific local cemetery. In the vicinities of mental institutions, legends often circulate concerning maniac escapees who were never recaptured but who still live as wild men in a woods or swamp.

Local historical legends have not been collected extensively in the United States, although American folk ballads based on historical events have long interested scholars. Such occurrences as lynchings, feuds, sensational crimes, scandals, fires and other natural disasters, Indian massacres, and labor disputes have generated legends that become formularized in characteristic ways as they pass in oral tradition and that eventually accumulate supernatural and other motifs. Probably because of their preoccupation with other forms of folklore or because such legends may seem to be simply garbled local history of little value, few collectors have awarded them the attention that, for example, Dorson did in the Upper Peninsula of Michigan with "The Lynching of the McDonald Boys" and "How Crystal Falls Stole the Courthouse from Iron River," or that William Ivey did in the same region with "The 1913 Disaster," a legend from the community of Calumet. Countless other legends based on local history could be collected and studied elsewhere.

Cycles of national legends tend to cluster around the most dramatic events in the country's history. Thus, in Norway for example, the most numerous historical legends are about the miracles of Saint Olaf, the medieval Great Plagues, the wars with Sweden, and the Nazi occupation. In the United States, legend cycles have developed about the settlement of the frontier, the Revolution, the Civil War (particularly in the South), the Indian wars, and all subsequent American military engagements, up to and including Vietnam and the Persian Gulf War.

BIBLIOGRAPHIC NOTES

For the analysis of legends, a basic survey is Wayland D. Hand's "Status of European and American Legend Study," CA 6 (1965): 439–46. Fourteen important papers from a conference on legends were edited by Hand as American Folk Legend: A Symposium (Berkeley and Los Angeles: University of California Press, 1971). Richard M. Dorson gathered American legends in a historical context in his anthology America in Legend: Folklore from the Colonial Period to the Present (New York: Pantheon Books, 1973). The quotation in this chapter from Timothy R. Tangherlini is from his article " 'It Happened Not Too Far From Here . . .': A Survey of Legend Theory and Characterization," WF 49 (1990): 371–90.

Reidar Th. Christensen proposed a list of international legend types and cataloged the Norwegian variants in his work "The Migratory Legends," FFC no. 175 (1958). Another important classification of widespread legends is Barbara Allen Woods's The Devil in Dog Form: A Partial Type-Index of Devil Legends, University of California Folklore Studies no. 11 (Berkeley, 1959). Wayland D. Hand surveyed "European Fairy Lore in the New World" in Folklore 92 (1981): 141–48, including such specific creatures as the leprechauns and such generalized forms as the "tooth fairy." A specific European story that appears as both folktale and legend is studied in terms of its special American adaptations in Butler H. Waugh's "The Child and the Snake in North America," Norveg 7 (1960): 153–82.

Frederic C. Tubach's "Index Exemplorum: A Handbook of Medieval Religious Tales," FFC no. 204 (1969), is a basic reference work on religious legends and tales with some fifty-four hundred examples identified in thirty-seven central collections. White Magic: An Introduction to the Folklore of Christian Legend (Cambridge, Mass.: Harvard University Press, 1948), by C. Grant Loomis, is a good folkloristic discussion of saints' legends; Loomis also wrote on "Legend and Folklore" in CFQ 2 (1943): 279–97. A Jewish-American folk group is studied largely in terms of its legendry in Jerome R. Mintz's Legends of the Hasidim (Chicago: University of Chicago Press, 1968). An international religious-legend complex is traced in George K. Anderson's The Legend of the Wandering Jew (Providence, R.I.: Brown University Press, 1965). A distinctly American religious-legend cycle is the subject of such studies as Hector Lee's The Three Nephites: The Substance and Significance of the Legend in Folklore, University of New Mexico Publications in Language and Literature no. 2 (Albuquerque, 1949), and William A. Wilson's "Mormon Legends of the Three Nephites Collected at Indiana University," IF 2 (1969): 3–35. F. L. Utley's "The Bible of the Folk" appeared in CFQ 4 (1945): 1–17.

Louis C. Jones analyzed "The Ghosts of New York" in JAF 57 (1944): 237–54. Rosalie Hankey did the same for California ghosts in CFQ 1 (1942): 155–77. Jones's anthology Things That Go Bump in the Night (New York: Hill and Wang, 1959) presents ghost beliefs and legends from New York. Two other anthologies of ghost stories from individual states are Ruth Ann Musick's The Telltale Lilac Bush and Other West Virginia Ghost Tales (Lexington: University of Kentucky Press, 1965) and William Lynwood Montell's Ghosts along the Cumberland: Deathlore in *the Kentucky Foothills* (Knoxville: University of Tennessee Press, 1975). A good collection of Canadian ghost legends is Helen Creighton's *Bluenose Ghosts* (Toronto: Ryerson Press, 1957). Ghost stories told by juveniles held in correctional facilities are found in Bess Lomax Hawes's "La Llorona in Juvenile Hall," *WF* 27 (1968): 153–70, and Craig Soland's two-part article "Ghost Stories from Cottage II," *AFFWord* 3 (July 1973): 1–24; 3 (January 1974): 1–33. A good survey of scholarship on the famous "weeping woman" legend of Hispanic Americans is Shirley L. Arora's "La Llorona: The Naturalization of a Legend," *SWF* 5 (1981): 23–40.

Roger E. Mitchell studies a woodsman alleged to have sold his soul to the Devil in *George Knox: From Man to Legend*, no. 11 of *NEF* (1969). In a related vein, Christine Goldberg compiled a catalog of "Traditional American Witch Legends" in *IF* 7 (1974): 77–108. William E. Lightfoot, in "Witchcraft Memorates from Eastern Kentucky," *IF* 11 (1978): 47–62, reports examples of all eight story types listed by Goldberg in 1974. Examining thirteen West Virginia witchcraft stories, Yvonne J. Milspaw shows how women called "witches" could use their supposed powers to manipulate people and gain certain benefits; see "Witchcraft in Appalachia: Protection for the Poor," *IF* 11 (1978): 71–86. (Further references to witchcraft beliefs are cited in the bibliographic notes to chapter 14.)

For modern cycles of supernatural legends see Thomas E. Bullard, "UFO Abduction Reports: The Supernatural Kidnap Narrative Returns in Technological Guise," *JAF* 102 (1989): 147–70, and Peter M. Rojcewicz, "The 'Men in Black' Experience and Tradition: Analogues with the Traditional Devil Hypothesis," *JAF* 100 (1987): 148–60. Carl Lindahl investigates belief in legends, both traditional and modern ones, in "Psychic Ambiguity at the Legend Core," *JFR* 23 (1986): 1–21.

An analysis of the formation of legendary narratives is Lauri Honko, "Memorates and the Study of Folk Beliefs," *JFI* 1 (1964): 5–19, which should be supplemented by Linda Dégh and Andrew Vázsonyi's article "The Memorate and the Proto-Memorate," *JAF* 87 (1974): 225–39. Patrick B. Mullen made two important contributions to the study of legend forms: "The Relationship of Legend and Folk Belief," *JAF* 84 (1971): 406–13, and "Modern Legend and Rumor Theory," *JFI* 9 (1972): 95–109. On rumor itself, see Tomotsu Shibutani, *Improvised News: A Sociological Study of Rumor* (Indianapolis: Bobbs-Merrill, 1966), and Ralph C. Rosnow and Gary Alan Fine, *Rumor and Gossip: The Social Psychology of Hearsay* (New York: Elsevier, 1976), both with good case studies and bibliographies. Joe Graham's "The Caso: An Emic Genre of Folk Narrative," in *"And Other Neighborly Names,"* ed. Richard Bauman and Roger D. Abrahams (Austin: University of Texas Press, 1981), pp. 11–43, shows how certain personal-experience stories told by Hispanic Americans are used to illustrate that "this kind of thing [often a supernatural event] happens."

Roger E. Mitchell studied folk and mass-cultural aspects of the accounts of the dreadful deeds of Wisconsinite Ed Gein (arrested in 1957 for murder, cannibalism, and other crimes) in "The Press, Rumor, and Legend Formation," *MJLF* 5, nos. 1–2 (1979). Other studies of legend formation are Helen Gilbert's "The Crack in the Abbey Floor: A Laboratory Analysis of a Legend," *IF* 8 (1975): 61–78; James Wise's "Tugging on Superman's Cape: The Making of a College Legend," *WF*

36 (1977): 227–38; and Bill Ellis's " 'Ralph and Rudy': The Audience's Role in Recreating a Camp Legend," WF 41 (1982): 169–91. For the use of rumor and legend to control black slaves, see Gladys-Marie Fry, Night Riders in Black Folk History (Knoxville: University of Tennessee Press, 1975).

The journal Indiana Folklore began with a volume devoted to studies of current legends (1 [1968]: 9–109); this interest continued with regular publication of such articles as John M. Vlach's "One Black Eye and Other Horrors: A Case for the Humorous Anti-Legend," IF 4 (1971): 95–140. Other studies of the legendary lore of American adolescents are Gary Alan Fine and Bruce Noel Johnson, "The Promiscuous Cheerleaders: An Adolescent Male Belief Legend," WF 39 (1980): 120–29, and Charlie Seemann, "The 'Char-Man': A Local Legend of the Ojai Valley," WF 40 (1981): 252–60.

The sizable scholarly and popular literature on urban legends is cited and sampled in five books of mine that also include comparative and historical notes plus a modicum of interpretation: see The Vanishing Hitchhiker: American Urban Legends and Their Meanings (New York: Norton, 1981), The Choking Doberman and Other "New" Urban Legends (New York: Norton, 1984), The Mexican Pet: More "New" Urban Legends and Some Old Favorites (New York: Norton, 1986), Curses! Broiled Again!: The Hottest Urban Legends Going (New York: Norton, 1989), and The Baby Train and Other Lusty Urban Legends (New York: Norton, 1993). Formed in 1988, the International Society for Contemporary Legend Research (ISCLR) holds an annual meeting and publishes a newsletter called FOAFTale News and a yearbook called Contemporary Legend (1991–). The ISCLR-sponsored Contemporary Legend: A Folklore Bibliography, Gillian Bennett and Paul Smith, eds. (New York: Garland, 1993), contains 1116 entries.

Introducing the topic of people's acting out of legend plots was Linda Dégh and Andrew Vázsonyi's "Does the Word 'Dog' Bite? Ostensive Action: A Means of Legend-Telling," JFR 20 (1983): 5–34. Bill Ellis edited a special issue of WF (49:1 [1990]) on "Contemporary Legends in Emergence," with seven papers from an American Folklore Society session. Among many other important articles of his, see also Ellis's " 'The Hook' Reconsidered: Problems in Classifying and Interpreting Adolescent Horror Legends," Folklore 105 (1994): 61–75. Significant book-length studies are Patricia A. Turner's I Heard It Through the Grapevine: Rumor in African-American Culture (Berkeley: University of California Press, 1993) and Gary Alan Fine's Manufacturing Tales: Sex and Money in Contemporary Legends (Knoxville: University of Tennessee Press, 1992). On urban legends inspired by recent disasters, see Elizabeth Simpson, "Mount St. Helens and the Evolution of Folklore," NWF 4 (1985): 43–47, and Regina Bendix, "Reflections on Earthquake Narratives," WF 49 (1990): 331–47.

Hero legends of European traditional literature are surveyed in Jan deVries's Heroic Song and Heroic Legend (paperback ed., London and New York: Oxford, 1963). The authentic versus the ersatz aspects of American heroic legendry have been discussed thoroughly in many publications, which are referred to in Dorson's American Folklore, pp. 199–243. The basic story of Paul Bunyan's origins is detailed in Daniel G. Hoffman's study Paul Bunyan, Last of the Frontier Demigods (Philadelphia: University of Pennsylvania Press, 1952; reissued by Columbia University Press, 1966, and repr. as a University of Nebraska Press paperback in 1983 with some updating and added illustrations). Howard W. Marshall documents the invention of a farmer's hero on the Paul Bunyan model in "The Heroic Urge in Kansas: The Creation of Johnny Kaw," *AFFWord* 1 (Oct. 1971): 11–21.

William Hugh Jansen's classic study of a Münchausen figure in America was reprinted from the original doctoral dissertation as *Abraham "Oregon" Smith: Pioneer, Folk Hero, and Tale-Teller* (New York: Arno, 1977). An article of mine describes a local liar, "Len Henry: North Idaho Münchausen," *NWF* 1 (1965): 11–19. Roger D. Abrahams surveys "Some Varieties of Heroes in America" in *JFI* 3 (1966): 343–62, and Michael Owen Jones suggests a formula for the development of a heroic figure, using it as his title: "(PC + CB) × SD (R + I + E) = Hero," *NYFQ* 27 (1971): 243–60. Bruce A. Rosenberg views the mythologizing of a character in history in his *Custer and the Epic of Defeat* (University Park: Pennsylvania State University Press, 1974). William E. Lightfoot investigates a modern hipster hero in "Charlie Parker: A Contemporary Folk Hero," *KFQ* 17 (1972): 51–62. A fine study of a notorious killer as something of a folk hero (or rather folk heroine) is Janet L. Langlois's *Belle Gunness: The Lady Bluebeard* (Bloomington: Indiana University Press, 1985). For a Northeast poacher as a folk hero, with revealing analysis of the hero-making process, see Edward D. Ives, *George Magoon and the Down East Game War: History, Folklore, and the Law* (Urbana: University of Illinois Press, 1993).

An excellent collection of American local legends that are fully representative of the genuine oral lore of their vicinity is Ronald L. Baker's *Hoosier Folk Legends* (Bloomington: Indiana University Press, 1982), which ranges from traditional supernatural stories, place-name legends, and the like to modern legends and even UFO stories. Another good regional collection of legends is volume 3 in the *Publications of the Texas Folklore Society*, ed. J. Frank Dobie, *Legends of Texas* (1924; repr. 1964). Ronald L. Baker discusses "The Role of Folk Legends in Place-Name Research" in *JAF* 85 (1972): 367–73. Richard M. Dorson's *Bloodstoppers and Bearwalkers* (Cambridge, Mass.: Harvard University Press, 1952; repr. in paperback, 1972) contains personal and local legends from the Upper Peninsula of Michigan: "sagamen" are discussed on pp. 249–72.

Family legends are studied by Kim S. Garrett in "Family Stories and Sayings," *PTFS* 30 (1961): 273–81; Mody Boatright in the title essay of *The Family Saga and Other Phases of American Folklore* (Urbana: University of Illinois Press, 1958), pp. 1–19; Patrick B. Mullen, "Folk Songs and Family Traditions," *PTFS* 37 (1972): 49–63; and Stanley H. Brandes, "Family Misfortune Stories in American Folklore," *JFI* 12 (1975): 5–17. Two studies focus on a specific genre of family story: Steven J. Zeitlin's " 'An Alchemy of Mind': The Family Courtship Story," *WF* 39 (1980): 17–33; and Patrick B. Mullen's "Two Courtship Stories from the Blue Ridge Mountains," *FFV* 2 (1980–81): 25–37. In "Did Great Grandpa Wood Really Talk about Tits in Church?" *SWF* 3 (1979): 29–35, Gordon S. Wood, Jr., examines a family anecdote about his ancestor and discovers it to be a well-traveled story, originally from Europe. (Other family-folklore references are given in the bibliographic notes to chapter 3, and family reunions are mentioned briefly, with one citation, in chapter 15.)

Personal-experience narratives were examined as a folklore form in a special double issue of *JFI* (vol. 14, nos. 1–2 [1977]); "The Personal Narrative in Literature" was discussed in a special issue of *WF* (vol. 5, no. 1 [1992]). Basic to the study of such stories is Sandra K. Dolby-Stahl's article "The Oral Personal Narrative in Its Generic Context," *Fabula* 18 (1977): 18–39, plus several other articles of hers and especially her book *Literary Folkloristics and the Personal Narrative* (Bloomington: Indiana University Press, 1989). Roger D. Abrahams discussed how "we represent, report, or replay" activities in "The Most Embarrassing Thing That Ever Happened: Conversational Stories in a Theory of Enactment," *FF* 10 (1977): 9–15. Yet another subcategory of the personal-experience story is featured in Eleanor Wachs's *Crime Victim Stories: New York City's Urban Folklore* (Bloomington: Indiana University Press, 1988); some related material was included in James P. Leary's "Fists and Foul Mouths: Fights and Fight Stories in Contemporary Rural American Bars," *JAF* 89 (1976): 27–39. Further theoretical insights are contained in Barbara Allen's "Personal Experience Narratives: Use and Meaning in Interaction," *FMS* 2 (1978): 5–7; and William M. Clements's "Personal Narrative, the Interview Context, and the Question of Tradition," *WF* 39 (1980): 106–12. In "The Life Story," *JAF* 93 (1980): 276–92, Jeff Todd Titon distinguishes the life history (a record of events presumed accurate) and the more fictitious life story (which focuses on personality and dramatic events). A related study is Elliott Oring's "Generating Lives: The Construction of an Autobiography," *JFR* 24 (1987): 241–62.

The Anatomy of the Anecdote (Chicago: University of Chicago Press, 1960), by Louis Brownlow, journalist, public servant, and educator, contains an informative discussion of the form and some good examples from the author's rich repertoire of family and political stories; the book was edited from tape-recorded talks by Brownlow. "Professor Einstein and the Chorus Girl" was traced by Jerah Johnson in *JAF* 73 (1960): 248–49. Sousa-name anecdotes were discussed by several correspondents, including Sousa's daughter, Helen Sousa Abert, in the "Letters to the Editor" columns of *Popular Mechanics* in July 1959. Other studies primarily of anecdotes are Wendy D. Caesar's "'Asking a Mouse Who His Favorite Cat Is': Musicians' Stories about Conductors," *WF* 84 (1975): 83–116; Henry E. Anderson's "The Folklore of Draft Resistance," *NYFQ* 28 (1971): 135–50; and Harry Joe Jaffe's "The Welfare Letter," *WF* 34 (1975): 144–48. Sandra K. D. Stahl provides an illuminating discussion in "The Local Character Anecdote," *Genre* 8 (1975): 283–302. Examples from a Canadian region are discussed in Diane Tye, "Local Character Anecdotes: A Nova Scotia Case Study," *WF* 48 (1989): 181–99. In "The Migratory Anecdote and the Folk Concept of Fame," *MSF* 4 (1976): 39–47, reprinted in *Readings in American Folklore*, pp. 279–88, Mac E. Barrick examines the human subjects of favorite anecdotes and concludes that they were often eccentric characters in real life, as well as being close to a "folk mentality" (like Lincoln, Truman, Davy Crockett, and so forth).

Legends about animals or about people who deal with animals are the subjects of three studies: David L. Wilson, "The Legend of the Pacing White Stallion," *Folklore* 90 (1979): 153–66; John W. Roberts, "Folklore of the Precocious Canine: Jim the Wonder Dog," *MFSJ* 3 (1981): 59–70; and Roger L. Welsch, *Mister, You Got Yourself a Horse: Tales of Old-Time Horse Trading* (Lincoln: University of Nebraska Press, 1981).

A general survey of "Comic Indian Anecdotes" by Richard M. Dorson appeared in *SFQ* 10 (1946): 113–28 (repr. in *Folklore and Fakelore*, pp. 269–82); see also Rayna D. Green, "Traits of Indian Character: The 'Indian' Anecdote in American Vernacular Tradition," *SFQ* 39 (1975): 233–62. The "Me All Face" story was traced in a note by Cecily Hancock in *JAF* 76 (1963): 340–42, and the "Membra Disjuncta" story was the subject of a note by Austin E. Fife in *WF* 22 (1963): 121–22. Colorado characters were treated in Levette J. Davidson's " 'Gassy' Thompson—and Others: Stories of Local Characters," *CFQ* 5 (1946): 339–49. Anecdotes about a Utah Mormon local character are collected in Thomas E. Cheney's *The Golden Legacy: A Folk History of J. Golden Kimball* (Salt Lake City: Peregrine Smith, 1974); see also William A. Wilson, "Trickster Tales and the Location of Cultural Boundaries: A Mormon Example," *JFR* 20 (1983): 55–66. Francis Haines published his study "Goldilocks on the Oregon Trail" in *IY* 9 (Winter 1965–66): 26–30.

Dorson collected New England local legends of Indian tragedies, haunts, buried treasure, and place-names in *Jonathan Draws the Long Bow* (Cambridge, Mass.: Harvard University Press, 1946), pp. 138–98. The Upper Peninsula historical legends appeared in Dorson's *Bloodstoppers and Bearwalkers*. See also William Ivey's " 'The 1913 Disaster': Michigan Local Legend," *FF* 3 (1970): 100–14. For a study linking an early American legend to classical prototypes, see Adrienne Mayor, "The Nessus Shirt in the New World: Smallpox Blankets in History and Legend," *JAF* 108 (1995): 54–77. "The Man Who Plucked the Gorbey" was studied by Edward D. Ives in *JAF* 74 (1961): 1–8. Barbara Allen's "The 'Image on Glass': Technology, Tradition, and the Emergence of Folklore" appeared in *WF* 41 (1982): 85–103. Other articles on local legends include Gerard T. Hurley's "Buried Treasure Tales in America," *WF* 10 (1951): 197–216; Patrick B. Mullen, "The Folk Idea of Unlimited Good in American Buried Treasure Legends," *JFI* 15 (1978): 209–20; Peter Gerhard's "The 'Lost Mission' of Baja California," *WF* 17 (1958): 97–106; Austin E. Fife's "The Bear Lake Monster," *UHR* 2 (1948): 99–106; Henry A. Person's "Bottomless Lakes in the Pacific Northwest," *WF* 19 (1960): 278–80; and Barre Toelken's "Traditional Water Narratives in Utah," *WF* 50 (1991): 191–200. A study of war legends collected from the Internet is Thomas E. Barden and John Provo's "Legends of the American Soldiers in the Vietnam War," *Fabula* 36 (1995): 217–29. (Entries on the legends of all past American wars are included in Jan Harold Brunvand, ed., *American Folklore: An Encyclopedia*, Reference Library of the Humanities vol. 1551 [New York: Garland, 1996].)

10

FOLKTALES

If legends are folk history, then **folktales** are the prose fiction of oral literature. Folktales are traditional narratives that are strictly fictional and told primarily for entertainment, although they may also illustrate a truth or a moral. Folktales range in length and subject matter from some European stories about fantastic wonders and magical events that take hours—even days—of narration, to brief American topical jokes with concentrated plots and snappy punch lines that are told in minutes. The term "folktale" usually connotes the complex, so-called fairy tale, familiar in children's literature. But there is no valid justification for ignoring recent tales that may have more realistic plots. Not only have these recent types of folktale replaced fairy tales in most American and many foreign oral traditions, but also, frequently these contemporary tales turn out upon investigation to have ancient parallels.

The folktales of the world, like the myths and legends, encompass a great variety of different narrative elements contained in a fairly limited array of basic forms, and both the details and the general outlines of specific folktales appear in widespread cultures and through great reaches of time. The recognition of these similarities spurred attempts in Europe in the early nineteenth century to organize comparative folktale research and to trace tales back to their origins. By the late nineteenth century a standard methodology had emerged, along with the first of several important reference publications; since analogous folktale materials and similar methods of study are found in the United States, it is appropriate to review this European background.

SOME CHARACTERISTICS OF
INDO-EUROPEAN FOLKTALES

A suitable general term for the "ordinary folktale" of broad Indo-European distribution is a basic problem, even though the characteristic style and form of such tales are easily recognized. Formularized openings and closings set off the items in this category; in English, they frequently begin with "Once upon a time" and end "They lived happily ever after." The setting is often some unnamed kingdom in a remote age; the characters usually include royalty; the structure of the tales tends to be based on threefold repetition; and some of the typical motifs are imaginary creatures (ogres, dragons, and giants), transformations, magic objects, helpful animals, and supernatural powers or knowledge. The hero in these tales is frequently a poor stepchild who rises to wealth, power, and authority through a combination of supernatural aid, good luck, and his own ingenuity and perseverance. In short, these "ordinary folktales" are the kind of stories that most people know best from reading (or being read to from) books of "fairy tales."

But "fairy tales" is a poor term for such stories, because they almost never are concerned with the "little people," or fairies, of legendary narratives. "Nursery tales" is an equally inappropriate term, since mostly adults have circulated them. "Wonder tales" is a reasonable term that has some currency among folklorists, but the German word *Märchen* is the most widely adopted scholarly term. That is the name that the Brothers Grimm used for their famous fairy-tale collection, first published in 1812, the *Kinder- und Hausmärchen*, or "Children's and Household Folktales."

As the collection of *Märchen* and other folktales spread, encouraged by nationalism, and as the study of these tales progressed, it became increasingly desirable to devise a uniform system of referring to individual tale plots. In the beginning, "catchword titles" alone were sufficient—"Cinderella," "Puss in Boots," "Jack the Giant

Killer," "Rumpelstiltzchen." In some early studies the numbers of the tales in the Grimm collection were used for reference purposes. But as large numbers of folktales were collected, serious drawbacks appeared in these systems. Titles vary greatly from country to country or even within an individual country. For instance, Cinderella is often a boy in Scandinavian tales with the nickname "Askeladden," or "the ash lad." (Cinderella sat in the cinders of the hearth, and Askeladden sat in the ashes; hence their names.) The helpful dwarf Rumpelstiltzchen is "Tom-Tit-Tot" in English folktales and has a different local name in each of the many countries from which that tale has been collected. Most tales are collected from oral tradition without titles being given to them by informants, and often several distinct tale plots are intermixed in one oral text. Obviously, the use of the Grimm numbers for classification was limited to the tale types that the Grimms had collected.

THE *TYPE-INDEX*

In Denmark, by the second half of the nineteenth century, the ballad scholar Svend Grundtvig had worked out a classification system for archiving Danish folktales for his own convenience in consulting them, but this was too narrow for general international use. However, in Finland in the late nineteenth century a folklorist devised a catalog based on most of the then-published European texts that introduced what has become the standard reference and classification system for *Märchen* and for some other kinds of European folktales as well. Kaarle Krohn, a founding father of modern folktale research, recognized the great need for an index of European folktale types when he experienced difficulties gathering from many countries variants of stories about the competition of a bear and a fox. He posed the problem to his student Antti Aarne, who undertook to solve it, producing in 1910 a catalog called *Verzeichnis der Märchentypen* (Folklore Fellows Communications no. 3), which was translated and enlarged in 1928 by the American folklorist Stith Thompson as *The Types of the Folktale* (FFC no. 74). In its second revision (FFC no. 184, 1961), the *Type-Index* is an essential tool for any collecting, archiving, or comparative analysis of Indo-European folktales throughout their present worldwide distribution.

The *Type-Index* should not be confused with the *Motif-Index*, introduced in chapter 8. The two works are cross-indexed to each other, but they are distinctly different references. The *Type-Index*, theoretically, classifies only whole plots, while the *Motif-Index* is an index of narrative elements—actions, actors, objects, settings, and the like. ("Cinderella" is Type 510A, but "Identification by fitting of slipper" is Motif H36.1., and merely one narrative element of some versions of that tale.) In reference to the scholars who developed the *Type-Index*, tales cataloged therein are frequently cited as "Aarne-Thompson" types (or simply "AT" or "AaTh" types, and sometimes in Europe "MT" for *Märchentypus*). The *Motif-Index* was Thompson's creation alone and was separately compiled; motifs are cited simply by their lettered chapters in Thompson's system, and with their individual numbers. Both indexes may be used to identify tales and their elements, to arrange archives, and to collect bibliographic references. But the *Type-Index* deals mainly with Indo-European folktales, especially *Märchen*, while the *Motif-Index* is international in scope and contains narrative elements from many kinds of texts besides folktales. There is some overlapping of the two indexes in the area of single-motif tales, which properly seem to belong in the *Type-Index*. The most important basic distinction between the two indexes is that while the designation of a "type" in the folktale catalog implies that all the items listed there are historically related, *Motif-Index* entries entail no such implication. To put it differently, one assumption in the *Type-Index* is that polygenesis of whole tales is unlikely; in the *Motif-Index* the assumption is that polygenesis does explain parallels among some individual, widely known narrative elements.

Even though it lacks many modern plots and variants of folktales, the *Type-Index* sets forth the basic kinds of tales found in Anglo-American folk tradition. This material is gathered under four major headings:

I. Animal Tales (Types 1 to 299)
II. Ordinary Folktales (Types 300 to 1199)
III. Jokes and Anecdotes (Types 1200 to 1999)
IV. Formula Tales (Types 2000 to 2399)

ANIMAL TALES AND FABLES

Animal tales have as their main characters domestic or wild animals that speak, reason, and otherwise behave like human beings. Usually these animals correspond to certain stock character types, such as the clever fox or rabbit, the stupid bear, the faithful dog, and the industrious ant. Frequently these tales describe conflicts between different animals or between animals and humans. A few animal tales are etiological—for example, Type 2, "The Tail-Fisher," which explains that the bear now has a short tail because he was once tricked by the fox into fishing through the ice with his original long one. Several of the favorite stories printed in children's books are traditional animal tales. "The Bremen Town Musicians," for example, is Type 130: "The Animals in Night Quarters"; "The Three Little Pigs" is Type 124: "Blowing the House In." Genuine oral versions of such tales, however, usually differ markedly from printed ones. For instance, in a Kentucky Mountain text of Type 124 the pigs are named "Mary, Martha, and Nancy" and they build their houses out of chips and clay, chips and hickory bark, and "steel and arn." When the wolf comes, he threatens "to get up on the house and fiddy, fiddy, faddy your house all down."

Popular published versions, at least in this country, now outnumber oral-traditional texts of animal tales, as well as of many other folktales. The best-known examples of animal tales in the United States come from Southern blacks, and these have been publicized mainly in the literary renderings of Joel Chandler Harris (the creator of "Uncle Remus") and in the cartoon treatments of Walt Disney. Both of these adaptations are somewhat removed from the actual oral specimens of such tales as Type 175, "The Tarbaby and the Rabbit," which has a wide international distribution.

Fables are sometimes regarded as a special subtype of animal tales, even though some fables have only human characters in them. A better term for fables might be *moral tales*, for their distinguishing quality is an explicit or implied lesson, often expressed as a proverbial moral to the story. Of the roughly five hundred to six hundred Greek and Indic fables known in literature, only about fifty have been collected from oral tradition. Such popular phrases as "the lion's share," "sour grapes," and "belling the cat" refer to such tales, these particular ones bearing the type numbers AT 51, 59, and 110, respectively.

Famous literary imitations of animal tales that have become children's classics should not be confused with stories in the oral tradition. Hans Christian Andersen's "The Ugly Duckling," for example, is not a folktale, although it might loosely be called a "fairy tale" in the popular or literary sense of the term. Similarly, "The Three Bears" was written by Robert Southey (1774–1843), the English poet laureate (from 1813 to 1843), probably in imitation of a folktale, and the story went through various literary revisions rather than oral changes. Parodies of "The Three Bears," however, do exist in modern folklore; in one of these, Mother Bear responds to the others' requests for their porridge, "Gripe, gripe, gripe, and I haven't even made breakfast yet!"

Joke fables (funny stories with a mock moral) and parodies of fables represent ways that the traditional folk fable adapts to the present. One such text, "The Fable of the Animal School" (often circulated as "Xeroxlore"), describes a group of animals determined "to do something heroic to meet the problems of a New World"; they decide to organize a school. The "activity curriculum" of their school includes all the means of animal movement (running, swimming, flying, etc.), but then all animals are required to take all the subjects, with the result that not one of them can master the school's demands. In the end the prairie dogs survive by fighting the tax levy because digging and burrowing are not in the curriculum, and they join the groundhogs and gophers to start a private school. The moral for modern educators is implied.

ORDINARY FOLKTALES

The **ordinary folktales** in part II of the Aarne-Thompson index include most of the *Märchen* proper, although the German term is sometimes used to refer to the entire contents of the *Type-Index*. But as Thompson writes in the preface of his last revision, "there are certainly many things in the index which are by no means *Märchen*." The "ordinary folktales," a poorly named category, constitute about one-half of the entire type catalog and include almost all of the

Märchen that are in it. Their characteristic features, as earlier stated, are formularized language and structure, supernatural motifs, and sympathy for the underdog or commoner.

All of the European immigrant groups in the United States, to some extent, carried their *Märchen* here with them, but these were seldom translated by the folk into English and thus have not usually persisted as oral tales in the second generation. The British *wonder-tale tradition*, however, with no language barrier to cross, became well established in this country, especially in the Southern Appalachian and Ozark Mountains. There, distinctive American adaptations took place, and the collected texts sometimes seem almost like native stories. Type 313, "The Girl as Helper in the Hero's Flight," became "The Devil's Pretty Daughter" in the Ozarks. In Kentucky, Type 425A, "The Monster as Bridegroom," was collected as "The Girl that Married a Flop-Eared Hound-Dog," and Type 326, "The Youth Who Wanted to Learn What Fear Is," was collected as "Johnny That Never Seen a Fraid." A North Carolina text that combines Type 330, "The Smith Outwits the Devil," and Type 332, "Godfather Death," is locally entitled "Whickety-Whack, Into My Sack." One cycle of Southern tales clustered around three brothers —Jack, Will, and Tom—with emphasis on the clever youngest one; these are known as "The Jack Tales."

Although the plots of Americanized *Märchen* may contain such unlikely motifs as royal characters, magical transportation, giants, ogres, and even unicorns, the language of the tellings is full of regional dialect. In her telling of "Jack and the Drill" for the Library of Congress, for example, Mrs. Maude Long of Hot Springs, North Carolina, used many local expressions, such as "bedads" (an exclamation), "bless me," "lit out," and "I reckon." She introduced such Southern terms as "ash cake" (bread baked directly in fireplace ashes) and "poke" (for a bag or sack). (Terms like "riddle," for a sieve, and "house plunder," for the necessities of housekeeping, are freely introduced in other mountain variants of *Märchen*.) As in the European versions of *Märchen*, the home life of royalty is described in very folksy terms: the hero may go down to "the king's house" and "holler him out"; and when the king summons the women in his family, in Mrs. Long's version, he calls out, "Hey old woman and girls! Come on over here."

FOCUS: KIND AND UNKIND

The Story of Salt and Pepper

Once upon a time there was a girl and a boy named Salt and Pepper. Their mother was really sick, and she asked Pepper to get her a drink out of the well. But he was a naughty boy and never did anything he was told to do, so he said "No." So she asked Salt, "Will you get me some water?" She was the best little girl, and she said, "Yes, Mother, I'd be glad to." So she went to the well, and as she went to get water she fell down and hit the bottom with a thump! She looked around, and all she could see was a glass door, so she went in.

It was like a glass department store inside with glass clothes and glass toys and glass floors. She saw another door that led to a street, so she went out. The cobblestones were made of gold, and the horses were all green. She decided that to get back to her mother she would have to get a job, so she started looking.

She knocked on one door, and a mean old lady came to the door. "What do you want?" she said. "I'm looking for work to get back home," but the lady slammed the door. So she went to the second house, and a tall man answered the door. He told her that he hated little girls. Then she went to the third house, knocked, and a nice lady answered the door. "I'm looking for work," said Salt, "and I can't find any." The nice lady said, "Well, I've been looking for somebody to help me, so you are just the one. Come in."

She gave Salt a bucket, a broom, and a rag. "Now, I'm going to the store, and I want this room spic-and-span when I come back." So Salt washed the walls until they shined, swept the floor, and cleaned the windows until they sparkled. She was just finishing when the lady came back, and she said, "Oh, what a beautiful job! Thank you so much," and she took Salt into the next room and brought in three boxes, a big one, a medium-sized one, and a small one. "Because you did such a good job, you may pick one box, but you must promise not to open it until you get home."

Salt promised and chose the small box. Then the woman told her to go to the bottom of the well, close her eyes, put her thumb by the side of her nose and say three times "I want to go home." She did as she was told, and when she opened her eyes she was standing beside the well with her box. And when she got home with it, she opened the box and it was filled with jewels. She ran to her mother and said, "Now the doctor can make you better!"

[Summary: Pepper then jumped down the well, went to the third house for work, did a poor job of cleaning, chose the largest box, and when he opened it a big mud ball hit him in the middle of his forehead, and a black-widow spider climbed out on his hand. The box was filled with snakes and bugs, and it smelled to high heaven.]

Source: Told by a fourteen-year-old girl in Salt Lake City in 1971; she learned it from her mother, who may have read published versions of this old European folktale.

DISCUSSION TOPICS:

1. This is Tale Type 480, a *Märchen* (fairy tale) variously titled "The Spinning Women by the Spring," "The Kind and Unkind Girls," or, with reference to the Grimm version, "Frau Holle." Use the Thompson and Baughman indexes to gather other versions of this story, both European and American, and compare their details (start of the journey, tasks, etc.).

2. Compare the traditional motifs in Type 480: unsuccessful repetition, impossible tasks, kindness rewarded, etc. In what other folktales do these motifs appear?

3. Besides the obvious lessons that kindness is rewarded and the modest choice may be the better one, variations of Type 480 set up oppositions that suggest further meanings. Examine these, including male versus female, black versus white, beauty versus ugliness, and home versus away. Also note the nature of the tasks assigned, generally being things related to needs of survival (food or shelter) or demands of civilization (kindess, order, cleanliness, etc.).

Like animal tales, parodies of *Märchen* circulate among sophisticated modern folk, who base them on book versions. For example, in a parody of Type 440, "The Frog King" (the first tale in the Grimm collection), set in a college dorm room, a woman says to the prince who has been transformed from a frog, "What is my housemother going to say?" Another form of "fractured fairy tale" found in modern tradition involves substituting soundalike words for every word of the familiar old story. For example, "Ladle Rat Rotten Hut" (Little Red Riding Hood) begins "Wants pawn term, dare worsted ladle gull hoe lift wetter murder inner ladle cordage honor itch offer lodge dock florist" (Once upon a time there was a little girl who lived with her mother in a little cottage on the edge of a large dark forest). As a tradition that requires writing for its transmission, this kind of parody belongs in the category of "Xeroxlore" as well.

JOKES AND ANECDOTES

The **jokes and anecdotes** section of the *Type-Index* also has a mis-leading title: no real difference between the two categories is estab-lished, and, as we have seen, the term "anecdotes" is usually applied to a subclass of personal legends. Simply "jokes" seems the best term for short, funny, fictional folktales, but only a few of the countless jokes told in modern tradition are included in the *Index*. This section of the *Index* is essentially a classification of the older European *jests*, or *merry tales*—humorous stories characterized by short, fairly sim-ple plots and by realistic settings. Some typical characters in the older jests were numskulls, married couples, and parsons; stories found in the *Type-Index* about such character types are still popular in the United States.

Numskull jokes (also called "noodle tales"), attribute absurd igno-rance to people, often to a particular group. In Denmark, for ex-ample, the traditional fools are the *Molbos*; in England they are the "Wise Men of Gotham," and in the United States they may be two Irishmen named "Pat and Mike." Some old favorite examples that have been collected frequently in this country are Type 1240, "Man Sitting on Branch of Tree Cuts It Off"; Type 1278, "Marking the Place on the Boat [Where an Object was Lost Overboard]"; and Type 1319, "Pumpkin Sold as Ass's Egg."

Many of the fad jokes of the twentieth century (moron jokes, Polish jokes, lightbulb jokes, etc.) contained numskull motifs, but in common with the many other fad jokes (elephant jokes, sick jokes, fruit jokes, etc.) they are really not narratives but question-and-answer routines (see the discussion of "riddle-jokes" in chapter 6).

The theme of stupidity manifests itself in many parallel jokes that are adapted to different groups. For instance, there is an airliner updating of the following characterization of how employees tell the time on four different divisions of the Illinois Central Railway:

Iowa Division: "Fifteen hundred."
Illinois Division: "Three o'clock."
Kentucky Division: "The big hand's on the twelve and the little hand's on the three."
Mississippi Division: "It's Tuesday."

In the airline version (in which the names change as airlines go out of business or merge with other companies) the pilots reply similarly to the question:

Pan American (or TWA): "Fifteen hundred."
United (or American): "Three o'clock."
Texas International: "The big hand's on the twelve . . ."

Stories about married couples, the next section of "Jokes and Anecdotes" in the *Index*, frequently deal with competition between husbands and their wives. For example, in Type 1351, "The Silence Wager," a husband and his wife become so angry that they refuse to speak to one another, even during a grave crisis. In Type 1365A, "Wife Falls into a Stream," the obstinate wife drowns, and her husband looks for the body upstream where he believes she would have drifted against the current. In a subtype of that tale the husband and wife had been arguing about whether to cut something with a knife or with scissors; the husband throws his wife into the stream, and as she drowns, she lifts her fingers out of the water and makes a clipping motion in order to have the last word in the dispute.

Jokes about parsons and religious orders make fools of the clergy. In Type 1791, "The Sexton Carries the Parson," one of the most popular anticlerical tales brought to the United States, thieves are overheard dividing their loot in a graveyard, and the two foolish listeners believe it is the Devil and the Lord dividing souls. In American versions, however, the listeners are not always specified as members of the clergy. In Type 1833, "The Boy Applies the Sermon," a parson's rhetorical question in a sermon receives a literal and absurd answer from someone in the congregation. For example, an American version has this dialogue:

Parson: "How shall we get to heaven?"
Baseball Player (just waking up): "Slide!"

Only a fraction of the oral jokes in American folk tradition are included in the Aarne-Thompson *Type-Index*. A few of them can be identified using Thompson's motif numbers, but the majority have not been entered in any catalog. Some may be original American

jests, but most of them probably have foreign parallels or counterparts. The full histories of these stories cannot be written until workable reference systems are published. Thus, the indexing of jokes is
a major future task for American folktale scholars, essential for further analysis. However, not even the basic framework for a classification has been developed. One possibility, employed in some
college archives, is to arrange texts according to their general subjects
under such headings as "Jokes about Religions," "Jokes about Nationalities," "Jokes about Sex." Another system is to group stories
according to stock character types: "Jokes about Hillbillies," "Jokes
about Musicians," "Jokes about Traveling Salesmen," "Jokes about
Politicians." The difficulty with such plans is obvious: many jokes
will fit several categories—for instance, a sexy joke about a hillbilly,
or a joke about an Irish politician. Some kind of plot-structure index
would seem to be the best option.

The *immigrant dialect story* has been identified as a distinctive
American folk creation, and it may be grouped by nationalities or
languages. The humorous point of such jokes is the immigrant's
broken English and resulting mistakes in using the language. The
impetus for their circulation is not necessarily prejudice, for immigrants themselves are the best raconteurs, but generally a humorous
reference is made to some of the group's problems in acculturation.
Some dialect stories reproduce the actual linguistic quirks of a nationality group, such as the "l"-"r" confusion among Japanese speaking English. Other tales adhere to different groups, as does the story
of the newly wealthy immigrant who orders a home built containing
a "Halo Statue." He finally explains, "You know. It rings; you pick
it up; you say, 'Halo, statue?'"

The consistent nature of immigrants' problems with the English
language, and the reworking of standard plot material in dialect
stories about different languages, is illustrated by two versions of the
same story from widely separated groups. In each joke the immigrant storytellers themselves display an awareness of the foolishness
of some of their own language problems and solutions. The first
example was told by a Norwegian settler in Alberta, Canada. The
story concerns an old Norwegian woman who is trying to buy some
matches in a store run by an Anglo-Canadian. Not knowing the
word "matches," she pantomimes striking a match, lighting an invisible pipe, and holding up the burning match. "Oh," says the store-

keeper, in fluent Norwegian, *"er det fyrestykker du vil ha?"* ("is it matches you want?"). The woman answers, astonished, *"Nei kan du snakke Norske? Og her staar jeg og snakker Engelsk!"* ("No, do you speak Norwegian? And here I stand speaking English!"). In a Mexican-American version of this joke, from Texas, as reported by Rosan A. Jordan (see the bibliographic notes to this chapter), two men speak to one another using English-accented Spanish until they discover that they are both Mexicans. "Then why are we speaking English?" they ask. Likely, the "speaking English" immigrant dialect story exists among other groups as well.

The *Jewish-American dialect story* is a particularly interesting subtype, since it humorously crystallizes the esoteric and exoteric attitudes of Jews and gentiles toward themselves and each other (and also attitudes toward the others' attitudes toward themselves), adding the dialect flavoring of an exaggerated form of Yiddish-American speech. The best informants, usually American-born offspring of European Jewish immigrants, become masters of the nasalized accent, stylized gesture, and dramatic role-playing typical of the form. The Jewish-American businessman in a joke asks the headmaster of Eton College, "Mine Jake, he's speaking de King's English now?" Then the narrator assumes the part of the headmaster to deliver the punch line. He hunches his shoulders, spreads his upturned palms wide, and says, "Netchally, vat else?"

FOCUS: THE J.A.M. (JEWISH-AMERICAN MOTHER) JOKE

The J.A.M. is such a stock character that she is virtually interchangeable within her cohort. Any Jewish Mother can serve in a crisis. This is beautifully illustrated in the following "big city" joke:
The telephone rings and the daughter answers.
"Hello?"
"How are you?" says the mother.
"Oh terrible, terrible."
"What's the matter?"
"The baby's sick, and the maid called in today, Ma, and she's not coming, and the place is a mess. There's nothing in the refrigerator and we're having company tonight for dinner. I'm supposed to go to the Hadassah meeting. I don't know what to do!"
"Don't worry. What's a mother for? I got plenty time. I've made gefilte fish; I've got a couple of chickens; I can bring them. I'll be right over.

I'll clean your apartment; I'll wait for the doctor to come over. You go to your Hadassah meeting, and I'll get dinner ready."

"Oh, Ma, that would be wonderful!"

"Listen, what's a mother for? Before you hang up, how's Stephen?"

"Stephen, who's Stephen?"

"What do you mean who's Stephen? He's your husband."

"My husband's name is Marvin."

(Long pause)

"Is this 841-5656?"

"No. It's 841-6565." (Pause) "Does this mean you're not coming?"

Source: Alan Dundes, "The J.A.P. and the J.A.M. in American Jokelore," *JAF* 98 (1985): 460.

DISCUSSION TOPICS:

1. What does J.A.P. refer to? Have you heard jokes based on either this stereotype or that of the J.A.M., or similar jokes based on other religious stereotypes?

2. What expression does the mother repeat, using it in almost a proverbial way?

3. What does use of the terms "Hadassah meeting" and "gefilte fish" suggest about the tellers of and audience for this joke? Why is this a "big city" joke?

4. In the article quoted above, Dundes discusses possible explanations of the Jewish-mother stereotype in such jokes. Review these, and decide which, if any, seems most plausible. How might such interpretations of modern jokelore be tested?

A study of the development of the *black dialect story* in America would yield insights into the psychology involved in the changing relationships between races. One past group of jokes, now nearly extinct, pictures the black person as a comical old darky—slow-moving, dull-witted, usually named something like Rastus or Liza, and always drawling in a thick Southern accent. (In the *protest jokes* of Southern blacks' own biracial folk humor, the same type of character—often John, the slave or hired man—manages to outsmart the white man.) Another cycle of urban white stories creates a vicious stereotype of the black as a crude, oversexed, automobile-loving maniac. The latest development was the *integration story*, in which the effects of the Civil Rights movement were directly mirrored. In these jokes white people seemed to be jolted into a belated recognition of new patterns in American life. In one such story a white librarian refused to censor books containing the word "nigger," pointing out that offensive words like "bastard" appear in books, too. The black person responds, "Yes, but us niggers is organized, and you bastards ain't." Another revealing story concerns the football coach in a Southern college who is forced to try out a black player. When the boy smashes through the team's best linemen, the coach shouts excitedly, "Will you look at that Mexican boy run!"

The whole complex of ethnic, religious, and racial folk humor in the United States deserves more investigation, but even separate studies of individual groups would not point up all the interrelationships. For example, a Jewish dialect joke concerns the Jewish person converted to Catholicism who is put upon at once by his family and friends. He grumbles, "I've only been a gentile for twenty minutes, and already I hate those Jews." The same story is told as a black dialect joke. Here a little black boy has smeared his face with flour or cold cream, and he runs home shouting, "I's white! I's white!" Criticized by his family, he declares that he already hates blacks. This theme of role shifting is also found in the integration story about a Southern black boy allowed to join a white gang. When a tire on their car has a blowout, he is the first to complain, "There's not a nigger for miles around to change it for us." The sometimes absurd basis for racial pride is illustrated in the joke about an Indian (that is, Native American) boy and a black boy arguing over who comes from the most notable race. The Indian wins the dispute when he points out that little white boys never play "cowboys and niggers." A related joke pits a white boy in debate against a boy from a black family that has just moved into the neighborhood. The black boy wins this round when he declares, "At least we don't live next door to no niggers."

One group of jokes, little collected or studied so far, involves children's misunderstandings of religious and patriotic texts. These not only allow for some criticism of these sensitive areas of life, but also may demonstrate a basic joke-making process. First a child's inadvertent error in language is related as an anecdote by his amused parents, but eventually the incident is described often enough to become an anonymous joke. This sequence would seem to explain the origins of such stories as the one about a child who wants to name his teddy bear "Gladly," because the people in church sing "Gladly, the Cross-eyed Bear"; or the one about the child's recitation in the Pledge of Allegiance to the Flag: "one nation, indigestible, with liver and juices for all."

A traditional story type usually told to children by adults—the *pictorial folktale*—has evolved mostly into joke form. In the older versions the storyteller would illustrate his or her tale with a simple sketch map of the tale's locale. The last line added would turn the drawing into a picture of the animal being described or hunted in the story, such as a wildcat or a duck. In modern pictorial jokes, usually told by children to other children, a teacher asks a group of grade-schoolers each to add a line to a drawing on the chalkboard. One draws an Indian teepee:

(1985)

The next adds a smokehole (or   decoration):

Another puts in the sun above:

But the fourth child draws an arc over the whole picture and calls it "My dad bending over the tub to wipe it out after he has taken a bath":

Another pictorial joke has one child drawing a simple representation of a lightbulb:

But another child turns the drawing around and says it is "My mom from the back pulling her girdle on":

A detailed classification has been published for one modern joke type, the *shaggy-dog story*. Some seven hundred texts were secured from both printed and oral sources, including the entries mailed in response to a radio program's nationwide contest. The following definition, based on the stories' humorous twists, was worked out for their classification into three major groups and some two hundred types and subtypes: "A nonsensical joke that employs in the punchline a psychological non sequitur, a punning variation of a familiar saying, or a hoax, to trick the listener who expects conventional wit or humor." On the basis of style, it was found that shaggy-dog stories "usually describe ridiculous characters and actions, and often are told (to heighten the effect of the final letdown) in a long drawn-out style with minute details, repetitions, and elaborations." The whole classification was lettered and numbered using decimal points, after the manner of the *Motif-Index*, so that new materials could be added at any point; but, like the *Type-Index*, it provided a brief summary of each plot, a list of versions, cross-references, and bibliographic and comparative notes. For example, the joke about a midget knight mounted on a large shaggy dog that has the punch line "I wouldn't send a knight out on a dog like that!" was classified C425., "The Midget Knight and his Mount," in a category with other stories that end with punning variations of popular sayings. Twenty-eight versions of the tale were reported, fifteen from the radio contest, six from a folklore archive, two from *Boys' Life* magazine, one each from a joke book, a mail-order catalog, a comic strip, *Today's Health* magazine, and a newspaper political cartoon. Other jokes in the index were related to literature; to historical persons; to traditional myths, tale types, and motifs; to popular poems and songs; and even to a Sumerian fable possibly five thousand years old.

Shaggy-dog stories continue to be invented, often to incorporate new characters or to allude to newly popular phrases. For instance, a shaggy-*frog* story was popular in the 1980s, with Kermit the Frog (of the Muppets) entering a bank and asking a teller named Miss Paddywhack for a loan. As collateral he offers an odd triangular-shaped piece of polished wood with some wires connected to it. Miss Paddywhack takes the object in to the loan officer, who glances at it and then stamps Kermit's application "Approved." When the teller in puzzlement asks what the object is, her boss replies, "It's a knickknack, Paddywhack, give the frog a loan." (This time the phrase is an *old* one—a line from the English children's song "This Old Man," the tune of which is used for the theme song of the children's TV program starring Barney the dinosaur.)

TALL TALES

Types 1875 to 1999 in the Aarne-Thompson index are *tales of lying*, commonly called **tall tales** (or "lies," or "windies") in the United States; this section is supplemented by a portion of chapter X (Humor) in the *Motif-Index*, Motifs X900. to X1899., "Humor of Lies and Exaggerations." Americans think of the tall tale as a peculiarly American product, just as Turks, Germans, and Scandinavians each think of it as peculiarly their national invention, all of them forgetting that tall tales existed before any of their nations was thought of.

Some of the best-known American windies are found in the *Type-Index*, among them Type 1889F, "Frozen Words Thaw"; Type 1889L, "The Split Dog"; Types 1890A through F, "The Wonderful Hunt"; and Type 1920B, often called "Too Busy to Tell a Lie." Even though a good number of lying tales are included in the *Type-Index*, they were formerly not considered numerous in most European countries. In the Norwegian standard-type catalog, for example, which was published in 1921, only four such tales were listed; but in 1959, when a marine-paint company in Norway offered prizes for good "skipper tales," some one hundred tall-tale texts were among the entries that sailors submitted. Some were Aarne-Thompson lying tales previously unlisted in the Norwegian catalog; others could be identified with motif numbers; and most of the new discoveries are known in some form in American folklore as well.

Tall tales may not be original with Americans, but they are certainly popular in the United States and fully characteristic of American folklore. Mody Boatright has written that they represent a sort of reverse bragging about the hardships of settling the continent and an exaggeration of natural features of the frontier. They flourished among frontiersmen, Boatright suggested, as a buoyant reaction to the wilderness itself and against the Eastern tourists' version of what life out West was like. Men were tough there, though not as tough as the Eastern emphasis on eye-gouging fights made them seem, and the tall tales made men even tougher. Danger and death were familiar, so the tales laughed at death. Westerners loved to gamble, and in tall tales gambling was pictured as mania. A folk story about the way a cowboy reported a man's death to the bereaved wife indicates the proper climate for tall tales.

He: "Howdy, Widow Jones."
She: "I'm not a widow."
He: "Bet you ten dollars you are!"

The latter example is really a local-character story, not a tall tale, but it is just that sort of narrator—the laconic, poker-faced, hardened, regional character—who specialized in telling tall tales (or "talking trash") to his cronies, youngsters, and tourists. Vance Randolph expressed the tone very well in the title of his book of Ozark tall tales: *We Always Lie to Strangers*. The success of tall tales does not depend on belief in the details of the story, but rather on a willingness to lie and be lied to while keeping a straight face. The humor of these tales consists of telling an outrageous falsehood in the sober accents of a truthful story. The best tall tales only improve upon reality: smart animals are made smarter, big mosquitoes are made bigger, bad weather is made worse, huge crops are made even larger. A smart dog hunts all kinds of game and even starts to dig worms when its master gets out a fishing pole one morning; mosquitoes eat a team of horses and pitch horseshoes for the harness; wind blows a suspended log chain out straight and snaps links off the end; a strawberry is so big that the cook won't cut it for only two orders of strawberry shortcake. (Tall-tale humor of this kind is often captured in postcard art created by using pasteups or trick photography.)

Although numerous other tall tales have been frequently collected and printed, they retain an appeal in oral transmission that quickly fades in reading printed versions. The art of the tall tale, like the art of the anecdote and the joke, is primarily a verbal one, deriving from the skill of the teller rather than from the originality of his or her material. When stretching the truth becomes second nature with

They claim to raise sizeable potatoes around here

A tall-tale postcard sold in Idaho.

a yarnspinner, he or she may rework traditional materials to create personalized remarks at the spur of the moment. A noted liar once got a jolt from a spark plug when an automobile engine was running. Someone asked, "Did it shock you, Len?" "Nope," the old-timer shot back, "I was too quick for it." He was merely borrowing from an older story about a person picking up and quickly dropping a hot horseshoe in a blacksmith's shop: "Did it burn you?" he was asked. "Nope, it just don't take me long to look at a horseshoe." (The punch line is also used as a family catchphrase to comment on someone's quickness in observing something: "It just don't take him long to look at a horseshoe.")

FOCUS: JIMMY CARTER, FOLKLORE COLLECTOR

About once a year my daddy took me on a fishing trip to a more distant place, usually farther south in Georgia. We made a couple of such visits to the Okefenokee Swamp in the southeastern corner of our state. . . . We stayed at the only fish camp around the western edge of the swamp, owned by a man named Lem Griffis. His simple pine-board bunkhouses, with screens instead of windowpanes, could accommodate about twenty guests. As we sat around an open fire at night, Lem was always eager to regale us with wild tales about the biggest bear, the prettiest woman, or a catch of so many fish they had to haul in water to fill up the hole left in the lake. His stories were honed by repetition so that the buildup and punch line equaled those of any professional entertainer. We listened and laughed for hours even when we were hearing the same yarn for the second or third time. His regular guests would urge, "Tell us about the city lady who thought her son might drown."

Lem would wait awhile until enough others joined in the request, and then describe in vivid and heart-rending tones the anguish of a mother who was afraid to let her only child near the swamp. "I finally said, 'Ma'am, I can guarantee you the boy won't drown. I've been here all my life and never heerd of anybody drowning in this here swamp.' The lady was quite relieved." There was always a long pause, until Lem finally added, "The 'gators always get them first."

Source: Jimmy Carter, *An Outdoor Journal: Adventures and Reflections* (New York: Bantam Books, 1988), pp. 29–30.

Future U.S. President Jimmy
Carter as a teenager, perhaps on his way to a fishing
trip with his "daddy."

DISCUSSION TOPICS:

1. Former president Carter here reveals himself to be an accomplished, if untrained, folklorist. What does he observe concerning
context, style, and audience involvement in Lem Griffis's storytelling?
(A second example of a similar tale is on p. 45 of *An Outdoor Journal.*)

2. What was Lem Griffis's status in relation to the other men, to
the city lady, and to the boy, Jimmy Carter?

3. Explain why this reminiscence records an instance of metafolklore, or folklore about folklore.

4. Lem Griffis as storyteller was discussed by Kay Cothran in
"Talking Trash in the Okefenokee Swamp Rim, Georgia," *JAF* 87
(1974): 340–56; repr. in J. Brunvand, ed., *Readings in American Folklore*, pp. 215–35. A racist version of the second tale recorded by
Jimmy Carter appears in that article; its punch line is "Is dis nigger
fishing, or am dat fish niggering?" rather than Carter's version: "First
time I ever seen a fish squirreling."

Georgia storyteller Luther A. Bailey, sometimes known as "Lying Bailey." He claims to be from south of Sycamore in Turner County.

FORMULA TALES

The **formula tales** in the last section of the *Type-Index* represent a very ancient category of folktales, those based on a strict pattern of development, usually involving repetition. Both *old* formula tales in several subclasses and *new* tales based on old formulas are known in the United States.

Cumulative tales, or "chains" (Types 2000 to 2199), are often based on the device of adding a further detail with each repetition of the plot. Familiar examples are Type 2030, "The Old Woman and Her Pig," and Type 2035, "House that Jack Built." Another group contains a series of alternate responses, as in Type 2014, "Chains Involving Contradictions or Extremes," which includes a dialogue based on the " 'That's good,' 'no, that's bad' " formula. A popular American collegiate example that has not been cataloged in any index of types contains sequences like the following, with the audience furnishing the responses:

"We've just built a new fraternity house!" (Yay!)
"With only one bar." (Boo!)
"A mile long!" (Yay!)

Catch tales (Types 2200 to 2205), like catch questions in riddling tradition, lead the listener on to be hoaxed; in this instance the trick consists of causing him or her to ask a question to which the storyteller returns a foolish answer. A favorite catch tale in the United States is Type 2205, "Teller Is Killed in His Own Story," sometimes with the following variation, in a story about being surrounded by Indians—Listener: "What did you do?" Storyteller: "What could I do? I bought a blanket." Another recent favorite, not specifically listed in the *Type-Index*, is a long, boring story involving the repeated line "Patience, little burro, patience." When an exasperated listener finally demands the point of the story, the narrator admonishes, "Patience, little burro, patience."

Two catch tales have become part of modern American women's folklore; both of them are narrated in a serious manner as accounts of personal experiences. The first gives a long circumstantial account of being pursued by a man with a cane or umbrella who at some point in the story supposedly strikes the narrator across the chest. When a shocked listener asks "What happened?" the storyteller replies, "Well, how do you suppose I got these two bumps here?" (A male version of the story, less commonly heard, says the blow caused "my big nose.") The second women's catch tale (which must be told to a woman) describes an encounter with another woman, who in anger, because of some favor that is not granted, throws a strong perfume on the narrator's throat that will, supposedly, cause her to become a lesbian. This time the storyteller stresses how strong the odor was and that it still lingers, and when the listener leans forward to try to smell it, the narrator kisses her on the forehead.

Endless tales (Type 2300) are formula tales that might continue indefinitely if the narrator had the will and the breath for it. These stories set up an action that is then repeated ad infinitum—sheep jumping over a fence, geese quacking, locusts carrying corn from a barn one grain at a time. *Rounds* (Type 2320) are endless stories that come back to their own starting points and then begin again. Often the situation is a tale within a tale within a tale, theoretically without any ending. One example is: "I laughed so hard I thought I'd die.

I did die. They buried me, and a flower grew on my grave. The roots grew down and tickled me. I laughed so hard I thought I'd die. I did die. . . ." Another popular round tells of the puppy who, when he walks outside in the winter, has the snow "pinch his paw." The puppy asks the big dog if snow is the strongest thing in the world, and he is directed to a series of items in the world, each of which can overpower the next: sun melts snow, clouds cover sun, wind moves clouds, etc. Eventually he gets back to the dog, but then he remembers that "the snow can pinch his paw." And around we go again!

One final tale form does not appear in the Aarne-Thompson index as a separate type, although several different animal tales and *Märchen* display its characteristic device—a song or rhyme interspersed with the prose narration. This is the so-called *cante fable*, or "singing tale." The narratives in which neck riddles are embedded suggest the *cante fable* form. Two of the best-known examples are often printed as nursery tales—"The Three Little Pigs" (Type 124) and "Jack and the Beanstalk" (Type 328). Type 480, quoted in Focus: Kind and Unkind, is often told as a *cante fable* with songs or verses included at two points in the plot. Another European-American tale frequently collected as a *cante fable* is Type 1360C, "Old Hildebrand." In some versions a man bets his fiddle against a ship captain's cargo that his wife can resist seduction for two hours; the man sings:

> Be true, my lover, be true, my lover,
> Be true for just two hours;
> Be true, my lover, be true, my lover,
> The cargo will soon be ours.

But the wife, from inside the captain's cabin, sings back:

> Too late, my lover, too late, my lover,
> He grabbed me round the middle;
> Too late my lover, too late my lover,
> You've lost your damned old fiddle.

An especially popular *cante fable* in the United States and Canada has to do with a man invited to supper who sees some very plain food replaced by better fare when the minister or other important guests arrive unexpectedly. The man then chants something like

> The Lord be praised,
> But I'm amazed,
> To see how things are mended.
> Applesauce and pumpkin pie,
> When pudding and milk were intended.

Or a prairie preacher, subtly protesting the sameness of all his meals out, may pray

> For rabbit roasted and rabbit fried,
> For rabbit cooked and rabbit dried,
> For rabbit young and rabbit old,
> For rabbit hot and rabbit cold,
> For rabbit tender and rabbit tough,
> We thank thee, Lord, that we have enough.

The humorous-grace *cante fable* involves more a curse than a blessing, a fact made clear in this verse collected from a Pennsylvania coal miner in the 1930s:

> May God above
> Send down a dove,
> With wings as sharp as razors;
> To cut the throats,
> Of those old bloats,
> Who cut the poor man's wages.

USING THE *TYPE-INDEX* AND THE *MOTIF-INDEX*

The identification of different classes and subclasses of folktales as well as the cataloging of types and motifs are only preliminary steps in the study of these narratives. The *Type-* and *Motif-Indexes* do not analyze tales, interpret them, or trace them to their origins; they simply organize the collected material in a systematic fashion, outline the usual forms, and provide bibliography. The two indexes used together render the tasks of identifying narratives, gathering variants, and analyzing them immeasurably easier than the process would be without such reference works. Thus, any folklorist working with traditional prose narratives should become familiar with these indexes. To illustrate their use, here is a verbatim entry from the *Type-Index*:

> 660. *The Three Doctors*. The hog's heart, the thief's hand, the cat's eye. The three doctors make a trial of their skill [H504.]. One removes one of his eyes, one his heart, and the other a hand [F668.1.]. They are to replace them without injury the next morning [E782.]. During the night they are eaten and others substituted [X1721.2. E780.2.], and one of the doctors thus acquires a cat's eye which sees best at night, one a thief's hand that wants to steal [E782.1.1.], and one a hog's heart that makes him want to root in the ground [E786.].
>   *BP II 552 (Grimm No. 118).—Finnish *50*; Finnish-Swedish *4*; Estonian *1*; Lithuanian *9*; Swedish *13* (Stockholm *2*; Göteborg *2*, Liungman *2*, misc. *7*); Norwegian *2*; Danish *3*; Irish *45*; French *7*; Flemish *3*; German: Ranke *6*; Czech: Tille Soupis II (2) 446f. *6*; Slovenian *3*; Polish *1*; Russian: Andrejev *1*.—Franco-American *4*.

Like all descriptions in the Aarne-Thompson index, this one begins with a numerical designation, a conventional title, and condensed description of the tale type. The tale is summarized next, with the appropriate motif numbers indicated in brackets. (For the more complex tales, a separate motif list is used, and subtypes may be established.) In this instance, the summary is based on the Grimm version. Last in the entry come abbreviated bibliographic references, including the total numbers of variants contained in national folktale archives and collections. The following entries in the *Motif-Index* correspond to the motifs cited:

H504. Test of skill in handwork.
F668.1. Skillful surgeon removes and replaces vital organs.
E782. Limbs successfully replaced.
X1721.2. Lie: man's organs replaced with animal's. He acts like animal.
E780.2. Animal bodily member transferred to person or other animal retains animal powers and habits.

E782.1.1. Substituted hand. Man exchanges his hand for that of
   another.
   E786. Heart successfully replaced.

For each of these motifs in the *Index* itself, cross-references to
other related motifs and to Type 660 are provided; also further bibliography is listed under most of them, although not all references
will necessarily be related to the tale type in question. To save space
and avoid repetition, only the numbers and descriptions are given
with the motifs above, but the bibliographic references quoted with
the Type 660 entry are typical items: The "*BP" refers to the voluminous notes by Bolte and Polívka for the Grimm tales (asterisks
are used throughout to mark the best reference sources); in this
instance the tale is number 118 in Grimm. Then follow a list of
sixteen countries or national groups in which this tale has been found
(including Swedes in Finland and French in America) and, in italics,
the totals for each country (158 in all). The full references for each
abbreviated item in the list are given in a bibliography at the beginning of the *Index*.
   Equipped with such indexes, folktale scholars are well prepared
to identify and annotate the texts they collect. Whether they begin
searching for a whole tale plot, for a characteristic motif, or for
details that may be in the alphabetical index to the *Motif-Index*, they
should eventually be able to pin down parallels from narrative folklore that have already been identified and classified. To do this,
however, they must not take type and motif entries too literally; the
indexes work best when they are flexibly applied. After all, indexers
cannot furnish the details of every text they have examined. In fact,
they usually cannot even examine all of the relevant texts. Instead,
for many items they must rely on catalogs and indexes made by
others using their own collected materials.
   Bearing these points in mind, it is not difficult to see that the
following paraphrased tale, heard orally in the West in 1961, is related to this complex of Type 660 and its related motifs.

   A cowboy is injured badly during a roundup, and a medical student is flagged down on a nearby highway to administer first aid.
   Finding an internal organ destroyed, the student calls for a wandering sheep to be dragged in, killed, and cut open. From the sheep's

insides he borrows the parts to patch up the man. A year later the same student drives down the same road and sees the same crew rounding up cattle again. Inquiring about the injured man, he is told, "He's all right now. 'Course he had quite a lot of trouble this spring. He brought a nice pair of twin lambs, and we sheared him—he sheared eight pounds."

That this tale is traditional and is related to Type 660 is supported by other variants. In 1956, for example, an informant in Maine said that his uncle had sheep's intestines substituted for his own in a hospital operation, and "every spring they had to shear the old devil." In a volume of Civil War reminiscences, a doctor is described as removing the liver of a soldier wounded in the field. A dog eats it, so the physician substitutes a sheep's liver. The soldier recovers, but he has a "hankering after grass." If it seems that these American tales deviate too far from the outlined type description, consider this summary of a version from a medieval collection, the *Gesta Romanorum* (Tale LXXVI): Two physicians alternate in removing and re-placing each other's eyes; a crow steals one, however, which must then be replaced with a goat's eye that thereafter persists in looking up at trees.

RESEARCHING AND ANALYZING FOLKTALES

Until the early 1960s the most typical form of folklore research was the gathering of all available variants of an international tale to try to discover, by means of comparative analysis, its original form, its most likely place of origin, and its probable routes of dissemination. This approach is often called the "Finnish method," in reference to the nineteenth-century Finns (Krohn, Aarne, and others) who de-veloped it, or the **historic-geographic method,** in reference to the plan of tale arrangement employed in it. The ultimate goals of this method were to write "life histories" of individual folktales and to reconstruct an *archetype*, or a hypothetical original form, for each tale. The method was based on the assumption that complex folk-tales have a single origin in one time and one place (rather than having resulted from polygenesis), and that each tale then spread throughout its present area of distribution by *automigration*—that is, from person to person, without needing large-scale folk migrations to carry it.

Although scholars employing the historic-geographic method were never able to make a definitive statement of exactly where a given tale began, their studies pointed to India as probably the most important center of folktale dissemination.

FOCUS: PARODIES OF FOLKLORE RESEARCH

They collected tons and tons of folktales and arranged them on a map in circles. This was known as the Finish Method, because it went around in circles and would never be finished. The Finish Method went on for a long time and is still not finished.

*

At the Indiana University Folklore Institute in the 1960s two bits of lore circulated relevant to the current essay. One was the title of an imaginary, mock study such as waggish graduate students concoct: "Frontier Humor in the Writings of Henry James." The other was the supposedly true story of a colleague who had undertaken to do a seminar paper on folklore in Ernest Hemingway's writings only to discover too late that he could discover none and that failure loomed.

Sources: Sabina Magliocco, "1846 And All That, A New History of Folkloristics Including Good Things, Bad Things, and One or Two Really Weird Things," *FF* 20 (1987): 128–37; and Frank de Caro, "The Three Great Lies: Riddles of Love and Death in a Postmodern Novel," *SF* 48 (1991): 235–54.

DISCUSSION TOPICS:

1. What published work does Magliocco's parody imitate? (Hint: the date in her model was 1066.) Would circulation of this parody among Indiana University graduate students (publishers of *Folklore Forum*) constitute a folklore phenomenon?

2. What categories of folk narrative might the "two bits of lore" in de Caro's statement belong to? What is the "folk group" that developed all three examples, and what seems to have been the function of these items? Is there any similar student folklore at your college or university?

3. Read de Caro's essay on the "postmodern novel" by Jay McInerney, *Story of My Life* (1988). How does he find that folklore is employed in this depiction of "upper class New York youth culture"?

In essence, the historic-geographic method involved the following steps:

1. Gather all available texts (using the indexes, corresponding with archives, field-collecting, etc.).
2. Label all texts (usually a letter code for the language group and a number for the specific text).
3. Arrange literary texts historically and oral texts geographically (often north to south within each country).
4. Identify the traits to be studied, and make a master outline of all traits found in the texts.
5. Summarize the traits in each individual text, referring to the outline of traits.
6. Compare all traits in texts, one by one, in order to:
    a. Establish subtypes (regional subclasses);
    b. Formulate the archetype (hypothetical original).
7. Reconstruct the life history of the tale that best explains all of the present texts and their variations.

Comparing the traits in families of folktales and reconstructing archetypal forms represent only one possible approach to studying the folktale. Another important method, the **structural approach to folktales,** seeks to establish a *synchronic* basis (viewed without reference to historical change) rather than a *diachronic* basis (viewed in terms of historical development) for comparing folktales. Following the method of structural linguistics, Alan Dundes, the chief proponent of this approach, began by defining *minimal units* of folktales that are distinct from the specific contents of the tales. Whether a tale is about animals, ogres, or numskulls should make no difference in a structural analysis as long as the *form* of the narratives is parallel. (Several similar tale-forms are widely separated in the *Type-Index,* Dundes has pointed out, simply because their cast of characters and other details differ.)

Borrowing terms from structural linguistics and adapting them to the system of the Russian structuralist Vladimir Propp, Dundes further suggests that if the phonetic level of linguistic analysis is the equivalent of what he calls the "etic" (nonstructural) approach of motif indexing, then the "emic" level would be reached by an index of the structural units, or *motifemes*. The Proppian approach, which leaves folktale elements in their original linear sequence as the tales are told, Dundes terms "syntagmatic," or analogous to the analysis of syntax in languages. A "paradigmatic" approach, akin to the use of paradigms (sample patterns) in language analysis, rearranges the folktale elements so as to reveal their underlying structure, usually as sets of oppositions: life/death, raw/cooked, good/evil, and so forth. The leading exponent of this method is the French anthropologist Claude Lévi-Strauss. Structural approaches, it is emphasized, would not eliminate the comparative approach or its long-established reference tools. Rather, both synchronic and diachronic studies are needed to fully explore folktale form and development.

As a counterbalance to the highly schematized and often largely statistical nature of both historic-geographic and structural analyses of folktale texts, modern folklorists see a strong need for more studies of the context, performance, and oral style of tale narrators. For this to be done requires first that collectors record much more than just the text and the informant's background. We need to know where, how, when, and to whom tales are told. Probably photographs—preferably motion pictures or videotapes—are necessary to record gestures and facial expressions, and it is desirable to observe good informants retelling tales to different audiences. We should take note of the dramatic role-playing of the teller, use of repetitions and other verbal formulas, personal or local references and other improvisations, and the responses that come from the audience. When data of this sort are collected and have been analyzed, it is possible to differentiate the styles characteristic of a specific tale, of a tale-teller, or of an individual culture. Moving beyond even these concerns, and rejecting past studies of story texts and their contents, Robert A. Georges, speaking as a "behavioral folklorist," advocates instead a holistic analysis, not of "stories" but of "storytelling events"—which are "communicative events . . . social experiences, and . . . unique expressions of human behavior."

BIBLIOGRAPHIC NOTES

Stith Thompson's *The Folktale* (see chapter 8) is the definitive survey of the field. Besides the original *Type-* and *Motif-Indexes* prepared by Thompson, American folklorists must consult the satellite work by Ernest W. Baughman, *A Type and Motif Index of the Folktales of England and North America* (The Hague: Indiana University Folklore Series no. 20, 1966). Advanced study of the folktale requires use of several reference works in foreign languages, especially Johannes Bolte and Georg Polívka, *Anmerkungen zu der Kinder- und Hausmärchen der Brüder Grimm*, 5 vols. (Leipzig, 1913–32). An important article translated from German for Alan Dundes's book *The Study of Folklore* is Axel Olrik's *Epische Gesetze der Volksdichtung* (Epic Laws of Folk Narrative) (1909). A good survey of older European folktale theories in English is in Emma Emily Kiefer's *Albert Wesselski and Recent Folktale Theories* (Bloomington: Indiana University Folklore Series no. 3, 1947).

European folktales in authentic texts, accurately translated and fully annotated, are available in the Folktales of the World series published under the general editorship of Richard M. Dorson by the University of Chicago Press. *Folktales of England*, edited for the series by Katharine M. Briggs and Ruth L. Tongue (Chicago, 1965), is of particular interest to American folklorists. Briggs also compiled the important reference work titled *A Dictionary of British Folktales in the English Language*; part A covers folk narratives, part B folk legends (Bloomington: Indiana University Press, 1970, 1971, 2 vols. each part).

Some representative non-English tales collected in the United States may be found in the following: Joseph Médard Carrière's *Tales from the French Folk-Lore of Missouri* (Evanston and Chicago, Ill.: Northwestern University Press, 1937); Thomas R. Brendle and William S. Troxell's *Pennsylvania German Folk-Tales, Legends, Once-Upon-a-Time Stories, Maxims, and Sayings* (Morristown: Pennsylvania German Society Publications no. 50, 1944); Richard M. Dorson's "Polish Wonder Tales of Joe Woods," *WF* 8 (1949): 25–52, 131–45; Rosemary Agonito's "Il Paisano: Immigrant Italian Folktales of Central New York," *NYFQ* 23 (1967): 52–64; Francine Pelly's "Gypsy Folktales from Philadelphia," *KFQ* 13 (1968): 83–102; Anthony Milanovich's "Serbian Tales from Blanford," *IF* 4 (1971): 1–60; and Elaine K. Miller's *Mexican Folk Narrative from the Los Angeles Area* (Austin, Tex.: AFS Memoir, vol. 56, 1973). Barry Jean Ancelet's book *Cajun and Creole Folktales* (New York: Garland, 1994) contains texts in the original French dialects and in English translations.

Robert B. Klymasz is only one field collector who has published non-English tales from Canada, in such works as *Folk Narratives among Ukrainian-Canadians in Western Canada* (Ottawa: Canadian Center for Folk Culture Studies, paper no. 4, 1973) and "The Ethnic Joke in Canada Today," *KFQ* 15 (1970): 167–73. A comprehensive anthology of Canadian oral narratives is Edith Fowke's *Tales Told in Canada* (Toronto: Doubleday Canada Ltd., 1986).

In 1957 (vol. 70), *JAF* published "The Folktale: A Symposium," with important articles by Warren E. Roberts—"Collections and Indexes: A Brief Review" (pp. 49–52); Richard M. Dorson—"Standards for Collecting and Publishing American Folktales" (pp. 53–57); and Herbert Halpert—"Problems and Projects in the American-English Folktale" (pp. 57–62). In a 1981 article, "*Märchen* to Fairy Tale: An Unmagical Transformation," *WF* 40: 232–44, Kay Stone shows how the reworkings of oral wonder tales in books and films have modified them for mass-media consumption. Her interviews with children and adults about such stories reveal that the stories seem more threatening to adults than to the children presumably protected by the rewriting. See also Bruno Bettelheim's influential book *The Uses of Enchantment: The Meaning and Importance of Fairy Tales* (New York: Knopf, 1976).

The Library of Congress published the useful bibliography by Barbara Quinnam, *Fables: From Incunabula to Modern Picture Books* (Washington, D.C., 1966). "Southey and 'The Three Bears' " was discussed by Mary I. Shamburger and Vera R. Lachman in *JAF* 59 (1946): 400–3. Alan C. Elms, in " 'The Three Bears': Four Interpretations," *JAF* 90 (1977): 257–73, reviews ritual, structural, psychoanalytic, and anal readings of the familiar story.

There are many reliable book-length collections of American folktales. Richard Chase's two books, *The Jack Tales* (Cambridge, Mass.: Houghton Mifflin, 1943) and *Grandfather Tales* (Boston: Houghton Mifflin, 1948), are important Southern Appalachian collections, especially the first with its notes by Herbert Halpert. All of Vance Randolph's Ozark collections, which contain a variety of folktale types and forms, are outstanding; these (all published by Columbia University Press) are *Who Blowed Up the Church House?* (1953), *The Devil's Pretty Daughter* (1955), *The Talking Turtle* (1957)—all with notes by Halpert—and *Sticks in the Knapsack* (1958), with notes by Ernest W. Baughman. Marie Campbell's collection *Tales from the Cloud Walking Country* (Bloomington: Indiana University Press, 1958) contains folktales from Kentucky. Ruth Ann Musick's *Green Hills of Magic* (Lexington: University of Kentucky Press, 1970) is subtitled *West Virginia Folktales from Europe*. Two excellent regional collections are Mariella Glenn Hartsfield's *Tall Betsy and Dunce Baby: South Georgia Folktales* (Athens: University of Georgia Press, 1987) and John A. Burrison's *Storytellers: Folktales and Legends from the South* (Athens: University of Georgia Press, 1989; paperback ed., 1991).

Leonard W. Roberts, premiere collector of Kentucky folktales, published numerous texts in journals such as *Mountain Life and Work*, *Kentucky Folklore Record*, and *Tennessee Folklore Society Bulletin*. His book *South from Hell-fer-Sartin* (Lexington: University of Kentucky Press, 1955; reissued in paperback, Berea, Ky.: Council of the Southern Mountains, 1964), like his subsequent collections, is rendered in absolutely verbatim oral style and has complete notes for all tales. Roberts's *Old Greasybeard: Tales from the Cumberland Gap* (Detroit: Folklore Associates, 1969) contains fifty tales; his *Sang Branch Settlers: Folksongs and Tales of a Kentucky Mountain Family* (Austin, Tex.: AFS Memoir, vol. 61, 1974) incorporates all the material previously published in book and microcard form as *Up Cutshin and Down Greasy* (Lexington: University of Kentucky Press, 1959).

Numerous folktales have been published in journal articles, only a few of which may be cited here. A double "Folk Narrative Issue" of *Midwest Folklore* (6 [1956]: 5–128) is a good example of such publications. Another is Helen Creighton and Edward D. Ives's "Eight Folktales from Miramichi as Told by Wilmot MacDonald," *NEF* 4 (1962): 3–70, a model of editing and annotation. Jan Harold Brunvand's "Folktales by Mail from Bond, Kentucky," *KFR* 6 (1960): 69–76, describes an unusual collecting method and provides several annotated texts. A variety of folk-narrative types is represented in Donald Allport Bird and James R. Dow's "Benjamin Kuhn: Life and Narratives of a Hoosier Farmer," *IF* 5 (1972): 137–63. Horace P. Beck discussed "The Acculturation of Old World Tales by the American Indian," using a "Jack Tale" as an example, in *MF* 8 (1958): 205–16.

Four "Jack Tales" were the focus of a special issue of *NCFJ* (vol. 26, 1978), which also featured four articles discussing the nature of the hero in the tales, and their structure, context, and style. W. F. H. Nicolaisen compared "English Jack and American Jack" in *MJLF* 4 (1978): 27–36, while Charles Thomas Davis III wrote of "The Changing World of the Jack Tales" in *TFSB* 45 (1979): 96–106. William Bernard McCarthy edited *Jack in Two Worlds* (Chapel Hill: University of North Carolina Press, 1994), which consists of essays containing texts and discussions by various scholars.

It is essential that folktales be heard, not just read, if they are to be fully appreciated. For the recorded performance of the Jack Tale from North Carolina mentioned in this chapter, consult "Jack Tales Told by Mrs. Maude Long of Hot Springs, N.C.," ed. Duncan Emrich (Washington, D.C.: Library of Congress Disc no. AAFS L47, 1957, now available as an audio cassette). See Alan Dundes's interpretation of her tale "Jack and the Drill" in "The Symbolic Equivalence of Allomotifs in the Rabbit-Herd (AT 570)," published in the Swedish yearbook of folktale studies, *ARV* (Uppsala, Sweden, 1982). Ray Hicks of Beech Mountain, N.C., among others, has recorded Jack Tales, the availability of which must be checked with sound-recording distributors. In *TFSB* 48 (1982): 68–82, W. K. McNeil and Kathy Nicol present "Folk Narratives of Jessie Hubert Wilkes," containing further stories and background on the narrator of seven folktales included on the recording *Not Far from Here: Traditional Tales and Songs Recorded in the Arkansas Ozarks* (Mt. View, Ark.: Arkansas Traditions, 1981).

A fully annotated collection of oral American jests is Vance Randolph's *Hot Springs and Hell* (Hatboro, Pa.: Folklore Associates, 1965), containing 460 brief items from the Ozarks and 130 pages of notes and bibliography. The erotic folktales collected by Vance Randolph, left out of his other books, were finally published in 1976 as *Pissing in the Snow and Other Ozark Folktales* (Urbana: University of Illinois Press, repr. as an Avon paperback), with annotations on the 101 texts by Frank A. Hoffman and an introduction by Rayna Green. Ronald L. Baker's *Jokelore: Humorous Folktales from Indiana* (Bloomington: Indiana University Press, 1986) contains 352 annotated jokes.

In "The Joke Fable," *SWF* 5 (1981): 1–10, Pack Carnes identifies a substantial group of oral narratives that mix two familiar forms; he quotes fables told as jokes, jokes with a moral, jokes masquerading as fables, and joking references to Aesop's fables. See also Steven Swann Jones, "Joking Transformations of Popular Fairy Tales: A Comparative Analysis of Five Jokes and their Fairy Tale Sources," *WF* 44 (1985): 97–114.

Richard M. Dorson called attention to "Dialect Stories of the Upper Peninsula: A New Form of American Folklore" in *JAF* 61 (1948): 113–50, an essay reprinted in his *Folklore and Folklife* (Chicago: University of Chicago Press, 1972), pp. 223–66. Two articles on dialect stories involving Mexican-Americans are María

Herrera-Sobek, "Verbal Play and Mexican Immigrant Jokes," *SWF* 4 (1980): 14–22; and Rosan A. Jordan, "Tension and Speech Play in Mexican-American Folklore," in *"And Other Neighborly Names . . . ,"* ed. Richard Bauman and Roger D. Abrahams (Austin: University of Texas Press, 1981), pp. 252–65. Keith Cunningham, in "Navajo Humor, Too," *SWF* 5 (1980): 1–15, gives examples of jokes told by Navajos, some of which he finds impossible to explain or appreciate.

Riddle-jokes, whether ethnic jokes or other numskull stories, are discussed in chapter 6; see the bibliographic notes there as well. Two articles by William M. Clements, however, take up larger issues of joking stereotypes and deserve mention here: "Cuing the Stereotype: The Verbal Strategy of the Ethnic Joke," *NYF* 5 (1979): 53–61; and "Braided Armpits, Clean Bowling Shirts, and the Feminine Mystique," *MJLF* 6 (1980): 34–40.

Richard M. Dorson presented "Jewish-American Dialect Stories on Tape" in *Studies in Biblical and Jewish Folklore*, ed. D. Noy, R. Patai, and F. L. Utley (Bloomington: Indiana University Folklore Series no. 13, 1960), pp. 111–74; further texts were published in *MF* 10 (1960): 133–46. The subclass of "Rabbi Trickster Tales" was the subject of an article by Ed Cray in *JAF* 77 (1964): 331–45. The following are analytical articles on Jewish dialect stories: Heda Jason, "The Jewish Joke: The Problem of Definition," *SFQ* 31 (1967): 48–54; Naomi and Eli Katz, "Tradition and Adaptation in American Jewish Humor," *JAF* 84 (1971): 215–20; and Dan Ben-Amos, "The 'Myth' of Jewish Humor," *WF* 32 (1973): 112–31.

The typical repertoire of Southern black folk narratives is surveyed by William R. Ferris, Jr., in "Black Prose Narrative in the Mississippi Delta," *JAF* 85 (1972): 140–51; a traditional vein of black jokelore is discussed by Harry Oster in "Negro Humor: John and Old Marster," *JFI* 5 (1968): 42–57. A brief discussion of some developments in dialect stories about blacks is in a note by Mac E. Barrick in *KFQ* 9 (1964): 166–68. Further study of black-white self-images and interrelationships as expressed in jokes may be found in such articles as Paulette Cross's "Jokes and Black Consciousness: A Collection with Interviews," *FF* 2 (1969): 140–61; Norine Dresser's "The Metamorphosis of the Humor of the Black Man," *NYFQ* 26 (1970): 216–28; and William R. Ferris, Jr.'s, "Racial Stereotypes in White Folklore," *KFQ* 15 (1970): 188–98. Two standard collections of black folk narratives with copious notes and bibliography are Richard M. Dorson's *Negro Folktales in Michigan* (Cambridge, Mass.: Harvard University Press, 1956) and *American Negro Folktales* (Greenwich, Conn.: Fawcett Premier Books, paperback, 1967), which incorporates part of the first-named collection.

G. Legman, the leading authority on sexual folklore, is the author of a combined collection, classification, and (mostly Freudian) analysis entitled *Rationale of the Dirty Joke: An Analysis of Sexual Humor*, First Series (New York: Grove Press, 1968); volume two, the second series, is titled *No Laughing Matter* (New York: Breaking Point, Inc., 1975). Vance Randolph's *Pissing in the Snow*, mentioned above, is a major collection of sexual jokes. Rosemary Zumwalt's "Plain and Fancy: A Content Analysis of Children's Jokes Dealing with Adult Sexuality," *WF* 35 (1976): 258–67, is reprinted in *Readings in American Folklore*, pp. 345–54. A related item is Sandra McCosh's "Aggression in Children's Jokes," *Maledicta* 1 (1977):

125–32. Carol A. Mitchell explores "The Sexual Perspective in the Appreciation and Interpretation of Jokes" in *WF* 36 (1977): 303–29; and C. W. Sullivan, III, studies a children's joke involving an off-color pun in "Johnny Says his ABCs," *WF* 46 (1987): 36–41.

Religious jokelore is studied in Jan Harold Brunvand's "As the Saints Go Marching By: Modern Jokelore Concerning Mormons," *JAF* 83 (1970): 53–60. See also Phyllis Potter's "St. Peter Jokes," *SWF* 3 (1979): 38–58. Mining another rich vein of modern oral humor, Michael J. Preston examines "A Year of Political Jokes (June 1973–June 1974); or, the Silent Majority Speaks Out," *WF* 34 (1975): 233–44. See also Holly Tanner and David Morris's "AIDS Jokes: Punishment, Retribution, and Renegotiation," *SF* 46 (1989): 147–57.

My note on "Jokes about Misunderstood Religious Texts" appeared in *WF* 24 (1965): 199–200. A "pictorial folktale" was noted by Maud G. Early in *JAF* 10 (1897): 80. Others are given by Simon J. Bronner in "Pictorial Jokes: A Traditional Combination of Verbal and Graphic Processes," *TFSB* 44 (1978): 189–96. My own "Classification for Shaggy Dog Stories," appeared in *JAF* 76 (1963): 42–68.

Three essays dealing with studies of traditional jokes in a broad context are Francis Lee Utley and Dudley Flamm's "The Urban and the Rural Jest (With an Excursus on the Shaggy Dog)," *JPC* 2 (1969): 563–77; Jan Harold Brunvand's "The Study of Contemporary Folklore: Jokes," *Fabula* 13 (1972): 1–19; and Frank Hall's "Conversational Joking: A Look at Applied Humor," *Folklore Annual* 6 (1974): 26–45. In an essay on "The Curious Case of the Wide-Mouth Frog," first published in 1977 (reprinted in *Interpreting Folklore*, pp. 62–68), Alan Dundes suggests that a joke about an animal's speech patterns is really concerned with white attitudes toward blacks during the 1970s. Lois A. Monteiro introduces a new joke type in "The Electronic Pocket Calculator: Joke 1," *WF* 35 (1976): 75; the punch line "Shell Oil" is seemingly spelled out on the calculator when the device is viewed upside down.

Innumerable joke studies may be found in the folklore journals. The following are but sample titles: Susan D. Rutherford, "Funny in Deaf—Not in Hearing," *JAF* 96 (1983): 310–22; James P. Leary, "Style in Jocular Communication: from the Cultural to the Personal," *JFR* 21 (1984): 29–46; Elliott Oring, "Jokes and the Discourse on Disaster," *JAF* 100 (1987): 276–86; Joseph P. Goodwin, "Unprintable Reactions to All the News that's Fit to Print," *SF* 46 (1989): 15–39; and Nancy A. Novotny, "Laughter on the Links: A Study of Golf Jokes," *NYF* 17 (1991): 63–81.

The Norwegian tall-tale contest referred to in this chapter was described by Gustav Henningsen in *Vestfold-Minne* in 1961 and was translated by Warren E. Roberts as "The Art of Perpendicular Lying" in *JFI* 2 (1965): 180–219. Mody Boatright's theory of frontier tall tales is contained in *Folk Laughter on the American Frontier* (New York: Macmillan, 1949; Collier Books paperback ed., 1961). A stylistic study of tall tales based on 233 texts of "The Wonderful Hunt" selected from a manuscript archive of more than two thousand American tall tales is reported in J. Russell Reaver's "From Reality to Fantasy: Opening-Closing Formulas in the Structures of American Tall Tales," *SFQ* 36 (1972): 369–82. Examining the tellers, contexts, and attitudes involved in traditional joking and lying, Kay Cothran wrote of "Talking Trash in the Okefenokee Swamp Rim, Georgia," *JAF* 87 (1974): 340–56, reprinted in *Readings in American Folklore*, pp. 215–35.

Stan Hoig's *The Humor of the American Cowboy* (Caldwell, Idaho: Caxton Press, 1958; Signet paperback ed., 1960) contains a good selection of Western occupational tall tales. A recent anthology is John O. West's *Cowboy Folk Humor: Life and Laughter in the American West* (Little Rock: August House, 1990). Mody Boatright's *Tall Tales from Texas* (Dallas: Southern Methodist University Press, 1934) selects examples from one state, as does Stephen Dow Beckham's *Tall Tales from Rogue River: The Yarns of Hathaway Jones* (Bloomington: Indiana University Press, 1974), in the latter case Oregon. Roger L. Welsch's *Shingling the Fog and Other Plains Lies: Tall Tales of the Great Plains* (Chicago: Swallow Press, 1972), the best annotated of this group, fills in part of the middle section of the West with tales from both oral and journalistic sources. Further examples from the Plains are in Welsch's *Catfish at the Pump: Humor and the Frontier* (Lincoln: Plains Heritage, 1982). *Man and Beast in American Comic Legend* by Richard M. Dorson (Bloomington: Indiana University Press, 1982) has ten chapters on fabulous animals in American folklore and eight chapters on tall-tale tellers. Two recent tall-tale studies are Carolyn S. Brown's *The Tall Tale in American Folklore and Literature* (Knoxville: University of Tennessee Press, 1987) and Richard Bauman's "Ed Bell, Texas Storyteller: The Framing and Reframing of Life Experience," *JFR* 24 (1987): 197–221

Vance Randolph's classic *We Always Lie to Strangers* was published in New York (Columbia University Press) in 1951. Lowell Thomas, who collected tall tales from his huge radio audiences by mail for many years, published *Tall Stories* in 1931 (Funk & Wagnalls), and it has been frequently reprinted. *Hoosier Tall Stories*, in the American Guide Series (Federal Writers' Project in Indiana, 1937), is a rare out-of-print book but a comprehensive collection. More Indiana tall tales are in my article in *MF* 11 (1961): 5–14. Samuel T. Farquhar reprinted a 1904 pamphlet of tall tales from Maine in *CFQ* 3 (1944): 177–84. An excellent collection from the same state is C. Richard K. Lunt's "Jones Tracy: Tall-Tale Hero from Mount Desert Island," *NEF* 10 (1968): 1–75. An important older collection recently made available again is James R. Masterson's *Tall Tales from Arkansas* (Boston: Chapman and Grimes, 1942; republished as *Arkansas Folklore* by Rose Publishing Company, Little Rock, 1974). Roger L. Welsch explores an area of folk/popular overlapping in "Bigger 'n Life: The Tall-Tale Postcard," *SFQ* 38 (1974): 311–24, adapted from the introduction to his book *The Tall-Tale Postcard: A Pictorial History* (New York: A. S. Barnes, 1976).

The *cante fable* in America has been collected and discussed in a series of articles, including two by Herbert Halpert in *SFQ* 5 (1941): 191–200 and *JAF* 55 (1942): 133–43; one by Leonard Roberts in *MF* 6 (1956): 69–88; and one by Edward D. Ives in *NEQ* 32 (1959): 226–37. Halpert provides rich annotation for one popular category of *cante fables*, "The Humorous Grace," in *MSF* 3 (1975): 71–82; and has "More on the Humorous Grace Cante Fable" in *MSF* 4 (1976): 77–86. Mac E. Barrick discussed "The Competitive Element in the Cante Fable" in *SFQ* 45 (1981): 123–34.

The chief theoretical underpinning for the historic-geographic method of folk-tale analysis, Kaarle Krohn's *Die Folkloristische Arbeitsmethode* (Oslo, 1926), was translated by Roger L. Welsch as *Folklore Methodology* (Austin, Texas: AFS Bibliographic and Special Series no. 21, 1971). Archer Taylor identified "Precursors of the Finnish Method of Folklore Study" in *MP* 25 (1927–28): 481–91. Taylor wrote that the method "is only common sense codified into a rigid procedure and not applied at random." He also published "The Black Ox," *FFC* no. 70 (1927) —a historic-geographic study of Finnish variants alone—as an exemplification of the method. A full-length study of worldwide distribution of a tale (Type 480, represented in Focus: Kind and Unkind) is Warren E. Roberts's "The Tale of the Kind and the Unkind Girls: Aa-Th 480 and Related Tales," in *Fabula*, Supplement, Series B, no. 1 (Berlin, 1958). Edwin C. Kirkland's "The American Redaction of Tale Type 922," *Fabula* 4 (1961): 248–59, is a comparative study of what is known here as "Pat and Mike and the Three Questions." Bruce A. Rosenberg and John B. Smith discuss "The Computer and the Finnish Historical-Geographical Method," marring their presentation with the questionable acronym FARTS (Folktale Analysis, Retrieval and Tabulating System) in *JAF* 87 (1974): 149–54.

Christine Goldberg surveyed "The Historic-Geographic Method: Past and Future" in *JFR* 21 (1984): 1–18. A historic-geographic study from the 1960s published thirty years later is Jan Harold Brunvand's *The Taming of the Shrew: A Comparative Study of Oral and Literary Versions* (New York: Garland, 1991). Studies that push outward the boundaries of conventional comparative studies are Bengt Holbek's *Interpretation of Fairy Tales: Danish Folklore in a European Perspective*, FFC no. 239 (Helsinki, 1987), and Steven Swann Jones's *The New Comparative Method: Structural and Symbolic Analysis of the Allomotifs of "Snow White,"* FFC no. 247 (Helsinki, 1990).

Two older survey articles on folktale studies are Anna Birgitta Rooth's "Scholarly Tradition in Folktale Research," *Fabula* 1 (1958): 193–200; and Jan DeVries's "The Problem of the Fairy Tale," *Diogenes* no. 22 (1958): 1–15. Surveys that projected sweeping changes in folktale studies are J. L. Fischer's "The Sociopsychological Analysis of Folktales," *CA* 4 (1963): 235–95; Melville Jacobs's "A Look Ahead in Oral Literature Research," *JAF* 79 (1966): 413–27; and Heda Jason's "A Multidimensional Approach to Oral Literature," *CA* 10 (1969): 413–26.

V. Propp's *Morphology of the Folktale*, first published in Russia in 1928 and the background for much modern structuralism in folklore, should be consulted in the second revised English translation (introduction by Alan Dundes), published both as AFS Bibliographical and Special Series vol. 9 (Austin, Texas, 1968) and as Indiana University Research Center in Anthropology, Folklore, and Linguistics, Publication no. 10 (Bloomington, 1968). Alan Dundes proposed the application of Propp's system to the structural study of tales in the Aarne-Thompson catalog in an article in *JAF* 75 (1962): 95–105, reprinted in *Analytic Essays in Folklore*, pp. 61–72, and he demonstrated its application in "The Binary Structure of 'Unsuccessful Repetition' in Lithuanian Folktales," *WF* 21 (1962): 165–74. For other structural studies, refer to the bibliographic notes to chapter 2 and to those for individual genre chapters. Alsace Yen offers a comparison "On Vladimir Propp and Albert B. Lord: Their Theoretical Differences," and criticizes the English translation of Propp's work, in *JAF* 86 (1973): 161–66.

Three articles discuss the distinctive American forms of European folktales: Wolfgang Mieder's "Modern Anglo-American Variants of the Frog Prince (AT 440)," *NYF* 6 (1980): 111–35; Yvonne J. Milspaw's "The Bride Test: Reflections on Changing Values in America," *KF*, NS vol. 1 (1982): 21–33; and Carl Lindahl's " 'Skallbone,' 'The Old Coon,' and the Persistence of Specialized Fantasy," *WF* 41 (1982): 192–204, a study of a black narrator retelling *Märchen* learned from her father.

The importance of studying storytelling rather than simply story plots is emphasized in Linda Dégh's important study (published first in German in 1962) *Folktales and Society: Story-Telling in a Hungarian Peasant Community* (Bloomington: Indiana University Press, 1969). Twenty of Dégh's essays are gathered in *Narratives in Society: A Performer-Centered Study of Narration*, FFC no. 255 (Helsinki, 1995). Another useful European study of a folk narrator, Mark Azadovskii's *"Eine Sibirische Märchenerzählerin,"* FFC no. 68 (1926), has been translated by James R. Dow and published as "A Siberian Tale Teller" by the Center for Intercultural Studies in Folklore and Ethnomusicology, Monograph Series no. 2 (Austin: University of Texas, 1974). An influential and inclusive essay taking this approach is Robert A. Georges's "Toward an Understanding of Storytelling Events," JAF 82 (1969): 313–28. Georges also asks "Do Narrators Really Digress?" in his article subtitled "A Reconsideration of 'Audience Asides' in Narrating," *WF* 40 (1981): 245–52.

John Ball's thoughts on "Style in the Folktale" appeared in *Folklore* 65 (1954): 170–72. William Hugh Jansen considered the problems of "Classifying Performance in the Study of Verbal Folklore" in *Studies in Folklore*, pp. 110–18. Richard M. Dorson analyzed the styles of six storytellers in "Oral Styles of American Folk Narrators," *Style in Language*, ed. Thomas A. Sebeok (Cambridge, Mass., New York, and London: Technology Press of MIT, 1960), pp. 27–51; the article was reprinted in *Folklore in Action*, pp. 77–100, and again (with four additional text samples) in Dorson's *Folklore: Selected Essays*, pp. 99–146. Dorson's 1961 study comparing the styles of two Maine storytellers, "Tales of Two Lobstermen," was reprinted in *Folklore and Fakelore*, pp. 212–22. Bruce A. Rosenberg considers the question of style in both written and oral storytelling in his essay "The Aesthetics of Traditional Narrative" in Stanley Weintraub and Philip Young's *Direction in Literary Criticism* (University Park: Pennsylvania State University Press, 1973), pp. 7–22. A practical example of the same subject is Willard B. Moore's "The Written and Oral Narratives of Sara Cowan," *IF* 10 (1977): 7–91, a good study of a writer for a weekly rural Kentucky newspaper using folk materials in her columns.

My Western text of Type 660, "The Two Doctors," with discussion of the variants that are mentioned in this chapter, appeared in "Some International Folktales from Northwest Tradition," *NWF* 1 (Winter 1966): 7–13. Luc Lacourcière studies nine French-Canadian texts of Type 660 in "Les Transplantations Fabuleuses: conte-Type 660," in *Cahiers d'Histoire* no. 22 (Québec: Archives de Folklore, Université Laval, 1970), pp. 194–204. A version from Italy retold as a sexy joke is reprinted in *European Anecdotes and Jests*, ed. Kurt Ranke (Copenhagen: Rosenkilde and Bagger, 1972), p. 10.

11

FOLKSONGS

PROBLEMS IN DEFINING THE FOLKSONG

The folksong, although long a popular subject for collection and research, has often eluded ventures at precise scholarly definition. The following attempt from A. H. Krappe's *The Science of Folklore* (1930) demonstrates the typical shortcomings of many in the past:

> The folksong is a song, i.e. a lyric poem with melody, which origi-
> nated anonymously, among unlettered folk in times past and which
> remained in currency for a considerable time, as a rule for centuries.

Not only is the logic here neatly circular (folksong = song of the folk), but also the criteria of illiterate origins and "considerable" age will simply not apply to the greater part of the materials accepted as folksongs by folklorists either of Krappe's time or later. American folksongs would seem to be ruled out entirely, and Krappe's own first example, named a few lines further on, does not fit the definition:

> the American *Kentucky Home*, though it is supposed to have origi-
> nated in circles of a somewhat darker hue than is popular in certain
> sections of the country, is a genuine folksong of both coloured and
> white people.

Krappe's remark was a racist one, and "My Old Kentucky Home," of course, is a Stephen Foster composition that has never achieved any oral circulation in variant versions.

On the one hand, we have the broad and vague popular concept that almost any folksy song performance qualifies as a folksong. On the other hand, we have narrow-minded antiquarian definitions such as Krappe's. But if we simply look at what the folk sing and what folklorists have collected and studied, we discover that **folksongs** consist of words and music that circulate orally in traditional variants among members of a particular group. Like other kinds of oral traditions, folksongs have come from several sources, have appeared in many different media, and have sometimes been lifted out of folk circulation for various professional or artistic uses. But all of those that qualify as true folksongs have variants found in oral transmission.

It is a common misconception that genuine folksongs can be detected by their style of performance; in fact, nonfolk performers may expertly imitate a traditional style. Nor can the age of a song determine its status as folk or nonfolk, for folksongs are still being created. Similarly, the specific origin of a song is not a reliable guide, because (as is shown in this chapter and the next) songs have entered the folk repertoire both from above (out of sophisticated music) and from below (rising from anonymous beginnings). Only the production of variants via communal re-creation, as a song remains for a time in the possession of a definite group, can justify the label "folksong."

The words and music of folksongs belong together, of course, and should be gathered and analyzed together. However, to facilitate a systematic survey of the kinds of American folksongs and ballads, and because the research methods for words and music are so different, tunes of folksongs (as well as instrumental music) are discussed separately in chapter 13.

Folksongs differ from nonfolksongs by their fluidity of form and content. This is apparent in contrast to the two other basic bodies of song—art songs and popular songs. Art songs are learned from printed scores exactly as their composers originally wrote them. Professional singers are expected to perform art songs in a manner in keeping with the musical conventions of the composer's own time, and usually in the composer's own language. Such songs as Schubert's *Lieder*, "Drink to Me Only with Thine Eyes," "Ave Maria," favorite arias from operas, musical settings of well-known texts (including in the United States "The Lord's Prayer," "Trees," and Roy Harris's setting of Sandburg's "Fog") are all familiar examples of art songs. They may follow any form the composer wishes to use, and they have a special, enduring intellectual or emotional (sometimes called "highbrow") appeal.

Popular songs are also printed or, more often, commercially recorded, and they, too, come from the pens of professional composers, sometimes people who are more businessmen and -women than artists, and sometimes from the performers themselves. Many popular-music artists (especially rock musicians) compose directly on their instruments, often in group sessions, thus participating in something akin to the folk process. Professional pop singers are expected to perform copyrighted songs more or less as they were written and to pay royalties for their use. Popular songs are generally more stereotyped in form than art songs, tending either to fit a rigid ABA pattern (like that of most older pop standards) or following some other mode (like the AAB twelve-bar blues form and blues diction used for some rock pieces). Most popular songs enjoy only a short but a very intense existence, being enormously popular with a broad, mostly adolescent, audience for weeks or at most months and then disappearing from radio and music-video shows. But a few popular songs become identified with the generational members of their eras—songs of World War II, of the '50s, the '60s, etc.—and are replayed as "golden oldies," both by individuals and on the airwaves, beyond the times of their initial popularity.

Folksongs as a group are even more widely accepted than art songs and popular songs, having circulated for generations, sometimes in different countries, among illiterate and semiliterate folk who had little knowledge of the other two bodies of song. Yet both middle-class and upper-class people know folksongs, too. Folksongs outlast most popular songs, and they may also be much older than art songs; for the latter generally go back to the eighteenth or nineteenth centuries at most, while some folksongs survive from the Middle Ages or earlier. Folksongs are unlimited in form and subject matter, ranging from very simple to relatively complex. But their chief distinction remains the manner by which they circulate and the resulting effect on their form: folksongs, unlike any other kind, are passed on mostly in oral tradition, and they develop traditional variants.

Since these song types are not defined primarily by their origin, folksongs may actually originate from either art songs or popular songs. As many scholars have emphasized, folksongs are *perpetuated* in oral tradition, but they need not have *originated* there. In fact, a song belonging to any one of the three groups may turn into one of the other two types, if we only apply our definitions a bit broadly.

The art songs, for instance, "O Promise Me" and the wedding march from Wagner's *Lohengrin* reached a popular-song audience when they began to be regularly sung at weddings. Then the wedding march achieved oral circulation as a folksong when words like the following were fitted to it:

> Here comes the bride,
> Big, fat, and wide.
> See how she wobbles from side to side.

In another such musical transformation, the theme melody from a Rachmaninoff piano concerto became a popular song, "Full Moon and Empty Arms." But the "Toreador Song" from *Carmen* is a folksong when it is sung this way:

> Oh Theodora,
> Don't spit on the floor-a;
> Use the cuspidor-a,
> That's-a what it's for-a.

By the same token, some popular songs outlive their typical brief careers to survive for generations as "standards." This is true especially of songs closely associated with particular singers like Bing Crosby ("White Christmas"), Judy Garland ("Over the Rainbow"), Mel Torme ("The Christmas Song"), or Frank Sinatra ("My Way"). Probably some popular songs also last because of the inherent high quality of their melodies and lyrics, and in a sense these are art songs in disguise. One thinks of "Stardust," "September Song," "Smoke Gets in Your Eyes," and such Beatles songs as "Eleanor Rigby" and "Yesterday," all of which have somewhat unconventional tunes and lyrics for popular songs. Other popular-song hits seem to cloy the public's taste eventually and are then cynically parodied in oral tradition, thus becoming folksongs: "Jealousy" turned into "Leprosy" (". . . is making a mess of me"), and "It's Magic" turned into "It's Tragic" ("You smile, your teeth fall out / Your hair looks just like sauerkraut . . ."). The popular song "Davy Crockett" spawned at least a dozen folk parodies with lines like "Born on a table top in Joe's Cafe, / Dirtiest place in the U.S.A."

When folksongs are "arranged" and enter the repertoires of professional singers and singing groups, they cease to behave like folksongs and become art songs. This has been the case especially with African-American spirituals ("Go Down, Moses," "Swing Low, Sweet Chariot," etc.), with some folk lyrics ("Black is the Color of My True Love's Hair" and "Shenandoah"), and with many foreign folksongs, which like foreign art songs are generally sung in the parent language. When folksongs catch the ears of a broad sector of the public, they may become popular songs for a brief period, as happened in the 1950s with "Goodnight, Irene" and "Tom Dooley." In the 1960s popular songs called "The Riddle Song" and "Scarborough Fair" were derived from Anglo-American folk ballads.

It should be evident now why folklorists cannot answer immediately when asked if "Barbara Allen" (or "Tom Dooley," or "Blue-tailed Fly") is a *folksong*. The only response they can give is "Which version?" Even knowing that, they might have to conclude, "Yes and no," because the decision must ultimately rest on the singer's performance and source—in short, on the singer's folk tradition, if any—rather than on any features of text and tune themselves. If words and music were learned orally from other traditional singers, if the performance is natural, and if oral variants exist, then there is a likelihood that we are dealing with folksong. Thorny problems, of course, do exist—the city fad for singing country folksongs, for instance, or the deliberate composition of popular songs in the folk style, or a song like "Greensleeves," which is widely regarded as a folksong, but which was actually revived professionally from a non-folk tradition. Such problems, however, are legitimate ones for investigation by folklorists. An example of the findings of such a study is the case of "Home on the Range." That song was first a piece of Kansas newspaper verse (in 1873), then an anonymous, somewhat fluid, cowboy folksong. It was finally tracked back to its written source, and now it is a "standard" that is invariably sung just as it is printed in songbooks.

The various ways by which folksongs have been transmitted are by no means limited solely to oral performance. Print, handwriting, sound recording, and broadcasting have all played a part in circulating folksongs among traditional singers. For example, many narrative songs (ballads) now regarded as folksongs originated as *broadsides*—crudely printed single sheets containing the lyrics for a new song and the name of a familiar tune to which it might be sung. Broadside ballads flourished in England from about the sixteenth to the early nineteenth century. They were sold on the streets, usually for a penny. Broadsides were printed in the United States until somewhat later, and have occasionally been revived in the twentieth century for such gatherings as labor-union rallies and pacifist or civil-rights demonstrations. (The general nature of Anglo-American broadside ballads is taken up in the next chapter.) *Songsters*—pamphlets of printed songs—became popular in the nineteenth century, and some are still printed now and then; their contents were generally miscellaneous, for they were compiled freely from all available sources, folk and otherwise. Songsters also were cheaply printed and sold, and, like broadsides, they were not preserved with any care either by their buyers or by early libraries. Today, however, intact broadsides and songsters are treasured library acquisitions. Countless American folksongs were also circulated in print by means of *periodicals*, especially local newspaper columns of old songs and poems. Sometimes readers were asked to submit the full texts for incomplete songs sent in by others, thus creating an informal folklore-collecting project. Some readers kept clippings of old song columns, and a few newspapers retained files of submitted songs for reference use; both kinds of collections can still occasionally be discovered.

Handwritten *"ballet books"* (*ballad* books, but spelled "ballet" to reflect a folk pronunciation) constitute another good source of folksongs ready-collected by informants themselves. The term "ballet book" has been applied to any notebook or scrapbook of songs kept by an individual for his own use. Some are in old copybooks or ledgers, while others are made out of printed books with blank paper pasted over the pages; the songs they contain usually were selected from all the songs that happened to be known to their compilers, some of whom even kept track of their own printed and oral sources.

Finally, *commercial recordings* have played an important role in folksong transmission. Beginning in 1923, when a recording company first put a "hillbilly" singer on a commercial 78 rpm disk, folksongs have been borrowed from oral tradition and then fed back into it through recordings. Other songs such as Vernon Dalhart's version of "The Death of Floyd Collins" or the Carter Family's "Worried Man Blues" originated from recording artists and their writers, and then passed on to an oral life.

FOCUS: "WILDWOOD FLOWER"

Written in 1860 by Maud Irving and J. P. Webster, a popular song-writing team, this is the original song the Carter Family remembered as "Wildwood Flower".—D. H.

> I'll twine 'mid the ringlets of my raven black hair
> The lilies so pale and the roses so fair
> The myrtle so bright with an emerald hue
> And the pale aronatus with eyes of bright blue.

[Four more stanzas follow.]

*

The first time I heard this song, I was just a kid. My mother sang it and her mother sang it. It has been handed down for years and years. It's the most popular song we ever recorded, and there's hardly a country group who doesn't use this song.—Mother Maybelle Carter, of the original Carter Family [who recorded it first in 1927]

1. Oh, I'll twine with my mingles and waving black hair
    With the roses so red and the lilies so fair
    And the myrtles so bright with emerald dew
    The pale and the leader and eyes look like blue.

[Two more stanzas, then . . .]

4. Oh, he taught me to love him and called me his flow'r
    That was blooming to cheer him thru life's dreary hour
    Oh, I'm longing to see him thru life's dark hour
    He's gone and neglected this pale wildwood flower.

*

I'll twine with my ring, made of raven black hair,
A rose so red and a lily so fair,
The myrtle so green with its emerald hue,
And pale Ermeta with eyes of dark blue.

[Three more stanzas follow.]

*

No title. From Mrs. Minnie Church, Heaton, Avery county [North
Carolina]. *A peculiarly corrupt and confused text, printed here as it stands
in the manuscript* . . .

Oh I whine with my mongles and waving black hair
With the roses so red and the lilies so fair
And moon shines so bright with the emblem of you.

[Three more stanzas, one fragmentary, follow.]

Sources: First and second from Dorothy Horstman, *Sing Your Heart Out, Country
Boy*, 3rd ed. (Nashville: Country Music Foundation Press, 1996). Third from Mel-
linger Edward Henry, *Beech Mountain* [North Carolina] *Folk-Songs and Ballads*, Set
15 (New York: G. Schirmer, Inc., 1936). Fourth from *The Frank C. Brown Collection
of North Carolina Folklore*, vol. III, no. 263, text D.

DISCUSSION TOPICS:

1. The first two texts are given in full by Dorothy Horstman.
Vance Randolph's *Ozark Folksongs* has two more, *The F. C. Brown
Collection* has four, and there are innumerable other folk texts, plus
versions sung or played as an instrumental by folksong revivalists
and bluegrass artists. Textual variations abound, especially of stanza
one. Gather and compare variant texts of this exceedingly popular
lyric. What skeletal plot is implied in most variants? Which folk
versions can probably be traced to the Carter Family's recordings?

2. The headnote to F. C. Brown's versions names the original as
"The Pale Amaranthus," a claim repeated by later commentators.
But the 1860 song by Irving and Webster reads "pale aronatus," a
flower [?] that cannot be identified. What is an "amaranthus," and
what might be appropriate about this as the intended flower reference? What literary and mythological associations does the amaranthus have? How have the "folk" mutated this line, reinterpreting it
in order to make some sense of the allusion?

The Carter Family singers: *(left to right)* Maybelle Addington, Alvin Pleasant ("A. P.") Carter, and Sara Carter (A. P.'s wife at the time). Maybelle
was Sara's first cousin; she became Maybelle Carter after marrying A. P.'s
brother Ezra, and in later years was called "Mother" Maybelle Carter.

3. Listen to recorded performances of "Wildwood Flower," perhaps by the
Carter Family, Joan Baez, David Grisman, various bluegrass artists, etc. Which
musical elements are consistent and which variable in such performances?

The preceding description represents a liberal, modern scholarly
concept of American folksong, but such has not always been the
accepted view of the subject. In 1897, nine years after the American
Folklore Society was founded, an early historian of American literature could write that we are a people "practically without folksongs." Nowadays, however, few surveys of American literature
would not contain at least a passing reference to native ballads and
folksongs, and contemporary folklorists are keenly interested in the
subject.

The first American folklorists in the late nineteenth century knew of almost no oral-traditional songs in the United States. Francis James Child, the great ballad editor, brought out his definitive edition of traditional British ballads at Harvard in the 1890s without doing any fieldwork and including only a handful of American versions that others had sent him. But the famous English collector Cecil J. Sharp, together with the American Olive Dame Campbell, found English folksongs of all kinds in abundance in the Southern Appalachians beginning in 1917, and their writings encouraged others to seek them, too.

Pioneering American collectors like Phillips Barry in the Northeast and John A. Lomax in the West and South began to publish native American folksongs at about the same time, and gradually academic folklorists accepted their finds and had to revise their own ideas about folksong types and dissemination. Widely respected scholars such as Louise Pound of the University of Nebraska and H. M. Belden of the University of Missouri were instrumental in promoting a broadened definition of American folksong, while such industrious collectors as George Korson (working among coal miners), Frank C. Brown (among North Carolina residents), and Vance Randolph (among Ozark mountaineers) gathered a widened spectrum of songs for analysis. In the 1950s and 1960s, John Greenway contended that American social-protest songs should be admitted into an inclusive definition of folksong, which he then phrased as follows:

> folksong is any song concerned with the interests of the folk and in the complete possession of the folk, who in turn are members of a homogeneous, unsophisticated, enclave living in but isolated from a surrounding sophisticated society by such features as geography, topography, race, religion, economic and educational deprivation, social inferiority, or even choice.

The historian of Anglo-American folksong studies, D. K. Wilgus, along with Greenway and others, took a rationalistic view of folksong tradition and emphasized the importance of the hillbilly-record influence upon American folksongs.

WORDLESS FOLKSONGS, NEAR-SONGS, AND FUNCTIONAL FOLKSONGS

So broad is the field of folksong that Wilgus conceded in his history of its scholarship: "It is doubtful that there will ever be a complete, not to speak of a consistent, outline of the varieties of folksong." Yet, classify we must; and if we borrow terms freely from many editions and studies, and invent a few new ones to fill gaps, we come up with something like the following scheme, with the large divisions based on form (arranged from simple to complex) and the subclasses organized by subject matter or function.

Since folksongs consist of oral-traditional words and music, we can imagine examples in which one element is stronger than the other or even exists without the other's presence at all. Such *proto-folksongs* do in fact occur in folk tradition. Vocal music without words—what we might call **wordless folksong**—is found in American folklore in such traditions as "chin music" (or "diddling," and in Ireland, "lilting"), when the voice imitates the sound of dance music played on a fiddle. The sound effect is similar to the nonsense refrains of some folk ballads, and it has a counterpart in jazz "scat singing." Some jazz instrumental styles derive from the early use of such partly vocal instruments as the Jew's harp, the jug, and the kazoo, developing into muted and "growl" effects produced on conventional band instruments. Yodeling, hollering, and African-American church "moaning," "humming," or "groaning," as it is variously called, are also examples of wordless folksong.

The musical as well as social aspects of a wordless folksong form are described in the following account of an Okefinokee swamp holler as observed by naturalist Francis Harper in 1912:

> Then I heard more of that strange music which always startles me—swamp hollering. I was unversed in the unwritten rules of the matter, and I assumed my friends at the upper end of the island were having fun. . . . [Later] Gator Joe asked me somewhat impatiently if I had heard them holler, and if so, why I hadn't answered. "When you hyear anybody hollerin', you holler back," he said with undisguised sternness. . . . And so Joe taught me rule one about the art of hollering. Even if I had been aware of what was required, I was

. . . totally incapable of producing a sound at all akin to the marvelous swamp yodeling . . . the exquisite music made by two masters, Gator Joe Saunders and Bryant Lee.

Another type of wordless folksong, known either as "eephing" or "hoodling," consists of breathy, grunting quasi-musical noises that sound somewhat like animal imitations. Wordless songs need not even necessarily be vocal; the "Johnny is a sissy!" three-note melody may be sung, hummed, whistled, or played on an instrument with the same insulting effect. The "wolf whistle" has an unmistakable meaning without any vocalizing of melody or words for it. However, the seven-stroke rhythmic pattern of one simple four-note melody does have traditional words associated with it: "Shave and a haircut, two bits." There can be no doubt that these items live orally, for no songbook contains them, yet everyone knows them. If you tap out the first five beats of "Shave and a haircut," someone will respond with "two bits"; if you hum "Johnny is a sissy" at a child, he will react. Similarly, the wolf whistle has no formal support as a greeting

Hamp Mizell demonstrates his two-mile Okefinokee swamp holler.

from etiquette books, but it speaks eloquently just the same because of its folk denotation.

When words predominate and melody is weak, we have what might be termed **near-songs.** The *cante fable*, as discussed in chapter 10, is half-and-half, and the verse may either be chanted or sung. The peddlers' cries, discussed earlier as rhymes, are often delivered in a singsong chant but sometimes are truly sung. Children's play-and-game rhymes fall into the same twilight zone between verse and song, as do many field hollers and work hollers. Square-dance calls, auctioneers' chants, and "talking blues" are all partly song, partly chant. For all of these materials, it could be said in general that the texts are fully traditional and formularized, but the tunes are improvised and free. They are nearly songs, but not quite.

The first group of true songs, with both traditional words and music, are those that closely match the rhythm of some special activity, and thus they have been called **functional songs.** Here we might classify *lullabies* that are smoothly rhythmical, peaceful, or repetitious ("Hush, Little Baby" is all three) so that they will induce sleep. Bess Lomax Hawes, who analyzed the "peculiar melange" of songs used as lullabies, also identified "happy vocalizing . . . a chatty style" and especially "the spatial isolation of the baby" as typical traits of content and performance.

Work songs belong in the functional-folksong category if they are regulated by the repeated pulses of chopping, hammering, marching, pulling on ropes, and so forth. Most American work songs are either African-American slave songs ("Take This Hammer" is perhaps the best-known example) or sailors' "sea chanteys" ("Hangman Johnny" and "Away to Rio"). A few still circulate as call-and-response songs or chants used when circus workers hoist a tent:

> Every time (Heave it!)
> Ding, dong, ring (Heave it!)
> Look on the table (Heave it!)
> Same damn old thing!

Play-party songs, which could be classified as functional songs, are discussed in chapter 16 in connection with folk dancing. Children's *game songs* belong in this category, too, for they are never sung apart from the playing of the game, and the words and melody closely follow the action of the game. A few songs are *mnemonic songs* used for remembering such lists as the presidents of the United States, the capitals of the states, multiplication tables, or basic geographical terms. A Utah example simply versifies the names of all the state's counties (adding two words at the end to fill out the rhyme), sung to the tune of the old song "Reuben and Rachel":

> Utah Train
> Beaver, Carbon, Davis, Morgan,
> Daggett, Millard, and Duchesne,
> Iron, Uintah, Rich, and Summit,
> Garfield, Cache, Piute, and Kane.
>
> Wasatch, Washington, and Weber,
> Sanpete, San Juan, Salt Lake, Wayne,
> Juab, Box Elder, Grand, Tooele,
> Sevier, Emery, Utah train.

LYRICAL FOLKSONGS

These first three broad divisions—wordless folksongs, near-songs, and functional folksongs—constitute clearly differentiated groups with easily recognizable contents. However, the folksongs that fit into them include only a small fraction of the whole. The last two divisions—lyrical folksongs and narrative folksongs—are much more complicated groups and involve many more texts. Narrative folksongs are discussed separately in the next chapter, leaving **lyrical folksongs** (the usual meaning of the simple term "folksongs") for the remainder of this one.

Some lyrical folksongs are true *folk lyrics*—that is, traditional songs devoted to expressing a mood or a feeling without telling any connected story. Many express despair for a lost or hopeless love, and these are sometimes developed as a series of impossible desires:

> Wisht I was a little fish,
> I'd swim to the bottom of the sea,
> And there I'd sing my sad little song,
> "There's nobody cares for me."

I wish I was a little sparrow,
Had wings, and oh! could fly so high.
I'd fly away to my false lover
And when he'd ask, I would deny.

Other folk lyrics have the thread of a story implied in them, as in "Down in the Valley" and "On Top of Old Smokey," while others simply take the form of warnings to lovers about the wiles of the opposite sex. Apart from the joys and sorrows of love, some folk lyrics refer to death ("Bury Me beneath the Willow"), homesickness ("The Indian Hunter" or "Let Me Go"), and general discontent ("Trouble in Mind"). A song that is probably of literary origin but circulates orally complains bitterly about household toil:

There's too much of worriment goes to a bonnet,
There's too much of ironing goes to a shirt,
There's nothing that pays for the time you waste on it,
There's nothing that lasts us but trouble and dirt.

Oh, life is toil and love is a trouble,
And beauty will fade and riches will flee;
And pleasures they dwindle and prices they double,
And nothing is what I wish it to be.

Another comic depiction of the drudgery of housework appears in these verses:

Everybody works but father,
He sets around all day,
Setting with his feet to the fire
Smoking his pipe of clay.

Mother takes in washing,
So does sister Ann.
Everybody works at our house,
But my old man.

A major category of American folk lyrical song is the African-American *blues*, a folk form based on field hollers and cries that developed countless fluid stanzas of emotional responses to life, en-

Roosevelt Holts, blues singer from Bogalusa, Louisiana, photographed in 1970.

tered a commercial and urban stage, and then profoundly influenced, both musically and textually, most of American popular music. In its classic form, the blues consists of a three-line twelve-bar pattern based on repeating one line of four musical bars twice and then rhyming a third line containing a complementary or responsive idea with it. A famous published example, based on the form of a folk verse, goes:

> I hate to see that evening sun go down,
> I hate to see that evening sun go down,
> Because my baby, she done left this town.

The spirit of the blues is often, although not necessarily, melancholy:

> Woke up this morning, blues all 'round my bed,
> Woke up this morning, blues all 'round my bed,
> Picked up my pillow, blues all under my head.

The subject matter of the blues is commonly disappointed love:

I want to know, why did my baby go,
I want to know, why did my baby go,
I love that woman, love her 'til it hurts me so.

And blues imagery is often frankly sexual, as shown in this Bessie Smith lyric, typical of folk blues, although from a commercial recording:

Bought me a coffee-grinder, got the best one I could find,
Bought me a coffee-grinder, got the best one I could find,
So he could grind my coffee, 'cause he has a brand new grind.

A black prisoner's blues, as recorded in Louisiana, is grippingly phrased:

Wonder why they electrocute a man at the one o'clock hour at night,
Wonder why they electrocute a man at the one o'clock hour at night,
The current much stronger, people turn out all the light.

Spirituals and other traditional *religious songs* may sometimes allude to a biblical story or a religious legend, or allegorize a lesson, but their narrative content is subordinate to their expression of strong feeling; they may be considered lyrical folksongs except for the relatively few that are "religious ballads." There are "white spirituals" as well as African-American ones, and the controversy over origins and precedence has filled several books. Religious songs exhibit much more variety than may be illustrated briefly, but the basic simplicity of many is seen in a stanza like "Where, oh, where are the good old patriarchs? [three times] / Safely over in the Promised Land." Some religious folksongs are infused with the imagery and fervor of revival meetings and fire-and-brimstone preaching. Scenes depicted frequently in others are crossing rivers, washing away sin, walking in heaven, and riding trains. Some folk hymns (like "Amazing Grace") derive from English Protestant hymns, which later appeared in the old American "shape-note" collections like *The Sacred Harp*, in which each tone of the scale was printed in one of four different shapes. The liveliest folk religious songs, such as "That Old Time Religion," anticipate the "gospel songs" that are still commercial country-music or bluegrass favorites on recordings and in broadcasts.

In the same spirit as religious songs are the secular *homiletic songs* that dispense advice like "Paddle Your Own Canoe," or ask embarrassing questions like "Why Do You Bob Your Hair, Girls?" But for every song that criticizes a life of "Puttin' on the Style," there are a dozen more that we might call *songs of gamblers, drinkers, ramblers, and prisoners.* Here the dissolute life, if not directly recommended for others, is often at least glorified by the singer. Witness "Old Rosin the Bow," who for his funeral wants to have his six pallbearers line up at the graveside and have one last drink to him, their burden. Some temperance songs circulate orally, like "Lips That Touch Liquor Must Never Touch Mine" and "I'll Never Get Drunk Anymore," but the more numerous variety of songs about drinking either describe the brewing process ("Moonshine" and "Mountain Dew") or revel in its product ("Pass 'round the Bottle" and "Pickle My Bones in Alcohol"). The most common song of the group is variously entitled "Jack of Diamonds," "Rye Whiskey," "On Top of Clinch Mountain," or "A Card-Player's Song." Typical verses, which may occur in any order, include:

> Jack of diamonds, Jack of diamonds
> I know you of old,
> You robbed my poor pockets
> Of silver and gold.
>
> For the work I'm too lazy
> And beggin's too low,
> Train robbin's too dangerous
> So to gamblin' I'll go.
>
> I eat when I'm hungry,
> I drink when I'm dry,
> And when I get thirsty,
> I lay down and cry.
>
> I've played cards in England,
> I've played cards in Spain,
> I'll bet you ten dollars,
> I'll beat you next game.

Focus: "Drunken Hiccups"

Jan Brunvand: Where did you learn the songs that you were singing for me Tuesday?

Mary Jane Fairbanks: Everywhere!

JB: Why don't you sing that whiskey song that you started with, and then tell me about it? . . . The one that has the hiccups in it.

MF: Oh, "Drunken Hiccups." [Sings]

Good whiskey, good whiskey, 'twill do you no harm,
I wish I had a bottle as long as my arm.
  Chorus: Hic-up and oh lordy, how bad I do feel
      Hic-up and oh lordy, how bad I do feel

I'm a rambler I'm a gambler and that's why I roam,
If people don't like me, they can let me alone. [Chorus]

I'll eat when I'm hungry, I'll drink when I'm dry,
And if whiskey don't kill me, I'll live 'til I die. [Chorus]

Rye whiskey, rye whiskey, rye whiskey, I cry,
If I don't get rye whiskey, I'll lay down and die . . . [no chorus]

MF: And that's all I know of it.

JB: Where did you learn it?

MF: Out in the cornfield one day. . . . My brother and I were hoeing corn for the man that we live on—where we lived on his place . . . and the hired man, and Ed, and I went up to a shade tree and sat under there and ate our dinners, and while we was there he learned me that song.

JB: How many times did he have to sing it before you learned it?

MF: Three or four times, and he learned me two of them . . . another way to sing the "Drunken Hiccups," but I've forgotten the other.

JB: Did the other way have the hiccups in it, too; do you remember?

MF: Yes, sir. It had the hiccups in it just the same.

JB: Have you ever heard the words "Jack of Diamonds" in that song?

MF: No.

Source: Jan Harold Brunvand interview with Mary Jane Fairbanks, age 95, December 3, 1965, in Edwardsville, Ill. (Another of Mrs. Fairbanks's songs is quoted in chapter 16.)

Jan Harold Brunvand interviews Mary Jane Fairbanks.

DISCUSSION TOPICS:

1. Mrs. Fairbanks called all of her songs "whiskey songs," whether they mentioned strong drink or not. This is the song from her extensive repertory that she always sang first. What did her term for her songs seem to mean to her?

2. Mrs. Fairbanks neither drank, rambled, nor gambled; she was confined to a nursing home at the time of this recording, and she had no nearby living relatives. Yet she sang this song enthusiastically, imitating the sounds of a drunkard's hiccups in the choruses and introducing a catch in her voice in the middle of the first line of each verse. What did her performance style indicate about what the song meant to her?

3. How many different verses and choruses can you find for this popular drinking song? Compile from the variants a rough biography and character sketch of the persona represented in the song.

Folksongs of courtship and marriage form a distinct group. These include songs that describe a courtship ("The Quaker's Wooing" and "The Old Man's Courtship," also known as "Old Boots and Leggings"), those that represent a courting dialogue ("I'll Give to You a Paper of Pins" and "Soldier, Soldier, Will You Marry Me?"), a few that express a desire for marriage ("I Love Little Willie, I Do" and "The Old Bachelor"), but many more that celebrate the single life ("Wish I Was Single Again" and "I Am Determined to Be an Old Maid").

The logical sequel to songs of courting and marriage is the group of *nursery and children's songs*, many of which derive their appeal and their easy memorability from the use of a simple repeated pattern. This is true of "Go Tell Aunt Rhody," "The Barnyard Song" (or "I Bought Me a Cat"), "There Was an Old Woman Had a Little Pig," "There's a Hole in the Bottom of the Sea," and a host of others. The last named item is a *cumulative song*, analogous to the cumulative folktales, and others involve imitations of animal sounds, dramatic dialogues (as in "Billy Boy"), gestures ("John Brown's Baby Had a Cold upon Its Chest"), and "jump" (or "scare") endings ("Old Woman All Skin and Bones"). This is also the place to mention three bodies of modern folksongs of childhood and adolescence that have not been collected or studied very systematically—*summer-camp songs, high school songs,* and *college songs.* Camp songs (which are sentimental, religious, homiletic, or simply funny) may be represented by these two samples, one a parody and the other pure nonsense:

> Let me call you sweetheart,
>   I'm in love with your machine.
> Let me hear you whisper
>   that you'll buy the gasoline.
> Keep your headlights burning,
>   and your hands upon the wheel.
> Let me call you sweetheart,
>   I'm in love with your automobile.

*

One bottle of pop, two bottles of pop
Three bottle of pop, four bottle of pop [up to seven bottles] . . .

Don't put your dust in my dustpan,
My dustpan, my dustpan,
Don't put your dust in my dustpan,
My dustpan's full

Fish and chips and vinegar,
Vinegar, vinegar,
Fish and chips and vinegar,
Pepper, pepper, pepper pot!

Although many folksongs (and a few ballads) are humorous, at least three kinds of funny songs might be separately noted. First, *dialect songs*, like dialect stories, derive their humor from an exaggeration of racial or national speech peculiarities. Those in Southern black dialect often stem from blackface minstrel shows, while "Chinese songs" from the West and "Swede songs" from the upper Midwest reflect regional settlement patterns and local prejudices. Second, *nonsense songs* take their comedy from a stream of purely meaningless verbiage, often delivered at a rapid-fire pace. Examples include "The Barefoot Boy with Shoes On," "It Was Midnight on the Ocean, Not a Streetcar Was in Sight," "The Soft Side of a Brick," and "The Billboard Song." Third, *parody songs*, seldom collected and studied, seem to cluster to a few old popular numbers, "My Bonny Lies over the Ocean" being the apparent favorite, and yielding versions like this:

My Bonny has tuberculosis;
My Bonny has only one lung;
She coughs up the blood and corruption,
And rolls it around on her tongue.

Evidence for the folk status of "Happy Birthday" are the many parodies of the familiar words:

Happy Birthday to you,
Happy Birthday to you,
You act like a baby,
But you look ninety-two.

*

Happy Birthday to you
You live in a zoo,
We're sure that you'll live there,
On your next birthday, too.

Regional and occupational folksongs are numerous in this country
and offer insights into the history of labor and of settlement that
few other sources give. *Cowboy songs* are now well known, thanks
largely to the early collecting efforts of N. Howard (Jack) Thorp
and John A. Lomax, who first started to collect and publish them
after 1908. There are also songs of loggers, railroaders, sailors, miners, military men, and other workers, and of such hobby groups as
mountain climbers, skiers, and surfers.

Proof that the creation of occupational folksongs has not died out
lies in a group of songs collected from American fighter pilots in
Southeast Asia in 1967 and 1968. Mostly parodies based on commercial hillbilly, folk, and popular songs, these were often heavy
with technical jargon and social protest, as this set of words for two
stanzas of "Wabash Cannonball" demonstrates:

"Hello, Cam Ranh Tower, this is Hammer 41;
My BLC light's glowing, I've just lost PC-1,
The engine's running roughly, the EGT is high,
Please clear me for a straight-in, this bird's about to die!"

"Hammer 41, this is Cam Ranh Tower here;
We'd like to let you in right now, but a senator is near;
He's here to please constituents, his plane is close at hand,
So please divert to Tuy Hoa, we can't clear you to land."

Verses from three songs of early American occupational groups
demonstrate how the working conditions and workers' attitudes
were mirrored in their singing then, too, and how the general
themes of songs, as well as details of texts, tended to be passed on
westward. One whalers' song contains this verse:

Some days we're catching whalefish, boys, and more days we're getting
   none,
With a twenty-foot oar placed in our hand from four o'clock in the
   morn.

But when the shade of night comes down we nod on our weary oar.
Oh, it's then I wished that I was dead, or back with the girls on shore!

A Northeast loggers' song describes similar conditions, even to the time of arising:

At four o'clock in the morning the boss he will shout,
"Heave out, my jolly teamsters; it's time to be on the route."
The teamsters they jump up all in a frightened way,
"Where is me boots? Where is me pants? Me socks is gone astray!"

And one cowboy song seems to be nothing more than a rewording of the above.

Oh early every morning you will hear the boss say,
"Get out boys, it's the breakin' of day."
Slowly you rise with your little sleepy eyes,
And the bright dreamy night's passed away.

. . . The cowboy's life is a very dreary life,
It's a ridin' through the heat and the cold.

The most prominent group of regional songs are those of early Western travel and settlement, which, like tall tales, seem to laugh at hardships with an ironic tone. One song cheerfully concerns "Starvin' to Death on My Government Claim," another celebrates "The Dreary Black Hills," and a third begins

I am looking rather seedy now,
While holding down my claim,
And my victuals are not always served the best;
And the mice play slyly round me,
As I nestle down to sleep
In my little old sod shanty in the West.

One ubiquitous Western song, sung to the tune of the old hymn "Beulah Land," has variants for many states—"Kansas Land," "Dakota Land," "Nebraska Land," etc., all with verses like

I've reached the land of wind and heat,
Where nothing grows for man to eat.
The wind it blows with feverish heat,
Across the plains so hard to beat.

O Dakota land, sweet Dakota land,
As on thy fiery soil I stand,
I look away across the plains
And wonder why it never rains,
Till Gabriel blows his trumpet sound
And says the rain's just gone around.

In the Northwest the same song appears as "Oregon, Wet Oregon"
or "Webfoot Land."

RESEARCHING FOLKSONGS

It would be an understatement to say that American folksongs have
been collected and published with more energy than has been devoted to their classification and study; as a matter of fact, considering
the vast numbers of texts and tunes available, they have hardly been
analyzed at all. Even classification remains a problem, since the few
categories for folksongs suggested in this chapter have counterparts
in almost every published collection, but the specific songs placed
under them vary widely. One person's "regional song" may be another's "comical song" and a third's "satirical song." Different
terms entirely—including "historical songs," "jingles," "martial and
political songs," and "dance songs"—appear in some collections, and
every system has its "miscellaneous" category, under which usually
appear what one scholar has called "sentimental balladlike pieces"
—songs like "In the Baggage Coach Ahead," "Christmas at the Poor
House," "Little Rosewood Casket," and "The Dream of the Miner's
Child."

The situation for folksong studies is even worse. Preceding his
study of one Anglo-American lyric, "Green Grows the Laurel,"
Tristram P. Coffin summed up some of the problems like this:

Lyric song offers a tremendous challenge to scholars interested in bibliographical and historical explanations of folk material. With its endlessly wandering groups of stanzas, interchange of cliché, and lack of plotted action, folk lyric often appears beyond definition and even description. As a field for study, it seems to have scared off and discouraged scholars.

Yet, as Coffin proceeded to demonstrate in his study, "If one isn't too bothered by the necessity of coming to concrete conclusions, one can learn much about oral transmission . . . particularly about folk-song travel, by tackling these lyrics one by one, group by group."

FOCUS: "GREEN GROW THE LILACS"

My mother sang this song while I was growing up, and she taught it to me and my sister. We would often sing it with her while she played the autoharp. She mentioned that it was a patriotic song, and that changing from green to red, white, and blue was like becoming an American citizen. She also said that "greengo" (which sounds like "green grow") was a nickname that Mexicans often called Americans.

> I once had a sweetheart but now I have none
> Since she's gone and left me, I care not for none.
> Since she's gone and left me, contented I'll be,
> For she loves another one better than me.
>
> Green grow the lilacs all sparklin' with dew,
> I'm lonely my darlin', since parting with you.
> But by our next meeting, I hope to be true,
> And change the green lilacs to red, white, and blue.

Source: A University of Utah student, about 1990.

DISCUSSION TOPICS:

1. This is merely one verse and the chorus of a song, often known as "Green Grow the Laurels," widely collected in both the U.S. and England. How does this text compare with others? What details of text and comments suggest that the Utah text may have been learned from a printed or commercially recorded source?

2. See the 1952 study of this lyric by Tristram P. Coffin, cited in the bibliographic notes. Does the Utah text tend either to confirm or deny any of Coffin's suggestions? What does Coffin have to say about the plants named, the "red, white, and blue" reference, and about the green grow/gringo idea?

3. The possible transformation of "green grow" to "gringo," a derogatory term used by Hispanics for Anglo-Americans, is mentioned by others, but regarded by lexicographers as a folk etymology of no merit. What is the generally accepted etymology for "gringo"?

American folksongs, therefore, seem to offer a particularly promising area for research. Hundreds of songs have been collected in possibly thousands of variants, and many of these are available in print. The broad outlines of a suitable classification system seem clear enough, but the details need to be worked out and published. Almost any song or song type that might be selected for study exists in enough variants from enough different regions to yield fascinating data, and both texts and tunes are usually intrinsically appealing in themselves. Questions of style, variation, function, and meaning would immediately present themselves in the study of any song. For all these reasons, and with the bibliographic aids and theoretical models now at hand and the many American folklorists interested in music, the study of American folksongs has the possibility of advancing quickly to the high level already achieved in the study of the Anglo-American ballad, which is discussed in the next chapter.

BIBLIOGRAPHIC NOTES

An excellent general introduction to the whole subject is George Herzog's essay "Song: Folk Song and the Music of Folk Song" in *Funk & Wagnalls Standard Dictionary of Folklore, Mythology, and Legend*, 2 (1949): 1032–50. Two comparable articles limited to the United States are Louise Pound's "American Folksong: Origins, Texts and Modes of Diffusion," *SFQ* 17 (1953): 114–21, reprinted in *Nebraska Folklore*, pp. 234–43, and Bruno Nettl's chapter "Words and Music: English Folksong in the United States" in Nettl, Charles Hamm, and Ronald Byrnside's *Contemporary Music and Music Cultures* (Englewood Cliffs, N.J.: Prentice-Hall, 1975), pp. 193–221. Among book-length surveys, Russell Ames's small *The Story of American Folksong* (New York: Grosset & Dunlap, 1955) is interestingly keyed to history, but the discussion is often too sketchy. Bruno Nettl's *An Introduction to Folk Music in the United States* (Detroit: Wayne State University

Studies no. 7, paperback ed., 1960; rev. 1962; 3rd ed. rev. by Helen Myers, *Folk Music in the United States: An Introduction*, 1976) is comprehensive, though short, and it is well documented. Nettl and Myers consider both texts and tunes. Edith Fowke presents "Anglo-Canadian Folksong: A Survey" in *EM* 16 (1972): 335–50.

MacEdward Leach introduced a symposium of seven writers on folksong studies with a note, "Folksong and Ballad—a New Emphasis," *JAF* 70 (1957): 205–7. He identified the shift in interest from collecting to analysis. A second important collection of articles, originally in the *Texas Folklore Society Publications* (33, 1964), includes papers on the literary and esthetic approach, the anthropological approach, the comparative approach, and the rationalistic approach; see Roger Abrahams's *Folksong and Folksong Scholarship: Changing Approaches and Attitudes* (Dallas: Southern Methodist University Press, 1964). The definitive historical work is D. K. Wilgus's *Anglo-American Folksong Scholarship since 1898* (New Brunswick, N.J.: Rutgers University Press, 1959). Wilgus offered his assessment of folksong research and ventured a look ahead in two important articles: " 'The Text Is the Thing,' " *JAF* 86 (1973): 241–52, and "The Future of American Folksong Scholarship," *SFQ* 37 (1973): 315–29.

Two books not primarily about American folksongs still have a great deal to contribute to analyzing and understanding them: Roger de V. Renwick, *English Folk Poetry: Structure and Meaning* (Philadelphia: University of Pennsylvania Press, 1980); and Barre Toelken, *Morning Dew and Roses: Nuance, Metaphor, and Meaning in Folksongs* (Urbana: University of Illinois Press, 1995).

Herzog and Nettl, cited above, discuss art, folk, and popular songs; see also Frank Howes's "A Critique of Folk, Popular, and 'Art' Music," *BJA* 2 (1962): 239–48; and Peter Stadlen's "The Aesthetics of Popular Music," *BJA* 2 (1962): 351–61.

Most folksong collections contain some texts from broadsides, songsters, clippings, "ballet books," and recordings. An interesting separate publication from a manuscript source is Harold W. Thompson and Edith E. Cutting's *A Pioneer Songster* (Ithaca, N.Y.: Cornell University Press, 1958); another is Ruth Ann Musick's "The Old Album of William A. Larkin," *JAF* 60 (1947): 201–51. In my article "Folk Song Studies in Idaho," *WF* 24 (1965): 231–48, a large Northwest newspaper collection of folksongs that went back some thirty years is described.

Questions concerning the popularization and commercialization of folksongs have been discussed many times in folklore journals and meetings. William Hugh Hansen presented "The Folksinger's Defense" in *HF* 9 (1950): 65–75, in which he discussed the repertoires of three young Kentucky singers and their tastes and preferences in folksongs compared to folklorists' usual categories and theories. Sven Eric Molin touched off an exchange of opinions with his article "Lead Belly, Burl Ives, and Sam Hinton," in *JAF* 71 (1958): 58–79. Three folklorists criticized in the article replied with notes in the same issue, followed by a rejoinder by Molin and a "last word" by Sam Hinton. An amusing reaction to citybilly singing from a country singer is Eugene Haun's "Lares and Penates, Once Removed," *JAF* 72 (1959): 243–47. Oscar Brand, a popular performer of folksongs, documented the rise of professional folksong singing in his book *The Ballad Mongers*

(New York: Funk & Wagnalls, 1962). In a related vein, see Norman Cohen's "Tin Pan Alley's Contribution to Folk Music," *WF* 29 (1970): 9–20. R. Raymond Allen's "Old-Time Music and the Urban Folk Revival," *NYF* 7 (1981): 65–81, criticizes folklorists for disregarding the music of the revival and makes some good suggestions for scholarly projects. On the whole subject of folklore revivalism, see Neil V. Rosenberg, *Transforming Tradition* (Urbana: University of Illinois Press, 1993). An intriguing memoir is Ronald D. Cohen, ed., *"Wasn't That a Time!": Firsthand Accounts of the Folk Music Revival* (Metuchen, N.J.: Scarecrow Press, 1995).

John Greenway's thesis was backed by his book *American Folksongs of Protest* (Philadelphia: University of Pennsylvania Press, 1953). But his ideas were attacked by Tristram P. Coffin in "Folksongs of Social Protest: A Musical Mirage," *NYFQ* 14 (1958): 3–9, with a brief rejoinder from Greenway, who then stated his position more fully in his article "Folksongs as Socio-Historical Documents," *WF* 19 (1960): 1–9, reprinted in *Folklore in Action*, pp. 112–19. A book that deals with some of the same materials without calling them folksongs is Josh Dunson's *Freedom in the Air: Song Movements of the Sixties* (New York: Little New World Paperbacks, LNW-7, 1965). Richard A. Reuss discusses a major figure in the social uses of folk and folklike music in his essay "Woody Guthrie and His Folk Tradition," *JAF* 83 (1970): 273–303; and provides an excellent historical survey in "American Folksongs and Left-Wing Politics: 1935–1956," *JFI* 12 (1975): 89–111. Reuss's essay on the "musical odyssey" of Charles Seeger appeared in *WF* 38 (1979): 221–38, the same year that Seeger died. A good survey is in Jens Lund and R. Serge Denisoff's "The Folk Music Revival and the Counter Culture: Contributions and Contradictions," *JAF* 84 (1971): 394–405. The other side of the coin is exposed in Marcello Truzzi's "The 100% American Songbag: Conservative Folksongs in America," *WF* 28 (1969): 27–40.

Wilgus and Greenway as coeditors blazed a new trail with the "Hillybilly Issue" of *JAF* (77 [July–September 1965]), which contains important articles and discography. Shortly thereafter the American Folklore Society published Bill C. Malone's book *Country Music: U.S.A.* as Volume 54 in the Memoir Series (Austin, Texas, 1968; rev. ed., 1985). Malone followed this with *Singing Cowboys and Musical Mountaineers: Southern Culture and the Roots of Country Music* (Athens: University of Georgia Press, 1993). Another folklore journal issue devoted to "commercialized folk music in general, and hillbilly music in particular" was *WF* 30 (1971): 171–246. Two separate articles of particular interest are Howard Wight Marshall's " 'Keep on the Sunny Side of Life': Pattern and Religious Expression in Bluegrass Gospel Music," *NYFQ* 30 (1974): 3–43 (expanded from a 1971 publication in *FF*); and Frederick E. Danker's "The Repertory and Style of a Country Singer: Johnny Cash," *JAF* 85 (1972): 309–29. A good general article on the whole subject of folksongs' mass popularity is Samuel P. Bayard's "Decline and 'Revival' of Anglo-American Folk Music," in *Folklore in Action*, pp. 21–29. Bayard describes how folksongs change musically into art or popular songs as they are reproduced by city singers in a synthetic atmosphere of folksiness.

There are far too many good general folksong collections to list them all, but

Wilgus's history offers a full bibliography. A few landmark volumes must be mentioned. Olive Dame Campbell and Cecil J. Sharp's *English Folksongs from the Southern Appalachians* first appeared in 1917 (New York and London: Oxford University Press). The two-volume edition, edited by Maud Karpeles, appeared in 1932 and was reissued in 1952. Louise Pound's anthology *American Ballads and Songs* (New York: Scribners, 1922) is a notable early book of native materials with a stunning introductory essay that manages to touch upon almost every important aspect of the pieces included. Midwestern states are well represented in collections such as Emelyn E. Gardner and Geraldine J. Chickering's *Ballads and Songs of Southern Michigan* (Ann Arbor: University of Michigan Press, 1939; repr. Hatboro, Pa.: Folklore Associates, 1967), Paul Brewster's *Ballads and Songs of Indiana* (Bloomington: Indiana University Folklore Series no. 1, 1940), George List's *Singing About It: Folk Song in Southern Indiana* (Bloomington: Indiana University Press, 1991), and H. M. Belden's *Ballads and Songs Collected by the Missouri Folk-Lore Society* (Columbia: University of Missouri Studies vol. 15, 1940).

Vance Randolph's four-volume *Ozark Folksongs* (Columbia, Mo.: State Historical Society, 1946–50) is as indispensable as his many excellent folktale publications. (A revised edition with an introduction by W. K. McNeil was published by the University of Missouri Press in 1980.) The folksong texts in *The Frank C. Brown Collection of North Carolina Folklore* are edited in vol. 3 (1952) by H. M. Belden and Arthur Palmer Hudson; tunes are in vol. 5 (1962). Book-length collections published since Wilgus's history include two from the West: Lester A. Hubbard's *Ballads and Songs from Utah* (Salt Lake City: University of Utah Press, 1961) and Ethel and Chauncey O. Moore's *Ballads and Folk Songs of the Southwest* (Norman: University of Oklahoma Press, 1964).

The rich African-American folksong heritage has been well documented, earlier in such studies and anthologies as Dorothy Scarborough's *On the Trail of Negro Folksongs* (Cambridge, Mass.: Harvard University Press, 1925; repr. Hatboro, Pa.: Folklore Associates, 1963) and N. I. White's *American Negro Folksongs* (Cambridge, Mass.: Harvard University Press, 1928), and later in such works as Harold Courlander's *Negro Folk Music, U.S.A.* (New York: Columbia University Press, 1963). Dana J. Epstein's *Sinful Tunes and Spirituals* (Urbana: University of Illinois Press, 1977) traces African-American music up to the Civil War. See also James Weldon Johnson's *The Book of American Negro Spirituals* (New York: Viking, 1969), and Erskine Peters's *Lyrics of the Afro-American Spiritual* (Westport, CT: Greenwood Press, 1993).

Social backgrounds of the blues are given in Frederic Ramsey, Jr.'s *Been Here and Gone* (New Brunswick, N.J.: Rutgers University Press, 1960), George Mitchell's *Blow My Blues Away* (Baton Rouge: Louisiana State University Press, 1971), and Alan Lomax's *The Land Where the Blues Began* (New York: Pantheon, 1993). For tracing further developments, see Samuel B. Charters's *The Country Blues* (New York: Rinehart, 1959), Harry Oster's *Living Country Blues* (Detroit: Folklore Associates, 1969), and Charles Keil's *Urban Blues* (Chicago: University of Chicago Press, 1966) and their discographies. Other aspects of blues tradition are discussed in William R. Ferris, Jr.'s "Racial Repertoires among Blues Performers," *EM* 14

(1970): 439–49; and David Evans, "Techniques of Blues Composition among Black Folksingers," *JAF* 87 (1974): 240–49. The special blues issue of *SFQ* (vol. 42 [1978]: 1–98), edited by Jeff Todd Titon, contained seven useful articles. Among the many other recent books on the blues are Jeff Todd Titon's *Early Downhome Blues* (Urbana: University of Illinois Press, 1977), David Evans's *Big Road Blues* (Berkeley: University of California Press, 1982), and Barry Lee Pearson's *Virginia Piedmont Blues* (Philadelphia: University of Pennsylvania Press, 1990).

The popular-cultural effects of blues tradition are described in John M. Hellmann, Jr.'s " 'I'm a Monkey': The Influence of Black American Blues Argot on the Rolling Stones," *JAF* 86 (1973): 367–73. Another important aspect of black folksongs is treated by Bruce Jackson in articles and in his book *Wake Up Dead Man: Afro-American Worksongs From Texas Prisons* (Cambridge, Mass.: Harvard University Press, 1972).

Pioneering collections of American occupational and industrial folksongs were made by George Korson and published in such works of his as *Songs and Ballads of the Anthracite Miner* (New York: Grafton Press, 1927), *Minstrels of the Mine Patch* (Philadelphia: University of Pennsylvania Press, 1938; reissued Hatboro, Pa.: Folklore Associates, 1964), and *Coal Dust on the Fiddle* (Philadelphia: University of Pennsylvania Press, 1943; reissued Hatboro, Pa.: Folklore Associates, 1965). A companion work is Archie Green's *Only a Miner: Studies in Recorded Coal-Mining Songs* (Urbana: University of Illinois Press, 1972). See "Labor Song: A Reappraisal," a special double issue of *JFR* (28:2–3 [1991]).

Collections of sea songs include W. Roy Mackenzie's *Ballads and Sea Songs from Nova Scotia* (Cambridge, Mass.: Harvard University Press, 1928; reprinted Hatboro, Pa.: Folklore Associates, 1963), Elisabeth Bristol Greenleaf and Grace Yarrow Mansfield's *Ballads and Sea Songs of Newfoundland* (Cambridge, Mass.: Harvard University Press, 1933; reprinted Hatboro, Pa.: Folklore Associates, 1968), and Frederick Pease Harlow's *Chanteying aboard American Ships* (Barre, Mass.: Barre Publishing Co., 1962). See also Elliott Oring, "Whalemen and Their Songs: A Study of Folklore and Culture," *NYFQ* 27 (1971): 130–52.

The interplay between the songs of sailors and of loggers is suggested in *Shantymen and Shantyboys* (New York: Macmillan, 1951) by William Main Doerflinger. For loggers' songs, see Edith Fowke, *Lumbering Songs from the Northern Woods* (Austin, Texas: AFS Memoir Series vol. 55, 1970). Hardrock miners' folksongs were first discussed by Duncan Emrich in *CFQ* 1 (1942): 213–32. A collection of "Songs of the Butte Miner" supplemented that pioneering article in *WF* 9 (1950): 1–49, by Wayland D. Hand, Charles Cutts, Robert C. Wylder, and Betty Wylder. S. Page Stegner discussed "Protest Songs from the Butte Mines" in *WF* 26 (1967): 157–67. Other articles on occupational folksong traditions are Ann Miller Carpenter, "The Railroad in American Folk Song, 1865–1920," *PTFS* 36 (1972): 103–19; "Big Tops Bloom, but Chanteys Disappear," reprinted from *Billboard* in *WF* 17 (1958): 57–60; and Marcello Truzzi, "Folksongs of the American Circus," *NYFQ* 24 (1968): 163–75. A major book is Norm Cohen's *Long Steel Rail: The Railroad in American Folk Song* (Urbana: University of Illinois Press, 1981).

Folksong collector John A. Lomax with his son Alan produced some of the most widely read—and sometimes controversial—general anthologies of folksongs in this country. The publication of Alan Lomax's *The Folk Songs of North America in the English Language* (New York: Doubleday, 1960) was the occasion for several reviews in professional journals that variously damned and praised all of the Lomax books. See reviews by G. Legman and D. K. Wilgus in *JAF* 74 (1961): 265–69; by Gene Bluestein in *TQ* 5 (1962): 49–59; and by David P. McAllester in *EM* 6 (1962): 233–38.

John Lomax's *Cowboy Songs and Other Frontier Ballads* of 1910 (New York: Sturgis and Walton) has been reprinted and expanded several times. Jack Thorp's pamphlet *Songs of the Cowboys* of 1908, to which Lomax was indebted for several of his texts, was reprinted with variants, commentary, notes, and a lexicon by Austin E. Fife and Alta Fife (New York: Clarkson N. Potter, 1966). In "Jack Thorp and John Lomax: Oral or Written Transmission?" *WF* 26 (1967): 113–18, John O. West reviews the evidence that Lomax had used nineteen out of the twenty-three songs Thorp earlier printed without giving credit. Professor and Mrs. Fife assembled at the Utah State University Library in Logan materials from print, recordings, and manuscripts for comprehensive analyses of most of the traditional songs of the cowboys. Two of their publications based on these data are *Cowboy and Western Songs: A Comprehensive Anthology* (New York: Clarkson N. Potter, 1969) with two hundred items, and *Heaven on Horseback: Revivalist Songs and Verse in the Cowboy Idiom* (Logan, Utah: Western Texts Society Series 1, 1970).

In an essay entitled "The Dying Cowboy Song," *WAL* 2 (1967): 50–57, John Barsness suggests that accounts of cowboy singing are greatly romanticized and that many collectors had little to do with real cowboys. A collection of seldom-collected items is Guy Logsdon's *"The Whorehouse Bells Were Ringing" and other Songs Cowboys Sing* (Urbana: University of Illinois Press, 1989). The actual folk-song repertoire of one real cowboy is given in Glenn Ohrlin's *The Hell-bound Train, a Cowboy Songbook* (Urbana: University of Illinois Press, 1973). John I. White, the composer of the song, gives the background for the Western-tinged "Great Grandma" in *WF* 27 (1968): 27–31. J. D. Robb provides examples in Spanish and English of another type of Western occupational song in " 'Whereof I Speak,' or Songs of the Western Sheep Camps," *NMFR* 12 (1969–70): 17–28.

Folksongs in scholarly journals are beyond counting, but some representative examples may be cited. Edward D. Ives has held to an exceptionally high standard of editing in his "Twenty-one Folksongs from Prince Edward Island," *NEF* 5 (1963): 1–87; and "Folksongs from Maine," *NEF* 7 (1965): 1–104. Another collection from this region is Richard M. Dorson, George List, and Neil Rosenberg's "Folksongs of the Maine Woods: Annotated Transcriptions," *FFMA* 8 (1965): 1–33. From the Midwest and West come "Songs I Sang on an Iowa Farm," collected by Eleanor T. Rogers with notes by Tristram P. Coffin and Samuel P. Bayard, *WF* 17 (1958): 229–47 (repr. in *Readings in American Folklore*, pp. 31–52); and Ben Gray Lumpkin, "Colorado Folk Songs," *WF* 19 (1960): 77–97. A small collection of items of a kind often ignored is given in Gloria Dickens's "Childhood Songs from North Carolina," *NCFJ* 21 (1973): 4–9.

Edward D. Ives's book *Larry Gorman, the Man Who Made the Songs* (Bloomington: Indiana University Press, 1964) exhaustively traces and analyzes the work of a woods poet responsible for some of the best folksongs of the Northeast. Ives followed this with *Lawrence Doyle: The Farmer Poet of Prince Edward Island* (Orono: University of Maine Studies no. 92, 1971), and *Joe Scott: The Woodsman-Songmaker* (Urbana: University of Illinois Press, 1978). Other studies that focus on the singer rather than the songs exclusively are Roger D. Abrahams's *A Singer and Her Songs: Almeda Riddle's Book of Ballads* (Baton Rouge: Louisiana State University Press, 1970) and Henry Glassie, Edward D. Ives, and John F. Szwed's *Folksongs and Their Makers* (Bowling Green, Ohio: Bowling Green State University Popular Press, 1970).

G. Legman deals with a long-neglected area of folksong in "The Bawdy Song in Fact and in Print," in *The Horn Book* (New Hyde Park, N.Y.: University Books, 1964), pp. 336–426. One such song is traced by Guthrie T. Meade, Jr., in "The Sea Crab," *MF* 8 (1958): 91–100; and Ed Cray has edited a sizeable anthology in *The Erotic Muse* (New York: Oak Publications, 1968; 2nd. ed. Urbana: University of Illinois Press, 1991).

Joseph Hickerson discussed college folksongs in two articles in *FFMA* 1 (1958): 2 and 6 (1963): 3–6. Some examples of camp songs are given by Linda Weaver in *NCFJ* 22 (1974): 75–79. Two nonsense songs ("The Soft Side of a Brick" and "She Was Built Like a Mississippi Shed") are given by Richard C. Poulsen in *AFFWord* 3 (1973): 11–15. Some military folksongs are given in an article by Gustave O. Arlt and Chandler Harris in *CFQ* 3 (1944): 36–40, and two by William Wallrich in *WF* 12 (1953): 270–82 and 13 (1954): 236–44. In the *FF* Bibliographic and Special Series no. 7 (1971), Major Joseph F. Tuso gathered thirty-three examples of "Folksongs of the American Fighter Pilot in Southeast Asia, 1967–68."

Good analytical studies of American folksongs (as opposed to studies of ballads) are relatively uncommon. Some early ones by Phillips Barry are contained in the *Bulletin of the Folksong Society of the Northeast*, reprinted by the American Folklore Society with an introduction by Samuel P. Bayard (Philadelphia: Bibliographic and Special Series no. 11, 1960). An important work is Roger D. Abrahams and George Foss, *Anglo-American Folksong Style* (Englewood Cliffs, N.J.: Prentice-Hall, 1968). Levette J. Davidson first summarized the investigation of "Home on the Range" in *CFQ* 3 (1944): 208–11. John Lomax added his observations on the song in "Half-Million Dollar Song," *Southwest Review* 31 (1945): 1–8. Probably the definitive account is John I. White's article on it in *TAW* 12 (Sept. 1975): 10–15, a chapter from his book *Git Along Little Dogies: Songs and Songmakers of the American West* (Urbana: University of Illinois Press, 1975). My own study " 'The Lane County Bachelor': Folksong or Not?" (the answer was "yes") appeared first in *Heritage of Kansas* 10 (1977) and was reprinted in *Readings in American Folklore*, pp. 289–308.

Tristram P. Coffin's "A Tentative Study of a Typical Folk Lyric: 'Green Grows the Laurel,' " *JAF* 65 (1952): 341–51, is unusual as a comparative study of a single nonnarrative song. Other approaches to specific genres of folksong are Peter T. Bartis's "An Examination of the Holler in North Carolina White Tradition," *SFQ* 39 (1975): 208–18; Bess Lomax Hawes, "Folksongs and Functions: Some Thoughts on the American Lullaby," *JAF* 87 (1974): 140–48 (repr. in *Readings in American Folklore*, pp. 203–14); D. K. Wilgus and Lynwood Montell, "Clure and Joe Williams: Legend and Blues Ballad," *JAF* 81 (1968): 295–315; and Américo Paredes, "The Décima on the Texas-Mexican Border: Folksong as an Adjunct to Legend," *JFI* 3 (1966): 154–67.

Two uncommon studies of the nature of folksong variation are John Quincy Wolf's "Folksingers and the Re-Creation of Folksongs," *WF* 26 (1967): 101–11; and Tom Burns's "A Model for Textual Variation in Folksong," *FF* 3 (1970): 49–56. Norman Cazden's article "Regional and Occupational Orientations of American Traditional Song," *JAF* 72 (1959): 310–44, offers an unusual statistical analysis of folksong distribution for various regions.

12

BALLADS

DEFINING AND CLASSIFYING BALLADS

A traditional ballad is a narrative folksong—a folksong that tells a story. To carry the basic definition any further, as most ballad collectors and scholars have been inclined to do, is asking for trouble; every other quality that might be listed as characteristic of some ballads requires a balancing list of other ballads that are exceptions to the rule. But because they all tell stories, a traditional ballad is a narrative folksong.

We have defined "folksong" in chapter 11. But how narrative is a "narrative"? At this point all folksong-versus-ballad distinctions become relative and arbitrary. For instance, the "folk lyric" called "On Top of Old Smokey," derived, in fact, from an English ballad called "The Wagoner's Lad" and tells a reasonably clear story, as the following stanza illustrates:

> Your parents are against me
> And mine are the same;
> So farewell, my true love
> I'll be on my way.

The same thing is true of "Careless Love," "The Dreary Black Hills," "The Lane County Bachelor," "Old Dan Tucker," and a host of other American folksongs; all of these have at least a modicum of plot. Conversely, some accepted ballads occur in scattered variants that have confusing story lines or extremely scant narrative content, so they seem more lyrical than narrative. At this point we need to look at what American ballad scholars have considered to be genuine ballads.

Some 850 Anglo-American narrative folksongs have been arranged by scholarly indexers in three categories: *British traditional ballads*, *British broadside ballads*, and *native American ballads*. The idea that these ballad classifications are canonical has been exaggerated by some past scholars. As recently as 1956 the noted Appalachian folklore collector Richard Chase declared in his popular anthology *American Folk Tales and Songs* that "the genuine *ballad* is only one type of folksong. Your 'ballad' is not a true *folk* ballad unless it is closely kin to one of the 305—no more, no less!—in Professor Child's great collection." (Italics in original.) So much for broadside and native American ballads!

It is true that Francis James Child wrote in 1882 that he had gathered "every valuable copy of every known ballad," but this was a good forty years before field-collecting of ballads in America had gotten well under way. All that the twentieth-century ballad indexer G. Malcolm Laws, Jr., claimed to offer was a "guide" and "bibliographical syllabus"; it is the users of these collections and indexes who have elevated them into canons and treated their rough groupings as if they were systematic classifications. All of which is preliminary to a warning that in the discussion that follows, the "three kinds of ballads," as well as generalizations offered about them, are merely to be regarded as convenient scholarly concepts that facilitate description and analysis. The last word has certainly not been said on ballad definition or classification, although D. K. Wilgus made some good progress toward an international Type Index with his proposal for a thematic catalog of the narrative units of traditional songs based on such events or actions as seductions, murders, punishments, and bereavements. However, his work has not been completed following Wilgus's death in 1989.

BRITISH TRADITIONAL BALLADS

The **British traditional ballads** are usually known as "the Child ballads," not because they are sung by children or have any connection whatever with children's folklore, but because they were gathered by Professor Francis James Child of Harvard University from hundreds of manuscript and printed sources in the late nineteenth century and published, together with voluminous notes, in his mon-

Francis James Child (1825–1896), compiler and editor of *The English and Scottish Popular Ballads*.

umental work, *The English and Scottish Popular Ballads* (5 volumes, 1882–98). These songs are called "Child ballads" only by scholars, of course, and not by folk informants, who would no more call them that than they would call "Jack, Will, and Tom tales" *Märchen* or refer to fairy tales by their Aarne-Thompson type numbers.

The Child ballads have been the folksong collectors' prime finds and the literary anthologists' favorite set pieces. Collectors went to the extreme at one time in this country of periodically tallying, state by state and county by county, the Child ballad variants "recovered" from oral tradition, either in complete or in fragmentary texts. The anthologists continue to reprint some eight or ten selected ballad versions from Child as examples of medieval popular poetry, notwithstanding the fact that most of these selections came from manuscript sources no earlier than the seventeenth century and the texts were often revised by ballad editors in the eighteenth century or later. The veneration that has surrounded the Child canon—the mystique of the 305 ballads that he included—is also seen in the typical "Child and other" arrangements of many printed folksong collections.

The editor's very choice of words in his title—*The* English and Scottish popular ballads—granted a false exclusiveness to his 305 ballads, when there are many other British popular ballads that Child either would not admit on esthetic grounds (because they were off-color or overly sentimental) or did not know. Yet his choices had considerable validity, too. These do constitute the oldest group of ballads in British tradition, and their basic form, at least, is found in medieval sources. These ballads are part of an international tradition in that they are related to corresponding narrative folksongs from the Continent, especially the Scandinavian ballads. The greatest influence upon Child was the edition of Danish ballads that came from the hand of Svend Grundtvig, beginning in 1853. Grundtvig's texts revealed numerous analogs to the English ballads. Furthermore, Grundtvig exerted direct influence on Child during their extended correspondence. Most important, these ballads serve as a norm against which other ballads are measured, for their treatments of subject matter, style, and narrative method are widely considered to be of a high poetic order, although within the limitations of a rigid set of traditional conventions.

BALLAD CHARACTERISTICS

The technique of comparing art songs and folksongs may be applied to literary poetry and ballad poetry. In literature we value originality—a fresh treatment of a universal theme, "What oft was thought, but ne'er so well expressed." But the traditional ballads, as Albert B. Friedman has written, are not literature but "illiterature"; they exist only in different oral performances, not in fixed written texts, and thus they abound in features that oral transmission creates and sustains. They use only a few simple stanza forms; their rhyme and meter seem irregular compared to conventional poetry; their language is stereotyped and cluttered with clichés; they freely repeat phrases, lines, and sometimes whole stanzas, often as refrains; and their texts are full of dialect terms, archaisms, and garbled usage. Despite all this, the best of the old traditional ballads have a unique charm and force that have not been equaled in literary imitations. Although no amount of description can replace hearing ballads sung by traditional performers, the characteristic features of ballad poetry may at least be illustrated in print.

The typical *ballad stanza* is the familiar one of many folk rhymes and jingles (including "Mary Had a Little Lamb") and of "common measure" in hymns. It is a quatrain rhyming "x, a, x, a" (that is, lines one and three do not rhyme), with lines measured "4, 3, 4, 3" (counting strong beats only), as shown in this typical opening verse from the ballad that Child called "James Harris" or "The Demon Lover" and that is frequently collected in this country as "The House Carpenter." It is Child's number 243:

"Well mét, well mét," said an óld true lóve,	(4, x)
"Well mét, well mét," said hé;	(3, a)
"I've júst retúrned from a fár foreign lánd,	(4, x)
And it's áll for the lóve of thée."	(3, a)

Other ballads, regarded by some scholars as the oldest ones, have a two-line stanza of four strong beats each, usually with refrain lines filling out a quatrain, such as in the following opening stanza from the Scottish ballad "Willie's Lyke-Wake" (Child 25):

"O Wíllie my són, what mákes you so sád?"
    As the sun shines over the valley.
"I lýe sarely síck for the lóve of a máid."
    Amang the blue flowers and the yellow.

There are other kinds of ballad stanzas—some say as many as a dozen—but the various forms cannot be fully established without reference to ballad music.

The *refrains* in ballads are often lyrical lines interspersed with story lines, as in the last example quoted above, or they may involve both lyrical lines and repetition, as in this opening stanza from "The Two Sisters" (Child 10):

Emma L. Dusenbury (1862–1941) of Mena, Arkansas, an outstanding singer of traditional ballads, who was recorded for the Library of Congress by John Lomax in 1936.

There was an old man in the North Countree,
  Bow down!
There was an old man in the North Countree,
  And a bow 'twas unto me.
There was an old man in the North Countree,
And he had daughters one, two, three.
  I'll be true to my love if my love be true to me.

Refrains like this suggest dance movements or directions. Others
are lists of plants, such as "Parsley, Sage, Rosemary and Thyme"
(which sometimes appears in variants like "Every rose grows merry
in time"). A number of refrains sound like pure nonsense, being
merely strings of syllables such as "hey nonny no," "derry, derry,
down," and "lillumwham, lillumwham."

Repetition alone in ballads may provide a refrain, usually through
the repeating of the last two lines of each quatrain to form a six-
line stanza, and there are numerous instances of repetition as a structural device in the plots themselves. Sometimes a question is repeated
in an answer or a command is repeated in action, with very little
change in wording, as shown in these typical commonplace lines
found in numerous ballads:

        "Who will shoe your pretty little foot,
        And who will glove your hand?"
        ". . . mother will shoe my pretty little foot,
        And father will glove my hand."

        "Go saddle me the black, the black,
        Go saddle me the brown,
        Go saddle me the fastest steed,
        That ever ran through town."

        She saddled him the black, the black,
        She saddled him the brown . . . (etc.)

The most typical form of ballad repetition is *incremental repetition*,
in which several lines are repeated with a slight "increment" (addition or change). Some ballads like "The Maid Freed from the

Gallows" (Child 95, also called "Hangman") and "Our Goodman" (or "Four Nights Drunk," Child 274) are developed entirely through this device.

Focus: Youthful Barnyard Humor

About forty years ago in a country town in Maine a group of boys, the writer among them, went to the woods in search of mayflowers. When the trailing arbutus proved to be more than usually elusive its absence was recompensed by an exchange of songs and stories, some of them of a nature not altogether suitable to the family circle. The youthful barnyard humor was in part familiar and is for the most part now forgotten, but one song clung and clings:

> As I came home the other night
> As drunk as I could be,
> I found a horse within the stall
> Where my horse ought to be.

> "Oh wife, dear wife,
> Why can't you be true to me?
> Whose horse is in the stall,
> Where my horse ought to be?"

> "You old fool, you damned fool,
> You son of a gun," said she.
> "That's nothing but a milking-cow
> My mother sent to me."

> I've travelled all around this world for twenty years,
> A hundred miles or more,
> But saddle on a milking-cow
> I never saw before.

There were more stanzas, increasingly forthright in expression and thanks in part to a repetitive pattern and thanks in part to impropriety I became then and there a link in the great chain of oral transmission, and also the collector of a popular ballad.

Source: Bartlett Jere Whiting, ed., *Traditional British Ballads* (New York: Appleton-Century-Crofts, 1955), p. v.

DISCUSSION TOPICS:

1. What is the ballad that Whiting learned as a boy usually called? How "forthright in expression" do the versions in Child and elsewhere become? Are there any unusual or unique wordings or details in Whiting's text?

2. What characteristic poetic features of British traditional ballads does this text display? What features seem to be weak or missing?

3. Whiting (who became a noted folklore scholar) wrote that his faculty advisor at Harvard, George Lyman Kittredge, published the version of "Lord Randall" (Child 12) that Whiting also knew, but said that the other ballad "was not in its entirety of a nature to lend itself readily to publication." Find other versions of this ballad in print; how have times changed with regard to publishing off-color or suggestive folklore?

Incremental repetition is also seen in two stanzas from "The Bonny Earl of Murray" (Child 181):

> He was a braw [fine] gallant,
> And he rid at the ring
> And the bonny Earl of Murray,
> Oh he might have been a king!

The next stanza is the same, except that the second line becomes "And he played at the ba' [ball]," while the last is altered to "Was the flower among them a' [all]."

The oft-repeated "shoe your foot," "saddle my horse," and other stanzas ("Oh, make my bed, mother . . . ," "Go dig my grave, father . . . ," etc.) are one kind of *commonplace*, or stereotyped diction, found in ballads. These are "commonplace stanzas," and there are also repeated phrases. Wine is always "blood-red"; steeds tend to be "milk-white" or "dapple grey"; knives are usually "wee penknives" (perhaps an alteration of "weapon knife"); and a frequent courtly servant is the "little foot page." Child ballads often begin conventionally (" 'Twas in the merry month of May") and express times in commonplace phraseology ("Two [or three] hours before it was day"). Such expressions certainly aid ballad singers' memories, for the performers can fall back on these phrases easily if other words escape them; but whether the words indicate the spontaneous "for-

mulaic composition" of ballads or are simply traditional poetic devices is debatable.

In the opening stanzas of traditional ballads quoted above, we can
see two other characteristic devices—ballads, like epics, often begin
abruptly, *in medias res* (in the middle of the story), and they are
highly *dramatic* in that they are told largely in terms of dialogue and
action. In "The House Carpenter," for instance, we do not know
who the "old true love" is who has returned saying "Well met, well
met" (a greeting like "Welcome," apparently). But as the ballad pro-
gresses in the dialogue of the next two stanzas, we can begin to piece
the background together:

> "Come in, come in, my old true love,
> And have a seat with me.
> It's been three-fourths of a long, long, year
> Since together we have been."
>
> "Well I can't come in or I can't sit down,
> For I haven't but a moment's time.
> They say you're married to a house carpenter,
> And your heart will never be mine."

Two of the most popular ballads in literary anthologies, "Lord
Randall" (Child 12) and "Edward" (Child 13), are told entirely in
dialogue, as are several others. Most, however, have stanzas of dialogue alternated with stanzas of action, with an occasional bit of
description. By this means ballads achieve the immediacy of real life,
of dramas, or, as one critic has suggested, of motion pictures. Another ballad characteristic that supports the film theory has been
called *leaping and lingering*—the tendency to make abrupt scene
changes and then "linger" in one place for several stanzas. The counterpart in film is the art of "montage," or selective cutting and splic-
ing of long, middle, and close-up shots.

Perhaps the most striking aspect of traditional ballad style (or
tone) is *impersonality*. Stories involving supernaturalism, stark tragedy, and bloody violence, often between lovers or family members,
are narrated with little intrusion of editorial comment or sentimentality. (A pleasant and uncomplicated tune often supports this kind
of thematic tone.) Like modern newspaper stories, which often deal

with the same kinds of subjects, the ballads tend to focus on the climax of an action and its result, relating the happenings in a straightforward, objective manner. In "Mary Hamilton" (Child 173), a lady of the Scottish court disposes of her illegitimate child thus:

> She's tyed it in her apron
> And she's thrown it in the sea;
> Says, "Sink ye, swim ye, bonny wee babe!
> You'll ne'er get mair o me."

In "Little Musgrave and the Lady Barnard" (Child 81, often called "Little Matty Groves" in the United States) a duel is described thus:

> The first stroke that Little Musgrave stroke,
> He hurt Lord Barnard sore;
> The next stroke that Lord Barnard stroke
> Little Musgrave nere struck more.

FOCUS: BALLADS AS LULLABIES

When on 8 April 1938 Alan Lomax walked into the comfortable, pleasant home of Thomas M. Bryant on East Gum Street in Evansville [Indiana] he found more music than he had anticipated. He and his wife, Elizabeth, were on a field trip collecting folk songs for the Archive of American Folk Song of the Library of Congress. They had come to see Mrs. Bryant [Mary Vandora McNeely Bryant] at the recommendation of Paul Brewster, to whom she had sent many texts of British and American ballads which she sang and which he later published in his Ballads and Songs of Indiana *(1940). Besides Mrs. Bryant there were her husband, who played the fiddle, and three of her four daughters [Esther, Kathleen, and Ethel] who sang ballads they had learned from their mother.*

Lomax set up his Presto instantaneous disc machine, plugged in the microphone, placed an acetate disc on the turntable, and began to record. Song succeeded song, intermixed with an occasional fiddle tune until late in the morning. Lomax returned again on 11 April, and when he left he still felt that there were more ballads that Dora, as she was usually called, could have sung for him. Actually, he had recorded twenty-eight songs, of which a dozen or so were old British ballads and of which at least three were fairly well known American ballads.

Dora told Lomax that she had never been a good singer and that her family never allowed her to sing when she was young. She had learned the songs from her mother and aunts and had always sung them around the house under her breath. This no longer applied when she had her own family. In the house on Gum Street two of her daughters, who were divorced, had their children with them so she sang not only to her daughters but also to her grandchildren.

Esther's daughter, Patsy Kixmiller of Evansville, remembers well Dora Bryant's ballad singing. Dora often sang ballads to the children as lullabies. "Some of the songs were absolutely, Oh my! they were brutal and harsh," she told me [i.e., George List]. "But when she sang them they were beautiful lullabies." Asked about this, Esther said that Dora's songs always seemed to deal with death. "People drowned, froze, were stabbed, or had their heads cut off with a sword. I don't think we thought much about the words. They were lullabies, they just put you to sleep at night."

Source: George List, *Singing About It: Folk Song in Southern Indiana* (Indianapolis: Indiana Historical Society, 1991), p. 11.

DISCUSSION TOPICS:

1. Look up the ballads sung by Dora Bryant, as published by Brewster and List. How "brutal and harsh" were the stories told in them?

2. If "ballad" is a category of folksong defined by the presence of narrative, how does "lullaby" seem to be defined, at least within this Indiana family? Is this definition typical of American lullabies? (In other words, are ballads of death traditionally sung to put children to sleep?)

3. Examine the published melodies of Dora Bryant's ballad singing. Presumably, the tunes, if not the texts, of these folksongs are what one might call "lulling" in their effect. Do you find them so?

BALLAD TRANSMISSION AND CHANGES

All of the ballad characteristics described so far are typical of English and Scottish texts, although the stanzas of "The House Carpenter" and "The Two Sisters" quoted above actually came from American variants. When we look more closely at traditional ballads collected in this country, a pattern of alteration becomes apparent. American versions of Child ballads tend to lose details of their stories, to slough off supernatural motifs, to become subjective in tone, to acquire local references, and to change their language.

The longer that ballads are transmitted orally, the more they tend to be reduced to what folklorist Tristram P. Coffin has termed the "emotional core" of the narrative; the focus is always on the climax of the story. Long ballads, originally sprinkled with circumstantial details, may eventually become lyrical folksongs. "Sir Lionel" (Child 18), for example, in older versions telling a complicated tale about a knight slaying both a wild boar and a giant, becomes in the United States "Old Bangum and the Boar," a comical song about a hunting expedition. "Little Sir Hugh" (Child 155), relating the same medieval legend as Chaucer's "Prioress's Tale" (part of the same tradition as the urban legend of "The Mutilated Boy"), loses its anti-Semitic plot in American versions and simply tells of a murder by a "Jeweler's daughter" or "gypsy lady." In "Mary Hamilton," Coffin's chief example of this process, the narrative is reduced to a five-stanza lament by the victim, and no story whatever is told.

Americans, presumably because they are hardheaded and practical, have tended especially to drop supernatural elements from British ballads. Little Sir Hugh no longer speaks miraculously after his murder; Sir Lionel faces no giant; James Harris is not a ghost (or the Devil) but merely a double-dealing sailor; and the ballad of "The Two Sisters" has lost its fascinating motif of a speaking harp being constructed from the dead girl's breastbone and strands of her hair. Ghosts, fairies, elves, and mermaids all drop out of most American texts. In the few variants in which the Devil still appears, he is a comic figure, not the Prince of Darkness.

American sentimentality and fundamentalist religion are credited with the alteration of the moral tone of many British traditional ballads. The most typical change is the addition of a concluding stanza that comments on the story. In "James Harris," the wife is persuaded to leave her husband and sail away with the returned lover. The ship sinks (in older British versions through magic), and this verse is then tacked on at the end:

> A curse be on the sea-faring men,
> Oh, curséd be their lives,
> For while they are robbing the House-Carpenter,
> And coaxing away their wives.

In some American versions of "Bonny Barbara Allen" (Child 84) the tragic heroine herself speaks:

> "Farewell ye virgins all," she said,
> "And shun the fault I've fell in;
> Henceforth take warning by the fall
> Of cruel Barbara Allen."

Unsavory subjects like incest are eliminated; cruel characters in ballads may return later and apologize for their behavior. In one of the most extreme examples of changed tone, the deeply moving British ballad "The Three Ravens" (Child 26; in Scotland "The Twa Corbies") became in the United States a rolicking nonsense song. The traditional British versions descend from one first printed in 1611 that began

> There were three ravens sat on a tree,
>   Downe a downe, hay downe, hay downe
> There were three ravens sat on a tree,
>   With a downe
> There were three ravens sat on a tree,
> They were as blacke as they might be,
>   With a downe derrie, derrie, derrie, downe, downe.

The story continues as a dialogue between the ravens that reveals how a knight lying "slain under his shield" is guarded by his hawks and hounds and is finally carried off for burial by a fallow doe, "great with child," who perishes from the effort. The ballad ends with the comment

> God send every gentleman
> Such hawks, such hounds, and such a leman [sweetheart].

In the Scottish version the hawks and hounds desert the knight, his lady takes another mate, and the ravens feast on his corpse. However, some American versions ignore pathos entirely, so that the song begins

>   There were three crows sat on a tree,
>   Oh Billy Magee Magaw!
>   There were three crows sat on a tree,
>   Oh Billy Magee Magaw!
>   There were three crows sat on a tree,
>   And they were black as crows could be;
>   And they all flapped their wings and cried,
>   "Caw! Caw! Caw!"
>   And they all flapped their wings and cried,
>   "Billy Magee Magaw!"

This time the three crows only pick out the eyes of an old dead horse, and the ballad sometimes ends:

>   O maybe you think there's another verse,
>   But there isn't.

Minor verbal variations in ballads may be the result of singers forgetting words, misunderstanding what they have heard, inserting a commonplace, or trying to improve on a story or to expand it. A frequent result is the creation of near nonsense—"a parrot sitting on a willow tree" becomes "exceeding on a willow tree," or instead of characters calling out "amain [vigorously], 'Unworthy Barbara Allen,'" they call "amen." The first of these changes possibly came about as a result of misunderstood pronunciation, the latter from the use of an unfamiliar archaic word. Names in the British ballads are particularly subject to change in American tradition. In "The Gypsy Laddie" (Child 200), for example, many variants occur, including Gypsy Davey, Gypsum Davey, Black Jack Davey, and Harrison Brady.

In many instances, verbal changes in American versions of British traditional ballads serve to relocalize the setting. Thus, in a logger's version of the ballad called "The Farmer's Curst Wife" (Child 278), the subject is a "woodsman's wife"; and Lord Randall in Virginia may be "Johnny Randolph," picking up the name of a prominent local family. References to "deep blue sea" sometimes change to "Tennessee." One of the most amusing relocalizations has appeared in the commonplace stanza that attaches a "rose-briar" ending to a tragic love story:

One was buried in the old churchyard,
The other in the choir.
And out of her grave grew a red, red, rose,
And out of his a briar.

They grew and they grew to the old church top,
'Til they couldn't grow any higher.
And there they locked in a true-lover's knot,
For all true lovers to admire.

A singer who evidently did not recognize "choir" as a part of a church in which bodies might be interred changed it to "Ohio."

BRITISH BROADSIDE BALLADS

British broadside ballads, as noted in chapter 11, are a more recent strain of balladry than the Child ballads. Also, in contrast to Child's 305 ballads, the plots of broadsides are even more sensational, their attitudes are more subjective, their stanza forms are more varied, and their language is less poetic. Broadside diction tends even more heavily than that in Child ballads toward stereotypes, drawing both on the same commonplaces found in the older ballads and on some new ones. (The "Come all ye" opening stanza, for example, is frequent.) Broadsides not only are like newspapers in general style and narrative method, but also, in common with the most sensational modern tabloids, they often dwell upon murders, robberies, scandals, love triangles, and like subjects.

Many thousands of such topical ballads were composed, printed on tens of thousands of broadside sheets, and sold on the streets, in both England and America, to a public eager for their lurid stories. But only a small number of these pieces passed into oral tradition and became folk ballads. The folk versions, in turn, continued to change in oral transmission in much the same way that Child ballads varied. Presumably, then, a broadside, too, can eventually be reduced to an "emotional core." Analysis of this whole process of ballad variation was greatly facilitated in 1957, when Professor G. Malcolm Laws, Jr., of the University of Pennsylvania published a classified bibliographic guide to some 290 common American ballads that had apparently derived from British broadsides, along with an illuminating discussion of their distribution, forms, and style. Laws's categories and some sample titles follow (letters A through I were reserved for Laws's index of "native American ballads" [i.e., those composed in the U.S.] discussed next):

J. War Ballads (A small group with few American versions; "The Drummer Boy of Waterloo" is J 1.)
K. Ballads of Sailors and the Sea ("The Sailor Boy" is K 12.)
L. Ballads of Crime and Criminals ("The Boston Burglar" is L 16 B.)
M. Ballads of Family Opposition to Lovers ("The Drowsy Sleeper" is M 4.)
N. Ballads of Lovers' Disguises and Tricks ("Jack Monroe" is N 7.)
O. Ballads of Faithful Lovers ("Molly Bawn" or "The Shooting of His Dear" is O 36.)
P. Ballads of Unfaithful Lovers ("The Butcher Boy" is P 24.)
Q. Humorous and Miscellaneous Ballads ("Father Grumble" is Q 1, and "The Babes in the Woods" is Q 34.)

Although ballads with broadside origins have not been so highly regarded by folklorists as have Child ballads, most traditional singers in America know more broadsides than any other kind of ballad. At any rate, in more than eighteen hundred folksong and ballad texts, Laws's analysis of the contents of six representative collections shows that the broadsides outnumber either Child or native American ballads by more than two to one. The fact that the collected variant texts of Child ballads outnumber either of the other two types in the same books is probably indicative of folklorists' rather than informants' preferences. In one other large and diversified printed collection, Frank C. Brown's *North Carolina Folklore*, a similar distribution among types is maintained. Among some 184 identifiable texts here, forty-nine are Child ballads, about seventy-five are broadsides, and about sixty are native American ballads. Another revealing statistic about this last collection is that the remaining printed texts—some 130 further ballads from North Carolina folk tradition—do not appear in any of the three published classifications of ballads in America, suggesting how incomplete these classifications actually are.

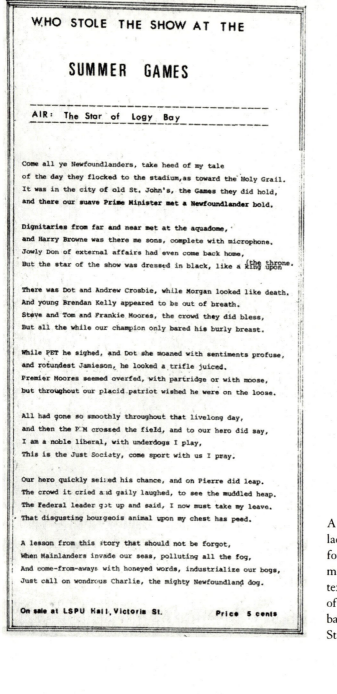

WHO STOLE THE SHOW AT THE

SUMMER GAMES

AIR: The Star of Logy Bay

Come all ye Newfoundlanders, take heed of my tale
of the day they flocked to the stadium,as toward the Holy Grail.
It was in the city of old St. John's, the Games they did hold,
and there our suave Prime Minister met a Newfoundlander bold.

Dignitaries from far and near met at the aquadome,
and Harry Browne was there me sons, complete with microphone.
Jowly Don of external affairs had even come back home,
But the star of the show was dressed in black, like a king upon (the throne.

There was Dot and Andrew Crosbie, while Morgan looked like death.
And young Brendan Kelly appeared to be out of breath.
Steve and Tom and Frankie Moores, the crowd they did bless,
But all the while our champion only bared his burly breast.

While PET he sighed, and Dot she moaned with sentiments profuse,
and rotundest Jamieson, he looked a trifle juiced.
Premier Moores seemed overfed, with partridge or with moose,
but throughout our placid patriot wished he were on the loose.

All had gone so smoothly throughout that livelong day,
and then the PM crossed the field, and to our hero did say,
I am a noble liberal, with underdogs I play,
This is the Just Society, come sport with us I pray.

Our hero quickly seized his chance, and on Pierre did leap.
The crowd it cried and gaily laughed, to see the muddled heap.
The Federal leader got up and said, I now must take my leave.
That disgusting bourgeois animal upon my chest has peed.

A lesson from this story that should not be forgot,
When Mainlanders invade our seas, polluting all the fog,
And come-from-aways with honeyed words, industrialize our bogs,
Just call on wondrous Charlie, the mighty Newfoundland dog.

On sale at LSPU Hall, Victoria St.   Price 5 cents

A broadside ballad from Newfoundland on a modern topic. The text fits the tune of a popular folk ballad called "The Star of Logy Bay."

Most other regional collections yield roughly similar figures. For example, when a miscellaneous group of some 730 folksongs and ballads (one thousand individual texts) from the Northwest was analyzed, about one-quarter of them were found to be ballads, and these fell into the following groups:

	INDIVIDUAL BALLADS	INDIVIDUAL TEXTS
Child	19	49
Laws Broadsides	41	71
(Other, prob. British)	12	36
Laws native American	57	83
(Other, prob. American)	38	65

Such statistics suggest that non-Child ballads are more common than Child ballads in American folk tradition, that many unclassified Anglo-American ballads still exist, and that, as a group, ballads are outnumbered in tradition by nonnarrative folksongs. Classifications, titles, and statistics, however, do not tell us anything about ballads themselves. Selected stanzas from the broadside ballads, whose titles and Laws numbers were listed above, give some notion of their characteristics; the versions quoted in the following summary are all taken from *The Frank C. Brown Collection of North Carolina Folklore*.

The broadside composers plodded grimly through their stories, getting the maximum pathos out of every situation and always taking the easiest way out to provide the rhymes. The following stanza of Laws J 1, given in the informant's own spelling, is typical:

> And when [his] lips his mother pressed
> And bid her noble boy adue
> With ringing hands and aching breast
> Behold a march for Waterloo.

Even when the characteristic rhetoric of the older ballads appears, it does little to elevate the general tone. The following use of incremental repetition from Laws K 12, for instance, is undistinguished:

> "Oh, father, go build me a boat,
> That over the ocean I may float."
> The father built her a boat
> And over the ocean she did float.

Further repetition appears in one later stanza of this ballad, from the beginning of which an alternate title is sometimes taken:

> "Oh, captain, captain, tell me true,
> Does my dear sailor boy sail with you?"
> "No, no, he does not sail with me;
> I fear he's drowned in the sea."

Frequently broadsides are narrated in the first person, but not usually with any improved poetic art. The burglar from Boston in Laws L 16 B merely begins with an obvious bid for sympathy (addressing himself directly to listeners) and then reels out the sequence of events in a pedestrian manner:

> I was born in the town of Boston,
> A town you all know well,
> Raised up by honest parents—
> The truth to you I will tell—
> Raised up by honest parents,
> Raised up most tenderly,
> Until I became a sporting man
> At the age of twenty-three.
>
> My character was taken
> And I was sent to jail.
> The people tried, but all in vain,
> To keep me out on trail [probably should be "out on bail"].
> The juror found me guilty,
> The clerk he wrote it down,
> The judge he passed the sentence
> To send me to Charlestown.

At times, however, the language becomes more inspired, as in the usual opening phrases of Laws M 4. In this particular version the first stanza is muddled, but the second one rescues the story. As in many fine old traditional ballads, things begin here *in medias res* and are carried on entirely in dialogue:

> "Awake, arise, you drowsy sleeper!
> Awake, arise; it's near about day.
> Awake, arise; go ask your father
> If you're my bride to be.
> And if you're not, come back and tell me;
> It's the very last time I'll bother thee."
>
> "I cannot go and ask my father,
> For he is on his bed of rest
> And in his hand he holds a weapon
> To kill the one I love the best."

This ballad often merges with the American "Silver Dagger," a kind of "climax of suicides" folksong:

> And he taken up that silver dagger
> And plunged it in his snowy white breast,
> Saying "Farewell, Bessie, farewell, darling;
> Sometimes the best of friends must part."
> And she taken up that bloody weapon
> And plunged it in her lily-white breast . . . (etc.)

Among the love ballads, external complications mar most romances, and tragic endings are the rule, with few exceptions. But lovers bring some problems on themselves, often as the result of their own attempts at tricks and disguises. One favorite device of broadsides is the return of a long-lost lover, in disguise, to his sweetheart. Another is the girl dressing in man's clothing in order to follow her lover into military service. From Laws N 7:

> She stepped into the tailor shop and dressed in men's array
> And enlisted with the captain to carry her away.
> "Before you get on board, sir, your name I'd like to know."
> She spoke with a pleasing countenance, "My name is Stephen Monroe."

"Your waist it is too slender, your fingers are too small,
Your cheeks too red and rosy to face a cannon ball."

"My waist is none too slender . . . (etc.)

Generally the name in the above ballad is "Jack Monroe," and
she is off to pursue "Jackie Frazier," from either of which character
the ballad may be named. Again in this passage, as well as the one
quoted just before, we observe incremental repetition developing in
the last partially quoted line.

An unintentional disguise led to the death of Molly Bawn (or
"Bond," Laws O 36), who is called "Polly Bonn" in the North Carolina version. She threw her apron over her head against the rain,
with this result:

> With her apron pinned around her
> The rain for to shun;
> Jimmy Randall he saw her
> And shot her for a swan.

In British versions Molly's ghost may return to defend Jimmy at
his murder trial, but American texts characteristically lose the
supernaturalism.

Broadside ballads of faithful lovers and unfaithful lovers run
about even in Laws's index (forty to forty-one), but sometimes the
classification of an individual piece is debatable. For instance, in
Laws P 24 we have a faithful girl with an unfaithful sweetheart,
and the ballad has been classified from her point of view:

> There lived a girl in that same town
> Where he would go and sit around.
> He'd take that girl upon his knee
> And tell her things that he wouldn't tell me.

Later she requests in her suicide note (using a commonplace
stanza):

> "So bury me both wide and deep,
> Place a marble stone at my head and feet,

And on my breast place a snow-white dove
To show to the world that I died for love."

The saving grace of humor seems to raise some of the ballads in
category Q a cut above most of the others in Laws's broadside index.
"Devilish Mary" (Q 4) is a comical antifeminist (or at least anti-
marriage) piece, "The Love-of-God Shave" (Q 15) has some felici-
tous wording for a very funny situation, and "Finnegan's Wake" (Q
17) deserves the respectability and immortality it achieved from
James Joyce's use of it. Another humorous success is Laws Q 1, in
which a farmer, variously named, takes an ill-considered oath:

Old Summerfield swore by the sun and the moon
And the green leaves on the tree
That he could do more work in one day
Than his wife could do in three.

Teeny the cow has to be milked during the man's day at home, and
she proves to be only one source of exasperation to him:

Teeny inched and Teeny winced
And Teeny curled her tail;
She gave the old man such a kick in the face
It made him drop his pail.

At the other extreme in the last category are some of the "miscellaneous" ballads—sad, trite orphans with no home elsewhere in
the index—like "The Babes in the Woods":

Oh, don't you remember, a long time ago,
Of two little children, their names I don't know.
They were stole on the way on a bright summer day [probably
    "stolen away"]
And lost in the woods, I've heard people say.

And when it was night so sad was their plight
The moon went down and the stars gave no light.
They sobbed and they sighed and they bitterly cried;
Poor babes in the woods, they lay down and died.

And when they were dead the robins so red
Brought strawberry leaves and over them spread
And sang a sweet song the whole day long.
Poor babes in the woods, they lay down and died.

These three verses, all that usually remain in many American versions, are based on a long and highly circumstantial ballad, which seems to have inspired one of Emily Dickinson's best-known poems. (It is number 9 in the standard numbering, and begins, "Through lane it lay—thro' bramble— / Through clearing and thro' wood—.") These verses also show that in broadside as well as Child ballads, repeated oral transmission tends to focus attention on the emotional core.

The broadsides have not stood up as good poetry under close examination of their texts alone, just as they did not under appraisal by Laws, who wrote, "The average or below average broadside is not so much composed as patched together from the materials at hand." However, we should bear in mind, as Laws also pointed out, that the poetic shortcomings of broadside ballads apply to them as printed literature only, not as oral folksongs. Most of these texts can be surprisingly appealing when they come from the lips of traditional singers. Such singers, at any rate, make no distinctions themselves between Child and non-Child ballads; they sing either kind (or non-narrative folksongs) interchangeably.

NATIVE AMERICAN BALLADS

The **native American ballads** are the most recent strain of all, coming largely from the last half of the nineteenth century. (Their name in the index merely indicates origination in the United States, not any connection to Native Americans' traditions.) In style these ballads are very similar to the British broadside ballads, and they have all their stereotypes of attitude and situation and most of their poetic flaws. Current events, especially scandals and tragedies, still are common topics, but American history and development add new subjects, as the following summary of Professor Laws's categories (from the 1964 revision of his *Native American Balladry*) shows:

A. War Ballads ("The Texas Rangers" is A 8.)
B. Ballads of Cowboys and Pioneers ("Joe Bowers" is B 14.)
C. Ballads of Lumberjacks ("Harry Bale" is C 13.)
D. Ballads of Sailors and the Sea ("The *Titanic*" is D 24.)
E. Ballads about Criminals and Outlaws ("Charles Guiteau" is E 11.)
F. Murder Ballads ("The Jealous Lover" is F 1.)
G. Ballads of Tragedies and Disasters ("Springfield Mountain" is G 16.)
H. Ballads on Various Topics ("The Young Man Who Wouldn't Hoe Corn" is H 13.)
I. Ballads of the Negro ("Frankie and Albert [or 'Johnny']" is I 3.)

Laws had indexed 256 native American ballads by 1964, far too many to be discussed in detail here. But again we can survey their characteristics by examining a group of sample stanzas. This time all but one are quoted from H. M. Belden's *Ballads and Songs Collected by the Missouri Folk-Lore Society*.

According to Laws's count, only two native American war ballads have remained in tradition from the colonial period, three from the Revolution, four from the War of 1812, two from the Indian wars, about a dozen from the Civil War, and none from World War I or later conflicts. This seems a very slim folk inheritance, but any valid generalization about American history in folk music would have to take folk*songs* into account as well; they survive in much greater numbers from all periods. A typical war ballad is a highly stereotyped account of some notable conflict, set off by patriotic sentiments or memories of mothers and sweethearts back home. The bare texts, as in the following stanzas from Laws A 8, convey little real sense of battle:

> I saw the Indians coming,
> I heard them give a yell.
> My feelings at that moment
> No human tongue can tell.
>
> Our bugle it was sounded,
> Our captain gave command.
> "To arms, to arms!" he shouted,
> "And by your horses stand."

("No tongue can tell" is a frequent cliché of the more recent ballads.)

The cowboy and pioneer ballads sometimes depict death and suffering in the Wild West, especially accidents in the cow camps— "When the Work's All Done This Fall" (B 3), "Utah Carroll" (B 4), "Little Joe the Wrangler" (B 5), and so forth. But many of the Western pieces laugh at the dangers instead, and they picture a group of adventurers who are high-spirited and ready to tackle anything. Joe Bowers, for instance, risks security back East for the sake of his sweetheart Sally:

> "Oh Sally, dearest Sally,
> Oh Sally, for your sake
> I'll go to California
> And try to raise a stake."
>
> Says she to me, "Joe Bowers,
> You are the man to win;
> Here's a kiss to bind the bargain,"
> And she hove a dozen in.

Sally, however, proves false; when Joe next hears from her, she is married to a red-haired butcher, and she has a baby with red hair.

Missouri is a good state for Western subjects, but would seem an unlikely place for loggers' ballads. Still, one example does appear in Belden's collection (from an Arkansas informant), illustrating that the topics of ballads do not necessarily limit their distribution. In this example, the original ballad about a logger named Harry Bahel, who was killed in a sawmill accident in Arcadia Township, Lapeer County, Michigan, appears here as one about "Harry Dale," killed in "Arcadia, Laneer County," no state specified. As in all versions, the ballad begins with a commonplace "Come all ye":

> Come all kind friends and parents,
> Come brothers one and all;
> Attention pay to what I say;
> 'Twill make your blood run cold.
> 'Tis about a poor unfortunate boy,
> Who was known both far and near.
> His parents raised him tenderly,
> Not many miles from here.

Then the story advances to a gory description of the tragic accident:

> In lowering the Vantle wheel [The reference is unclear.]
> He threw the carriage in its gear.
> It drew him into the saw
> And it sawed him all severe.
>
> It sawed him through the shoulder blade
> And half-way down his back,
> And he fell upon the floor
> As the carriage it rolled back.

Woods accidents dominate the lumberjack ballads as a group, the most typical ones being drownings or deaths by crushing during a river drive. Probably the best known of these is number C 1, "The Jam on Gerry's Rock" or "Foreman Young Monroe."

For a ballad of the sea, we must turn to another anthology, for Belden has none that are indexed in Laws. From the Frank C. Brown collection, however, come these typical stanzas and chorus of "The *Titanic*" (as written out by an informant):

> It was on one Monday morning about one o'clock
> When the great Titanic began to reel and rock.
> All the people began to cry saying lord I have to die.
> It was sad when that great ship went down.
>
> Oh it was sad when that great ship went down.
> There were husbands and their wives,
> Little children lost their lives.
> It was sad when that great ship went down.
>
> You know it was ofel out on the sea.
> The people were singing nearer my god to thee.
> Some were homeward bound, sixteen hundred had to dround.
> It was sad when that great ship went down.

The sinkings of many ships—both saltwater and Great Lakes vessels—have been celebrated in balladry, but few have so gripped the folk imagination as did the sinking of the *Titanic* on her maiden voyage in 1912. Besides the serious version of the ballad, a comic version sung to a jolly tune still survives in American collegiate tradition, there are distinctive black variants (some of them recited as "toasts"), and there are at least four other *Titanic* ballads of more limited folk distribution.

Criminals and outlaws are the subjects of some of the most popular and widely distributed of the native American ballads. Their typical motifs include the Robin Hood tradition, the tenderhearted criminal, the regretful "boy gone wrong," and sometimes the defiant captive. Perhaps the best known is "Jesse James," about whom there are two distinct ballads (E 1 and 2), as well as one about his cohort "Cole Younger" (E 3). President Garfield's assassin, like several other criminals of balladry, speaks for himself, using commonplace lines borrowed from older ballads and appealing for his listeners' sympathy.

> Come all ye Christian people,
> Wherever you may be,
> And likewise pay attention
> To these few words from me.
> For the murder of James A. Garfield
> I am condemned to die
> On the thirteenth of June
> Upon the scaffold high.
>
> For my name is Charles Guiteau,
> And the name I'll never deny,
> Tho I leave my aged parents
> In sorrow for to die.
> Oh! little did they think
> While in my youthful bloom
> I'd be taken to the scaffold
> To meet my fatal doom.

The favorite American ballad topic is the murder of an innocent girl. Naomi Wise, murdered in Randolph County, North Carolina, in 1808, has been described in Laws ballad number F 4. Laura Foster (Laws F 36) was stabbed to death in Wilkes County, North Carolina, in 1866, by Tom Dula, or "Tom Dooley," as the ballad tells it. Pearl Bryan of Greencastle, Indiana, was murdered by her lover, Scott Jackson, in 1896, and is celebrated in Laws F 2 and 3. Leo Frank, according to folk tradition, beat little Mary Phagan to death as she

walked home from working at The National Pencil Company factory in Atlanta, Georgia, in 1913, and that is the subject of number
F 20. (Frank, a Jewish pencilmaker, was convicted of the crime
partly on the testimony of fourteen-year-old Alonzo Mann and was
lynched by a mob in 1915. But in 1982 Mann, now eighty-three years
old, came forward and said he was sure that Frank was innocent of
the murder and that Jim Conley, the chief witness against Frank,
had killed the girl. Conley had died in 1962.)

Several other ballads are associated with specific female victims,
and many more are generalized. Most of them, as a study by Anne
B. Cohen shows, develop in stereotypic ways common also to sensational journalism. One of these ballads is about the killing of "fair
Ellen," who is often called "Florella" or "Floella"; the ballad is usually entitled "The Jealous Lover":

> One evening when the moon shone brightly
> There fell a gentle dew,
> When out of a cottage
> A jealous lover drew.
>
> Says he to fair young Ellen:
> "Down on the sparkling brook
> We'll wait and watch and wonder
> Upon our wedding day."

This unfortunate girl, like so many others, is most cruelly murdered; yet she forgives the killer:

> "Oh Edward, I'll forgive thee,
> Though this be my last breath.
> I never was deceiving,
> Though I close my eyes in death."

The ballads in category G concern railroad accidents (like "Casey
Jones," G 1), mine fires and other subterranean tragedies (like "The
Avondale Disaster," G 6 and 7), floods (like "The Johnstown Flood,"
G 14), fires, suicides, explosions, cyclones, death by freezing, and
even a spelunking accident ("Floyd Collins," G 22).

Focus: "Young Charlotte"

[In this lengthy and extremely popular American ballad, Charlotte, riding to a New Year's Eve ball in a sleigh with her sweetheart, Charles, refuses to dress warmly or to fold a blanket about her. Following are some climactic verses from an Ozark version.]

On an' on they went throughout
The clear, cold starry night,
Until now five more weary miles
An' the ballroom was in sight.

They reached the door an' Charles jumped out,
To give his hand to her.
"Why sit you there like a monument
That has no power to stir?"

He asked her once, he asked her twice,
Yet she answered not a word;
He asked her for her hand again,
An' yet she never stirred.

The mantle from her neck he tore,
An' the cold stars on her shone,
An' up into the lighted hall
Her lifeless form he bore. . . .

*

[A parody of "Young Charlotte," changing her name to Hannah, was recorded by a popular musical group in the 1940s.]

So o'er the hills and faster o'er,
And by the cold starlight.
'Til Charles in these well frozen words,
At last the silence broke.

"Why sit you like a monument
Which has no power to stir?"
He called her name again and again,
But she answered not a word.
    No, she answered not a word.

So Charles turned 'round to go back home
And as they reached the door,
Poor Hannah being frozen,
Fell exhausted to the floor.

Young Charlie wept with bitter tears
On seeing her this way.
He held her hand and stroked her brow,
And tenderly did say:

"Get up off'n that floor, Hannah,
Them hogs has got to be fed!
Why there ain't no one to do the chores
With you a playin' dead.

"Why there's ducks and geese in the parlor,
And the dog's been in your bed.
So get up off'n that floor, Hannah,
Them hogs has got to be fed!"
[Chorus repeated with slight variations and musical hokum.]

Source: Vance Randolph, *Ozark Folksongs*, edited and abridged by Norm Cohen (Urbana: University of Illinois Press, 1982). Parody composed and recorded by Red Ingle and the Natural Seven (Capitol 15123); copy supplied by Norm Cohen from his personal record collection.

DISCUSSION TOPICS:

1. The origin and history of "Young Charlotte" is well documented. See Cohen's note in the source cited above for references, plus the discussion in George List's *Singing About It* (cited in Focus: Ballads as Lullabies). Compare texts to see how the ballad story and language evolved from an 1843 newspaper poem to a folksong and finally to a parody.

2. Presumably, "folk" singers of "Young Charlotte" regarded the ballad as seriously moving, not overly sentimental or laughable. How might this be accounted for from the collected texts of the ballad, or explained from singers' comments?

3. Can you find other recorded or published parodies of traditional ballads? How would you modify another popular ballad to create a humorous parody?

One more example of a characteristic development in American balladry—stemming from one of the oldest native ballads—is seen in "Springfield Mountain." This once-serious ballad describing an agricultural accident in New England in 1761 has turned into a funny song with a nonsense chorus, from which the following sequence is typical:

> "Oh, Mollie dear, do come and see
> What a venomous viper did bite me."
>   With a bumble bumble dick a ri dum
>   Able de dinctum day
>
> "Oh, Johnnie dear, why did you go
> Away down yonder in the field to mow?"
>
> "Oh, Mollie, dear, I thought you knowed
> 'Twas Daddy's hay and it had to be mowed."

The miscellaneous classification includes ballads about wanderers, gamblers, and sportsmen, plus a few religious, romantic, and humorous pieces. One ballad (Laws H 13) even comments upon the unlikely poetic topic of hoeing corn. A lazy young man never hoes his corn, with this result:

> He went to the fence and he peeped in.
> The grass and the weeds were up to his chin.
> The careless weeds they grow so high
> Caused this young man for to sigh.

Even worse, he finds that his sweetheart will no longer have him:

> "Then what makes you ask me to wed
> When you can't raise your own corn bread?
> Single I am, single I'll remain.
> A lazy man I won't maintain."

In disgust—with her rather than with himself—the lazy farmer takes his leave:

He picked up his hat and he went away,
Saying, "Madam, you'll rue the day,
Rue the day as sure as you're born,
Giving me the mitten 'cause I didn't hoe my corn."

Finally, the ballads in category I are distinguished by their presumed African-American origin or their subject matter, although
many of them have become generally familiar throughout the United
States, including "John Henry" (I 1), "The Boll Weevil" (I 17), and
"The Blue-tailed Fly" (I 19). The best known of all is, of course,
"Frankie and Johnny" (I 3, "Albert" in older versions), which has
passed into literary drama, popular song, and jazz. Repeated attempts to identify the principals in the story with real-life figures
have met with failure. The ballad, with its familiar "He done her
wrong" chorus, is too common to need quoting at any length; Belden's text, however, is an unusual one, being a long composite of
various stanzas known to his informant, interspersed with lines of
commentary and explanation. The informant at one point said,
"Then they go to the city, and for a while all is lovely. But Albert
gets 'onery' and don't work and spends money on other women."
Then follows:

"Frankie, she shot Albert,
And I'll tell the reason why.
Ever' dollar bill she give Albert,
He'd give to Alice Blye [also "Nelly Bly" and "Alice Frye"].

"Frankie and Johnny" has developed a group of near-common-
places of its own; these are the chorus, Frankie's "forty-four" that
goes "roota toot toot," and this "graveyard stanza":

They took him to that cemet'ry
In a rubber-tired hack,
They took him to that cemet'ry
But they did not bring him back.

In many versions ten men go to the funeral in that "rubber-tired
hack," but only nine come back.

RESEARCHING AND STUDYING BALLADS

Ballads, especially the oldest British-American group, have attracted detailed and voluminous study since the beginning of British and American folklore research in the nineteenth century. Surveys of this scholarship by Sigurd B. Hustvedt, D. K. Wilgus, and Albert B. Friedman eliminate the necessity to do any more here than sketch out trends and rough outlines and indicate some areas for future studies.

One curious fact about ballad scholarship is that a "definitive" publication—the Child ballads—came before field-collecting had been well established or had even been begun in this country. A period of broad theorizing about ballad origins followed, with the "communalists" (led by F. B. Gummere) disputing with the supporters of individual origins (dominated by Louise Pound). The Pound group eventually prevailed, but the skirmishes of this "ballad war" made clear that further analyses would depend on more collection and classification of American materials. It was then, too, that Phillips Barry's useful term "communal re-creation" was coined. (See "Theories of the Folk and Folk Groups" in chapter 3.) Subsequently, many brilliant collectors and editors of ballads emerged in the United States.

Child's notes for *The English and Scottish Popular Ballads* were themselves international studies of individual ballads, and further such studies followed, notably of "Edward," "The Two Sisters," and "Lady Isabel and the Elf Knight." Another approach, popular for generations, was the isolation of one particular aspect of many ballads—superstitions, place-names, proverbs, commonplaces, and the like. As American collecting progressed, comparative studies of British and American versions of ballads followed, with results like tracing the descendants of "The Unfortunate Rake," a British broadside, in such new forms as "The Young Girl Cut Down in Her Prime" (Laws Q 26) and "The Cowboy's Lament" (Laws B 1).

A favorite research topic of the past was searching for historical origins. Louise Pound, for instance, was able to show that John A. Stone, an early author of songster texts, probably composed "Joe Bowers." Austin E. Fife traced the cowboy ballad "The Trail to Mexico" from a seventeenth-century broadside, "The Seaman's

Focus: Burying "The Unfortunate Rake/Dying Cowboy"

[The dissolute young man, or "rake" as he is sometimes called in the old British broadside versions of this ballad, is found dying by a passing comrade. He lives long enough to order his funeral, variously described.]

From a nineteenth-century broadside text:

> "Get six young soldiers to carry my coffin,
> Six young girls to sing me a song,
> And each of them carry a bunch of green laurel
> So they don't smell me as they bear me along.
>
> "Don't muffle your drums and play your fifes merrily,
> Play a quick march as you carry me along,
> And fire your bright muskets all over my coffin,
> Saying There goes an unfortunate lad to his home."

*

From a Scottish version:

> Go send for my brother to play the pipes slowly,
> And play the dead march as they carry me along.
>
> There's a bunch of roses to lay on my coffin,
> There's a bunch of roses for my head and my feet,
> There's a bunch of roses to lay in the churchyard,
> To perfume the way as they carry me along.

*

From a Canadian version:

> So beat your drums and play the fife lowly,
> And play the dead march as you carry me along;
> Take me to the churchyard and lay the sod over me,
> I am a young maid and I know I've done wrong.

*

From a Virginia version:

> I want four young ladies to bear up my coffin,
> I want three young maidens to carry me on,
> And each of them carry a bunch of wild roses,
> To lay on my body as I pass along.

*

From a Virgin Islands version:

> Six jolly young sailors to carry my coffin,
> Six jolly young ladies to walk by my side
> With a bunch of green roses to place on my coffin,
> That the people might smell me while passing along.

*

From a version of "The Streets of Laredo":

> "Get sixteen cowboys to carry my coffin,
> Get sixteen pretty ladies to bear up my pall,
> Put roses all over the top of my coffin
> To deaden the smell as they bear me along.

> "Oh, swing the rope slowly and ring your spurs lowly,
> And play the dead march as you bear me along;
> Take me to the green valley, there lay the sod o'er me
> 'Cause I'm a poor cowboy and I know I've done wrong."

*

From a version of "Gambler's Blues":

> I want six crap shooters for pall bearers,
> A chorus girl to sing me a song;
> Put a jazz band on my hearse wagon,
> Raise hell as I stroll along.

*

From a skier's parody of "Streets of Laredo":

> Get six from the ski school to carry my coffin,
> Get six little bunnies to sing me a song;
> Oh lower me gently and sprinkle Schnee o'er me,
> For I was a skier, my life was not long.

Source: The Unfortunate Rake: A Study in the Evolution of a Ballad, recording and booklet, edited by Kenneth S. Goldstein (New York: Folkways Records, 1960), now available from the Smithsonian Institution's Center for Folklife Programs and Cultural Studies.

DISCUSSION TOPIC:

There are myriad variations and parodies of this ever-popular ballad, twenty of which are included on the above-cited recording, which also has historical/comparative notes and a selected bibliography. Plenty of material—both printed and recorded—is available for comparison and analysis.

Complaint," to its later evolution into "Early, Early in the Spring" (Laws M 1), and finally to numerous versions and parodies in the American West.

Generally speaking, American ballad studies in the beginning were oriented toward literature and later were inclined to folkloristic and historic approaches. The strongest current trend is toward deeper studies of ballad music, performance contexts, and the interdependence of texts and tunes (see chapter 13). Interesting findings are also likely to come from the anthropological (or "functional") approach to ballads as "socio-historical documents" and from symbolic, psychological, or structural approaches to ballads. When these various possibilities are considered along with the continuing need for better and more-inclusive editions and classifications of ballads, it is apparent that, despite numerous ballad studies of the past, American folklorists may pursue the subject for many years to come without running short of research topics. For the amateur or beginning folklorist, the history and the basic problems and broad approaches of ballad scholarship suggest many small-scale projects worth carrying out.

For example, students might teach themselves a great deal about ballad variation, and perhaps even make some original discoveries, by preparing an annotated edition of all readily available texts of a native or recent ballad. A good study of narrative method in ballads might also be done without any elaborate bibliographic materials. Another possibility is a full explication of the background, function, and meaning to the informant of a ballad that a student has collected from oral tradition. Psychological or structural discussions of ballads need not refer to every extant variant, but might be based on a fairly limited corpus from easily available library sources. There is also much to be learned from a close critical evaluation of a ballad study, an old 78 rpm "hillbilly" record of a ballad, or perhaps a recent disk that purports to be "authentic" folk music.

BIBLIOGRAPHIC NOTES

General works on folksongs, cited in the notes to chapter 11, by Herzog, Nettl, Pound, Ames, and Wilgus are all pertinent to ballads as well. The earlier history of ballad studies was treated in two books by Sigurd B. Hustvedt: *Ballad Criticism in Scandinavia and Great Britain during the Eighteenth Century* (New York: The American-Scandinavian Foundation, 1916) and *Ballad Books and Ballad Men* (Cambridge, Mass: Harvard University Press, 1930). An invaluable resource is W. Edson Richmond's *Ballad Scholarship: An Annotated Bibliography* (New York: Garland, 1989).

Two good general introductions are Gordon Hall Gerould's *The Ballad of Tradition* (Oxford: Oxford University Press, 1932; Galaxy paperback ed., 1957) and M. J. C. Hodgart's *The Ballads* (London: Hutchinson's University Library, 1950; Norton Library paperback ed., 1962). A useful compilation is Dianne Dugaw's *The Anglo-American Ballad: A Folklore Casebook* (New York: Garland, 1995).

MacEdward Leach and Tristram P. Coffin edited *The Critics and the Ballad* (Carbondale: Southern Illinois University Press, 1961; paperback reprint, 1973), which contains fifteen articles (one a previously unpublished one by Phillips Barry) concerning ballad origins, definitions, meter and music, and the literary tradition of ballads. Two of the most important articles included here are Thelma G. James's "The English and Scottish Popular Ballads of Francis J. Child" and Coffin's "'Mary Hamilton' and the Anglo-American Ballad as an Art Form" (repr. in *Readings in American Folklore*, pp. 309–18), both originally published in *JAF*. Another important set of ballad studies is *Narrative Folksong: New Directions (Essays in Appreciation of W. Edson Richmond)*, ed. Carol L. Edwards and Kathleen E. B. Manley (Boulder, Colo.: Westview Press, 1985) with eighteen essays, including some on international ballad tradition.

The three basic American-ballad syllabi described in this chapter were all published by the American Folklore Society in the "Bibliographic and Special Series": Laws's *Native American Balladry* was volume 1 in the series (1950), revised in 1964; Coffin's *The British Traditional Ballad in North America* was volume 2 (1950), revised in 1963 (reissued with a supplement by Roger deV. Renwick in 1977); and Laws's *American Balladry from British Broadsides* was volume 8 (1957). D. K. Wilgus outlined problems and progress in improving ballad classifications in "A Type-Index of Anglo-American Traditional Narrative Songs," *JFI* 7 (1970): 161–76.

Statements by two prominent ballad scholars, D. K. Wilgus (a "textualist") and Barre Toelken (a "contextualist") appeared in *The Ballad and the Scholars: Approaches to Ballad Study* (Los Angeles: UCLA William Andrews Clark Memorial Library, 1986). In the same year, in the "Ballad in Context" special issue of *WF* (45:2), Toelken's essay "Figurative Language and Cultural Contexts in the Traditional Ballads" appeared, with a response from Wilgus. (The issue also contains an introduction by the editor, Carol L. Edwards, and three further essays with responses.) This and other interpretive ballad studies by Toelken are expanded and revised as chapters in his book *Morning Dew and Roses: Nuance, Metaphor and Meaning in Folksongs* (Urbana: University of Illinois Press, 1995).

There are several general anthologies of ballads, most with useful introductions; unfortunately, three of the best, mentioned here, have gone out of print. Bartlett Jere Whiting edited *Traditional British Ballads* for "Crofts Classics" (paperback; New York, 1955), containing forty Child texts with notes. MacEdward Leach's *The Ballad Book* (New York: Harper, 1955) and Albert B. Friedman's *The Viking Book of Folk Ballads of the English Speaking World* (New York: Viking Press, 1956; Compass Books paperback, 1963; reissued by Penguin in 1976) both contain many ballads, both Child and non-Child.

Folk ballads were gathered in volume 2 (1952) of *The Frank C. Brown Collection of North Carolina Folklore*, ed. H. M. Belden and Arthur Palmer Hudson. Ballad tunes are in volume 4 (1957). The Northwest ballad and folksong collection mentioned in this chapter are described in my article "Folk Song Studies in Idaho," *WF* 24 (1965): 231–48; repr. in *Idaho Folklife: Homesteads to Headstones*, ed. Louie W. Attebery (Salt Lake City: University of Utah Press, 1985), pp. 37–45.

Child's own theories about ballads were discussed by Michael J. Bell in " 'No Borders to the Ballad Maker's Art': Francis James Child and the Politics of the People," *WF* 47 (1988): 285–307. The thorny question of actual oral credentials for Child's selections is taken up in two articles: J. Barre Toelken, "An Oral Canon for the Child Ballads: Construction and Application," *JFI* 4 (1967): 75–101; and Kenneth A. Thigpen, Jr., "An Index to the Known Oral Sources of the Child Collection," *FF* 5 (1972): 55–69.

Literary aspects of the ballads have interested both folklorists and literary critics. Louise Pound examined the treatment of ballads in some popular anthologies of literature in her article in *SFQ* 6 (1942): 127–41. Arthur K. Moore took the literary point of view in an article in *CL* 10 (1958): 1–20. Holger Olof Nygard discussed a subject of importance to the question of literary ballad analogs in "Ballads and the Middle Ages," *TSL* 5 (1960): 85–96. Central to the whole subject is Albert B. Friedman's book *The Ballad Revival: Studies in the Influence of Popular on Sophisticated Poetry* (Chicago: University of Chicago Press, 1961).

MacEdward Leach, an advocate of a literary approach to ballads, provided a good survey of the goals of such studies in "The Singer or the Song," *PTFS* 30 (1961): 30–45. His student Tristram P. Coffin has written many important articles from this point of view, including "The Folk Ballad and the Literary Ballad: An Essay in Classification," *MF* 9 (1959): 5–18 (reprinted in *Folklore in Action*, pp. 58–70), and "Remarks Preliminary to a Study of Ballad Meter and Ballad Singing," *JAF* 78 (1965): 149–53.

An important general introduction to the international body of ballads is W. J. Entwistle's *European Balladry* (Oxford: Oxford University Press, 1939). Archer Taylor discussed "The Themes Common to English and German Balladry" in *MLQ* 1 (1940): 23–35, and he published an important individual study of "Edward" and "Sven i Rosengnard" (Chicago: University of Chicago Press, 1931).

Paul G. Brewster studied "The Two Sisters" in *FFC* no. 147 (1953). The best study of "Lady Isabel" is by Holger Olof Nygard in *FFC* no. 169 (1958).

Three representative studies that draw material from many different ballads are L. C. Wimberly's *Folklore in the English and Scottish Ballads* (Chicago: University of Chicago Press, 1928); W. Edson Richmond's "Ballad Place Names," *JAF* 59 (1946): 263–67; and William E. Sellers's "Kinship in the British Ballads: The Historical Evidence," *SFQ* 20 (1956): 199–215.

There are a number of studies of variation in the American tradition of a particular ballad, including Foster B. Gresham's "The Jew's Daughter: An Example of Ballad Variation," *JAF* 47 (1934): 358–61; Frances C. Stamper and William Hugh Jansen's " 'Water Birch': An American Variant of 'Hugh of Lincoln,' " *JAF* 71 (1958): 16–22; Tristram P. Coffin's "The Problem of Ballad-Story Variation and Eugene Haun's 'The Drowsy Sleeper,' " *SFQ* 14 (1950): 87–96; Alisoun Gardner-Medwin's "The Ancestry of 'The House Carpenter': A Study of the Family History of the American Forms of Child 243," *JAF* 84 (1971): 414–27; Charles Clay Doyle and Charles Greg Kelley's "Moses Platt and the Regeneration of 'Barbara Allen,' " *WF* 50 (1991): 151–69; and a study that compares folk and popular traditions, Howard Wight Marshall's " 'Black Jack David' on Wax: Child 200 and Recorded Hillbilly Music," *KFQ* 17 (1972): 133–43. Christine A. Cartwright, in "Johnny Faa and Black Jack Davey: Cultural Values and Change in Scots and American Balladry," *JAF* 93 (1980): 397–416, demonstrates how changing concepts of an ideal marriage in the 1960s–1970s made the story told in Child 200 more acceptable to American singers.

A "formulaic improvisation" theory of ballad tradition was proposed by James H. Jones in *JAF* 74 (1961): 97–112, and opposed by Albert B. Friedman in the same issue of the journal, pp. 113–15.

Journalistic reporting of news was compared to broadside ballad style in Winifred Johnston's article "Newspaper Balladry," *AS* 10 (1935): 119–21. A longer and more detailed treatment of the same idea appeared in Helen MacGill Hughes's *News and the Human Interest Story* (Chicago: University of Chicago Press, 1940), pp. 126–49 and passim. Two books that have treated broadsides in general are Leslie Shepard's *The Broadside Ballad: A Study in Origins and Meaning* (London: Herbert Jenkins, 1962) and Claude M. Simpson's *The British Broadside Ballad and Its Music* (New Brunswick, N.J.: Rutgers University Press, 1966).

Phillips Barry, the best early student of American folksongs, discussed "Native Balladry in America" in *JAF* 22 (1909): 365–73. Louise Pound, another pioneer in this area, published a landmark essay, "The Southwestern Cowboy Songs and English and Scottish Popular Ballads," *MP* 11 (1913): 195–207; reprinted in *Nebraska Folklore*, pp. 156–70. Austin E. Fife provides a detailed study of 147 known versions of a cowboy ballad in "The Trail to Mexico," *MSF* 1 (1973): 85–102. Louise Pound's study of the composer of "Joe Bowers," originally published in *WF* 16 (1957): 111–20, was reprinted in *Nebraska Folklore*, pp. 171–83. A further study of the origin of that ballad was published by John Quincy Wolf in *WF* 29

(1970): 77–89. In " 'Rose Connoley': An Irish Ballad," *JAF* 92 (1979): 172–95, D. K. Wilgus establishes the foreign source of Laws F 6, also known as "Down in the Willow Garden." John Foster West provides the full history behind one of the most popular ballads of the folksong revival in *The Ballad of Tom Dula* (Durham, N.C.: Moore Publishing Co., 1977).

Bill Ellis, in two articles, studied sentimental ballads usually disregarded by American folklorists: " 'The "Blind" Girl' and the Rhetoric of Sentimental Heroism," *JAF* 91 (1978): 657–74; and " 'I Wonder, Wonder, Mother': Death and the Angels in Native American Balladry," *WF* 38 (1979): 170–85. The folk, Ellis points out, take the emotions of such ballads seriously, even if folklorists do not. Barton Levi St. Armand analyzed a major American poet's reworking of such a ballad in "Emily Dickinson's 'Babes in the Wood': A Ballad Reborn," *JAF* 90 (1977): 430–41.

Two general articles of interest to the study of native balladry are Robert D. Bethke's "Narrative Obituary Verse and Native American Balladry," *JAF* 83 (1970): 61–68; and Tristram P. Coffin's "American Balladry: The Term and the Canon," *KF* 19 (1974): 3–10.

Geraldine J. Chickering, in "The Origin of a Ballad," *MLN* 50 (1935): 465–68, reviewed the evidence for authorship of "Jack Haggerty" (Laws C 25). Arthur Field proposed some interesting interpretive answers to his question "Why Is the 'Murdered Girl' So Popular?" in *MF* 1 (1951): 113–19. But the definitive study in this genre is Anne B. Cohen's book *Poor Pearl, Poor Girl!: The Murdered Girl Stereotype in Ballad and Newspaper* (Austin, Tex.: AFS Memoir Series, vol. 58, 1973). Further studies of American ballad origins are Daniel G. Hoffman's "Historic Truth and Ballad Truth: Two Versions of the Capture of New Orleans," *JAF* 65 (1952): 295–303; Peter R. Aceves's "The Hillsville Tragedy in Court Record, Mass Media, and Folk Ballads: A Problem in Historical Documentation," *KFQ* 16 (1971): 1–38; Edward D. Ives's " 'Ben Deane' and Joe Scott: A Ballad and Its Probable Author," *JAF* 72 (1959): 52–66; as well as two articles by Norm Cohen: " 'Casey Jones': At the Crossroads of Two Ballad Traditions," *WF* 32 (1973): 77–103; and "Robert W. Gordon and the Second Wreck of 'Old 97,' " *JAF* 87 (1974): 12–38.

In " 'Railroad Bill' and the American Outlaw Tradition," *WF* 40 (1981): 315–28, John W. Roberts compares African-American with Anglo-American ballad tradition and finds it similar as to meaning but different in structure. The ballad story of Morris Slater, also known as "Railroad Bill," has some Robin Hood traits, but the plot pictures him more as an avenger—selling stolen goods to the poor at lower prices than those charged at the company store in Alabama—than as a noble robber in the Jesse James tradition. On an African-American badman ballad, see Roberts's "Stackolee and the Development of a Black Heroic Idea," *WF* 42 (1983): 179–90.

Non-English ballad traditions in the United States may be sampled in such works as Américo Paredes, *"With His Pistol in His Hand": A Border Ballad and Its*

Hero (Austin: University of Texas Press, 1958) and Joan B. Purcell, "Traditional Ballads among the Portuguese in California," *WF* 28 (1969): 1–20 and 77–90. An important collection and study is María Herrera-Sobek's *Northward Bound: The Mexican Immigrant Experience in Ballad and Song* (Bloomington: Indiana University Press, 1993). The non-Anglo ballad and folksong tradition in the United States is vast, however, and requires bibliographic aids beyond the scope of this survey.

13

FOLK MUSIC

In 1898, when the publication of Francis James Child's edition of British traditional ballads was finally completed, the last section to leave the press (volume 5, part 10) contained the only reference in the entire work to the music of the ballads—a short index of published tunes for ballads, and fifty-five "Ballad Airs from Manuscript." Child made no analysis whatever of these melodies, in contrast to his erudite and extremely detailed comments that had accompanied each group of ballad texts. The proportion of space devoted to tunes as opposed to texts (twenty pages out of about twenty-five hundred) is a good measure of the relative interest folklorists had in the words versus music of folksongs at the end of the nineteenth century.

In 1905, Phillips Barry, a forerunner of more-diversified American folksong specialists of the twentieth century, delivered what he called later "the first shot fired in the thirty years' war for the rights of ballad music." He asserted then what has now become a commonplace in folklore scholarship—that "the words constitute but one-half of a folksong; the air is no less an essential part." While this generalization has long been accepted, the practice, especially by ballad editors, has changed slowly. In 1944, Bertrand H. Bronson, one of the most thorough and systematic of musical folklorists himself, warned again, "If the student of the ballad is not prepared to give equal attention to the musical, as to the verbal, side of his subject, his knowledge of it will in the end be only half-knowledge."

Barry's metaphor proved inappropriate. There never was any protracted "ballad war" over the issue of the significance of music. Instead, most folklorists in the past, while granting the importance of tunes, remained untrained either to collect or to study them. Editors of ballad and folksong collections continued to present mostly texts, and they published very little tune analysis. But by 1950 the study of traditional music had become sufficiently advanced to justify a special term for it—**ethnomusicology.**

Detailed technical research in folk music is complex; to master it requires devoting much time to developing the skills of a specialist. But anyone who desires more than a superficial understanding of American folklore and who wishes to avoid the kind of "half-knowledge" that Bronson cautioned against, should understand, in general terms at least, what the basic form and styles of American folk music are, how folk music is collected, and by what means music is analyzed.

STYLES AND FORMS

In large part, with regard to style, American folk music is folk singing. Characteristically, in the oldest white tradition, it is solo singing, without accompaniment, of either lyrical or narrative matter (that is, of "folksongs" or "ballads") by an amateur performer before a close-knit family or community audience. The songs are usually "strophic"—that is, arranged in stanzas—and the melody of the first stanza is used again and again with little conscious change until all the stanzas have been sung. A four-line stanza is common, but couplets, triplets, and stanzas of five, six, or more lines also occur. Many folksongs, as discussed in chapters 11 and 12, have "refrains"—that is, regularly repeated independent elements attached to each stanza. The melodies to which folksongs are sung are not frozen to particular texts, so that one song text may be sung to several melodies or one melody may be attached to various songs. Furthermore, the general tone of a folksong text may seem to clash with the melodies sometimes used for it, so that what strikes us as a "jolly" tune may be employed for a tragic ballad. Whenever American folksingers have been known to make up new song texts, these generally have been sung to old folk tunes.

FOCUS: THE OZARK BALLAD-SINGING STYLE

In order fully to appreciate just how seriously the old songs are taken by the hill folk, one must note the reactions of the audience as well as the behavior of the singer. I have seen tears coursing down many a cheek, and have more than once heard sobs and something near to bellowings as the minstrel sang of some more or less pathetic incident, which may have occurred in England three or four hundred years ago. . . .

A ballad is sometimes broken by long pauses at the end of certain stanzas, so as to enable the singer to take a drink of whiskey or a chew of tobacco, or to reply to his critics, or to introduce some explanatory comment about the subject of his song. One old man, when he concludes the eighth stanza of "Molly Vaughn"—

> Up stepped his old father, whose hair was quite gray,
> Sayin' "Son, oh dearest son, you must not run away;
> Stay in your own country till the trial is at hand,
> An' you may be cleared by the law of the land,"

always adds: "The old feller knowed what he was a-doin'!"

Another senile ballad-singer of my acquaintance is so full of sharp comments and bucolic wisecracks that he talks almost as much as he sings, and is very apt to lose track of the melody altogether. The following is a fair sample of his version of the "Orange and Blue" song, with the spoken interpolations in italics:

> I oft-times have wondered why women love men,
> *Mostly for whut they can git out'n em!*
> But more times I wonder how men can love them,
> *Now he's a-talkin' sense!*
> They're men's ruination an' sudden downfall,
> An' they cause men to labor behind the stone wall,
> *They shore do, now!*

I have known two or three quiet, soft-spoken men who, for some reason or other, always shout the old songs at the very top of their voices. Another old fellow always leans back with closed eyes and sings in a peculiar quavering falsetto, until he reaches certain particularly moving lines, when he opens his eyes and shouts in a very loud voice, looking about as if he expected some comment from his audience.

Source: Vance Randolph, *Ozark Folksongs*, edited and abridged by Norm Cohen (Urbana: University of Illinois Press, 1982).

DISCUSSION TOPICS:

1. Randolph collected Ozark folksongs mostly from 1924 to 1942; his four-volume collection was published between 1946 and 1950. The singing styles he describes here may be outdated or eccentric, but what confirmation can you find that similar styles existed elsewhere in the United States, or that Ozark style has changed in more-recent years?

2. What might explain the speaking of the last line of ballads in the Northeast or the shouting of certain lines in this Ozark description? Why don't more informants simply recite ballads (a very rare practice, indeed)?

3. Further in this section Randolph writes that instrumental accompaniment for singing of old songs was not common. How has that changed in more-recent years, and for what likely reasons? (If possible, listen to some recordings of traditional Ozark singers, some of which were made by Randolph for the Library of Congress.)

Al Hopkins and the Hillbillies (1925), the first group to attach the term *hillbilly* to music: *(left to right)* Tony Alderman, John Hopkins, Charlie Bowman, and Al Hopkins.

Singing style in Anglo-American tradition varies somewhat from region to region and group to group, but everywhere it differs radically both from concert-hall art-song style and from popular singing. To the ear that is not accustomed to traditional singing, it may at first sound like merely an inept job of amateur vocalizing—the tone may be nasalized, the meter might not be maintained evenly, the pitch and tempo may waver in the first one or two stanzas or gradually shift from one point at the beginning of a song to another at the end. Unlike the professional singer, who tends to "act out" his material with appropriate facial expressions, gestures, and volume changes, traditional white American folksingers usually maintain an even volume level and are passive, sometimes even to the extent of tilting the head back, staring into space, and holding the face mask-like. Black folksingers, in contrast, often perform in chorus and with instruments, may improvise more freely on the melodic or rhythmic base, introduce more personal feeling into their singing, and often slur words or notes and intersperse whoops, slides, or falsetto passages into the basic text, all of which are features probably derived from African tradition.

A broad sampling of genuine traditional folk singing will reveal that most of these techniques and mannerisms (or lack of mannerisms), as well as others, are regular features of a definite folk style that has been maintained by oral transmission through unselfconscious imitation of other singers. The singing style is largely traditional, not personal. The practice of speaking the last phrase in a ballad instead of singing it, for instance, which is common in the Northeast, is not just an individual habit or the result of the singer running out of breath; it is a distinct characteristic of the regional style—a kind of traditional local custom. Similarly, the way some singers "lead up" to a note, using a nasalized slur ("Nnnh-It was in the merry month of May") is a device passed in oral transmission and by example from person to person, possibly influenced by traditional fiddle-playing technique. In general terms, singers who hold closely to an even meter—often with one note for each syllable of text—and with very few musical ornaments, are said to have a *tempo giusto* (strict tempo) style, while those who deviate widely from an established meter, and who ornament the melody freely with trills, slurs, and glides, are said to be using a *parlando rubato* (free, "speaking" rhythm) style.

The melodies themselves of old traditional songs may seem peculiar to unaccustomed listeners. That is because their ears are used to hearing music based only on a *diatonic scale*—that is, a series of tones separated by intervals of "seconds," or one-note jumps, as represented by the white keys on the piano from C to C. Cultivated music, on the whole, is based on such scales in "major" and "minor" keys. But many old folksongs have melodies drawn from scales with larger intervals between some tones—the so-called *gapped scales*— or from scales with fewer than the usual seven tones ("do" to "do," as they are usually learned). These may be five-tone (*pentatonic*) or six-tone (*hexatonic*) scales. Even if a folksong is based on a seven-tone (*heptatonic*) scale, its intervals may be differently arranged so that its character is neither major nor minor but "modal," or corresponding to the "church modes" of the Middle Ages that are generally referred to by Greek names. (As it happens, the original Greek names became scrambled between the classical period and the Middle Ages!) A folklorist without technical training in music may learn to recognize at least the general character of modal music by listening to the melodies of Gregorian chants and by playing the white keys of a piano as follows: C to C (*Ionian*, or "natural major"), D to D (*Dorian*), E to E (*Phrygian*), F to F (*Lydian*), G to G (*Mixolydian*), and A to A (*Aeolian*, or "natural minor").

The folk singing described so far has all been "monophonic," or single-toned, for in unaccompanied solo singing only one note of a melody can be produced at a time. But in group singing or when instruments are played to accompany songs, there occurs what may loosely be termed "polyphony," or more than one tone at a time. (This is not to be confused with formal polyphony in art music, in which two or more thematically related melodic parts are heard simultaneously.) In American multivoiced tradition, listeners may join in singing the refrain of a song, or a whole group may sing work songs, game songs, or party songs—usually in unison (all singing the same note) rather than in harmony. Traditional religious songs, especially in the South, may be rendered either in harmony or in unison by the congregation, with a leader to "line out," or recite, each line of the text in advance, a procedure sometimes referred to as "deaconing." Black congregations still sometimes refer to certain hymns regularly "lined out" as "Doctor Watts," in reference to Isaac Watts (1674–1748), the English composer of many

At the Clarks Creek Progressive Primitive Baptist Church in rural Virginia, Fred Brim plays the piano while the congregation sings.

still-popular hymns. The typical accompanying instruments in American folk-singing tradition are from the plucked-string family —the guitar, five-string banjo, and dulcimer—but sometimes the fiddle is also employed.

A bridge between vocal and purely instrumental music is formed by what were termed "wordless folksongs" in chapter 11—"diddling" or chin music, nonsense chants, "scat singing," and so forth. From the other direction, we might think of clapping, "clogging" (rhythmic beating time with the feet), and rattling spoons or "bones" (polished slats of bone or wood) as the simplest kind of instrumental folk music, closely followed by the near-vocal effects produced on instruments such as the kazoo, Jew's harp, and harmonica (or "French harp"). Highly complicated solo-instrumental music developed in American folk tradition on several of these instruments. For instance, harmonica players often perfected various "talking" pieces, fox chases, train sounds, and even narratives incorporating their "mouth organ" music. Early country string bands worked out solo techniques that later flowered in commercial country-western and bluegrass music, not only using the traditional fiddle, guitar, and banjo, but adding mandolins, autoharps, and electrified instruments of various kinds. Jazz instrumental virtuosity—along with blues-inspired jazz singing—provides another rich example of American folk-musical trends that reach high levels of achievement and large international audiences.

The student of instrumental American folk music should learn to approach the subject using its own terms and recognizing its own special techniques. For example, the "left-hand pizzicato" method of producing notes on a guitar or banjo by plucking strings with fingers of the upper, rather than the picking, hand has been called "pulling-off" in folk music, and its opposite is "hammering-on," or adding upper-hand notes by striking down sharply on selected strings. Folk guitar- and banjo-picking styles include patterns with names like "church lick," "lullaby lick," "Carter lick" (named for the Carter Family's guitar style heard on 1920s and 1930s records), "double thumbing," "Cotten picking" (named for the guitar style of Elizabeth Cotten), "frailing," "clawhammer," and "Scruggs style." Most folk instrumentalists play in several tunings besides the standard one for their instruments, and these have acquired such names as "mountain minor," "natural flat," "cross key," and "discord." Stringed instruments may be grouped for playing dance music, but the traditional melodies played are often called simply "fiddle tunes." The names of these tunes are wildly diverse, but their typical form is regular. There are usually two sections of eight measures each, with a "first and second ending" so that one part is played twice, then the other part twice, then the first, and so on until the musicians or the dancers are tired. Then some kind of concluding figure (often the "shave and a haircut" pattern) is used for a sign-off. Some fiddlers will refer to one part of a fiddle tune as the "coarse" (played on lower strings) and the other as the "fine" (played on upper strings). Some players have learned instruments left-handed or "upside down." A final matter that may be taken up with instrumentalists is how they learned to play and how long they practiced to master their first tune. To such an inquiry, answers from one large group of traditional fiddlers ranged from "just picked up the fiddle and played it" to "I can't do very good even now."

(*Above*) John R. Griffin of Lenox, Georgia, plays fiddle while his brother Arthur "beats a straw" on the fiddle strings for rhythm. From the South-Central Georgia Folklife Project, 1977. (*Below*) Elizabeth Cotten (1896–1987), folk singer, composer, and originator of the guitar-playing style called "Cotten picking."

FOCUS: LEARNING BLUEGRASS FROM BILL MONROE

[In the early 1960s, as a folklore graduate student at Indiana University, Neil V. Rosenberg led a second life as a banjo player haunting the Brown County Jamboree in Bean Blossom, Indiana, and learning from, among others, the "Father of Bluegrass," Bill Monroe (1911–1996), owner of this country-music park.]

My musical learning was largely by osmosis and example. For a start I simply had to be able to play the music, from old-time fiddle tunes to the latest country hits, in the standard keys and proper arrangements and be able to take the role of a featured soloist when my turn came.

The next step in my education came when Bill Monroe returned for another show in September, without a banjoist. As I was coming off stage after playing with Shorty and Juanita, his fiddler told me, "Bill'd like you to play with us." I was both excited and scared—this was big-league stuff and I was by no means familiar with Monroe's repertoire. . . . As the show began, I asked the guitar player to tell me after each piece the key of the next, because I knew Monroe's shows moved along briskly and for me any change of key meant retuning the fifth string and moving the capo. . . . What I didn't know (and no one told me) was Bill Monroe's efficient system of communicating the key of the next piece directly to everyone on stage at the end of each number by briskly "chopping" the tonic chord of the key for the next song on his mandolin. After one such signal the guitarist deliberately misinformed me about the key—what I now realize was an act of on-the-job hazing.

Ironically, at the time I interpreted another of Monroe's actions toward me on stage as a kind of on-the-job hazing when, in fact, it was one of his musical training techniques. During several songs he came and stood next to me and loudly beat mandolin chords in rhythmic variation to the song being played. . . . I later discovered that this was something that Monroe did with fledgling musicians to help them feel his rhythm. He was, as others have said, beating the rhythm into me. After the show he graciously dismissed my apology for all the clunkers with "You done your best."

That was practically all Monroe said to me at the time, and in fact he rarely spoke to me about music.

Source: Neil V. Rosenberg, "Picking Myself Apart: A Hoosier Memoir," *JAF* 108 (1995): 277–86. The essay was part of a forum titled "A Conversation between Two Disciplines: What Do We Learn When We Learn Music from Our 'Informants'?"

Bill Monroe.

DISCUSSION TOPICS:

1. Besides "osmosis and example," what teaching techniques are evident in this account? What did Rosenberg already know about playing the music, and what did he have to be taught? How are similar techniques used in teaching folk arts and crafts or other traditions?

2. Rosenberg introduced himself to Grand Ole Opry star Monroe and his house band as "a newlywed . . . just moved to Bloomington . . . starting graduate work at 'the university.'" How did these professional musicians initiate the newcomer?

3. Rosenberg mentions later in the essay how his experiences as a musician, plus his Ph.D. training in folklore, was reflected in his later analytical writings. See his book *Bluegrass: A History* (Urbana: University of Illinois Press, 1985) for the full fruits of that combination.

FIELDWORK: USING THE TAPE RECORDER

The collector of folk music must develop a few more skills than just the ability to operate a tape recorder and adjust its sound level properly. Successful fieldwork, as the ethnomusicologist Bruno Nettl has remarked, sometimes resembles "a combination of public relations and mental therapy." As in any folklore field project, the collector must be able to identify and locate good informants, to put them at their ease, and to encourage them to perform naturally and without inhibitions. The following advice applies to all collecting of folklore with a sound-recording device, but folk-music collecting also involves some special problems and techniques.

Folklorists of the past had to be technically trained in musical transcription before they could collect folk music; then they simply wrote out the tones they heard while a performer repeated his material several times. However, since different listeners tended to hear slightly different things, and standard musical notation cannot adequately represent all of the effects that occur in folk music anyway, these field transcripts were of uneven quality. Furthermore, there was no way to go back and verify field notes after an informant or a collector died.

The tape recorder is the standard—and the ideal—tool for fieldwork in folk music, and it quickly replaced the cylinder, disk, and wire recorders that had preceded it. Modern high-fidelity recorders that operate from house current, batteries, or even from spring-wound motors are available today at prices that allow all folklorists either to have their own equipment or to have access to that belonging to universities, archives, and other institutions. But even the modern magnetic tape recorder has its quirks. Tapes may fade or the magnetic backing may crumble, destroying irreplaceable field data, and a tape recorder improperly handled may yield nearly useless results.

Collectors must become thoroughly familiar with the equipment they will use *before* they get into the field to use it, but a few general techniques apply to all machines. The slow speeds of 1⅞ and 3¾ inches per second found on many home reel-to-reel recorders are suitable for recording the speaking voice alone, but nothing slower than 7½ ips should ever be used for music, because the faster speed reproduces a wider range of "cycles" or sound waves. (Home cassette-tape recorders are the least desirable choice for collecting music, since these machines lack either speed variation or adequate metering and tone controls.) Whatever the machine used, a speed of 15 ips, available on larger studio tape recorders, is needed for high-fidelity recording, and for the very best recordings a crystal-controlled recorder or a machine producing Digital Audio Tape (DAT) is needed.

An independent field-worker may not have access to the highest-level equipment, but at least the recorder available should be used carefully. The sound-level adjustment on the tape machine should be set for a trial recording at the normal volume an informant uses for performance and then checked periodically to assure that the results are "loud and clear," but not overrecorded so that interference is created. If it is possible to do so without distracting the informant, the collector should "label" items by announcing the facts of the session at the beginning of each tape and then identifying each selection with a title or description just before or after it is performed. To provide a reference point, a pitch-pipe A should be sounded just after each performance—not before, when it might predetermine an informant's choice of pitch. If instruments are played, the tuning of the individual strings should be recorded, with the order of strings announced as each one is played. It is also advisable to record an informant's actual tuning process from time to time. If the music is polyphonic, the microphone should be moved up to emphasize the role of each voice or instrument as a tune is repeated, and careful notes should be kept on where the microphone is situated at all times. Whenever possible, performers should be recorded several times on different days and perhaps before different audiences, in order to document their varying styles and techniques.

When the finished tapes are brought to an archive, backup copies should be made on separate reels of tape of all material recorded on "both sides" (really both "tracks") of the tapes. In that way, editing may be done without chance of disturbing the verbatim record of the original session. Duplicate tapes might be "dubbed" for storage purposes, especially if one copy is to be played repeatedly for transcription or perhaps in the classroom. Some archives file disk dubbings of all tapes to guard against tape fading, but careful temperature and humidity control will assure reasonably long life for tape recordings if quality tapes are used at the start.

TRANSCRIBING FOLK MUSIC

The ranscription of the field tapes—that is, the writing-out of them in musical notation—is a long and complicated process involving hours of careful listening and a firm technical grasp of music. The basic problems may be merely physical to begin with. For instance, Professor Jan Philip Schinhan, editor of the more than one thousand tunes in the Frank C. Brown Collection from North Carolina, found that Brown had played his original wax cylinders over and over again for college classes until many of them were badly worn and scratched. Even the most sensitive dubbing in the sound lab retained all the static and scratches that had been engraved into the originals. In addition, during the copying process, a number of labels were mixed up. These were hard errors to compensate for, because in some instances even the texts of songs were nearly inaudible and the music was next to impossible to hear clearly.

The traditional folksinger's flexible style and unorthodox techniques make it difficult for even expert ethnomusicologists to reduce the sounds they hear to standard transcription. In order to stretch the possibilities of the system of notation, some special symbols have been introduced—a plus sign or an arrow pointing upward for a tone slightly higher than notated, a minus sign or a downward arrow for a slightly lower tone, small-head notes for indefinite pitches, and barring according to a melody's own internal structure rather than in a standard meter. The transcriber may find help in such mechanical devices as the oscillograph, which visually represents musical pitches on a graph; the stroboscope, which helps to identify individual pitches; and the "instantaneous musical notator," which produces a complete transcription from a sound recording, although a specially coded one that cannot substitute fully for standard written notation.

RESEARCHING AND ANALYZING FOLK MUSIC

Any folklorist can learn to record folk music clearly enough for study purposes, and any collector with some basic musical ability and training can learn to produce a fair transcription from tapes. But when it comes to close technical analysis of folk music, we enter

the true specialist's territory. Only the broad theoretical outlines need
be sketched here. If collectors acquire some idea of what ethnomusicologists may wish to investigate, they can bring in the best
possible field data for analysis.

Even preparing a complete transcription of a piece of folk music
involves certain theoretical matters, such as how freely the modal
scales should be interpreted, whether melodies should be transcribed
to a common key signature, and how detailed a transcript need be
for comparative purposes. Beyond such questions, the "first principles" of folk-musical analysis are generally as follows.

Tonality, determined by the kind of scale upon which a melody
is based, may be indicated by a major or minor key signature or by
one of the modal names, if applicable. "Gapped scales" are identified
by the number of tones they contain—pentatonic (five), hexatonic
(six), etc. The *range* of tones that occurs in a particular piece is
sometimes indicated by the special terms "authentic" (all tones between the "tonic," or keynote, and the octave above) and "plagal"
(some tones occur below the tonic). *Tempo* in a performance is represented in a transcription by the number of quarter-note beats per
minute. *Meter* is stated as a standard "time signature" (4/4, 6/8, etc.)
if appropriate, or simply by assigning time values to each tone, using
the standard musical symbols, and then marking off musical phrases
with bar lines. If the melody of a tune has been transcribed to a
standard key, the original *pitch* of the tonic should be stated.

Once a tune has been carefully transcribed, the *phrasal pattern* of
the melody may be determined—that is, the musical "statements"
may be counted and identified. (Some typical patterns in Anglo-
American folksongs are AABA, AABB, ABAB, and ABBA.) The
number of "bars" or measures in each melodic phrase is represented
in parentheses, such as (4,3,4,3). Most ethnomusicologists have found
it useful to go beyond this stage to define the *melodic contour* of a
piece. This is done by removing all ornaments to the basic melody,
then all repeated tones, until only a "skeletal melody" remains,
which may be characterized (according to its notated shape on the
page) as descending, ascending, arc (or "triangular"), undulating, or
the like. From such skeletal abstracts of many melodies, combined
with all of the other data, *tune families* may be recognized.

All of this technical data (which have been simplified above) lend
themselves perfectly to computer analysis, a technique pioneered

with the Child ballad melodies by Bertrand H. Bronson of the University of California. Bronson employed an IBM 5081 punch card, which provided twelve rows of eighty units each for data storage, with extra space for printed information. He coded into each card —representing one variant melody—nine categories of musicological information, and he imprinted on the cards certain bibliographic and historical notes. The cards were then sorted in various ways, thus greatly speeding comparisons and analyses of melodies. Computer analysis, however, has advanced greatly since the days of punch-card data input. Perhaps the opposite approach is represented by the ethnomusicologist Samuel P. Bayard, who urges that "the investigator must, by immersing himself in the tunes, have impressed on his mind the identifying features of various members of perhaps many different tune families." Yet even Bronson has written that "the essence of melodic identity [is] . . . almost a metaphysical idea."

The widely held concept of "tune families," which Bayard had characterized roughly as including tunes "presumably owing their mutual likeness to descent from a single air that has assumed multiple forms through processes of variation, imitation, and assimilation," was refined by ethnomusicologist James R. Cowdery in a 1984 essay. Cowdery proposed, in place of the "family" metaphor, an approach based on three principles pointing to "a whole complex 'society' of a living music culture in which each tune can stand alone as an individual and still be seen as 'related' to various other tunes or groups of tunes." Cowdery's principles he titled "outlining" (similarities in tune contours), "conjoining" (tunes with sections in common and other sections that differ), and "recombining" (sections compared to sections and wholes to wholes).

Classifying Anglo-American folksongs into meaningful musical categories is still progressing. However, as George Herzog, one of the earliest American ethnomusicologists, wrote in 1937, "The study of a melody *begins* after it has been placed in some system or index; it does not end there." Probably the next logical step is a return to the text—a close comparison of the "wedding" of folksong texts and tunes. But, as Herzog also wrote, "The marriage has often been rather modernistic; melodies as well as texts have frequently gone their own way."

Text-tune fit proved to be a fascinating subject for research, although relatively few folklorists have pursued the topic very far.

Numerous questions suggest themselves. How much does textual-verse meter alter a melody, and in what ways? Is there a corresponding effect the other way? Do the phrasal patterns of words and music match, or does one sometimes crosscut the other? Can the wandering tunes as well as the floating verbal stanzas of folksongs help to explain their histories? What kinds of symbolic functions, if any, do tunes contribute to their texts? What aspects of conscious creative art may be identified in the whole text-tune relationship in folksongs? The full explication of folksongs, comparable to what is done in musical analysis of art songs, depends upon securing answers to such questions.

Some revolutionary ideas in Anglo-American ethnomusicology are those of Alan Lomax, who, backed by his years of field and editorial experience, proposed a "new science of musical ethnography." Lomax regarded formal musical elements as merely one small and abstract segment of a total "folksong style," which, more importantly, includes such factors as the relationship between musicians and their audience, the physical behavior of musicians, the vocal timbre and pitch favored by different cultures, the social functions of music, and the psychological and emotional content of texts. Applying these criteria, Lomax first made a broad survey of world musical styles (in his enlarged sense of the term "style"), listening to all available recordings of singers, until he could organize a rough grouping of musical families. From this background he listed fundamental factors in stylistic analysis, including the degree to which singing is communal or individualistic in a culture, the quality of voice and the mode of production used, the prevailing mood of the music, the content of texts, and the social and emotional factors present in the culture. Lomax made field observations of these criteria in Spain in 1953 and tested his hypothesis concerning the relationship between culture and singing styles in Italy in 1955. Finding a "positive correlation between the musical style and the sexual mores of the communities," Lomax studied the mechanics of this relationship in Italian lullabies, noting the relationships between mothers and children, the roles in society of women and children, and the customs surrounding the singing of lullabies. He concluded that "in those societies considered, the sexual code, the position of women, and the treatment of children seem to be the social patterns most clearly linked with musical style." He explored these ideas further in the introduction and notes of his anthology *The Folk Songs of North America in the English Language* (1960). Here he asserted that "after many years of collecting in both countries, I am profoundly impressed by the comparative paganism and resignation of Britain, as contrasted with the Puritanism and free aggressiveness of America."

Perhaps the "last word" on Anglo-American ethnomusicology may be quoted from Charles Seeger, who was one of the most specific critics of Lomax's proposal. Seeger suggested that the task of studies might be to "refine music theory" and to "coarsen technological aids" until some kind of pragmatic middle ground is reached.

BIBLIOGRAPHIC NOTES

Many of the general works on folksongs and ballads cited fully in the notes to chapters 11 and 12 contain discussions of music. The ballad anthologies edited by Leach and Friedman, for instance, treat ballad music briefly in their introductions. D. K. Wilgus surveys "Tune Scholarship" on pages 326–36 of his *Anglo-American Folksong Scholarship since 1898*. In Bruno Nettl and Helen Myers's *Folk Music in the United States: An Introduction*, the technical aspects of music are discussed throughout. An enduring older general survey of the subject is George Herzog's article "Song: Folk Song and the Music of Folk Song" in *Funk & Wagnalls Standard Dictionary of Folklore, Mythology, and Legend*. For a more recent general work, see Philip V. Bohlman's *The Study of Folk Music in the Modern World* (Bloomington: Indiana University Press, 1988).

In Bruno Nettl's *Folk and Traditional Music of the Western Continents* (Englewood Cliffs, N.J.: Prentice-Hall, 1965), most pertinent are chapter 2, "Studying the Structure of Folk Music" (pp. 15–32) and chapter 3, "The General Character of European Folk Music" (pp. 33–52). Nettl has also written the introductory textbook *Theory and Method in Ethnomusicology* (London: Free Press of Glencoe, 1964), wherein he discusses fieldwork, transcription, description of musical forms, style, instrumental music, and music in culture. He also provides guidance in the bibliography and an appendix of exercises and problems designed for the reader with no advanced formal training in music.

Charles Seeger's essay "Professionalism and Amateurism in the Study of Folk Music" is recommended reading for any student embarking on such study for the first time. It appeared in *JAF* 62 (1949): 107–13 and was reprinted in MacEdward Leach and Tristram P. Coffin, *The Critics and the Ballad* (Carbondale: Southern Illinois University Press, 1961; paperback, Arcturus Books, 1973), pp. 151–60. Another good summary of studies and approaches is Samuel P. Bayard's essay "American Folksongs and Their Music," *SFQ* 17 (1953): 122–39.

A basis for studies of fiddle tunes is Ira W. Ford's collection *Traditional Music of America* (New York, 1940; reissued with an introduction by Judith McCulloh, Hatboro, Pa.: Folklore Associates, 1965). Vance Randolph listed "The Names of Ozark Fiddle Tunes" in *MF* 4 (1954): 81–86. Winston Wilkinson discussed some "Virginia Dance Tunes" in *SFQ* 6 (1942): 1–10. Samuel P. Bayard provided a detailed study of selected American fiddle tunes in his *Hill Country Tunes* (Philadelphia: AFS Memoir no. 39, 1944) and "Some Folk Fiddlers' Habits and Styles in Western Pennsylvania," *JIFMC* 8 (1956): 15–18. Bayard's major work on this subject is *Dance to the Fiddle, March to the Fife: Instrumental Folk Tunes in Pennsylvania* (University Park: Penn State University Press, 1982). An interesting cross-genre analysis is Louie W. Attebery's article "The Fiddle Tune: An American Artifact," *NWF* 2 (1967): 22–29 (repr. in *Readings in American Folklore*, pp. 324–33).

A questionnaire survey of traditional fiddlers was reported by Marion Unger Thede in *EM* 6 (1962): 19–24. Thede also published *The Fiddle Book* (New York: Oak Publications, 1967), a self-instructor for would-be folk fiddlers containing music for 150 traditional fiddle tunes, a chatty discussion of fiddling, and some very fine photographs. Linda C. Burman's article "The Technique of Variation in an American Fiddle Tune," *EM* 12 (1968): 49–71, provides a detailed transcription and analysis of a 1926 recording of "Sail Away Lady," comparing the variations to those of Elizabethan virginalists. Burt Feintuch's "Notes on a Fiddle Run: Formulaic Composition in the Music of an Old Time Fiddler," *KF* 21 (1976): 3–10, studies the role of memory and improvisation in learning and performing fiddle tunes. Eugene Wiggins discusses fiddlers' contests and folklore in literature in "Benéts' 'Mountain Whipoorwill': Folklore Atop Folklore," *TFSB* 41 (1975): 99–114.

Religious folk music in America was studied by George P. Jackson, beginning with his *White Spirituals in the Southern Uplands* (Chapel Hill: University of North Carolina Press, 1933); see Wilgus for references to Jackson's other works as well as those of other scholars. Sacred-harp shape-note singing has attracted the major attention in this area. Richard D. Wetzel, for example, treats "Some Music Notation Systems in Early American Hymn-Tune Books" in *KFQ* 12 (1967): 247–60. Brett Sutton, in "Shape-Note Tune Books and Primitive Hymns," *EM* 26 (1982): 11–26, shows the relationship between published books and the oral tradition of hymns in the rural South. A good description of sacred-harp singing in east Texas may be found in Francis Edward Abernethy's "Singing All Day & Dinner on the Grounds," *PTFS* 37 (1972): 131–40. David Stanley's "The Gospelsinging Convention in South Georgia," *JAF* 95 (1982): 1–32, describes the setting and occasion for a gospel-singing convention in 1977 that has been held every July since 1893; the bibliography here is extensive. See also William H. Tallmadge, "Dr. Watts and Mahalia Jackson—the Development, Decline, and Survival of a Folk Style in America," *EM* 5 (1961): 95–99; and Joe Dan Boyd, "Negro Sacred Harp Songsters in Mississippi," *MFR* 5 (1971): 60–83.

For a useful recent assessment of the riches of black American folk music, see John F. Szwed, "Musical Adaptation among Afro-Americans," *JAF* 82 (1969): 112–21. Robert Ladner, Jr., classifies the major types of black traditional music and traces its adaptation and imitation by whites in "Folk Music, Pholk Music and the Angry Children of Malcolm X," *SFQ* 34 (1970): 131–45. Patrick B. Mullen describes "A Negro Street Performer: Tradition and Innovation" in *WF* 29 (1970): 91–103. For structure and meaning in the blues, see John Barnie's "Formulaic Lines and Stanzas in the Country Blues," *EM* 22 (1978): 457–73; and Harriet J. Ottenheimer, "Catharsis, Communication, and Evocation: Alternative Views of the Sociopsychological Functions of Blues Singing," *EM* 23 (1979): 75–86. The partially traditional music of the American minstrel show has been studied by Hans Nathan; see "The First Negro Minstrel Band and Its Origin," *SFQ* 16 (1952): 132–44; and "Early Banjo Tunes and American Syncopation," *MQ* 42 (1956): 455–72. On the larger tradition of black American banjo music see Cecelia Conway's *African Banjo Echoes in Appalachia: A Study of Folk Tradition* (Knoxville: University of Tennessee Press, 1995). Rap music is discussed in several writings by Cheryl L. Keyes, most recently in "At the Crossroads: Rap Music and Its African Nexus," *EM* 40 (1996): 223–48.

Richard Blaustein cites "musical punning" and the association of performances with lower-class musicians to answer the question raised in his article "Jugs, Washboards and Spoons: Why Improvised Musical Instruments Make Us Laugh," *TFSB* 47 (1981): 76–79. An inexpensive musical instrument much loved by folk but largely neglected by folklorists—the ten-hole diatonic harmonica—is the subject of Michael S. Licht's "Harmonica Magic: Virtuoso Display in American Folk Music," *EM* 24 (1980): 211–21. Articles on the history and construction of folk instruments are listed in the notes to chapter 21. For a survey of the varied instrumental traditions of one state, see James P. Leary et al., *In Tune with Tradition: Wisconsin Folk Musical Instruments* (Cedarburg, Wisc.: Cedarburg Cultural Center, 1990).

Few publications deal specifically with the field recording of traditional music. Bruno Nettl had a useful note, "Recording Primitive and Folk Music in the Field," in *AA* 56 (1954): 1101–2, from which several suggestions in the present chapter were taken. Maud Karpeles prepared a small but helpful manual called *The Collecting of Folk Music and Other Ethnomusicological Material* (London: International Folk Music Council, 1958). George List discussed "Documenting Recordings" in *FFMA* 3 (Fall 1960): 2–3 and "The Reliability of Transcription" in *EM* 18 (1974): 353–77. The latter is accompanied by a small-disk recording of the examples presented. Frances M. Farrell proposed another way to transcribe folk music in "Heightened Graphic Neumes," *FMS* 3 (1979): 33–38, illustrating the method with a transcription of a 1959 sacred song from Kentucky, "Lend Me a Hand, Dear Lord, and Guide Me." Charles Seeger evaluated the uses of an instantaneous music notator in "Prescriptive and Descriptive Music-Writing," *MQ* 44 (1958): 184–95, while various "Electronic Aids to Aural Transcription" were discussed by Nazir A. Jairazbhoy and Hal Balyoz in *EM* 21 (1977): 275–82.

Classic studies of American folk music are represented by the work of Cecil J. Sharp and Phillips Barry. Sharp's *English Folk-Song: Some Conclusions* (London: Simpkin and Co., 1907) still merits study, and Barry's approach may be seen in such articles as "Folk-Music in America," *JAF* 22 (1909): 72–81; "The Origin of

Folk-Melodies," *JAF* 23 (1910): 440–45; and "American Folk Music," *SFQ* 1 (1937): 29–47.

An excellent summary of ethnomusicological approaches to analyzing American folksong is provided by George Foss in his essay "The Transcription and Analysis of Folk Music" in *Folksong and Folksong Scholarship*, ed. Roger D. Abrahams (Dallas: Southern Methodist University Press, 1964), pp. 39–71. In another valuable essay, Foss describes "A Methodology for the Description and Classification of Anglo-American Traditional Tunes," *JFI* 4 (1967): 102–26. Donald M. Winkleman's article "Musicological Techniques of Ballad Analysis," in *MF* 10 (Winter 1960–61): 197–205, provides a clear introduction by means of generalizations and examples. The individual approaches of two major scholars are seen in Samuel P. Bayard's "Prolegomena to a Study of the Principal Melodic Families of British-American Folk Songs," *JAF* 63 (1950): 1–44, reprinted in *The Critics and the Ballad*, pp. 103–50, and Bertrand H. Bronson's "Some Observations about Melodic Variation in British-American Folk Tunes," *JAMS* 3 (1950): 120–34. James R. Cowdery's essay discussed in this chapter was published as "A Fresh Look at the Concept of Tune Family" in *EM* 28 (1984): 495–504.

Bronson's theories and working methods may be traced through his important series of articles, eighteen of which are gathered in *The Ballad as Song* (Berkeley: University of California Press, 1969). The culmination of Bronson's work appeared in his *The Traditional Tunes of the Child Ballads*, 4 vols. (Princeton: Princeton University Press, 1959–72).

Two other folksong editions contain important technical studies of their music. Jan Philip Schinhan edited and analyzed "The Music of the Ballads" and "The Music of the Folksongs" for *The Frank C. Brown Collection of North Carolina Folklore* (4, 1957; 5, 1962). In Helen Hartness Flanders's *Ancient Ballads Traditionally Sung in New England*, 4 vols. (Philadelphia: University of Pennsylvania Press, 1960–65), the musical annotations are by Bruno Nettl.

An early discussion of the problems of folk-music classification was George Herzog's "Musical Typology in Folksong," *SFQ* 1 (1937): 49–55. A practical system is described by George List in "An Approach to the Indexing of Ballad Tunes," *FFMA* 6 (Spring 1963): 7–16.

Bronson discussed text-tune relationships in two articles: "The Interdependence of Ballad Tunes and Texts," *CFQ* 3 (1944): 185–207, reprinted in *The Critics and The Ballad*, pp. 77–102, and *The Ballad as Song* (see above); and "On the Union of Words and Music in the 'Child' Ballads," *WF* 11 (1952): 233–49, reprinted in his *The Ballad as Song*, pp. 112–32. A detailed individual study is found in George List's "An Ideal Marriage of Ballad Text and Tune," *MF* 7 (1957): 95–112. George W. Boswell provides a good general discussion of the subject in chapter 23 of his and J. Russell Reaver's *Fundamentals of Folk Literature* (Oosterhout, The Netherlands: Anthropological Publications, 1962), pp. 188–95, and he has a closer study of the matter in his article "Reciprocal Controls Exerted by Ballad Texts and Tunes," *JAF* 80 (1967): 169–74.

Musical analysis of commercial and popularized folk music has advanced in such articles as Judith McCulloh's "Hillbilly Records and Tune Transcriptions,"

WF 26 (1967): 225–44; Neil V. Rosenberg's "From Sound to Style: The Emergence of Bluegrass," *JAF* 80 (1967): 143–50; and especially Anne and Norm Cohen's "Tune Evolution as an Indicator of Traditional Musical Norms," *JAF* 86 (1973): 37–47. The definitive work on its subject is *Bluegrass: A History* by Neil V. Rosenberg (Urbana: University of Illinois Press, 1985). Documenting an interesting mix of musical traditions, W. H. Bass, in "McDonald Craig's Blues: Black and White Traditions in Context," *TFSB* 48 (1982): 46–61, writes of a black singer who has introduced songs learned from recordings by the white singer Jimmy Rodgers (who had himself incorporated black material) into his own oral tradition.

Bill C. Malone provides a rich historical and contextual survey of folk and popular musical traditions in *Southern Music. American Music* (Lexington: The University Press of Kentucky, 1979). Concentrating on a single southern state is Charles K. Wolfe's *Kentucky Country: Folk and Country Music of Kentucky* (Lexington: The University Press of Kentucky, 1982). Louis M. "Grandpa" Jones, with Charles K. Wolfe, wrote an account of his own development from "folk" to professional in *Everybody's Grandpa: Fifty Years Behind the Mike* (Knoxville: University of Tennessee Press, 1984).

For selected ethnic-American musical traditions see Nicholas Tawa's *A Sound of Strangers: Musical Culture, Acculturation, and the Post–Civil War Ethnic Americans* (Metuchen, N.J.: Scarecrow Press, 1982). The musics surveyed are from southern Italy, the Middle East, Eastern Europe (including Jewish music), China, and Japan. Essays on various musical traditions of a single state are included in the special issue of *NYF* (14:3–4 [1988]), "Folk and Traditional Music in New York State," edited by Ray Allen and Nancy Groce. Another ethnic tradition is discussed in Paula Savaglio's "Polka Bands and Choral Groups: The Musical Self-Representations of Polish-Americans in Detroit," *EM* 40 (1996): 35–47. An unusual approach is taken in the sixteen essays collected in George O. Carney, ed., *The Sounds of People and Places: Readings in the Geography of American Folk and Popular Music* (Lanham, Md.: University Press of America, 1987). Bruce Harrah-Conforth appraised a popular genre for its traditional aspects in "Rock and Roll, Process, and Tradition," *WF* 49 (1990): 306–13.

Alan Lomax proposed his concept of "Folk Song Style" in an article by that title in *JIFMC* 8 (1956): 48–50. Charles Seeger offered a rebuttal and proposals of his own in "Singing Style," *WF* 17 (1958): 3–11. A more extended treatment of Lomax's ideas then appeared in his "Musical Style and Social Context," *AA* 61 (1959): 927–54; and in the introduction and notes to his anthology *The Folk Songs of North America in the English Language* (New York: Doubleday, 1960). Important reviews of that work are cited in the notes to chapter 11. Alan Lomax's work in "cantometrics" yielded "The Good and the Beautiful in Folksong," *JAF* 80 (1967): 213–35 (an article replete with both field anecdotes and highly technical analysis of data), and the survey of world traditional song styles entitled *Folk Song Style and Culture* (Washington, D.C.: American Association for the Advancement of Science, publication no. 88, 1968). For the background of this work and a concise summary of its method, see William R. Ferris, Jr., "Folk Song and Culture: Charles Seeger and Alan Lomax," *NYFQ* 29 (1973): 206–18. Bess Lomax Hawes,

John Lomax's daughter and Alan's sister, who had worked with Charles Seeger as well, provided a fascinating autobiographical statement in "Reminiscences and Exhortations: Growing Up in American Folk Music," *EM* 39 (1995): 179–92.

It is important that beginning students of folk music not confine themselves to studying printed materials alone, but also become familiar with recorded examples. A problem in this area, however, is the great profusion of popularized or semi-original material on records and the relative obscurity of companies that issue authentic recordings. Several of the general books cited here and in chapters 11 and 12 contain discographies. Wilgus offers an especially good annotated one on pages 365–82 of his work. Another problem, however, is that as audio cassettes and compact disks supplanted vinyl disks, many of the older releases were allowed to go out of print, and many recording companies went out of business, changed names, or merged with other companies.

III

CUSTOMARY FOLKLORE

While there is often a verbal component to the folk traditions described in this section, and sometimes even a material component, customary folklore is essentially a matter of traditional habit and behavior. Some customs are characteristically employed for communicating directly to other individuals (as when gesturing in greeting or leave-taking), some are practiced by varisized family or community groups (as in folk festivals), and some may involve set numbers of performers (as in most folk dances). The "audiences" for such traditional performances may be participants themselves (as in a game), the community (folk dramas), or even, perhaps, "the gods" (superstitions). Its practitioners typically regard customary folklore as "just entertainment," but folklorists often can show that it has overtones of magic, ritual, or traditional science.

In some past studies, behavioral lore has been treated much like oral lore (collecting game or superstition "texts," etc.), but special approaches and techniques are needed to do the job of behavioral and belief analysis more fully. Therefore, each type of customary folklore presented here is put into the framework of the most reliable recent studies, whatever direction they have taken.

14

SUPERSTITIONS

WHAT ARE SUPERSTITIONS?

Superstitions are often thought of as naive popular beliefs, usually concerning chance, magic, or the supernatural, that are logically or scientifically untenable. Hence, the alternate term "folk belief" is often employed, carrying with it the equally negative connotations of unsophistication and ignorance that the word "folk" has in popular usage. Such a substitution seems mistaken on at least three counts. First, superstitions include not only belief, but also behavior and experiences, sometimes equipment, and usually sayings or rhymes. Second, no one is immune from the assumptions that underlie superstition, nor from holding or practicing superstitions to some degree. Third, the term "superstition" is now so well entrenched in folklore study that it probably should continue to be used, despite its traditional suggestions of ignorance and fear. While it may seem more precise, as some folklorists have suggested, to speak of "folk (or 'traditional') science" or of "conventional wisdom" rather than "superstition," it is under the latter name that most such items have been collected and published, and the habits of mind underlying them are the same in any case.

Superstitions involve beliefs, practices, and procedures based upon conscious or unconscious assumptions, usually concerned with the nature of cause and effect. Even though superstitions are not essentially just verbal statements, it is as such that they are usually transmitted and have often been collected by folklorists. Alan Dundes described these characteristics in a typical compilation of "superstitious sayings." The sayings describe *conditions* (either *signs* or *causes*) and their supposed *results*: "If there's a ring around the moon (*sign*), it will rain (*result*)" or "Turn a dead snake belly up (*cause*), and it will rain soon (*result*)." Superstitions like the last example, in which deliberate human actions "*cause*" the *result*, are termed *magic* by folklorists (referring not to stage illusions, but to the assumption that supernatural effects have been humanly caused). Other superstitious sayings describe *conversions*—that is, when a *sign* is right, a certain *act* will convert the conventionally expected *result*: "If you break a mirror (*sign*), you'll have seven years bad luck (*result*), unless you gather up the pieces and throw them into running water (*conversion*)." Another example is "If you see a shooting star (*sign*), you should say 'money' three times before it disappears (*conversion*), and then you'll have good luck (*result*)." Incorporating these characteristics into one description, Dundes proposed as a definition: "Superstitions are traditional expressions of one or more conditions and one or more results with some of the conditions, signs and others causes."

While this definition seems more satisfactory than many older ones that simply branded superstitions as nonreligious beliefs, bad logic, or (in Sir James G. Frazer's term) "false science," there are other objections to it. Mainly, it is a definition of the "expressions" of superstition, not of superstitious beliefs and practices themselves. As Michael Owen Jones pointed out, Dundes's approach did not allow for considering "the meaning and function of the material or the nature of the folk mind." A better concept of superstition— much harder, however, to phrase in a concise description—would take into account the social contexts in which folk beliefs occur and also reflect the fact that informants themselves distinguish between useful traditional knowledge and harmful or foolish "superstitions." Dundes himself also suggested using the term *folk ideas* for simple statements of popular misconception that are neither signs, magic, or conversions, but which do appear in folklorists' collections of superstitions: "Lightning never strikes twice in the same place" or "Dragon flies feed [or cure] snakes," for example.

SUPERSTITIONS IN MODERN LIFE

However unsound the assumptions underlying superstitious beliefs and behavior, they are generally couched in sound logic and are remarkably widespread at every level of society. (Some traditional superstitions have even turned out to be fairly reliable, perhaps as cures, weather signs, planting lore, etc.) Thus, even among the best-educated segments of society, we may find superstitions known and to some degree believed.

Since 1907, various American professors have investigated the degree of superstition found among their students. The published results of these surveys (listed in the bibliographic notes), which spanned the country geographically and reached students from a variety of backgrounds, indicated that many students are significantly superstitious, and that as a group they have become neither more nor less superstitious more recently; only details of their belief and practice vary.

At the University of California at Berkeley in 1907, nine hundred psychology students were asked to list and comment upon their own superstitions. A total of seven thousand items was submitted: four thousand were superstitions known but not believed, two thousand were recognized as superstitions but still partly believed, and one thousand were superstitions trusted fully. More than one-half of the test group believed in some superstitions, the most common being good- and bad-luck signs involving Friday the thirteenth (or other occurrences of thirteen), breaking mirrors, opening an umbrella in the house, finding a horseshoe, hearing a dog howl, seeing the moon over the left shoulder, or dropping silverware.

In 1923, forty-five students at Vassar College recorded 186 items of superstitious belief and practice from their personal knowledge. Most of the items had to do with good and bad luck, love and marriage, and wishing. Some unusual examples turned up: "Say the word 'hare' last on the last day of one month, and the word 'rabbit' first the next morning, and you will have good luck"; "A pause in conversation that occurs twenty minutes before or after an hour signifies that an angel is passing by"; "Count the cars in a passing freight train like daisy petals, 'Loves me, loves me not,' etc."

FOCUS: FIRST-OF-THE-MONTH RITUAL

Dear Dad:

Did you know that if you say "rabbits" first thing in the morning on the first day of a month, it's good luck? If the month has an "r" in it, say "white rabbit." This is what all the girls do here in my school in New Zealand.

*

"On the first morning of the month," notes a typical informant, "before speaking to anyone else, one must say 'White rabbits, white rabbits, white rabbits' for luck." Subject to minor modifications the utterance of this spell appears to be the accepted routine throughout Britain. Some children feel it is enough just to cry "Rabbits," as long as it is the first word they pronounce. Others, though not many, believe it is necessary to say "Hares" last thing the previous night, as well as saying "Rabbits" in the morning. In Romford a boy says that "White Rabbits" must be intoned three times, "after the first foot has touched the floor when getting out of bed, and not after the second foot has touched the floor or it will bring bad luck." In Liverpool the first of the month is known as "Bunny Rabbit Day." In Luncarty, near Perth, it is considered especially lucky if "Rabbits" is cried on the first of May. Others in Perthshire hold that it is important to say "Rabbits" when there is an R in the month. Radnorshire children, or some of them, assert that "Black rabbit" should be shouted on the eve of the new month, and "White Rabbit" shouted in the morning; and the same view appears to be held in parts of Devon, for a South Molton girl warns that while it is lucky to say "White rabbit," [that] if you say black rabbit on the first day of the month you have bad luck all the month."

Sources: A letter home in 1983 from an American daughter on a high school exchange in Dunedin, New Zealand; Iona and Peter Opie, *The Lore and Language of Schoolchildren* (New York: Oxford University Press, 1959), pp. 299–300.

DISCUSSION TOPICS:

1. What hypotheses about origin, distribution, and meaning or function might be drawn from the appearance of this similar superstitious custom among Vassar College women in 1923 (see text above), among British schoolchildren in the 1950s, and in a New Zealand private girls' school in 1983?

2. Catalog all the varying details of text and performance of this good-luck spell, along with any similar items you can locate. In what other superstitious practices may similar patterns be observed?

3. Dunedin is a strongly Scottish-influenced city. Do the Scottish

variants of the First-of-the-Month Ritual in the Opies' book (from Perth and Perthshire) seem especially close to the New Zealand items?

At about the same time as the Vassar collection, a Harvard professor of anthropology, who published his results in 1932, secured a large number of superstitions from students at Harvard and elsewhere. By having the students write papers about their personal superstitions, this investigator received comments as well as the items themselves. The results suggested that 70 to 75 percent of undergraduates "carried out certain acts or refrained from carrying them out in the hope that something good would follow or something evil would be prevented." About one-quarter of those questioned owned "fetishes"—lucky objects of some kind, such as coins, pens, clothing, or amulets. A large number of superstitions were associated with examinations, athletics, and games of chance. Although some of the student writers strongly protested that superstition was dead in the twentieth century, and some even complained that college students should not be required to write such nonsense in an enlightened age, others described elaborate personal rituals that they were convinced had brought them luck. If they failed to practice these acts, the students suffered "a distinct feeling of uneasiness."

In 1950, an anthropologist at Indiana University submitted a questionnaire based on the Harvard study to 175 of his students and analyzed the results statistically. His conclusions, the most scientifically controlled thus far reported, showed that students were just as superstitious as ever. Some believed firmly in one-half of the thirty-three items listed, but the average number of items believed by an individual was 5.1. Women seemed to be generally more superstitious than men, and the freshman-sophomore group more superstitious than juniors and seniors. Although the last finding seems to suggest that education erases superstition, the study also indicated that the more educated the parents, the more superstitious their children. Furthermore, no significant relationship was indicated between the number of superstitions believed by urban versus rural students, who presumably should be closer to the roots of "folk wisdom."

(On the suggestion of women being more superstitious than men, a widely publicized 1993 Harris Poll seemed to confirm this. The pollsters found that women are more apt than men to do such things as pick up a penny or knock on wood for good luck, avoid walking under a ladder, or throw spilled salt over the left shoulder.)

In 1961, fifty freshmen in English composition at the University of Idaho were assigned to write papers on their personal superstitions, and not a single student lacked for subject matter. (However, no alternate topic was offered the classes.) Not only did many of the students admit to certain irrational practices to assure themselves good luck in examinations, athletics, or dangerous situations, but also most of the writers could cite personal experiences (that is, relate "memorates") that seemed to uphold the validity of their actions. The subjects of the papers included lucky items of clothing, ski accidents, wart cures, three on a match, logging and traffic dangers, farm and ranch work, and even a student's wife's pregnancy, supposedly guaranteed by the couple's residence in a lucky apartment and through the magic of the number three.

Surveys in many undergraduate folklore courses continue to yield the same kind of information about students' superstitions, but one need not have a captive experimental group of college students to show that modern educated people are superstitious. The popular press is rich in examples. Winners of contests, lotteries, and athletic events are frequently quoted in news stories describing their good-luck charms; medical and advice columnists regularly answer queries about common superstitions; victims of serious diseases, when publicized, often are sent numerous folk cures, which are later reported back to the press. For example, when President John F. Kennedy was suffering from his back ailment someone reportedly wrote to him, "Just get an old pair of shoes and put them under your bed upside down."

In 1964, Mrs. Kathryn O'Hay Granahan, then treasurer of the United States, published a plea in a Sunday supplement magazine that had nationwide distribution, urging Americans to accept the two-dollar bill instead of rejecting it because of the bad luck that is supposed to attend that denomination, and not to tear off a corner to "let the bad luck drain out." In 1976, when printing and distribution of two-dollar bills was resumed, a spate of traditional and superstitious lore about them again appeared in the press. Just as this chapter was first being written (in 1967), the following statements appeared in the health column of the *St. Louis Post-Dispatch*: "My son is a year old and has asthma. Several people have told me that if I get a Chihuahua it will cure the asthma. My husband won't get the dog until you answer."

A modern example of supernatural "tourist folklore" is documented from Hawaii in a study by Joyce D. Hammond published in 1995. Her first paragraph concisely sums up the tradition:

> Every year hundreds of packages and letters are sent to tourist bureaus, travel agencies, hotels, and national parks in the Hawaiian Islands from people who have visited the islands as tourists. The packages, sent most frequently from the U.S. mainland, contain volcanic rock, sand, or articles made from volcanic material. Many of the packages also contain confessional letters which explain that at the time of their visit, the senders either did not believe in or did not know of the curse attributed to Pele, Hawaiian "goddess of volcanoes." Subsequently, however, the tourists, and sometimes those upon whom they bestowed the souvenirs, suffered a series of misfortunes, often enumerated in great detail in the letters, which confirm the belief that Pele causes bad luck for those who take volcanic rock from her islands. According to the tourist folklore, only by returning the rock to Pele can the negative consequences be arrested or avoided.

Hammond's study contrasts native Hawaiian Pele lore with that of the tourists, and points out that the media and "hosting agencies" in Hawaii encourage tourists' beliefs by displaying collections of returned souvenir rocks and the letters that accompanied them. (Similar confessional letters and returned materials are displayed at several American mainland sites noted for geology, volcanic activity, or petrified wood.)

Further examples of superstitions in modern life are easy to find. For example, when the popular newspaper advice columnist Ann Landers wrote that there was no way to guarantee the sex of a child a woman would bear, an irate reader wrote:

> You are wrong. My great-grandmother told me the secret of producing a boy or a girl baby . . . and it works! (I have two of each.)
>
> The left ovary produces boys, the right ovary produces girls. The minute a woman discovers she is pregnant (or even suspects it) she

should start to sleep on her left side if she wants a boy and her right side if she wants a girl. It's as easy as that!

—Lucky Me

But Landers had the right answer on this one:

Lucky is the word, all right. . . . The sex of a child is determined at the moment of conception. Once a woman is pregnant she can sleep on her head and it won't affect the sex of her unborn child.

(See also "the Drāno test" in chapter 15.)

The survival of old superstitions, or at least the knowledge of them, is apparent in some familiar contemporary practices. Hotel owners will skip thirteen when numbering floors, or use that floor only for storage. Manufacturers of billfolds sometimes put a piece of imitation money in each one so that it may safely be given as a gift, for "Giving an empty billfold or purse will spoil your friendship." People who believe that spitting, in certain situations, is good luck, or who belong to ethnic groups that may spit to avoid giving the evil eye, may only pretend to spit if the time and place happen to be wrong for the actual gesture. Other people, lacking a piece of wood to knock on, will playfully knock on their own heads if they utter a statement that suggests some future good fortune. And otherwise perfectly sane and reasonable people will detour around a ladder, postpone business deals or trips that fall on a Friday or on the thirteenth of a month, or carefully date a check written on Sunday to the next day. The rationale for most superstitions such as these is that they may not help, but they won't hurt either. (The proverbial rationalization is "Can't hurt; might help.") A news story about a sufferer from chronic hiccups, who was about to try hypnosis as a last resort, put the matter this way: "Desperate for relief, [she] already had tried surgery, shock therapy, more than 200 home remedies, chiropractic treatment, and prayer." Thus, superstitions ("home remedies") thrive side by side with modern medical science, psychology, and religion.

The "proof" that certain superstitions work seems to come from personal experience. Case histories, expressed as memorates, such as the following, from everyday life are common in student folklore collections:

Elevator buttons in a large office building in New York City indicate that thirteen was skipped when the floors were numbered.

Last December four of us were playing bridge and the first time a two, three, and four came up on an ace, one guy muttered "Wish trick". Since I considered anything worth a try, every time another wish trick came up after that I wished I would get engaged. And that same night at 11:00 Bob proposed!

*

Whenever I play a slot machine in Nevada I leave a few coins in the pay-off tray for good luck. Money in the machine will then be attracted down there. I made my biggest winning ever when I was doing this faithfully.

*

When my grandfather had been working all day in the fields and was really tired—when he'd come home at night, he'd stick one shoe inside the other and put it under the bed. That made it so he wouldn't toss and turn at night, and he said he'd always sleep well. I have three aunts that all still swear by this.

Many superstitions probably arose from faulty reasoning based on personal experiences such as these. An event is assumed to be the cause of certain later happenings—the familiar logical fallacy of *post hoc, ergo propter hoc* ("after this, therefore because of this"). In a classic account of early travel on the Santa Fe Trail, Josiah Gregg's *Commerce of the Prairies* (1844), just such an instance was described:

> There is but little rain throughout the year, except from July to October—known as the rainy season; and as the Missouri traders usually arrive about its commencement, the coincidence has given rise to a superstition, quite prevalent among the vulgar, that the Americans bring the rain with them.

The line of reasoning is no different when modern students do well on an examination and then credit their "luck" to the T-shirt they wore or the pen they used. Psychology favors them further when they retain the same fetish for later examinations. But if their luck holds, then the superstition, rather than their understanding of how their own minds work, is reinforced. Such practices are further encouraged by the human tendencies to ignore negative evidence, to want to believe in the supernatural, and to be able to predict or control events.

Since individual superstitions may be generated by fallacious reasoning from personal experiences and reinforced by coincidences, it is possible that countless private beliefs and practices never pass into folklore circulation at all. Nevertheless, even people's personal superstitions tend to follow traditional patterns involving luck, divination, magic, dreams, colors, numbers, and so forth. This largely explains why it is that while new collections of superstitions invariably contain many items previously unrecorded in printed collections, the existing classification schemes can readily accommodate them. Also, frequently, older superstitions have simply been modernized: a belief about a buggy, for example, is transferred to automobiles, or one about farming is applied to home gardening.

THE WAYLAND D. HAND SYSTEM OF
CLASSIFYING SUPERSTITIONS

There are numerous collections of American superstitions, and some of them are voluminous. They have come from widespread sources, and although there is still much to be collected from regions and folk groups, a comprehensive study of American superstitions has begun. The basis for this study is at the University of California at Los Angeles in the files of the late scholar Wayland D. Hand, editor of the section on superstitions in *The Frank C. Brown Collection of North Carolina Folklore* (volumes 6 and 7). Hand assembled a master file of hundreds of thousands of individual statements of American superstitions taken from all published collections and many archives. He arranged them in one systematic classification system, and individual folklorists in many other states and in several provinces of Canada collected and published superstitions from their own regions in order to broaden the base of Hand's data for his planned *Encyclopedia of American Popular Beliefs and Superstitions*, still being edited in the 1990s following Hand's death in 1986. Thus, it is important to outline Hand's widely followed classification system for superstitions—as demonstrated in the North Carolina collection—as a guide to published and archived superstitions. Even though much future work on superstitions will put greater stress on the social contexts and functions of the items, all major collections of American superstitions published since the North Carolina collection appear to have used some form of Hand's classification for their arrangement.

The system Hand devised for the Frank C. Brown collection contained fourteen major categories, grouped under four broad headings: *the cycle of human life, the supernatural, cosmology and the natural world*, and *miscellaneous superstitions.*

SUPERSTITIONS ABOUT THE LIFE CYCLE

Superstitions related to the cycle of human life fall into the first seven categories of Hand's system as follows:

I. Birth, Infancy, Childhood
II. Human Body, Folk Medicine

Many items in sections I, VI, and VII correspond to three of the four kinds of ceremonies to mark changes in the life cycle (*rites de passage*, or "rites of passage") commonly practiced in "primitive" cultures. By means of these rituals, people "pass" safely from one stage of their existence to the next—from prelife to birth, from childhood to adulthood (at puberty), from a single to a married state, and from life to death. Folk superstitions such as putting an ax under the mother's bed to ease childbirth, having a bride wear or carry certain objects to ensure her future happiness, or guarding a corpse from cats at a wake are modern equivalents for the primitive's complex rituals at the same stages in life. For initiation to adulthood we have such formalized events as graduation, confirmation, and bar mitzvah, but few folk superstitions. A rare exception is the traditional belief that the ribbon on a diploma must not be cut or broken, but must be slipped off whole to preserve one's luck.

Numerous current superstitions associated with *birth, infancy, and childhood* (category I) display concepts and habits of reasoning also associated with primitive cultures. Although it is unreasonable to adopt a "survivals" explanation for all such items, the origins of at least some of them may be so traced. The belief in prenatal influence, for example, is essentially no different whether it exists among modern Americans or among aborigines: the pregnant mother's experiences are supposedly manifested in marks on or habits of her child. If the mother is struck with something, the baby has a birthmark in the shape of that object; if she craves a particular food, that will turn out to be the baby's favorite food, too, or the baby may be "marked" in a related way. (So-called strawberry birthmarks are often explained from such events.) The term "harelip" for the deformity that looks like a hare's cleft lip hints at the superstition that the sight of a hare can cause a pregnant woman to bear a child with that mark. Similarly, personal names are frequently regarded with awe and surrounded with magic among primitives; modern people retain vestiges of the same attitude in such beliefs as that if an unnamed baby is sick, he will recover as soon as he is given a name, or that good luck attends a person whose initials spell a word. (This makes my brothers Tor Arne Brunvand [tab] and Richard Olav Brunvand [rob] luckier than I.)

Folk medicine (category II) is another area in which primitive practices may survive in modern times. In sickness, as during other crises, people almost instinctively rely on traditional cures, even if medical science has been consulted. Thus, a person may secure a salve or ointment with a doctor's prescription and then carefully apply it with the middle finger to improve its effectiveness; here magic and science combine to the detriment of neither. Or, knowing that a nosebleed may be stopped by pressing a blood vessel, a traditionally inclined person chooses "brown paper" as the compress and "under the upper lip" as the pressure point. (In the nursery rhyme "Jack and Jill" it is "vinegar and brown paper" that Jack uses to "mend his head," and some people say a brown paper bag placed against the stomach is a cure or a preventative for car sickness.) The less that medical science knows about an ailment, the more likely it is that folk remedies will survive. For this reason, hiccups, sties, warts, fever blisters ("cold sores"), rheumatism, cancer, and the common cold are among the ailments most frequently treated with folk cures.

Typical cures for warts illustrate some characteristic patterns in folk cures. "Measuring" as a curative device is demonstrated in superstitions requiring that the number of warts be represented by knots on a string or notches in a stick. "Plugging" is used when something that has been rubbed on the warts or pricked into them is driven into a hole in a tree or buried in the ground. "Transfer" is a common device for removing warts by passing them on, through a ritual or a saying, to someone else or even to an animal or object. The same devices appear in many cures for different ailments, and all of them are based on the principle that something may be invisibly removed from the infected area and magically disposed of somewhere else. (Since warts, like colds, appear and disappear with baffling illogic, folk cures for them seem destined to live on for many generations to come.)

The common sensation of ear-ringing, or "tinnitus," may sometimes precede an actual loss of hearing or be associated with other symptoms, such as dizziness. But for most sufferers (including the author of this book) "false tinnitus"—a sporadic ringing sound not actually detectable by a doctor with a stethoscope—is merely an occasional annoyance with no known cure. Published collections of superstitions, surprisingly, offer no traditional remedies, but only supposed "meanings" of ear-ringing, ranging from "Someone is thinking of you" to "You may expect rain." (Earaches, on the other hand, according to American folk beliefs, may be cured by introducing such things as olive oil, onion juice, salt water, or cigarette smoke into the ear.) However, popular nonprescription remedies of no proven medical value, but similar in their makeup to folk cures, are sold. For example, an advertisement for "Bio-Ear" drops costing $15.00 per half ounce claims that this supposedly Swedish formula contains "all natural ingredients including aloe, ginseng root, bitter orange, dandelion root, myrrh, saffron and more." A like appeal to the modern desire to find "natural cures" for common ailments occurs in advertising for an encyclopedia containing "the wisdom of Amish folk medicine." Beginning with the unproven premise that the Amish are healthier than average Americans, yet rely solely on home remedies, this book promises to reveal the Amish secrets for curing everything from poor memory, allergies, thinning hair, and prostate trouble to sleep problems, age spots, and even overweight, all with the use of "simple items you have around your home like vinegar, salt, soda, onions—even olive oil."

"Faith healers," semiprofessional folk specialists in traditional medicine, usually employ a combination of personal and religious power, sometimes in combination with certain herbs or nostrums. Their concepts of diseases and cures may reflect popular writings on medicine of many decades earlier, and they generally also display folk attitudes held by their particular regional or ethnic group. For instance, the Mexican-American *curanderos* may be called upon to treat *mal puesto* (afflictions involving magic or witchcraft) or *males natural* (natural diseases, unknown among Anglo-Americans and not treated by physicians) such as *empacho* (a form of indigestion), *mal ojo* (evil eye), *susto* (fright sickness), and *caída de la mollera* (fallen fontanel).

Just as the traditional belief systems of folk healing deserve study, so do the traditional aspects of professional medical care. For example, one common piece of hospital lore is that deaths come in threes, and there may be elaborate rules about which deaths to count and about other signs or conditions related to the deaths. Hospital taboos include not pushing a patient feet first on a stretcher and never mixing red and white flowers in a vase to be put in a patient's room. A related area of modern folklore is the way people make use of commercial medications, such as taking pills in a certain sequence or swallowing them only with beer or milk.

Superstitions associated with *home and domestic pursuits* (category III) usually concern cooking, clothing, housekeeping, and changing households. Many people, without considering themselves superstitious, will avoid such taboos as seating thirteen at a table, mending clothes while someone is wearing them, or allowing someone to enter the house, if accidentally locked out, through a window without exiting through the same route. Stirring cake batter clockwise, eating the point of a wedge of pie last, or crumpling up (rather than folding neatly) one's dinner napkin may seem meaningless habits, but to some informants they are lucky acts. Similar superstitions also survive as habits of thought in *economic and social relations* (category IV). Store owners sense—even if they are not aware of a superstition—that if the first customer of the day buys nothing, they will have bad sales all day. People walking together will avoid allowing a post or tree to come between them, perhaps not realizing that some consider it a bad-luck sign or a condition that will allow wishes to come true after a dialogue is repeated that begins "Bread and butter—Come to supper." The superstitions of games and sports also fall under this category, and these constitute a rich area, especially when gambling is involved. Horse bettors, poker players, and slot-machine addicts are notoriously superstitious, but even hardheaded bridge players may think their luck is improved if they can manage to sit lined up with their partner the same way as the bathtub is positioned in the house.

FOCUS: ST. JOSEPH SELLS REAL ESTATE

Home Sellers Plant Statues of St. Joseph to Lure Buyers
By Kyung M. Song, Business Writer

He outsells his closest competitor, the Blessed Virgin, five to one in the downtown Tonini Church Supply Co. He is sought by people who can't tell a scapular from a rosary.

He is St. Joseph, the patron saint of family and household needs —and underground real estate agent.

More and more Louisville-area home sellers and agents are burying statues of St. Joseph in yards and asking for his intercession to bring buyers. The practice—which is popular in Chicago and on the East and West coasts—is spreading locally by word of mouth. . . .

Source: The Louisville, Kentucky, *Courier-Journal*, April 12, 1991.

DISCUSSION TOPICS:

1. The appearance of this practice in autumn 1990 in several American cities, as reported by media and correspondence, is chronicled in Jan Harold Brunvand, *The Baby Train and Other Lusty Urban Legends* (New York: W. W. Norton, 1993), pp. 181–84. Compare variations on the theme, as reported here and elsewhere. Ask local realtors and individual home sellers if they know of the practice. Is there any reason for this particular saint to become associated with home selling?

2. Notice in the various reports how the simple idea of burying the statue has been elaborated and ritualized by the folk, adding specific details about where and in what manner the statue must be buried. Some people, for example, say that as the statue is buried the hopeful sellers should promise St. Joseph that they will dig him up after a sale and display him in a place of honor in their new home. Is this "folk religion"?

3. In addition to traveling by "word of mouth," the St. Joseph story has been repeated in tabloids, by humor columnists, and as a "News of the Weird" item syndicated to many newspapers. The ritual has been commodified by various statue and For Sale–sign kits sold via mail-order catalogs. Gather some examples and analyze this merging of folk- and popular-culture elements.

Travel and communications (category V) is another "danger area" (like birth, sickness, and gambling), for which superstition may provide a safeguard. This often takes the form of auspicious days and times for beginning a trip, signs of future trips or of visitors to come, and procedures for traveling or for returning to fetch something forgotten at home. Recent superstitions about mail, telegrams, telephones, and the like conveniently fit into this category, too. These include items such as "If a letter falls to the ground when you mail it, bad luck will attend it" or "Talking on the telephone during a storm may give you an electric shock."

Superstitions of *love, courtship, and marriage* (category VI) concern

aphrodisiacs and other love charms, divinations, and various practices to predict or ensure marital or sexual happiness. Although few
Americans probably believe in divination nowadays, some young
women still pretend to determine their future mates by consulting
objects ranging from buttons (which are counted "doctor, lawyer,
merchant, thief"), an apple peel pared in a whole strip (which is
thrown over the left shoulder to fall in the shape of the man's initial),
or a drinking straw (which is pinched into a pattern and then flat-
tened until one of the initialed ends is intact and thus indicates the
spouse's name). The old taboo against trying on another person's
engagement ring lest you never get married yourself is perhaps today
as much a matter of courtesy as an item of actual belief.

Anyone who has taken part in weddings knows the care that some
brides will take to secure the required "Something old, something
new, something borrowed, something blue." The suggestion that the
bride might see the bridegroom shortly before the wedding is met
with horror in some quarters. Other brides will go to the extreme
of being sure that they are not married while standing with their
feet aligned at right angles to the floorboard in the church. After
marriage, a tradition that supposedly reveals which partner is the
boss in the family involves having the person fold his or her hands;
the thumb that comes out on top signifies who has the power in the
home, though people disagree on which thumb signifies each
partner.

Superstitious *death and funereal customs* (category VII) reflect our
fear of all things associated with death. A bird flying into the house,
a red spider, a dog howling at night, an empty rocking chair that
is moving, a picture falling off the wall—these are only a few of
the signs that were once widely regarded as sure omens of a coming
death and that still may occasion a good deal of anxiety. When there
is a death in the house, people may stop the clocks, throw out water
in flower vases, or perform other traditional acts for which there is
no rational explanation, only the authority of traditional usage. Once
it was considered bad luck to break through a funeral procession,
while today it is merely bad manners (or, in many states, illegal). In
any case, doing it accidentally leads one not only to a feeling of
personal regret, but also to a definite twinge of uneasiness for offending the dead.

SUPERSTITIONS ABOUT THE SUPERNATURAL

Superstitions concerned exclusively with the supernatural are gathered in category VIII of Hand's system, *Witchcraft, Ghosts, Magical Practices*. Although the Anglo-American witch is now mostly a semi-comical figure of cartoons and Halloween decorations in the urban United States, one does not have to go too far into the backwoods or among ethnic groups to find flourishing beliefs in midnight witch-riding, conjuring, hoodoo, cursing, casting spells, haunts, shape shifting, and the like. Collections and studies of American superstitions are rich in supernatural lore, too voluminous to be summarized here. Ghost lore is still extremely active in the United States, encouraged in large part by film and television productions probing "unsolved mysteries" and supposed psychic phenomena. "Second sight" and other forms of supernatural communication through time or space are still trusted by some. The modern Americans' habits of carrying lucky charms, knocking on wood, crossing their fingers, and cursing things that offend them all point back to supernaturalism that is medieval, if not much more ancient.

Probably not best considered part of supernaturalism (although their popular name suggests that they are) are "water witches" (or "dowsers"), who seek groundwater sources by magical means. Such practitioners, walking back and forth across an area with their forked sticks or "doodlebugs" (for locating minerals), are a kind of traditional or folk scientist found in many rural counties in America and in most urban ones as well. As one Western big-city newspaper commented in a feature about local dowsers, "Even skeptics often consult them to be on the safe side before they drill a well." In 1992, complicated instructions for a "Missing Person Locater" circulated on the Internet; they consisted of some traditional dowsing techniques redirected via a photograph or some other "specimen" of the missing person so as to reveal whether the person still lived and in what direction he or she should be sought. It was suggested that the technique be used to find "missing children, kidnap victims, MIAs, or lost pets."

Ozzie Waters of Concord, Contra Costa County, California, witches wells using a forked branch

FOLK RELIGION

Although Wayland Hand's extensive classification system for the
thousands of isolated superstitions gathered in North Carolina by
Frank C. Brown cannot incorporate the much more structured nature of folk religion, this is an appropriate place to mention the
subject in this book. Many people, perhaps most, engage in some
aspects of **folk religion,** which comprises, in folklorist Don Yoder's
words, "views and practices of religion that exist among the people
apart from and alongside the strictly theological and liturgical forms
of the official religion." These traditional unofficial religious attitudes and actions may range in complexity from simple aspects of
prayer, veneration of religious objects, blessings, faith-promoting stories, and the like, up to elaborate folk-religious organizations such
as the voodoo practiced in New Orleans, which derives from Haitian
traditions, and the Southern snake-handling cults, which take their
inspiration from the literal interpretation of biblical passages.

Folklorist William Clements developed a useful set of distinctions
to identify the traditional elements in American folk Protestantism,
and, though his focus was northeast Arkansas, most of his terms
could apply elsewhere. This variety of the folk church, Clements
found, is oriented to the past, accepts the Scriptures literally, believes
that providence works in everyday life, and strongly emphasizes
evangelism. The groups' services (often held in buildings relatively
isolated from mainstream churches) are characterized by informality
and emotionalism. The group follows a rigorous moral code, and
the church organization tends to be sectarian (split off from some
orthodox congregation) and egalitarian (admitting to membership all
professed believers). Clearly, many of these features may also be
found among popular religious movements (such as the followings
that faith healers and television evangelists enjoy), and different traits
might be identified for such groups as the Unification Church, the
transcendental meditators, or the American converts to Eastern
religions.

SUPERSTITIONS ABOUT COSMOLOGY AND THE NATURAL WORLD

Superstitions related to cosmology and the natural world fall into the following five categories in Hand's system:

   IX. Cosmic Phenomena: Times, Numbers, Seasons
    X. Weather
   XI. Animals, Animal Husbandry
  XII. Fishing and Hunting
 XIII. Plants, Plant Husbandry

Such *cosmic phenomena* (category IX) as tides, winds, rainbows, and the movements of heavenly bodies have long been studied and regarded as possible portents, often of wars or of natural disasters. The more unusual the phenomenon, the more likely it will be read as an omen. As a result, eclipses, comets, and meteors ("shooting stars") occasion more superstitions than do phases of the moon, shifting patterns of stars, and bright colors of sunsets. General superstitions of this kind, as well as those dealing with times, numbers, and seasons, when they are unrelated to other areas of folk belief, fall into this group. Examples include "Seeing the moon over the right (or left) shoulder is good luck"; "Sing before breakfast; cry before dinner"; "Trouble always comes in threes"; and "Nothing made of leather at Christmas time will last."

As Mark Twain pointed out, people talk about the weather, but they *do* very little about it—not even predict it with complete reliability—despite the science of meteorology, with its orbiting weather satellites and computer models. The natural result is survival of an enormous number of weather superstitions. Most items in category X are signs: "If you see a dog eating grass, it is going to rain soon"; or "If it snows on Christmas day, Easter will be green." Others are magic: "Sit in the middle of the room and hold a glass of water in your hand and you won't be struck by lightning during a storm"; or "Sleep with a flower under your pillow and the weather will be fair the next day." Only a few are conversions, such as "Every flash of lightning is accompanied by a thunderbolt; if you can find one (a thunderbolt) and keep it in your house, it will never be struck by lightning."

Superstitions concerning *animals and animal husbandry* (category XI) or *plants and plant husbandry* (category XIII) include all the beliefs and practices used to enhance agricultural success. Even in an age of farm advisers in every county, government bulletins to cover all problems, and technological advances for every need, many farmers still plant by the "signs," consult almanacs, treat sick animals with home cures, and follow countless other traditional usages. One of the most whimsical animal beliefs carried to the New World from the Old is that rats may be induced to leave a building by writing them a polite note that suggests another abode nearby and stuffing it into a rat hole. Traditional ways of controlling threatening animals include "Hold your breath and bees won't sting you"; "A rattlesnake won't cross a hair rope"; "Cut off the tip of a dog's tail and carry it with you and that dog will never harm you"; and "If you see a stray dog out on your lawn, cross your fingers and hold them tight and he won't defecate there." (A related practice, said to keep dogs from fouling the lawn, is placing clear-plastic soft-drink bottles filled with water around the yard.) The familiar children's rhyme "Ladybug, ladybug, fly away home" is said to have been used by hop growers to spare the useful little beetles when the vines were burnt off.

The most common agricultural superstitions are those that deal with the best time to perform farm work such as planting, harvesting, dehorning, castrating, and slaughtering. Some farm traditions seem to have fairly logical explanations—such as the rules for animal surgery that correlate with the times of year naturally best suited for healing (i.e., months without an "r," that is, the summer months, are sometimes taboo for castration)—while others are strictly magic—such as the belief that thanking the giver will cause a gift plant to wither and die, or the belief that only if a hen is set on an even number of eggs will they all hatch.

Fishing and hunting superstitions (category XII) exist because, as with gambling, sports, sickness, crops, weather, and the like, success cannot be predicted or guaranteed. As a result, there are traditional signs for the good-luck days and places, and traditional magic for the best methodology of the hunt. Members of hunting or fishing parties may be excessively sensitive about such acts as sticking an ax into the ground (it will throw the dog's scent off) or stepping over a fishing pole (it will ruin the luck). Other sportsmen are convinced by years of experience that a big opossum will always go up a little tree and vice versa, or that the behavior of a small fish kept in a tank at home will indicate how good the fishing will be that day in the waters from which the captive fish was taken. Commercial fishermen have many folk signs and practices associated both with increased production and better individual protection against storms and accidents.

FOCUS: TEXAS FISHERMEN'S BELIEFS

"And it was rough, you know, a southeaster was blowing. And he said, 'You've whistled in the wind. And if you hadn't whistled, this wind wouldn't a blowed.' And he turned around and went back to the dock, and I got fired." . . .

"I was loading ice, threw the hatches off, and one of them flipped over on the deck. My brother came down and told me to never let that happen again, that that damn boat was going to sink. The next night it did." . . .

"I never did like nobody to say 'alligator' on board. That's something that you heard, and it seems like every time that I was ever on a boat and anybody said it on there, I'd go out and tear my net or just something or another would go wrong."

The alligator, hatch cover, and whistling superstitions are all examples of magic beliefs. . . . [These are] found mainly among sea fishermen and include taboos, omens, good-luck devices and customs, control devices and aids, and several miscellaneous beliefs. . . . Magic beliefs have no rational explanation in the fishermen's minds; these are the practices that seem to be based on some mysterious element ordinarily beyond human control.

Source: Excerpted from Patrick B. Mullen, "I Heard the Old Fishermen Say": Folklore of the Texas Gulf Coast (Austin: University of Texas Press, 1978; 2nd. ed. Logan: Utah State University Press, 1988), pp. 3–4.

DISCUSSION TOPICS:

1. Besides magical beliefs, Mullen distinguishes "empirical beliefs," including weather signs and fishing aids often "based on tradition and on observation and experience of nature." Mullen's many examples of these two categories and his analysis are well worth reading in full. Would his categories work for other bodies of occupational folk belief?

2. How should the term "belief" be understood in the context in which these and similar items are transmitted? Are some of them

really "artistic superstitions" preserved more for their entertainment or esthetic appeal than for any actual serious belief? How might the degree of literal belief be estimated when collecting folklore?

3. In his book's conclusion, Mullen suggests that folklore (legends and anecdotes, as well as beliefs) "is chiefly an occupational expression for Gulf fishermen and a regional expression for bay fishermen." What evidence and analysis supports this view? Can this idea be applied to other occupational folklore?

As in almost every classification in the study of folklore, there remains a group of very general items that may be no better labeled than simply *Miscellaneous*. This category (XIV) contains the lore of wishing, general good and bad luck, and a small but interesting group of modern beliefs. One of the most persistent contemporary superstitions, for example, is that to save enough of an apparently worthless item will result in some kind of reward. The items saved may be ticket stubs, cigarette packages (or the red opening-tabs from the packages), beer-bottle labels, tea-bag tabs, or the red trademark tags from Levi's. Generally the assumption is that "a million of them" (or some other large number) will be good for some charitable gift such as a Seeing Eye dog for a blind person, a wheelchair for a physically disabled one, or hospital care for a poor child. Probably the publicity given to a few actual prize contests based on saving "proofs of purchase" has done much to keep alive beliefs in non-existent redemption schemes.

Just as American children attach some significance to finding the words "Hershey Kisses" printed three times on an opening tab or an entire Indian pictured on a Tootsie Pop wrapper, adults have traditions associated with the number of dots on an Olympia Beer label or the number of stars on a *Playboy* magazine cover. Other items for this miscellaneous category might be the beliefs that too much exposure to television or to a computer monitor may cause sterility, or that stones grow.

THEORIES OF SUPERSTITIONS

The preceding discussion of the persistence of superstitions and of their definition, classification, and folk rationalization has also introduced several *theoretical aspects* of superstitious behavior. These include faulty reasoning, coincidence, psychological predilection to believe in the supernatural, rites of passage, the theory of survival, the uncertainty of some desired ends, fear of the abnormal or of the risky, fear of the dead, modernization of superstitions, and the power of magic to persist traditionally side by side with officially maintained science and religion. Two other important theories still sometimes invoked in superstition studies deserve mention.

The famous theory of **sympathetic magic** proposed by Sir James G. Frazer in his twelve-volume work *The Golden Bough*, although discredited by modern anthropologists, provided terminology still in use for explaining some superstitions. Frazer believed that many primitive beliefs in magic were founded on the assumption of an inherent "sympathy" between unconnected objects. This could take the form either of *homeopathic magic* (magic of similarity), based on the idea that like objects may affect each other, or *contagious magic* (magic of touch), based on the idea that objects formerly in contact with each other continue to have an invisible connection. The theory was applied beyond primitive cultures to explain many superstitions, both ancient and modern. When the witches in *Macbeth* stir up waves in their kettle to make waves rise at sea, or when a primitive person fears that his or her likeness in a photograph will steal his or her soul away, or when planting lore implies a parallel between the crescent moon enlarging and crops increasing, homeopathic magic is said to be at work. In each instance an event *like* the desired one is involved. But when a nail or knife that caused a wound is treated along with the wound, or when a person's footprint may be molested to harm that person, or when the spittle of someone who has delivered the "evil eye" is used in the curative ritual, contagious magic is said to be at work. Here each event involves something formerly *in touch* with the subject of the magic.

Both kinds of sympathetic magic are involved in such rites as a curse performed with a voodoo doll made as an image of the victim that also contains bits of his or her hair, nail parings, or clothing. In a wart cure, if a stolen dishrag is simply buried "to rot the wart away," only homeopathic magic is used; but if it must first be touched to the wart, contagious magic is at work also. Part of the difficulty in accepting wholly Frazer's "false science" approach is that when a magical act is followed by the desired result, there may be nothing defective in either the logic or its application: some "superstitions," in other words, seem to be true and useful—at least part of the time. Conversely, the institutionalized religious "magic" of blessings, prayer, or good works may or may not prove effective and thus may or may not (depending on one's belief) be accepted as "true." In other words, Frazer's explanation is ethnocentric (see chapter 15), and most folklorists using his terminology do not completely accept his underlying theory.

The theory of **gesunkenes Kulturgut** proposed by German scholar Hans Naumann never gained much academic support after it was introduced in the 1920s. The theory held that some modern folklore may represent surviving fragments of learned traditions (rather than only "savage" ones) that have "sunken down" from a high stratum of society among the educated to a lower level in the peasant class. (The theory was the direct opposite of that held by the "survivals" school.) *Gesunkenes Kulturgut*, however, is an apt explanation for certain important bodies of superstition, mainly astrology and witchcraft. In each of these areas, what were once the trusted beliefs of the best-educated people of earlier times have become present-day folk superstitions. Rulers of nations once consulted astrologers before making important decisions (some, in fact, still do), and courts of law once seriously tried and condemned witches, but only traditional practice maintains these beliefs in the United States now.

Theories concerning superstitions, like all theories of folklore, should not be formulated too rigorously or applied too mechanically without full regard for the social contexts and field data on which they are based. In many instances more than one theory may apply. For example, the placing of an ax under the bed during childbirth might be alternately explained as part of a rite of passage, as the survival of primitive veneration for valuable tools, as an instance of homeopathic magic (the sharp edge "cutting" the pain), or as a safety precaution to counter the fear of a dangerous situation. An alert listener can detect the theoretical basis in explanations sometimes offered for common superstitions. "Three on a match" is usually explained as a survival from a wartime safety measure, "step on a crack and break your mother's back" involves homeopathic magic, putting a piece of the desired mineral on a "doodlebug" (miner's divining rod) draws on contagious magic, and most personal validations for superstitions involve fallacious reasoning. In addition, explanations for superstitions, like those for proverbs, may themselves be traditional, and when such explanations become sufficiently formularized, they become legends.

As Barre Toelken pointed out in reference to college students' "superstitions," some statements of alleged folk belief are passed on merely because they appeal humorously or esthetically to the group; these are, in his terms, "artistic superstitions," not to be mistaken for the more seriously taken "religious superstitions." (The term "artistic" is used here to mean formularized in a pleasing way, while "religious" here refers to serious believing practice of an item.) Whether a superstition is artistic or religious is largely a matter of individual attitude—one person's religiously believed tradition may be another's mere whimsical saying—but other items in the *form* of folk belief are clearly not believed by anyone who repeats them, such as the following supposed cure for a cold:

> Get in bed with your hat hanging on the bedpost, and drink whiskey until you see two hats; then you can sleep your cold off.

This American mock folk cure has its counterpart in the Norwegian so-called Coffee Doctor:

> Put a coin in a cup and pour in black coffee until you can't see it; then add whiskey until you can see it again. Drink this and you'll cure your cold.

RESEARCH IN SUPERSTITIONS

Research approaches to superstitions have generally taken the form of collecting projects, classifications, attempts at framing better definitions, determining the functions of superstitions, and theoretical studies. Another promising approach, so far only touched upon, is experimentation. An experiment with superstitions might be designed to field-test a theoretical explanation, to determine the efficacy of a superstition, to study variations that occur in transmission, or for other purposes. An experiment on a very simple level that shows how coincidence reinforces belief was performed by the columnist Allan M. Trout of the *Courier-Journal* (Louisville, Kentucky) in 1960.

(It was reported in that newspaper while I was a graduate student at Indiana University and caught my eye as an example of someone testing a traditional belief.) After hearing the first katydid on July 20, Trout calculated by means of folk prognostication that the first frost would come ninety days later, on October 20. He then proceeded to write his column for that date in advance, boldly predicting the weather that the katydids had promised. What did his readers find on the morning of October 20? A light frost—the first of the season!

The katydid experiment, of course, was uncontrolled and unscientific; it demonstrated more about how superstitions arise through coincidence than about the natural causes that might underlie them. An experiment on a higher plane was reported in 1962 in the *Journal of American Folklore*. Pigeons were confined in boxes where food was delivered and colored lights were flashed in a random pattern. The birds, however, tended to react as if their own bodily movements or the appearances of the lights had a real connection with the delivery of food. They learned to respond to the supposed light patterns or to attempt to control the appearance of food by their movements; in short, they became what is termed "superstitious." The experimenters concluded that the basic conditions that may lead to superstitions are deprivation and the uncertain appearance of a desired commodity, "accidental reinforcement" of behavior that supposedly leads to success, and the continued maintenance of such behavior even without much positive encouragement. Whether such stimulus-response experimentation tells us much about the psychological state of superstitious humans is open to question.

BIBLIOGRAPHIC NOTES

Alan Dundes compared definitions of superstitions and proposed the one quoted in this chapter in his "Brown County Superstitions," *MF* 11 (1961): 25–56; repr. in *Analytic Essays in Folklore*, pp. 88–94. In "Folk Beliefs: Knowledge and Action," *SFQ* 31 (1967): 304–9, Michael Owen Jones commented on Dundes's definition and suggested a need for an improved approach to better account for meanings and functions of superstitions and for the workings of the "folk mind."

Dundes offered the term "folk ideas" for items of traditional attitude and assumption not easily included under "folk belief" or superstition; see "Folk Ideas as Units of World View," *JAF* 84 (1971): 93–103. He collected examples of these ideas in such articles as "The Number Three in American Culture," in his anthology *Every Man His Way* (Englewood Cliffs, N.J.: Prentice-Hall, 1968), pp. 401–24 (repr. in *Analytic Essays in Folklore*, pp. 206–25); "Thinking Ahead: A Folkloristic Reflection of the Future Orientation in American Worldview," *Anthropological Quarterly* 42 (1969): 53–72 (repr. in *Analytic Essays in Folklore*, pp. 226–38); and in an article on the primacy of sight data in American folk speech and folk belief entitled "Seeing Is Believing," *Natural History* 81 (May 1972): 8–12, 86–87.

Studies of collegiate superstitions referred to in this chapter are as follows: Fletcher Bascom Dresslar's *Superstitions and Education*, University of California Publications in Education no. 5 (Berkeley, 1907); Martha Warren Beckwith's "Signs and Superstitions Collected from American College Girls," *JAF* 36 (1923): 1–15; Alfred Marston Tozzer's *Social Origins and Social Continuities* (New York: Macmillan, 1932), pp. 225–30, 242–66; Harold E. Driver's "A Method of Investigating Individual Differences in Folkloristic Beliefs and Practices," *MF* 1 (1951): 99–105; and Jan Harold Brunvand's "Folklore and Superstitions in Idaho," *IY* 6 (1962): 20–24 (see also a note in *WF* 22 [1963]: 202–3).

Two other notes on student superstitions are Martin L. Wine's "Superstitions Collected in Chicago," *MF* 7 (1957): 149–59 (175 items from nineteen students at Austin High School), and Charles A. Huguenin's "A Prayer for Examinations," *NYFQ* 18 (1962): 145–48 (appeals to St. Joseph of Cupertino, "The patron saint of the stupid"). Gustav Jahoda reports several other studies of student superstitions in *The Psychology of Superstition* (Baltimore: Penguin Books, 1970), pp. 31–32. An article by L. Michael Bell contains numerous folk beliefs concerning a popular soft drink, collected from college students; see "Cokelore," *WF* 35 (1976): 59–65 (repr. in *Readings in American Folklore*, pp. 99–105).

Joyce D. Hammond's essay quoted in this chapter is titled "The Tourist Folklore of Pele: Encounters with the Other" and appears in Barbara Walker, ed., *Out of the Ordinary: Folklore and the Supernatural* (Logan: Utah State University Press, 1995), pp. 159–79.

Mark Graubard compared ancient and modern attitudes toward superstitions in "Some Contemporary Observations on Ancient Superstitions," *JAF* 59 (1946): 124–33. A discussion of the truthfulness of some superstitions is E. H. Lucas's "The Role of Folklore in the Discovery and Rediscovery of Plant Drugs," *Centennial Review of Arts and Science* 3 (1959): 173–88. Bergen Evans's *The Natural History of Nonsense* (New York: Knopf, 1946; Vintage Books paperback ed., 1958) debunked many popular delusions. Ray B. Browne's "Superstitions Used as Propaganda in the American Revolution," *NYFQ* 17 (1961): 202–11, illustrated the appearance of such delusions in an earlier period.

Collections of American superstitions are listed in the bibliographies of both volumes of the North Carolina collection, and Wayland D. Hand's introduction in volume 6 is a comprehensive survey of theories of superstitions and problems of research as they apply to the 8,569 items he has arranged and annotated here. Besides this invaluable work, a key European reference source is the *Handwörterbuch des deutschen Aberglaubens*, ed. Eduard von Hoffman-Krayer and Hanns

Bächtold-Stäubli, 10 vols. (Berlin and Leipzig: W. deGruyter, 1927–42). Space permits listing only four other important American collections: Harry Hyatt's *Folklore from Adams County, Illinois* (New York: Alma Egan Hyatt Foundation, 1935; 2nd rev. ed., 1965); Vance Randolph's *Ozark Superstitions* (New York: Columbia University Press, 1947; Dover Books paperback ed., 1964); Ray B. Browne's *Popular Beliefs and Practices from Alabama*, University of California Folklore Studies no. 9 (Berkeley and Los Angeles, 1958); and a volume edited from several collectors' materials by Wayland Hand and Jeannine E. Talley, *Popular Beliefs and Superstitions from Utah* (Salt Lake City: University of Utah Press, 1984).

Two enormous collections of American superstitions published in their entirety greatly broaden the base for studies in this area. Harry Middleton Hyatt's *Hoodoo-Conjuration-Witchcraft-Rootwork* was issued in five volumes by Western Publishing Company of St. Louis, Missouri (1970–78). Newbell Niles Puckett's *Popular Beliefs and Superstitions*, including more than thirty-six thousand items collected in Ohio, was edited for publication in three volumes by Wayland D. Hand, Anna Casetta, and Sondra B. Thiederman (Boston: G. K. Hall, 1981). The system established for the Brown collection was somewhat modified and reorganized for this work.

A good collection from Canada with bibliographic references to others is Helen Creighton's *Bluenose Magic: Popular Beliefs and Superstitions in Nova Scotia* (Toronto: Ryerson Press, 1968).

For the particular folk beliefs of African-American culture, begin with Newbell Niles Puckett's *Folk Beliefs of the Southern Negro* (Chapel Hill: University of North Carolina Press, 1926). An important early study is Zora Hurston's "Hoodoo in America," *JAF* 64 (1931): 317–417.

Confronting the vast materials available for classification and study, Samuel J. Sackett proposed "Using a Computer on a Belief Collection" in *WF* 29 (1970): 105–10. A reader offered a correction to Sackett's methodology in *WF* 30 (1971): 55, but little progress has been made in computerizing superstition studies since.

In the folklore of childbirth, the curious practice of giving the husband medical care after his wife has given birth is discussed in historic and geographic perspective by Wayland D. Hand in "American Analogues of the Couvade," *Studies in Folklore*, pp. 213–29. Lucile F. Newman presents a large classified collection in "Folklore of Pregnancy: Wives' Tales in Contra Costa County, California," *WF* 28 (1969): 112–35.

A general approach to the subject of folk medicine may be made via the collection *American Folk Medicine: A Symposium*, ed. Wayland D. Hand (Los Angeles, Calif.: UCLA Center for Study of Comparative Folklore and Mythology, pub. 4, 1976). Many techniques of folk medicine (plugging, nailing, transfer, passing through, animal sacrifice, etc.) are analyzed in the twenty-three essays by Wayland D. Hand gathered in his *Magical Medicine* (Berkeley: University of California Press, 1980). Jack Santino edited a special issue of *Western Folklore* (44:3 [1985]) devoted to "Healing, Magic, and Religion."

Cures using "madstones" (hair or fiber balls from the stomachs of ruminants) are discussed in a special issue of *NCFJ* (24:1 [1976]). Articles on folk herbalists and their cures are found in *NCFJ* 27 (1979): 20–25 and in *TFSB* 48 (1982): 61–

65. A major collection of studies is James Kirkland et al., eds., *Herbal and Magical Medicine: Traditional Healing Today* (Durham, N.C.: Duke University Press, 1992).

Data on faith healing are contained in such articles as Terry M. Carbo, "The Faith Healing Beliefs of a New Orleans Family," *LFM* 2 (August 1968): 91–100; and Gopalan V. Gopalan and Bruce Nickerson, "Faith Healing in Indiana and Illinois," *IF* 6 (1973): 33–99. More analysis is given in Wayland D. Hand, "The Folk Healer: Calling and Endowment," *Journal of the History of Medicine and Allied Sciences* 26 (1971): 263–75; and Michael Owen Jones, *Why Faith Healing?* (Ottawa: Canadian Centre for Folk Culture Studies, paper no. 3, 1972). In an overview, Greg Johnson charts strategies of faith healing in "A Classification of Faith Healing Practices," *NYF* 1 (1975): 91–96. In "Faith Healing Narratives from Northeast Arkansas," *IF* 9 (1976): 15–39, William M. Clements discusses the theology of healing among Pentacostals (from the power of the Holy Ghost) and examines some themes of faith-healing stories (crisis conversions, spirit baptisms, exorcisms, prophecies, etc.).

Occurrences of a curious belief concerning the human body are recorded in "Measuring for Short Growth," *HF* 7 (1948): 15–19. For instance, children may be considered undersized if their heights are not found to be seven times the length of their feet. For further data, see Barbara Ann Townsend and Donald Allport Bird, "The Miracle of String Measurement," *IF* 3 (1970): 147–62, with an additional account supplied in *IF* 4 (1971): 89–94.

Of particular interest in the general area of folk cures is Richard M. Dorson's "Blood Stoppers," *SFQ* 11 (1947): 105–18, which was reprinted with some additions as chapter 7 of *Bloodstoppers and Bearwalkers* (Cambridge, Mass.: Harvard University Press, 1952). Another area of folk cures is presented in Frank M. Paulsen's "A Hair of the Dog and Some Other Hangover Cures from Popular Tradition," *JAF* 74 (1961): 152–68. Articles on folk veterinary medicine in Tennessee were published in *TFSB* 43 (1977): 140–48 and 44 (1978): 55–65. A related item, "Communicating with Critters," *FFV* 1 (1979): 52–59, by Elmer L. Smith, concerns various notes and verbal charms directed to insects, rats, and the like in order to repel or eliminate them.

As background for a Spanish-American pattern of faith healing and folk medicine, see Irwin Press, "The Urban Curandero," *AA* 73 (1971): 741–56. On the nature of ailments for which magical aid is sought, see Keith A. Neighbors, "Mexican-American Folk Diseases," *WF* 28 (1969): 249–59. A local study in this area is E. Ferol Benavides, "The Saints among the Saints: A Study of Curanderismo in Utah," *UHQ* 41 (1973): 373–92; and a book-length study is Beatrice A. Roeder's *Chicano Folk Medicine from Los Angeles, California* (Berkeley: University of California Press, 1988).

Folk practices and beliefs concerning sex are discussed in three articles: Eleanor Long, "Aphrodisiacs, Charms, and Philtres," *WF* 32 (1973): 153–63; George W. Rich and David F. Jacobs, "Saltpeter: A Folkloric Adjustment to Acculturation Stress," *WF* 32 (1973): 164–79; and Lydia Fish, "The Old Wife in the Dormitory—Sexual Folklore and Magical Practices from State University College," *NYFQ* 28 (1972): 30–36.

Folk beliefs and superstitions of various occupations constitute a fascinating but largely uncollected body of material. Actors' superstitions are found in Ralph Freud's "George Spelvin Says the Tag: Folklore of the Theater," *WF* 13 (1954): 245–50; Dan Gross's "Folklore of the Theater," *WF* 20 (1961): 257–63; and Wayland D. Hand's "Folk Beliefs and Customs of the American Theater: A Survey," *SFQ* 38 (1974): 23–48. Other occupational studies include Lee Allen, "The Superstitions of Baseball Players," *NYFQ* 20 (1964): 98–109; Henry Winfred Splitter, "Miner's Luck," *WF* 15 (1956): 229–46; and two studies by Patrick B. Mullen— "The Function of Magic Folk Belief among Texas Coastal Fishermen," *JAF* 82 (1969): 214–25; and "The Function of Folk Belief among Negro Fishermen of the Texas Coast," *SFQ* 33 (1969): 80–91. Another study of fishermen's superstitions is John J. Poggie, Jr., and Carl Gersung, "Risk and Ritual: An Interpretation of Fishermen's Folklore in a New England Community," *JAF* 85 (1972): 66–72. An unusual study of urban black folk belief is David J. Winslow's "Occupational Superstitions of Negro Prostitutes in an Upstate New York City," *NYFQ* 24 (1968): 294–301.

A body of European-American beliefs and practices is described by Aili K. Johnson in "Lore of the Finnish-American Sauna," *MF* 1 (1951): 33–39 (repr. in *Readings in American Folklore*, pp. 91–98). Louis C. Jones traced "The Evil Eye among European-Americans" in *WF* 10 (1951): 11–25, but found no evidence of survival among English or Scottish stocks.

A basic study of Anglo-American supernatural folklore is George Lyman Kittredge's book *Witchcraft in Old and New England* (Cambridge, Mass.: Harvard University Press, 1929; republished New York: Russell and Russell, 1956). Patricia K. Rickels collected "Some Accounts of Witch Riding" from a black college student who had been witchridden—see *LFM* 2 (August 1961): 1–17 and the reprint in *Readings in American Folklore*, pp. 53–63. The major study of witch riding (or "the old hag") is by David J. Hufford, *The Terror That Comes in the Night*, AFS publications, new series, vol. 7 (Philadelphia, 1982).

On the basis of an interview with a "good" witch living in Philadelphia, Jane C. Beck published "A Traditional Witch of the Twentieth Century," *NYFQ* 30 (1974): 101–16. A catalog of American witch legends is cited in the notes to chapter 9.

The practice of dowsing or "water witching" has attracted numerous studies; the most comprehensive is Evon Z. Vogt and Ray Hyman's *Water Witching U.S.A.* (Chicago: University of Chicago Press, 2nd. ed., 1979). A fascinating review of the first edition of the book by a practicing "witch" is R. Carlyle Buley's "Water (?) Witching Can Be Fun," *IMH* 56 (1960): 65–77. Vogt also cowrote "Some Aspects of the Folklore of Water Witching in the United States," *JAF* 71 (1958): 519–31, with Peggy Golde; and "The Urban American Dowser," *JAF* 82 (1969): 195–213, with Linda K. Barrett. A study of dowsing in a regional context is Hilda Webb's "Water Witching as Part of Folklife in Southern Indiana," *JFI* 3 (1966): 10–29.

A "Symposium on Folk Religion," ed. Don Yoder, appeared in *WF* 33 (1974): 1–87. Steven M. Kane's "Ritual Possession in a Southern Appalachian Religious Sect," *JAF* 87 (1974): 293–302, deals with snake handling in a six-state area. Articles on African-American folk religion include David J. Winslow, "Bishop E. E. Everett and Some Aspects of Occultism and Folk Religion in Negro Philadelphia," *KFQ* 14 (1969): 59–80; James F. Byers, "Voodoo: Tropical Pharmacology or Psychosomatic Psychology?" *NYFQ* 26 (1970): 305–12; Loudell F. Snow, " 'I Was Born Just Exactly with the Gift': An Interview with a Voodoo Practitioner," *JAF* 86 (1973): 272–81; and Claude F. Jacobs, "Spirit Guides and Possession in the New Orleans Black Spiritual Churches," *JAF* 102 (1989): 45–67.

William M. Clements deplored the neglect of folk religion by American folklorists in an essay published in *JFI* 15 (1978): 161–80. He proposed the list of folk-religious elements referred to in this chapter. Two articles on folk varieties of Catholicism appeared in *IF* 9 (1976): 147–74. *NYF* 8: 3–4 (1982) was a special issue containing seven essays on folklore and religious belief. See also *Diversities of Gifts: Field Studies in Southern Religion*, ed. Ruel W. Tyson, Jr., James L. Peacock, and Daniel W. Patterson (Urbana: University of Illinois Press, 1988). Just at this writing, further studies on religion in America are beginning to appear.

An early government publication, Edward B. Garriott's *Weather Folk-Lore and Local Weather Signs*, attempted to "segregate from the mass of available data the true sayings that are applicable to the United States." Material was drawn from two late-nineteenth-century collections; the work was published as *U.S. Dept. of Agriculture, Weather Bureau, Bulletin No. 33—W. B. No. 294* (Washington, D.C., 1903; Superintendent of Documents Index No. A29.3:33). Another interesting older collection is W. J. Humphreys's *Weather Proverbs and Paradoxes* (Baltimore: Williams & Wilkins, 1923; 2nd ed., 1934). Louise Pound surveyed the history of attempts to make rain on the Great Plains in her article "Nebraska Rain Lore and Rain Making," *CFQ* 5 (1946): 129–42, reprinted in *Nebraska Folklore*, pp. 41–60. Background material from eighteenth-century New England for the study of a popular reference work on weather lore and other agricultural and domestic traditions is George Lyman Kittredge's *The Old Farmer and His Almanack* (Cambridge, Mass.: Harvard University Press, 1904).

Except that it becomes excessively ritualistic in its interpretations, W. W. Newell's "Conjuring Rats," in *JAF* 5 (1892): 23–32, is a good discussion of the old superstition concerning writing a note to rid a building of rats (see also "Communicating with Critters," cited earlier in these notes). Two items of recent folk belief are described in Michael J. Preston's "Olympia Beer Comes to Colorado: The Spread of a Tradition," *WF* 32 (1973): 281–83 (supposed significance of the dots on the backs of labels); and Harry Joe Jaffee's "The Stars of Playboy," *WF* 31 (1972): 122–23 (traditions about stars printed on the magazine cover).

Allan M. Trout's experiment was described in the *Courier-Journal* on October 20, 1960. The pigeon experiment was described by Arthur J. Bachrach in "An Experimental Approach to Superstitious Behavior," *JAF* 75 (1962): 1–9. In "Superstitious Pigeons, Hydrophobia, and Conventional Wisdom," *WF* 30 (1971): 1–18, Kenneth Ketner, with reference to such experiments, asserts that notions of folk groups and their supposed beliefs are useless for defining superstition. Instead he advocates study of the "psychological state of individuals" and prefers the term "conventional wisdom" to "superstition." An article that deals further with the habits of mind that permeate superstition is Eric Berne's "The Mythology of Dark and Fair: Psychiatric Use of Folklore," *JAF* 72 (1959): 1–13. Gustav Jahoda's *The Psychology of Superstition*, mentioned earlier in these notes, is the only book-length survey of modern psychological theories as they apply to folk beliefs.

15

CUSTOMS AND FESTIVALS

WHAT ARE CUSTOMS?

Possibly no other category of American folklore has been so frequently referred to, yet so vaguely defined, so ill classified, and so little understood or studied, as folk customs have been. While few proposed definitions of American folklore would exclude customs, nowhere is there a comprehensive explication of the term, nor is it consistently employed. Tolerably rich materials are scattered through such sources as state and local historical journals, but there is no definitive folklore study of them as a genre. Customs have sometimes been presented in folklore collections under such labels as "folkways," "usages," or "social institutions," or they are included in collections together with superstitions or material folklore. Some folklore anthologies that list "customs" among their contents actually contain few or none, while others that do include customs have no special terms for them. Indexers and bibliographers of American folklore usually group customs with other "minor areas" of traditional materials. Social historians and folklorists who may be dealing with the same customs seem to be unaware of each other's publications. For all of these reasons, this chapter attempts to integrate various points of view by extracting some generally useful terms, concepts, and examples.

To begin with, many customs are closely associated with superstitions. Hence, the typical combination "Beliefs and Customs" is used as a section title in *The Frank C. Brown Collection of North Carolina Folklore* and other major collections. Like superstitions, customs involve both verbal and nonverbal elements traditionally applied in specific circumstances. But unlike superstitions, customs do not usually involve faith in the magical results of application. Thus, the "customs" that incorporate traditional belief in the supernatural are usually classified by folklorists as "superstitions."

A **custom** is a traditional *practice*—a mode of individual behavior or a habit of social life—transmitted by word of mouth or imitation, then ingrained by social pressure, common usage, and parental or other authority. When customs are associated with holidays, they become *calendar customs*; and when such events are celebrated annually by a whole community, and especially over a period of several days, they become *festivals*.

Transmitting folklore is itself customary. Storytelling, ballad singing, riddle posing, game playing and prank playing, and the like all depend for their survival on traditional performance and acceptance rather than on official control. Generally, folklorists have not separated the customary contexts from folklore texts, except perhaps when studying something like quilting bees or barn raisings rather than quilt patterns or the barns themselves, or when researching a "liars' contest" rather than merely collecting texts of tall tales. But there are more subtle behavioral patterns, integral parts of folklore-performance situations, that folklorists also study: "framing" devices that initiate and conclude folk transmissions, postural and gestural clues to meaning, audience-response codes, nonverbalized folk beliefs, and the like.

This expanded sense of the term "custom" involves the folklorist in what anthropologists term **ethnography**—the descriptive study of all traditions in a particular group or region. Ethnographic descriptions of different cultures make possible comparative studies, or **ethnology.** Since the terms "ethnography" and "ethnology" are sometimes used synonymously, especially in Europe, and both terms tend to be associated with studies of primitive cultures, the term "folklife" (from Scandinavian *folkliv*) deserves the increased American usage it has had lately. **Folklife** refers to the full traditional lore, behavior, and material culture of any folk group, with emphasis on the customary and material categories (see chapter 19). For verbal folklore the term **folk literature** has some currency, although whether "folklife" includes "folk literature" is not always clear. A safe generalization is that American folklorists have accepted the European concept of folklife as constituting their subject matter, and that they are borrowing from ethnography and ethnology for new field methods and theories. In both respects, customs are important data.

Not all customs are still-living folklore. Those that have become a fixed part of national behavior and are practiced unvaryingly throughout a country (or sometimes several countries) are termed *manners* or *mores*, although their origins may lie in folklore and their sustaining power may still be that of tradition. The domestic manners that characterize Americans include switching the fork from hand to hand while eating, serving certain drinks iced, and maintaining a high degree of informality in social life. Manners may involve different levels of awareness, however; we switch fork hands as a matter of course, but icing drinks is a deliberate act, and social informality may be either studied or "natural."

Mores are traditional modes of behavior that have achieved the status of moral requirements, often being institutionalized in laws. These include such practices as monogamous marriages, the patterns of family naming, and the age when adulthood begins. *Ethnocentrism* is the assumption that one's own customs, manners, and mores are the "right" ones, and that all others are scaled out in degrees of "wrongness" from this center. Ethnocentrism accounts for feelings among Americans, for example, that range from intolerance of some other culture's religion (or lack of religion) to mild annoyance at having to drive on the "wrong" side of the highway in some other countries, or being expected to bow as a greeting in Japan. That contacts with other cultures may lead to voluntary changes as well as to hostility is demonstrated by the spread of American courtship customs throughout much of the Old World.

National manners and mores, ethnocentrism, acculturation, and related subjects are the concerns of anthropologists and especially sociologists; folklorists have been concerned mostly with customs that are both traditional and variable, being sustained informally in specific folk groups rather than nationally among the whole population. By the time traditional frontier hospitality evolved into the "Welcome Wagon" and the political candidate's barbecue became the $1,000-a-plate fundraising dinner, these "folkways" had ceased to have much folkloristic significance, although they still might interest other students of American behavior.

RITE-OF-PASSAGE CUSTOMS

Most true folk customs in the United States are associated with special events, especially those that require "rites of passage"—birth and adolescence, coming of age, courtship and marriage, and death. They begin at once when a child is born. Boy babies are customarily dressed in blue and girls in pink, but sometimes only the first child of each sex in a family is so clothed, while later arrivals must make do with hand-me-down infantwear or may appear in other pastel shades. Father is expected to hand out cigars, a custom that may repeat itself after promotions in his occupation as well. (In Mormon-dominated Utah and perhaps elsewhere from other influences, instead of cigars a new father passes out Tootsie Rolls or bubblegum cigars.) None of these practices is required by any authority other than local custom, which varies from region to region or even from family to family. Some families have special clothes for the baby's homecoming or christening, or heirloom furniture for the baby's room.

Celebrations of birthday anniversaries may begin as early as the first year in some families, and they may continue through one's entire life. More commonly, however, birthday parties are dropped at about high school age, sometimes to be revived once at the symbolic age of maturity (twenty-one years) and again as an annual celebration in later middle age. A person's fortieth birthday is often the occasion for a celebration in the form of a mock funeral, wake, or other somber ceremony, to make that person's now being "over the hill."

Children's birthdays almost invariably are the occasion for spanking—one spank for each year, with extras "to grow on" or "for good measure." Children in some regions maintain a fairly rigid schedule of extra-punishment days before and after the birthday anniversary—"pinch day," "hit day," "kiss day," and so forth. Blowing out birthday-cake candles and wishing are standard cus-

An African-immigrant naming ceremony performed at the 1995 Festival of American Folklife in Washington, D.C.

toms, sometimes varied by naming the candles for possible marriage partners and assuming that the last candle smoking marks the mate. Birthday gifts at a party may be held over the head of the celebrating child for him or her to guess the donor or to announce the use to which that gift is to be put. For each correct guess the child is granted a wish.

Even the standard birthday congratulatory song, "Happy Birthday," has its variations, most commonly in the form of humorous parody verses. Other versions of the song may be performed by the birthday person ("Happy birthday to me / I'm sweet as can be"), or else the parody turns the cheery greeting into a dismal comment, as in this one, sung to the tune of "The Volga Boatman":

> Happy birthday, happy birthday,
> People dying everywhere, not a one without a care,
> Happy birthday, happy birthday.

Many families allow the birthday person to rule as "King (or Queen) for the day," and some families celebrate birthdays of pets or of favorite dolls with the usual human traditions. Birthday customs, in general, comprise ceremonies that unite a family or peer group, sometimes setting up temporary new relationships at home or work, and that offer in the familiar elements of cake, candles, wishes, presents, etc., plenty of opportunities for local or individual variation.

FOCUS: FAMILY BIRTHDAY CUSTOMS

In my family whenever it was someone's birthday you would get up before they got up and put butter on their nose when they were still asleep. My mother always thought this was a really fun tradition, but it led to a lot of fights. There was nothing you could do about it because it was traditional. It's true, it's true, there was nothing you could do. It was the tyranny of tradition.

Cathy Condon
St. Louis, Missouri

*

We had a tradition just in our immediate family that I really liked. On my brother's birthday and on my birthday, the family always has dinner together. And Dad used to sit down with a drink and recount the day of our birth: what happened, how he felt, how my mother felt, what was going on that day. He did it every year. My father died about five years ago but my brother and I have kind of carried that on. On my birthday, my brother will say, "Well, twenty-seven years ago at this time," or I'll say, "Twenty-nine years ago at this time . . ."

Virginia A. Heasley, Age 27
Philadelphia, Pennsylvania

*

When I was little—I was one of six—my mother would come up with some day out of the year that was really far away from Christmas and your birthday, you know, that endless stretch. You'd come home from school and she'd tell you it was your unbirthday. She'd cook your favorite dinner, whatever it was—even hot dogs. And you could watch all your favorite television programs. Nobody could argue with you about it. People sang happy unbirthday to you. There was a cake sometimes and presents, but it wasn't like a birthday when you got real presents. It wasn't every year that everybody had one. It was just kind of spontaneous. It

came from Alice in Wonderland. *Remember the Madhatter's teaparty?*
"Have a happy unbirthday!"
 Wendy Roges, Age 23
 Washington, D.C.

Source: Steven J. Zeitlin, Amy J. Kotkin, and Holly Cutting-Baker, eds., *A Celebration of American Family Folklore* (New York: Pantheon, 1982), pp. 179–80.

DISCUSSION TOPICS:

1. These three items were among many recorded by visitors to the Smithsonian Institution's Festival of American Folklife. Although each of these informants seems to regard her own family birthday tradition as unique (or at least unusual), another "Butter-Nosed Birthday" custom was recorded during the same event by a visitor from Washington, D.C., and the custom of recounting events on one's day of birth is practiced in many families. What other variations of these or other birthday customs can you locate in your own family or in others' families?

2. Who seems to be responsible for carrying out these traditions in each family? What are the sources of their inspiration? How do the participants regard "tradition" as a reason for preserving the customs?

3. Discuss the functions of these and other family birthday traditions.

The loss of "baby teeth" provides another occasion in a child's life when folk customs are followed. The most common practice is for the child to sleep with the tooth under his or her pillow for the "tooth fairy" to buy for a quarter (prices vary). School customs are practiced to some degree in most communities, often being channeled eventually by teachers and principals into well-regulated events. "Dress-up day" or "hillbilly day" under various names are begun informally by students to vary the routine of regulated school dress, but eventually become sanctioned and controlled by school officials and are placed on the activities calendar. A school custom of possible folk origin is the backwards prom, or "morp," to which girls ask boys for dates, and at which people are often expected to dress in some respects "backwards." One school custom certainly remains a folk one—the designation of a certain day (often Thursday) as "queer day," when the wearing of a certain color (often green, yellow, or purple) marks the supposed homosexuals. In the past, many unsuspecting teachers were ridiculed behind their backs for unwittingly violating the taboo. Nowadays the politically incorrect and offensive nature of the custom has led to its well-deserved demise in most schools.

The hazing of freshmen, initiation into clubs, and "tapping" for honorary societies are further school occasions for which the establishment has forged ersatz "traditions" to supplant or forestall folk customs, although these seldom catch on as group traditions, and when they do the participants tend to modify them back in the direction of earlier folk behavior. Few regret the passing of older customs of violent and often dangerous initiation rituals for school groups that sometimes resulted in injury and even death.

Some customs followed at school have no real connection with school itself. The passing around of autograph books for inscriptions (see chapter 7) often goes on there, as does the passing of "slam books"—homemade albums for the entry of negative remarks about one's classmates and against oneself by others. On the other side of the coin, various "friendship customs," usually involving the exchange of articles of clothing or jewelry, are equally popular. One practice is to give others sets of "friendship beads," tiny glass beads strung into safety pins and worn on the recipients' shoelaces. A variation of this is the "friendship bracelet" woven of colored string and given to one's best friend.

A more elaborate adolescent custom is "legend-tripping." During the years when "cruising" in automobiles is popular (roughly from when one gets a learner's permit until one reaches legal drinking age), a favorite destination for nighttime drives is some locally famous site associated with a supernatural legend (see chapter 9). Teenagers will "cruise" to a place said to be haunted, cursed, inhabited by witches or maniacs, the scene of a terrible accident, or the like, and there retell the legends while half-hoping that something supernatural will take place. Sometimes pranks resembling initiations are performed, and often the trips are associated with drinking, drugs, sex, or vandalism. In Rhode Island, another form of adolescent legend-tripping has developed. Students in Tiverton High School there commemorate a long-ago teenager named Paddy (or "Patty") Murphy who, according to local legend, skipped school on a Friday in May to go for a swim on Horseneck Beach and was drowned. Although school officials assert that the story is pure fiction, some students continue to observe Paddy Murphy Day by skipping school on the first Friday in May. At least three generations of students are aware of the story, according to a recent newspaper account, and the name mentioned in the custom may derive from a college song popular in the 1940s that began

The night that Paddy Murphy died, I never shall forget.
The whole damned town got stinking drunk, and some ain't sober yet.
The only thing they did that night that filled my heart with fear,
They took the ice right off the corpse and put it on the beer.

In St. Louis an unusual local variation of the cruising trip has developed called "finarking" (or "fernarking") the birds. Adolescents drive to the St. Louis Zoo on summer nights, park up close to the big birdcage there, and shout "Finark! Finark!" in an attempt to get the birds, and ultimately the whole zoo population, to screech and howl back at them. "Finarking the birds" itself has a legendary basis: some postadolescents claim that it began in the late 1930s or early 1940s, when the zoo had one exotic bird whose distinctive cry was "Finark!"

Customs associated with reaching maturity (coming of age) are often institutionalized according to the ethnic group, educational level, or religious affiliations of the family. But the kinds of celebrations, gifts, and possible pranks provided for the confirmation, graduation, or bar mitzvah may involve folk traditions. These can include the choice of gifts, the manner of opening them, the photos that are taken (or the activities recorded and videotaped), the people invited, the dress and food deemed correct, the stories told and songs sung, and perhaps other behavioral patterns. Folklorists have largely failed to document such events, so student projects in this area would be valuable. Other possible studies might be done of practices associated with buying one's first car, going away to college, entering the military service, reaching the legal age to drink or to vote, or reaching the age of forty.

Courtship and engagement begin a new round of customs that may lead to marriage, the most tradition-regulated personal ceremony in American life, or, more recently, to other arrangements of living together that may have their own folk traditions. Here, time has changed but not diminished the role of folklore. Couples formerly were granted the family parlor or porch swing for courting; today they have the automobile. Bundling as a courting custom gave way to "necking" or "petting" in the 1940s and 1950s, "making out" and "scoring" later. Ice-cream socials or church "sings" were replaced by drive-ins (both movies and restaurants). Customs of "going Dutch," "blind dates," "double-dating," "study dates," and the like depended on individual finances and desires as well as on local practices. "Going steady" with one partner became a well-entrenched dating pattern surrounded with customary devices for signaling whether one is attached or free (exchanging rings, leaving certain buttons or buckles open, placement of jewelry, etc.). But under the influence of feminism by the late 1960s women were less often willing to display signs of "belonging" to a man, and they were as likely to initiate dates as to wait to be asked. In some high schools and colleges a so-called virgin pin was once worn, supposedly indicating by its position or shape whether a girl was or wasn't. Today the decline of a desire to "save one's virginity for marriage" has rendered the "virgin pin" obsolete; instead, a lore of aphrodisiacs and folk birth-control methods circulates. Formally engaged couples still often have the time-payment diamond ring to advertise and seal their promises, but custom may decree the exchange of other special gifts as well.

Wedding customs begin with the "shower," often several of them, to emphasize different kinds of needed gifts. Shower parties were once customarily for women only, but more recently men friends, too, are invited. Friends of the bridegroom may hold a "stag party" for him, while the bride's friends may organize a "bachelorette party." Certain recreations are reserved exclusively for showers. A favorite is writing down the words of the future bride as she opens gifts. Her remarks are read aloud later as "what she will say to her husband on their wedding night."

Customs of the wedding itself are numerous and largely regulated by tradition. They include the dress of participants, the seating of guests, the choice of attendants, kissing the bride, throwing rice, playing pranks on the married couple, and decorating the car. Some of the more esoteric American wedding customs originated in the Old World. The passing around of the bride's shoe in order to collect money from the guests is known in one form or another in several

European countries. When the advice columnist Abigail Van Buren ("Dear Abby") once asked her readers for an explanation, she got at least half a dozen different responses: people claimed that the custom was German (money for the bride), French (for the cook), Polish (for the couple or for the first-baby's crib), Hungarian (as payment to dance with the bride), and Yugoslavian (so the husband would have to match the amount collected, give it to the bride, and thus prove he was not flat broke). The varying explanations, of course, may be regarded as part of the folklore of the custom.

Noisy harassment of brides and bridegrooms is an old custom in the United States. First it was the "shivaree," derived from the Old World word and custom of the "charivari." A crowd of friends and neighbors would awaken a bridal couple with "rough music" and shouting, subjecting them to various indignities, and pestering them until the husband surrendered and provided refreshments. The shivaree was also known as "belling," "warmer," "serenade," "collathump," "skimmilton," and "going for a one-way ride" (dropping the groom off far from home). In 1946, a folklore journal reported that a recently married couple in Oregon was awakened and the husband dunked in a rain barrel, then forced to push his wife around in a wheelbarrow while the celebrants threw firecrackers at him; afterward he was expected to treat the crowd to refreshments. Many Americans can describe similar customs firsthand, and shivarees still occur; but the typical custom of post-wedding harassment today is to decorate and sabotage the honeymoon car. Crepe-paper decorations, signs on the car, additives to the gasoline, a note in the fueltank cap ("Help, I'm being kidnapped!") are among the usual tricks. Car inscriptions may include pictures, sayings, ribald rhymes, hearts and arrows (similar to tree carvings), and such formulas as "1 + 1 = 3." Sometimes pranks are directed at the newlyweds' home. A favorite is removing the labels from all of their canned goods or tying bells to their bedsprings.

The "Mock Wedding" is a parody of a couple's wedding in dramatic form put on as an anniversary celebration, usually at a milestone date such as the twenty-fifth anniversary. Popular in the Great Plains states of the U.S. and Canada, mock weddings pretend to reenact the marriage ceremony of the honored couple, using men in all of the roles, and with all participants costumed in a humorously undignified way. The ring bearer may wear a suit covered with

A prankster at a 1994 Catholic wedding in Orange, California, has sabotaged the groom's shoes.

canning-jar rings, for example, or the minister may wear a funny hat and have a jug of whiskey dangling from his belt. The actors in the mock wedding exaggerate their gestures and speeches, and they incorporate such inappropriate props into the drama as a shotgun in the hands of the bride's father, a roll of toilet paper for the weeping mother to dry her eyes with, and a telephone book or a copy of *Playboy* magazine instead of the Bible in the minister's hands. The vows exchanged by the couple in the mock wedding, rather than of the "love, honor, and obey" variety, refer to ordinary real-life matters, such as "Do you promise to keep her dressed in the finest of jeans, even if they are beyond your means?"

Once children begin to arrive in a marriage, the birth customs start anew. Baby showers for the mother-to-be, for example, have as much tradition associated with them as bridal showers. The refreshments, decorations, kinds of gifts "showered" on the woman, and the games played are all likely to be suggested by folk practices. Favorite games may be based on buying baby needs (often requiring unscrambling letters that spell out "powder," "diapers," etc.) or naming the baby (sometimes asking the players to construct appropriate names out of the letters of the parents' names). Such recreations are photocopied and passed from mother to mother through the years. Another favorite practice at baby showers is to try the folk prognostication to determine the sex of the unborn child using observation (the way the baby is being carried or how the mother-to-be moves), magic (i.e., with a ring or needle suspended on a thread), or pseudoscience (the test with Drāno that is wet with the woman's urine).

Customs associated with death are generally fraught with suggestions of fear or superstition. Pouring water out of vases, covering mirrors, and stopping the clocks in a house in which death has occurred seem to mask some superstitious fear. Draping the furniture in the room in which a corpse lies or leaving the digging tools by the grave for some days after the burial are marks of respect—or propitiation. The custom of "telling the bees" about a death in the family lest the insects swarm and fly away is the subject of a poem by John Greenleaf Whittier (1807–1892). Sometimes the disposal of the small personal belongings of the deceased is governed by custom rather than a formal will, and many families commemorate the anniversaries of a beloved's passing by printing annual poems or notices in the classified columns of a newspaper. In some communities the funeral is organized by a traditionally appointed "arranger"; Southern and Southwestern writers have described family or community "decoration days," "memorial days," or days for "graveyard working" on which people gather at the cemetery for clean-up work and to remember those who have passed away. Special foods may be served, and the names of those who died since the last memorial day are read aloud.

OTHER CUSTOMS

Apart from the cycle of life and the "rites of passage," customs tend to cluster around work, recreation, or social events. Family reunions (in Utah, also "missionary reunions"), "Old Home Weeks," and "Homecomings" may be structured around special customs, foods, or entertainments. Communal-labor parties, important to frontier survival, have largely disappeared from American life, except in recent experimental communities or among such religious sects as the

Amish, who have deliberately maintained them. But in the past there was a great variety of work parties—quilting bees, apple peelings, corn shuckings, ice cuttings, log rollings, house raisings, turkey drives, rabbit drives (followed by a community "rabbit dance"), and threshings. Another persistent occupational custom is that of attaching a small evergreen tree to the top of the highest beam of the new building when the structural steel has been erected.

A domestic work ritual of the past—the weekly washday—is described in the following text from North Carolina, which, although published as a pioneer tradition, actually seems to be a fairly modern composition projected back in time and employing quaint terms and spellings:

WASHDAY RECEET

1. bilt fire in backyard to heet kettle of rain water.
2. set tubs so smoke won't blow in eyes if wind is pert.
3. shave one hole cake lie soap in bilin water.
4. sort things. make three piles. 1 pile white, 1 pile cullord, 1 pile work britches and rags.
5. stir flour in cold water to smooth, then thin down with billin water. rub dirty sheets on board, scrub hard, then bile. Rub cullard, don't bile, just rench in starch.
6. spread tee towels on grass.
7. hang old rags on fence.
8. pore rench water in flour beds.
9. scrub porch with hot soapy water.
10. turn tubs upside down to dreen.

Several other versions of the "Washday Receet," sometimes titled "Grandma's Washday," have turned up on restaurant menus and place mats, in locally compiled recipe books, and elsewhere; at least one version was printed in *Reader's Digest*, and it has been preserved and displayed in museums and archives, although never in a reliably dated copy that goes back much further than about 1950. All of these versions include misspellings and errors in capitalization and punctuation, but not always the same errors; sometimes the line numbers are omitted, lines are combined, or the order of items is slightly changed. Many of the texts end with a further step, some variation of this: "brew cup of tee, set and rest a spell and count blessins."

While the text of the above "receet" may be doubtful as a pioneer tradition, certainly the general description of washdays of the past is accurate. In later years the typical washday routine required only that each housewife had her clean laundry hanging on the line to dry every Monday, preferably earlier than any other woman on the block. Today we simply do the wash when we wish to, and we do it entirely indoors. But perhaps a weekly washing of the family car has for some families substituted for the older washday custom.

Nowadays, although neighbors may willingly "pitch in" to help others in emergencies, these are spontaneous and improvised occasions, usually not traditional ones. One such communal-aid tradition, still fairly common in small-town neighborhoods, however, is the so-called pound party, in which every participant brings a pound of some commodity to help set up housekeeping for a new neighbor or member of the clergy. An urban counterpart is the "rent party." Certain occupations, such as auctioneering, livestock trading, rodeo work, and the like have rich traditional backgrounds, and many continuing folk practices are associated with them.

Most traditional American frontier amusements were lost or greatly altered in later years. No longer do we enjoy the likes of bearbaiting or gander pulling as recreations. Dogfighting and cockfighting persist illegally, while target-shooting matches (turkey shoots, etc.) have changed their character to survive. Spelling bees, hayrides, taffy pulls, and ice-cream socials survive to some degree. Hunting and fishing are still very popular pursuits and retain some customary traces, such as marking the forehead of the hunter with the blood of his first kill or having the game divided among the participants of the hunt by a blindfolded outsider. Traditions have also developed in modern sports and children's games: choosing sides by odd or even fingers, choosing the server in tennis by spinning the racket, rallying for the serve in Ping-Pong, deciding the order of play in baseball by placing hand over hand on the bat, tossing a coin for the kickoff in football.

FOCUS: A SURPRISING ANNOUNCEMENT

TACO BELL BUYS THE LIBERTY BELL.

IN AN EFFORT TO HELP THE NATIONAL DEBT, TACO BELL IS PLEASED TO ANNOUNCE THAT WE HAVE AGREED TO PURCHASE THE LIBERTY BELL, ONE OF OUR COUNTRY'S MOST HISTORIC TREASURES. IT WILL NOW BE CALLED THE "TACO LIBERTY BELL" AND WILL STILL BE ACCESSIBLE TO THE AMERICAN PUBLIC FOR VIEWING. WHILE SOME MAY FIND THIS CONTROVERSIAL, WE HOPE OUR MOVE WILL PROMPT OTHER CORPORATIONS TO TAKE SIMILAR ACTION TO DO THEIR PART TO REDUCE THE COUNTRY'S DEBT.

NOTHING ORDINARY ABOUT IT.

Source: Full-page advertisement in *The New York Times* on April 1, 1996.

DISCUSSION TOPICS:

1. Media pranks on the first of April, as well as individuals' April Fool jokes, are common. Look at various publications dated April 1

for the past few years and see what you can find. Are these pranks ever retracted or apologized for?

2. Was there any media follow-up, in *The New York Times* or elsewhere, that jokingly (in the spirit of the tradition) proposed other corporate purchases of American icons?

3. What was the commercial and cultural context of spring 1996 in the United States that helped make the Taco Bell prank especially effective?

CALENDAR CUSTOMS

Calendar customs in the United States cluster around a few annual events, unlike those in Europe and elsewhere abroad that are linked to many more occasions. (Large collections of British folklore, for example, have been devoted to descriptions of nothing but such annual customs.) American tradition has retained few Old World celebrations and has originated even fewer native ones. In chronological summary, some common general American calendar customs are: *St. Patrick's Day*, wearing green; *April Fools' Day*, playing pranks; *Easter* (both standard Christian and Orthodox), dyeing eggs and wearing new clothes; *Memorial Day*, visiting the cemetery and decorating family graves; *Independence Day*, shooting fireworks and giving patriotic speeches; *Halloween*, "trick-or-treating"; *Thanksgiving*, feasting and giving thanks; *Christmas*, caroling and hanging mistletoe; and *New Year's Eve*, attending a "watch party" at which there is much noisemaking and general congratulations at the stroke of midnight. Of course, numerous holidays of specific religious and ethnic groups are also fairly well known, and sometimes commemorated, in general American tradition; among these are *Cinco de Mayo*, Day of the Dead, Bastille Day, Ramadan, Chinese New Year's, and several Jewish holidays, especially Hanukkah. Also, various official holidays of individual states as well as provinces of Canada deserve mention, although they are too numerous and varied to be listed and discussed here. A special case is Sadie Hawkins Day, which originated in the comic strip "Li'l Abner," then spun off to become a pseudoholiday actually celebrated in a few locations (mostly by high school students, with a dance for which the girls invite boys to attend).

There are many regional and family variations of standard American holiday customs. St. Patrick's Day and Columbus Day, for example, are celebrated with much more vigor and variety in regions that have a large Irish or Italian population, respectively, than in other parts of the country. Decorating an "Easter tree" with real or plastic colored eggs is a custom known in several parts of Europe and originally practiced in the United States probably by immigrants, either English or German. But Easter trees are now found in many regions where the custom seems to have no relation to national background.

Some official American holidays, such as Presidents' Day, Flag Day, Armed Forces Day, and Veterans Day, while commemorated officially, seem to have few or no folk aspects. Celebrations of some traditional holidays, such as May Day, Shrove Tuesday (apart from Mardi Gras), and Arbor Day, have waned almost to the point of extinction, while other holidays on the American calendar—whether religious, patriotic, or folk in origin—tend to have only sporadic or commercially stereotyped customs associated with them. Valentine's Day card exchanging is a good example, for without the elementary schools' and the merchants' emphasis of it, the custom would probably long since have died out. Groundhog Day can hardly be thought of as an occasion for folk celebration, since practically the only observance of it nowadays is in newspaper feature articles. Mother's Day and Father's Day are officially established occasions only for further gift giving; but another such holiday, Labor Day, has become the traditional time in some regions for "closing the summer cottage" or ending the season with one last beach party, as well as organized events commemorating American laborers. A few recently created holidays, such as Kwanzaa, Secretaries' Day, Bosses' Day, Grandparents' Day, and Martin Luther King Jr. Day, may still be developing their traditional aspects, while one older African-American holiday, Juneteenth (commemorating the emancipation of the slaves) has emerged from a regional celebration to one known in many parts of the country.

Halloween, one of the favorite folk holidays for American children, has suffered an image problem as stories (many, undoubtedly, just legends) circulate annually about tainted foods being given to children. The "razor blades in apples" legends, coupled with a few actual crimes like the 1982 Tylenol killings, have made parents wary of sending their children out on the streets to go from door to door trick-or-treating on Halloween. Thus, in many communities other activities (such as adult-supervised "Spook Alleys," trick-or-treating in shopping malls, or collecting money for UNICEF) are substituted, or else special hotlines or X-ray units are made available for reporting suspicious foods or checking the foods before they are eaten. Halloween has evolved into an extremely popular adult holiday, particularly among gay people, and an occasion for parties, costuming, and parades. Detroit's notorious Devil's Night Halloween activities, centering on acts of vandalism and arson, are publicized nationwide each year, and they were part of the background of the popular 1994 film *The Crow*.

The most typical and original American holiday is certainly Thanksgiving—a combination of the traditional European peasant harvest festival and the first New England settlers' day of giving thanks to God. The Pilgrims' "first Thanksgiving," so often depicted in popular culture, had more of the former character than the latter, while the special meal we eat on Thanksgiving is more Victorian than colonial in its choice of foods and modes of preparation. The televised professional football games of today's holiday had their counterparts in the games and contests of early New England holidays. (Canadian Thanksgiving falls on the second Monday in October, about one month before the holiday in the United States.)

Other festive gatherings in which the sharing of food promotes social interaction are not tied to a calendar date the way Thanksgiving is. Folklorist Linda T. Humphrey has proposed distinguishing from calendric events, work-centered gatherings, and fund-raisings (like box socials) other such "Small Group Festive Gatherings" (SGFGs) as picnics, potlucks, taffy pulls, fish fries, and cocktail parties. Sociability alone is the purpose of SGFGs, and to her list we may easily add office parties, après-ski activities, tailgate parties, clambakes, wine tastings, progressive dinners (each course served in a different home), gatherings to watch television specials or to view videotapes of favorite movies, mortgage burnings, TGIF parties, sack-lunch breaks from work, and divorce celebrations.

FOLK FESTIVALS

There is little more to distinguish calendar customs definitively from true **folk festivals,** perhaps, than the degree of community involvement in them and the elaboration of the celebrations. In fact, the large-scale general commemorations, both commercial and "folk," of such holidays as Easter, Halloween, and especially Christmas, justify considering these times as "festival" occasions.

The religious folk dramas mentioned in chapter 16 and the aspects of folk religion discussed in chapter 14 may also be considered in the context of folk festivals. Some of the most interesting American festivals are immigrant-group seasonal traditions uniquely developed in the United States. The commercialized Mardi Gras of New Orleans, for example, is much more elaborate than most Old World carnival days or than the traditional celebrations of the start of Lent in some parts of rural Louisiana, where a party of masked riders travels from farm to farm singing and begging for food. The processions of the *penitente* brotherhood (carrying Christ's cross and receiving His whippings on their own backs), which originated in Spain centuries ago, differ markedly in the American Spanish Southwest, where they have evolved along new lines, even absorbing some Indian elements. The gradual change in the nature of Czech and Slovak harvest festivals as they were revived and sustained in the United States is typical of other such efforts at retention of Old World celebrations. Here, because the participants were no longer farmers, the spontaneous community ritual of Europe became a well-organized public drama with clearly defined actors and spectators. Whether there are any purely American festivals is uncertain, but probably the best case could be made for the rodeo. All others seem to have clear foreign prototypes: the county fair with harvest festivals, the circus with its ancient Roman ancestor, the family reunion with tribal and clan gatherings.

One unusual American celebration, probably derived from German festivals, is the "New Year's Shoot," as it is called in North Carolina, or the "New Year's Sermon" of Missouri. A party of riders travels from house to house, beginning at midnight of New Year's Eve, pausing at each one for the leader or "preacher" to deliver a set speech. Afterward, firearms are discharged and the party is invited into the house for a treat. The custom has elements in common with English "mumming," which is still found in vigorous tradition in Nova Scotia, and resembles the customs of "belsnickles and shanghais" followed in the late nineteenth century in Virginia. The procedure is also very much like the country Mardi Gras of Cajun Louisiana, and has a dim parallel perhaps in the traditional Southern holiday greeting "Christmas gift!"

FOCUS: NORWEGIAN-AMERICAN *JULEBUKK*

If you grew up in rural Minnesota, Wisconsin, the Dakotas or Iowa, you may have participated in—or been terrorized by—the custom of going julebukk. *Any time between December 26 and Epiphany, an unannounced group of raunchy revelers, looking like no one you would willingly invite, invades your home. Refusing to let you know who they are—you have to guess—they demand to sample your Christmas fare. . . .*

In earlier times, julebukkers disguised themselves as goats, covered themselves with real animal skins, and followed a leader who sported a genuine goat's head held in place by a pole under his goatskin costume. Today's julebukkers more often appear in old cast-off clothing or a wide variety of quickly-improvised disguises reminiscent of American Halloween garb. . . .

Veteran julebukkers know that hands can be as revealing as faces, so they wear gloves or mittens; to avoid being identified by their characteristic movements, they adopt a limp or slouch, or otherwise disguise their walk and stance; they also abandon their usual coats and boots since these, too, can quickly give them away.

We learned these indispensable tips in Spring Grove, Minn., where the julebukk custom not only survives, it thrives.

Source: Kathleen Stokker, "*Julebukk* (The Norwegian Art of Christmas Fooling)," *The Sons of Norway Viking Magazine* (December 1990), pp. 10–13.

DISCUSSION TOPICS:

1. Kathleen Stokker mentions that *julebukking* has been incorporated into the annual Christmas celebration held at Vesterheim, the Norwegian-American Museum in Decorah, Iowa. Thus, a folk custom has become part of a community festival. Can you find examples of similar incorporations of custom into festival among ethnic or immigrant groups in the United States?

2. Three "observers from Decorah's Vesterheim Museum," after studying the tradition, actually went out *julebukking* accompanied by a Spring Grove, Minn., resident. This experiment in participant-

observation fieldwork was highly successful, both in providing further data and by incorporating other community members into their group. Try a similar project with any seasonal custom practiced in your own community.

3. Stokker identifies two phases to *julebukking*, first a reversal of normal behavior, and second the unmasking of the revelers and their incorporation into the household, with refreshments and conversation. What functions seem to be revealed by this or another analysis of Christmas mumming customs? See Stokker's further treatment of this topic in an essay published in *Norwegian-American Essays*, ed. Knut Djupedal et al. (Oslo, Hamar, Stavanger [Norway]: The Norwegian Emigrant Museum, 1993), pp. 28–39.

The observance of Passover by East European Jews in the United States is one of the few imported festivals that has been systematically compared by a folklorist to its original form. The changes are characteristic of America—the traditional "search for leaven," formerly conducted with a candle and a quill, may now be performed with a flashlight and brush; shopping for new clothing replaces the "visit to the tailor"; the ritual cleansing of dishes and utensils is rendered unnecessary by ownership of a special set of them for exclusive holiday use; and the careful handwork in the baking of matzoh has been automated out of existence by the invention of the matzoh machine. New quasi customs have appeared in the United States—the "Third Seder" (Passover meal) held outside the family circle, individual-brand preferences among the various commercially prepared Passover foods, new games played with the traditional old-country food (nuts), and songs sung in English (including the black spiritual "Go Down, Moses") after the Seder.

A further transplanting of holiday celebrations is exhibited in the Americanized Christmas customs that took root in Japan as early as the middle of the nineteenth century and flourished there, especially since the Allied Occupation following World War II. So pervasive is the celebration now that it is even marked on calendars issued by Shinto and Buddhist organizations, and there have been proposals either to make Christmas a new national holiday or to designate December 25 as "International Goodwill Day." Japanese merchants display Christmas decorations; families put up Christmas trees, or printed pictures of them; Christmas carols are played, parties held,

(Above) Laotian immigrant Shoua Her of Oskaloosa, Iowa, displays Hmong needle art at the 1996 Festival of American Folklife in Washington, D.C.
(Below) Steve Kerper of New Vienna, Iowa, proprietor of the Kerper Country Store, carves a duck decoy at the 1996 Festival of American Folklife in Washington, D.C.

and gifts exchanged. Lacking a fireplace chimney on which to attach their Christmas stockings, many Japanese children find presents placed near their pillows in the morning. Some youngsters, however, fasten their stockings on the pipe of the bathroom stove on Christmas Eve.

The term "folk festival" has been applied since the 1930s in the United States to annually sponsored public performances of folklore, generally folksongs and dances. Folklorists began attending them, studying them, and later planning them, or even taking part in some of them. Only on the current folk-festival stage—whether devoted to bluegrass music, storytelling, country music, handicrafts, or another topic—have the folk, the folklore enthusiast, and the folklorist all met face-to-face and begun to try to understand one another in some depth. The oldest consecutive American folk festival is the "National Folk Festival," first held in St. Louis in 1934 with strictly American performers but eventually branching out into all manner of immigrant and "ethnic" acts. Other folk festivals have sprung up (and some have died) in many regions; these events have ranged from glossy extravaganzas with celebrity performers to the more rustic "Arkansas Folk Festival" in Mountain View, Arkansas, with its largely homegrown talent and audience. Another development in the revivalist folk-festival field, and a very promising one, was the appearance of university-sponsored annual events (at the University of Chicago and the University of California at Los Angeles, for instance), where the enthusiastic collegiate folklore buff could rub elbows and share ideas with academic students of folklore and with practitioners of the genuine material itself. The Smithsonian Institution's "Festival of American Folklife," founded in 1967, has also successfully combined education with entertainment by employing folklorists and folklore students to locate talented folk artisans and performers, who are brought to Washington, D.C., for the annual event.

BIBLIOGRAPHIC NOTES

Funk & Wagnalls Standard Dictionary of Folklore, Mythology, and Legend, often a good guide for separate genres of folklore, has no general headings for either customs or festivals. The original index to the *Journal of American Folklore* grouped "Customs, Beliefs, and Superstitions," but the articles cited were mostly about superstitions; the 1988 centennial index to *JAF* had no subject entry for "custom," although nine title entries began with that word. The annual bibliographies once published by the American Folklore Society used the heading "Customs," placing under it "Festivals and Rites of Passage," but also "Social Relationships, Planting, etc." The Swiss folklorist and museum director Robert Wildhaber included a section on customs in his "Bibliographical Introduction to American Folklife," *NYFQ* 21 (1965): 259–302. He also discussed the European concept of "folklife" in his introduction. In an effort to bring some order to the chaotic treatment of custom as a folklore genre, *American Folklore: An Encyclopedia* has both a general entry for the term as well as a number of related entries and cross-references.

William Graham Sumner introduced the term "folkways" in his classic book of that title (Boston, Mass.: Ginn and Co., 1907; Mentor Book paperback, 1960). He outlined the basic process of customs becoming "mores" (another term he coined) and mores becoming laws. Theodore Blegen urged historians' attention to "traditional beliefs, customs, folk art, ideas, and practices" in his *Grass Roots History* (Minneapolis: University of Minnesota Press, 1947). His section on "Pioneer Folkways" (pp. 81–102) demonstrated the approach with data from Norwegian-American immigrant life.

Paul G. Brewster edited "Beliefs and Customs" for *The Frank C. Brown Collection of North Carolina Folklore* (vol. 1: pp. 221–82). However, not only beliefs, but also material folklore are described; most of the customs that appear here are related to superstitions. Wayland D. Hand seems to have used most of the same items plus many more in volumes 6 and 7 of the same collection, "Popular Beliefs and Superstitions," in some cases citing as the only comparative reference the identical item in volume 1. Hand's article "Anglo-American Folk Belief and Custom: The Old World's Legacy to the New," in *JFI* 7 (1970): 136–55, is a good example of thorough annotation of customary lore, using as examples mainly the "dumb cake" or "dumb supper" customs.

Three chapters in Everett Dick's *Sod-House Frontier, 1854–1890* (Lincoln, Neb.: Johnsen Pub. Co., 1954) illustrate the treasury of customs to be found in some social histories. They are chapter 20, "Sports"; chapter 26, "Amusements"; and chapter 35, "Crude Frontier Customs." A few special collections of customs exist: Afton Wynn's "Pioneer Folk Ways," *PTFS* 13 (1937): 190–238; Louise Pound's "Old Nebraska Folk Customs," *NH* 28 (1947): 3–31, reprinted in *Nebraska Folklore*, pp. 184–208; and "Customs," by S. J. Sackett, pp. 182–208 of *Kansas Folklore*, ed. Sackett (Lincoln: University of Nebraska Press, 1961). Norbert F. Riedl and Carol K. Buckles compiled a bibliography and an interesting study of "House Customs and Beliefs in East Tennessee," in *TFSB* 41 (1975): 47–56. In "The Finlinson Family Reunion Tradition," *AFFWord* 4 (Spring 1974): 37–39, Jill Kelly describes a typical Mormon family celebration taking place in Oak City, Utah. And in " 'We Did Everything Together' . . . Farming Customs of the Mountain West," *NWF* 4 (1985): 23–30, William A. Wilson reviews material from the same region.

Allen Walker Read outlined the background of an American school custom in his article "The Spelling Bee: A Linguistic Institution of the American Folk," *PMLA* 56 (1941): 495–512. Iona and Peter Opie, in *The Lore and Language of*

Schoolchildren (New York: Oxford University Press, 1959), give a "Children's Calendar" and describe British children's "Occasional Customs" (pp. 232–305), some of which have parallels among American children. Herbert Halpert discussed the custom of sending "chain letters" in *WF* 15 (1956): 287–89; Alan Dundes added a foreign reference and provided further examples in an article in *NWF* 1 (Winter 1966): 14–19; and Michael J. Preston traces some examples back to the 1930s in the United States and earlier in Europe in an article in *TFSB* 42 (1976): 1–14 (Preston is the only author to analyze the mathematics involved in the chain letters' promises of riches).

An excellent essay on birthday celebrations is Theodore C. Humphrey's "A Family Celebrates a Birthday: Of Life and Cakes," in *"We Gather Together"— Food and Festival in American Life*, ed. Theodore and Linda T. Humphrey (Logan: Utah State University Press, 1988), pp. 19–26.

An essay by Julia Woodbridge Oxreider, "The Slumber Party: Transition into Adolescence," *TFSB* 43 (1977): 128–34, is a rare one taking up a traditional ritual/recreation of young American women on the threshold of maturity. She discusses games, songs, dances, and the pranks played on the first one to fall asleep.

"Adolescent Legend-Tripping" was a tradition identified and a phrase coined by Bill Ellis in a note published in *Psychology Today* (August 1983): 68–69. Ellis wrote further on the topic in an essay on "ostension" (the acting out of legend themes) published in *WF* 48 (1989): 201–20, and in an essay published in *The Satanism Scare*, ed. James T. Richardson, Joel Best, and David G. Bromley (New York: Aldine De Gruyter, 1991), pp. 229–95. See also Patricia M. Meley, "Adolescent Legend Trips as Teenage Cultural Response: A Study of Lore in Context," *MAF* 18 (1990): 1–26.

Courtship and wedding customs in Utah were listed by Thomas E. Cheney in *WF* 19 (1960): 106, and some from the Ohio Valley were discussed by Lawrence S. Thompson in *KFR* 9 (1963): 47–50. Some modern campus courtship rituals were the subject of Michael J. Preston's "The Traditional Ringing at Temple Buell College," *WF* 32 (1973): 271–74. Another aspect of wedding lore appears in Joyce Thompson and Phyllis Bridges, "West Texas Wedding Cars," *WF* 30 (1971): 123–26. One article on ethnic-group customs is Philip V. R. Tilney, "The Immigrant Macedonian Wedding in Ft. Wayne," *IF* 3 (1970): 3–34. E. Bagby Atwood discussed "Shivarees and Charivaris: Variations on a Theme" in *PTFS* 32 (1964): 64–71. Other discussions of the history of the term and its variations appeared in *AS* 8 (1933): 22–26 and *AS* 15 (1940): 109–10. The 1946 Oregon shivaree mentioned in this chapter was described by Rex Gunn in "An Oregon Charivari," *WF* 13 (1954): 206–7. See also Alan Dundes, " 'Jumping the Broom': On the Origin and Meaning of an African American Wedding Custom," *JAF* 109 (1996): 324–29.

On the customary aspects of American funerals and cemeteries, see such works as Lawrence S. Thompson's "Rites of Sepulcher in the Bluegrass," *KFR* 9 (1963): 25–28; J. Frank Lee's "The Informal Organization of White Southern Protestant Funerals: The Role of the Arranger," *TFSB* 33 (1967): 36–40; and Donald B. Ball's "Social Activities Associated with Two Rural Cemeteries in Coffee County, Tennessee," *TFSB* 41 (1975): 93–98. Kentucky family memorial ceremonies have been described in Thelma Lynn Lamkin's "Spring Hill Decoration Day," *MF* 3 (1953): 157–60; and Harry Harrison Kroll's "Licking River Revisited," *SFQ* 26 (1962): 246–51. Similar traditions from other regions are found in Ted-Larry Pebworth's "Graveyard-Working: The Passing of a Custom," *LFM* 2 (August 1961): 44–49; and Robert Cowser, "Community Memorial Day Observances in Northeast Texas," *WF* 31 (1972): 120–21.

The version of the "Washday Receet" or "Grandma's Washday" quoted in this chapter was reprinted from a 1975 newspaper article in *NCFJ* 29 (1981): 42–43. Typical of the many other versions that circulate are those printed on a place mat at the Crane Orchards Cider Mill and Pie Pantry Restaurant in Fennville, Michigan; one posted on a building at Silver Dollar City in Branson, Missouri; another displayed in the historical museum in Arrowtown, New Zealand; and one (titled "Receet for Washin Cloes") published in Louise Henderson's booklet *Luizie Sez: A Book of Receets fer Country Cookin* (Cassville, Missouri: Litho Printers, 1969), p. 62.

The following works treat various occupational customs: Henning Henningsen, *Crossing the Equator* (Copenhagen: Munksgaard, 1961); Wayland D. Hand, "The Folklore, Customs, and Traditions of the Butte Miner," *CFQ* 5 (1946): 1–25; Donald J. Ward, "The 'Carny' in the Winter" (carnival concessions workers), *WF* 21 (1962): 190–92; John Solomon Otto, "Traditional Cattle-Herding Practices in Southern Florida," *JAF* 97 (1984): 291–309; and Maggie Holtzberg-Call, *The Lost World of the Craft Printer* (Urbana: University of Illinois Press, 1992). Customs in a contemporary scientific context are discussed in David Hufford's "Customary Observances in Modern Medicine," *WF* 48 (1989): 129–43.

Articles on traditional group-work customs include William Marion Miller, "A Threshing Ring in Southern Ohio," *HF* 5 (1946): 3–13; Mrs. Arthur Turner, "Turkey Drives: South Mississippi, Greene County," *MFR* 3 (1969): 31–32; David Rhys Roberts, "Ice Harvesting," *NYFQ* 26 (1970): 114–26; and Celia M. Benton, "Corn Shuckings in Sampson County," *NCFJ* 22 (1974): 131–39. Studies of food-gathering occupations from water sources are Diane Tebbetts, "Earl Ott: Fishing on the Arkansas," *MSF* 5 (1977): 101–12; and Paul Valvo, "Clamming in the Great South Bay," *NYF* 1 (1975): 169–82. Two book-length studies are Timothy C. Lloyd and Patrick B. Mullen, *Lake Erie Fishermen: Work, Tradition, and Identity* (Urbana: University of Illinois Press, 1990) and Paula J. Johnson, ed., *Working the Water: The Commercial Fisheries of Maryland's Patuxent River* (Charlottesville: University Press of Virginia, 1988).

Auctioneers' traditions were collected in William Hugh Jansen's "Down Our Way: Who'll Bid Twenty?" *KFR* 2 (1956): 113–21; Anne Marsh and William Aspinall, Jr., "Harold E. Leightley: Portrait of an Auctioneer and His Craft," *KFQ* 16 (1971): 133–50; William R. Ferris, Jr., "Ray Lum: Muletrader," *NCFJ* 21 (1973): 105–19; and Mac E. Barrick, "The Folklore Repertory of a Pennsylvania Auctioneer," *KF* 19 (1974): 27–42. Further examples of Ray Lum's lore, also reported by William Ferris, appeared in *MSF* 6 (1978): 15–26 and 43–50. A survey of Indiana auctioneering, ". . . No Two Sales the Same," was published by Phyllis Harrison in *IF* 12 (1979): 101–19. See also Geoffrey Miller, " 'Are You All Unhappy at a Twenty Dollar Bill?': Text, Tune, and Context at Antique Auctions," *EM* 38 (1984): 187–208; and Amanda Dargan and Steven Zeitlin, "American Talkers: Expressive Styles and Occupational Choice," *JAF* 96 (1983): 3–33. A similar form of commercial tradition was treated by Alex S. Freedman in "Garage Sale Folklore," *NYF* 2 (1976): 167–76.

Aspects of occupational lore still largely unexplored are documented in Don Boles, "Some Gypsy Occupations in America," *JGLS* 37 (1958): 103–10; Sandra Bennett, "Rodeo," *AFFWord* 2 (Sept. 1972): 1–10; and Albert B. Friedman, "The Scatological Rites of Burglars," *WF* 27 (1968): 171–79.

For three systematic and detailed presentations of a highly ritualized and illegal sporting event, see Gerald E. Parsons, Jr., "Cockfighting: A Potential Field of Research," *NYFQ* 25 (1969): 265–88; Steven L. Del Sesto, "Roles, Rules, and Organization: A Descriptive Account of Cockfighting in Rural Louisiana," *SFQ* 39 (1975): 1–14; and Charles R. Gunter, Jr., "Cockfighting in East Tennessee and Western North Carolina," *TFSB* 44 (1978): 160–69. Another fascinating area of sporting tradition is covered in Mary T. Hufford's *Chaseworld: Foxhunting and Storytelling in New Jersey's Pine Barrens* (Philadelphia: University of Pennsylvania Press, 1992).

The American Book of Days by George William Douglas (1938; rev. ed. by Helen Douglas Compton, New York: H. W. Wilson, 1948) is a useful reference source on American holidays, their origins and celebration. George R. Stewart's completely engaging book *American Ways of Life* (Garden City, N.Y.: Dolphin paperback, 1954) includes an excellent chapter on holidays (pp. 222–48). Two important general sources are Hennig Cohen and Tristram Potter Coffin's *The Folklore of American Holidays*, 2nd ed. (Detroit: Gale Research, 1991); and Jack Santino's *All Around the Year: Holidays and Celebrations in American Life* (Urbana: University of Illinois Press, 1994). A recent wartime tradition is analyzed by Jack Santino in "Yellow Ribbons and Seasonal Flags: The Folk Assemblages of War," *JAF* 105 (992): 18–33.

Kelsie B. Harder's note "Just an April Fool," *TFSB* 27 (1961): 5–7, describes the custom of sending April Fool letters. On another holiday see Maurice A. Mook, "Halloween in Central Pennsylvania," *KFQ* 14 (1969): 124–29; Catharine Harris Ainsworth, "Hallowe'en," *NYFQ* 29 (1973): 163–93; Jack Kugelman, "Wishes Come True: Designing the Greenwich Village Halloween Parade," *JAF* 104 (1991): 443–65; and especially Jack Santino, ed., *Halloween and Other Festivals of Death and Life* (Knoxville: University of Tennessee Press, 1994). An excellent work on a single international holiday is Venetia Newall's *An Egg at Easter, a Folklore Study* (Bloomington: Indiana University Press, 1971), where the "Easter tree" is discussed in chapter 13. Perhaps the best general essay on the larger topic is Robert J. Smith's chapter "Festivals and Celebrations," in *Folklore and Folklife: An Introduction*, ed. Richard M. Dorson (Chicago: University of Chicago Press, 1972), pp. 159–72.

The Louisiana Federal Writers Project publication *Gumbo Ya Ya*, ed. Lyle Saxon, Edward Dreyer, and Robert Tallant (Boston: Houghton Mifflin, 1945), has much interesting information on superstitions, customs, and festivals of that state. Two general books on foreign festivals in the United States do not carefully distinguish natural survivals from self-conscious revivals, but they are, nevertheless, informative: Allen H. Eaton's *Immigrant Gifts to American Life* (New York: Russell Sage Foundation, 1932) and Helen R. Coates's *The American Festival Guide* (New York: Exposition Press, 1956). The "Festival Issue" of *WF* (31:4 [1972]) contains studies of four regions. See also Robert H. Lavenda, "Minnesota Queen Pageants: Play, Fun, and Dead Seriousness in a Festive Mode," *JAF* 100 (1988): 168–75.

Articles on individual foreign festivals in the United States appeared with some frequency in the journal of the California Folklore Society; these included Wayland D. Hand's "Schweizer Schwingen: Swiss Wrestling in California," *CFQ* 2 (1943): 77–84; William Hoy's "Native Festivals of the California Chinese," *WF* 7 (1948): 240–50; Charles Speroni's "California Fishermen's Festivals," *WF* 14 (1955): 77–91; and Father John B. Terbovich's "Religious Folklore among the German-Russians in Ellis County, Kansas," *WF* 22 (1963): 79–88. In other journals, see Roslynn Plemer, "The Feast of St. Joseph," *LFM* 2 (Aug. 1968): 85–90; and Laurie Kay Sommers, "Symbol and Style in *Cinco de Mayo*," *JAF* 98 (1985): 476–82. A similar subject treated in book-length form and fully illustrated with photographs is *The Amish Year* by Charles S. Rice and Rollin C. Steinmetz (New Brunswick, N.J.: Rutgers University Press, 1956).

Two original essays on Louisiana Cajun customary life were included in Richard M. Dorson's *Buying the Wind*: Harry Oster's "Country Mardi Gras" (pp. 274–81) and Calvin Claudel's "Folkways of Avoyelles Parish" (pp. 235–45). John Rowe described "Cornish Emigrants in America" and their traditions in *Folk Life* 3 (1965): 25–38. For another group's traditions see Norine Dresser, " 'Is It Fresh?': An Examination of Jewish-American Shopping Habits," *NYFQ* 27 (1971): 153–60.

Penitente ceremonies are treated in George C. Barker's "Some Aspects of Penitential Processions in Spain and the American Southwest," *JAF* 70 (1957): 137–42; Juan Hernandez's "Cactus Whips and Wooden Crosses," *JAF* 76 (1963): 216–24; and Marta Weigle's book *Brothers of Light, Brothers of Blood* (Albuquerque: University of New Mexico Press, 1976). Svatava Pirkova-Jakobson described "Harvest Festivals among Czechs and Slovaks in America" in *JAF* 69 (1956): 266–80.

John E. Baur's *Christmas on the American Frontier, 1800–1900* (Caldwell, Idaho: Caxton Press, 1961) sketches a broad view of the adaptation of European customs in the American wilderness; Elizabeth Bacon Custer, widow of General Custer, described her own Western army-camp Christmases in a manuscript edited by Walter F. Peterson as "Christmas on the Plains" and published in *TAW* 1 (Fall 1964): 52–57. David W. Plath studied "The Japanese Popular Christmas: Coping with Modernity" in *JAF* 76 (1963): 309–17. The November 1971 issue of *NCF* (19: 4) contains several articles on Christmas customs and beliefs in North Carolina. Sue Samuelson's *Christmas: An Annotated Bibliography* (New York: Garland, 1982) is essential for research on this holiday. For a Mexican-American Catholic Christmas festival, see Mary MacGregor-Villarreal's "Celebrating Los Posados in Los Angeles," *WF* 39 (1980): 71–105.

Shooting the anvil, a noisy custom once commonly practiced in American communities to celebrate various holidays, was the subject of a study by Bill Harrison and Charles Wolfe in *TFSB* 43 (1977): 1–13. One blacksmith's anvil was placed atop another with gunpowder between them; ignition provided a satisfyingly ear-splitting bang. The North Carolina "New Year's Shoot" is included in Brewster's chapter in *North Carolina Folklore* (vol. 1, pp. 241–43). H. M. Belden gave a partial text of the Missouri "New Year's Sermon" in *Ballads and Songs Collected by the Missouri Folk-Lore Society*, University of Missouri Studies 15 (Columbia, 1940), p. 514. Ruth H. Cline described "Belsnickles and Shanghais" in *JAF* 71 (1958): 164–65. For information on similar celebrations in various states see Walter L. Robbins's note "Christmas Shooting Rounds in America and Their Background," *JAF* 86 (1973): 48–52. On related traditions see Charles E. Welch, Jr., " 'Oh Dem Golden Slippers': The Philadelphia Mummers Parade," *JAF* 79 (1966): 523–36; Herbert Halpert and G. M. Story, eds., *Christmas Mumming in Newfoundland* (Toronto: University of Toronto Press, 1969); and Marcia Gaudet, "Christmas Bonfires in South Louisiana: Tradition and Innovation," *SF* 47 (1990): 195–206.

John F. Moe, in "Folk Festivals and Community Consciousness: Categories of the Festival Genre," *FF* 10 (1977): 33–40, proposes three large groupings of festivals—participatory (such as haying, marriages, and Thanksgiving dinner), semiparticipatory (such as community fairs and bluegrass festivals), and nonpar-ticipatory (such as the Smithsonian Institution's festivals of American folklife). In an article on what he calls the "protofestival," John A. Gutowski traces the origins of a particular Midwestern community celebration as an example of an emerging festival; see *JFI* 15 (1978): 113–32. Linda T. Humphrey's essay on "Small Group Festive Gatherings" (SGFGs), referred to in this chapter, appeared in *JFI* 16 (1979): 190–201.

At the same time that many folk festivals seem to be fading out, American folklorists were finding them interesting to study. Three such publications are Laurel Doucette's "Folk Festival: The Gatineau Valley Church Picnic," *C&T* 1 (1976): 55–62; Richard Blaustein's "The Old Time Country Radio Reunion: A Different Kind of Folk Festival," *TFSB* 47 (1981): 105–18; and James L. Evans's "Frog Jumping Contests," *MFSJ* 3 (1981): 3–28.

Beatrice S. Weinreich analyzed "The Americanization of Passover" in *Studies in Biblical and Jewish Folklore*, ed. Raphael Patai et al., Indiana University Folklore Series no. 13 (Bloomington, 1960), pp. 329–66. See also Sharon R. Sherman, " 'That's How the Seder Looks': A Fieldwork Account of Videotaping Family Folklore," *JFR* 23 (1986): 53–70.

Sarah Gertrude Knott, a founder and leading force of the National Folk Festival, described her early problems and experiences with it in "The National Folk Festival after Twelve Years," *CFQ* 5 (1946): 83–93. An address by Stith Thompson on "Folklore and Folk Festivals" delivered to the annual conference of the National Folk Festival Association in 1953 was published in *MF* 4 (1954): 5–12.

A local folk-music festival and its folkloristic significance is analyzed in Barre Toelken's "Traditional Fiddling in Idaho," *WF* 24 (1965): 259–62. Gerald Weales wrote a humorous description of the 1952 Georgia Tech Homecoming Game as "an annual semi-religious festival" in his article "Ritual in Georgia," *SFQ* 21

(1957): 104–9. His observations on dress, symbols, decoration, the parade, cheers, and ecstatic responses to the game would apply easily to many other American sporting events.

16

FOLK DANCES AND DRAMAS

Dances and dramas began in ritual and developed into entertainment. They have, in common with superstitions, customs, festivals, and games, significant oral and behavioral elements. Both dance and drama are essentially performances in which participants assume certain active roles, but also utter the speeches and songs, or sometimes directions, that accompany the action. Dance has been associated with drama since its ancient origins, so it may not be stretching Aristotle's definition too far to suggest that the list of six elements he proposed for the drama could fit dance almost as well: action, character, thought, language, spectacle, and music. To some degree, the student of folk dances and dramas will be concerned with all of these elements, as well as with such other aspects as structure, function, dissemination, and variation.

American folk dances and dramas long constituted a decidedly minor field of folklore research. Folk dances of the early settlers in this country persisted in the twentieth century largely in the form of revivals, while folk dramas, replaced by commercial entertainments, are represented only in a few amateur forms or as survivals. Despite recent interest in folk dance and drama, including those of immigrant and ethnic groups, there are questions that remain unanswered, reference works that should be compiled, theories awaiting better analysis, and further collecting that might be done, even in the Anglo-American field.

FOLK DANCES

"The dance," wrote Curt Sachs, historian of the subject, "is the mother of the arts." In its basic form of a rhythmic, stylized pattern of individual or group movement performed with or without music in response to a religious or creative urge, dance has existed in every known culture, including the most primitive, and it occurs, some would claim, even among animals. From the movements of dancing, Sachs suggested, were derived the other means of artistic expression, all of which eventually drifted away from close involvement with worship and the cycle of life to their current connections largely with self-expression and entertainment. **Folk dances** are those dances that are transmitted in a traditional manner, whatever their origin, and that have developed traditional variants, whatever their other developments. Perhaps more than in any other field of folklore, such distinctions are extremely difficult to apply. Probably it is best, as Curt Sachs suggested, for ethnological purposes simply to treat all dances equally.

Gertrude P. Kurath, a leading American student of dance, distinguished primitive dance from folk dance in terms of the relationship of dancing to the rest of a given culture: "Natural cultures," she wrote, "dance from the cradle to the grave; mechanized society, for sociability and diversion." Certainly this holds true in the United States, for although we still hold dances as a matter of custom at graduations, holidays, and weddings, all of our dancing, whether folk or not, is performed for "sociability and diversion" and not as ritual. Still, the potential student of folk dance has a good deal to learn from the authority on primitive dance.

Kurath answered very specifically the questions "What does a field-worker record during the study of native dances?" and "What can a nonspecialist do in the presence of unexpected festivities?" The three fundamental matters to observe, she said, are the *ground plan* (location, participants, arrangements, geometry, progression), the *body movements* (steps, posture, arms), and the *structure* (repetition, combination). Observations should be made in the above order, and the observer finally should participate in the dance he or she is describing, especially for the fullest understanding of its structure.

Complex systems of precise dance notation have been created, perhaps the most widely accepted and elaborate being the "Labanotation" invented by Rudolf von Laban in 1920. For the nonspecialist collector, the minimal technique required is simply the employment of video recorder, camera, or sketch pad whenever possible, and the consistent use of a standardized vocabulary for descriptions. As Kurath showed, such a term as "step" is misleading and vague, unless the collector distinguishes such variations as the shuffle, run, trot, slide, gallop, skip, leap, jump, and hop. The last three terms can serve to illustrate just how precise dance descriptions should be, for a *leap* is springing from one foot to the other, a *jump* is springing up with both feet simultaneously and landing on both feet, and a *hop* is springing up on one foot and landing on the same foot again.

Given an interest in collecting folk dances and having established a list of questions and a vocabulary for field use, what is there for the modern student of American folk dance to observe? Regrettably, there is little in a purely traditional context. The two primary forms of Americanized folk dances—square dances and play-parties—had died out in most localities by the 1930s. A few dance songs were later popularized by professional folksingers, and square dancing and other traditional forms have enjoyed a vigorous revival as an organized recreation, but neither of these developments is part of a pure folk process. However, American folk-dance scholars should investigate the nature of the revival movement itself, and also devote themselves to discovering, analyzing, and classifying historic accounts of folk dancing. Native Americans and immigrant groups still provide opportunities for fieldwork in dance ethnography, as do regional styles of social dancing. Even the lore of professional dance companies, including customs and superstitions of rehearsals and performances, might be studied.

Both square dances and play-parties developed from British traditions, the former from "country dances," and the latter seemingly from children's games. The terminology of early forms, however, is somewhat confused. English **country dances** were usually either *rounds* (dancers standing in a circle) or *longways* (dancers in

The Bell Telephone Pioneers square-dance group performing in Louisville, Kentucky, 1939.

two lines facing each other). But the French, who had similar folk dances, associated the English word "country" with their term *contre* ("against") to produce the name *contredanse* for the "longways" type. The term then became Anglicized as "contradance." The country dances throughout Europe probably all represent, at least in part, inheritances via *gesunkenes Kulturgut* of such popular nineteenth-century social dances as the spirited *cotillion*, in which partners were exchanged, and the *quadrille*, a dance for four couples. Neither rounds nor longways persisted in American folk dancing proper, although both formations are found in children's games, and the still-popular "Virginia Reel" is a longways.

FOCUS: A JEWISH-AMERICAN HOEDOWN

The headline over the small notice in the newspaper caught my eye. "Purim Begins Saturday," it read. As an anthropologist interested in ethnic folklore, I read on. After a brief description of the traditional origins of the holiday, the article continued:

an old-fashioned "Purim hoe-down" will begin at 8:15 Saturday. . . . Square dancing lessons will be led by a caller. Western dress is suggested. . . . A reading of the Megillah will follow the celebration.

Even though I know little of Jewish holiday customs, I suspect that this "traditional" means of celebration may not be exactly kosher. Moreover, I believe it is not an isolated phenomenon. Today, traditions such as square dancing and Western dress, along with concomitant "real" American values, seem to be increasingly popular within an increasingly wider audience. Why? Is the entire nation going "country"? Is the entire nation "goin' to the dawgs"?

Judging by contemporary trends in American culture, such seems to be the case.

Source: John M. Coggeshall, "Goin' to the Dawgs?: The Rustication of American Culture," *WF* 44 (1985): 122. The quoted notice was from *Southern Illinoisan*, March 16, 1984.

DISCUSSION TOPICS:

1. How is the holiday of Purim traditionally celebrated among Jews? What is the "Megillah"?

2. What is the likely etymology and meaning of "hoedown"? Is it an American term? What seems to be the function of this announced hoedown at the Purim celebration?

3. Can you find examples in your own community of the American "rustication" of Old World traditional dances or other customs?

4. Coggeshall continues by commenting that Americans "seem to be reverting to often blatantly artificial 'country' roots." He suggests that "the rustication of American culture may be the barometer of another forthcoming wave of nationalism." Is his reading of the situation convincing, and was his concern for the results of this rustication borne out by later events?

Some traditional American solo dancing—like clogging and tap dancing—has been identified, although the major folk types of American dance are the social dances for couples and larger groups.

And despite the emphasis in research among folklorists on the older folk-dance forms, attention should also be encouraged toward the various contemporary social dance forms and fads such as the "bunny hop," the "chicken dance," the "hokey pokey," disco, break dancing, "raves," western swing, line dances, the Macarena, and many others.

The **square dance** is an authentic American folk development of the Old World four-couple dance. The terms "New England Quadrille," "Kentucky Running Set," and "Cowboy Square Dance" indicate the principal centers of development—the Northeast, the Midwest and Southern mountains, and the Far West. The three most distinctive features of the square dance are the shuffling-gliding-running step, the handclapping done by both dancers and bystanders, and the chanted or sung "calls" giving directions for the steps. New England square dancing was rather restrained and formal, but the shuffling step or *sashay* (from French *chassé*, "dance") was already present. In the Midwest, handclapping was added, calls were formalized as part of the dance, and new figures such as "Birdy in the Cage" and "Grand Right and Left" became popular. The West introduced hybrid steps from other social dances for "sashaying," as well as the device of occasionally having boys lift their partners from the ground during the "swing." Eventually all of these movements backtracked and merged to a degree that renders it impossible to sort out the origins of such colorfully named figures as "Box the Gnat," "Georgia Rang Tang," "Dip for the Oyster," "Ocean Wave," "Shoot the Owl," "Grapevine Twist," and "Wring the Dishrag."

FOCUS: MORMON FIDDLERS AT A MEXICAN-AMERICAN *BAILE*

Sometime in 1902, Concho leaders sent young Teodoro Lopez on horseback the thirty-five miles to Snowflake for the purpose of engaging the Youngblood and Kartchner dance orchestra for a three-day fiesta celebration. This was something new and we wondered about adjusting our music to their type and tempo of dances. [Concho and Snowflake are towns in northern Arizona, the former settled by Mexican-Americans, the latter by Utah Mormons. Snowflake's name combines the surnames of Apostle Erastus Snow and settler William J. Flake.

The "orchestra" consisted of fiddlers Claude T. Youngblood and Kenner C. Kartchner, the latter the author of this memoir. In 1902 Kartchner was sixteen years old and Youngblood was twenty-three. On this occasion they also engaged the blind guitarist Antolino Tafoya of Saint Johns, Arizona.]

    . . . *Carrying a violin on horseback is tiresome, but we were somewhat used to it and didn't mind too much. Topping the hill west of town we rode into Concho that afternoon amid cheers from the populace. People shouted* "Los Musicos Mormitos" *(The Mormon Musicians) in obvious anticipation of events to come. . . .*

    We musicians sat on an improvised platform at the back of the hall, conspicuous for all to see. Wide-eyed youngsters stared at Claude and me as if we might have come from Mars. Older people were curious. Floor manager Federico Sandoval called for "un vals," *which we played in duet form faster than ordinary, as coached by Antolino in preliminary rehearsal. The two-violin combination was a hit here no less than elsewhere, especially with Antolino's expert accompaniment. Next was a Spanish polka also in faster tempo. Dancers and wallflowers alike seemed delighted and encored vigorously. Then came a cotillion, a term I never understood, pronounced* "koteelio." *This was a Spanish quadrille similar to a square dance but without a caller. Our stepped-up hoedowns proved ideal for time, and we marveled at the grace and perfect rhythm with which the dance was executed. Beginners were few and rarely was there an error on the part of individual dancers. These three numbers are mentioned in particular, since they occupied most of the agenda. Less frequent were dances of the Anglos—schottishe, two-step, even Comin' Through the Rye (rye waltz). Their manner of closing was another new feature to us. At about 11 p.m. the different family heads rounded up their broods, lit the lanterns, and simply left for home. There was no announcement or request for the* "Home Waltz," *to which we were accustomed. They just quietly cleared the hall and the* baile *was over until the following evening.*

Source: Kenner Casteel Kartchner, *Frontier Fiddler: The Life of a Northern Arizona Pioneer*, ed. Larry V. Shumway (Tucson: University of Arizona Press, 1990), selected from pp. 84–86.

DISCUSSION TOPICS:

    1. Kartchner mentions several dance forms played for the *baile*. How many can you perform, describe, or at least recognize? Perhaps there are older people in your community who can help you with this. (Shumway's appendix C, pp. 262–64, describes the dance forms of the period and region.)

2. Is there other evidence in published sources of fiddle duets serving as the accompaniment for frontier dancing?

3. In what ways did these Anglo fiddlers have to adapt their playing for the Mexican-Americans, and what differences did they note in the way the dance was carried on?

PLAY-PARTIES

In communities where religious influences prohibited all forms of dancing, as well as the "sinful" fiddle music that accompanied them, the play-party became popular as a substitute, at least according to one traditional explanation. **Play-parties** were usually organized as rounds rather than squares and were performed to songs sung by the participants themselves rather than to instrumental music and a caller. In most regions, face-to-face waist swinging was forbidden, and boys held their partners by the hand instead. By such means the ban against dancing was circumvented. The terms employed for the two kinds of activities were kept carefully separated. Play-parties were "plays," "games," or even "bounce-arounds," and they were always "played," never "danced." But square-dancing parties were "hoedowns," "barn dances," "house dances," "kitchen dances," "shindigs," or even "hog wrassles." It should be emphasized that both of these kinds of activities were part of the social life of adults or adolescents of courting age, but not until recently were they held exclusively for children.

As ballroom couple-dancing became more acceptable and popular among Americans, square dances nearly died out, and their organized revival, part of the general rise in folklore interest beginning in the late 1930s, was in full swing by the time scholars had begun to notice the form. Play-parties lasted longer in folk tradition but were not revived on a large scale. Also, the play-party song leaves more of a text to be remembered and collected than does the square-dance call. As a result, many more play-party songs and descriptions are available in reliable folklore sources than there are detailed accounts of square dances. The most pressing need in square-dance studies is to uncover more published and unpublished early accounts of dances so that a better idea of historical development may be gained. But in play-party studies the time is ripe for a basic reference

A play-party in progress in McIntosh County, Oklahoma, 1940.

work to be compiled, along the lines of Child's great ballad anthology, in order to organize and facilitate comparisons of the numerous play-party texts already in print. Both endeavors would contribute to the verification or replacement of the unproven play-party origin theory mentioned earlier.

Play-party movements and songs may seem simple and rather repetitious, but they have been very popular in folk tradition and have evolved into both children's games and fiddle tunes of lasting popularity. The texts and formations themselves are not without interest. A careful classification of play-parties would have to take into account that a few of them are archway formations, longways, and even squares, as well as round games. Although most play-parties require only skipping around and singing, some also involve dialogue and dramatic action, choosing, kissing, and progressive figures. Sometimes dance directions are embedded literally in the song, as in this one, called "Miller Boy":

> Happy is the miller boy, that lives by the mill;
> He takes his toll with a free good will.
> One hand in the hopper and the other in the sack,
> *The ladies step forward and the gents step back.*

Note that the first three lines of the verse contain a traditional criticism of unscrupulous millers who extract a double toll from customers: "One hand in the hopper and the other in the sack." And "Miller Boy" also stands up well as folk poetry; after a close study of this play-party—text, tune, and dance—Keith Cunningham concluded that "the poetics fit the action of the game."

In other play-parties, such as "Go in and out the Window" and "The Needle's Eye," the dance movement is metaphorically suggested. Some songs sketch a character type—"Captain Jinks," "Old Dan Tucker," or "Cincinnati Girls"—while others mirror frontier life—"Shoot the Buffalo," "Wait for the Wagon," or "Weevily Wheat." A number of puzzling but strangely effective lines and verses in old play-party songs have yet to be explained. These include:

> Water, water, wine-flower
> Growing up so high.
> We are all young ladies,
> And we are sure to die.
> > (An American play-party derived from the
> > British children's game "Wallflowers.")

> *

> Coffee grows in the white oak tree,
> The rivers run with brandy.
> My little gal is a blue-eyed gal,
> As sweet as any candy.
> > (The first line is the common title.)

> *

> The higher up the cherry tree,
> The finer grow the cherries;

> The more you hug and kiss the girls,
> The sooner will they marry.
>   (From "Weevily Wheat.")

For pure, straightforward defiance of logic, however, nothing can beat the popular line from "Skip to My Lou" that goes "Little red wagon painted blue."

Sometimes a play-party or other dance song will tell a story and thereby suggest an incipient ballad, or a dramatic game of children. In the "Hog Drivers" play-party the players take the roles of various characters. First, the hog drivers march in and sing to a tavern keeper:

> Hog drivers, hog drivers, hog drivers are we,
> A-courting your daughter so fair and so free.
> Can we get lodging here, oh here?
> Can we get lodging here?

To which he responds:

> I have a fair daughter who sits by my side,
> But no hog driver can get her for a bride.
> You can't get lodging here, oh here;
> You can't get lodging here.

The hog drivers then angrily sing:

> Fair is your daughter, but ugly yourself;
> We'll travel on farther and seek better wealth.
> We don't want lodging here, oh here;
> We don't want lodging here.

The conclusion of the play is that the tavern keeper's daughter whispers her choice of husband to her father, who then stops the hog drivers' march and allows the lucky young man to stay on. While this play-party is certainly related to other dramatic courtship games such as "Three Knights from Spain," it also reflects social life of eastern Tennessee and western North Carolina during the heyday of hog raising and driving in the late nineteenth century.

Another good example of a dramatic dance song is the following text collected in Edwardsville, Illinois, from an elderly woman. She sang it in a spirited manner to the tune often used for the dance song "Great Big 'Taters in Sandy Land," also known as "Sally Ann."

> "Hey, old man, where you been at?"
> "Down the mountainside shootin' craps."
>
> "I told you once, I told you twice,
> You can't make a livin' throwin' dice.
>
> "Get out of my house and go to town,
> Make that wooden leg jar the ground.
>
> "Sift your meal and save the bran,
> You can't make a livin' on rocky land."

THE DRAMATIC ELEMENT IN FOLKLORE

The **dramatic element in folklore** has been demonstrated several times in previous chapters. The Wellerism, for example, is a dramatic vignette containing both speech and action. Riddles involve two roles—the questioner's and the respondent's. In asking non-oral riddles, the poser adds a dramatic gesture to his question. Such riddle-jokes as the "knock-knocks" have separate speaking roles for each participant. The skillful narrator of folktales must impersonate many characters, and there are distinct dramatic techniques for narrating different kinds of tales—the deadpan of the tall-tale artist, the broken English of the dialect-joke raconteur, the imitative sounds of the animal-tale teller, and so forth. One American fiddle tune, "The Arkansaw Traveler," has a dramatic skit associated with it. In this sketch, not to be confused with the ballad "An Arkansaw Traveler," or "The State of Arkansas" (Laws H 1), there is a dialogue between a man who gets lost traveling through the Arkansas countryside and a hillbilly fiddler that includes exchanges such as these:

Traveler: Where does this road go to?
Fiddler: I been livin' here twenty years, and it ain't gone nowhere yet.

Traveler: You're pretty dumb, aren't you?
Fiddler: I ain't lost!

Most traditional ballads are dramatic, and those based on incremental repetition are usually related entirely in dialogue. A remarkable fluidity of dramatic form is illustrated in the American versions of "The Maid Freed from the Gallows" (or "Hangman"). Here, a condemned girl is standing on the scaffold waiting to be hanged and repeatedly asking her relatives, and finally her sweetheart, if they have come to set her free or merely "to see me hanged on the gallow's tree." Tristram P. Coffin has observed:

> The story itself has taken a number of forms in America. It is, particularly with Negroes, popular as a drama and is also found as a children's game. It exists as a prose tale in the United States and West Indies and upon occasion has been developed as a cante fable.

Folk games, too, are often dramatic, as discussed in chapter 18. One game, "Mother, Mother, the Milk's Boiling Over," is a fairly complex playlet with ten distinct roles—mother, hired girl (or nurse), a thief (or witch), and seven children who are named for the days of the week. Each time the mother goes out, the thief distracts the hired girl and steals a child; the mother is summoned repeatedly by the cry "The milk's boiling over!" and she contrives, when the last child is gone, to win them all back, one by one, from the thief. In common with most older dramatic games, this one goes back to an English prototype. "Charades" is a popular parlor game that is entirely dramatic, while "Poppy Show" is an old amusement of little girls that consisted of arranging poppy petals between small sheets of glass and then charging one pin for a look. The shower chanted:

> Pinny, pinny, poppy-show,
> Give me a pin and I'll let you know.

FOLK DRAMA

Although the dramatic element in folklore is common, full-scale folk drama is less well known in the United States. **Folk drama** includes plays that are traditionally transmitted, usually for regular performance at such occasions as initiations, seasonal celebrations, festivals, and religious holidays. Traditional transmission, as with some folk rhymes, may in this case include handwritten manuscripts. To qualify as true drama, these performances must involve some imitation of actions (mimesis or mimicry), the assignment of roles among different players, and, of course, transmission in a folk group. What makes such pieces folkloric—whether preserved orally or in writing—is that they vary from region to region and generation to generation, that they originate in an unself-conscious folk milieu rather than from a sophisticated artistic background, and that they remain part of folk-group tradition in some variation.

One living tradition of folk drama in the United States is part of the religious pageantry of the Spanish Southwest, especially at Christmastime, but also at Easter. The Christmas play of the shepherds (*Los Pastores*) exists in the Southwest in many versions, and it has been collected and studied by three generations of American folklorists.

Performance of the *Los Pastores* folk drama in Santa Fe, New Mexico, about 1915.

The traditional English Christmas drama, *The Mummers' Play*, with its masked band of begging participants, was known in the New World in the eighteenth century. (It is further related to the New Year's "shoots" and "belsnickles" described in the previous chapter.) The drama itself, although still found in Canada, never became firmly established in the U.S. as a folk custom; today's elaborate New Year's parade in Philadelphia is the only organized outgrowth of English mumming in the United States. The Philadelphia parade, which stems from traditional backgrounds, was granted official civic support in 1900. Only two instances of genuine mummers' *plays* have been recorded from American informants since then. The first was in 1909, when a text was collected in St. Louis from an immigrant from Worcestershire, England, who had taken part in it as a boy thirty-five years earlier.

The play had the familiar stock characters of the English tradition—Father Christmas, St. George, the Turkish Knight, the Italian Doctor, and others. The plot unfolded in the manner of a pageant, each grotesquely costumed character coming forth to announce himself before engaging in the simple ritualistic action, the sequence of which is suggested by the conventional identification of the parts as presentation, combat, lament, cure, and quête (the collection of a reward for the actors). In 1930 a group of Kentucky mountaineers performed a mummers' play for folklorist Marie Campbell, to show her how these plays had formerly been acted. The announcer began with this revealing notice:

We air now aiming to give a dumb show for to pleasure the little teacher for not going off to level country to keep Christmas with her kin. Hit ain't noways perfect the way we act this here dumb show, but hit ain't been acted out amongst our settlement for upward of twenty or thirty year, maybe more. I reckon folks all knows hit air bad luck to talk with the dumb show folks or guess who they air.

Few native American folk plays of any significance have developed. The use of the term for written dramas based on folk themes is misleading, but, beginning in the 1920s, a so-designated school of folk drama centered around the Carolina Playmakers. Outstanding among this group's work were the plays of Paul Green, set in a regional framework, such as *In Abraham's Bosom* (1912) and *The House of Connelly* (1931). These plays, however, are literature, not folklore. Another group of outdoor dramas or pageants are sometimes billed as "folk" productions; these include *Tecumseh!* in Ohio, *The Stephen Foster Story* in Kentucky, *Vicksburg* in Mississippi, and a pageant about Joseph Smith in Palmyra, New York. Closer to the folk level are many nonliterary amateur church plays, Passion plays, parades, and small-town festivals.

A case might be made for the blackface minstrel show, the vaudeville show, or the entertainments of some medicine shows, carnivals, and riverboats as American folk drama. But a better candidate is a now-obscure traveling tent comedy that survived until recently in some parts of the Midwest—the "Toby shows." Named for their stereotyped lead character, a red-haired, freckle-faced country bumpkin named Toby, these shows appealed to a rural carnival audience with a play based on wholesome, homespun, slapstick humor. The Toby character had emerged by 1911, and Toby shows were common throughout the Mississippi Valley and the Southwest during the 1930s. Only a few, however, were revived after World War II. The texts for Toby shows were usually based on nineteenth-century popular drama, but extemporaneous dialogue and stage business were common. At least one Toby show was reported still traveling in 1964, providing folklorists with a rare example of native folk drama in action.

Popular juvenile skits, some of which seem to derive from vaudeville or other stage comedy, are other shreds of folk drama to be found in the United States. Many of these playlets are popular at children's summer camps, Boy Scout and Girl Scout meetings, Sunday-school picnics, and the like, and similar original skits are sometimes composed for lodges, office parties, and family reunions. The best known of the traditional skits is probably "You Must Pay the Rent," a farcical melodrama involving the classic figures of villain, his victim (a beautiful young girl), and the hero. Often this skit is performed as a monologue, with the actor using a ribbon bow alternately as the girl's hair ribbon, the hero's bow tie, and the villain's drooping mustache.

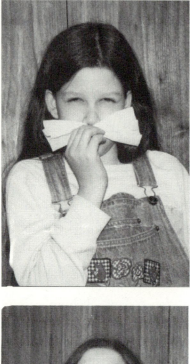

Three stages of the melodramatic skit "You Must Pay the Rent": *(clockwise from top left)* first the villain, next the heroine, and third the hero, who declares, "I will pay the rent." "Curses! Foiled Again!" responds the villain.

FOCUS: THREE CAMP SKITS

Pebbles in the Pond

A person with a pretend microphone goes up to the front of the room or stage. Another person walks by. The reporter asks him the question, "What's your favorite thing to do here at Little Eden Camp?"

The passerby answers, "Throwing pebbles in the pond."

As five or six people walk by the reporter, the reporter asks them their names and the question, "What is your favorite thing to do at Little Eden Camp?"

All of them answer, "Throwing pebbles in the pond."

Finally, a completely drenched girl walks by. The reporter asks, "What's your name?"

She replies, "Pebbles."

Collected by Rita Rychener; contributed by Kelly Schmucker, camper, Little Eden Camp, c. 1983.

*

Water in Your Ear

All the guys line up straight across the stage. On one end, someone pretends to brush his teeth.

After the person is done, he takes a drink of water from a glass that was there before on stage.

Instead of spitting out the water, he pretends to squirt it into the ear of the person next to him.

That person makes his cheeks fill out as if the water was going into his mouth.

This continues all the way down the line, until the last person spits the water out into a glass and then drinks it.

(Only the first and last person really have any water in their mouths.)

Collected by David Tijerina; contributed by Chad Sears, who learned it from his mother, Goshen, Indiana, c. 1989. In a variation, the campers chew up an Oreo cookie and pass it down.

*

No Skit

The first person goes on stage. She just stands there and cries and cries.

Another person comes out and says, "What's the matter with you?"

So the first person whispers in the second person's ear, and then the two of them just stand there and bawl their eyes out, just sobbing.

The third person walks out and pretty soon there is a whole row of girls, standing up there and sobbing.

The last person comes out and says, "What's the matter? What's everybody crying about?"

And they all say together, "We don't have any skit for skit night!"

(This skit is usually performed by girls.)

Collected by Paula Brunk Kuhns; contributed by Beth Landis Weaver, camper, Camp Menno Haven, 1970.

Source: Telissa J. Yoder-Sickler, *J. C. Penny & Other Camp Skits* (Goshen, Ind.: Pinch-penny Press, 1994). These skits were collected by Goshen College students, and most were performed at summer camps sponsored by the Mennonite Church.

DISCUSSION TOPICS:

1. What are the dramatic elements in the texts or performances of these simple skits?

2. The first skit above is categorized by the editor as "Pun," the second as "Gross-Out," and the third as "Surprise." Other skits in the collection are categorized as "Catch," "Moron," or "Mime," with two items left over as "Other." How well do these classifications apply to other camp skits that you know?

3. Note that two of these skits involve water; why should this be a favorite stage prop of camp skits? What other props, costumes, actions, or themes are popular and why?

Another favorite skit, "Baby Can Spell," is based on the everyday humor of a small child understanding the words that adults spell out in conversations to keep secrets from the infant—"c-a-n-d-y," "b-a-b-y," and "s-e-x," for instance. A skit called "The Nut Buying Cider" embodies an old folk jest about a fool who tries to carry a beverage home in his hat. When the hat has been poured full, he flops it over to fill the other side. "The Balky Flivver" skit makes use of six children crouched down to represent an automobile's wheels, motor, and spare tire; while in "The Murder of the Light-house Keeper" a circular staircase is suggested simply by having all the actors run around the central figure several times—one way for up, the other for down. One of these skits, "The King of Beasts," resembles a traditional frontier prank. In the skit a group of brawny boys pulls a long rope across the stage to which is supposed to be attached the "king." Instead, a small child riding a kiddy-car finally emerges tied to the end of the rope. In the old prank called "The

Badger Fight," a greenhorn on the frontier would be given the honor of pulling the fierce badger out of his box to do battle with a dog. When the "greeny" pulled on the leash, a chamber pot slid into view.

Folklorist Jay Mechling has made a good case for Boy Scout campfire programs as folk drama. These have a compelling combination of darkness at the edges and flickering light within the circle, of skits and songs (some of them sexually suggestive), and of such behavior as urinating on the fire at the end of the session. Mechling sees in such performances "a ritual dramatization of male solidarity and male world view." The next question, obviously, is "What kind of campfire programs do the Girl Scouts have at their camps?"

BIBLIOGRAPHIC NOTES

Curt Sachs's *World History of the Dance* (New York: Norton, 1937; Norton Library paperback, 1963) is a basic study with emphasis on the development of movements, themes, and forms from ancient to modern types of dance. The essay "Dance: Folk and Primitive" by Gertrude P. Kurath is a comprehensive survey and a scholarly article in itself, although it appeared as an entry in *Funk & Wagnalls Standard Dictionary of Folklore, Mythology, and Legend*, volume 1 (1949), pp. 276–96. The sketch of the development of square dances in this chapter is based largely on this article.

Kurath published "A Choreographic Questionnaire" in *MF* 2 (1952): 53–55, and her note "A Basic Vocabulary for Dance Descriptions" was in *AA* 56 (1954): 1, 102–3. She dealt with another field technique in "Photography for Dance Recording," *FFMA* 5 (Winter 1963): 1, 4. Labanotation as a folkloristic tool was discussed by Juana de Laban in "Movement Notation: Its Significance to the Folklorist," *JAF* 67 (1954): 291–95, and by Nadia Chilkovsky in "Dance Notation for Field Work," *FFMA* 2 (Fall 1959): 2–3. A useful reference is Andrea Greenberg's "The Notation of Folk Dance: A Survey," *FF* 5 (1972): 1–10.

Kurath began a dance department in Ethnomusicology in 1956 (Newsletter No. 7); it is a valuable source for bibliographic references. Her article "Panorama of Dance Ethnology," in *CA* 1 (1960): 233–54, was based on eighteen months of correspondence with scholars the world over; a bibliography is appended, along with a list of dance studies then in progress and of dance films. An analytical article by Kurath demonstrates the possibilities of dance ethnology: "Dance Relatives of Mid-Europe and Middle America: A Venture in Comparative Choreology," *JAF* 69 (1956): 286–98.

Other professional students of folk dance were once rare in the United States; the 1965 "Works in Progress" report published by the American Folklore Society listed only two besides Gertrude Kurath engaged in dance research, and both were writing historical studies. Such a work, with implications for folklore studies, is Marshall and Jean Stearns's *Jazz Dance: The Story of American Vernacular Dance* (New York: Macmillan, 1972). The situation in folk drama was no better. Five scholars were listed, but three were concerned with the use of folklore in literary drama, one was restricted to Spanish-American plays, and only one was studying general folk drama. In later years, both folk dance and drama have attracted many folklorists' attention. Three illustrated articles on African-American "stepping" appeared in *NCFJ* 43 (1996): 82–119; the authors are Amy Davis, Alicia J. Rouverol, and Lisa J. Yarger.

The American folk-dance revival movement can be traced back to the English Folk Dance Society, founded by Cecil Sharp in 1911, which merged with the Folk Song Society (founded in 1898) in 1930. An American branch was organized in 1915 and later took the name the Country Dance Society of America. Ralph Vaughn Williams outlined the history of the English societies in an article in *EM* 2 (1958): 108–12; see also the similar article by S. R. S. Pratt in *JFI* 2 (1965): 294–99. Anyone interested in these movements should study the back numbers not only of the *Journal of the English Folk Dance and Song Society* and *English Dance and Song*, but also the *Folk Dancer and the Folklorist*, and the American periodicals *Folk Dance Guide* and *American Squares*. *Dance Magazine* also occasionally publishes articles on folk dancing.

Books associated with the revival of square dancing are too numerous to list in detail. A typical early one was Grace L. Ryan's *Dances of Our Pioneers* (New York: A. S. Barnes, 1939). Lloyd Shaw wrote two influential works: *Cowboy Dances: A Collection of Western Square Dances* (rev. ed., Caldwell, Idaho: Caxton Press, 1952) and *The Round Dance Book: A Century of Waltzing* (Caldwell, Idaho: Caxton Press, 1950). A book that features a brief opening note by folklorist Louise Pound is Cornelia F. Putney and Jesse B. Flood's *Square Dance, U.S.A.* (Dubuque, Iowa: W. C. Brown Co., 1955). Most revivalist collections do not state their sources, but David S. McIntosh's *Singing Games and Dances* (New York: National Board of Young Men's Christian Associations, 1957) does—his own fieldwork in southern Illinois. An account of folk-dance revival and dance festivals in California is Virginia C. Anderson's "It All Began Anew: The Revival of Folk Dancing," *WF* 7 (1948): 162–64. Another regional survey is Betty Casey's *Dances Across Texas* (Austin: University of Texas Press, 1985).

There are few scholarly studies of square dances in American folklore journals, but an aid for such studies was published in J. Olcutt Sanders's article "Finding List of Southeastern Square Dance Figures," *SFQ* 6 (1942): 263–75. Sanders began by commenting on the meager list of reliable sources available for information on old-time square dancing. A type of needed historical work is represented by John Q. Wolf's "A Country Dance in the Ozarks in 1874," *SFQ* 29 (1965): 319–21; and Robert D. Bethke's "Old-Time Fiddling and Social Dance in Central St. Lawrence County," *NYFQ* 30 (1974): 164–84. Good studies of square dances in context are Thomas A. Burns and Doris Mack's "Social Symbolism in a Rural Square Dance Event," *SFQ* 42 (1978): 295–327; and Burt Feintuch's "Dancing to the Music:

Domestic Square Dances and Community in Southcentral Kentucky (1800–1940)," *JFI* 18 (1981): 49–68. An important work on Canadian folk dance is Colin Quigley's *Close to the Floor: Folk Dance in Newfoundland* (St. John's: Memorial University of Newfoundland, 1985).

The danger of an overenthusiastic folklore revival movement not having a solid background of scholarly knowledge was illustrated in an exchange published in *Western Folklore* in 1956 and 1957. A "Cowpuncher's Square Dance Call" was printed in one issue (15: 125–26) as a previously unpublished example of the "real thing" and as a contrast to the "cheap imitations" of today. But folklorist Sam Hinton pointed out later (16: 129–31) that not only had the same stanzas been published several times earlier, but they were not a dance call at all, but a poem by a known author describing a dance, and the verses could not possibly function as a square-dance call.

The pioneering book on play-parties was Leah Jackson Wolford's *The Play-Party in Indiana* (Indianapolis, 1917). It was revised by W. Edson Richmond and William Tillson and republished in 1959 as volume 20 of the *Indiana Historical Society Publications*, pp. 103–326. The discussion in this chapter of the classification of play-parties is partly drawn from Wolford's introduction in the revised edition of her book. Wolford drew all of her examples from Ripley County, Indiana. B. A. Botkin collected Oklahoma play-parties for his study *The American Play-Party Song* (Lincoln: University of Nebraska, 1937; reissued, New York, 1963). A third collection is drawn entirely from another state—S. J. Sackett's *Play-Party Games from Kansas*, in *Heritage of Kansas* 5 (Emporia, Sept. 1961). The Sackett work should be supplemented by the chapter "Dances and Games" in the same author's *Kansas Folklore* (Lincoln: University of Nebraska Press, 1961), pp. 209–25, as well as by Alan Dundes's review in *JAF* 76 (1963): 251–52, which adds several Kansas references.

Numerous play-parties from other regions have been published in *JAF*, including texts from western Maryland—54 (1941): 162–66; eastern Illinois—32 (1919): 486–96; the Midwest generally—25 (1912): 268–73 and 28 (1915): 262–89; and Idaho—44 (1931): 1–26. Richard Chase included some square dances and play-parties in his paperback anthology *American Folk Tales and Songs* (New York: New American Library of World Literature, 1956; Dover Publications repr., 1971). The basic tool for bringing together many of the available texts is Altha Lea McLendon's "A Finding List of Play-Party Games," *SFQ* 8 (1944): 201–34.

A good analytic review of publications on play-parties was published by Keith Cunningham in *AFFWord* 2 (April 1972): 12–23. An excellent study of the historical background of a play-party is John Q. Anderson's " 'Miller Boy,' One of the First and Last of the Play-Party Games," *NCFJ* 21 (1973): 171–76 (repr. in *Readings in American Folklore*, pp. 319–23). Some interesting contextual and comparative notes on another example, published by a nonfolklorist, is Edmund Cody Burnett's "The Hog Drivers' Play-Song and Some of Its Relatives," *Agricultural History* 23 (1949): 161–68.

The dramatic dance song in this chapter was collected from Mrs. Mary Jane Fairbanks, age ninety-five, residing at the Anna Henry Nursing Home in Edwardsville, Illinois, on December 3, 1965. (Another of Mrs. Fairbanks's songs is quoted in chapter 11, Focus: "Drunken Hiccups.") George Morey Miller discussed "The Dramatic Element in the Popular Ballad" in *University Studies of the University of Cincinnati*, Series 2, vol. 1, no. 1 (1905). The quotation from Tristram P. Coffin is from *The British Traditional Ballad in North America*, discussed in chapter 12. "Poppy Show" was described in W. W. Newell's *Games and Songs of American Children* and in Lady Gomme's collection of English games, both cited in chapter 18.

Richard M. Dorson discussed *Los Pastores* in his book *American Folklore* (Chicago: University of Chicago Press, 1959), pp. 103–7. He cited the basic bibliography of Spanish-American folk drama on page 293. A translation of some scenes of the shepherd's play is given in Dorson's *Buying the Wind* (Chicago: University of Chicago Press, 1964), pp. 466–79. To Dorson's list of sources should be added John E. Englekirk's two-part article "The Passion Play in New Mexico," *WF* 25 (1966): 17–33, 105–21. An article that sets Spanish-American folk drama in a modern context is Nicolás Kanellos, "Folklore in Chicano Theater and Chicano Theater as Folklore," *JFI* 15 (1978): 57–82.

Standard works on the English mummers' play are R. J. E. Tiddy's *The Mummers' Play* (Oxford: Oxford University Press, 1923); E. K. Chambers's *The English Folk-Play* (Oxford: Oxford University Press, 1933); and Violet Alford's *Sword Dance and Drama* (London: Merlin Press, 1962). Charles E. Welch, Jr., traced the history of the Philadelphia Mummers' Parade in *KFQ* 8 (1963): 95–106; related material is cited in the notes to the previous chapter. The mummers' texts collected in the United States were published in Antoinette Taylor's "An English Christmas Play," *JAF* 22 (1909): 389–94; and Marie Campbell's "Survivals of Old Folk Drama in the Kentucky Mountains," *JAF* 51 (1938): 10–24.

James F. Hoy's article "A Modern Analogue to Medieval Staging," *JAF* 90 (1977): 179–87, compared the local festival called "Biblesta" performed in Humboldt, Kansas, to the medieval English Corpus Christi processions and plays.

Information on the "school of folk drama" may be found in Robert E. Spiller et al., *Literary History of the United States*, 4th ed., rev. (New York: Macmillan, 1974), pp. 722–24, and bibliography, p. 200. Charles G. Zug III evaluated this material and its relationship to traditional folk drama in an article in *SFQ* 32 (1968): 279–94.

Larry Dale Clark submitted his study "Toby Shows: A Form of American Popular Theatre" as his Ph.D. dissertation at the University of Illinois in 1963; see *Dissertation Abstracts* 24 (May 1964): 4, 858. Carol Pennepacker described "A Surviving Toby Show: Bisbee's Comedians" in *TFSB* 30 (1964): 49–52, and Jere C. Mickel published "The Genesis of Toby: A Folk Hero of the American Theater" in *JAF* 80 (1967): 334–40.

An interesting Southern African-American religious drama was described in Redding S. Sugg, Jr., "Heaven Bound," *SFQ* 27 (1963): 249–66.

A collection of eleven popular skits was compiled by Norris Yates as "Children's Folk Plays in Western Oregon," *WF* 9 (1951): 55–62, but these playlets are by no means peculiar to that region, nor does this article exhaust the list of such skits.

For a large collection citing sources, see Margaret Read MacDonald's *The Skit Book: 101 Skits from Kids* (Hamden, Conn.: Shoestring Press, 1990). Anne C. Burson drew on some satiric medical skits for her theoretical essay "Model and Text in Folk Drama," *JAF* 93 (1980): 305–16; she treated similar material in her "Pomp and Circumcision: A Parodic Skit in a Medical Community," *KF*, New Series, 1 (1982): 28–40. Skits, songs, and ritual behavior interact in Jay Mechling's analysis of "The Magic of the Boy Scout Campfire," *JAF* 93 (1980): 35–56.

Thomas A. Green pioneered in redefining folk drama (or refining older definitions) in "Toward a Definition of Folk Drama," *JAF* 91 (1978): 843–50, and also in the special folk-drama issue of *JAF* (94:374 [1981]), which he edited.

17

FOLK GESTURES

GESTURES AND MEANING

Gestures are a silent language made up of movements of the body, or a part of it, used to communicate emotions or ideas. As such, they are an important aspect of informants' total performances, and, as MacEdward Leach emphasized in a classic essay on folklore collecting, we should try to record everything, the "voice—tone and inflection—gestures, facial expressions, [and] attitudes as well as words." To retain the fullest possible report, field collectors sometimes photograph or videotape the typical gestures informants use, or they describe them, as in the following passage from Richard M. Dorson's discussion of African-American storytellers:

> When the rabbit scoots away from the fox, or John runs from the Lord, the narrator slaps his hands sharply together, with the left sliding off the right palm in a forward direction—a manual trademark of the Negro raconteur.

Gestures that accompany folktales may be stylized, like these raconteurs', or like snapping the fingers to emphasize "Just like that!" They may also be introduced from everyday behavior—shrugging the shoulders to indicate doubt, flexing a bicep to show strength, shading the eyes when looking for something, raising an imaginary gun to shoot—whatever fits the action occurring in the tale. However, some folktale plots include specific gestures that are a necessary part of the performance. For example, Aarne-Thompson Type 924, "Discussion by Sign Language," and its subtypes concern manual-sign conversations that are sometimes mutually misunderstood but still are finished to the complete satisfaction of both parties.

FOCUS: SIGN OF THE DOUBLE-CROSS

The Nun and the Little Boy

A little boy was going down the street crossing himself. A nun walked by and saw him making the sign of the cross and thought, "What a nice little boy." She said to him, "Does your mother send you to church all of the time?" "No, she just sent me to the store, and I'm trying to remember what she wanted—a head of lettuce, two jugs of milk and a package of wieners."

Collected in May 1971 from a nineteen-year-old female student from Greencastle.

*

Generalized castration anxiety moves all over the body, in these various symbolizations, not knowing exactly where to center itself, and unable to search specifically in the genital area since the actual fear of being castrated, or of being endangered by castration, has been repressed from consciousness. This is strikingly seen in a popular American gesture-story, collected in numerous forms, almost always involving the Jew. A Jewish woman coming out of a nightclub is seen by a friend crossing herself as she gets into the taxi. The friend expresses surprise at her conversion to the Catholic religion. "Converted? Who's converted? I'm just checking on my jewels (with gestures): Tiara, brooch, clip, clip." *(N.Y. 1949. It is perhaps relevant that "jewels" or "family jewels" are used in both English and French to refer to the testicles.) The male form:* A Jewish commuter is noticed by another Jew crossing himself on the Long Island train, just as the train pulls into his station at Great Neck. He denies that he is crossing himself. "Just checking," he says, "hat, wallet, fountain-pen, zipper." *(N.Y. 1951.)*

. . . A version . . . "localized" in the Korean war, collected in Los Angeles, Calif. 1957. The rabbi is accused by the Catholic chaplain of having found the "true religion" when a shell explodes. The rabbi

looks at him and says, "Oh, no. Just checking: spectacles, wallet, watch, and testicles."

Sources: Ronald L. Baker, joke no. 284 in *Jokelore: Humorous Folktales from Indiana* (Bloomington: Indiana University Press, 1986), p. 164; G. Legman, *No Laughing Matter: An Analysis of Sexual Humor* (Bloomington: Indiana University Press, 1975), vol. 2, pp. 575–76.

DISCUSSION TOPICS:

1. How is the Catholic Church's sign of the cross correctly performed? In which, if any, of these jokes is the gesture performed thus, and why is it done as it is in each joke?

2. Probably the correct form of the "spectacles" punch line is "spectacles, testicles, wallet, and watch." First, the rhyme and rhythm of the line is smoother, and second, the gesture then is actually performed correctly. (This is the most common form of the joke known to the author of this textbook.)

3. Legman also includes the "shopping list" version of this gesture joke with the third gesture actually touching the crotch, the last gesture going back to the head, and the punch line "a head of lettuce, two quarts of milk, and a pound of weenies." He calls this "the ultimate castratory statement." What do you think of Legman's sexual (Freudian) interpretation of these jokes? How may they also be interpreted as religious jokes?

In one riddle-joke with gestures, the question asked is why a stupid fellow has hunched shoulders and a dent in the middle of his forehead. The answer is that when you ask him a question he "goes like this" (shrugging the shoulders), and when you explain it he "does this" (slapping the palm of one hand to the forehead). The non-oral riddles described in chapter 6 are other traditional questions involving gestures, and among children's chants, rhymes, and songs are further gesture pieces. (Favorite gesture songs of children are "Eensy, Weensy Spider," "I'm a Little Teapot," "Do Your Ears Hang Low," and "John Brown's Baby.")

Superstitions, too, often involve traditional gestures. Crossing the fingers, tossing spilled salt over the left shoulder, and knocking on wood for good luck are familiar ones, as are the actions sometimes performed to seal a pact between children—crossing one's heart, raising the right hand in imitation of courtroom swearing, and spitting on the ground. When two Americans say the same words at the same time, they may hook little fingers and say "Needles-Pins," and make a wish; Spaniards hook the same finger, but say "Cervantes." Rituals of witchcraft make use of special gestures and symbols, and some body movements are believed to have the power to cast the "evil eye" on someone else or to avert its power from oneself. An ancient one for the latter purpose is made by extending the forefinger and little finger of one hand and clenching the others—the "Devil's Horns," although this gesture has other meanings and other names, including "Hook 'em Horns," the slogan of the University of Texas football team. The sign of the cross is commonly made, outside of any formal religious context, to ward off bad luck.

A folk game involving gestures is "Rocks, Paper, and Scissors." Manual imitations of these three objects are given by several players sitting in a circle, gesturing in unison, and keeping time to a strict rhythmic beat. Penalties fall to players according to the formula that "paper covers rock, rocks break scissors, and scissors cut paper." Thus those who have signed "paper" win over rock, while rock wins over scissors, and scissors over paper. The punishment is a sharp slap on the wrist dealt by winners to losers, using the first two fingers of one hand held together, and dampened with the tongue before striking; play continues until a player's wrist is too sore to go on.

Although gestures often accompany speech, a simple and familiar one by itself can communicate eloquently to those who know its customary meaning. Functionally, these gestures (such as holding one's nose or pretending to slash one's throat) are comparable to proverbs, since they succinctly summarize "how things are." President Ronald Reagan demonstrated this principle beautifully in July 1985 after undergoing the surgical removal of a tumor from his colon. No signs of cancer were found, and the President in his first public appearance from Bethesda Medical Center declared himself "fit as a fiddle." He held aloft one hand with the thumb and index finger forming a circle while closing his eyes, in a common American gesture of "OK."

Even animals seem to employ such gestures—the friendly dog wagging its tail, or the cat rolling over on its back for a tummy rub, for instance. Such "proverbial-gesture" use partly explains the long-term effectiveness of the famous United States Army recruiting poster that shows Uncle Sam pointing directly at the viewer. Similarly, a profile representation of a pointing finger was once a com-

President Ronald Reagan gives an "OK" sign from the window of his hospital room at the Naval Medical Center in Bethesda, Maryland, on July 18, 1985. Reagan was recovering from surgery to remove a cancerous polyp in his intestines.

mon American direction sign, while the picture showing a forefinger laid across the lips, once posted in libraries, commanded, "Silence!" Advertisers, fashion photographers, and drama directors still make use of such well-known conventional gestures to convey desired feelings to their audiences. Conversely, many proverbial phrases contain references to gestures that have unambiguous meanings, such as "to turn up one's nose at" (scorn), "to keep a stiff upper lip" (courage), "to tear one's hair" (rage), and "to raise an eyebrow" (surprise, shock, or skepticism). The very word "supercilious" derives from the Latin terms for the gesture of raising eyebrows to denote haughtiness.

FOCUS: THUMBS UP

You probably think we make the thumbs-up gesture because that's what the Romans used to do when they wanted to spare a fallen gladiator, right? Wrong—that's a myth based on a succession of mistranslations. The truth is when the Romans were feeling merciful they hid their thumbs in their clenched fists (symbolically sheathing their swords, some historians believe). To have a guy offed they didn't turn thumbs down but rather extended their thumbs in a stabbing gesture. For whatever reason, though, thumbs-up today means OK just about everywhere— except in Sardinia or Greece, where it means "screw you." I'm told that for rookie travelers this makes hitchhiking in Athens a pretty lively experience. Caveat viator.

*

Romans did not give a thumbs-up sign in the arena as an indication that the downed gladiator should be spared death. There is some question as to just what the Latin expression verso pollice, *"to turn the thumb," means exactly. But according to Kevin Guinagh's* Dictionary of Foreign Phrases and Abbreviations *(New York, 1971), the popular interpretation is quite the reverse of the ancient Romans'. Says Guinagh (p. 289): "Actually the Romans pointed the thumb upward toward the chest when they wanted the vanquished slain, and down when they wanted the victor to spare his opponent."*

*

*It is not certain just what was done with the thumb in this famous gesture, but it is certain that the modern American assumption that "thumbs up" was favorable, "thumbs down" unfavorable, is wrong. From passages in Horace, Juvenal, Prudentius and others, it is plain that the thumb was turned some way (*verso pollice *and* converso pollice*) and that its being up was unfavorable. The evidence suggests that the thumb was turned up and back and possibly rotated in the unfavorable verdict and folded down into the fist for the favorable. But this is not absolutely certain. The American interpretation is very new. Throughout the 19th century, "thumbs up" was in England an expression of disapprobation.*

Sources: Top—Cecil Adams, *More of the Straight Dope* (New York: Ballantine Books, 1988), p. 452. Middle—Tom Burnam, *The Dictionary of Misinformation* (1975; first Ballantine Books ed., 1977), pp. 289–90. Bottom—Bergen Evans, *Dictionary of Quotations* (New York: Delacorte Press, 1968), p. 692.

DISCUSSION TOPICS:

1. Collect traditional explanations for other common gestures such as sticking out the tongue, thumbing the nose, making the "Devil's Horns," saluting, and rubbing thumb and index finger together to suggest money or payment.

2. Although the above explanations of "thumbs up" vary slightly, and they differ in style, each sounds authoritative. They were published over a period of twenty years in relatively popular works. Why, then, do most people still believe that "thumbs up" was a Roman gesture for sparing a gladiator's life and "thumbs down" condemned one to death?

3. Cecil Adams also published a reader's letter pointing out that an 1874 painting by French artist Jean-Léon Gérôme, showing a gladiator standing over a fallen opponent, had popularized the traditional

explanations for the thumb gestures. Try to locate a reproduction of this painting and some information on Gérôme's sources and influence.

Any mannerism or behavioral pattern associated with passing on oral traditions may interest the folklore collector, but not all gestures are true folk gestures. Some body movements are merely **autistic,** or **nervous, personal gestures;** these include drumming with the fingers, jingling change, fussing with hair or clothing, biting the lips or fingernails, and cracking knuckles. Only a few of these—such as "twiddling" the thumbs, or stroking the chin or beard—may become stereotyped signs for certain attitudes, and then begin to circulate traditionally. Closely related to autistic gestures are **culture-induced gestures**—aspects of sitting, walking, hand movements, and stance that are learned unconsciously from one's cultural surroundings and employed as a subconscious symbolic code. Other movements belong to **technical gesture systems** that are usually taught by formal methods. The military salute is a good example of this: it is described precisely, with its proper use, in military manuals, and its correct form is instilled in every new member of the group. But a traditional mock version of the salute, which turns into the derisive gesture of "thumbing the nose," can be considered a folk gesture. The saying associated with this variation goes "I salute the captain of the ship; / Pardon me, my finger slipped."

Complex systems of technical gestures are important for special uses; the best known is communication between deaf-mutes. Native American sign language constitutes another highly developed system, as do religious gestures for prayer and worship, and gestures used for communication within certain monastic orders. Many occupations require that a special gesture language be flawlessly learned and consistently performed time after time. Umpires and referees of various sports have their strict systems, as do radio and television performers, land surveyors, music conductors, traffic and airport directors, auctioneers, some heavy-machinery operators, and even surgeons, who use some hand signals during operations to request instruments from a nurse.

These occupational gestures learned from manuals or special instructors have their folk counterparts in others used in the same occupations that pass on through tradition. For example, the railroad worker's operating rulebooks show only a few official hand signals, but railroad men have other gestures of their own invention used for special purposes. If an inspector or other company authority is on a train, the signal may be given with the thumbs stuck into an imaginary vest. Another is the gesture of pretending to scratch one's head a few inches out in the air to indicate that the "big heads" are approaching. Similarly, truck drivers long used the two-finger "V" sign, not to signify "victory," but to signal other drivers that a police patrol car is ahead. Automobile drivers picked up the same signal for a time, using it to warn oncoming cars of a radar speed-trap ahead.

Some systems of gesturing, such as those used for bidding in different kinds of auction sales, may have been folk gestures originally that were later regularized and formally adopted. Other systems, such as those used by a particular athletic team or coach to signal strategy, may be largely individual and secret. Whenever an occupation demands communicating in secrecy (as in professional baseball), or above the sound of loud noises (as in sawmills), or across a considerable distance (as when fencing a farm or ranch), then both systematized and informal gestures can be expected to develop. And within a technical system of gestures like American Sign Language used by the deaf, various jokes, abbreviations, and "dialects" of the standard gestures inevitably develop.

FOLK GESTURES

A true **folk gesture** is kept alive by tradition and exhibits some variation in action or meaning. Most obscene gestures clearly qualify as "folk." Like customs, folk gestures tend to pattern themselves within national boundaries. Americans wave good-bye with the palm out; Italians keep the palm turned in. Americans "thumb" a ride, while many Europeans wave the whole hand up and down when hitchhiking. Western peoples tend to point to themselves at chest level; some Asians point to their own noses. To signify that something is "just right," a French person places the right index fingertip on the right thumb tip and kisses them both, while an American (such as President Reagan, mentioned above) forms a circle with the same two fingers, holds that hand up, closes his or her eyes, and gives the hand a little shake. In Sicily the same idea is conveyed by pinching the cheek, in Brazil by tugging on an earlobe, and in Colombia by pulling down a lower eyelid. Kissing, considered as a gesture, displays several variations; where the kiss is applied is significant—on the lips, cheek, forehead, back of the hand; "blown" from the fingers or palm; and so forth. A greeting that consists of two kisses rapidly applied, one to each cheek, immediately seems to identify the performer as French, even though several other European cultures use this greeting, too. Kissing a ring, a Bible, a piece of someone's clothing, or a photograph is a widespread sign of extreme devotion, and the image of the Pope kissing the ground at an airport after landing in a new country is a familiar one from the media.

An excellent example of a culturally significant gesture having a secret communications use was described in a news story during the Korean War (1950–1953). An American Air Force captain recounting his experiences as a prisoner in North Korea told how he was photographed with other prisoners in a mock library, presumably to show the world how well they were being treated. To counter the propaganda value of the pictures, he made the sign of the "Devil's Horns" in each one, which to Americans is usually interpreted as the "bull sign" or "baloney." To his captors, the gesture was innocuous, and the pictures were released to the press. In 1968 some members of the captured United States vessel *Pueblo* managed to repeat this trick, using an obscene gesture—the "bird" (extended middle finger), when they, too, were photographed. Another notable use of the "Devil's Horns" sign came in November 1989, when the California mass murderer Richard Ramirez, known as "The Night Stalker," was sentenced to death. As he left the courthouse, Ramirez flashed the sign to the press and spectators.

Gestures of greeting have become well established in different cultures and seldom change much, but the degree of formality in a social situation may allow for some variation in the greeting employed. Thus, a firm handshake is "correct" in some situations, while a hearty slap on the back or playful rumpling of the other's hair is better for others. Beginning with jazz musicians, and quickly spreading to other Americans, was an exaggerated handshake that began with a dramatic "windup" and the remark "Give me some skin,

(*Above*) Crewmen of the U.S.S. *Pueblo*, captured by the North Koreans in 1968, in a propaganda picture released by their captors, display what *Time* magazine referred to as "the U.S. hand signal of obscene derisiveness and contempt." (*Below*) The "Night Stalker" serial killer Richard Ramirez gives the "devil's horn" sign as he is led from the courthouse in Los Angeles after being sentenced to death for the murder of thirteen people.

FOCUS: RUDE GESTURES

At present rude gestures seem to be in a state of flux, the following being currently regarded as the most offensive:

1. The first and second fingers, extended and slightly parted, are jerked upwards, the back of the hand facing outwards.

2. The nose is pressed upwards with thumb, and the tongue put out.

3. Ears are twisted, or thumbs placed in ear-holes and fingers fluttered, a gesticulation known as "elephant ears".

4. The nose is held while an imaginary lavatory chain is pulled.

5. Air is forced through the pursed lips to make a juicy noise known as a "raspberry".

They also continue to make the well-known schoolboy "face" by inserting their thumbs in the corners of their mouth and tugging sideways while simultaneously plucking downward the undersides of their eyes with their forefingers.

Source: Iona and Peter Opie, *The Lore and Language of Schoolchildren* (Oxford: Oxford University Press, 1959), pp. 319–20.

DISCUSSION TOPICS:

1. These were the rude gestures of British schoolchildren in the 1950s. Which of them have, or had, counterparts among American children? Are there names for these gestures?

2. Are American children's rude gestures of the present also in "a state of flux"? Which gestures are currently regarded as the most offensive, whether among children or adults?

3. Is No. 5 above really a "gesture," or is it a rude sound, similar to laughing, groaning, or hissing? (Or are these sounds also gestures, in some instances?)

man!" and culminated with the hands or fingers barely touching. Another playful American greeting is the manual imitation of shooting a revolver at someone else, usually accompanied by a wink, and sometimes by the expression "Gottcha!" There are also mock handshakes, supposedly appropriate for different occupations: the "farmers' handshake" has the thumbs of one person turned down and being "milked" by the second person, and the "politicians' handshake" begins with great enthusiasm and ends with the two parties reaching over each other's shoulders to pick each other's pockets.

Many athletic teams and other groups (probably learning to do so from African-American members) use complicated little palm-slapping patterns as gestures of greeting, or greet others with a "high five" over-the-head handshake.

CLASSIFYING AND STUDYING GESTURES

No standard system of classifying folk gestures has been adopted. Some collectors have used the parts of the body as a basis for arrangement, while others classify in terms of meanings expressed. Some collections have not been put in any special order, but were simply published as random lists. A better possibility may lie in trying to establish categories based on the *nature* of different gestures. As has been shown, some are parodies of technical gestures or derivations from autistic gestures. Others imitate letters of the alphabet (forming a "C" with the hand to invite someone to have coffee with you), or they signify numbers (gestures to hot-dog salesmen in grandstands). It might be noted that even the procedure for counting on the fingers is culturally determined. Germans, for example, begin counting with the thumb, so an American tourist holding up an index finger to order one beer is actually ordering two.

There are gestures borrowed for general folk use from a specialized application (the prizefighters' victory sign of hands joined over the head, wagging in jubilation and triumph). Some gestures come directly to the point, such as touching a wristwatch or cupping a hand behind the ear as signals to a speaker, or holding the nose as a reaction to an idea. Other gestures are more abstract, such as that of circling the forefinger around one ear to mean "crazy" (something loose in the head?) or rubbing one forefinger held at right angles against the other toward another person for "shame" (shedding the "dirt"?). A large group of folk gestures could be classed as *pantomimic*—that is, they act out the intended message. We gesture and say "Chalk one up" in the air with imaginary chalk against an invisible blackboard, as if keeping score of our "goofs"; and we pretend to slash the throat with a finger to show that a certain kind of trouble has occurred or is soon expected. Other pantomime gestures are those of playing an invisible violin, for mock sympathy; mopping the brow, for great exertion; breathing on and pretending to polish the fingernails, for self-pride; and smoothing an eyebrow with a dampened little finger, used by males to denote effeminacy in other males.

Gestures can be studied historically, geographically, comparatively, contextually, and structurally, like any other kind of folklore, although only a few such investigations have been made. Most published studies of gestures are physiological, linguistic, or psychological, and thus beyond the scope of this survey. Two, however, deserve further mention.

In 1944 a psychologist published his detailed study of the "V for Victory" campaign among the Allied nations during World War II, an outstanding instance of morale boosting by means of symbolism. To anyone who remembers the war years, the image of Winston Churchill flashing the "V" gesture with his two fingers raised immediately comes to mind. But the sign was carried much further during the war—in posters, advertising, the "dot-dot-dot-dash" of Morse code, and even through allusion to the code "V" by playing or humming the first phrase of Beethoven's *Fifth Symphony* (da, da, da, DA). The study traced the history of the campaign, schematized the communications process involved in it, analyzed the types of symbolism found, and described the degeneration of the symbol as it was widely applied apart from its original context. More recently, of course, the "V" sign, while retaining its "victory" meaning among athletes, politicians running for office, etc., also became a greeting of recognition, implying "peace," among young people, and it has an entirely separate function in the Cub Scouts organization, calling meetings to order and signifying ideals of the group.

The continuing effectiveness of the "V"-sign gesture was demonstrated vividly in the spring of 1990 as the Communist governments of Eastern Europe disintegrated. For weeks the news media carried photographs of the citizens of these countries demonstrating against their leaders and flashing the "V" sign defiantly. David Turnley, of the *Detroit Free Press*, won the Pulitzer Prize for feature photography for his portfolio, including a memorable shot of a Romanian man weeping tears of joy in a crowd and holding two fingers aloft in the "V" gesture. President Richard M. Nixon had become so identified with his personal version of the same gesture—both hands in a "V" and both arms upraised in a larger "V"—that throughout his career, even to the day he left office, he continued

Richard M. Nixon, boarding a helicopter for Andrews Air Force Base after resigning the presidency on August 9, 1974, bids good-bye to his staff with his personal version of the "V" gesture.

to use it and was frequently caricatured by political cartoonists in that posture. At the time of Nixon's death in 1994 one cartoonist represented him entering the Pearly Gates, still flashing the big triple "V" sign; even though the drawing showed Nixon from the back, there was no doubt who was portrayed.

Folklorist Archer Taylor produced the only full-length folkloristic study of an individual gesture in English in his work on the so-called Shanghai Gesture, also called thumbing the nose, "cocking a snook," "Queen Anne's fan," "taking a sight," and other names. After an exhaustive survey of the gesture in art, literature, news media, and oral tradition, Taylor concluded that it originated in Western Europe and had been known in Great Britain during the sixteenth century. It did not become faddish in England until early in the nineteenth century. In the United States it was first described by Washington Irving in *Diedrich Knickerbocker's History of New York* (1809), and it was well known by 1862, when Mark Twain made it the basis of his hoax in "The Petrified Man." Ezra Pound alluded to it in a poem in 1917, and since then numerous American writers and illustrators have continued to describe and picture it. Only recently, Taylor felt, has the gesture acquired an obscene connotation—the end result of its becoming increasingly more insulting as time passed.

Since 1956, when Taylor's study was published, the gesture has continued to be popular—and insulting. In 1959–60, for example, which was designated World Refugee Year, some English people became alarmed when postmarks depicting the symbol for that year—an outstretched, empty hand—occasionally became imprinted on canceled stamps bearing Queen Elizabeth's picture so as to show Her Majesty delivering a perfect Shanghai Gesture. In 1983, President Ronald Reagan provided news photographers with a memorable picture when he delivered the related derisive gesture of sticking his thumbs in his ears and wiggling his fingers directly into the television cameras. No American needed an explanation of what he meant, and for a moment, perhaps, we were all one big folk group.

President George Bush may have inherited his mentor's—Reagan's—use of folk speech combined with a gesture. Following his own annual checkup in April 1990, Bush declared that he felt "like a spring colt," while giving a double "thumbs up" sign to the press. A few months earlier, in October 1989, the President narrowly avoided being caught by press photographers performing a well-known obscene gesture, but the situation was entirely accidental and benign. Bush had just had a small cyst removed from his middle finger, which was still bandaged. A journalist asked him to hold up the injured finger, but Bush immediately caught on and declined to hold up the finger. However, he did have to turn to a foreign visitor accompanying him on the occasion to explain why everyone was laughing. Imagine! The President of the United States giving the "bird" sign for photographers!

BIBLIOGRAPHIC NOTES

There are a few small collections of American gestures but few studies of them, although groundwork for analysis has been laid. No "Gestures" heading exists in the index to *JAF* for volumes 1 to 70 (1888–1958). Finally, a study appeared in *JAF* 89 (1976): 294–309, namely John A. Rickford and Angela E. Rickford's essay "Cut-Eye and Suck-Teeth: African Words and Gestures in a New World Guise," reprinted in *Readings in American Folklore*, pp. 355–73. A key work elsewhere was Francis C. Hayes's "Gestures: A Working Bibliography," *SFQ* 21 (1957): 218–317. Hayes's bibliography included both foreign and English references, popular articles as well as scholarly ones, and some descriptions of specific gestures from literature and popular media. Obscure and unpublished items were included, and many entries were annotated, with their presence in four American libraries indicated.

Survey articles on gestures as folklore are rare. Charles Francis Potter's work in *Funk & Wagnalls Standard Dictionary of Folklore, Mythology, and Legend* (1,451–53) is largely anthropological and religious in its orientation. A better survey is Levette J. Davidson's "Some Current Folk Gestures and Sign Languages," *AS* 25 (1950): 3–9; a more detailed one is Robert A. Barakat's "Gesture Systems" in *KFQ* 14 (1969): 105–21. Barakat also provides a detailed discussion of more than two hundred "Arabic Gestures" in *JPC* 6 (1973): 749–93, which could serve as a model for similar surveys in other cultures.

MacEdward Leach's comment quoted at the beginning of this chapter is from "Problems of Collecting Oral Literature," *PMLA* 77 (1962): 335–40. Richard M. Dorson described gestures of African-American storytellers in *Negro Folktales in Michigan* (Cambridge, Mass.: Harvard University Press, 1956), p. 24. The gestures of Austrian storytellers are discussed and pictured in Karl Haiding's *"Von der Gebärdensprache der Märchenerzähler,"* *FFC* no. 155 (1955).

A comprehensive treatment of gestures, written by a neurologist, is MacDonald Critchley's *The Language of Gesture* (London: E. Arnold Co., 1939). Ernest Thompson Seton's book *Sign Talk* (Garden City, N.Y.: Doubleday, 1918) proposed an ingenious "universal signal code without apparatus" that borrowed gestures freely from various technical systems as well as from folk usage. An ambitious theoretical work, fully illustrated, that involved gestures in part, was Jurgen Ruesch and Weldon Kees's *Nonverbal Communication: Notes on the Visual Perception of Human Relations* (Berkeley and Los Angeles: University of California Press, 1961).

Francis C. Hayes distinguished technical, autistic, and folk gestures in his essay "Should We Have a Dictionary of Gestures?" in *SFQ* 4 (1940): 239–45. Exactly that—*A Dictionary of Gestures*—edited by Betty J. and Franz H. Bäuml, was published in 1975 (Metuchen, N.J.: Scarecrow Press).

Two articles that present occupational folk gestures are Charles Carpenter's "The Sign Language of Railroad Men," *American Mercury* 25 (Feb. 1932): 211–13; and C. Grant Loomis's "Sign Language of Truck Drivers," *WF* 15 (1956): 205–6.

Mario Pei discussed different nationalities and their typical gestures in *The Story of Language* (Philadelphia: Lippincott, 1949). Some of his findings were illustrated with photographs of people performing the gestures in "Gesture Language," *Life* (January 9, 1950), pp. 79–81. An article in German by Lutz Röhrich contained thirty-seven plates illustrating historical gestures. See *"Gebärdensprache und Sprachgebärde,"* in *Humaniora: Essays in Literature, Folklore, Bibliography Honoring Archer Taylor on His Seventieth Birthday*, ed. Wayland D. Hand and Gustave O. Arlt (Locust Valley, N.Y.: J. J. Augustin, 1960), pp. 121–49. Characteristic gestures of Spanish-speaking peoples were described in Walter Vincent Kaulfers's "Curiosities of Colloquial Gestures," *Hispania* 14 (1931): 249–64. The North Korean incident described in this chapter was reported in Captain Harold E. Fischer, Jr.'s "My Case as a Prisoner Was Different," *Life* (June 27, 1955), pp. 147–60. A photograph of Fischer making the gesture (which *Life* termed "the whammy sign") is found on page 157 of that issue of *Life*.

Three lists of gestures from California have appeared: Charlotte McCord described thirty collected from the Berkeley campus of the University of California in *WF* 7 (1948): 290–92; William S. King added ten more in *WF* 8 (1949): 263–64; and Jean Cooke published a strangely mistitled list of forty more gestures from Berkeley in "A Few Gestures Encountered in a Virtually Gestureless Society," *WF* 18 (1959): 233–37. None of these notes had bibliography. Many instances of gestures used by English children are cross-referenced under "gesture" in the index to Peter Opie and Iona Opie's *The Lore and Language of Schoolchildren* (Oxford: Oxford University Press, 1959). A curiosity is Michael J. Preston's note "A Gesture Rebus," showing how two brands of whiskey are represented by folk gestures, published in *SWF* 5 (1981): 42–45.

A major study unfortunately treats only gestures in Europe and North Africa. See Desmond Morris, Peter Collett, Peter Marsh, and Marie O'Shaughnessy, *Gestures: Their Origins and Distribution* (London: Jonathan Cape, 1979). Twenty key gestures in forty sites surveyed are discussed with regard to meanings, origins, and variations. The bibliography here is impressive, and the methodology should be repeated for the United States.

Edgar A. Schuler's article "V for Victory: A Study in Symbolic Social Control" appeared in *JSP* 19 (1944): 283–99. Some further developments in the uses and meanings of the "V" sign are illustrated in Jan Harold Brunvand, "Popular Culture in the Folklore Course," in Ray B. Browne and Ronald J. Ambrosetti, *Popular Culture and Curricula* (Bowling Green, Ohio: Bowling Green University Popular Press, 1970), pp. 59–72. Archer Taylor's "The Shanghai Gesture" was published in *FFC* no. 166 (1956). Taylor added an English description of the gesture from shortly after 1810 in "The Shanghai Gesture in England," *WF* 23 (1964): 114. Wirephotos of canceled stamps from England, with and without the embarrassing juxtaposition of open hand and royal nose, were distributed by the Associated Press in 1959 and printed in many American newspapers.

18

FOLK GAMES

GAME LORE

Children's traditional games offer an ideal topic for folklore research. They are passed from child to child in almost pure oral tradition, with little reference to print and probably negligible influence from teachers, parents, or recreation leaders. The players are naturally conservative about their texts and will strive to maintain the "right way" of playing against all variations. Thus, old games may survive, little altered, through many generations of children. Children's games also develop clear regional subtypes. When families change neighborhoods or move to other communities, the children will soon discover whether their old versions are played in the new home or whether they must adopt new ones, for seldom do newcomers succeed in converting their playmates to outside games. Finally, children are usually excellent informants—easy to locate, eager to perform, and uninhibited with their responses.

The folk games all people play, whether children, adolescents, or adults, may be based on the movements of the body (stepping, running, hopping, jumping, etc.), on simple social activities (chasing, hiding, fighting, dramatizing, etc.), on chance (the fall of dice, cards, bones, coins, etc.), or on elementary mathematics or mechanics (counting, sorting, balancing, throwing, handling equipment, etc.). These common foundation blocks help to explain the similarity of certain games through long periods of time and in widespread cultures, or the diffusion of folklore may better account for some similar forms. (It is the question once again of polygenesis versus diffusion from a single origin.) Only detailed studies of many versions of different games can suggest answers to such questions.

By their very nature as voluntary recreations with rules fixed only by custom and tradition, folk games reveal much about the societies in which they are played and about the individuals who play them. Game preferences, the forms of games, local variations, attitudes toward play, and play behavior are all valuable cultural, sociological, and psychological data to be documented and analyzed. In such research, the nonverbal elements of games are significant along with such verbal ones as traditional sayings, rhymes, or songs associated with games. Good fieldwork in folk games requires that one describe the action clearly and logically; secure all variations in names, rules, and texts; sketch or photograph all diagrams or equipment; and collect the full social and contextual background of the game along with the text. Useful projects in game study would include collecting the games of one family, neighborhood, school class, or season.

It is not surprising that the first American folklorists were interested in collecting and studying folk games. For example, W. W. Newell, charter member of the American Folklore Society in 1888 and first editor of its journal, had already published a classic study, *Games and Songs of American Children*, five years earlier. But this early interest declined when folklorists assumed that children had abandoned folk games. Only a scattering of articles and notes on folk games appeared in this country until Paul G. Brewster's book, *American Non-Singing Games*, published in 1953, balanced the picture Newell had given by describing the games without songs that Newell had ignored. Since then there has been increasing interest in game analysis among American scholars, and a comprehensive sociopsychological, anthropological, and folkloristic theory of play and games emerged as studies illuminated how role-playing and competition in games reveal underlying motives and reflect on other behavior.

The problem of classifying games, basic to further research, has not been completely solved. The singing or nonsinging dichotomy suggested by Newell's and Brewster's works is no better than other proposed systems that separate games of boys from those of girls, or indoor from outdoor games, or games of different age groups. One writer suggests grouping games into four classes, depending upon the elements of competition, chance, mimicry, or vertigo (motion alone, i.e., teeter-tottering). But these categories are too broad for classification purposes, and it is not clear that the last two represent games at all. A better grouping, made by anthropologists, classifies games according to their requirements for either physical skill, strategy, or chance. This has proved meaningful for studying the relationship of games to cultural and environmental factors. But for folklore purposes—especially folklore archiving—a more workable classification might be made on the basis of the primary kind of play activity involved—whether physical action, manipulation of objects, or mental activity.

First, **pastimes** (or "amusements") must be distinguished from true games. A pastime, as the name suggests, is a traditional recreation performed simply to pass the time away. It lacks what true games have—the element of competition, the possibility of winning or losing, and a measure of organization with some kind of controlling rules. Most pastimes are solo activities such as bouncing a ball, juggling, balancing oneself or an object, swinging, walking on stilts, spinning a top, operating a yo-yo, and making cat's cradles (string patterns on one's fingers). When two or more individuals toss a ball about, they are engaging in a mere pastime as long as they introduce no rules and no way of distinguishing a winner. Yo-yoing, top spinning, rope jumping, or other such activities may lead to a contest of skill or of endurance and thus turn into true games. Two people balance on a teeter-totter more commonly than just one (in the middle of the board), and sometimes two may swing together with one seated and the other standing and "pumping"; these activities, however, remain pastimes. There are also four-handed cat's cradles in which the ever-changing design in the string loop is passed back and forth from one person to another.

A solo recreation, on the other hand, may be a game—solitaire, for instance, is played against an imaginary opponent, and the player may win, or (more commonly) lose. Puzzle solving is something of a game if one thinks of "winning" by finishing the picture or word pattern in a specified time with no outside help. We even bribe ourselves to finish unpleasant or tiresome tasks by "making a game of it" or by promising ourselves a reward upon completion.

GAMES OF ACTION

Games of physical action may be subdivided by the principal action involved. There are hopping games (hopscotch), chasing games (Red Rover), hiding games (hide-and-seek), battle games (prisoner's base), and dramatic games (farmer in the dell), to list only the major kinds. At their simplest level, such games are merely outlets for high spirits and a means of getting lively exercise. They provide healthy competitions in strength and skill between individuals or teams. Games like running races, leapfrog, tag, Johnny on the pony, and king on the hill satisfy these needs, but they have other dimensions, too. In tag, for instance, if "it" is thought of as a fearsome aggressor, possibly the Devil, the safety gained by touching iron (long used to avert evil spirits) or wood (the cross), and the truce cry "King's X" (royal pardon plus the cross) are all readily understood. (Probably the game and the basic symbolism are pre-Christian.) Any doubts that children's games might contain such underlying themes are shaken by

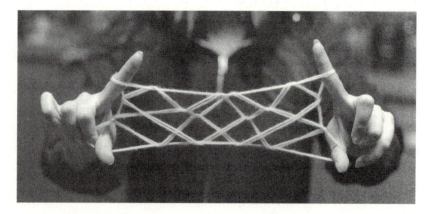

Patsy Bedonie, a Navajo woman from Black Mesa, Arizona, makes the traditional Navajo string figure of Dilyéhé (the Pleiades), 1975.

the actual appearance of the names "black man" or "Devil" for "it" in some games that are still in current circulation. Also, hopscotch patterns that have "Heaven" at one boundary and "Hell" at the other are not unusual, even today, although "Dead End" is perhaps a more popular marker.

Some types of hiding games illustrate the variety of play that is possible on the basis of one simple concept. In many of these all but one player hide and the person who is "it" searches; various rules govern "its" activities while finding other players. In other games one person hides and the others search, and in one game, sardines, the searchers join the hider one by one as they discover him or her, until all are crammed into one hiding place. Still other varieties of hiding games involve a whole team of players hiding and another team searching, or an object or objects are hidden and the players search. The swimming-pool game called Marco Polo is a kind of tag-hiding game, since "it" must locate other players with his or her eyes closed; whenever "it" calls out "Marco," the others are obliged to answer "Polo." Truce terms and sanctuary terms in all such recreations differ from game to game and region to region.

Adults are often nostalgic about the action games of their childhood, believing them to have completely died out, and being taken by surprise to overhear modern children playing them. The grownups forget that in most cases games are passed from child to child, not adult to child, and that even while they themselves were growing out of childhood, other and younger children were transmitting the games. Still, adults may remember their childhood games quite well. For example, I once observed a worker at an upscale Rocky Mountain ski resort directing traffic coming from two different sides toward the loading area of a ski lift using the calls "red light!" and "green light!" to summon each line forward in turn. Most adult skiers immediately recognized his allusion to a children's game, and they adopted the pattern of play. Some of them even discussed other such games and local names for them as they waited their turns to board the lift.

Most of the active games involve a certain amount of mimicry of life situations, although it is only the most complex of these recreations that are usually called *dramatic games*. Little children play a game that begins with all but one player in a "jam pile"—everyone falls down in a heap with limbs tangled. Then they cry "Doctor, doctor, we need help!" and the remaining child hurries to untangle them. The game is a simple, playful enactment of a horrible scene that might occur in accidents. In Mother, may I? the "it" player (who may be male or female) assumes the role of a demanding "mother," who dictates movement toward a goal by calling for types and numbers of rather grotesque steps, and then only if the children remember to say "May I?" and "Thank you." Cheating by sneaking ahead, or distracting "mother" while others inch forward, however, are regular features of the game as it is actually played. The game of fox hunt (or hare and hounds) imitates hunting, with bits of scattered paper instead of a scent as the trail. The city child's counterpart game, arrow chase (or chalk walk), is an adaptation for sidewalk playing with detectivelike overtones. Nineteenth-century children, girls especially, enjoyed courtship games such as knights of Spain or Here come three dukes a-riding, but these have mostly died out now as the more aggressive kissing and party-mixer games (discussed below) flourish. Many courtship games, as well as others that involve singing, are related to the play-parties discussed in chapter 16, and some of the old Anglo-American games have passed into the tradition of African-American children, surviving there more as dances than as actual games.

FOCUS: "LITTLE SALLY WALKER"

For another example of how a European game can be changed into ring play, here is "Little Sally Walker," long a favorite among British and American children. It is a very old play. In what are perhaps the oldest versions, little Sally's last name is "Water" instead of "Walker" and she is "crying for a young man." Some writers suggest that this play may have grown out of purification ceremonies in ancient British marriage rites.

In sin-conscious early America, however, "Little Sally Walker" became a brief drama about the joys of release from shame; black children undoubtedly learned it from their white neighbors.

FORM: Ring of Children standing; center player sits or kneels in
the middle of the ring.

ALL VOICES EXCEPT CENTER PLAYER	ACTION
Little Sally Walker,	Center player puts head in hands
Sitting in a saucer,	as though crying.
Crying and a-weeping	
Over all she has done.	
Rise, Sally, rise.	Center player stands; wipes eyes;
Wipe out your eyes.	arms outstretched and waving,
Fly to the east, Sally,	walks to right;
Fly to the west, Sally,	as above walks to left; as above,
Fly to the very one that you love the best.	goes to face chosen partner.
(Begin strong offbeat clap)	
Now Miss Sally, won't you jump for joy,	Center player and partner jump for joy.
Jump for joy, jump for joy.	
Now Miss Sally, won't you jump for joy,	Center player bows; partner takes
And now, Miss Sally, won't you bow.	place in center while first Little Sally joins the ring.

Source: Bessie Jones and Bess Lomax Hawes, *Step It Down: Games, Plays, Songs, and Stories from the Afro-American Heritage* (1972; 2nd printing, Athens: University of Georgia Press, 1987), pp. 107–08. Bessie Jones (1902–1984), source of this game, grew up in the rural south. The headnote is by folklorist Bess Lomax Hawes.

DISCUSSION TOPICS:

1. Hawes lists British and American versions of this game published in, among others, books by Gomme, Newell, and Brown cited in this chapter or its notes. Compare the Anglo- and African-American versions.

2. For the origin theory mentioned by Hawes, see the full discussion of "Sally Water" in Iona and Peter Opie's book *The Singing Game* (Oxford: Oxford University Press, 1985), pp. 167–71. Do the Opies subscribe to this theory? How do you evaluate it?

3. In what mood or spirit do children play such games? Here is Hawes's general advice to parents and teachers who may want to teach them to children: "Enjoy yourself. This is a beautiful and democratic tradition, full of joy and the juices of life. Don't be too solemn, or too organized; these are for *play*."

Battle games, like cops and robbers or cowboys and Indians, are dramatic imitations of adult conflicts that have survived even in the age of space exploration. Children have also been reported playing a game with as old-fashioned a title (perhaps learned from TV or from the name of a major bank) as Wells Fargo. Here the "Indians" are identified by strips of adhesive tape on their foreheads. When they storm the office or stagecoach, they may be "killed" by yanking the tape away.

That children are imaginative and have extremely good memories for the things that interest them is demonstrated by the fanciful forfeits sometimes proposed in games like Tappy-on-the-icebox and the complicated dialogue preserved in one like The Old Witch. That children have boundless stamina is shown by the hours they will spend in snowball fighting or playing a chasing game like fox and geese over a pattern stamped in the snow. And that children are adaptable was strikingly demonstrated after the devastating Alaskan earthquake on Good Friday 1964, when, only a few days later, amid the wreckage, the children of Kodiak were playing new games called earthquake and tidal wave.

GAMES WITH OBJECTS

Games involving manipulation of objects may be classified by the objects that are used, whether "found" items like stones, sticks, seeds, and plants, or manufactured objects like marbles, jacks, balls, and knives. In these games, strategy or dexterity is usually more important than physical strength. Some of the games involve trading and winning the objects used. The most fully collected aspect of games with objects is the terminology, which may be both elaborate and lengthy. The games played with marbles, for instance, have given rise to such terms as *fudgies, stickies, changies, roundsies, clearsies, lagging, steelie, dogob, vint, one knuckle down,* and *cateye.* Jacks players use terms such as *pig pens, around the world, taps, baskets, behind the fence,* and *lefties.* All too often, however, collectors stopped with such vocabulary, failing to document the rules and customs of play sufficiently. Thus, we have no full descriptions of knife games beyond the familiar mumbletypeg (others include baseball, territories, and chicken), and we have little data on the age groups, seasons, regions,

Boys playing marbles at the Farm Security Administration farm
workers' mobile unit, Friendly Corners, Arizona, 1942.

and individual places in which such games are played or about the
different rules or equipment appropriate for each.

Another area of equipped folk games little studied as yet is that
of variations of organized sports. Baseball or softball, for instance,
in folk groups are seldom played with full teams, game officials,
standard-size playing fields, and the like, Little League notwithstanding. Instead, neighborhood children will use their baseballs,
bats, and gloves for games like flies and grounders, scrub, work-up,
and stickball, adapting the rules to the terrain available and to the
prevailing customs. Similarly, in driveway and backyard basketball
games, there is only one basket, not two, and the game may range
all the way from simple basket shooting and scrambling for re-
bounds to elaborate spelling or mathematical contests controlled by
the drops of shots into the basket. ("C-o-w" is used for a short game,
"h-o-r-s-e" for a medium-length one, and "M-i-s-s-i-s-s-i-p-p-i" for
a long one.) The influence of playground supervisors may be felt on
group ball games such as dodge ball, but other games, such as Anthony Over (or anti over, rain on the roof, etc.), played by opposing
"sides" (teams) of from one on up, are completely traditional.

The survival of older folk games in play equipment now produced
by manufacturers also deserves study. Checkers, Parcheesi, and other
board games; darts, beanbags, and other target games; and most card
games have traditional ancestors on their family trees. At least two

manufactured toys—Frisbees and hackeysacks—are used frequently for playing traditional games, perhaps the most elaborate being "ultimate Frisbee," a game popular with college students. (There may also be games played with skateboards and snowboards, although none has been collected, so far.) The game of tiddlywinks, now commercially produced, probably had its origin in earlier play with homemade equipment. A counterpart folk game is still played by little girls in India with broken fragments of glass bangles (worn in bunches as bracelets), which they find washed out of the village dust after rainstorms and which they gamble with, attempting to win by snapping each other's bangle fragments out of a circle scratched in the ground. Marbles and jacks, on the other hand, are folk games played now with factory-made equipment. The former, moreover, has increasingly been normalized and regulated in organized tournaments by contest officials.

MENTAL GAMES

Games of mental activity are characterized by guessing, figuring, choosing, and the like, although they usually also involve some physical action as well, and often manipulation of objects. It is difficult to classify a game like lemonade (also called New Orleans, dumb trades, the dumbies' trade, etc.) that involves dialogue, acting, guessing, and chasing. But the heart of the game, emphasized in several of the variant names for it, is the procedure of one team acting out a kind of work and the other team guessing what it is. When the correct trade is named, the guessers chase the actors, and the game continues with different trades being imitated until all players have been caught. The game of statues is a similar active-mental combination game. A leader whirls and releases each player, who must then "freeze" in whatever posture the motion leaves him or her. Sometimes each statue is "turned on" so that it can come to life and behave like the person it represents. Then the leader selects the best "statue," or the funniest, to be next leader.

A few other games of mental activity are played outdoors—stone school on the front steps of a house, for instance, with each child advancing up through the grades (i.e., a step) by guessing which of "teacher's" hands holds a stone. But most are indoor games, called frequently *parlor games* or *party games*. Charades and twenty questions are two of these that eventually found their way into television "game shows," but a more complex one in folk tradition is Botticelli, often played by college students or faculty. It requires a leader to give the initials only of a personality, recent or past—real or fictional—in art, music, literature, history, etc. The group guesses at his or her identification by listing credentials that fit such figures with the same initials. Each time the leader cannot come up with the name that another player has in mind, the leader must answer truthfully a direct "yes or no" question about the person he or she is thinking of. Another popular guessing game is based on a kind of story riddle sometimes termed "logic problems." These are often mini murder mysteries "solved" by spotting such slips in the story as the murderer buying a round-trip ticket for himself or herself and a one-way for the victim, or using an icicle for a weapon that will melt without a clue. (So he or she thinks; it leaves a telltale puddle.)

Games involving drawn diagrams are usually called *pencil-and-paper games*, although they may occasionally be played on a blackboard or even scratched into the earth or sand. Ticktacktoe is the simplest and best known, and is often played as a triple contest, each player recording the games won as well as those that went to "the old cat" as ties. Another similar game is squares, or completing squares; the players alternate connecting dots in a pattern, and they win a point for each square they complete and initial. Battleship is similar, but requires two diagrams containing various hidden "ships," which the players attempt to "sink" by calling out the grid coordinates where they believe the ships are located. (This game and others have been adapted for commercial sale and mass production either as table games or video games.) Another game, hangman, ends when one player has been "hanged" by missing a guess (usually of letters in a person's name) for each line of a stick-figure drawing of a hanging man. (I saw a variation of hangman played with chalk on a sidewalk in Bucharest, Romania, in the 1970s. Instead of a hanging man, the players drew a small propane tank—commonly used for cooking—and a box of matches. If the full striking match was drawn by the winner of the game, the loser was said to be "blown up" by the exploding propane.)

Traditional letter and number puzzles, tricks, and amusements

A B C D E F G H I J K L
M N O P Q R S T U V W
X Y Z

A L F _ ED E. N EW _ AN

Hangman.

(such as those discussed in chapter 6) occasionally come close to being
games. Those played in automobiles, for example, have rules and
winners—the child wins who sees a whole alphabet in initial letters
of words on billboards or who sees the most distant state license
plate or the most out-of-state plates. (No fair counting except on
your own side of the car!) A similar adult amusement is the popular
office game of paycheck poker (or cribbage), in which the "kitty"
(cash) goes to the person whose paycheck serial number represents
the highest-scoring hand of cards. (These paycheck games have declined as workers more often than not have direct deposit of their
salaries into their bank accounts, but my father and his coworkers
in a Michigan office used to play the game faithfully every payday
during the 1940s and '50s.)

OTHER FOLK RECREATIONS

Several kinds of folk recreations will not fit clearly into any of the
above categories and must simply be grouped last. These include
practical jokes, kissing games, and drinking games.

Practical jokes do not qualify as true games because, in Richard
S. Tallman's definition, they consist of "a competitive play activity
in which only one of two opposing sides is consciously aware of the
fact that a state of play exists. . . . The unknowing side is made to
seem foolish or is caused some physical and/or mental discomfort."
Usually practical jokes require that all participants but one be in on
the joke. The dupe may be told that the group is going to play a
game called barnyard chorus; each player is assigned the name of

a farm animal whose sound he or she is to imitate loudly when a signal is given. What the dupe does not know is that everybody else will keep silent, and the unsuspecting person alone is left calling out the assigned animal sound—the bray of a donkey. Sometimes this trick is set up with the players blindfolded and assigned the animal sounds in pairs. Then when all the others have found their partners and removed their blindfolds, the poor "donkey" is still lonesomely braying and stumbling around the room. Other similar practical jokes are a trip to the dentist, during which the dupe receives a dash of pepper in his or her open mouth, and a mock contest involving a nickel balanced on the forehead, which is supposedly to be flipped down into a funnel stuck into the pants. The victim receives a glass of water poured into the funnel. In a variation of this prank a quarter is used, first being traced around with a soft pencil to create a "target." When the dupe rolls the quarter down his or her nose, the pencil lead on the coin's edge leaves a black streak on the person's face.

Many popular practical jokes take the form of the "fool's errand"—the newcomer to a job is sent searching and asking for a variety of nonexistent tools, materials, or other items. Among the best known of these "beguilers" are the "left-handed monkey wrench," the "skyhook," and the pilot's "bucket of prop-wash." Other terms suggest a more advanced technical knowledge of a trade: the banker's "key to the clearinghouse," for example.

One of the most venerable pranks is the snipe hunt, which remains a successful trick on an occasional youthful camper or club member. The other hunters explain the habits of the elusive snipe —prowling nocturnally for food and responding to a soft call or whistle. The victim is to hold a bag open and make the proper sound (sometimes also hold a flashlight or lantern), while the others will fan out in the woods to drive the snipe toward him. But all the tricksters simply go home, leaving the poor hunter dolefully "holding the bag" until realizing he or she has been fooled. Other old practical jokes are begun as elaborate ceremonies of initiation. In Introducing to the King and Queen, the butt of the joke is solemnly presented to a boy and girl who are seated on two chairs placed a chair's width apart and covered with a blanket or sheet. When the dupe is invited to sit between them, the royal figures rise, dropping their guest to the floor or into a tub of water.

Some practical jokes are individual gags pulled by a "trickster" on an unsuspecting audience, and only a few of these may be traditional. One prank that seems to be traditional is the "surprising drink" gambit. The prankster writes for a long time in a crowded library reading room, dipping his steel pen into a supposed well of ink (really grape juice). Suddenly he is seized with a fit of coughing so severe that it seems he will strangle unless he has a drink. Without blinking an eye, he takes up the "ink" and drinks it down. Or the trickster may carry his sample of urine (really ginger ale) into a doctor's waiting room. He examines it critically, then remarks "Looks a little thin; I'll run it through again," and drinks. Whatever their forms, pranks and practical jokes seem to have created another traditional form, the "practical-joke story," which describes past pranks and pranksters. Any of these might be analyzed, using Tallman's adaptation of the outline developed by Oliver H. P. Ferris, in terms of The Actors (prankster or pranksters versus victim or victims) and The Action (nature, intent, and result of the prank). For further pranks, see the discussion of school customs in chapter 15.

Focus: A Folklore Quiz

People in American Folklore

Identify each of the following in terms of his or her significance in American folklore.

> Ambrose Merton
> Polly Genesis
> Roy G. Biv
> Isaac Watts
> Len Henry
> Frank C. Brown
> Oliver H. P. Ferris
> O. J. Simpson
> Leonard Roberts

Source: A pop quiz given to a folklore class on April 1, 1996.

DISCUSSION TOPICS:

1. What proves that this quiz was an April Fool prank? Hint: the name O. J. Simpson was included in order to provide another "O."

2. All of these names may be found in *The Study of American Folklore*. Ambrose Merton, for example, is in the bibliographic notes to chapter 1. The next two names, of course, are not actual names of persons. Oliver H. P. Ferris, although mentioned in the book, is itself a hoax name, created as part of a prank at an American Folklore Society meeting. Why was it placed where it is in the book?

3. Hoax tests are traditional in higher education. (Perhaps you can collect some examples.) A mock Ph.D. folklore qualifying exam at Indiana University, for example, asked such questions as these: "Discuss the proverb 'There's many a slip 'twixt the cup and the lip' in the context of advanced graduate study in folklore" and "What books would you consult in preparing an introductory lecture on 'Structuralism and Deconstructionism in the History of Folkloristics' for *Sesame Street?*" What aspects of folklore study do such questions mock?

Kissing games take three different forms: *chasing kiss games* (like kiss in the ring), in which the kiss is a reward for catching a partner; *mixing kiss games* (like post office), in which pairing of couples occurs temporarily during the course of the game; and *couple kiss games* (like flashlight), in which couples are established beforehand and the game allows them to kiss each other repeatedly (partner exchanging may occur later in the game). The popularity of these three types with different age groups, at least in the past, was roughly equivalent to the first type with secondary-school pupils, the second type with junior- and senior-high school students, and the third with senior-high school and college students. Flashlight (or willpower, spotlight, etc.) illustrates the most actively companionable level of such games. "It" is seated in the center of a room holding a flashlight, and couples sit all around the darkened room. When "it" flashes the light on, he or she points it to a couple, and if they are not kissing, he or she changes places with the appropriate member. A few kissing games are more like couple amusements than true games. In perdiddle, for instance, the boy may kiss his girl companion if he sees a car with one headlight burned out and says "perdiddle" first. If she wins, she slaps him. In show kiss, a boy and girl attend a movie with a love plot, and every time the screen characters kiss, they do, too.

Drinking games are popular in many college and high school party groups, but they seldom surface for any public recognition, either by school administrators or folklorists. Only the gag sweatshirts lettered "Olympic Drinking Team" and the red-eyed, sleepy students in early-morning classes allude to them. Most drinking games are transparent excuses to "chug-a-lug"—that is, to down a drink of beer or liquor in one draught. The players supply themselves with drinks and then go through a complicated routine of some kind involving numbers, a speech, a series of actions, or a rhythmic chant. Whoever misses must chug-a-lug, refill his or her glass, and start over. The more often a player misses some requirement such as saying "Buzz" for all sevens and multiples of seven ("Buzz-buzz" for seventy-seven, etc.), the more that person drinks, and the more he or she tends to go on missing. Among the popular drinking games are quarters, Hi Bob!, categories, Cardinal Puff, and Colonel Powwow; in the latter two a mock title is conferred upon the player who successfully completes the game.

STUDYING AND ANALYZING GAMES

The first students of American children's folk games—who would have been scandalized at the idea of drinking games—believed that they were rescuing the last remaining fragments of an "expiring custom," as W. W. Newell expressed it. Newell wrote regretfully in his 1883 introduction:

> The vine of oral tradition, of popular poetry, which for a thousand years has twined and bloomed on English soil, in other days enriching with color and fragrance equally the castle and the cottage, is perishing at the roots; its prouder branches have long since been blasted, and children's song, its humble but longest-flowering offshoot, will soon have shared their fate.

Newell's explanations of the origins of children's games were typical of late-nineteenth-century folklore theories. He regarded them as belonging to the peasantry recently, but earlier descended from an upper-class source; they came, "from above, from the intelligent class." He also believed, somewhat contradictively, that some games contained survivals of ancient rites and customs. Thus, he singled out eleven for special discussion as "mythological games." The familiar London Bridge, for example, was not only "a representation of the antagonism of celestial and infernal powers," but also an enactment of the human sacrifice once practiced to placate "the elemental spirit of the land, who detests any interference with the solitude he loves, [and] has an especial antipathy to bridges." (Newell's counterpart in England, Lady Alice B. Gomme, went even further with a survivals explanation for the game London Bridge, comparing several sacrifices associated with building foundations in the "actual facts of contemporary savagery" to traditions about London associated with the game.) But despite the romanticism of Newell's attitude toward games, the frills in his writing style, and the doubtful nature of his theories, his published texts and notes on American children's singing games were the groundwork for later studies.

FOCUS: ARE CHILDREN'S GAMES DYING OUT?

That the old-time ring and round games, such as children and, not so long ago, grown people, have played of summer evenings since human memory reaches, are gradually dying out, it is very generally acknowledged by every one who takes an interest in children's pastimes.

Twenty, or even ten years ago, our city streets and country greens were musical with voices of children in the refrains:

As we go round the mulberry bush
The mulberry bush, the mulberry bush,
As we go round the mulberry bush,
So early in the morning.

or

Green grow the rushes, oh,
Green grow the rushes, oh.
He who will my true love be
Come and sit by the side of me.

and that other, so well known:

Ring a round a rosy,
A bottle full of posy,
All the girls in our town
Ring for little Josie.

Nowadays, if we wish to hear these quaint, childish rhymes sung in play, we must go down to the poorest quarters of the city, where the shrill voices of the gamins still may be heard occasionally piping these fragments of songs, as they indulge in games which once amused kings and courtiers. But even the slum children are fast abandoning old-time plays, and the indications are that but a few years are needed for Time, like an auctioneer, to have cried out for the last time, "Going, going, gone!" and, finding no bidder, ring down the curtain, and pack away these abandoned games in one of oblivion's dark corners, where no children will ever think to look for them, and where only an occasional student of folk-lore will have the hardihood to bring them to light.

Source: E. Leslie Gilliams, "Folk-Lore of Children's Games," *The Peterson Magazine*, n.s. 5 (Nov. 1895), pp. 1184–92.

DISCUSSION TOPICS:

1. The demise of older folklore has repeatedly been announced. Do you recognize the games quoted, or others mentioned in the article, such as London Bridge; Miss Jennie O'Jones; Here come three ducks a-roving; and oats, peas, beans, and barley grow? Do modern American children play any traditional singing games?

2. What explanation of the games' origin is suggested in this passage? (Other parts of the article claim some games are "survivals of religious customs [or of] primitive customs which have now died out.") What proofs do authors of this period offer for such interpretations?

3. Where does the author assume that the last of the old games might still be played? Is this idea supported by recent folklore collecting among children?

In analyses of children's games, American folklorists seem to have bypassed the stage that was so important in folktale studies—that of historic-geographic studies. There are no monographs on American games to compare with one by a Finnish scholar on the European "Game of Rich and Poor" that was done according to the classic "Finnish method" of Aarne and Krohn. Instead of this, folkgame scholars in the United States have proceeded directly from classification and annotation to studies of the meaning, function, and structure of games. Some investigators have begun simply by asking children what their games mean to them and why they like them —always an interesting line of inquiry. In general it appears that

what many children like most about games is the dramatic element.
They tend to identify with the situations and characters represented
in games, and they especially prefer games that suit their own personalities best. Often the children's comments will be gems of analysis (or "oral-literary criticism") in themselves. One shy child wrote
for a folklorist who visited her class, "The game which I love best
is grean gravel because it is not plaid ruffly." Another, responding
to the delight of a collector in a rare game, said quietly, "I like this
one best because you like it."

The game preferences of American children since the 1890s have
been fairly closely documented in folklore studies. One survey covering the years 1895 to 1944 for the city of St. Louis pointed out the
gradual disappearance there of the older English games, the increasing influence of school games, and the occasional invention of new
folk games. A more recent study extended the data in both time and
space, including surveys from 1896, 1898, 1921, and 1959, in Massachusetts, South Carolina, San Francisco, and Ohio, respectively.
Fully 180 different games or pastimes were involved, and conclusions
were drawn concerning changing boy-girl game preferences and the
changes in types of games played. One interesting finding in the
study was that girls have definitely tended toward the traditional
male roles in games (perhaps to match the emancipation of women
in American society). At the same time, boys have tended increasingly to reject roles in games that they feel smack of femininity
(hopscotch, jacks, jump rope, etc.), retreating instead to the rougher
masculine sports where girls could traditionally follow only as cheerleaders or spectators. Another suggestion of the study was that formal games of a traditional nature may at last be dying out, as the
organized and commercialized distractions of American society take
over.

As the structural movement in folktale studies influenced game
studies, Alan Dundes suggested that a folktale may be described as
"a two-dimensional series of actions displayed on a one-dimensional
track," and a game as "structurally speaking, a two-dimensional
folktale." In other words, the hero and villain "motifemes" (see
chapter 10), which are simply narrated one at a time in a folktale,
are assumed as dramatic characterizations in many folk games and
then acted out to a conclusion. But whereas in tales the hero always
wins, in games either side may conquer. Interestingly, there are also

parallels in special forms of tales and games; for example, the cumulative tale has its counterpart in a game like link tag, and the trickster tale is reflected in practical jokes.

Another development in game studies came from what has been called the behavioral or contextual approach to folklore. Expressing the dissatisfaction of some folklorists with "merely collecting and annotating [game] texts and studying them within diffusionist and survivalist frameworks," and so drawing instead upon "the work of social scientists who are interested in dynamic processes," Robert A. Georges proposed using behavioral models as a device for a holistic analysis of what he preferred to call "traditional play activities." Postulating that such activities are social events involving person-to-person communication as well as cognitive experiences that are clearly recognized by all players as "play," Georges has drawn up three proposed models to represent schematically some kinds of communication and interaction that occur during play. For example:

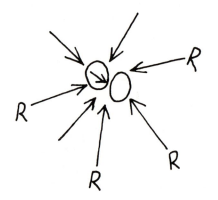

One social entity encodes and transmits to the other(s) a message, indicating his or her desire to engage in a particular traditional play activity. (The outside arrows represent general social rules; those marked "R" are specifically "play rules" that define this particular play activity.)

The above may seem like an overly jargonistic and complex way of representing a common situation, such as when one child says to others, "Hey, let's play kick-the-can!" It should be remembered, however, that such "game models" are only analytic devices drawn up in hopes of understanding the much more complex nature of traditional play itself. They serve as analogies or schematic representations of patterns of social interaction that constitute a clear basis for comparisons and further analysis. Also, such analyses ultimately derive from the same basic fieldwork and reference work in folklore as did earlier studies; as Georges put it, his data are from "personal observation . . . participation . . . [and] printed descriptions and texts of traditional play activities." But whether viewed from a comparative, psychological, structural, or behavioral approach, certainly folk games still offer a fertile and partly untilled field for folklore collectors, classifiers, and analysts.

BIBLIOGRAPHIC NOTES

The new and enlarged edition (1903) of W. W. Newell's *Games and Songs of American Children* became the standard one. It was reprinted in paperback by Dover Books (New York) in 1963. Lady Alice B. Gomme's important collection *The Traditional Games of England, Scotland, and Ireland*, published in two volumes in 1894 and 1898, was published as a Dover paperback in 1964. The introductions by Carl Withers for Newell and Dorothy Howard for Gomme are important essays on game study.

Paul G. Brewster's article "Games and Sports in Sixteenth- and Seventeenth-Century English Literature," *WF* (1947): 143–56, helps to give historical depth to studies of modern games. Brewster's work in collecting, classifying, and annotating games has been prolific and important, especially in his book *American Non-Singing Games* (Norman: University of Oklahoma Press, 1953), and his editing of the games in *The Frank C. Brown Collection of North Carolina Folklore* (1: 29–159). A varied and well-annotated collection in a folklore journal is Warren E. Roberts's "Children's Games and Game Rhymes," *HF* 8 (1949): 7–34. Iona and Peter Opie's book *Children's Games in Street and Playground* (New York: Oxford University Press, 1969) contains British children's games, many of which have parallels in the United States.

Several scholars proposed sweeping theories concerning games and the impulse to play. Outstanding among them is Roger Caillois, editor of *Diogenes*, who published in that journal "The Structure and Classification of Games" (12 [1955]: 62–75) and "Unity of Play: Diversity of Games" (19 [1957]: 92–121). Both articles were stages leading up to his book *Man, Play, and Games* (New York: Free Press of Glencoe, 1961). An anthropological approach is represented in John M. Roberts, Malcolm J. Arth, and Robert R. Bush, "Games in Culture," *AA* 61 (1959): 597–605. Roberts collaborated with Brian Sutton-Smith and Adam Kendon in a special application of this theory in "Strategy in Games and Folk Tales," *JSP* 61 (1963): 185–99. Starting with the observation that "conflicts induced by child training . . . lead to involvement in games . . . which in turn provide[s] . . . learning important both to players and their societies," these scholars confirmed their hypothesis that "folktales with strategic outcomes would be found in the same cultural setting as games of strategy." They did this by comparing games and tales from several cultures, sorted on the basis of whether strategy was present, and correlating these with other data on the cultures.

Pastimes have seldom been treated in separate folklore studies. For articles on cat's cradle we must turn to British publications—W. Innes Pocock's article in *Folklore* 17 (1906): 73–93, 351–73; and Dorothy Howard's in the same journal, 72 (1961): 385–87. A fascinating little booklet, Kathleen Haddon's *String Games for Beginners*, first published in 1934, was still in print until recently. The forty-page pamphlet contains descriptions of twenty-eight string figures from various native cultures, with instructions for learning them, and even a piece of string with which to practice. The pamphlet was published by W. Heffer and Sons, Ltd., Cambridge, England. The 1906 book by Caroline Furness Jayne, *String Figures and How to Make Them*, with an introduction by A. C. Haddon, was republished in paperback by Dover Books (New York, 1962). See also Lyn Harrington, "Eskimo String Figures," *School Arts* 50 (May 1951): 319–21, which has some good photographs although limited discussion.

Ray B. Browne's article on California jump-rope rhymes, cited in the notes to chapter 7, analyzes the various actions of this popular pastime as well as the rhymes that are chanted with them. A much more analytical study of this tradition is Marjorie Harness Goodwin's "The Serious Side of Jump Rope: Conversational Practice and Social Organization in the Frame of Play," *JAF* 98 (1985): 315–30.

The pastime called Chinese jump rope, which started to be popular in the United States about 1963, has been described in Ruth Hawthorne's "Classifying Jump-Rope Games," *KFQ* 11 (1966): 113–26; and Michael Owen Jones's "Chinese Jumprope," *SFQ* 30 (1966): 256–63. The pastime is performed with two players holding a long elastic loop stretched between their ankles while a third player, jumping in and out of it, stretches it into patterns with his or her toes. The same pastime with the same name (*Kinesersjip*) was reported from Copenhagen; see Erik Kaas Nielsen's *Det lille Folk* (Forlaget Fremad, 1965). Roger Welsch discussed a group of "Nebraska Finger Games" (mostly pastimes) in *WF* 25 (1966): 173–94.

A reminiscent study of children's neighborhood play is Thomas S. Yukic's "Niagara River Playground: The Allen Avenue Gang, 1925–1946 (An Historical Glance at a Boyhood on the Niagara River)," *NYF* 1 (1975): 210–28.

A good survey of some older games is found in Mac E. Barrick's chapter "Games from the Little Red School House" in *Two Penny Ballads and Four Dollar Whiskey*, ed. Kenneth S. Goldstein and Robert H. Byington (Hatboro, Pa.: Folklore Associates, 1966), pp. 95–120. Another such article, Gilbert C. Kettelkamp's "Country School Games in the Past," *MAF* 8 (1981): 113–23, discusses early-twentieth-century games from south-central Illinois called blackman, darebase, hatball, sowhole, and longtown.

Various games of physical action are described in Eugenia L. Millard's "Racing, Chasing, and Marching with the Children of the Hudson-Champlain Valleys," *NYFQ* 15 (1959): 132–50. Vance Randolph and Nancy Clemens's article "Ozark Mountain Party-Games," in *JAF* 49 (1936): 199–206, describes a variety of guessing games, forfeit games, courtship games, kissing games, and active games in a regional folk culture. John Harrington Cox printed forty texts of singing games from West Virginia with bibliography and musical notation in *SFQ* 6 (1942): 183–261. Active games of city children were early collected by Steward Culin in "Street Games of Boys in Brooklyn, N.Y.," *JAF* 4 (1891): 221–37. Excellent candid photographs of New York City children playing five popular street games were published in "Youths' Concrete Joys," *Sports Illustrated* (August 17, 1959), pp. 18–22.

Some games of racial and ethnic minorities are studied in Bessie Jones and Bess Lomax Hawes, *Step It Down: Games, Plays, Songs, and Stories from the Afro-American Heritage* (cited in Focus: "Little Sally Walker"; in Margaret K. Brady, " 'Gonna Shimmy Shimmy 'til the Sun Goes Down': Aspects of Verbal and Nonverbal Socialization in the Play of Black Girls," *Folklore Annual* 6 (1974): 1–16; and in Clement L. Valetta, "Friendship and Games in Italian-American Life," *KFQ* 15 (1970): 174–87.

An essay on a game played with objects is J. W. Ashton's "Marble Playing in Lewiston [Maine] Fifty Years Ago," *NEF* 3 (1960): 24–27. A more rigorously statistical article along the same lines (but concerning New Zealand) is Brian Sutton-Smith's "Marbles Are In," *WF* 12 (1953): 186–93. (This essay is reprinted in Sutton-Smith's *The Folkgames of Children*, mentioned below, pp. 455–64.) An extremely thorough study of the history of one ball game is Erwin Mehl's article "Baseball in the Stone Age," *WF* 7 (1948): 145–61, supplemented by further notes in *WF* 8 (1949): 152–56. Robert Cochran's "The Interlude of Game: A Study of Washers," *WF* 38 (1979): 71–82, describes a pitching game, somewhat like horseshoes, played by adults using metal washers about two inches in diameter.

Games based on mental activity are seldom treated separately from other games. Three exceptions are Eugenia L. Millard's article "A Sampling of Guessing Games," in *NYFQ* 13 (1957): 135–43, and two articles on games played by college teachers or students: Michael Dane Moore, "Linguistic Aggression and Literary Allusion," *WF* 38 (1979): 259–66; and John William Johnson, "Killer: An American Campus Folk Game," *IF* 13 (1980): 81–101. An interesting popular piece is Martin Gardner's "Mathematical Games. A Bit of Foolishness for April Fools' Day," in *Scientific American* 208 (April 1963): 156–66.

Practical jokes have attracted several studies. Anne Penick described six favorite pranks in "Look Out, Newcomer!" *MF* 4 (1954): 239–43. Kelsie Harder discussed introductions to the King and Queen under the title "The Preacher's Seat," in *TFSB* 23 (1957): 38–39. The prank called going to see the widow has been the subject of several notes, which were consolidated and supplemented by Wayland D. Hand in *WF* 17 (1958): 275–76. An interesting example of a practical joke apparently growing out of a folktale was described by James Ralston Caldwell in "A Tale Actualized in a Game," *JAF* 54 (1945): 50. Some pranks involving use of the telephone are discussed by Norine Dresser in *NYFQ* 29 (1973): 121–30; and Marilyn Jorgensen, "A Social-Interactional Analysis of Phone Pranks," *WF* 43 (1984): 104–16.

Pranks concerning automobiles may be found in an article by M. Licht in *NYFQ* 30 (1974): 44–65. A special issue of *SFQ*, edited by Richard S. Tallman and devoted to studies of practical jokes, contains a note and five extended essays on such subjects as definitions of the genre, wedding pranks, and summer-camp pranks; see the December 1974 issue (38: 251–331). Pranks are an important part of the behavior described by Robert S. McCarl, Jr., in "Smokejumper Initiation: Ritualized Communication in a Modern Occupation," *JAF* 89 (1976): 49–66.

A number of important studies by Brian Sutton-Smith, a leading student of children's games, has been printed in the AFS Bibliographical and Special Series (No. 24) as *The Folkgames of Children* (Austin: University of Texas Press, 1972). Among these is his 1959 essay "The Kissing Games of Adolescents in Ohio," which furnished the terminology used in this chapter. Richard M. Dorson discussed college drinking games in chapter 7 of *American Folklore*, pp. 265–66.

The historic-geographic study of the dramatic European "Game of Rich and Poor" was published by Mrs. Elsa Enäjärvi Haavio in *FFC* no. 100 (1932). An important early study of American children's games and the attitudes of their players was made by Jean Olive Heck, "Folk Poetry and Folk Criticism, as Illustrated by Cincinnati Children in Their Singing Games and Their Thoughts about These Games," *JAF* 40 (1927): 1–77. Leah Rachel Clara Yoffie published her study "Three Generations of Children's Singing Games in St. Louis" in *JAF* 60 (1947): 1–51; Brian Sutton-Smith's more comprehensive article along similar lines was the 1961 publication "Sixty Years of Historical Change in the Game Preferences of American Children," reprinted in *The Folkgames of Children*, pp. 258–81. Alan Dundes, who proposed the structural approach to folktales, has applied his theories to games in "On Game Morphology: A Study of the Structure of Non-Verbal Folklore," *NYFQ* 20 (1964): 276–88, reprinted in *Analytic Essays in Folklore*, pp. 80–87, and in *Readings in American Folklore*, pp. 334–44. Robert A. Georges outlined the contextual-behavioral approach referred to at the end of this chapter in "The Relevance of Models for Analyses of Traditional Play Activities," *SFQ* 33 (1969): 1–23. A more recent analytical article is Jay Mechling, "Patois and Paradox in a Boy Scout Treasure Hunt," *JAF* 97 (1984): 24–42.

IV

MATERIAL FOLK
TRADITIONS

Essentially, the order of subjects presented in this book follows the general history of studies of American folk traditions, from the folk*lore* interest begun in the late nineteenth century to the folk*life* studies from the 1960s up to today. These final chapters deal with material folk traditions, which constitute the largest part of the field of folklife and, in the United States, perhaps the fastest-growing branch. Material folk traditions are too diverse to be covered in a few pages, so the following chapters are mainly an outline of materials, representative examples, and a summary of what present studies suggest, along with some technical guidelines on recording, documenting, and analyzing material traditions. Following a general introduction to folklife studies, the areas surveyed are folk architecture, folk handicrafts and art, folk costumes, and folk foods.

19

FOLKLIFE

FOLKLIFE AND FOLKLORE

The concept of "folklife," introduced in chapter 15 in connection with customs and festivals, offers a promising area for original research in American folklore. Offsetting generations of literature-oriented text-dominated folklore studies, the students of American folklife now examine the whole range of traditional verbal lore, behavior, and material creations in folk circulation, especially the latter category. In most instances, the term "folklife" as used in American folklore study refers to traditional material culture.

In theory, the term "folklore" would seem to be synonymous with "folklife," and, in fact, many American folklorists in their publications have employed the term in this way. For example, in the foreword to his 1959 book *American Folklore* Richard M. Dorson wrote that

> "folklore" usually suggests the oral traditions channeled across the centuries through human mouths. In its flexible uses folklore may refer to types of barns, bread molds, or quilts; to orally inherited tales, songs, sayings, and beliefs; or to village festivals, household customs, and peasant rituals.

We recognize here the familiar triad (in Dorson's order of listing) of material traditions, oral traditions, and customary traditions. Yet Dorson's book itself barely touched upon a few material traditions, and none of them was illustrated, except for a photograph of a rail fence on the dust jacket of the book.

Alan Dundes's book *The Study of Folklore* (1965) contained chapters on painted hex marks ("barn stars") and on the practice of water witching as well as on several forms of oral folk traditions, but the book never used the term "folklife." Obviously, the present book is similar, having the word "folklore" in its title, but equally surveying "folklife." Even though the material-culture component of the book has grown steadily since the first edition in 1968, the book has not been retitled *The Study of American Folklife*, as it well might be. "Folklore" is still assumed to be the broader term, encompassing "folklife."

Richard M. Dorson's book *Folklore and Folklife: An Introduction* (1972) reflected in its contents as well as its title the growing attention to material folk traditions. But in a brief comparison of the two words in his preface, Dorson pictured them as competing for the name of the discipline:

> In recent years another term, folklife, has vied with and even threatened to dominate folklore. The supporters of folklife studies claim that folklorists are too narrowly preoccupied with verbal forms and neglect the tangible products of folk artisans. They maintain that folklife embraces the whole panorama of traditional culture, including oral folklore. Conversely, the champions of folklore stoutly maintain that their term includes traditional arts and crafts. The following chapters give equal time and space to the two terms, recognizing their nuances and their partnership.

Published in 1983, Dorson's important *Handbook of American Folklore* (like *Folklore and Folklife*, it is an anthology containing chapters by many scholars) failed even to mention "folklife" by name, either in the preface or the index. Yet the term was prominent in separate chapters on artifacts and folk museums, and most notably in Charles Camp's essay "Developing a State Folklife Program." Archie Green, in his chapter "Interpreting Folklore Ideologically," offered this capsule account of the spread and use of the term "folk-life" among American scholars:

> In 1967 the [Festival of American Folklife's] director Ralph Rinzler had borrowed the label "folklife" from Professor Don Yoder, who had learned it in European usage (material culture, regional ethnology). Smithsonian staff members extended "folklife" broadly to encompass dramatic and musical performance, craft demonstration, decorative art, and ritualistic behavior by a wide variety of people. Through four Congresses (91, 92, 93, 94), individual legislators equated the words "folklore" and "folklife," and defined each largely in commonsense terms of rurality, ethnicity, and artisanship.

So "folklore" continues to be the general term of choice, even though "folklife" has its distinctive usage as well. As discussed in chapter 1, when a national institution to preserve and study American folk traditions was established in 1976, the enabling legislation was called the American Folklife Preservation Act, and the office created took the name American Folklife Center. Still, the leading independent scholarly group devoted to the study of American folk traditions retains the name American Folklore Society, and its quarterly is the *Journal of American Folklore*. Almost without exception, the researchers who pursue these studies, whatever their affiliations, call themselves "folklorists."

University of Pennsylvania folklorist Don Yoder, a specialist in Pennsylvania German traditions and in folk religion, is credited with introducing the term "folklife" to American folklore studies in a 1963 article titled "The Folklife Studies Movement." Better known and highly influential was Yoder's 1976 anthology *American Folklife*, which contained important historical and theoretical statements on the "new" field. Contributors to the volume discussed topics including folk architecture, boatbuilding, basketry, and various customs and rituals. As for the basic terminology, Yoder wrote, "I prefer to follow [others] in subsuming folklore (defining it after William Bascom as the verbal arts of a society) under folklife, as only one aspect of folk culture." However, since American folklorists as a group did not adopt "folklife" full scale for their journals, scholarly societies, and teaching, we continue to define "folklife," as Yoder wrote in 1976, "by default," to mean only customary and material folk traditions, even though there seems to be good reason to substitute the word immediately and permanently for the much-abused term "folklore." And in practice, as a strategy for defining "folklife" itself, many folklorists tend to rely on a mere list of examples.

FOCUS: WHAT IS FOLKLIFE?

Folklife is reflected in the names we bear from birth, invoking affinities with saints, ancestors, or cultural heroes. Folklife is the secret languages of children, the codenames of CB operators, and the working slang of watermen and doctors. It is the shaping of everyday experiences in stories swapped around kitchen tables or parables told from pulpits. It is the African-American rhythms embedded in gospel hymns, bluegrass music, and hip-hop, and the Lakota flutist rendering anew his people's ancient courtship songs.

Folklife is the sung parodies of the "Battle Hymn of the Republic" and the variety of ways there are to skin a muskrat, preserve string beans, or join two pieces of wood. Folklife is society welcoming new members at bris and christening, and keeping the dead incorporated on All Saints Day. It is the marking of the Jewish New Year at Rosh Hashanah and the Persian New Year at Noruz. It is the evolution of vaqueros into buckaroos, and the riderless horse, its stirrups backward, in the funeral processions of high military commanders.

Folklife is the thundering of foxhunters across the rolling Rappahannock countryside and the listening of hilltoppers to hounds crying fox in the Tennessee mountains. It is the twirling of lariats at western rodeos, and the spinning of double-dutch jumpropes in West Philadelphia. It is scattered across the landscape in Finnish saunas and Italian vineyards; engraved in the split rail boundaries of Appalachian "hollers" and the stone fences around Catskill "cloves"; scrawled on urban streetscapes by graffiti artists; and projected onto skylines by the tapering steeples of churches, mosques, and temples.

Source: Mary Hufford, *American Folklife: A Commonwealth of Cultures* (Washington, D.C.: American Folklife Center, 1991), title page.

DISCUSSION TOPICS:

1. How many specific genres of folklife are mentioned here, and which are verbal, customary, and material? (Note that Hufford does not use the word "folklore" here, though on the next page she mentions that the two terms "often are used interchangeably.")

2. Which ethnic, regional, occupational, religious, and age-related groups are alluded to here?

3. Are any examples listed, either of folklife topics or of folk groups, that seem to you questionable as "folk"? Why are they included?

Another preliminary problem is the lack of widely accepted procedures and theories for American folklife studies, many of which in the past have been simply descriptive approaches to individual artifacts or artisans. Again, Don Yoder offered early guidance, identifying in *American Folklife* "three essentially different approaches": Historical Folklife Studies, Folklife Studies and Survivals, and Folklife Studies and the Ethnographic Present. One example of the first approach is Theodore Blegen's documenting of the "grass-roots history" of Norwegian-American folk culture; of the second, the efforts to preserve examples of early American folk architecture; and of the third, questionnaire surveys of existing traditional crafts, such as quilting.

The usual direction in which American scholars looked for a model of folklife studies was to Europe, especially Scandinavia, where systematic research of this kind began. In Sweden, for example, folklife study dates from the end of the nineteenth century, with the establishment of museums of folk architecture and folk artifacts. The distinctive Scandinavian format for presentation of research to the public became the open-air collection of old farmhouses and outbuildings, the earliest museum being *Skansen* (part of a large park near Stockholm), which was shortly imitated in Norway, Denmark, Finland, and eventually in many central and eastern European countries.

Leading American folklife scholar Warren E. Roberts, of Indiana University, has written about how he was personally influenced by the Norwegian example:

When the time for my first sabbatical leave approached, I applied for and received a Fulbright Research Award to Norway. I left with my family in the fall of 1959 and spent nearly a full year working in the Norwegian Folklore Archives in Oslo.

I also visited the Norwegian National Folk Museum at Bygdøy

near Oslo. These visits had a profound influence on me. It is no exaggeration to say that I went to Norway as a folktale scholar but that I returned to the United States as a folklife researcher. I was fascinated by the way that Norwegian scholars had studied the old way of life of the Norwegian countryside and had preserved buildings and other artifacts in the folk museums.

While the organized study of folklife in the United States began in the 1960s, the term itself has deeper roots. In Germany both *Volksleben* (folklife) and *Volkskunde* (folk art) were used from the early 1800s, while the Swedish *folkliv* (folklife) and its counterpart terms in Norwegian and Danish were in use by the mid-nineteenth century. But it was not until 1937 that the Swedes formally launched their term for the whole field by beginning publication of the journal *Folk-Liv*, helpfully printing all of its articles in English. The Swedish classification system for archiving folklife was soon widely adopted, and, as it happened, the most convenient sources in English based on the Swedish pattern dealt with Irish folklife. Thus, the official collectors' guide used in Ireland, *A Handbook of Irish Folklore* (Dublin: Irish Folklore Commission, 1942; reprint, Hatboro, Pa.: Folklore Associates, 1963), summarized all the materials to be investigated, while a book like E. Estyn Evans's *Irish Folk Ways* (New York: Devin-Adair, 1957) gave a systematic discussion of the findings of fieldwork and research. The Swedish example, partly mediated through Irish publications, shaped the American field of folklife studies.

CONCEPTIONS AND MISCONCEPTIONS

Before the word "folklife" entered the general vocabulary of American folklorists, a considerable number of what might be termed folklife studies were done in the United States from the point of view of art history and centering on folk crafts and folk art. Some art historians continue to use the term "folk art" in the special sense of work by artists lacking formal training and reflecting everyday life. (Other terms sometimes used for such art are "vernacular," "primitive," and "outsider.") An important task of American folklife research, then, has been to locate, evaluate, and synthesize these borderline studies in order to establish a critical bibliography for the field and to determine what genuinely traditional material has already been described. The beginning student must recognize that not every publication about handicrafts or "folk art" takes a folkloristic approach; indeed, some folklorists now prefer to ignore terms like "folk" and "tradition" in their studies of objects that ordinary people create and embellish in their own individual ways. A review of two representative older publications—one a period survey and the other concerning a particular group—illustrates some of the differences between these writings and modern folklife research on similar material.

To a degree the popular interest in folk arts and crafts that arose in the 1920s and 1930s was a reaction against nonrepresentational modern art, but at the same time, ironically, the modern-art movement claimed folk art as part of its own background. In 1932 The Museum of Modern Art, in New York, arranged an exhibition called American Folk Art, the subtitle of which—The Art of the Common Man in America, 1750–1900—revealed two typical attitudes toward the subject. The first implication was that "folk art" must be the work of "common" people or, as the text explained, "people with little book learning in art techniques, and no academic training." The second implication was that the golden age of such art in America extended from the middle of the eighteenth century to the beginning of the twentieth. Further, the classification of the works by medium (oil, pastel, watercolor, velvet painting, wood sculpture, metal sculpture, etc.) suggested that folk art, like academic art, should be viewed as mainly "creative" rather than utilitarian. That is, the artifacts chosen for display were judged significant for their decorative, not their functional, qualities. Yet many of the works illustrated were definitely useful (and, it may be hoped, effective), such as weather vanes, advertising symbols (like cigar-store Indians), and signs. So it seems that once these kinds of things were admitted as "art," the door should have been opened for needlework, quilting, basketry, pottery, toymaking, and many other crafts now studied by folklife scholars, and valued (by folk and folklorists alike) for both their beauty and their utility. Unfortunately, few of these folk-art scholars pursued such crafts seriously, and now it seems doubtful that the media and period classifications of such art histories serve a useful purpose in folklife studies.

Numerous books and articles were based on a similar conception of American folk art, although there is much diversity in the examples to which they refer. A broader scope is found in works on folk groups and their artifacts, such as the studies of Pennsylvania German (or "Dutch") material traditions. All the distinctive forms of building, handicrafts, and decorative art in this regional-immigrant group were the subject of attention, but the approaches and findings here were usually not applicable to other American folk groups. The very impressive fruits of Pennsylvania German folklife studies inspire students of Anglo-American materials, but they cannot say much about what the students will find elsewhere or how they should approach it.

A second early "folklife" survey was Frances Lichten's *Folk Art of Rural Pennsylvania*, published in 1946. The folk art shown here was "rural," and it flourished, according to Lichten's discussion, from the middle of the eighteenth century to about 1850. "Art" here was taken to include such disparate items as coverlets, butter molds, stove plates, and decorated barns (i.e., those bearing "hex marks"). The arrangement of items was again by medium, but this time keyed to the close relationship of old-time farm life with the land—its raw materials, its crops, and its supported animals. Such a classification brought together some odd combinations: stone houses or foundations for houses were grouped with gravestones ("from beneath the surface of the earth"); wood houses were placed with cabinetmaking and ornamental carving ("from the woodland"); and thatching was paired with basketry ("from the surface of the earth"). The book, with its many good illustrations, presented a nostalgic picture of the arts and crafts of a special group in a bygone era, but a different presentation was required for scholars who wanted to investigate American folklife more generally, particularly if they intended to study modern instances of material folk tradition.

There is some question, however, whether folklife studies should properly include contemporary traditions at all. Warren Roberts insists on the necessity of focusing on what he terms "the old traditional way of life" and of studying mainly the traditions belonging to or deriving from "the great mass of people in the pre-industrial era." Roberts explains:

The Industrial Revolution was a great upheaval that drastically altered the way of life of vast numbers of people, a way of life that
had persisted for centuries. . . . The pre-industrial way of life was
predominantly rural . . . [and] because rural people in earlier times
left few written records, the folklife researcher concentrates on
fieldwork.

Other prominent folklife scholars—including several trained by
Roberts at Indiana University—assert that descriptive fieldwork concentrating on the old traditional way of life (sometimes abbreviated
OTWOL) is insufficient, and that theories must precede collection
of data, while modern urban life may yield such traditional artifacts
for study as individually made curbside trashcan holders, homemade
basketball hoops, and decorated inner-city townhouses. They also
contend that even as older folklife patterns fade from use, new forms
appear.

FOCUS: CHANGING FOLKLIFE IN NORTH CAROLINA

*The folklife of the old North Carolina disappears. Tobacco barns sag
and rot beneath mounds of trumpet vines. Past them the highway crews
lay sand-white bands of concrete that roll over successive hilltops between
the towns of the Triangle and the Triad. The towns themselves soon
follow after the roads, spreading and meshing with one another. Service
to tourists replaces the family farm. Developers turn the textile mill into
a shopping mall. Rock videos resound on the commercial airwaves, while
the Center for Public Broadcasting wafts out British comedies and glossy
National Geographic "specials" on the costumes of ptarmigans. An enter-
prising Texan suddenly beams down a giant emerald skyscraper onto a
piney hilltop in Durham.*

*But all these changes give rise to new tensions and new folklife. The
corridors of the skyscraper rustle with acidic jokes bred by the tedium and
jockeying for power in corporate America. Outside, resentful neighbors
pass a rumor that the building has a tilt and will have to be torn down.
At a nearby college campus a gathering of young Lumbees encircles a
drum, chanting powwow songs learned in the Great Plains. In Raleigh,
a few miles downhill from the capitol building, a new gospel choir of
black and white "inmates" in a "women's correctional facility" sing in
call-and-response their discovery of God's love. In nearby counties Mex-
ican-born workers tend dairy cattle and on weekends dance to the music*

of the Fuerza Quatro at a baile. Scattered through the piedmont, pockets of Hmong and Montagnard refugees displaced from highland villages of Vietnam or Laos struggle to make room for themselves in a world of alien ways. Meanwhile sheriffs in Wilkes and Mecklenburg counties report calls from parents terrified by rumors of cults that plan to kidnap a hundred blond boys. And a journalist in North Carolina's largest and most cosmopolitan city hears of a shooting and speeds into print with a news story headlined "Murder Charge Dismissed Against Woman Under 'Spell.'"

Source: Daniel W. Patterson and Charles G. Zug III, eds., *Arts in Earnest: North Carolina Folklife* (Durham, N.C.: Duke University Press, 1990), pp. 23–24. (The Triangle and Triad are large areas of North Carolina where various high-tech laboratories and think tanks are located; the Texan's giant skyscraper, though futuristic in design, was built normally—from the ground up. The PBS nature special alluded to was about seasonal color changes in a northern bird.)

DISCUSSION TOPICS:

1. What forces have caused old North Carolina folklife to disappear? How does the author of this section seem to regard some elements of modern life in North Carolina?

2. What genres of new folklife have developed, and within what folk groups?

3. Can you compose a similar list of modern influences, disappearing traditions, and new traditions applicable to your own area?

Whatever materials are documented in fieldwork, they must be classified in some manner to be useful to scholars. The principle of classification for folklife materials developed in Sweden and followed in Ireland and elsewhere in Europe was not by medium or materials used but by the needs to which customs and artifacts were applied, beginning with land use, cultivation, housing, settlement, and subsistence crafts, and proceeding through furniture, domestic handwork, leisure-time handicrafts, decorative arts, representational art, musical instruments, folk toys, and the like. Basically, it is a logical arrangement of the whole gamut of traditional customs and materials, ranging from the necessities of life to the luxuries and pleasures.

For the purpose of a systematic presentation of the kinds of folklife, we have already dealt briefly with the customary traditions in section III. The study of material traditions (*folk artifacts*) presents special problems, however, which are best taken up separately. When studying them, researchers will still collect, classify, and analyze data (see chapter 2), but must also learn some new techniques. Folk artifacts must be photographed or sketched, even if they are going to be brought in physically from the field for an archive or a museum. For most field-workers, then, this means the ability to make simple measured drawings and the acquisition of at least the rudiments of good documentary still photography and perhaps some skills in film or video documentation as well.

FIELDWORK: USING THE CAMERA

Camera equipment varies so much in features, and changes so often and so quickly, that it is difficult to give general advice that will not soon be outdated. Until recently, the best type of camera for all-around folklife fieldwork was a good single-lens-reflex (SLR) camera taking 35-mm film, with a built-in coupled exposure meter. Such cameras were available at a wide range of prices and with a variety of attachments and accessories; many field-workers still prefer them, despite the development of 35-mm cameras with automatic electronic focusing and exposure controls. The chief advantage of the SLR was that the photographer sighted on the subject and focused the image directly through the camera lens, thus seeing at the time exactly what would be in the picture. Since lenses in all but the cheapest SLR models were detachable and the metering system was read directly through the focusing and viewing window, this camera system offered great flexibility and ease of operation at fairly moderate costs. The automatic electronic models are somewhat more limiting, but faster to use, and most of them allow the user to "lock" onto a specific part of the image for focusing and exposure.

It is not necessary to master the technical details behind the inner workings of any camera to use it well. But if photographers acquire the essentials of photographic theory (as contained in the owner's manual, for example), their results will be far superior to those obtained with any fixed-focus snapshot camera, and they will get the most out of their more expensive equipment. Whatever the camera used, the photographer should always practice with it and see the results at home before using it for fieldwork.

The 35-mm film size, of course, is the standard one for transparencies, from which color prints of publishable quality may also be

Marilyn Banuelos *(right)* photographs Connie Romero as she interviews Corpus Gallegos on the *vega*, a publicly owned piece of grazing land in San Luis, Colorado, 1994.

made. Black-and-white 35-mm negatives, even on sensitive film, are also sufficiently free of "grain" (image coarseness) to make excellent enlargements. Since both slides and monochrome prints are useful for different purposes, and since 35-mm film comes only in twenty-four- or thirty-six-exposure rolls, field photographers often carry either two cameras or two identical camera bodies on which they may interchange their basic lenses, loading each camera or camera body with a different film type. Naturally, it is essential to mark and remember which camera contains which type of film!

Besides the "normal" lens supplied with most cameras, the two most useful extras are a wide-angle lens and a zoom-telephoto lens.

(Many recent camera models, however, have a zoom-telephoto lens as the fixed standard lens.) The wide-angle lens is useful especially when walls, shrubbery, or topography prevent getting far enough back to take the subject in with a normal lens. The photographer must be careful, however, not to tip the camera off a straight vertical plane; this introduces distortion. The zoom lens offers in a single accessory a range of possibilities for magnifying a selected portion of the subject. Such magnification is useful not only for bringing in, say, distant buildings, but also for taking close detail shots of remote features like chimney tops or cornice moldings. In addition, with this lens an SLR camera may be used as a telescope, to determine whether distant features on the landscape are worth hiking to for close examination.

Both black-and-white and color films are produced with sensitivities to accommodate the existing illumination in most field conditions on relatively light days. For unusually dark conditions or subjects, the photographer should have a supplementary flash unit, a feature built into many recent camera models. The only other basic equipment needed is a medium-yellow filter for darkening sky tone in black-and-white photography (since some black-and-white films are oversensitive to blue and will produce skies that look white on very light gray), and a tripod for any exposures slower than 1/60 of a second, particularly for telephoto shots. A cable release should be used for tripod shots, or the photographer may set the camera's self-timer to snap the picture, in order to avoid camera movement and achieve maximum sharpness.

Sharp, clear, and well-exposed pictures rather than artistic compositions or "trick" shots are needed for documentary purposes. Generally, the photographer should take many pictures, given that film is cheaper than travel and that the building or other artifact might subsequently change in appearance or cease to exist. Long, medium, and close-up shots should always be taken, along with an indicator of scale in some pictures—a yardstick, ruler, pencil, hand, or person at one side of the shot for size comparison. Other "in-frame documentation" might include a meaningful inscription or sign, the informant demonstrating use of the artifact, or the tools and ingredients for a subject. For any traditional process, such as the steps of construction, a series of pictures illustrating the sequence should be taken.

Negatives, slides, and prints should be systematically filed and carefully preserved after they are processed. The 35-mm size allows for easy printing of one full black-and-white roll on a single 8 × 10 proofsheet and subsequent filing of these proofs, plus the negatives (in strips of five or six frames), in loose-leaf binders. Photographers or their helpers should keep a log of data on all shots taken, information used to label and annotate the picture file. It is essential at the time of taking pictures to ask all persons appearing in them to sign a release form allowing possible later publication.

STUDYING FOLKLIFE

Folk artifacts must be measured carefully, and the materials from which they are constructed must be identified. Maps and atlases should be made up for recording the locations of finds. Sometimes it is desirable and possible to collect the artifact itself—a complex task when buildings, fencing, farm equipment, and the like are involved. Artifacts may need repairs before they can be moved or studied, and large-scale restoration and reconstruction may be necessary, using historical records or old plans as guides.

Preserving diverse material objects is much more complicated than filing manuscript sheets or tape recordings of oral folklore in an archive. The usual archive for manuscript folklore can adequately accept photographs, sketches, or descriptions of material traditions, but museum facilities and techniques are required for storing and displaying the original objects themselves. Analysis of folk artifacts requires, first, that the truly traditional variations be distinguished from individual innovations that are not transmitted to other people, and, second, that the significant traditional variations that define classes and subclasses be identified for the purpose of accurate classification.

Students of American material folk traditions have had fewer indexes and bibliographies to guide them than did the folklorist working with verbal or customary lore, although this situation has improved recently. They also have had to become familiar with a large number of foreign folklife studies, and to search for descriptions of earlier American folk artifacts in nonscholarly publications and in local histories, diaries, collections of letters, travelers' accounts, and pioneer reminiscences. Regional literature may yield folklife data, too, such as this brief description of a log stile from Mark Twain's *Adventures of Huckleberry Finn* (1884):

> A rail fence round a two-acre yard; a stile, made out of logs sawed off and up-ended, in steps, like barrels of a different length, to climb over the fence with, and for the women to stand on when they are going to jump onto a horse. (Chapter XXXII)

The ideal institution for carrying on folklife studies is a combination museum and research center, such as the Norwegian Folk Museum at Bygdøy (near Oslo), the Nordic Museum in Stockholm, or the Village Museum in Bucharest, Romania. There are many other examples elsewhere in Europe of such museums, but two of particular relevance for American-immigrant folklife studies are the Welsh Folk Museum at St. Fagans (near Cardiff) and the Ulster Folk and Transport Museum at Holywood, Northern Ireland. The closest American equivalent to these is the Farmers' Museum in Cooperstown, New York, a fine re-creation of an early-nineteenth-century New York farm and village. Some other notable American museums containing some folklife materials, also built around a village reconstruction, are Old Sturbridge Village, Massachusetts; the Stuhr Museum of the Prairie Pioneer, Grand Island, Nebraska; Old Mystic Seaport, Connecticut; and New Salem Village, Illinois. Oriented more to town life than rural folk culture are such establishments as Colonial Williamsburg, Virginia, and Greenfield Village in Dearborn, Michigan. Other notable collections are in the Shelburne Museum, Burlington, Vermont; the International Folk Art Museum, Santa Fe, New Mexico; the Norwegian-American Museum, Decorah, Iowa; and the Du Pont Museum in Winterthur, Delaware. "Living Farm" museums exist near Des Moines, Iowa; Minneapolis, Minnesota; Atlanta, Georgia; and elsewhere. An accurate reproduction of "Plimoth Plantation" as it was in the early seventeenth century has been constructed in Massachusetts, and during the commemoration of the United States Bicentennial many similar projects and existing museums received grants to establish or expand facilities. Some Canadian museums with folklife materials are Black

Creek Village and Upper Canada Village in Ontario and Pioneer Heritage Park in Calgary, Alberta. To some degree in such institutions the casual visitor may observe displays of artifacts often housed in traditional buildings and see demonstrations of traditional work techniques, while a visiting scholar has access to stored collections of objects and to reference sources.

Since no unified approach to American material traditions has been established, each museum, publication, or research project tends to have its own emphasis and its own peculiarities. Many people conducting research that falls into the field of American folklife seem unaware of similar European studies, and even those who know the work in Europe find that European methods are not fully adaptable to American materials. For instance, here we have no single national culture, but instead a merging of numerous foreign elements in a confusing number of regional settings. Pioneering put immigrants into a unique relationship with the wilderness continent, but technological change has been so rapid during the short history of the United States that pioneer methods and materials either changed drastically or were lost entirely before there was any interest in studying or preserving them. The social equality, political democracy, and economic opportunity of the New World, with the resulting effects on labor and crafts, were not matched in the Old World.

FOCUS: AN IDAHO HOMESTEAD

Cartter Hilliard helped swell the number of Missouri emigrants, arriving by train from a small place near St. Louis in 1911 and settling near Weiser [Idaho]. He was then too young to file a homestead claim, but in 1914 he found a site on Sheep Creek, and since he was then old enough, he filed on the place he only recently sold but still lives on. . . .

When asked how he made a go of it while other homesteaders were losing their land, Mr. Hilliard sets forth a recipe for survival involving unceasing work, thrift, the use and reuse of homemade articles, and making every aspect of the farm venture produce at least something. . . . Until he recently sold his place, [Mr. Hilliard] could say, "The sun never caught me in bed." . . .

Every structure on the place except the house was built by Mr. Hilliard. Many of the building components were fashioned by him. He designed and forged the hinges; he made the fastenings for most of the doors. When asked where he got the idea for the pattern, he replies, "Oh, I just made it." . . .

The full context of Cartter Hilliard's life and work must allow room for other aspects of his role as tradition bearer. He butchered his own meat—sheep, beef, hogs—and salted and smoked the pork, using alder from the nearby creek. He stacked long hay with a derrick and a Jackson fork. He is well attuned to folk beliefs. Coyotes, for example, predict the weather. When they howl a great deal, a storm is coming. The third of December is supposed to rule the winter; that is, the kind of weather that prevails on that day is the kind of weather that will prevail all winter.

In addition to all this, Mr. Hilliard is a water witch. . . . His method has never failed.

Source: Louie W. Attebery, "A Contextual Survey of Selected Homestead Sites in Washington County," in Attebery, ed., *Idaho Folklife: Homesteads to Headstones* (Salt Lake City: University of Utah Press, 1985), pp. 129–42.

A derelict homestead shack, built around 1914, located about one quarter of a mile below the Cartter Hilliard place on the Jenkins Creek Road, roughly nine miles north of Weiser, Idaho, 1979.

DISCUSSION TOPICS:

1. This is a short portion of one description of three Idaho homesteads settled between 1903 and 1914 and, until recently, still occupied by the settlers or their direct descendants. Attebery characterizes each

as "a climax homestead, to borrow a term from ecology." What is the meaning of this borrowed term, and how does it apply to homesteads?

2. How do Cartter Hilliard's survival skills typify the "old traditional way of life" identified by Warren E. Roberts as the proper concern of folklife scholars? (This becomes even clearer if one reads the entire description of all three Idaho homesteads in Attebery's essay.)

3. Concerning another homestead's house Attebery wrote that "the roof was made of shakes that Mr. Wavrick rived out with a froe." What are shakes and a froe? How is a froe used?

Despite these conditions, the key to studies of American folk artifacts remains the same as for all folklore—it is *tradition*. We may investigate in artifacts, as well as in texts of verbal lore or descriptions of customs, the kinds of things that are transmitted in repeated but varying forms casually by word of mouth or by demonstration. We may attempt to discover how traditional materials originated, how changes occurred, and in what manner traditional variants related to the rest of the folk culture from which they came. We can recognize in material traditions not only survivals from the past, but also recent folk creations, and we should be prepared to admit that traditional "folk" methods of work may be followed by professional craftspeople and artists as well as by amateurs. Above all, we should not be misled in our studies by the notion that *every* artifact that is rural or old-fashioned or handmade is a piece of three-dimensional folklore, any more than we think that every amateur poem is a *folk* poem or that every picturesque remark is a *folk* saying.

BIBLIOGRAPHIC NOTES

An anthology that proves there were American folklife studies before "folklife" was a familiar term is Simon J. Bronner's *Folklife Studies from the Gilded Age: Object, Rite, and Custom in Victorian America* (Ann Arbor, Mich.: UMI Research Press, 1987). Usually credited with introducing the term and the formal study of folklife is Don Yoder's important survey "The Folklife Studies Movement," *PF* 13 (July 1963): 43–56.

There followed shortly several appeals for scholars to devote more attention to American folklife. See, for example, two by Norbert F. Riedl—"Folklore vs. *Volkskunde*: A Plea for More Concern with the Study of American Folk Culture on the Part of Anthropologists," *TFSB* 31 (1965): 47–53; and "Folklore and the Study of Material Aspects of Folk Culture," *JAF* 79 (1966): 557–63. An important guide for such studies is Robert Wildhaber's "A Bibliographical Introduction to American Folklife," *NYFQ* 21 (1965): 259–302. Wildhaber mainly listed books, and he included works on folk architecture, furniture, "imagery and popular painting," tools and utensils, wood carving, metalwork, pottery, glassware, signs, and scrimshaw.

An indication of progress in the next decade was W. F. H. Nicolaisen's report "Surveying and Mapping North American Culture," *MSF* 3 (1975): 35–39. This article furnished the background of efforts to establish an American Folklore Atlas, beginning with a pilot study of foodways. See also *Approaches to the Study of Material Aspects of American Culture*, a special issue of *FF* (12:2–3 [1979]), ed. Simon J. Bronner and Stephen P. Poyser.

The volume of essays *American Folklife* (Austin: University of Texas Press, 1976), edited by Don Yoder (several times quoted in this chapter), contained important historical and theoretical statements as well as several excellent studies. Contributors discussed anthropological, esthetic, historic, and geographical perspectives. Important collections of studies by leading American folklife scholars, both published by UMI Research Press in Ann Arbor, Mich., in 1988, are Warren E. Roberts, *Viewpoints on Folklife: Looking at the Overlooked*, and Austin E. Fife, *Exploring Western Americana* (edited by Alta Fife). Simon J. Bronner's *Grasping Things: Folk Material Culture and Mass Society in America* (Lexington: The University Press of Kentucky, 1986) is a comprehensive work of history, methodology, and examples in American folklife study; and his *American Material Culture and Folklife: A Prologue and Dialogue* (1985; 2nd ed., Logan: Utah State University Press, 1992), involves several important American folklife scholars. Bronner's entry "Folklife Movement" in *American Folklore: An Encyclopedia* gives a concise up-to-date account of the topic.

Most American folklore journals did not in the past publish much on material tradition, but useful semischolarly articles may be found in back issues of periodicals such as *Ozark Guide*, *Mountain Life and Work*, *Antiques*, and *Hobbies*. Folklife studies are sometimes also published in the journals of historians and geographers. An important journal for studies of American material traditions is *Pennsylvania Folklife*, published quarterly under that name since 1957 but preceded by other variously titled publications of the Pennsylvania Folklife Society. Articles in this journal go beyond Pennsylvania German material, and they are generally well documented and always excellently illustrated. More recently, the journal *Pioneer America* (later renamed *Material Culture*) entered the field; the student should look here for Thomas J. Schlereth's statement "American Studies and American Things," *PA* 14 (1982): 47–66.

As an introduction to European folklife studies, besides works mentioned in this chapter, one should consult such journals as *Scottish Studies*, *Ulster Folk Life*, the Swedish *Folk-Liv*, and the English *Folk Life*. Sigurd Erixon's study "West European Connections and Culture Relations," *Folk-Liv* 2 (1938): 137–72, is a basic one. Specifically, for the British backgrounds, see Ronald H. Buchanan's "Geography and Folk Life," *Folk Life* 1 (1963): 5–15; Alexander Fenton's "An Approach to Folklife Studies," *KFQ* 12 (1967): 5–21; and the essays gathered in *Studies in Folk Life*, ed. Geraint Jenkins (New York: Barnes & Noble, 1969). Richard M. Dorson was the special editor of an issue of *JFI* (2:3 [1965]: 239–366), devoted to "Folklore and Folklife Studies in Great Britain and Ireland." R. W. Brunskill's *Illustrated Handbook of Vernacular Architecture* (New York: Universe Books, 1970) clarifies the architectural terminology and has some direct relevance to American houses, although its scope is mostly British. In "Some Similarities between American and European Folk Houses," *PA* 3 (1971): 8–14, Eugene M. Wilson surveyed European antecedents for the central-passage ("dogtrot") house type.

Two important essays on the role of museums in folklife research are Howard Wight Marshall's "Folklife and the Rise of American Folk Museums," *JAF* 90 (1977): 391–413; and Ormond Loomis's "Sources on Folk Museums and Living Historical Farms," *FF* Bibliographic and Special Series, no. 16 (1977).

An interesting early survey of American folklife is found in *Lewis Miller: Sketches and Chronicles. The Reflections of a Nineteenth Century Pennsylvania German Folk Artist* (York, Pa.: Historical Society of York County, 1966). Some 160 selections from a total of about two thousand drawings and watercolors are reproduced, illustrating many diverse aspects of everyday life. Perhaps a comparable effort, documented with camera and sketches, is the series called *Foxfire* (Garden City, N.Y.: Doubleday, 1 [1972], 2 [1973], 3 [1975], and beyond), edited by Eliot Wigginton, a Georgia high school teacher who inspired his students to study the folk culture of their own region and who parlayed a small periodical into book-length publications, government grants, and many spinoff *Foxfire*-like projects. Log-cabin building is covered in the original *Foxfire Book*, and a subject index is included in *Foxfire 3*.

The wide range of traditional talents and skills that characterize American folklife, and the national recognition given them, is documented in a beautifully illustrated book, *American Folk Masters: The National Heritage Fellows*, text by Steve Siporin (New York: Harry N. Abrams, Inc., 1992). The Folklife in the South series, edited by Lynwood Montell, contains individual volumes on the Cajun, Kentucky Bluegrass, Upper Cumberland, South Florida, and Ozark regions. The latest volume is Michael Ann Williams's *Great Smoky Mountains Folklife* (Jackson: University Press of Mississippi, 1995). See also Janet C. Gilmore, *The World of the Oregon Fishboat: A Study in Maritime Folklife* (Ann Arbor, Mich.: UMI Research Press, 1986).

The cultural-geography approach to American folklife materials may be seen in such works as Amos Rapoport's *House Form and Culture* (Foundations of Cultural Geography Series; Englewood Cliffs, N.J.: Prentice-Hall, 1969) and in such regional surveys as Peter O. Wacker's *The Muconetcong Valley of New Jersey: A Historical Geography* (New Brunswick, N.J.: Rutgers University Press, 1968) and Malcolm L. Comeaux's *Atchafalaya Swamp Life: Settlement and Folk Occupations* (Geoscience and Man, vol. 2; Baton Rouge: Louisiana State University, 1972). Milton B. Newton, Jr., a geographer, has published a useful booklet as *Mélanges*, no. 2 (Museum of Geoscience publication), *Louisiana House Types: A Field Guide*

(Baton Rouge: Louisiana State University, 1971). Another example of folk architecture discussed by a geographer is in Joseph E. Spencer's "House Types in Southern Utah," *GR* 35 (1945): 444–57. Two good studies of folk architecture appear in the "Material Culture in the South" special issue of *SFQ* (39 [Dec. 1975]: 303–406).

Austin and Alta Fife, together with Henry H. Glassie, edited *Forms upon the Frontier: Folklife and Folk Arts in the United States*, containing several papers on Western folk architecture and folk arts and crafts from a conference held at Logan, Utah (Utah State University Monograph Series 16 [April 1969]). A collection of fifteen essays by various contributors comprises *Arts in Earnest: North Carolina Folklife*, ed. Daniel W. Patterson and Charles G. Zug III (Durham, N.C.: Duke University Press, 1990). Eight essays, two previously unpublished, plus a bibliography by John Michael Vlach are in *By the Work of Their Hands: Studies in Afro-American Folklife* (Charlottesville: University Press of Virginia, 1991).

20

FOLK ARCHITECTURE

Folk architecture, sometimes called "vernacular architecture" (that which is common or native in a given area), includes all traditional nonacademic building types. In particular, these consist of cabins and houses, barns, smokehouses, washhouses, summer kitchens, springhouses, privies, stables, and other agricultural outbuildings; some taverns, shops, offices, churches, and other meeting houses; and numerous minor building types such as carriage houses, sheds, garages, hunting blinds, ice-fishing shacks, icehouses, boathouses, tree houses, playhouses, mills, and covered bridges. Folk architecture, and especially folk housing, is the most basic aspect of traditional material culture, being both a three-dimensional product of folk-cultural concepts and an important continuing influence on these same concepts. The placement of traditional buildings in relation to one another and to the landscape, the buildings' floor plans and heights, their construction techniques, the volumes enclosed in them, the light admitted and views afforded by them, the materials of their construction and decoration, their functional qualities, and many other factors all constitute statements of certain human values, and at the same time they are pervasive forces preserving these values.

Folk housing in the United States was typified during the settlement period by the use of the most easily available local materials for building in inherited traditional forms. The teepees, wigwams, and lodges of the Native Americans; the first log, frame, or half-timbered houses in the Eastern half of the country; the forts, dug-outs, and lean-tos of explorers, pioneers, and homesteaders; the sod houses of the Great Plains; the adobe houses of the Southwest; and many other vernacular forms all followed this principle. Interest in studying American folk architecture has burgeoned in the second half of the twentieth century, after decades of folklorists either ig-noring the subject or leaving it to the attention of cultural geogra-phers and architectural historians. The bibliography of scholarship is enormous now, and the findings are so voluminous that this chap-ter may only sample some prominent examples and conclusions. (The first edition of this textbook in 1968 combined folk architecture, arts, and crafts in one chapter and grouped folk costumes and food in another, with a mere thirty-four pages sufficient to present all of these topics, including the bibliographic notes. Reflecting the re-markable growth of American material-culture studies in all genres, a current complete listing of published American folk-architectural studies alone might fill a volume.)

FOCUS: CONNECTED FARM BUILDINGS IN NEW ENGLAND

Although there is considerable visual variation, most connected farms throughout New England were organized and functioned similarly and, like the Sawyer-Black farm, contain four distinct buildings. A children's verse from the nineteenth century describes the most typical organization: "Big house, little house, back house, barn." It is a refrain often repeated by old timers when asked to describe the unusual building arrangement. A few even recall childhood games played to its rhythmic cadence.

During lectures I have conducted at various Maine historical societies, over fifty elderly listeners indicated their familiarity with the verse. Most said it was a childhood rhyme. Charlotte Lawrence of Yarmouth, Maine, remembers the verse repeated to children's games. An old farmer from Greenwood, Maine, recalled a satirical version comparing playmates' farms. Richard Lunt, author of The Maine Folklife Index, *was told the verse in the children's mate selection game, "She love me, she loves me not."*

Source: Thomas C. Hubka, *Big House, Little House, Back House, Barn: The Connected Farm Buildings of New England* (Hanover, N.H.: University Press of New England, 1984), pp. 5–6 and footnote no. 1, p. 205.

The Sawyer-Black Farm of Sweden, Maine. Its units were constructed and altered from the early to the mid 1800s.

DISCUSSION TOPICS:

1. Can you find other examples of "house" rhymes, songs, or sayings in oral folklore? Do they reflect aspects of folk architecture or other house tradition?

2. What might be reasons for connected farms in New England? (Check Hubka's conclusions to see what reasons he deduced.)

3. The parlor and sleeping rooms were in the big house, the kitchen and woodshed in the little house; various work spaces and storage, plus a privy, were in the back house; and the barn was just a barn. What is the progression of functions in such an arrangement? Does this pattern hold true for any other kinds of connected buildings?

ARCHITECTURAL FORM

Folk tradition in vernacular architecture may be evident in the form, the construction techniques and materials, and the uses of buildings, but it is **form** that serves best to identify genuine folk architecture and to establish its types and subtypes. In other words, a log cabin is "folk" not because it is made of log, but because it is a traditionally laid-out cabin. As leading folk architecture scholar Henry Glassie has written, a cabin comprises "a single construction unit . . . less than two stories high." While a true folk cabin may be made of many kinds or combinations of material, other nonfolk house types (that is, nontraditional forms) might be constructed out of logs joined in traditional ways—a hunting lodge, a ski lodge, or a motel, for example. Just because a building is made of log does not necessarily make it "folk." By the same token, folk or nonfolk buildings might be put to traditional or nontraditional uses; for example, an amateur art show might be mounted in a genuine pioneer cabin or a fiddling contest might be held in a football stadium.

Since form is the basic criterion, close description and accurate measurement are the chief requirements of good folk-architectural fieldwork. A building under study as a possible example of folk architecture should be measured carefully along each outside wall with a long tape measure, measured again inside from the corners up to and then across each opening, and finally measured for height and for the thickness of walls. A drawn floor plan should indicate the placement of all openings, chimneys, and stairways, besides giving either a clear graphic indication of scale or stating the measurements themselves. An "elevation" drawing, also showing scale, or else a photograph can document the building's overall appearance, height, and roof shape. It is important to remember during such documentary fieldwork to include all additions ("appendages") to the basic house (porches, shed, "wings," "ells," etc.) and to record all details of ornamentation. However, during the formal analysis of the building, the researcher should disregard all but the essential construction units to establish the building's type. The level of further details to be taken down will depend upon the needs and interests of the researcher, but a good general rule is to "keep track of everything," insofar as the time and the facilities allow.

The specific data of field observations and measurements are combined and generalized to describe the patterns of folk housing. For example, the Southern Mountains cabins' *primary characteristics*, according to Glassie, are approximate height, shape, general floor plan, and roof form; while their *secondary characteristics* are the exact measurements, construction details, interior partitions, and types of appendages (if any). In general, for folk-architectural analysis the floor plan and the height of the building are the prime considerations. The placement of doors and chimney are considered primary for classification, while the placement of windows and stairs, these being more variable and subject to the builders' whims or skills, are secondary. One advantage of folklorists' concern with the building's essential form rather than with the other criteria is that whatever the additions to or the condition of a structure, the form remains. Asbestos-shingle siding or galvanized-metal roofing may disguise the log and wood-shingle construction of a cabin, for example, but these additions do not hide the square shape, the height, or the gable-end chimney placement of the original cabin.

Folk builders of such cabins were *truly* following traditions, not merely making up the house forms as they went along. After all, the builders could just as well have followed a circular floor plan (like that of a Navajo hogan), built an L-shaped house, or placed the chimney centrally or away from a gable end; yet seldom did they vary cabin design even to the point of exceeding the typical dimensions of cabins. Nor were these sizes merely dictated by the length of available tree trunks, for approximately the same size cabins reappear in all regions, whatever their forest resources, and even in frame and adobe. Furthermore, logs were often spliced together for larger structures than cabins, such as barns and stables. Another point to remember is that some self-taught builders did in fact construct unique log buildings inspired only by their own needs and tastes; also, there exist such regional forms as the "Rocky Mountain Cabin," which has a gable-end doorway, with a roof extension to protect the entrance.

CABIN TYPES

Since the cabin—especially the log cabin—is such an important icon of American history and culture, it is important to recognize what features are traditional in cabin architecture. Glassie's analysis in the Southern Mountains (verified by other studies) revealed only two basic cabin forms beneath the many surface features and appendages of individual cabins. These two were the **square cabin** and the **rectangular cabin,** both of which have external centered gable-end chimneys and have at least one dimension very close to sixteen feet. Thus, the kind of old homemade family housing most traditional in the area surveyed was characterized by a small, neatly square-cornered, single unit (or "single pen," as the log structure is called), with very specific and quite limited variations in the placement of openings. Although small, such a cabin was often referred to simply as "the house" or even "the big house." The traditional cabin was a conservative and functional kind of housing, which provided little separation among family members, and with little relationship to the vast areas of American landscape. Not only were the cabin's dimensions and floor plan bound by tradition, but so was the use of interior space.

FOCUS: LIFE IN A ONE-ROOM OR TWO-ROOM HOUSE

When the kitchen was removed from the big house, the use of space was more fluid. Depending on need, beds were more evenly distributed around the room. The chimney corners were popular locations for beds; still, enough room was always allowed around the hearth for family and social activities. Memories of family life are therefore frequently tied to the hearth, the social and symbolic center of the household. "[Mother would] sing Rock of Ages, Lord Thomas, oh, lots of different songs. Pappy, he'd help her. We'd sit in the chimney corner, us little ones would. They'd get in front and they'd sit there and chew their tobacco and sing and spit in the fire." . . .

The individual who chose to build a double pen house (without a separate kitchen) was accepting a system of spatial use which was different from that of the person whose two rooms were a "big house and kitchen." Both single pen and double pen plans did share a single intensively used room. . . . In the double pen plan this room was referred to as "the room we lived in," "the house," or "the fireplace room." The other room of the double pen plan was traditionally the parlor. Unlike the small "other room" of the partitioned single pen dwelling, the room ostensibly had a formal purpose. . . . One of the features most commonly associated with the double pen plan is the presence of two fireplaces in the main block of the house. The presence of a second hearth was critical in separating formal functions away from the main hearth. It was the presence of this hearth, and not the size of the rooms, that functionally distinguished the double pen from the partitioned single pen house.

Source: Michael Ann Williams, *Homeplace: The Social Use and Meaning of the Folk Dwelling in Southwestern North Carolina* (Athens: University of Georgia Press, 1991), pp. 52, 78–79.

DISCUSSION TOPICS:

1. The term "big house" here refers to use of living space rather than to the actual house. Generally, Williams explains, it means "the main dwelling unit," distinct from the kitchen, whether the kitchen is attached or detached from the house. How is "big house" also used in reference to large Southern plantations, and in the criminal world? What house terms or room terms are commonly used in America today?

2. Is there a "social and symbolic center" to the modern American home? Is it perhaps the kitchen, the deck or patio, or the television set for some dwellings? Or is it sometimes the fireplace? Do "memories of family life" refer to certain dwelling places or spaces more than to others?

3. Do any modern Americans—possibly ethnic or immigrant families—maintain a formal seldom-used area of the dwelling as a counterpart to the old-fashioned "parlor"?

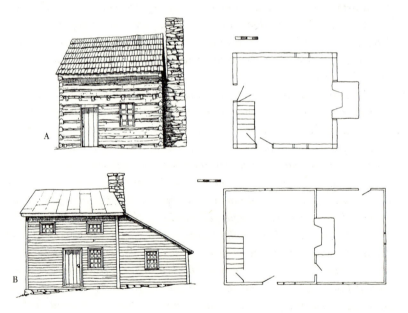

A. V-notched cabin situated south of Fletcher, near Hood, Green County, Virginia (July 1963). By May 1966 this cabin had fallen to ruins. B. This cabin was built of balloon (light, sawed, nailed together) frame covered with vertical boards. When the shed was added to the chimney end, both parts were covered with weatherboards. It is situated between Crozet and Whitehall, Albemarle County, Virginia (August 1964).

Single-pen cabins sometimes had interior partitions—often merely hanging blankets or quilts—and there were also two-room traditional house types, which followed their own strict pattern of layout and construction. Additions to one-room cabins were usually built only at the gable end and generally with the same traditional proportions for the add-ons as full cabins had. When such a "double-pen" house was formed by an addition to the chimney end, it became a "saddlebag" house; when the addition (with a second chimney) was to the opposite end and a breezeway was left open, it became a "dogtrot" house. (Both of these house types, however, were also constructed separately, not just as additions to existing cabins.) Despite the folksy ring of its name, the "dogtrot" house (also sometimes

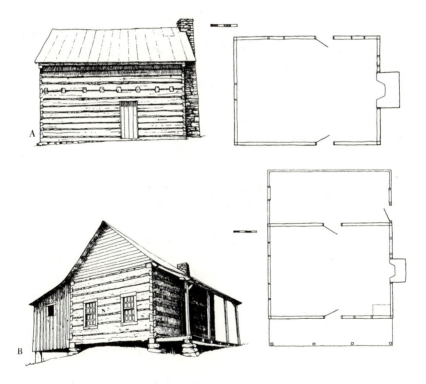

A. Half-dovetail cabin located west of Allen Gap, Greene County, Tennessee (August 1964). This is one of the few observed mountain cabins that has an earth floor. Like many other early log houses, this cabin has been converted into a tobacco barn. B. Half-dovetail cabin with front porch and rear shed additions situated in the Shelton Laurel area north of Marshall, Madison County, North Carolina (June 1963).

called "possum trot" or "turkey trot") seems to be descended from a one-story, central-hall, two-chimney frame house type called the "hall and parlor." Another variation of the single-unit folk house, termed the "stack house" by folklorist Howard Wight Marshall, consists of two units—either square or slightly rectangular—stacked on top of each other. Marshall found such houses built most often on smaller lots in Midwest towns.

FOCUS: DINNER IN A DEEP-SOUTH DOGTROT HOUSE

The farm of the Deep South is a seemingly pattern-less composite of many separate buildings, each with its special use; frequently such a farm is organized about a dogtrot house lying parallel to the road with a transverse-crib barn behind it and off to one side. In addition to the transverse-crib, the farm often includes a small single-crib barn—a corncrib of log or vertical board flanked by sheds. . . . If the house is not a dogtrot . . . it might be a cabin of one room fitted with a shed on the rear for a kitchen, but it probably is a one-story two-room house with two front doors and a chimney in the center or on one end. . . . In such houses, built generally of frame but sometimes of light pine logs, the family sits down today to a noontime dinner of field peas cooked with fat meat and sprinkled with "pepper sauce" from a 7-Up bottle filled with vinegar and sun-dried peppers. Depending upon how long it has been since hog-killing, there might be a pork chop, some ham, bacon, or sausage on the side of the plate. To sop the juices there are buttermilk biscuits thickly spread with butter which the lady of the house churned while she rocked, and afterward there is cornbread soaked in syrup. Whether made from sugar cane or sorghum, syrup is manufactured in the same way, with the same devices, on small farms throughout the South. The butt ends of the cane are fed into the syrup mill powered by a mule walking a slow circle. The juice crushed out of the cane is caught in a tub, poured into a pan over a wood fire, boiled down to syrup, strained through a cloth, and put up in jars or cans.

Source: Henry Glassie, *Pattern in the Material Folk Culture of the Eastern United States* (Philadelphia: University of Pennsylvania Press, 1968), pp. 101–07.

DISCUSSION TOPICS:

1. In this "seemingly pattern-less" setting, Henry Glassie finds patterns. What elements does he identify as part of the traditional structure of the setting?

2. What justifies calling these observations about life in a Deep-South dogtrot house a "folklife" summary?

3. This short section of Glassie's book has six footnotes citing sources and two sections of illustrations comprising twenty-four individual examples, all of them from Glassie's own fieldwork. The footnote on syrup-making alone contains eight references. (The whole 241-page book has 361 footnotes and seventy-three pages of bibliography.) What do these numbers say about the study of folklife, as well as the expertise of Henry Glassie, even back in 1968?

Larger traditional houses often repeated and extended the square and rectangular principles underlying cabin plans. The "I house," for example, said to have been identified as a traditional type in states whose names begin with "I" (but also said to be shaped like an "I" at the gable ends), is two stories tall, one room deep, and two rooms wide. In New England it had a central chimney, in the Mid-Atlantic region two inside chimneys at the gable ends, and in the South usually two external gable-end chimneys. The four basic interior volumes of an "I house" are recognizable as the identical square or rectangular units of traditional cabins. However, under the influence of the academic architectural model called "Georgian," "I houses" and other folk houses acquired a central hall and often Greek Revival trim (such as "return cornices"). When the roof height of a house is two stories in front and slopes down as a "lean-to" or "shed" to one story in the rear, the form is called a "saltbox" (characteristic of, and often named for, New England, but by no means original or peculiar to that region). Putting all our descriptive terminology together, we can say that a saltbox (supposedly shaped like an old-time salt box, which was fastened to the kitchen wall near the stove) is a central-chimney hall-and-parlor (two main rooms) "I house" with an integral rear shed consisting (usually) of three smaller rooms on the first floor. Also, from the "I house" base, a possible variation is "two-thirds of an 'I house,'" the equivalent of removing one square or rectangular unit of the floor plan, leaving only one main room (with chimney) and the "hall." Another possibility is the "four-over-four" design, which simply doubles the house size, usually also retaining the Georgian central hall and with either central or end, internal or external chimneys, depending upon the region.

BARN TYPES

Some traditional barns conform to the patterning principles of simple American house types. A basic barn type is the **double-crib design,** with two cabinlike units side by side, joined by one roof, and with gable ends closed and the main doors on the long side. These barns could be covered with siding, and barns of the same proportions were built as large single units. A **four-crib barn** has two such structures side by side under a single roof, possibly with doors on all four sides. The **transverse-crib barn** of the Deep South is the evolutionary result of closing off the passage that transects the longer side of a four-crib barn. Often in transverse-crib barns there are no doors between the remaining passage that runs parallel to the roof ridge, and the stalls face each other across the middle space. Sometimes these larger barns had more than two "cribs" to a side, and often they were entirely sided over or (as with double-crib barns) could be built as one large unit. Any of these barn types (like the cabin types) might have lean-to appendages, usually extending from the long sides, but sometimes even on all four sides.

Some house and barn types, usually of regional or ethnic origin, stand apart from these general patterns. Examples are the "Cape Cod" house, an English derivative, which has two front rooms on either side of a central chimney and a row of three or more rooms along the back; the Southern "shotgun" house, possibly an African derivative via Haiti, which has a gable-end entrance and is one room wide and three or more rooms deep; and the Mormon "polygamy house," which served to provide "equal comforts" for several wives of one man. Three major barn types are the "English barn," a three-bay structure with stables, hay mow, and a central threshing floor; the "New England barn," with its major entrance at a gable end; and the Pennsylvania "bank barn" (based on Swiss prototypes), which is built into a hillside, with an overhanging "forebay" extending over the farmyard on the opposite side from the bank. Limited in their distribution, both in time and place, are various round and polyhedral barns.

BUILDING MATERIALS

While construction techniques and materials are not used to identify traditional architectural types, they certainly should be investigated, being interesting in themselves as well as important for determining the national origins and paths of diffusion of folk buildings. Although many Americans tend to visualize log construction employing round logs stacked with their ends protruding, this was only an early and short-lived method of building. Most American log construction is typified by horizontal placement of hewn logs (trimmed to a square or rectangular cross section) fitted at the corners with V-notch, half-dovetail, and dovetail joints, and finished with "chinking" between the logs. (Other log-notching techniques sometimes used were saddle notch, square notch, and diamond notch, and a few buildings employed a "hooked half-dovetail" system that secured the logs even more tightly together.) The antecedents of the

Log ends sawn from a derelict house employing the "hooked half-dovetail" notching technique, held by Lester Severson, a Norwegian-Canadian of the "Bardo District," near Round Hill, Alberta, Canada, 1972.

most common log construction techniques seem to be in Pennsylvania German tradition (ultimately from central and eastern Europe), not English (where log construction is not traditional) nor Scandinavian (where logs are shaped and more tightly fitted without chinking and have their notched logs extending at the corners rather than being trimmed off square).

Log buildings may have clapboard siding, either original to the construction or added at a later time. Early timber-framed buildings used older joinery techniques (like pegged laps or mortise-and-tenon joints) rather than nailing. After the Civil War, a lighter system called "balloon framing," composed of vertical studs covered with siding, was introduced, and virtually all of the traditional American house types were also built in this manner.

Popular fashions in architecture tend to reject some of the functional qualities of folk architecture. Sod houses, for example, despite some obvious disadvantages, were cheap, fireproof, and well insulated, but few prairie pioneers continued to build them or use them once wood became more easily available. Log houses are strong, fairly simpler to build, and better insulated without any special ma-

Sod-house home of the J. C. Cram family, Loup County, Nebraska, 1886.

terials than are most balloon-framed houses, but they came to be considered rustic and outmoded. As a result, people who continued to live in traditional log houses sometimes painted or shingled them as a kind of disguise, while city people who built log houses for nostalgia purposes preferred to leave many of the natural wood surfaces—walls, posts, beams, etc.—to remain exposed.

In the late twentieth century, log dwellings have boomed in popularity, largely for their rustic appeal; they are built as homes, summer cottages, and vacation resorts. For reasons of pure nostalgia, newly constructed buildings or park structures often are made out of round logs, even though square-hewn logs that fit together more securely and need less chinking are more efficient, both in terms of insulation and solidity. The most degenerate stage of this log-house revival might be the attachment of false half-logs to the outside of a balloon-framed building or even to the sides of a "park-model" mobile home (i.e., a home designed to be left on site in an RV park and not towed on the highway).

Two square-hewn log houses joined in the "saddlebag" style with a central chimney, Mercer County, Kentucky, photographed between 1890 and 1903.

FOCUS: HEWN LOGS VERSUS ROUND LOGS, AND PREFAB LOG HOUSES

There is a parallelism between the type of log preparation and the interior finish of the cabin. While the hewn logs represented an attempt to remove the material from its natural state—squared timbers with notched ends instead of round, bark-covered tree trunks—the round logs are closer to a natural state, even though the bark is removed.* The interiors of older log houses were usually painted, white-washed, plastered or even papered in the later years of the useful life. The older log dwellers came to avoid the very appearance of wood surfaces; they painted furniture in solid colors or gave it an unnatural form of imitative graining (wood pretending to be wood). . . .

The most recent chapter in log building in central Pennsylvania, a chapter not even close to completion, begins with the energy crisis of the late 1970s. Rising oil prices and other factors led to the reevaluation of fuel consumption and the recognition of log buildings as energy-efficient housing. As it became socially desirable to conserve energy, compact cars and log houses acquired a certain amount of snob appeal, short-lived in the case of the cars but less so regarding the houses. Prefabricated log buildings with all modern conveniences became available as a popular house form, completely removed from the folk tradition. The cost factor alone meant that most traditional log-house dwellers were priced out of the market. These modern log houses enable their owners to occupy an image of the American frontier with none of the disadvantages. The individualism of original log housing, dependent as it was on the size and type of materials available and on the level of skill of its builders, has been eliminated, replaced by machine-processed standardization.

Source: Mac E. Barrick, "The Log House as Cultural Symbol," *Material Culture* 18 (1986): 1–19.

---

* Structural anthropologists might find a relationship between the use of carefully prepared logs by a previous generation whose taste in food also ran to carefully pared and fully cooked items in contrast to the more recent inhabitants of round-log cabins whose diet includes fresh fruits and vegetables, raw or cold foods, and potatoes baked or boiled in their skins.

DISCUSSION TOPICS:

1. Most traditional American log construction employed hewn logs with notched corners cut off flush, but many popular-culture images of pioneer log construction depict round logs with saddle notching

and the log ends protruding at the corners. Look in the media for illustrations of both types, as well as for illustrations of modern "designer" log construction.

2. Can Barrick's suggested comparison of different log-building styles to the preferred food types of inhabitants be carried further, say to drinks, dress, or other social customs?

3. What other recent trends in home-building materials are motivated by a desire for energy efficiency plus a rustic "back to nature" appeal? (One example is construction using automobile tires packed with dirt.)

RESEARCHING AND STUDYING FOLK ARCHITECTURE

As close studies of folk architecture in specific regions were finished, it became possible to describe characteristic regional distributions of building types and to chart the cultural contacts they represent. Henry Glassie's important early book *Pattern in the Material Folk Culture of the Eastern United States* (1968) identified the most typical house and barn types (among other artifacts) as they appear in four folk-cultural regions—the Mid-Atlantic, Upland South, Deep South, and North. There are, of course, many subregional distinctions to be made, as well as studies of the other major sections of the country where various ethnic or sectional "islands" of folk architecture may exist. The Mormon settlers of Utah, for instance, brought with them as cultural baggage mainly the forms of traditional Eastern and Midwestern American architecture, but these houses were constructed of local materials such as adobe, mud concrete, and various stones. Some were made by immigrant craftsmen who had been converted to Mormonism. Thus, what are called in Utah "Old Mormon Houses" may simply be variations of traditional Eastern central-hall plans constructed of locally quarried stone by a Welsh stonemason and enhanced by a modest addition of Greek Revival trim or sometimes an indigenous Utah "Alpine" decor.

While we have described some major American folk architectural forms here, we have only scratched the surface. The principles set forth, however, should enable beginning students to start making field studies of their own. Left out of consideration here have been such technical matters as chronologies of nails and other hardware, methods of raising houses or barns and roofing them, cutting (or "riving") shingles, building stone chimneys, making adobe, and decorating the interior. We need to study the social contexts of traditional housing expressed in folk speech, folk narratives, folksongs, and other genres. There are also a number of "exotic" traditional building materials, including hay bales, railroad ties, bottles (set in concrete-filled forms), and wooden packing cases. Even pretentious nineteenth-century urban houses may have traditional elements associated with them, such as hand-cut scrollwork, sometimes called "Carpenter's Gothic." And in modern building the essential construction jobs such as excavating, stonework, carpentry, masonry, plastering, plumbing, and roofing could be investigated in detail for traditional elements. Practitioners of these jobs, or new ones, such as installing electrical wiring, automatic heating, or air-conditioning, may have a traditional vocabulary or retain some folk techniques in their work.

BIBLIOGRAPHIC NOTES

For American folk architecture generally, see Wildhaber's bibliography mentioned in the notes to chapter 19. A selection of 23 important articles is reprinted in *Common Places: Readings in American Vernacular Architecture*, ed. Dell Upton and John Michael Vlach (Athens: University of Georgia Press, 1986).

Everett Dick's *Sod-House Frontier*, cited in the notes to chapter 15, includes one chapter on building and maintaining the sod house. Roger L. Welsch discussed "The Nebraska Soddy" in *NH* 48 (1967): 335–42; his extended study is *Sod Walls: The Story of the Nebraska Sod House* (Broken Bow, Neb.: Purcells, Inc., 1968). Many of the same sod-house photographs are reproduced in John L. White's "Pages from a Nebraska Album: The Sod House Photographs of Solomon D. Butcher," *TAW* 12 (1975): 30–39. Good photographs and a bibliography accompany Tim Turner's article "Sod Houses in Nebraska," *Association of Preservation Technology Bulletin* 7 (1975): 20–37. In "The Meaning of Folk Architecture: The Sod House Example," *KF* 21 (1976–77): 34–49, Roger L. Welsch suggests that at least in part sod houses were "a response to psychological needs," such as to shut out nature and to enforce social life inside the houses. Allen G. Noble presents an annotated bibliography of sod-house scholarship in *PA* 13 (1981): 61–66.

Other Plains building materials are presented in Roger Welsch's "Sandhill Baled-Hay Construction," *KFQ* 15 (1970): 16–34; and "Railroad-Tie Construction on the Pioneer Plains," *WF* 35 (1976): 149–56. A useful "Adobe Bibliography" by

Mark R. Barnes appears in the *Association of Preservation Technology Bulletin* 7 (1975): 89–101. John F. O'Conner's *The Adobe Book* (Santa Fe, N.M.: Ancient City Press, 1973), although oriented mainly to the contemporary builder of modern adobe houses, has very good practical information and fine photographic details.

An early and well-illustrated general survey on American log architecture was C. A. Weslager's *The Log Cabin in America from Pioneer Days to the Present* (New Brunswick, N.J.: Rutgers University Press, 1969), but it is superseded by Terry G. Jordan's *American Log Buildings: An Old World Heritage* (Chapel Hill: University of North Carolina Press, 1985). Peter O. Wacker and Roger T. Trindell studied "The Log House in New Jersey: Origin and Diffusion" in *KFQ* 13 (1968): 248–68, demonstrating effective use of maps, plates, and historical citations. Log cabins from the upper Midwest are illustrated in Paul W. Klammer's "Collecting Log Cabins: A Photographer's Hobby," *MH* 37 (1960): 71–77. A portfolio of excellent photographs of log buildings in Jackson Hole, Wyoming, was printed in *TAW* 1 (1964): 21–30. Another attractive nontechnical publication is Clemson Donovan's *Living with Logs: British Columbia's Log Buildings and Rail Fences* (Saanichton, B.C., Canada: Hancock House, 1974). For a brief explanation of the "Rocky Mountain Cabin" see Jennifer Eastman Attebery, *Building Idaho: An Architectural History* (Moscow: University of Idaho Press, 1991), p. 111.

Two articles on log-cabin construction in *IF* 13 (1980): 46–80 are well illustrated and very systematic in their approaches. Charles F. Gritzner wrote of "Log Housing in New Mexico" in *PA* 3 (1971): 54–62, while Jennifer Eastman Attebery's topic was "Log Construction in the Sawtooth Valley of Idaho" in *PA* 8 (1976): 36–46. Going beyond articles merely on log buildings themselves, Warren E. Roberts has a comprehensive piece on "The Tools Used in Building Log Houses in Indiana" in *PA* 9 (1977): 32–61, reprinted in *Common Places* (see above). Among many other publications on regional log construction, see Roberts's *Log Buildings of Southern Indiana* (Bloomington, Ind.: Trickster Press, 1984) and John Morgan, *The Log House in East Tennessee* (Knoxville: University of Tennessee Press, 1990).

An article tracing one European house form as it was adapted in the United States, Albert J. Petersen's "The German-Russian House in Kansas," *PA* 8 (1976): 19–27, was reprinted in *Readings in American Folklore*, pp. 374–86. Compare Alvar W. Carlson's "German-Russian Houses in Western North Dakota," *PA* 13 (1981): 49–60. Lászlo Kurti treats "Hungarian Settlement and Building Practices in Pennsylvania and Hungary" in *PA* 12 (1980): 35–53.

The identification of the Southern "shotgun house" as an African architectural form was provided in great detail by John Michael Vlach in a two-part essay in *PA* 8 (1976): 47–70. Jay Edwards similarly traced the Louisiana Creole cottage to French, Haitian, and West African roots in an article in *LFM* 4 (1976–80): 9–40. See also Vlach's important study *Back of the Big House: The Architecture of Plantation Slavery* (Chapel Hill: University of North Carolina Press, 1993).

Stone houses of northern Utah were surveyed in an article of that title by Austin E. Fife in *UHQ* 40 (1972): 6–23. Teddy Griffith covered one community in the same region in "A Heritage of Stone in Willard," *UHQ* 43 (1975): 286–300; and Richard C. Poulsen turned to a community farther south in Utah in his study

"Stone Buildings of Beaver City," *UHQ* 43 (1975): 278–85. On Utah folk architecture in general, see Jan Harold Brunvand, "The Architecture of Zion," in *TAW* 13 (1976): 28–35.

Noting a nine-by-eight-foot shelter built by transients is Ted Daniels's "A Philadelphia Squatter's Shack: Urban Pioneering," *PA* 13 (1981): 43–46. D. C. Beard's 1914 book *Shelters, Shacks and Shanties* contains over three hundred drawings and instructions intended to instruct "boys of all ages" in constructing simple shelters; it was reprinted in 1992 by Shelter Publications of Bolinas, California. See also Kathy Smith Antenat, *American Tree Houses and Play Houses* (White Hall, Va.: Betterway Publications, 1991).

For studies in American traditional house designs beyond the simplest forms, see William R. Ferris, Jr., "Mississippi Folk Architecture: A Sampling," *MSF* 1 (1973): 71–83; James R. O'Malley, "Functional Aspects of Folk Housing: A Case for the 'I' House, Union County, Tennessee," *TFSB* 38 (1972): 1–4; Alice Reed Morrison, "Rediscovering Roots through a Material Artifact: An Indiana I-House," *IF* 12 (1979): 146–64; Richard Pillsbury, "Patterns in the Folk and Vernacular House Forms of the Pennsylvania Culture Region," *PA* 9 (1977): 12–31; Henry Chandlee Forman, *Early Nantucket and Its Whale Houses* (New York: Hastings House, 1966); and Henry Glassie's brilliant study *Folk Housing in Middle Virginia: A Structural Analysis of Historic Artifacts* (Knoxville: University of Tennessee Press, 1975). Glassie's influence is apparent in such recent works as Howard Wight Marshall's *Folk Architecture in Little Dixie: A Regional Culture in Missouri* (Columbia: University of Missouri Press, 1981).

In common with Marshall, William Lynwood Montell and Michael Lynn Morse discuss barns and other farm outbuildings as well as houses in their *Kentucky Folk Architecture* (Lexington: University Press of Kentucky, 1976). Barns have also been studied in such works as Wilbur Zelinsky's "The New England Connecting Barn," *GR* 48 (1958): 540–53; Henry Glassie, "The Variation of Concepts within Tradition: Barn Building in Otsego County, New York," in *Man and Cultural Heritage: Papers in Honor of Fred B. Kniffen, Geoscience and Man* 5, ed. H. J. Walker and W. G. Haag (Baton Rouge: Louisiana State University School of Geoscience, 1974), pp. 177–235; Glassie's "Barns across Southern England: A Note on Transatlantic Comparisons and Architectural Meanings," *PA* 7 (1975): 9–19; Allen G. Noble's "Barns as Elements of the Settlement Landscape of Rural Ohio," *PA* 9 (1977): 63–79; Theodore H. M. Prudon's "The Dutch Barn in America: Survival of a Medieval Structural Frame," *NYF* 2 (1976): 123–42; and Robert F. Ensminger's *The Pennsylvania Barn: Its Origins, Evolution, and Distribution in North America* (Baltimore: Johns Hopkins University Press, 1992).

A fine survey of barn types (including ethnic examples, round barns, and polygonal barns), barn-construction details, and barn-building tools and materials appeared in a special section by Lee Hartman, "Michigan Barns, Our Vanishing Landscape," *Michigan Natural Resources* 45 (March–April 1976): 17–32. Alvar W. Carlson provided a "Bibliography on Barns in the United States and Canada" in *PA* 10 (1978): 65–71. The round barn was actually an advanced design that was commercially advertised and produced, though it is considered "vernacular" by some scholars today. See two essays by Roger L. Welsch—"The Nebraska Round Barn," *JPC* 1 (1967): 403–9; and "Nebraska's Round Barn," *NH* 51 (1970): 49–92 —and especially John T. Hanou's book *A Round Indiana: Round Barns in the Hoosier State* (West Lafayette, Ind.: Purdue University Press, 1993).

Allen G. Noble and Richard K. Cleek tackled the thorny problem of "Sorting Out the Nomenclature of English Barns" in *MC* 26 (1994): 49–63, but their proposals were disputed by John Fraser Hart in his essay "On the Classification of Barns," *MC* 26 (1994): 37–46.

David R. Lee and Hector H. Lee document the "Thatched Cowsheds of the Mormon Country" in *WF* 40 (1981): 171–87; these simple structures found in parts of Utah, Idaho, and Nevada are used to protect livestock from rain, snow, and cold. In a supplementary note, Charles S. Peterson compared such cowsheds to the pioneer bowery, and the "Old Tabernacle" of the Mormons to "The Grove" erected in Nauvoo, Illinois, and to "speaking stands" used by Brigham Young during the Western trek—see *WF* 41 (1982): 145–47.

In *Hollybush: Folk Building and Social Change in an Appalachian Community* (Knoxville: University of Tennessee Press, 1984), Charles E. Martin uses fieldwork and oral history to reconstruct the folklife of a remote mountain community in eastern Kentucky that lasted from 1881 to 1960. In its focus on social and cultural aspects of folk architecture, it is comparable to Michael Ann Williams's *Homeplace* (cited in Focus: Life in a One-Room or Two-Room House). Another study of the uses of rather than forms of folk architecture is Gerald Thomas's "Functions of the Newfoundland Outhouse," *WF* 48 (1989): 221–43.

In a unique folklife study, published in *IF* 4 (1971): 61–88, John M. Vlach made a detailed survey of two Parke County, Indiana, covered-bridge builders' works (thirty-six out of Indiana's 130 examples). Covered bridges, however, like round barns, were often built by professionals following plans developed by engineers. Mainly it is their rustic quality and nostalgic evocation of early America—plus the fact that they were built only during a limited past time—that leads us to classify them as "vernacular" structures.

21

FOLK CRAFTS
AND ART

FOLK CRAFTS

The artifacts of American folk design and creation are an engaging and worthwhile subject for study, but a unified theoretical basis for such study is difficult to formulate. Perhaps even more than with other types of folk tradition, it is extremely problematic to categorize the artifacts themselves as "folk" or "nonfolk" and to describe their production as "craft" or "art." How can we distinguish the impulse to create and to decorate objects as essentially different in a "folk" sense from a supposedly higher "art" sense? Where does a utilitarian *craft* leave off and an *art* begin? The usual assumptions underlying studies of folklife are not much help. **Folk crafts,** for instance, are usually thought of as amateur labor resulting in traditional home-made objects that are primarily functional. But these "folk" items may also be made by professional or semiprofessional artisans well aware of their creative abilities, and often the artifacts produced are decorative as well as useful.

Fencing farm and ranch fields, for example, is a necessary stage in the settlement and use of land; pioneer fences, like houses, were at first made from the nearest resources. Thus, stone fences, wooden fences, hedges, and ditches are common in different topography or in different parts of the country. The proper construction techniques for each type were traditionally passed on, along with such variant names as "snake fence," "worm fence," or "zigzag fence" for those made of interlocking split rails. The simplest fences, usually also the earliest, were rows of the waste material generated from clearing land for cultivation—brush, stones, or branches and stumps (generally interwoven into a "rip gut" or "bull" fence). Such fences were picturesque and fairly functional, although somewhat wasteful of land; their meanders prevented cultivation to the edge of the cleared plot. Later, as time permitted and esthetic considerations prevailed, more-attractive rail or "post-and-rider" fences were put up, and these were often contracted for with local builders or carpenters. Solid, well-aligned, and often painted, wooden fencing is still a high-prestige consideration for many property owners, both rural and suburban, so the folk fence may be considered simultaneously an adjunct to architecture and landscaping, a useful craft, and a commonplace work of art. When barbed wire became readily available for fencing, devices employing the levering principle were invented for tightening the strands, and rock-filled frames were made for supporting posts in hard ground where postholes could not easily be dug or drilled.

Gateways and stiles in fences range from the simplest openings —just the removal of some rails or the leaving of a small crack to slip through—to elaborate arrangements that allow the gate to be opened from horseback or in a buggy and that have an automatic self-closing feature. Traditional American fence and gate makers demonstrated their taste and ingenuity in the uses to which they put old wagon wheels. Some wheels were lined up in rows, forming the fence itself; others served as the pivot point of a gate or were merely fastened to the gate as decoration. The theme was sometimes carried indoors, when a wagon wheel was used as a chandelier or its hub alone became a lamp base.

Western cattle guards (which occasionally also used old wagon wheels as the "wings" to span the area between road and fence) are other folk artifacts that demonstrate both ingenuity and considerable variation. Blocking ranch animals' passage along a roadway (no one is sure exactly *why* they work!), cattle guards were made of wood rails, metal pipes, or other materials, either with or without a pit;

Stockade fencing at the Warburton Ranch in the Grouse Creek area of extreme Northwestern Utah (1985).

they could be elaborate or very simple, and sometimes nowadays on modern highways are simply represented by stripes painted on the pavement.

Stands for rural mailboxes show similar patterns of development. The basic needs, to support the box at a suitable level and to identify its owner, can be solved simply by nailing the box to a post and painting a name on it. But people have gone to great lengths to improve on this solution with handcrafted, and often quite decorative, traditional devices made of welded chain links, bent pipes, driftwood, and other materials. A favorite traditional American mailbox stand is the plywood Uncle Sam, which is painted red, white, and blue, with the box placed in the figure's hands. Another common mailbox holder is the old piece of discarded farm equipment—milk can, cream separator, wagon wheel, hand plow, or the like—or a potbellied stove. The last sometimes appears supporting a box marked "mail," the smoke pipe marked "newspapers," and the door to the stove marked "bills." A variation on the "joke" mailbox has an extra receptacle mounted on a pole some ten or more feet high; it is marked "airmail."

A rural mailbox decorated with old automobile wheels
(place and date unknown).

FOLK CRAFTS AND ART: PROBLEMS IN IDENTITY

In folklife studies, **folk art** is usually thought of as the purely decorative or representational items produced by traditional means. But
much folk art is very close to handicraft, and it is difficult to distinguish the two fields. Stenciling, for example, was once a favorite
decorative medium for house floors and walls, and it is often displayed or pictured as an early American "folk art." But except for
the original creative drawing and cutting of the design in the stencil
pattern, the application of it to a surface was a mere mechanical
matter of moving it along, holding it down, and applying paint to

the cutout opening. Fancy sewing, quilting, rug hooking, and weaving also satisfy the creative urge and go beyond just holding textiles together or making bodies, beds, or floors warm; they might be considered both folk craft and folk art. If a "craft" piece, like a duck decoy or a quilt, is displayed on a shelf or hung on a wall as decoration, then it would seem to have become "art."

Folklorist Simon J. Bronner, in his 1985 book *American Material Culture and Folklife* (cited in chapter 19), made these distinctions on the folk or nonfolk aspects of handmade quilts:

> The woman making quilts for her grandchildren the way her grandmother made one for her grabs the attention of the folklorist. When a woman makes quilts for art shows and clubs, or learns to make quilts from a kit or class, the object attracts the student of popular culture. When the woman becomes a "textile artist" with creations proudly protected in a refined gallery, the art historian and critic are usually nearby.
>
> More often than not, though, students from the disciplines find themselves side by side considering the complex workings of tradition in American culture.

In his book *Folk Art and Art Worlds*, Bronner distinguished the two "art worlds"—first, that of dealers, collectors, and gallery professionals (who focus on the art objects themselves); second, "the world of academe" (where the focus is on the folk).

As with building trades and handicrafts, mere amateur status does not define the folk artist, for traditional creations have come from many professional artists—portraitists, carvers, calligraphers, metalworkers, and the like. In fact, only artisans or artists producing things solely for their own or their family's use can, strictly speaking, be called amateurs. But the vast majority of such creators are specialists who produce only one kind of artifact and then sell or barter it with others; professionalism is the rule, not the exception, in folk crafts and arts.

The particularly loose terminology of many folk-art studies, whether among art collectors or folklore scholars, further confuses the matter of definitions. We find "primitive art," "popular art," "schoolgirl art," "provincial art," "outsider art," and several other terms in use for essentially the same materials. The most consistent use of the term "folk art" is for untrained ("nonacademic") representational artists, primarily painters, who depicted traditional subjects, like barn raisings or harvesting, in traditional styles. Some, but not all of them, were itinerant artists, but none of them (at least it has never been proved) painted bodies on canvases all winter and traveled around adding the heads of their customers in the summer. This notion is merely a folk legend of considerable tenacity.

As broadly conceived by folklorists, American "folk art" includes a wide variety of miscellaneous decorative traditions. In a schoolroom, for instance, drowsy children may amuse themselves by tracing repetitious looped patterns on scratchpaper or on flyleaves of books. Others like to carve a checkerboard pattern down the length of a new pencil and all the way around it. Some people fold long paper chains out of gum wrappers or one-dollar bills, while others fold bills into origamilike patterns. Some folk artists specialize in carving wooden chains or a "ball in cage" from one piece of wood. Cattails, dried milkweed pods, and other weeds may be gathered and painted for decorations.

A prolific source of contemporary folk crafts and art, already touched on in the discussion of rural mailboxes and the reuse of old wagon wheels, is the modern continuation of what W. F. H. Nicolaisen called "distorted function." Adaptation of old durable parts from outmoded equipment for new purposes was formerly, as Nicolaisen wrote, "part of a campaign of thriftiness." But in today's suburban context such adaptation of old artifacts for new purposes has less an economic motivation than a symbolic one, expressing the modern person's attitude toward the rural past.

FOCUS: REINVENTING THE WHEEL'S FUNCTION

Stronger in its function as a reminder of a squandered, unrecoverable past than all the material items listed so far and unending in its invocation of non-urban folkiness and so-called peasant simplicity, is the wheel. Indeed, it is probably not too extravagant to claim that the wheel has become the suburban symbol of American rusticity, decorative in its smooth roundness and symmetrical radiation of its spokes, usually painted in the innocent white of an untainted past. Sometimes wheels are simply left standing in contrived abandon, either leaning against a building (significantly often a garage!) or against a pile of stones, but mostly they have

*been placed more deliberately at the end of a driveway or entrance, some-
times singly, but more often in pairs giving visual emphasis to an additional lateral symmetry, or rarely in even larger mumbers employed as
boundary markers or delimiting property. Sometimes their dominating
decorativeness is also exploited functionally beyond the mere marking of
driveways and property lines, in so far as they may serve as nameplates,
advertisements for antique stores, and as ornamental additions to, or supporting props of, mailboxes.*

*Although the wooden cartwheel predominates, iron wheels not infre-
quently serve the same purpose. Sometimes, millstones take their place,
providing not only acceptable stone-made alternatives considered pleasing
to the eye, but through their connection with the other aspects of milling,
their own special category of pre-industrial symbolism.*

Source: W. F. H. Nicolaisen, " 'Distorted Function' In Material Aspects of Culture,"
FF 12 (1979): 223–35.

DISCUSSION TOPICS:

1. How does Nicolaisen interpret the shape, symmetry, placement,
materials, color, and various functions of old wheels used as suburban
decoration? Why is it significant that wheels are sometimes displayed
leaning against a garage?

2. What other items left over from the past may serve similar
functions and provide comparable symbolism in the modern suburb?

3. Prepare an annotated display of photos showing old rural items
serving a new "distorted function" in a modern suburb.

Just as an outmoded or leftover piece of rain guttering or hot-
water heater may be converted into a planter, older bits of verbal
lore (such as sea chanteys) may later reappear as entertainment (i.e.,
be sung in a folk-music concert). Similarly, plastic bleach jugs, tin
cans, and milk cartons are turned into baskets, banks, or toys.
Wreaths are woven of wool, feathers, or human hair and may be
fashioned from coat hangers and plastic bags. Modern wreaths might
even be formed out of the plastic holders for six-packs of canned
soda or beer, twisted into patterns and stapled onto old wooden
gravemarkers as decorations.

The enhancement of "found objects" may also produce a form of
folk art. For example, in one Western sawmill the "chopper saw-
yers," whose job it is to cut knots out of second-grade to fourth-
grade lumber, specialize in decorating knots with a pencil or pen
and sending their artwork down the line for the other men to ad-

mire. The drawings may be animal figures, caricatures of fellow workmen, or scenes. Even appreciation and acceptance by the folk may qualify an item as folk art: folklife specialist Roger Welsch went so far as to suggest that the brilliant autumn color of a prominent tree in a Nebraska small town—much appreciated by the residents and closely watched each year—is perhaps an object of "folk art" for that community.

However simple some of these items may seem, they are certainly more valid as instances of genuine folk art than are, say, pieces of ersatz tole painting (decorated tinware), fake plastic scrimshaw (whale-ivory decorating), or Navajo-like sand-painting designs produced by professional artisans or by amateurs from factory-made kits. Such artifacts belong to popular culture, not folk tradition, even though they take their inspiration from traditional designs. The colors and design of an artifact do not make it authentic folk art, no matter how closely these features follow a folk prototype; the traditional construction and use of an artifact, however, do establish it as "folk." Stressing the importance of tradition in the production of folk art, folklorist John Michael Vlach wrote, in *Folk Art and Art Worlds* (1986; reissued 1992):

> No genuine folk artist can ever be completely self-taught. Certainly folk artists may work alone, even in seclusion, but they will work within a socially sanctioned set of rules for artistic production which they expect will insure the acceptability of their completed pieces. Thus they are mentally connected even if physically isolated.

FOLK CRAFTS AND ART: STUDIES AND EXAMPLES

Another American folklorist who has given these matters a great deal of thought, Michael Owen Jones, in a 1975 study of Kentucky chairmakers (reissued in 1989), proposed this definition of art in general, which describes folk art insofar as the individual creator works within a group or regional tradition that is transmitted informally:

> skill in the making or doing of that which functions as (among other things) a stimulus to appreciation of an individual's mastery of tools

and materials apparent in what he has made, the output of that skill; and the activity manifesting the use of that skill. . . . [Art] is something thought to be special (usually because of the skill required), generating an appreciative, contemplative response in the percipient.

In practice, Jones's informants recognized both the functional and the esthetic qualities of well-made objects; one man referred to the "beauty part" and the "lasting part." John O. Livingston, a basket-maker of Mount Pleasant, York County, Pennsylvania, made the same point in different words, as reported by Henry Glassie in *The Spirit of Folk Art* (1989):

> Livingston discusses his baskets in terms of utility and strength. "Them babies are strong," he says, dropkicking one the length of his shop. But his baskets are unnecessarily beautiful. He chooses their wood carefully and arranges it by color. He finishes them fastidiously, burning off all the fine splinters that disrupt their smooth, clean appearance. More important, he takes delight in the elaborate process of their creation, felling young oak trees, splitting them into long strips, shaving the strips round in a machine of his own invention, then weaving baskets that match perfectly the models in his mind. "From a Tree to a Basket," a sign in his shop proclaims, telling you directly where his joy lies: in the wonder of technological manipulation through which he masters both the nature that lies beyond and the nature that rises within himself.

Following this lead, we may use the terms "craft" and "art" synonymously when studying traditional artifacts. Consequently, the goals for fieldwork in folk artifacts (in common with those for folk architecture) require several different kinds of data: careful description and picturing of the items themselves, facts about the raw materials used and the stages of construction, information about how the skills were acquired and to what uses the finished items are put, psychological profiles of the builders and the users, and statements by the individual makers and their community regarding the "esthetic" appeal of the finished products.

Traditional handcrafted devices for home, farm, and ranch are numerous, and many are still being constructed and are in regular use. Outside the house proper, there are weather vanes, whirligigs, door knockers, wells, and yard ornaments to investigate. Another interesting category is the identification devices for dwellings, including signs for family and residence names (especially on ranches and summer cottages). Some people handmake items that have long since been replaced by factory-produced ones—wooden scoop shovels, lawn furniture, and garden tools are examples.

In one well-known study of a homemade rural piece of folk technology, Central Western hay derricks were investigated by Austin and James Fife in research that considered the classification and distribution of the objects, the need for them, and their probable history. When they realized that light rainfall in the region allowed for the year-round outdoor storage of hay, Great Basin pioneer farmers created devices to stack their hay into high, compact formations that would shed what rain did fall. First they just dragged the hay up by means of a rope rigged to a "flagpole," but soon they constructed more complex derricks with pivoted booms and sometimes even wheels for moving them from job to job. Neighbors borrowed ideas from one another as the hay-derrick idea spread through the region, and so successful was this traditional manufacture that only recently have any mass-produced devices begun to replace the homemade ones.

Similar studies might be made of traditional fruit-boxing equipment, berry pickers, rattraps, harvesting tools (corn knives, husking pegs, etc.), rope-twisters, bits, spurs, rawhide equipment, scarecrows, and other agricultural artifacts. Homemade hunting, fishing, and camping equipment may also be traditional. These objects include shelters, boats, traps, animal calls, fishing lures, some trout flies, decoys (used for ducks, geese, swans, and even fish), and camp lanterns, all of which are commercially produced in great variety but which also linger in some folk forms. A good example of a folk invention incorporating a manufactured product is the fishing lure made from the aluminum snap-top of a beer or soft-drink can. This appeared in the West for steelhead fishing in the mid-1960s, only about one year after the pop-top beverage can was introduced to the market.

Household or domestic arts and crafts, sometimes subsumed under the inaccurate label of "women's art," form another large category of material for documentation and study. While it is true that certain clichéd themes of art were stressed in the "female academies" of the eighteenth and nineteenth centuries (still-life paintings, pastoral scenes, memorial pictures, etc.) and that crafts like needlework

Interior of a cabin in Harlan County, Kentucky, photographed between 1890 and 1903. Note the homemade quilts both on the beds and in storage above them.

are almost entirely the province of women, not every such work can be positively identified as a woman's production. Conversely, American women and men did occasionally cross over and engage in art or craft work that was not usually associated with their respective sex. Just who painted all the early American decorated fireplace screens, window shades, furniture, and kitchenware, for example, is not at all clear, although in many instances it may be guessed (as one art historian put it) that "anonymous was a woman." Most stitched samplers, embroidered bed rugs, and woven coverlets were certainly made by women, though men were also known to do some kinds of needlework in special circumstances (such as when they went to sea for long periods). Women also occasionally invaded such "hard" crafts as carpentry and blacksmithing.

Some of the old subsistence crafts like spinning, dyeing, braiding, soapmaking and candlemaking, and quilting are practiced nowadays solely as recreational pastimes. Among them, only quilting has been the subject of much study, perhaps partly because the picturesque names for the many colorful quilt patterns provide both linguistic and artistic matter for consideration. As Austin Fife pointed out, these names may be simply *descriptive* ("Turkey Tracks"), or they may be *romantic* ("Steps to the Altar"), *biblical* ("Jacob's Ladder"), *ancestral* ("Grandmother's Fan"), *exotic* ("Arabic Lattice"), or *evocative of the pioneering experience* ("Road to California").

A large number of professional crafts with formal apprenticeships provided useful objects for the home and farm through much of the nineteenth century. The list includes woodworking, cabinetmaking, furniture making, blacksmithing and other metalworking, glazing and glassblowing, pottery, basketry, and broommaking. Such production has largely been transferred to factories now, although small-scale individual-shop manufacture does continue and, in the case of some crafts like stained- and leaded-glass making, has begun to flourish again in recent years. The other side of the picture— traditional aspects of modern manufacturing—is represented by a skill such as sheet-metal working (producing downspouts and gutters, air-conditioning and heating ducts, and the like). With its background in the traditional tinkers' trade, this industrial craft, studied by David Shuldiner, retains some aspects of the old folk practices, and the same is probably true of other modern industries.

FOCUS: CHARLESTON BLACKSMITH

At least one celebrated blacksmith is still around, Philip Simmons. "If you see a beautiful iron gate with meticulous curves," Alphonso Brown said, "it was made by one of the master blacksmiths of two hundred years ago—or it was made by Philip Simmons." . . .

We went to see Philip Simmons. He is a kindly man of eighty-two whose forge is in a ramshackle tin building behind his house on Blake Street. It doesn't look like the workshop of a National Treasure, but that's what Mr. Simmons is, officially certified by the Smithsonian Institution.

I asked him how he got started.

"When I was thirteen," he said, "I used to stand in the door of the blacksmith shop and see the red-hot fire and see the sparks flying, and I liked that. The blacksmith let me help out, hold the horse while he was putting the shoe on, turn the hand forge, clean up the shop. After a while, he learned me the names of everything. If he said, 'Boy, hand me that three-inch swage,' I had to know what he wanted. I learned that way." . . .

There is an old saying among blacksmiths that the two ways a blacksmith can go to hell are by hammering cold iron and not charging enough.

It appeared to me from his modest living conditions that Mr. Simmons hadn't charged enough.

Source: Charles Kuralt, *Charles Kuralt's America* (New York: G. P. Putnam's Sons, 1995), pp. 68–69.

DISCUSSION TOPICS:

1. Kuralt, the late popular CBS newsman, captures the "feel" of Philip Simmons's work and personality, while folklife scholar John Michael Vlach has documented the exact details of the work and career of Philip Simmons. (See chapter 5 of *By the Work of their Hands*, cited in chapter 19, and Vlach's book *Charleston Blacksmith*, cited in the bibliographic notes to this chapter.) Contrast these treatments by a journalist and a folklorist; for example, how does each man describe the blacksmith's shop and his apprenticeship?

2. Philip Simmons was named a National Heritage Fellow in 1982. What other American folk crafts and arts—and what other artisans and performers—have been so honored? (See the book *American Folk Masters*, cited in chapter 19.)

3. Simmons mentioned a "swage" to Charles Kuralt, and Vlach listed "anvil tools (swages, hardies, fullers, etc.)" in his inventory of Simmons's tools. What are these devices, and how are they used by blacksmiths?

Of surviving traditional crafts, basketry stands out as a prime example. Although baskets have been largely replaced as everyday containers by cartons, bottles, bags, and the like, whatever baskets are still made almost invariably are folk products. There are several good practical reasons for the continuing production of baskets: in addition to being durable, inexpensive, light but strong, and reusable, they may be constructed in a variety of pleasing shapes and handy sizes. American baskets are usually made of splints (or "splits") of pliant wood, such as white oak or ash, woven around bentwood hoops or ribs. Different sizes and shapes of baskets are made for marketing, for food harvest or storage, or for use as picnic baskets, magazine baskets, laundry baskets, fishing creels, or pack baskets. African-American basketry is of the "coil" type, made from bundles of "sweet grass" and long-leafed pine needles coiled around and upward to form the bottom and sides, and sewn together with thin strips made from fronds of palmetto trees.

Focus: Making a Palmetto Hat

Martha McMillin Roberts. *Mrs. Louis Brunet, of the Bayou Cane Community, Plaiting Strips of Bleached Palmetto for a Palmetto Hat.* 1947. Courtesy of University of Louisville Photographic Archives, Standard Oil Collection, neg. no. 50741.

Palmetto has been used in the folk arts of various Louisiana ethnic groups. Artifacts made with palmetto have included hats, fans, mats, purses, baskets, and sandals. Palmetto weaving was a fairly common craft in America generally in the nineteenth century, widely practiced in the South, where palmetto was readily at hand, but also in other places, such as New England, where the palm had to be imported. In Louisiana the Acadian Handicrafts Project directed by Louise Olivier of the LSU extension service promoted the art during the 1930s, and in recent years Acadian Elvina Kidder of Arnaudville has been recognized as a promising practitioner of this type of weaving.

Source: Frank de Caro, *Folklife in Louisiana Photography: Images of Tradition* (Baton Rouge: Louisiana State University Press, 1991), photograph no. 82, p. 82, and note, p. 183.

DISCUSSION TOPICS:

1. What else can you see in this 1947 photograph of possible folk-life interest?

2. What is palmetto and where does it grow? (Frank de Caro offers a brief explanation in his note to photograph no. 13, p. 175.)

3. Can you find other illustrations of braiding with palmetto strips, or of similar folk crafts, either in local museums or in other published sources?

Folk pottery making, once widely practiced in the United States, is a more complex and diversified craft involving chemistry and physics, special equipment, numerous designs, and different marketing traditions. The investigator must study the raw materials (clays and glazes), equipment (wheels, mills for grinding materials, kilns), the potter's shop layout, decorative elements (colors, shapes, handles, lids, inscriptions, etc.), and the great variety of artifacts produced, which include syrup jugs, whiskey jugs, pickling crocks, bowls, mugs, plates, and churns. Most of the few truly traditional potters that remain (apart from Native American potters) are in the South.

The craft of barrelmaking no longer involves individual "coopers" turning out entire barrels, but traditional work methods persist in the remaining modern cooperages, which supply the relatively few wooden vessels of staves and hoops that are still in use. While barrels and kegs were once commonly employed for flour, crackers, nails, lard, gunpowder, wine, beer, and many other commodities, and coopers also made tubs, buckets, and churns, nowadays the principal use for barrels in the United States is for aging bourbon whiskey. The industry's need for tight, charred, white-oak barrels keeps the craft alive, and modern coopers face the same problems of shaping their staves, "raising" a barrel, fitting the hoops and heads, and assuring its tightness as their predecessors did.

The traditional craft of handmaking skis would provide for an interesting study. It would require a great deal of searching through early accounts of life in northern parts of the country, including Alaska, and making careful distinctions between skis and snowshoes, both of which were frequently called snowshoes in some regions in the nineteenth century. A character called "Snowshoe" Thompson, for example, wore long, homemade skis when he carried mail in the

California mountains in 1856. A Colorado minister in the 1860s wrote in his autobiography:

> I made me a pair of snow-shoes, and, of course, was not an expert. . . . [They] were of the Norway style, from nine to eleven feet in length, and ran well when the snow was just right, but very heavy when they gathered snow. I carried a pole to jar the sticking snow off.

A man who settled in Boise, Idaho, in 1869, referred to homemade skis in his reminiscences as "Idaho snowshoes." Were such skis made in other regions, and were they called "snowshoes" or something else there? Does the term "Norway style" indicate that Norwegians taught others to make skis in this country? What materials and techniques were used to make skis? How were they employed? The answers to such questions might well be found in a thorough research project, and the next step might be to inquire about traditional aspects of the modern high-tech manufacture of skis and snowboards.

Folk toys existed in the past and still exist in great variety. They are made both by parents and by children. Some are made from natural materials (willow whistles, cornstalk "fiddles," apple-head dolls, burr baskets, and dandelion chains), while others begin with manufactured items (clothespin dolls, spool window-rattlers and "tanks," and tobacco-can "harmonicas"). A whole family of toys is made simply from folded paper—"cootie catchers" (a toy for the mock capture of "cooties" from a person's scalp), airplanes, noise-makers, and hats—while toy weaponry forms another large class (slingshots, hairpin launchers, peashooters, and rubber-band guns with spring-clothespin triggers). Some children in the past made an effective—and dangerous—substitute for fireworks by screwing a machine bolt halfway into a nut, filling the cavity with tips cut from wooden "kitchen matches," and then screwing a second bolt in from the other end. The device is thrown into the air so it will come down on a sidewalk or pavement, and when a bolt head strikes, the whole arrangement blasts apart with a loud report.

Musical instruments of folk construction have benefited from the widespread interest in folk music in this country and, thus, have received considerably more study than many other kinds of material tradition. A number of very simple instruments are found in African-American tradition—a "rattler," made of bottle tops loosely nailed to a paddle; "quills," or the panpipe, fashioned of hollow reeds tied together; the "diddly bow" (or "bow diddly"), a single string stretched along a board, broom, or house wall (sometimes also called a "jitterbug"); and the slightly more elaborate washtub bass. Much more highly developed, both physically and musically, from African roots is the American five-string banjo. The unfretted fifth string on the folk banjo contributes a drone sound in some strumming styles and takes a more active role in fingerpicking. Another distinctive American instrument is the Southern Mountain plucked dulcimer. Enjoying a revival in the twentieth century, the plucked dulcimer is not to be confused with the rarer (and usually German or eastern European) hammered dulcimer. The plucked dulcimer derives from the European family of folk instruments that includes the Norwegian *langeleik*, the Swedish *humle*, the German *Scheitholt*, and the French *espinette des vosges*, all instruments with drone strings that are played while being rested horizontally on a table or on the lap. The American mountain dulcimer generally has three strings —a melody string and two drones—and is shaped in graceful curves along the sides, with sound holes (often heart-shaped) on the top surface. Traditionally, the dulcimer is played with a quill or "feather pick."

Forms of purely decorative and representational American folk art already mentioned include whittling, needlework, stenciling, and painting. Other examples are scrimshaw (carving and decorating objects of whalebone or ivory), tattooing, gravestone carving, door- and window-screen painting (practiced in Baltimore, Maryland), and what have been called "dendroglyphs" (patterns, inscriptions, and pictures carved on trees), particularly common on the white bark of birches and aspens. Folk artisans sometimes make special "art" objects, such as face jugs and figurines by potters and toy furniture or miniature farm equipment by woodworkers. In African-American folk art, alligators, heads, and grotesque skulls are found in clay sculpture and wood carving. Carved and painted canes (walking sticks) depict a wide variety of designs and creatures—from snakes, lizards, frogs, and birds to political and patriotic symbols and human figures ranging from Adam and Eve to Elvis. Even the making of snowmen and other snow sculpture may be considered a folk-art form, although snow-sculpture contests with professional entrants once again illustrate the disparity between folk, popular, and elite levels of performance.

Just as musical expression, too, has been identified at folk, popular, and art levels, comparisons might be made of such forms as portraiture, still life, the grotesque, or caricature as they appear in folk art, popular art, and "high" art. Or a historical subject, such as "Custer's Last Stand," might be compared in American folk expressions, in popular media such as magazine illustrations or Currier and Ives prints, and in serious academic art. Some scholars, however, argue against the utility of identifying such "levels" of art, and they prefer to drop the terms "folk art" and "primitive art" in favor of something like Michael Owen Jones's formulation "units or structures of expressive behavior learned and manifested primarily in situations of firsthand interaction." Still, some kind of esthetic and comparative evaluations of art levels seems necessary, if only to provide a good foundation for supporting or rebutting such provocative generalizations as these from an art historian writing in the 1950s, but representing a viewpoint sometimes still heard:

> Folk art is naïve, crude, clumsy and old-fashioned, popular art often skillful and technically apt, though vulgar, subject to superficial and rapid transformation, but incapable of achieving either more radical change or finer discrimination. Genuine art is used up, disintegrated, and simplified by folk art; it is watered down, botched and bowdlerized by popular art.

The notion of "genuine art" being threatened and debased by both folk art and popular art results from the viewer examining only the artifacts themselves (the art) and neglecting the creators (the artists, including the folk) while applying standards of formal academic art criticism. The folklorist's antidote to such judgments is to reemphasize the folk behind the artifacts. Promoting this viewpoint, here are the statements of three leading modern specialists in American folk crafts and art:

Aspen-tree carving showing a horse with brand "TH" and the name "Tony" in fancy script. This and other carvings signed "Tony Herrara" and dated in the early 1950s were photographed in 1968 in Millcreek Canyon, on the Dog Lake Trail, Wasatch Mountains, just east of Salt Lake City, Utah.

John Michael Vlach:

The study of American folk art needs to find its center—its center of meaning—so that it may grow and develop in an orderly and productive fashion. That center is, I believe, where it has always been, in its folk artists. Generally folk art has been pursued as a set of things, important things to be sure, but the current generation of scholars and collectors now find themselves pondering much folk art that has no folk attached to it. . . . The study of folk art can be reoriented so that our efforts center on the people who create this art. (From "The Need for Plain Talk about Folk Art," in *Folk Art and Art Worlds*)

Michael Owen Jones:

It seems to me that as significant as objects, artifacts, and things are, they should not be elevated to supremacy over the people who made and used them. If the tangible products of human imagination become a center of attention, and the ideas, feelings, needs, and desires manifested by them are ignored, then both appreciation and understanding of those very artifacts are, ironically, diminished. Therefore, material culture studies and folk art research might achieve their purposes most fully when the makers and users as well as the processes of conceptualization, implementation, and utilization—rather than the artifacts per se—are the object of inquiry. (From "Epilogue," in *Exploring Folk Art: Twenty Years of Thought on Craft, Work, and Aesthetics*)

Henry Glassie:

Folk art demands a different context, not a context conditioned by Kandinsky and Picasso and shaped by dealers and scholars, but a context constructed by the people who made the art. In its own context, when the weaver sits at her loom, when the supplicant touches his forehead to the prayer rug, folk art is not a corollary or critique of modern art, it is a part of the experience of life. At life's center, in the midst of common work, people always have found and always will find ways to create things that simultaneously enfold themselves, present their social affinities, and mutter about the enormity of the universe. In that context these things are not folk. They are art. (From "The Idea of Folk Art," in *Folk Art and Art Worlds*)

BIBLIOGRAPHIC NOTES

The following are general older surveys of American handicrafts, all containing some illustrations and useful descriptions, although their analyses are out of date: *Hands That Built New Hampshire*, published by the Work Projects Administration Writers' Program (Brattleboro, Vt., 1940); Ella Shannon Bowles, *Homespun Handicrafts* (Philadelphia, 1931; reissued, New York: Benjamin Blom, 1972); Allen H. Eaton, *Handicrafts of the Southern Highlands* (New York: Russell Sage Foundation, 1937; paperback reprint, New York: Dover Publications, 1973); Rollin C. Steinmetz and Charles S. Rice, *Vanishing Crafts and Their Craftsmen* (New Brunswick, N.J.: Rutgers University Press, 1959); and Erwin O. Christensen, *American Crafts and Folk Arts*, America Today Series, no. 4 (Washington, D.C.: Robert B. Luce, 1964).

Mamie Meredith collected "The Nomenclature of American Pioneer Fences" in *SFQ* 15 (1951): 109–51. Two studies with more depth are H. F. Raup's "The Fence in the Cultural Landscape," *WF* 6 (1947): 1–12; and E. C. Mather and J. F. Hart's "Fences and Farms," *GR* 44 (1954): 201–23. A unique fence, "the lopped tree fence," was described by Mary Catharine Davis in *SFQ* 21 (1957): 174–75. Patricia Mastick writes of "Dry Stone Walling," the construction technique that proceeds without mortar between the stones, in an article in *IF* 9 (1976): 113–33, based on interviews with an Indiana master of the form. James F. Hoy's *The Cattle Guard: Its History and Lore* (Lawrence: University Press of Kansas, 1982) is a book-length study of a familiar kind of Western folk technology.

The Fifes' hay-derrick study was published in *WF* 7 (1948): 225–39, with addenda in *WF* 10 (1951): 320–22. A distributional study of a particular type of homemade hair- or rope-twister was Fred Kniffen's "The Western Cattle Complex: Notes on Differentiation and Diffusion," *WF* 12 (1953): 179–85. On a related craft, see Robert and Martha Cochran, with Christopher Pierle, "The Preparation and Use of Bear Grass Rope: An Interview with Robert Simmons, Mississippi Folk Craftsman," *NYFQ* 30 (1974): 185–96. An interview with a Finnish "tie-hacker" of McCall, Idaho, was published by H. J. Swinney in *WF* 24 (1965): 271–73; while "Tiehacking in the Northeast Arkansas Bottomlands" was documented by Larry D. Ball and William M. Clements in *SF* 49 (1992): 157–71. On traditional blacksmithing techniques, see Mody C. Boatright, "How Will Boatright Made Bits and Spurs," *JAF* 83 (1970): 77–80; and John M. Vlach, "The Fabrication of a Traditional Fire Tool," *JAF* 86 (1973): 54–57, which deals with a black craftsman who is the subject of Vlach's 1981 book *Charleston Blacksmith: The Work of Philip Simmons* (Athens: University of Georgia Press; rev. ed., Columbia: University of South Carolina Press, 1992). Vlach surveyed "Afro-American Folk Crafts in Nineteenth Century Texas" in *WF* 40 (1981): 149–61. A special double issue of *SFQ* (42:2–3 [1978]) concerned African-American material culture (basketry, pottery, fifes and flutes, wood carving, etc.)

The Colorado skiing minister quoted in this chapter was the Reverend John L. Dyer, whose autobiography, *The Snow-Shoe Itinerant*, was published in Cincinnati in 1890. "Idaho snowshoes" were described by Thomas Corwin Donaldson in *Idaho of Yesterday* (Caldwell, Idaho: Caxton Press, 1941).

Three studies that related folk craftsmanship to larger-scale production were Carlos C. Drake, "Traditional Elements in the Cooperage Industry," *KFQ* 14 (1969): 81–96; Robert S. McCarl, Jr., "The Production Welder: Product, Process and the Industrial Craftsman," *NYFQ* 30 (1974): 243–53; and David Shuldiner, "The Art of Sheet Metal Work: Traditional Craft in a Modern Industrial Setting," *SWF* 4 (1980): 37–41.

Several books offer general illustrated surveys of household and farm crafts. Jared van Wagenen, Jr., in *The Golden Age of Homespun* (New York: American Century Series, 1963), provided "a record of the lore and the methods by which our forebears lived upon the land" in upper New York State from the Revolution to the Civil War. Works by Eric Sloane, beautifully illustrated with line drawings of museum pieces, include *American Yesterday* (New York: W. Funk, 1956), *The Seasons of America Past* (New York: W. Funk, 1958), *Diary of an Early American Boy: Noah Blake, 1805* (1962; repr. Ballantine paperback, 1974), *A Reverence for Wood* (1965; repr. Ballantine, 1973), and *A Museum of Early American Tools* (1964; repr. Ballantine, 1974).

In "An Indiana Subsistence Craftsman," *PA* 8 (1976): 107–18, Willard B. Moore documented the work of a part-time craftsman, not well known in his community, who makes and repairs various artifacts for personal or local use—gambrel sticks (to hang hogs for butchering), well drops (to retrieve lost buckets from wells), clevises (to secure chains), corn knives, foot-adze handles, sledge runners, wheels, and the like. In "Flag and Rush Industry of Savannah, New York," *NYF* 7 (1981): 1–46, Hugo Freund and Amy Rashap showed both the use of swamp plants (of the cattail family) as gaskets in barrels and the folk industry that supplied them.

Special studies of particular crafts include Mac E. Barrick, "Pennsylvania Corn Knives and Husking Pegs," *KFQ* 15 (1970): 128–37; Laurence Clayton, "How Litt Perkins Treats Hides and Makes Leather Goods," *WF* 40 (1981): 162–71; and four articles on basketmaking—Henry Glassie, "William Houck, Maker of Pounded Ash Adirondack Pack-Baskets," *KFQ* 12 (1967): 23–54; Howard Wight Marshall, "Mr. Westfall's Baskets: Traditional Craftsmanship in Northcentral Missouri," *MSF* 2 (1974): 43–60 (reprinted in *Readings in American Folklore*, pp. 168–91); Glenn Hinson, "An Interview with Leon Berry, Maker of Baskets," *NCFJ* 27 (1979): 56–60; and Charlene E. Gates, " 'The Work Is Afraid of Its Master': Proverb as Metaphor for a Basketmaker's Art," *WF* 50 (1991): 255–76. A book-length study is Rosemary O. Joyce's *A Bearer of Tradition: Dwight Stump, Basketmaker* (Athens: University of Georgia Press, 1989).

Kentucky's Age of Wood, by Kenneth Clarke and Ira Kohn (Lexington: University Press of Kentucky, 1976), deals with many artifacts traditionally made of the same material. Other articles on craftsmen in wood include Sylvia Ann Grider and Barbara Ann Allen, "Howard Taylor, Cane Maker and Handle Shaver," *IF* 7 (1974): 5–25; James R. Dow, "The Hand Carved Walking Canes of William Baurichter," *KFQ* 15 (1970): 138–47; Frank Reuter, "John Arnold's Link Chains: A Study in Folk Art," *MSF* 5 (1977): 41–52; and three articles on woodworkers and carvers in *IF* 13 (1980): 1–45. Three important book-length studies are Charles L. Briggs's *The Wood Carvers of Cordova, New Mexico: Social Dimensions of an Artistic "Revival"* (Knoxville: University of Tennessee Press, 1980), Simon J. Bronner's *Chain Carvers: Old Men Crafting Meaning* (Lexington: University Press of Kentucky, 1985), and George H. Meyer's *American Folk Art Canes: Personal Sculpture* (Bloomfield Hills, Mich.: Sandringham Press, 1992).

Beulah M. D'Olive Price described "Riving Shingles in Alcorn County" in *MFR* 6 (1972): 108–14, while David J. Winslow's topic was "New York Duck Decoys" in *KFQ* 17 (1972): 119–32. Two essays on traditional boatbuilding are Howard Wight Marshall and David H. Stanley, "Homemade Boats in South Georgia," *MFR* 12 (1978): 75–94; and Malcolm L. Lomeaux, "Origins and Evolution of Mississippi River Fishing Craft," *PA* 10 (1978): 73–97. See also Charles G. Zug III, "Little Boats: Making Ship Models on the North Carolina Coast," *NCFJ* 39 (1992): 1–42.

Southern American folk-pottery tradition is discussed in Charles G. Zug III, "Pursuing Pots: On Writing a History of North Carolina Folk Pottery," *NCFJ* 27 (1979): 35–55; and in Zug's book *Turners and Burners: The Folk Potters of North Carolina* (Chapel Hill: University of North Carolina Press, 1986). John A. Burrison's interest in Southern pottery, expressed in "Alkaline-glazed Stoneware: A Deep-South Pottery Tradition," *SFQ* 39 (1975): 377–403, flowered into his book *Brothers in Clay: The Story of Georgia Folk Pottery* (Athens: University of Georgia Press, 1983). For another region, see C. Kurt Dewhurst, *Grand Ledge* [Michigan] *Folk Pottery: Traditions at Work* (Ann Arbor, Mich.: UMI Research Press, 1986).

A general list of household handicrafts was given in the article by Afton Wynn cited in the notes to chapter 15. Paul Brewster included information on quilt patterns, dyeing, and folk toys in volume 1 of *The Frank C. Brown Collection of North Carolina Folklore*. For related studies, see Annie Louise D'Olive, "Folk Implements Used for Cleaning," *MFR* 2 (1968): 125–34; and Annelen Archbold, "Percy Beeson, a Kentucky Broommaker," *MSF* 3 (1975): 41–45.

There are many books on quilt patterns, most of them offering instructions for making quilts and providing historical notes. A good one is Carrie A. Hall and Rose G. Kretsinger's *The Romance of the Patchwork Quilt in America* (Caldwell, Idaho: Caxton Press, 1936; reissued, New York [n.d.]). Carrie Hall's large collection of quilt patches and patterns is deposited in the Museum of Art at the University of Kansas in Lawrence, which has a major collection of American quilts. Commenting on a list of quilt-pattern names submitted by Paul Brewster to *CFQ* 3 (1944): 61, Wayland D. Hand pointed out the interplay of folk and commercial patterns fostered by companies that sold quilt battings wrapped with advertising for their own lines of quilt patterns: see *CFQ* 3 (1944): 151–52. Useful for further studies are Andrea Greenberg's survey "American Quilting," in *IF* 5 (1972): 264–79, and a bibliography of American quilt making compiled by Susan Roach and Lorre M. Weidlich and published in *FFemC* 3 (Spring 1974): 17–28. For the work of individual artisans, see Joanne Farb, "Piecin' and Quiltin': Two Quilters in Southwest Arkansas," *SFQ* 39 (1975): 363–75.

Quilt studies continue to flourish, perhaps in part because quilting has a secure status as a revival craft in urban environments, although the focus of most studies is rural or small town. *Kentucky Quilts and Their Makers*, by Mary Washington Clarke (Lexington: University Press of Kentucky, 1976), offers a compact history and analysis. Articles include Sandra K. D. Stahl, "Quilts and a Quiltmaker's Aesthetics," *IF* 11 (1978): 105–32; Elizabeth Smith Schabel, "The Historical Significance of Patchwork Quilt Names as a Reflection of the Emerging Social Consciousness of the American Woman," *TFSB* 47 (1981): 1–16; Geraldine N. Johnson, "'More for Warmth Than for Looks': Quilts of the Blue Ridge Mountains," *NCFJ* 30 (1982): 55–84; and Laurel Horton, "Nineteenth-Century Quiltmaking Traditions in South Carolina," *SF* 46 (1989): 101–15.

Representative works on other textile crafts (among many that could be cited) are Gerald L. Pocius, "Hooked Rugs in Newfoundland: The Representation of Social Structure in Design," *JAF* 92 (1979): 273–84; Ann Williams, "The Alexander Family 'Kentucky Beauty': The Unraveling of a Coverlet Draft" [about weaving], *NCFJ* 29 (1981): 94–105; Joseph E. Sanders, "Woven Bed Covers of Central Indiana and Illinois," *MAF* 11 (1983): 1–12; and C. Kurt Dewhurst and Marsha MacDowell, *Michigan Hmong Arts: Textiles in Transition* (East Lansing: Michigan State University Museum, 1984).

Michael Owen Jones has written a number of important studies of American furniture making, such as "The Study of Traditional Furniture: Review and Preview," *KFQ* 12 (1967): 233–45; "'They Made Them for the Lasting Part': A 'Folk' Typology of Traditional Furniture Makers," *SFQ* 35 (1971): 44–61; and "'For Myself I Like a Decent, Plain-made Chair': The Concept of Taste and the Traditional Arts in America," *WF* 31 (1972): 27–52. Jones's work in these and other articles is incorporated into his book *The Hand Made Object and Its Maker* (Los Angeles: University of California Press, 1975), revised and reissued as *Craftsman of the Cumberlands* (Lexington: University Press of Kentucky, 1989). A lengthy study of a family of rural and urban chairmakers is Warren E. Roberts's "Turpin Chairs and the Turpin Family: Chairmaking in Southern Indiana," *MJLF* 7 (1981): 57–106.

American folk toys have been included in general books on folk crafts, but have had little individual scholarly treatment. A popular, nostalgic book that deals largely with simple folk toys is Robert Paul Smith's *How to Do Nothing with Nobody, All Alone by Yourself* (New York: W. W. Norton, 1958). An article describing a small local industry for manufacturing copies of folk toys is Henry B. Comstock's "Folk Toys Are Back Again," *Popular Science* (March 1960): 144–47. Two instruction books on folk-toy making are Joan Joseph's *Folk Toys around the World and How to Make Them* (New York: Parents Magazine Press in cooperation with the U.S. Committee for UNICEF, 1972) and Dick Schnache, *American Folk Toys: How to Make Them* (Baltimore: Penguin Books, 1973).

Andrea Koss studied the making of apple-head dolls in an article in *IF* 12 (1979): 38–54. In "The Cooties Complex," *WF* 39 (1980): 198–210, Sue Samuelson discussed children's play centering on an imaginary invisible germ or bug, but failed to mention the folded-paper toy known as a "cootie catcher." Donald B. Ball wrote of "The 'Spoke Gun' and 'Match Gun': Examples of Two Southern

Folk Toys" in *TFSB* 42 (1976): 181–83. A broader view of folk toys was taken in Mark I. West's "Meaning in the Making: The Toys of Young Folk," *TFSB* 48 (1982): 105–10. One folklorist's survey for a single state is Francis Edward Abernethy's *Texas Toys and Games*, *PTFS* 48 (Dallas: SMU Press, 1989).

Roger Welsch discussed "The Cornstalk Fiddle" (a toy, not an instrument) in *JAF* 77 (1964): 262–63 (repr. in *Readings in American Folklore*, pp. 106–7). Another widely distributed folk noisemaker is described by John C. McConnell in "The Dumbull or Scrauncher," *TFSB* 25 (1959): 89.

Louise Scruggs gave a brief and sketchy "History of the 5-String Banjo" in *TFSB* 27 (1961): 1–5. More-detailed studies are Gene Bluestein's "America's Folk Instrument: Notes on the Five-String Banjo," *WF* 23 (1964): 241–48; C. P. Heaton's "The 5-String Banjo in North Carolina," *SFQ* 35 (1971): 62–82; and Jay Bailey's "Historical Origin and Stylistic Developments of the Five-String Banjo," *JAF* 85 (1972): 58–65. Information on an even simpler class of traditional stringed instruments is given by David Evans in "Afro-American One-stringed Instruments," *WF* 29 (1970): 229–45. Charles Seeger submitted "The Appalachian Dulcimer" to a full historical treatment in *JAF* 71 (1958): 40–51; and S. E. Hastings reported on one notable old instrument in his article "Construction Techniques in an Old Appalachian Mountain Dulcimer," *JAF* 83 (1970): 462–68. A good regional survey is Charles W. Joyner's "Dulcimer Making in Western North Carolina: Creativity in a Traditional Mountain Craft," *SFQ* 39 (1975): 341–61. Other useful information on dulcimer playing in the Southern Mountains is found in the following popular works: John F. Putnam's "The Plucked Dulcimer," *MLW* 34 (1958): 7–13; Putnam's booklet *The Plucked Dulcimer and How to Play It* (Berea, Ky.: Council of the Southern Mountains, 1961); and Jean Ritchie's *The Dulcimer Book* (New York: Oak Publications, 1963). L. Allen Smith reports on his comprehensive and systematic study in "Toward a Reconstruction of the Development of the Appalachian Dulcimer: What the Instruments Suggest," *JAF* 93 (1980): 385–96. A book-length study is R. Gerald Alvey's *Dulcimer Maker: The Craft of Homer Ledford* (Lexington: University Press of Kentucky, 1984).

S. J. Sackett discussed "The Hammered Dulcimer in Ellis County, Kansas" in *JIFMC* 14 (1962): 61–64. A study of the folk use made of a commercial musical instrument is A. Doyle Moore's "The Autoharp: Its Origins and Development from a Popular to a Folk Instrument," *NYFQ* 19 (1963): 261–74.

There are numerous books and publications on folk art, using either that term or another. Two important exhibition catalogs were *The Abby Aldrich Rockefeller Folk Art Collection: A Descriptive Catalog*, by Nina Fletcher Little (Colonial Williamsburg, Va., 1957) and *New-found Folk Art of the Young Republic*, by Agnes Halsey Jones and Louis C. Jones (Cooperstown, N.Y.: New York State Historical Association, 1960). Among well-illustrated works on nonacademic representational and decorative art are Janet Waring, *Early American Stencils on Walls and Furniture* (1937; reprinted, New York: Dover Publications, 1968); Jean Lipman, *American Primitive Painting* (London and New York: Oxford University Press, 1942); Henry J. Kauffman, *Pennsylvania Dutch American Folk Art* (1946; rev. and enlarged ed., New York: Dover Publications, 1964); Alice Ford, *Pictorial Folk Art: New England to California* (London and New York: Studio Publications, 1949); and Nina Fletcher Little, *American Decorative Wall Painting 1700–1850* (Sturbridge, Mass., and New York: Old Sturbridge Village and Studio Publications, 1952).

Essential to investigating the whole topic of American folk crafts and art are Simon J. Bronner's *American Folk Art: A Guide to Sources* (New York: Garland, 1984) and Henry Glassie's *The Spirit of Folk Art: The Girard Collection at the Museum of International Folk Art* (New York: Harry N. Abrams, 1989), both quoted in this chapter. Other catalogs of folk-art exhibits and published anthologies of folk-art illustrations are far too numerous to mention, but may be located via library bibliographic searches or through reviews in folklore journals.

An important picture book on American folk crafts and art is Erwin O. Christensen's *The Index of American Design*, published by the Smithsonian Institution (Washington, D.C., 1950). The index was part of the Federal Art Project of the 1930s and is now housed in the National Gallery of Art. It includes photographs and drawings of designs, weather vanes, utensils, costumes, and pictorial art. Some good examples of its riches are used as illustrations in Duncan Emrich's article "America's Folkways," *Holiday* 18 (July 1955): 60–63 and following.

Jean Lipman's book *American Folk Art in Wood, Metal, and Stone* (New York: Pantheon, 1948) is another well-illustrated survey volume, as is her work done in collaboration with Alice Winchester, *The Flowering of American Folk Art (1776–1876)* (New York: Viking Press, 1974). The book *America's Arts and Skills*, published by the editors of *Life* (New York, 1957), although neither wholly art nor folk, contains some folk art and is magnificently illustrated. It surveys American popular art and design from colonial times to the present, as do similar works, too numerous to list here, produced by state historical societies and arts councils to commemorate the United States Bicentennial.

Kenneth L. Ames's *Beyond Necessity: Art in the Folk Tradition* (Winterthur, Del.: Winterthur Museum, 1977), part of the catalog of an exhibit, sought to dispel some "myths about folk art" and bring the thinking of art historians closer to that of modern folklorists. The dialogue was continued (in what some called "the shootout at Winterthur") in a conference published as *Perspectives on American Folk Art* (Winterthur Museum, 1980), ed. Ian M. G. Quimby and Scott T. Swank. Folklorist Henry Glassie was much quoted here, and American folklorists were represented in person by Roger Welsch, Marsha MacDowell, Kurt Dewhurst, John Michael Vlach, and Michael Owen Jones, all of whom contributed strong papers that are required reading for anyone working in this field.

Two articles on the work of individual painters are John Michael Vlach's "Quaker Tradition and the Paintings of Edward Hicks: A Strategy for the Study of Folk Art," *JAF* 94 (1981): 145–65; and Simon J. Bronner's " 'We Live What I Paint and I Paint What I See': A Mennonite Artist in Northern Indiana," *IF* 12 (1979): 5–17. Rosemary O. Joyce was guest editor for a special section of *NYF* (12 [1986]: 43–112) on "Marketing Folk Art," which contained five articles.

American women's folk art, a long-neglected topic, was treated in two 1979 publications—Mirra Bank, *Anonymous Was a Woman* (New York: St. Martins) and C. Kurt Dewhurst, Betty MacDowell, and Marsha MacDowell, *Artists in*

Aprons: Folk Art by American Women (New York: E. P. Dutton)—both well illustrated but only the latter with any in-depth discussion of the topic and with a large bibliography.

Some byways of folk art are charted in articles such as Geoffrey Cortelyon and Kathleen Green's study "Pop Owen," concerning an amateur artist in rural New York State, in *KFQ* 28 (1972): 293–304; Alan B. Govenar's "Leonard L. 'Stoney' St. Clair, Tattooist," *JOFS* 3 (1975): 9–14; Charles L. Perdue, Jr.'s "Steve Ashby: Virginia Folk Artist," concerning a black creator of various "constructions," in *FFV* 2 (1980–81): 53–66; E. N. Anderson, Jr.'s "On the Folk Art of Landscaping," *WF* 31 (1972): 179–88; and Jo Mueller, "I Brake for Art Cars: A First Look at Decorated Cars in Seattle," *NWF* 8 (1989): 10–37.

Michael Owen Jones has published a number of thoughtful studies of methodology and analysis of American folk arts and crafts, beginning with "Two Directions for Folkloristics in the Study of American Art," *SFQ* 32 (1968): 249–59. Jones's essays were gathered in his book *Exploring Folk Art: Twenty Years of Thought on Craft, Work, and Aesthetics* (Logan: Utah State University Press, 1987), which is quoted in this chapter. A related essay is Elizabeth Mosby Adler's "Direction in the Study of American Folk Art," *NYF* 1 (1975): 31–44.

Three studies of the whalers' art of ivory carving are Marius Barbeau, "All Hands Aboard Scrimshawing," *The American Neptune* 12 (1952): 99–122 (reprinted by the Peabody Museum of Salem [Mass.], 1966); Walter K. Earle, *Scrimshaw: Folk Art of the Whalers* (Cold Spring Harbor, N.Y.: Whaling Museum Society, Inc., 1957); and Edouard A. Stackpole, *Scrimshaw at Mystic Seaport* (Mystic, Conn.: The Marine Historical Assoc., 1958). A brief note on a domestic art/craft form is Ila A. Wright's "Hair Watch Chains and Flowers," *WF* 18 (1959): 114–17.

American gravestones have been treated as folk art in a number of illustrated books of various degrees of scholarly merit and in numerous articles. For some good studies and many references, see two recent books edited by Richard E. Meyer, *Cemeteries and Gravemarkers: Voices of American Culture* (Logan: Utah State University Press, 1992) and *Ethnicity and the American Cemetery* (Bowling Green, Ohio: Bowling Green State University Popular Press, 1993).

African-American folk art has had some special study in such works as William R. Ferris, Jr., "Vision in Afro-American Folk Art: The Sculpture of James Thomas," *JAF* 88 (1975): 115–31 (which expands upon a 1970 article); and David Evans, "Afro-American Folk Sculpture from Parchman Penitentiary [Miss.]," *MFR* 6 (1972): 141–52. Both writers provide good bibliographic guidance for background reading in this area.

Designs carved on aspen trees by Western sheepherders and vacationers were first documented with photographs by Ansel Adams and Paul Hassel in *TAW* 1 (Spring 1964): 37–45. Since then such studies have appeared as Jan Harold Brunvand and John C. Abramson, "Aspen Tree Doodlings in the Wasatch Mountains: A Preliminary Survey of Traditional Tree Carvings," in *Forms upon the Frontier*, ed. Austin Fife, Alta Fife, and Henry H. Glassie, Monograph Series 16:2 (Logan: Utah State University, 1969), pp. 89–102; James B. DeKorne, *Aspen Art in the New Mexico Highlands* (Santa Fe: Museum of New Mexico Press, 1970); and Kenneth

I. Periman, "Aspen Tree Carvings," *SWF* 3 (1979): 1–10. The best study so far of tree carving is Jose Mallea-Olaetxe's "History that Grows on Trees: Basque Aspen Carving in Nevada," *Nevada Historical Society Quarterly* 35 (1992): 21–39. Other rather-obscure folk-art expressions are depicted and discussed in general terms in Avon Neal and Ann Parker, *Ephemeral Folk Figures: Scarecrows, Harvest Figures, and Snowmen* (New York: Clarkson N. Potter, 1969).

The closing quotations in this chapter came from Arnold Hauser's "Popular Art and Folk Art," *Dissent* 5 (Summer 1958): 229–37, reprinted in *The Philosophy of Art History* (New York: Knopf, 1959), p. 347; from a book by Michael Owen Jones cited earlier; and from the important anthology of studies and essays edited by Simon J. Bronner and John Michael Vlach, *Folk Art and Art Worlds* (Ann Arbor, Mich: UMI Research, 1986; reissued in 1992, with a new introduction, by Utah State University Press in Logan, Utah).

22

FOLK COSTUMES

Traditional costumes hold a prominent place in European folklife research, and consequently they are often featured there in publications, archives, museums, and folk festivals. Vestiges of folk costume still linger in the everyday life of some rural regions in almost all European countries, and elsewhere in the world distinctive traditional clothing traditions are well maintained, despite the influx of Western fashions. Many city people in Europe and beyond put on national or regional garb at festive occasions, and Americans have become familiar with foreign folk costumes through folksong and dance groups from abroad, publications and television broadcasts, and travel. We understand certain clichés of clothing as being nationally symbolic—the German in *Lederhosen*, the Scot in kilts, and the Russian in a fur cap and high boots, for example. But we tend to assume that the United States really has no distinctive costume traditions, recognizing, perhaps, only a comical American tourist stereotype of a man in shorts, a loud sport shirt, sandals or tennis shoes, and a baseball cap, with a camera dangling around his neck; or an Indian chief with beaded buckskins and full headdress.

As folklorist Patricia A. Turner has shown in her analysis of African-American "contemptible collectibles," the kind of clothing —or lack of clothes—depicted for blacks in numerous popular-culture images maintained the "Topsy and Uncle Tom" stereotypes familiar from Harriet Beecher Stowe's antislavery novel *Uncle Tom's Cabin* (1852). Turner writes:

> When real children played with black dolls, the dolls were made from fabric, not bisque, and had rough wooly hair, thick cherry-red lips, and patched clothing. The 1945 Sears catalog featured a black doll whose outfit was held together by a safety pin. The costume on a 1937 puppet has a prominent patch. If a boy is shown in overalls, they are either too short or one of the shoulder straps droops. The dresses worn by little girls are either torn or too short, or both. Even when a child is wearing a complete, clean outfit, some portion of it is out of place. . . . The Gold Dust Twins [advertising trademarks] had plenty of gold but no clothes. A wine crate label depicts a naked black infant sitting in the middle of a field, while a souvenir bank consists of a naked black infant sitting on two bananas. Contemptible collectibles seldom depict a clean well-dressed black child.

The typical depiction of adult black women in popular culture of the past was the "mammy" stereotype, familiar in the older "Aunt Jemima" product advertising. Adult black men, if not shown as "Uncle Toms," were shown as overdressed dandies, a stereotype featured in the blackface minstrel shows, whose performers were white men wearing black makeup and clothed in outlandish styles:

> The suits, shirts, hats, gloves, and pants they were shown in were always overdone. If a white lace ruffle around the cuff was the style white men were adopting, the black-faced figures would be depicted with four rows of ruffles, so many that the fabric would fall into their food.

Despite the recognition of such clothing stereotypes as false and demeaning, and despite the pervasive influence of international fashion and the easy accessibility of ready-made mass-produced clothing, some traditional influences continue to be apparent in both *what* Americans wear and *how* they wear it. While we have never had a national peasant class with distinctive folk attire, and though mobility and mass communications have wiped out many regional clothing styles, some folk-group differentiation is created just as much by costume choices as by folk speech, customs, beliefs, or other traditional forms. Examples of clothing traditions include special clothing, such as a tennis or ski "outfit"; holiday costumes, such as for Halloween or the custom of wearing green on St. Patrick's Day; ethnic clothing styles; and the custom of "dressing up" for special occasions, such as first Communion, graduation, marriage, or appearances in a courtroom.

Costumes worn for Halloween, now widely seen on adults as well as children, have evolved from one set of traditions to another, as folklorist Sylvia Ann Grider noted:

> Halloween costumes used to represent the supernatural beings of the underworld, but contemporary advertising and the entertainment media have substantially expanded the range of costume possibilities. For the past several years, some of the most common Halloween costumes have depicted media creations, such as characters from *Star Wars*, *Batman*, *ET*, or from whatever new Disney animated feature film is current. Such developments have almost eliminated the custom of children fashioning their own costumes out of old clothes and other odds and ends lying around the house and garage.

FOCUS: WHAT TO WEAR SQUARE DANCING

One Saturday evening when my husband and I were at our farm in the Missouri Ozarks, he suggested we go square dancing. He'd seen a dance advertised at a place called Fosters Outback somewhere near the town of Willow Springs. Why not? We'd learned to square dance in gym class long ago. Hadn't everyone? Couldn't we do-si-do? He put on a T-shirt and jeans. I put on a T-shirt and denim skirt and slipped into the bowling shoes that I always go dancing in because they have slick soles and jingle bells.

. . . The 50 or so dancers were all dressed in costume. The men wore fancy Western outfits with shirts cut from material to match their wives' skirts. The women wore ruffled peasant blouses with puffed sleeves, knee-length skirts held aloft by elaborate petticoats, lacy pettipants and high-heeled dancing shoes. Both men and women jingled with strings of metal badges from festivals, conventions and other clubs at which they had danced.

We joined in a square that was just beginning to form. Larry [Foster] launched into a singsong call that had very little do-si-do in it, and we promenaded not at all. We hadn't the least notion of what we were to do and immediately snarled the dancing pattern. The others began pushing us though, first in amusement, but only at first. Panting, ashamed, badly

dressed, we sat down and waited until a waltz was put on the record
player before sneaking back out onto the dance floor.

Source: Sue Hubbell, "Farewell 'Do-si-do,' hello 'Scooot and counter . . . Perco-
late!' " *Smithsonian* 26 (February 1996): 92–99.

DISCUSSION TOPICS:

1. Later Sue Hubbell learned from the caller's wife, Reda Foster,
that rather than traditional square dancing, this was "modern Western square dancing." What can you learn from reading or interviews
about the dance, musical, and clothing styles of this modern dancing
tradition?

2. Among other dancers, Hubbell interviewed female twins who
dress alike. In the rapid, complex style of modern square dancing,
however, identical costumes may cause problems. What do you suppose the problems are?

3. Hubbell also met a couple "dressed in coordinated red-white-
and-blue outfits . . . carrying a white toy poodle who sports a blue
skirt with a red petticoat, to match." Other dog owners train their
pets to dance with them as part of a group called "Do Si Dogs." In
what other contexts do people dress up their pets, sometimes in outfits
to match the owners' clothing?

Just as with folk music, where traditional material mingles with
commercialism, clothing-fashion leaders sometimes borrow and exploit ideas from folk practice. For instance, a style called "folkloric,"
popular in the mid-1970s, supposedly used elements from European
peasant and gypsy costumes to design and market styles for the
middle-class masses. Since there is considerable published work on
cycles in the history of fashionable and popular styles, and these are
not clearly "folk" aspects of costume, we confine ourselves in this
chapter to outlining some possibilities in identifying and studying
traditional American dress. Very little such research has been done,
so far.

Folk-costume research involves identifying and classifying details
of *traditional* dress and adornment among the standardized general
aspects, relating these traditions to the larger structure of folk-group
behavior, and interpreting the meanings of these patterns. Probably
in clothing research we have even greater problems sorting out folk,
popular, and elite influences than with any other aspect of folklore.
Clothing manufacture, after all, is a gigantic international industry

that is quick to respond both to the dictates of "high fashion" and to hints of future fads in current folk practices. So rapid are these changes that to cite specific examples risks dating this chapter, but two styles prominent in store displays at the time of this writing may be mentioned: first, platform shoes, dictated by fashion despite their awkwardness and even health hazards, and second, in a style based on traditional practice, faded and even ripped jeans, now available as ready-made garments.

HISTORICAL STUDY

One useful avenue of approach to American folk-costume research is the historical, tracing the development of today's clothing styles out of the medley of national and ethnic styles that settlers brought to the New World. We may identify historical differences and developments in costume according to age, sex, national origin, region, occupation, economic and social status, and whether people are dressing for every day or for a special occasion.

The first settlers, of course, came to the New World wearing the ordinary clothes of their homelands and bringing whatever fine clothes they could, according to their wealth and social status. Colonial costume, as historical research reveals, preserved considerable diversity in dress, depending upon the national origins, religions, occupations, and other cultural traits of the settlers. Soon, however, modes of dress more appropriate for a frontier society developed, influenced by the physical environment, the available raw materials and means of production, and to some extent by the Native Americans' example.

The characteristic frontiersmen's outfit—a distinctive American costume—was made from the typical native material, buckskin, from the neck right down to the moccasins. The trousers were close-cut without cuffs, but sometimes had long fringes down the sides; the upper garment was a tunic, slit part way down the front and laced, with a sort of cape-shawl shoulder piece. The sleeve edges and cape were also fringed. A coonskin or other fur hat topped the rig, and a belt—usually worn with buckle to the rear to prevent sun glare or snagging—completed it. The explanations offered for the fringing on the outfit sound suspicious. One is that the longer the

Undated illustration of a frontier couple taking refuge from the Indians in the woods. Their costume is characteristic of the early settlement period.

fringes, the better the rainwater would drip off a man. Another story is that the fringes provided a ready source of buckskin thongs for tying. Cases are also on record of mountain men deriving nourishment, or at least believing that they did, from chewing the fringes from their clothing. Probably the fringe came first as a mere decorative device, and its various practical uses developed later and were orally transmitted.

The settlers who followed the trailblazers on the Great Plains and beyond were farmers from "back East," and they wore the homemade clothing common to all of the settlements. As Francis Parkman described them in *The Oregon Trail*, from his observations in 1846, the men wore broad-brimmed hats, and "their long angular proportions [were] enveloped in brown homespun, evidently cut and adjusted by the hands of a domestic female tailor." The women wore homespun or "linsey-woolsey" dresses, sometimes supplemented by an apron or a shawl, and sunbonnets. A fine description of part of the process of a family making most of its clothing is included on the Library of Congress recording "Jack Tales Told by Mrs. Maude Long of Hot Springs, N.C." (AAFS L47). Mrs. Long described the family setting in which the "Jack Tales" were told:

It would be on a long, winter evening when, after supper, all of us were gathered before the big open fire, my mother taking care of the baby or else the baby was in the cradle very near to mother, and she would be sewing or carding.

My father would be mending someone's shoes or maybe a bit of harness. The older girls were helping with the carding or the sewing. And all of us little ones would either have a lapful or a basket full of wool out of which we must pick all the burrs and the Spanish needles and the bits of briars and dirt against the next day's carding.

For my mother wove all of this wool that had been shorn from the backs of our own sheep—raised there on the farm that was in the heart of the Great Smoky Mountains in North Carolina—into linsey-woolsey, for hers and our dresses, or into blue jeans for my father's and brothers' suits, or into blankets to keep us warm, or into the beautiful patterned coverlets, to say nothing of all the socks and stockings and mitts and hoods that it took for a large family of nine children. And so she needed every bit of the wool that she could get ready.

As settlers became adjusted to the Far West, they modified their costume. In *Roughing It*, Mark Twain described himself, only a year after he had arrived there in 1861 as a typical greenhorn, as dressed in miner's garb, "rusty looking . . . coatless, slouch hat, blue woolen shirt, pantaloons stuffed into boot-tops, whiskered half down to the waist, and the universal navy revolver slung to my belt." The blue or red color of the shirt was evidently a traditional touch; an 1859 guidebook for overland travel stated that "the shirt [should be] of red or blue flannel, such as can be found in almost all the shops on the frontier." Bandanna handkerchiefs, too, were until recently made only in blue or red, and as late as 1966 the L. L. Bean Company, of Freeport, Maine, longtime outfitter of hunting, fishing, and camping parties, advised in its catalog, "A good blue flannel shirt cannot be beaten for all around wear." In response to my inquiry at the time about this supposed utility, a company executive lamely explained in a letter, "Traditionally red-blue is worn out of doors and those colors do not show dirt as do tans." (One wonders if black or dark green might not be equally impervious to stains and dirt.) By 1976, however, the old blue flannel shirt was featured only in the fall catalog of L. L. Bean, and with a different caption. Today's outdoor-wear catalogs, of course, are dominated by references to materials such as organic cotton, Gore-tex, Thinsulite, and Polar-fleece.

The changes in Mormon pioneer dress during the first thirty-odd years of settlement in the West illustrate a unique case of adaptation of important styles. The Latter-day Saints numbered among them Midwesterners and Easterners, as well as many European converts, all of whom brought elements of their clothing traditions with them to Utah when they first began to arrive there in 1847. But in their eagerness to become "real Americans," most immigrants quickly discarded peasant styles. (One exception may be the Mormon pioneer men's "barn-door trousers," possibly developed from northern European peasant breeches; these had a front-buttoned flap, somewhat like that on the traditional sailors' pants.) The American fashions of the time influenced women to substitute pasteboard, folded newspapers, or wooden slats for starch and the whalebone stiffeners used in bonnets and skirts. The climate in the mountain settlements dictated warmer clothing—including quilted petticoats—than was common back East. The desire for adornment on clothing was filled partly by weaving straw flowers out of native grasses and making dyes from wild plants. Special religious rituals and beliefs led to the everyday wearing of sacred underclothing ("Temple Garments") and to robes used exclusively in temple ceremonies. Unlike several other American sects, however, the Mormons developed no uniform outer clothing as a mark of membership and piety, although a women's work costume with wide pants, a short skirt, and wide-brimmed straw hat ("The Deseret Costume") was proposed at one time. Currently in Utah many of the ethnic groups, whether Mormon or not, are returning to national costumes for festive occasions, and the Mormon women and girls have a strong preference for long "Pioneer style" dresses to wear for church or going out. A Latter-day Saint splinter group, the Order of Aaron, has adopted a conservative sectarian costume discreetly embroidered with symbols of their group for general everyday use.

OCCUPATIONAL DRESS

Most early American occupational groups had traditional costume elements, such as a leather apron for a cobbler or blacksmith, a miller's smock, or the nineteenth-century farmer's outfit with its heavy shoes, vest, suspenders, and wide-brimmed hat (later replaced by denim bib-overalls, and still later by matching pant and shirt sets in green, blue, or gray). Merchant sailors of all nations tended to have some distinctive garb, just as different navies of the world still do. American loggers wore checkered shirts, pants that were "stagged" (cut off above the cuffs), sometimes a sash around the waist, and always hobnailed and well-greased boots. The cowboy's distinctive outfit, much improvised upon, has become a national symbol. Originally it was characterized by the smooth leather (later sometimes fur) "chaps," a dull-colored shirt set off by a red scarf, vest, gunbelt, gloves, high-heeled boots, and wide-brimmed hat. Some of the cowboy-hat styles first associated with different parts of the West are still named for these regions, and these styles sell better in some places than others. The first cowboy trousers were usually of brown or naturally colored canvas, but the blue Levi's were introduced by the 1860s, and the copper rivets at stress points arrived in 1872 or 1873, although cowboys declined to accept them until about the 1890s.

Clothing researcher Laurel Wilson investigated the contrast between what cowboys actually wore on the job and what they wore in photographers' studios. She learned that:

> The cowboys themselves helped to create the image which eventually appeared on stage. Rather than posing for photographs in clothing they actually wore while doing their work, they dressed in garb they knew would be recognized as cowboy dress, that is large hats, bandannas, revolvers in holsters, chaps, boots, and spurs. While many of these articles of clothing were used on the job part of the time, the photographic evidence indicates that the revolvers, bandannas, and chaps were used only occasionally.

Other occupational traditions in dress may be distinguished, as well as the prestige values of different modes, as suggested in such verses from folksongs as this:

> I would not marry the farmer,
> He's always in the dirt;

I'd rather marry the railroader
Who wears the striped shirt.

IMMIGRANT DRESS

The later immigrants to the United States and Canada from southern and eastern Europe repeated even more rapidly the earliest settlers' practice of discarding native styles in preference for
Westernized fashions. They sensed at once as they mingled with
their new compatriots how clearly one's clothes projected a personal
image, identifying the outsider as a foreigner.

M. E. Ravage, a Romanian-Jewish immigrant, arrived in New
York City in 1900; he commented frequently on his awareness of
how "clothes made the man" in his book *An American in the Making*
(1917). He soon discovered that many of his fellow Romanians mixed
their clothing styles as badly as they did their languages; some he
saw were "clad in an absurd medley of Rumanian sheep-pelts and
American red sweaters." Real Americans, he felt, showed more taste
and "obvious wealth (judging from their clothes)." It amused him
to recall that in his home village in Moldavia "none but young ladies
of marriageable age wore gloves; for any one else the article would
have been regarded as silly dandyism." But in New York, he wrote,
"even teamsters and street laborers wore gloves at their work, to
preserve, I supposed, their dainty hands." After many rebuffs during
his first job-seeking, Ravage mustered up the courage to ask a potential employer what was lacking in him:

> He looked me over from head to foot, and then, with a contemp-
> tuous glance at my shabby foreign shoes (the alien's shoes are his
> Judas), he asked me whether I supposed he wanted a greenhorn in
> his store. . . . In order to have a job one must have American clothes,
> and the only way to get American clothes was to find a job and earn
> the price.

Ravage finally managed to break out of this vicious circle by borrowing money and some articles of clothing to create a better appearance and win a position. With his first earnings he purchased a

Homeless Italian earthquake refugees wearing their everyday clothes on their way to America (date unknown).

new suit, new shoes, and derby hat; thus (in about three months' time) began to evolve an "American in the making."

The speed with which Norwegian immigrant girls abandoned their traditional garb is indicated in a young Norwegian-American's letter home, quoted by Theodore Blegen in his history *Norwegian Migration to America* (1940):

> I am sure you will laugh but, believe it or not, the servant girls have certainly come into their own here. The first Sunday after their arrival in America they still wear their usual old Norwegian clothes;

the next Sunday, it's a new dress; the third, a hat, a parasol, a silk shawl, new clothes from top to toe.

Now, of course, when descendants of these very immigrants form folksong and -dance groups they like to put on a semblance of national costume for their performances.

There is ample evidence that ethnic Americans' "dressing up" in folk costumes for festive occasions has important symbolic value in identifying cultural backgrounds, despite seldom being accurate in terms of specific style or details. In southern Illinois, for example, folklorist John M. Coggeshall found that "the few so-called ethnic festivals in the area, such as Belleville's Deutschfest or Germantown's Spassfest, are not considered truly ethnic by local residents. . . . The superficial trappings of German culture, such as polka bands, German costumes, German dance clubs, and German food and beer, add [a kind of] authenticity but not validity as ethnic markers." Similarly, in small Norwegian-settled towns of Alberta, Canada, I found that women frequently wore Norwegian costumes to banquets and holiday celebrations, but these outfits were almost always recently purchased and especially made for them in Norway, with the design chosen according to the taste of the wearer rather than the actual regional background. One woman who showed me her beautiful custom-made costume admitted that she was not even sure what part of Norway it represented.

In Hawaiian hula competitions, as reported by Amy Ku'uleialoha Stillman, the standard costume rule for the "ancient hula" division (*hula kahiko*) is that only natural materials may be used—no plastic flowers or cellophane skirts. But for competition in the "modern hula" (*hula 'auana*) division, the costuming takes a different slant:

Many favorite hula songs [for modern hula] are about the late monarchy era of the late 1800s. Part of the attraction for participants in women's groups who select such songs for their hula 'auana contest number is the opportunity to wear elegant Victorian-period styles of dress, especially "Gibson Girl" shirtwaists with leg-o'-mutton sleeves. While such dress styles are certainly historically accurate to the period and while the choice of fashion is often justified by citing photographic portraits of members of the nobility in such attire, there is a dearth of evidence that hula was actually performed in such attire during the late 1800s.

FOCUS: FOLKLIFE REVIVAL VISITED BY TIME TRAVELERS

If a man and woman living a hundred years ago in the Great Smoky Mountains were somehow transported to the present day, they would indeed be mystified by much of what is now presented as authentic traditional mountain culture. As they watch young clogging groups, the couple might ask why these children are dressed in identical outfits, the little girls with so many petticoats that you see their underpants (discreetly made to match their dresses) when they turn, or why they are clogging in uniform step in square dance figures. Listening to the music, the couple might find some of the tunes to be familiar, as would be the fiddle and probably the banjo, but the rhythm and the pacing of the music, as well as several of the instruments in the band, would be strange.

If the bewildered couple were to venture into a craft store, even one purporting to sell authentic mountain crafts, much of what they would see would be unrecognizable to them. It is quite likely that they would never have set eyes on the Appalachian dulcimer (more often purchased than played by those modern folks who wander into the crafts store). The handwoven coverlet, that enduring symbol of Appalachian craftsmanship, might be more familiar, although some of the designs and colors would seem odd to the couple, as would the perfectly matched seams.

Source: Michael Ann Williams, *Great Smoky Mountain Folklife* (Jackson: University Press of Mississippi, 1995), p. xv.

DISCUSSION TOPICS:

1. Look in sources listed in the bibliographic notes for illustrations of actual period clothing of this region. What did children wear in the Great Smoky Mountains one hundred years ago?

2. How many of the folk activities and artifacts mentioned here have you encountered in a revivalist context? Did the performers or presenters of these displays claim them to be authentic?

3. How would "the rhythm and the pacing" of the dance music differ from old-time music? Compare recordings of older traditional musicians with recent revivalists. What can you learn about the Appalachian dulcimer as a folk instrument?

RESEARCHING FOLK COSTUMES

Besides historical developments in traditional dress and the special garb of a few nationality or sectarian groups, other possibilities exist for research in traditional American costumes. Standardized uniforms (as for monastic orders, schools, military units, law-enforcement agencies, or bands) are not folk costumes, but probably less formal dress-markers indicating one's role or status are, such as the medical student's lab coat, the chef's tall white hat, the motorcyclist's leather jacket, the clogger's or square dancer's performance outfit, or the ballet dancer's favorite well-worn warm-up clothes. The sense of what constitutes "dressing up" in what were once referred to as "Sunday go-to-meeting" clothes, and which occasions call for such garb, would seem to be a traditional matter with variation through time and from one period to another or from region to region. People sometimes deliberately "dress down" to show rejection of society's clothing standards and to signal their alliance with like-minded individuals, whether "hippies," "freaks," "punks," environmentalists, rappers, or others. (These examples illustrate that even within nonconformity there is conformity with another set of standards. Some dissident youth—often dedicated antimilitarists—favor old military uniforms as their badge of rebellion. On the other hand, "skinheads," who often promote or practice violent confrontations, also like to wear militarylike outfits.) Patchwork and embroidered decoration on denim clothing and the modification of jeans and bib overalls into other garments has developed as a modern clothing craft of great variation and popularity. The supposed and actual dress of homosexuals might also be studied. The degree of belief and practice involved with lucky clothing, for which basketball coaches are notorious, is another open question.

FOCUS: THE LETTER SWEATERS OF WAR

One of the most visible forms of material culture of the GI experience in Vietnam were the embroidered jackets known as "Pleiku" jackets—decorated jackets featuring dragon designs, stylized maps, flags, eagles, and verses. Decorated "tour" jackets, whether they be "Pleiku" jackets (named

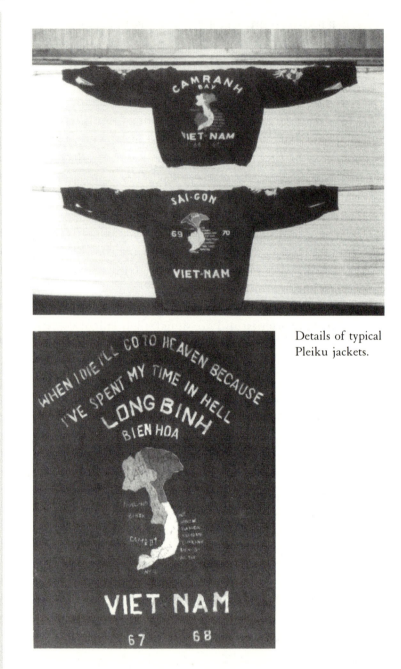

Details of typical
Pleiku jackets.

for the established practice of making these jackets in Pleiku, Vietnam)
or decorated working jackets worn by sailors, were visual testaments to
membership in both a branch of service and a distinct smaller unit.
   . . . Jackets were decorated with patches with such expressions as "Par-

*ticipant in South East Asia War Games," "Viet Cong Hunting Club,"
"Peace-Hell-Bomb," and "The Tonkin Gulf Yacht Club." . . . Among
the most poignant verses on patches and slogans embroidered on jackets
was "When I die I'll go to Heaven Because I've Spent My Time in
Hell."*

*

*Readers should note that such jackets were sold primarily to rear ech-
elon personnel with little exposure to war. Those personnel had much
greater access to souvenir stores and tailors than did combat veterans, and
perhaps sought to dramatize their service. Dewhurst takes too seriously
the almost universal slogan on tour jackets, "When I die I'll go to heaven,
because I've spent my time in hell," followed by the city in which one
served and the years of one's tour. The irony apparent to a Vietnam
veteran is that Danang, Pleiku, Saigon, and the other cities commonly
found embroidered on such jackets were generally extremely safe.*

Sources: C. Kurt Dewhurst, "Pleiku Jackets, Tour Jackets, and Working Jackets:
'The Letter Sweaters of War,'" JAF 101 (1988): 48–52; Stephen Sossaman, "More
on Pleiku Jackets in Vietnam," JAF 102 (1989): 76.

DISCUSSION TOPICS:

1. Can you find other illustrations of Pleiku jackets, or perhaps
even actual jackets in the possession of Vietnam veterans or in military museums?

2. How and why did the original author possibly misread the
meaning of the decorated jackets? What aspects of the artifacts themselves were interpreted, and what did context contribute to
interpretation?

3. What are "letter sweaters," and how is their form or use possibly "traditional"?

The popularity of "Come as you are" or period-dress parties could
be studied, as could the visual clichés of pioneer costumes concocted
for use in local historical parades and pageants. Even not wearing
something (going braless, shoeless, or tieless) or wearing something
in an unintended manner (a backwards baseball cap or untied shoes)
constitutes a statement about a tradition made via one's mode of
dress, and there are traditional associations between the age of a
person and what he or she wears. Some metaphoric proverbial language refers to clothing: "to give the shirt off one's back," "to bet

one's boots," "to throw one's hat in the ring," "if the shoe fits, wear it," "to wear the pants in the family," and "to beat the socks off someone" are examples. Perhaps a good beginning for costume research would be simply to inventory one's own wardrobe to see what traditional elements are present, then to look more closely at one's friends and acquaintances for a time, to see what their clothes seem to be saying about them and to what degree these are traditional statements or are made by some traditional means.

Finally, the symbolic use of certain garments by politicians may be noted. (For foreign examples, think of Fidel Castro's military fatigues or Yassir Arafat's head scarf.) The frontier-American coonskin hat was an effective political trademark for Senator Estes Kefauver of Tennessee in the early 1950s, then briefly became a fashion in children's wear (thanks also to the Walt Disney TV series *Davy Crockett*). President Jimmy Carter during his term of office (1977–81) appeared for televised statements wearing a cardigan sweater, which gave him the appearance of chatting with friends. In the 1996 presidential primary race, Republican hopeful Lamar Alexander made a down-to-earth red-and-black plaid shirt his trademark. And Bill Clinton seems to have been the first American president seen jogging in well-worn T-shirts and skimpy running shorts—a natural outfit for the occasion, but a marked departure from the presidential "uniform" of dark suit and white shirt. (Ronald Reagan, "the great communicator," never went further than to don jeans, a cowboy shirt, and boots during his vacation breaks.)

BIBLIOGRAPHIC NOTES

Since there are very few studies in American folk costume, two survey articles by Don Yoder are especially valuable. One is "Sectarian Costume Research in the United States," in *Forms upon the Frontier*, ed. Austin Fife, Alta Fife, and Henry H. Glassie, Monograph Series 16:2 (Logan: Utah State University Press, 1969), pp. 41–75; the other is Yoder's chapter "Folk Costume" in *Folklore and Folklife: An Introduction*, pp. 295–323. Robert Wildhaber's bibliography (mentioned in the notes to chapter 19) had a short section on costume and textiles. Some studies of customs (see chapter 15) touch on costumes as well, and there is an entry for costume in *American Folklore: An Encyclopedia*.

An important recent set of papers is *Dress in American Culture*, eds. Patricia A. Cunningham and Susan Voso Lab (Bowling Green, Ohio: Bowling Green State

University Popular Press, 1993). The editors and authors of the nine essays included there explore clothing "as a record of the struggles, changes, and adjustments experienced by various people in the process of becoming Americans." Two of the essayists quoted in this chapter are Laurel Wilson, "The American Cowboy: Development of the Mythic Image" (pp. 80–94) and Patricia Williams, "From Folk to Fashion: Dress Adaptations of Norwegian Immigrant Women in the Midwest" (pp. 95–108).

Patricia A. Turner's book quoted in this chapter is *Ceramic Uncles and Celluloid Mammies: Black Images and their Influence on Culture* (New York: Anchor Books, 1994). An essay titled "Nineteenth-Century African-American Dress" by Barbara M. Starke appears in *Dress in American Culture*, mentioned above (pp. 66–79).

Sylvia Ann Grider's article quoted in this chapter is "Conservatism and Dynamism in the Contemporary Celebration of Halloween: Institutionalization, Commercialization, Gentrification," *SF* 53 (1996): 3–16. See also John McDowell's "Halloween Costuming Among Young Adults in Bloomington, Indiana: A Local Exotic," *Indiana Folklore and Oral History* 14 (1985): 1–18.

General histories of American dress were often published for the use of stage-costume designers. Some that contain good illustrations and discussion are Elisabeth McClelland, *History of American Costume, 1607–1870* (1937; repr., New York: Tudor, 1969); Douglas Gorsline, *What People Wore: A Visual History of Dress from Ancient Times to Twentieth-Century America* (New York and London: B. T. Batsford, 1952); R. Turner Wilcox, *Five Centuries of American Costume* (New York: Scribners, 1963); and Edward Warwick, Henry C. Pitz, and Alexander Wyckoff, *Early American Dress: The History of American Dress*, vol. 2 (New York: B. Blom, 1965). Joan L. Severa's book *Dressed for the Photographer: Ordinary Americans and Fashion, 1840–1900* (Kent, Ohio: Kent State University Press, 1995) contains a large and important sampling of richly captioned and dated illustrations, and the book is thoroughly indexed by items of apparel, hairstyles, age groups, etc.

Many illustrated works on American occupations and trades (cattle raising, railroading, seafaring, farming, etc.) are good sources of information on distinctive forms of work costume and uniform. Diana de Marly's book *Working Dress: A History of Occupational Costume* (New York: Holmes and Meier, 1986), although British in its inclusion, depicts some kinds of clothing probably worn by American workers of the past as well. See also E. Lisle Reedstrom's *Authentic Costumes and Characters of the Wild West* (New York: Sterling, 1992).

The article "Fashion on the Frontier" by Hazel Stein in *SFQ* 21 (1957): 160–64 is poorly documented and of slight scholarly value. Much better is Fairfax Proudfit Walkup's study "The Sunbonnet Woman: Fashions in Utah Pioneer Costume," *UHR* 1 (1947): 201–22, which is carefully documented and well illustrated.

John M. Coggeshall's essay quoted in this chapter is " 'One of those Intangibles': The Manifestation of Ethnic Identity in Southwestern Illinois," *JAF* 99 (1986): 177–207. On hula competitions, see the article by Amy Ku'uleialoha Stillman, "Hawaiian Hula Competitions: Event, Repertoire, Performance, Tradition," *JAF* 109 (1996): 357–80.

A rare book-length study of an American costume tradition, Melvin Gingerich's *Mennonite Attire through Four Centuries* (Breiningsville, Pa.: The Pennsylvania-German Society, 1970), is highly detailed and very well illustrated.

The decoration of students' shirts and jeans with embroidery is the subject of Patricia Kemerer Downey's article "Current Trends in Decorative Embroidery: Folklore or Fakelore," *TFSB* 42 (1976): 108–24. Fifty illustrations of stitches and designs are included here; the conclusion, however, is that this does not represent true folklore, a finding that might well be disputed from the evidence presented.

The advice quoted in this chapter about buying red or blue shirts for Western travel was given in Randolph B. Marcy's *The Prairie Traveler: A Handbook for Overland Expeditions* (1859; republished by West Virginia Pulp and Paper Company, 1961). This book contains various interesting references to clothing and food for Western living, as might other early travel books.

23

FOLK FOODS

Folk foods are the only traditional product to be quickly and wholly consumed, usually in a short time after preparation. Folksongs and stories may be forgotten, traditional houses may deteriorate and burn down, and folk costumes may eventually wear out or be discarded; but only folk foods disappear regularly with such speed and completeness. The study of folk foods, therefore, should include the entire process of traditional food handling and consumption: what is eaten, how and when it is eaten, food preparation and preservation, seasoning and serving food, ethnic and regional foods, religious food taboos and other requirements, food terminology and beliefs, kitchens and cookware, table manners, and so forth. Such studies, as with most folklife subjects, are more advanced in Europe than in the United States; European foodways specialists have prepared atlases of food traditions, studies of national and festival foods, films on food preparation, and, since 1979, have gathered at international conferences of "Ethnological Food Research" or "Ethnogastronomy" in order to plan and coordinate such research. (Other suggested names for folk-foods research are "Foodways," "Folk Cookery," and "Ethnocuisine.") It is clear that anything as basic as eating, with so many traditional attitudes and techniques associated with it, deserves serious study.

HISTORICAL STUDY

As with American folk costume, a historical approach to national food traditions is a good place to start, although only a brief sketch is possible here. The first settlers took some hints from the Native Americans about how to use the resources of the new land. As discussed in earlier chapters, Native American culture had a negligible influence on settlers in terms of verbal folklore; but for solving the practical problem of subsisting in a wilderness, it contributed much more. For example, the term "Indian corn" that the English settlers used for *maize* (the Spanish-derived word for it) indicated a debt to the natives, as do the Indian-derived names for some corn dishes, such as corn *pone*, *hominy*, and *succotash*. Traditionally, in the Northern states the European-peasant staple food—oat or wheat porridge—was modified into corn mush (called hasty pudding); in the South corn was traditionally processed into hominy (by treating the whole kernels with lye) or else coarsely ground and cooked in salted water as grits and eaten with butter or gravy.

White trappers and hunters learned from the Native Americans how to prepare lightweight survival rations like pemmican and "jerked" beef. Jerky was often made by overland emigrants simply by hanging strips of raw meat on the outside of their wagon covers and allowing the sun to dry them out. But one emigrant's guidebook described a more elaborate process:

> The meat is sliced thin and a scaffold prepared by setting forked sticks in the ground, about three feet high, and laying small poles or sticks crosswise upon them. The meat is laid upon those pieces, and a slow fire built beneath; the heat and smoke completes the process in half a day; and with an occasional sunning the meat will keep for months.

Nowadays, most jerky is prepared, packaged, and sold commercially, but a few Westerners still make their own at home, often from venison, and offer it for sale at highway rest stops. These entrepreneurs often advertise "Fresh Jerky Ahead" on a series of homemade signs along the road, although the specific meaning of "fresh" in the context of dried meat is none too clear.

The "Mountain Men" of the Western fur trade developed tastes for the Natives' favorite wild meats—both cooked and raw—and even for dog meat. A rendezvous feast of buffalo meat was described in these terms:

> The Mountain Men often began their repast by drinking some of the blood, which reminded them of warm milk. Then the liver was eaten raw, flavored with the contents of the gall bladder. If the cow buffalo was pregnant they savored one of the trappers' most exotic luxuries: the raw legs of unborn calves. . . . After these delicacies, the trappers were ready for their feast. This always included the hump ribs, which were pulled away by hand and the fat meat gulped down, while grease dripped over the face and clothing. These might be alternated with strips of the tenderloin, partially roasted or boiled, or by chunks of the tongue. Another prized portion was the "fleece," the inch-thick layer of fat that lay just beneath the buffalo hide. Scarcely less tempting were the intestines, or *boudins*, which were roasted in the fire until puffed with heat and fat, then coiled on a blanket and gulped down without chewing. On such an occasion two trappers would start on the opposite ends of a pile of intestines and work their way toward the middle, each eating faster and faster to get his share, and shouting to the other to "feed fair."

In the Northeast, as late as the 1850s, Henry David Thoreau learned from a Native American companion how to make tea from the "creeping snowberry"; it was "better than the black tea which we had brought," he wrote in *The Maine Woods*. Thoreau mused in his journal in 1859: "I think that a wise and independent self-reliant man will have a complete list of the edibles to be found in a primitive country or wilderness. . . . He will know what are the permanent resources of the land and be prepared for the hardest of times."

If not from Native American lore or systematic study of the wilderness, at least from their own ingenuity and desperation, the tamers of the American frontier sooner or later ate every kind of meat that the land offered. An examination of the literature of early Western exploration and travel turned up reports of eating not just the standard fare of game animals, but also badgers, coyotes, insects, lizards, prairie dogs, wolves, many other beasts, skins and pelts (either as soup or simply chewed upon), and even, in extreme circumstances, human beings. One Western army veteran wrote that when his unit was out of provisions and forced to devour the mules one by one, a bit of extra flavor could be added to the unseasoned meat by burning the mule steaks on the outside and sprinkling gunpowder over them.

Although rattlesnakes were never a preferred food on the American frontier, they were consumed on rare occasions of extreme food shortage. Even today, at the Sweetwater, Texas, Rattlesnake Roundup, fried rattlers are eaten by many of the participants. Sponsored by local Jaycees since 1959 as a fund-raiser for charity, the roundup takes place annually during the second weekend of March and has attracted crowds of up to thirty thousand. Hundreds of Western Diamondback rattlers are flushed from their dens by spraying gasoline inside, and after appraisal of the size and number of snakes captured, the rattlers are "milked" of their venom, beheaded, skinned, cleaned, and fried. As folklorist Charlie McCormick interprets this custom, it is related to humans' long-term fascination with all kinds of snakes, but reflects specifically Americans' attitudes toward snakes in general and rattlers in particular. "The Rattlesnake Roundup," he writes, ". . . foregrounds the tension between life and death in a way that is meaningful for the community given their shared knowledge, assumptions, and history."

Among the vanguards of the frontier, the diet prescribed by available resources and field expediency became, to a degree, traditional. From such practices perhaps we might trace at least part of some modern Americans' continued passion for hunting wild game and for liking meat cooked rare and served in large portions. Also, the early use of such a variety of animals for food probably underlies the current humorous folklore of mock recipes for preparing tough or undesirable game. The cook is directed to put the meat on a plank, season it well, cook it carefully and slowly, and then to discard the meat and eat the plank. Related items are the jesting recipe for "Shadow Soup," which is supposedly made from only the shadow of a fowl that is hung over the cooking pot, and the "Stone Soup" of traditional folktales, for which a generous variety of edible ingredients supplements the supposed contribution to the recipe of the special "soup stone."

The food of typical frontier occupations also developed along traditional lines, limited by what was most readily available and what could be preserved easily. Native folksongs contain some records of these menus. In "The Buffalo Skinners" (a parody of "Canaday I O"), for example, the singer complains,

We lived on rotten buffalo hump and damned old iron-wedge bread,
Strong coffee, croton water to drink, and a bull hide for a bed.

In another version the fare is "old jerked beef, croton coffee, and sour bread." ("Croton water" is probably a reference, surviving from the older song, to water coming from the Croton River in Westchester County, New York, first tapped for the New York City water supply in 1842; various early references to "Croton water" show that there was some difference of opinion then about its drinking qualities and appearance. One writer referred to the New York City town pumps, located at street corners, "so that no person who is athirst need perish. . . . If he stand in need of physic at the same time, the pump will furnish that also." Perhaps the suggestion in the song is just "river water," or the cathartic "Croton oil" may be implied.)

The housekeeping of a "Lane County [Kansas] Bachelor" is described in a song of that title that is also known as "Starving to Death on a Government Claim."

My clothes are all ragged, my language is rough,
My bread is case-hardened, both solid and tough. . . .

The dishes are scattered all over the bed,
All covered with sorghum, and government bread.
Still I have a good time, and I live at my ease,
On common sop sorghum, an' bacon an' cheese.

What the bachelor yearned for in the song was a comfortable home elsewhere and three square meals every day, prepared by someone else:

Farewell to Lane County, farewell to the West,
I'll travel back East to the girl I love best,
I'll stop at Missouri and get me a wife,
And live on corn dodgers, the rest of my life.

"Corn dodgers" (a term applied to a variety of cornmeal cakes) represent relative luxury in other songs, too, but the long-term bad effect of the unbalanced diet is pictured in "The State of Arkansas," or "An Arkansaw Traveler":

> He fed me on corn dodger that was hard as any rock,
> Till my teeth began to loosen and my knees began to knock.
> And I got so thin on sassafras tea I could hide behind a straw,
> You bet I was a different lad when I left old Arkansaw.

Another popular folksong that pictures the crudeness of bachelor life on the frontier is directed as a warning to young ladies not to marry Kansas boys, Cheyenne boys, Mormon boys, boys of many other places, and, in the following version, "Texan Boys":

> Come all ye Missouri girls and listen to my noise;
> You must not marry these Texan boys.
> For if you do your portion will be
> Cold Johnnycake [corn bread] and venison is all you'll see. . . .

> When the boys get hungry they bake their bread.
> They build up a fire as high as your head,
> Shovel up the ashes and roll in the dough;
> The name that they give it is dough, boys, dough!

FOCUS: WHO EATS TURTLE SOUP, AND WHY?

Canons of taste differ. An example is a story of turtle soup consumption. Sister Carrie [in Theodore Dreiser's 1900 novel] noticed it in her chic restaurant, but it is not on most menus today. It is one commodity that has resisted mass consumption. Rather, turtle consumption is relegated to either informal use, often in isolated, poor, and rural areas of the country, or to epicurean, elite tastes. . . .

In Dubois County [Indiana], the church picnic is a celebration combining the ritual preparation and sale of turtle soup by men, assistance by women, and the value placed on family togetherness and community visiting associated with Sunday dinners on the grounds. . . .

After butchering, family members or neighbors begin preparing the soup. Each person contributes garden vegetables, homemade wine, beef, chicken, and pork. "Everything in the garden is thrown in," Edwin said. "The meats are there to kill the turtle taste. You can't taste the turtle when you fry it though; it tastes just like chicken. The turtle has seven different meat tastes." Few can name all seven, but they're sure seven or nine tastes are there.

Source: Simon J. Bronner, *Grasping Things: Folk Material Culture and Mass Society in America* (Lexington: The University Press of Kentucky, 1986); selections above are from pages 160–77, where turtle-soup preparation and consumption is discussed and illustrated in great detail.

DISCUSSION TOPICS:

1. Bronner writes that "few of the people I talked to reported actually liking the taste of turtle meat or even recognizing it . . . and even fewer enjoyed the work required to hunt, butcher, and prepare the turtles." Why, then, do some rural Americans continue to consume turtles? Bronner offers several possible reasons that are interesting to compare and evaluate.

2. Can you discover when the Campbell's Soup Company produced "Mock Turtle" soup, how it was advertised, and when (plus why) it was discontinued? Is turtle soup or mock turtle soup commercially available in the United States today?

3. William Alexander Percy, in *Lanterns on the Levee: Recollections of a Planter's Son* (New York: Knopf, 1941), also describes home butchering and cooking of turtles in the Mississippi delta of his childhood. How does his concluding comment agree with one of Bronner's main points in the quotation above? Percy wrote, "Turtle soup indeed! I don't miss it and I hope not to meet up with it unexpectedly in elegant surroundings."

4. What other meats are said to "taste just like chicken"? Are there any other animals whose flesh is said to taste like several other meats?

On the nineteenth-century American sailing ships, as described in R. H. Dana's *Two Years before the Mast* (1840), the diet was a tiresome repetition of meals consisting mostly of weak tea, tough salt beef, and hard biscuits. The shipboard meat barrels were picked over for the officers' meals first, so the ration that reached the crew was bad enough to inspire a chant, called "The Sailor's Grace," which began "Old horse! old horse! what brought you here?" A rare treat was "scouse," made of pieces of salt beef boiled up with pounded biscuits and a few potatoes. Pudding, or "duff," made of flour, water, and molasses, with a little dried fruit added for Christmas, was an occasional dessert treat.

American cowboys and loggers ate a little better than this, although still without much variety. A local song from Maine describes the food supplies of a typical camp in these terms:

> They tote in all their flour and pork
>   their beans, oat, peas, and straw,
> Their beef it comes from Bangor, boys,
>   and some from Canada;
> They haul it to our good cook Lou
>   who cooks it in a pot
> And serves it on the table
>   when it is nice and hot.

Staples of the cowboy diet were similar, although not usually stewed. The Westerners consumed large meals of fried steak, sourdough biscuits, and strong coffee, with canned or dried foods included if available. Although one verse of the widely sung "Old Chisholm Trail" declared "Oh it's bacon and beans 'most every day / I'd as soon be a-eatin' Prairie hay," the cowboys appreciated their cooks' good efforts and got what they could when they could from the countryside to vary the diet. They traded beef for vegetables, fruit, or melons whenever possible, hunted up wild birds' eggs, tried to shoot game, and, if nothing else was available, just referred to their bacon as "fried chicken" and gulped it down. There seems to be no truth to the story that in logging and cow camps the men took turns being amateur cooks, each being replaced whenever a man complained, and the complainer taking over. (One punch line of this story is "That tastes like moose turd pie, and by God I like it!")

The Dutch oven (a cast-iron kettle with a heavy lid), which allowed controlled baking to be done by an open fire or over a bed of coals, saved cowboy cookery from the tyranny of the frying pan and the stewing pot. A good-food company was sometimes referred to as "strictly a Dutch-oven outfit," and its cook could be counted on to prepare dried-apple pies regularly, and other kinds of treats when supplies were on hand. (The term "Dutch oven" is probably a national slur, like "Dutch treat.") Sourdough cookery, about which a whole book might be written concerning both its cowboy and many other Western specialists, provided a staple for the menus of

Plenty of Meat, Potatoes, Frijoles and Coffee about to be consumed

A cowboys' feast, pictured on an old undated tinted postcard. Note the dutch ovens and other cooking implements, the chuck wagon, and the simple hearty menu implied by the caption. The back of the card indicated that a one-cent stamp was needed for mailing.

all meals, only occasionally varied with salt-rising bread. The latter, one cowboy commented, "tasted mighty good, but smelled something like old dirty socks."

American men's cooking in their own work camps almost always concentrated on solid fundamentals that stuck to the ribs. As women settled on the frontier they began to exercise their talents to supply the frills, often having no more to work with than the foods that would keep or could be gathered from the land. Their traditional recipes were passed on from mother to daughter or exchanged with neighbors. The continued transmission of favorite recipes through the generations is a subject that ought to be studied in more detail by foodways scholars.

Frontier men had already learned to settle for substitutes when supplies ran out—"Horsemint tea" for coffee, or shredded red-willow bark for tobacco. But it seems to have been women who invented a way of stretching the coffee supply by baking cornmeal in molasses and stirring it into the grounds. Another method was to burn coffee dregs for reuse; in fact, nearly every berry, grain, weed, or seed that could be roasted and ground seems to have been tried at one time or another as a substitute for coffee. Sweetenings, always in short supply and expensive, were another challenge to housewives. Sugar, maple sugar, sorghum, and honey were used when readily available, and when they were not, the cook fell back on corncob syrup to stretch the supply of sweetening, or watermelon syrup to replace it. Other ingenious culinary gimmicks included "Lengthened Eggs" (with milk and flour) for breakfast omelets, "Mock Strawberries" made from chunks of peaches and apples, and "Casserole of Rabbit," which was designed to make something worthwhile out of those pesky creatures. (The recipe was revived during the Dust Bowl period.)

It was with the "Nothing-in-the-house Pies" that the early American housewife showed her best form, and some of her creations are still favorites. These pies were either concocted from marginally tasty fruits—green currants or elderberries, for instance—or from unlikely ones such as grapes. The out-and-out "mock" pies required the greatest daring—cream pie flavored with either vinegar or field sorrel might pass for lemon, and crushed crackers could be made to taste like an apple filling, with the proper seasoning. (In 1991, when the Nabisco company resumed printing the recipe for mock apple pie on the back of its Ritz Cracker packages, one newspaper columnist, deploring the whole idea, noted that mock apple pie cost more to make and required four times the sugar of a real apple pie. He concluded that the high sugar content could endear the fake pies to many people, and he recommended that we "abandon apple pie and circle the wagons around the flag and motherhood.")

One mock mincemeat pie was made from green tomatoes, and another from rolled crackers and raisins properly seasoned. It is apparent in such examples that the frontier settlers were intent upon serving the status foods associated with Eastern or Old World menus, even in preference to some of the succulent wild fruits and berries that the new land provided. (By the same reasoning, few white settlers really seemed to relish the Native American foods they tried, and ate them only during periods of shortage.) In some families a traditional pie-top design, often a monogram, was cut or punched into the top crusts as a last flourish—another pie tradition still preserved by some cooks.

Apart from frontier food traditions, many other historical foodways might be studied, only a few examples of which may be mentioned here. These topics include wild-food gathering (greens, mushrooms, honey, maple sap), traditional food processing (molasses-making, moonshining), and several kinds of food preservation (smoking, pickling, salting, drying, canning, and freezing, plus boiling fruit down into "butter" or drying it as "leather"). More studies of American festival foods need to be done, including those eaten for birthdays, weddings, or other special occasions. Ethnic foodways among a few groups have been largely maintained, but in most immigrant groups they are relegated to special occasions. Commenting on one immigrant tradition in the city where he lived at the time, folklorist Henry Glassie wrote:

> Back home in Philadelphia, in the region below South Street, where the mood is dominated by people of Italian descent, food attracts thought. A market for fresh produce marks the community's center. Small shops fill with savory fragrance. People gather at home or in restaurants for long dinners. Consider the Easter cake, a sweet ring studded with dyed eggs. Its making occupied its creator's attention. It is a gift, an idea received from others, given to others. It is a celebration of Resurrection, a reminder of sacrifice and the hope for immortality. This cake that was a pleasure to make, a pleasure to behold, to give, to eat, to think about—a cake with God as its topic—is a South Philly work of art.

FOCUS: NORWEGIAN SOUL FOOD—LUTEFISK

Norwegian Americans seem indelibly linked with lutefisk, a boardlike, salt-preserved, imported codfish which is treated with lye, repeatedly rinsed, and boiled. The result, sometimes flaky but often gelatinous, is a feast that tends to polarize those who discuss it: One either loves lutefisk or detests it; either reaction reinforces a relatively visible Norwegian-American ethnic profile. A "survival food" for Norwegian immigrants and early pioneers, lutefisk continues to lend that group an image of cultural tenacity in the face of hardship. . . .

Not only does lutefisk stand as a complex symbol in Norwegian-American foodways, but it is also one of many dishes about which young

Norwegians, visiting this country for the first time, know little or nothing. Many Americans are surprised to learn that lutefisk does not enjoy in Norway the attention it receives on this side of the Atlantic. And it probably never did. . . . Minnesotans of Norwegian ancestry insist that their forebears brought lutefisk with them on the ships during emigration. Others believe that lutefisk is all they had to eat at first on the frontier. In any event, the fish is linked symbolically with hardship and courage in Minnesota.

Source: Anne R. Kaplan, Marjorie A. Hoover, and Willard B. Moore, eds., *The Minnesota Ethnic Food Book* (St. Paul: Minnesota Historical Society Press, 1986), pp. 103 and 115.

DISCUSSION TOPICS:

1. In a footnote to the above passage lutefisk is dubbed "Norwegian Soul Food" while the liquor called akevitt ("distilled from grains or potatoes and flavored with caraway seeds") is known as "Norwegian Drāno." Both terms connote foods that are "strong, harsh, earthy, and barely palatable." Why, then, are they consumed?

2. Are other American-immigrant foods more popular in the New World than in the immigrants' home countries? Consider the "Irishness" of soda bread, or corned beef and cabbage; or the "Italianness" of pizza. Or compare Mexican foodways with Mexican-American, Tex-Mex, and fast-food versions of tacos, enchiladas, burritos, etc.

3. What does it add to the understanding of Norwegian-Americans' reasons for consuming lutefisk and akevitt that these foods are offered almost exclusively at holiday times, particularly Christmas? (There are even comic monologues and songs about eating lutefisk at Christmas, available on recordings of ethnic humor in the Midwest.)

REGIONAL FOODS

The development of regional food specialties and preferences deserves study. The identification of baked beans with Boston, one kind of clam chowder with New England and another with Manhattan, black-eyed peas and fried chicken and many other foods with the South, corn on the cob with the Midwest, and Mexican specialties with the Southwest are partly traditional matters, especially in a day and age in which any region's food can be delivered to any other region with ease, and in which one can declare that chicken cooked anywhere (and in several ways) is "Southern fried." Perhaps the best-known and most thoroughly documented regional food tradition is that of Creole and Cajun cooking in Louisiana.

A unique instance of urban food regionalizing is the "Cincinnati Chili Culinary Complex" described by folklorist Timothy Lloyd. Served now in dozens of chain-operated chili parlors, Cincinnati Chili ingredients typically include such spices as cinnamon, allspice, and bay leaves, presumably because the original recipe was invented by a Greek cook who wanted something different in the way of chili but tasting familiar (to him) as a meat dish. Even more distinctive is the terminology of serving chili: there is "a bowl of plain," two-way (served over spaghetti, as are all subsequent "ways"), three-way (cheese added), four-way (onions added), and five-way (beans added). The protocol of ordering requires that one state the highest "way" involved, then possibly subtract lower-ranking ingredients: thus, never "three-way with onions," but possibly "four-way, no cheese." Chili, of course, is loaded with regional and personal quirks in preparation all through the South and Southwest, and it deserves a full study by a food specialist with a big appetite and an iron stomach.

The varying names for similar foods in different regions have folkloristic overtones, too. When the columnist Allan M. Trout, of the *Courier-Journal* of Louisville, Kentucky, described a traditional stew made at hog-killing time, his readers wrote in to say that it was called "Pluck" (or "Pluck and Plunder"), "All Sorts," "Scrap-ple," "Liver Mush," "Giblets," and "Monroe County Stew." (Other regional names for it are "Cowboy Stew," "Son of a Bitch [or Gun]," "Forest Ranger Stew," "Boss-Man Stew," and "Mother-in-Law Stew.") Doughnuts are variously termed "Fried Cakes," "Sinkers," "Crullers," and "Ginger Nuts," in different parts of the country. Green beans may be called "String Beans" or "Snap Beans," and pancakes appear on menus across the land as "Hotcakes," "Griddle Cakes," "Flapjacks" or "Wheat Cakes." Some similar situations occur with soft drinks ("soda," "pop," "soda-pop," "tonic," etc.). Also from our regional cooks have come terms like "Hopping John," "Snickerdoodle," "Hush-Puppies," "Apple Slump," "Brown Betty," "Soggy Coconut Cake," "Cinnamon Flop," "Red-Eye Gravy," and "Red-Flannel Hash."

St. Joseph's Day feast at St. Therese's Roman Catholic Church, Pueblo, Colorado, 1990.

THE FOLK MEAL

The basic characteristics of the American folk meal seem to be large quantities, great variety, and the use of regional specialties. This is true whether it is a family meal, a "company meal," or the fixings for a special festival or gathering being described.

FOCUS: COMPANY MEALS AND EVERYDAY FARE IN ARKANSAS

Fast-food chains such as McDonald's, Pizza Hut, and Kentucky Fried Chicken create the illusion that there is a uniform American cuisine. This illusion can be quickly dispelled by having a "company" meal with an Arkansas family: it might include fried chicken, potatoes and gravy, corn-on-the-cob, a fresh garden salad or "garden sass," homemade pickled beets, and fresh apple pie, or perhaps baked ham, red-eyed gravy, rice, baked sweet potatoes, fried okra, steaming hot rolls, and peach cobbler or pecan pie. Everyday fare, of course, is not quite so sumptuous. Although food preferences change when a greater variety of foods becomes available, many Arkansans still enjoy an everyday meal of boiled beans and turnip

greens, both heavily seasoned with a chunk of fat pork, and cornbread.
The popularity of this meal, called a "poorboy supper" when sponsored
by churches and civic clubs as a fund raiser, attests to our continued taste
preference for the staples in the diet of our ancestors.

Source: Earl F. Schrock, Jr., "Traditional Arkansas Foodways," in W. K. McNeil
and William M. Clements, eds., *An Arkansas Folklore Sourcebook* (Fayetteville: University of Arkansas Press, 1992), pp. 173–211.

DISCUSSION TOPICS:

1. Are there any foods mentioned in this selection with which you
are not familiar, or which you have not eaten? (Schrock's chapter is
rich in details of Arkansas food history, names, preparation, and preservation, plus customs of consumption.)

2. What would constitute a typical "company" meal in your family
or your region? What "everyday" foods might not be served to company? What local or traditional foods are served at church suppers
or fund-raisers?

3. What attempts are made by the fast-food chains mentioned
above—or other franchise restaurants—to make their menus seem
more like authentic regional or "home" cooking?

Descriptions of the varied offerings at gargantuan American feasts
have been a commonplace of our literature since the Pilgrims' "First
Thanksgiving," and the following two are merely a pair of less familiar examples. From Kentucky, this is given as an everyday meal
at about the turn of the century:

The meat was fried old ham, with red gravy. Also on the table were
chicken and dumplins, corn, beans, sweet potatoes, okra, candied apples, sliced tomatoes, potato salad, miscellaneous pickles and relishes,
hot chess pie topped with whipped cream, and chocolate pie with
deep meringue.

And this one is from H. L. Davis's novel *Honey in the Horn*, set in
Oregon in 1905:

The supper was all everyday victuals, but there were plenty of them.
There was fried deerliver with onions, a little greasier than it needed
to be; beefsteak, excellent cuts but infernal cooking, with all the juice
fried out and made into flour-and-milk gravy; potatoes, baked so the
jackets burst open and showed the white; string beans, their flavor

and nutritive value well oiled with a big hunk of salt pork; baked squash soaked in butter; a salad of lettuce whittled into shoestrings, wilted in hot water, and doped with vinegar and bacon grease; tomatoes stewed with dumplings of cold bread; yellow corn mowed off the cob and boiled in milk; cold beet-pickles, a jar of piccalilli, and a couple of panloads of hot sourdough biscuits. For sweets there were tomato preserves, peach butter, wild blackcap jam, and wild blackberry and wild crabapple jelly. For dessert there was a red-apple cobbler with lumpy cream, and two kinds of pie, one of blue huckleberry, and the other of red. The country fed well, what with wild game and livestock and gardens, milk and butter and orchards and wild fruits; and no man was ever liable to starve in it unless his digestion broke down from overstrain.

The same American tendency to dream of much good eating is reflected in traditional songs such as "Big Rock Candy Mountain," the metaphorical suggestions of "Pie in the Sky" (labor organizer and martyr Joe Hill's famous parody of "In the Sweet By and By"), and in stanzas from hillbilly favorites such as

> Bile 'em cabbage down;
> Bake 'em hoecake brown.
> The only song that I can sing,
> Is "Bile 'em cabbage down."
>
> *
>
> Gonna buy me a sack of flour,
> Bake me a hoecake every hour,
> Keep that skillet good and greasy all the time.

Other appearances of this theme occur in the phrase "chicken every Sunday" and the political slogan "A chicken in every pot."

"PLAYING WITH YOUR FOOD"

"Playing with your food" represents a fairly strong American taboo that is, in fact, frequently broken. For example, some people eat a chocolate-cream sandwich cookie by "screwing apart" the two halves and licking off the filling; the principle here is "best first." But "best last" is the game when the frosted end of a wedge of cake is set

Family homecoming meal near Live Oak Church, Turner County, Georgia, photographed about 1920 to 1930.

aside, possibly also with the rest of the frosting and filling. (Similarly, some people will eat all around the yolk of an egg that is fried "sunny side up" and eat this part last.) Mashed potatoes with gravy may be sculpted into a miniature volcano (or is it a lake or a well?), and then the food is manipulated until the gravy flows over the plate as the potatoes are eaten.

Another sort of food recreation is represented in various playful recipes for special cakes, the simplest and most common of which is for "Upside-Down Cake." Sometimes this is a matter of ingredients, as with "Tomato Soup Cake" and "Sauerkraut Cake" (in which relatively small amounts of the "odd" ingredient are used). In another set of funny directions we find "Wacky Cake" (in which the moist ingredients are placed atop mounds of the dry ones before mixing), "1-2-3-4 Cake" (in which the portions of the first four ingredients are in units from one to four), and "Scripture Cake" (in which Bible verses are referenced where the necessary ingredients are mentioned). And, recalling the urban legends of chapter 9, the recipe for "Red Velvet Cake" contains the surprising addition of a large dollop of red food coloring as the cook's supposed "secret."

RESEARCHING FOLK FOODS

Modern American foodways offer a real challenge to the folklife scholar: while there are traditional qualities in virtually every aspect of eating and drinking, the most obvious factors influencing these acts are now commercial and professional ones. For instance, ethnic and regional tastes are reflected even in some of the fast-food chains (e.g., Taco Bell and Kentucky Fried Chicken, now simply "KFC") and even in microwavable TV dinners. Mixtures of traditions are apparent in such restaurant names as "Mexican-American Smorgasbord" or "Der Wienerschnitzel" (which serves no actual "schnitzels," but mostly varieties of hot dogs). The foods people prefer for breakfast, while mainly of commercial origin, group themselves in traditional ways: Continental breakfasts, hot versus cold foods, meat versus cereals, fruit and sweets, pie, side dishes of potatoes or grits, and so forth. The names, timing, and foods considered appropriate for other meals and snacks, as well as for camping or picnics, could be studied. Foods for backpacking range from the commercial freeze-dried products to homemade jerky and pemmican, as well as the ubiquitous mixtures of dried fruits, nuts, candy, etc., usually called simply "gorp." (Similar trail mixes are called "scroggin" by New Zealand "trampers," that is, hikers.) "Natural" or "organic" food devotees, similarly, may either produce their own foodstuffs or buy them in special shops. The concept of "soul food"—including both what is eaten and how it interrelates with other traditional aspects of a subculture—would be a useful piece of research, as would the idea of eating "lighter" or more healthy foods and how this is accomplished by different individuals.

Kay Cothran viewed "participation in tradition" in food preferences of Deep South (piney woods) "cracker culture." The four categories of foods she identified were those appropriate whenever eating itself is, those that follow "situational food rules" (e.g., curative foods), foods to be avoided in certain circumstances (e.g., just after childbirth), and things never to be eaten (some regarded by her informants as "nigger foods"). Such food rules could be studied closer to a student's home, and the results would likely involve taboos against talking with one's mouth full or wasting food, and attitudes toward mixing certain foods in one meal or even mixing them up on one plate.

Probably any American could add something to the following list of other prospective subjects for studies of traditional eating and drinking in the United States: folk-speech references to food, such as "in apple-pie order," "not worth his salt," "to eat crow," and "in a stew"; traditions of the "potluck" or "pitch-in" dinner; varieties of alcoholic mixed drinks; types of ice-cream sundaes; dandelion and other homemade wines; rhymed recipes; "Tuna Wiggle," "Barf on a Board," and other traditional names for institutionalized cooking; "Adam and Eve on a Raft" (meaning poached eggs on toast), "CB" (meaning "cardboard" for the "to go" containers), and other hash-slingers' (food servers') terms; hobos' recipes; and superstitious food taboos. No folklorist need starve for ideas when so many juicy tidbits remain.

BIBLIOGRAPHIC NOTES

The study of American foodways (ethnocuisine, ethnogastronomy, etc.) got a good early start among folklorists, but was a long time developing, finally coming into its own fairly recently as a viable subspecialty of research. The only full-length article on food published early in *JAF* was John G. Bourke's "Folk-Foods of the Rio Grande Valley and of Northern Mexico," *JAF* 8 (1895): 41–71. A good indication of progress was the "Special Food Issue" of *KFQ* (16 [1971]: 153–214); with five articles edited and introduced by foodways specialist Jay Anderson, it contained studies of foodways research, Native American foods, soul food, and the organic-foods movement, plus a report on an international ethnological food-research symposium.

Thirty-three papers representing the proceedings of the Third International Conference on Ethnological Food Research, which met in Cardiff, Wales, in 1977, provide a good cross section of approaches. See Alexander Fenton and Trefor M. Owen, eds., *Food in Perspective* (Edinburgh: John Donald, 1981). Among American folklorists attending the conference whose papers were published here were Jay Anderson, Roger L. Welsch, and Don Yoder. American anthropologist Robert J. Theodoratus presented a paper on Greek immigrant cuisine in America, which is also relevant to this chapter. (See also G. James Patterson, *The Greeks of Vancouver: A Study in the Preservation of Ethnicity* [Ottawa, Canada: National Museum of Man, Mercury Series No. 18, 1976.])

A special issue of *JAC* (2:3 [1979]) offered a "Focus on American Food and Foodways," ed. Kay Mussell and Linda Keller Brown. The most useful articles to folklorists were Angus K. Gillespie's "Toward a Method for the Study of Food in American Culture" (pp. 393–406) and Charles Camp's "Food in American Culture: A Bibliographic Essay" (pp. 559–70). Camp has also published the useful volume *American Foodways* (Little Rock, Ark.: August House, 1989).

The Brown/Mussell compilation was expanded as a book titled *Ethnic and Regional Foodways in the United States* (Knoxville: University of Tennessee Press, 1984). Another important anthology is Theodore C. Humphrey and Lin T. Humphrey, eds., *"We Gather Together"—Food and Festival in American Life* (Logan: Utah State University Press, 1988). See also Lin T. Humphrey's essay "Traditional Foods? Traditional Values?" *WF* 48 (1989): 169–77.

Cookbooks and popular works on American foods may be useful in foodways research. There are literally hundreds of such books, so only a few with particular ethnographic value may be mentioned. *The American Heritage Cookbook and Illustrated History of American Eating & Drinking* (New York: American Heritage Publishing Co. and Simon and Schuster, 1964), for example, is well written, informative, and also magnificently illustrated in both black and white and color. A similar publication is *American Cooking*, by Dale Brown (New York: Time-Life Books, 1968), particularly its chapter "Two Hundred Years in the Kitchen," pp. 184–99. *The Minnesota Ethnic Food Book*, quoted in Focus: Norwegian Soul Food—*Lutefisk*, is an excellent and inclusive regional cookbook containing both analyses of foodways and actual recipes. With individual essays on regional foodways written by folklorists, the *Smithsonian Folklife Cookbook* (Washington, D.C.: Smithsonian Institution, 1991) is a unique volume of recipes and studies. Compiled by Katherine S. and Thomas M. Kirlin, this book includes a summary of all Smithsonian Festival of American Folklife sessions from 1967 to 1991 plus photographs of participants, who were the sources of the foodways described.

The description of Mountain Men eating buffalo meat quoted in this chapter is from Ray Allen Billington's *The Far Western Frontier, 1830–1860* (New York: Harper, 1956; Harper Torchbook paperback edition, 1962), p. 51. Martin Schmitt surveyed Western food traditions in " 'Meat's Meat': An Account of the Flesh-eating Habits of Western Americans," *WF* 11 (1952): 185–203. The description of making jerky on the frontier is quoted from Jacqueline Williams's *Wagon Wheel Kitchens: Food on the Oregon Trail* (Lawrence: University Press of Kansas, 1993). Charlie McCormick's essay "Eating Fried Rattler: The Symbolic Significance of the Rattlesnake Roundup" appeared in *SF* 53 (1996): 41–54. My note on a Western tradition of "Mock Recipes for 'Planked' Game" appeared in *WF* 2 (1962): 45–46, and a similar item of food jokelore is described in Mac E. Barrick's "Texas Chicken" [fried fatback], *NCFJ* 27 (1979): 88–92.

Three articles concern the preparation of sweetenings by folk methods: William E. Lightfoot, " 'I Hardly Ever Miss a Meal without Eating Just a Little': Traditional Sorghum-Making in Western Kentucky," *MSF* 1 (1973): 7–17; Nora Leonard Roy, "Maple Sugaring in Southern Indiana: A Descriptive Study of the Technology of Four Maple Sugar Makers," *IF* 9 (1976): 197–234; and Suzanne Stiegelbauer, "A Folk Craft as a Folk Art: An Example of Cane Syrup Production in East Texas," *MFR* 12 (1978): 118–30.

Sylvie Howbart describes "A Hog Killing in Eastern North Carolina," *NCFJ* 28 (1980): 42–55, while Howard Wight Marshall takes the process further in "Meat Preservation on the Farm in Missouri's 'Little Dixie,' " *JAF* 92 (1979): 400–17. On regional barbecue, see John Marshall, "Traditional Barbecue Methodology in Hickman County, Kentucky," *MAF* 11 (1983): 21–28. Another food-preparation study is Marlene Schroeder's "George DeMeyer: Belgian-American Wine-Maker," *IF* 11 (1978): 193–200.

The frontier folksongs referred to in this chapter appear in many collections. Several of these texts are from H. M. Belden's *Ballads and Songs Collected by the Missouri Folk-Lore Society*, University of Missouri Studies 15 (Columbia, 1940). Logger's stew is described in "The Depot Camp" quoted in "Folksongs from Maine," *NEF* 7 (1965): 15–22. Roger L. Welsch gives a number of folksong references to frontier foods, plus other interesting data, in his article " 'Sorry Chuck': Pioneer Foodways," *NH* 53 (1972): 99–113 (repr. in *Readings in American Folklore*, pp. 152–67). The food of sailors and cowboys was compared in my own article "Sailors' and Cowboys' Folklore in Two Popular Classics," *SFQ* 29 (1965): 266–83. Edward Everett Dale's *Frontier Ways: Sketches of Life in the Old West* (Austin: University of Texas Press, 1959) has chapters on "Cowboy Cookery" (pp. 25–42) and "Food on the Frontier" (pp. 111–31). An extended study of the former topic is Ramon F. Adams's *Come an' Get It: The Story of the Old Cowboy Cook* (Norman: University of Oklahoma Press, 1952; reissued, 1972). Rose P. White discussed that staple of Western cooking in "The Sourdough Biscuit," *WF* 15 (1956): 93–94; Peter Tamony explored the terminology, mystique, and history of "Sourdough and French Bread" in his Western Words section of *WF* 32 (1973): 265–70. A revealing project that suggests other possibilities with other groups is Charlie Seemann's paper "Bacon, Biscuits, and Beans: Food of the Cattle Trails as Found in American Cowboy Songs," *AFFWord* 4 (Oct. 1974): 24–39.

Three early notes in *JAF* concerned recipes for substitutes. These were "Traditionary American Local Dishes," *JAF* 13 (1900): 65–66; "Some Homely Viands," *JAF* 13 (1900): 292–94; and "Blood-Root 'Chocolate,' " *JAF* 19 (1906): 347–48. Miriam B. Webster's "Maine Winter Menus: A Study in Ingenuity," *NEF* 1 (1958): 7–9, has some similar recipes, as do several of the works on pioneer foods mentioned previously. Comments on Ritz Cracker mock apple pie quoted in this chapter are from Steve Rubenstein's column titled "Six and 30 Crackers Baked in a Pie" in the *San Francisco Chronicle* in early spring 1991. Henry Glassie's comments on Italian-American Easter cake appeared in *Folk Art and Art Worlds*, cited in chapter 21, pp. 270–71.

A query for variant terms and shapes for doughnuts was published by Charles Peabody in *JAF* 18 (1905): 166, but apparently no responses were ever printed. Students may pursue the subject, however, in several studies of folk dialect.

B. A. Botkin included sections on regional foods in *A Treasury of New England Folklore* (New York: Crown, 1947) and *A Treasury of Southern Folklore* (New York: Crown, 1949). Southern traditional recipes were discussed by George W. Boswell in two articles appearing in *MFR* 5 (1971): 1–9 and *MSF* 3 (1975): 13–20. Early American recipes from New York and elsewhere in the East are given in articles by Janet R. MacFarlane in *NYFQ* 10 (1954): 135–40 and 218–25, and in *NYFQ* 11 (1955): 305–9. The latter contains one rhymed recipe. For other regional food traditions, see Kathy Newstadt, *Clambake: A History and Celebration of an American Tradition* (Amherst: University of Massachusetts Press, 1992); Grahm Tomlinson, "The Encoding of Subcultural Features in a Culinary Item: The Case of the Boiled Peanut," *MAF* 14 (1986): 1–17; and especially the fine study by C. Paige Gutierrez, *Cajun Foodways* (Jackson: University of Mississippi Press, 1992).

In a study of "Children's Food Preferences," *NYF* 5 (1979): 189–96, A. J. Lamme III and Linda Leonard Lamme summarized the results of a questionnaire given to one thousand children at the 1976 Smithsonian Festival of American Folklife —cake and ice cream, corn, peanut butter and jelly sandwiches, and cereal led the choices here. In "The Cincinnati Chili Culinary Complex," *WF* 40 (1981): 28–40, Timothy Charles Lloyd traced the history and varieties of this regional speciality. A query by the editor of *PA* on "Sliced Tomatoes for Breakfast" (vol. 9 [1977]: 11) asked for information on the eating of sliced fresh tomatoes instead of grits or potatoes with eggs and meat as a breakfast dish. A (somewhat) related item was a note and reply entitled "Were Tomatoes Considered Poisonous?" *PA* 11 (1979): 112–13; while some early references describe the eating of tomatoes, others seem to reflect suspicions about them, so the point is still moot.

On the Thanksgiving meal, see James Deetz and Jay Anderson, "The Ethnogastronomy of Thanksgiving," *Saturday Review* (November 25, 1972), pp. 29–39. "Soggy Coconut Cake" in a family tradition is described in Mary Hufford, Marjorie Hunt, and Steven Zeitlin, *The Grand Generation: Memory, Mastery, Legacy* (Washington, D.C.: Smithsonian Institution, 1987).

The description of a Kentucky meal in this chapter is quoted from Allan M. Trout's *Greetings from Old Kentucky, Volume Two* (Frankfort, Ky., 1959), p. 71. A food item from another Southern state was described in James W. Byrd's "Poke Sallet [a dish made of pokeweed greens, bacon drippings, and eggs] from Tennessee to Texas," *TFSB* 32 (1966): 48–54. Paul Brewster included cooking, preserving, and beverage making in volume 1 of *The Frank C. Brown Collection of North Carolina Folklore*, pp. 266–75.

The description of the Oregon meal in this chapter is quoted from H. L. Davis's novel *Honey in the Horn* (New York: Harper, 1935; Avon paperback ed., [n.d.]), p. 19. Some Utah folk foods were included in Jan Harold Brunvand, *A Guide for Collectors of Folklore in Utah* (Salt Lake City: University of Utah Press, 1971), pp. 118–19; but with much better context in Janet Alm Anderson's *Bounty: A Harvest of Foodlore and Country Memories from Utah's Past* (Boulder, Colo.: Pruett Pub. Co., 1990). Anderson also wrote *A Taste of Kentucky* (Lexington: University Press of Kentucky, 1986). Marjorie Sackett discussed Kansas folk recipes in *Kansas Folklore*, ed. S. J. Sackett (Lincoln: University of Nebraska Press, 1961), pp. 226–38; in *MF* 12 (1962): 81–86; and in *WF* 22 (1963): 103–6.

Ethnic American foodways offer many good subjects for study. Three fine examples of published work are Don Yoder's articles "Sauerkraut in the Pennsylvania Folk-Culture," *PF* 12 (Summer 1961): 56–69; "Schnitz in the Pennsylvania Folk-Culture," *PF* 12 (Fall 1961): 44–53; and "Pennsylvanians Called It Mush," *PF* 13 (Winter 1962–63): 27–49. Other studies are Elaine J. Abboud and Jean A. Sarrazin, "New Orleans Lenten Recipes: A Multi-Ethnic Sampling," *LFM* (April 1970): 55–69; Janet Langlois, "Moon Cake in Chinatown, New York City: Continuity and Change," *NYFQ* 28 (1972): 83–117; Craig Soland, "How to Make a Sve-te-Saba [Serbian food]," *AFFWord* 3 (Spring 1974): 1–7; and William G. and Yvonne R. Lockwood, "The Cornish Pasty in Northern Michigan," in C. Kurt Dewhurst and Yvonne Lockwood, eds., *Michigan Folklife Reader* (East Lansing: Michigan State University Press, 1987), pp. 359–74.

Marjorie Sackett investigated "the recipe as a measure of the extent to which neighboring cultures influence each other" in her note "Folk Recipes as a Measure of Intercultural Penetration," *JAF* 85 (1972): 77–81. Robert A. Georges made some unique observations on his own family foodways in an essay titled "You Often Eat What Others Think You Are: Food as an Index of Others' Conception of Who One Is," *WF* 43 (1984): 249–56.

Since 1971, when the journal began publication, *AFFWord*, the organ of the Arizona Friends of Folklore, has periodically had an "Ethno Cuisine" section. The subjects have included Western cooking techniques (Dutch ovens, the goat roast, pit barbecue), food specialties (flour tortillas, son-of-a-bitch stew, cactus jelly), ethnic foods (Norwegian, Serbian, Flemish, Mexican, German of Transylvania), playful recipes (wacky cake), and even pseudo-recipes or food hoaxes (rattlesnake steak). This journal, however, has since terminated publication.

A good example of modern foodways research merging with recent folklore theory is Kay L. Cothran's thought-provoking article "Talking with Your Mouth Full: A Communications Approach to Food Rules," *TFSB* 38 (1972): 33–38. An extended summary of an important piece of European food research is provided by Roger L. Welsch in *KFQ* 16 (1971): 189–212; the work is Gunter Wiegelmann's *Alltags- und Festspeisen: Wandel und gegenwartige Stellung* [Daily and Festival Foods: Migration and Present Situation] (Marburg: N. G. Elwert Verlag, 1967).

An imaginative project that yielded fine results was reported in Carter W. Craigie's "The Picnic Experience," *TFSB* 45 (1979): 161–65; he drew on oral and written accounts of picnics in Chester County, Pennsylvania, from 1870 to 1925 to show how formalities of everyday life were relaxed and new social-interaction patterns developed while people were attending picnics. Similar studies might be done of backyard barbecues, brown-bag lunches, company parties, fish fries, and so forth. In a brief but suggestive note, Melissa Caswell Mason wrote of "Food and Food-related Metaphors in Folkspeech" (such as "You said a mouthful!") in *FMS* 6 (1982): 29–33.

An important general publication on American folk foodways was the special issue of *WF* (vol. 40 [1981]) edited by Michael Owen Jones, Bruce Giuliano, and Roberta Krell. A prologue, thirteen articles, and an epilogue took up such diverse topics as playing with food, food aversions, customs relating to food portions, carnival food, compiled cookbooks, and food-related speech.

PERMISSIONS ACKNOWLEDGMENTS

The author and publisher wish to thank the libraries, museums, publishers, and private collectors for permitting the reproduction of works in their collections and supplying the necessary photographs. Any changes to this information would be gratefully acknowledged.

Chapter 1
Paul Bunyan: Reprinted by permission of the University of Pennsylvania Press.
Four women: Photograph by Neil Ryder Hoos.
Ray Hicks: Fresh Air Photographics/Tom Raymond. Reprinted by permission.
Times Square: Photo by Todd Plitt. AP/Wide World Photos.
Chapter 2
Louie Attebery: Reprinted by permission of Jan Boles, © 1997.
Herbert Halpert: Reprinted by permission of Violetta and Herbert Halpert.
Robert Winslow Gordon: The American Folklife Center, Library of Congress.
Chapter 3
Navajo "codetalkers": U.S. Marine Corps photo, The National Archives.
Doc Grant Doll Carriage Parade: Photo by Madeleine de Sinety. Reprinted by permission of *The Rangeley Highlander.*
Chapter 4
Dialect boundaries: Hans Kurath, *A World Geography of the Eastern United States*, The University of Michigan Press, © 1966. Reprinted by permission of The University of Michigan Press.
DARE entry: Reprinted by permission of the publisher from *Dictionary of American Regional English, Volume II*, edited by Frederic G. Cassidy and Joan Houston Hall, Cambridge, Mass.: Harvard University Press, Copyright © 1991 by the President and Fellows of Harvard College.
Committeeman and Minister: From *Roughing It* by Mark Twain. The New York Public Library.
Loggers: Photo by J. Mullen. The Photographic Archives, University of Louisville. Reprinted by permission.
Chapter 5
Advertisement: Reprinted by permission of America First Credit Union.
Cartoon: From *The Chronicle of Higher Education*, 1/20/95. Reprinted by permission of Ed Fisher, © 1995.
Roseanne: Photo by Joan Fahrenthold. AP/Wide World Photos.
Napkin: Reprinted by permission of Marie Callender's Restaurants and Bakeries.
Chapter 7
Fourth graders: Photo by Patrick Mullen. The American Folklife Center, Library of Congress.
"Old Rags": Bettmann.
Rhyme: The American Folklife Center, Library of Congress.
Chapter 8
Johnnie Moses: Fresh Air Photographics/Tom Raymond. Reprinted by permission.
"Devil with Chicken's Feet": Originally printed in the *Texas Monthly*, October 1978. Reprinted by permission of Kirsten Soderlind.
Chapter 9
Bronko Nagurski: AP/Wide World Photos.
Chapter 10
Postcard: Copyright 1973 by Mike Roberts.
Jimmy Carter: Reprinted by permission of Charles M. Rafshoon.
"Lying Bailey": The American Folklife Center, Library of Congress.
Chapter 11
The Carter Family: From the Gid Tanner Artist File #NF 1996, The Southern Folklife Collection, Wilson Library, The University of North Carolina at Chapel Hill. Reprinted by permission.
Hamp Mizell: Photo by Francis Harper. Reprinted by permission of Robin Harper.
Roosevelt Holts: Reprinted by permission of Carol Thurber.
Chapter 12
Francis James Child: The Library of Congress.
Emma L. Dusnebery: Photo by Vance Randolph. From the Gid Tanner Artist File #NF 1996, The Southern Folklife Collection, Wilson Library, The University of North Carolina at Chapel Hill. Reprinted by permission.
"Focus: Ballads as Lullabies": Excerpt from page 11 of George List, *Singing About It: Folk Song in Southern Indiana* (Indianapolis: Indiana Historical Society, 1991). Reprinted by permission of the publisher.
Broadside ballad: Courtesy of Wilson Library, University of North Carolina Library.
Chapter 13
Al Hopkins and the Hillbillies: From the Gid Tanner Artist File #NF 1996, The Southern Folklife Collection, Wilson Library, The University of North Carolina at Chapel Hill. Reprinted by permission.
Baptist church: Photo by Thomas A. Adler. The American Folklife Center, Library of Congress, BR8-20398-34.
John R. Griffin: Photo by Carl Fleishhauer. The American Folklife Center, Library of Congress.
Elizabeth Cotton: Photo by Johsel Namkung. The American Folklife Center, Library of Congress.
Bill Monroe: From the Gid Tanner Artist File #NF 1996, The Southern Folklife Collection, Wilson Library, The University of North Carolina at Chapel Hill. Reprinted by permission.

Chapter 14
Elevator buttons: Photograph by Neil Ryder Hoos.
Ozzie Waters: The American Folklife Center, Library of Congress.
Chapter 15
African-immigrant naming ceremony: Photograph courtesy of the Center for Folklife Programs & Cultural Studies, Smithsonian Institution.
"Focus: Family Birthday Customs": From *A Celebration of American Family Folklore* by Stephen Zeitlin, Amy J. Kotkin, Holly Cutting-Baker, editors. Copyright © 1982 by Smithsonian Institution. Reprinted by permission of Pantheon Books, a division of Random House, Inc.
Prankster at a wedding: Photograph by Ben Wexler.
Advertisement: Reprinted by permission of the Taco Bell Corporation.
Shoua Her: Photograph courtesy of the Center for Folklife Programs & Cultural Studies, Smithsonian Institution.
Steve Kerper: Photograph courtesy of the Center for Folklife Programs & Cultural Studies, Smithsonian Institution.
Chapter 16
The Bell Telephone Pioneers: Photographic Archives, University of Louisville. Reprinted by permission.
Play-party: Photo by Russell Lee. The Library of Congress.
Los Pastores: Photograph by Aaron B. Claycraft. Courtesy Museum of New Mexico, Neg. No. 13695.
"You Must Pay the Rent": Photographs by Neil Ryder Hoos.
Chapter 17
Ronald Reagan: AP/Wide World Photos.
Crewmen of the U.S.S. *Pueblo*: AP/Wide World Photos.
Richard Ramirez: Photo by Jim Ruymen. Bettmann.
Richard M. Nixon: AP/Wide World Photos.
Chapter 18
Patsy Bedonie: Reprinted by permission of Barre Toelken.
Boys playing: Photo by Russell Lee. The Library of Congress.
Chapter 19
Marilyn Banuelos: Photo by James Hardin. The American Folklife Center, Library of Congress.
Derelict homestead shack: Reprinted by permission of Louie Attebery.
Chapter 20
Sawyer-Black Farm: Thomas C. Hubka photo *Sawyer-Black* from p. 5, *Big House, Little House, Black House, Barn* © 1984 Trustees of Dartmouth College, by permission of University Press of New England.
V-notched cabin and cabin of balloon frame; two half-dovetail cabins: Reprinted by permission of Henry Glassie.
Log ends held by Lester Severson: Reprinted by permission of the Canadian Museum of Civilization, image number: 72-17468.
Sod-house home: Photo by Solomon D. Butcher. Courtesy of the Nebraska State Historical Society, B983-1059. Reprinted by permission.
Two square-hewn log houses: Photo by A. B. Rue. Photographic Archives, University of Louisville. Reprinted by permission.
Chapter 21
Stockade fencing: Photo by Tom Carter. The American Folklife Center's Grouse Creek (Utah) Cultural Survey, Fife Folklore Archives, Utah State University. Reprinted by permission.
Rural mailbox: Joseph Sohm/ChromoSohm Inc./Corbis.
Interior of cabin: Photo by J. Mullen. Photographic Archives, University of Louisville. Reprinted by permission.
Mrs. Louis Brunet: Photo by Martha McMillin Roberts. Photographic Archives, University of Louisville. Reprinted by permission.
Aspen tree-carving: Photo by Jan Brunvand.
Chapter 22
Frontier couple: The Library of Congress.
Homeless refugees: The Library of Congress.
Details of Pleiku jackets: Copyright by the Michigan State University Board of Trustees. Courtesy of the Michigan State University Museum.
Chapter 23
A cowboys' feast. Photo by Jan Brunvand.
St. Joseph's Day: Photo by Myron Wood. The American Folklife Center, Library of Congress.
Family homecoming: Photo by Carlos Ross. The American Folklife Center, Library of Congress.

INDEX